Dungeons and Desktops

Dungeons and Desktops

The History of Computer Role-Playing Games

Second Edition

Matt Barton
Shane Stacks

CRC Press
Taylor & Francis Group
Boca Raton London New York

CRC Press is an imprint of the
Taylor & Francis Group, an **informa** business

AN A K PETERS BOOK

CRC Press
Taylor & Francis Group
6000 Broken Sound Parkway NW, Suite 300
Boca Raton, FL 33487-2742

© 2019 by Taylor & Francis Group, LLC
CRC Press is an imprint of Taylor & Francis Group, an Informa business

No claim to original U.S. Government works

Printed on acid-free paper

International Standard Book Number-13: 978-1-138-57464-9 (paperback)
978-1-138-57467-0 (hardback)

Library of Congress Cataloging-in-Publication Data

Names: Barton, Matt, author. | Stacks, Shane, author.
Title: Dungeons and desktops: the history of computer role-playing games / Matt Barton and Shane Stacks.
Description: [2nd edition]. | Boca Raton: Taylor & Francis, [2018] | Includes bibliographical references and index.
Identifiers: LCCN 2018054591| ISBN 9781138574649 (pbk. : alk. paper) | ISBN 9781138574670 (hardback: alk. paper)
Subjects: LCSH: Fantasy games—History. | Computer games—History.
Classification: LCC GV1469.6 .B37 2018 | DDC 794.809—dc23
LC record available at https://lccn.loc.gov/2018054591

Visit the Taylor & Francis Web site at
http://www.taylorandfrancis.com

and the CRC Press Web site at
http://www.crcpress.com

From Shane

I would be doing a disservice to my personal history with CRPGs if I didn't dedicate my efforts on this book to my friend and game developer Johnny Wood, who first introduced me to Pool of Radiance *in high school (not to mention* Red Dwarf, Doctor Who, *and* Blake's 7*!).*

Also, most likely to their surprise, a nod to my friends at the RPG Codex. The faint of heart fear to tread their forums (and rightly so), but they collectively have a true love of CRPGs and have done their part to keep the genre alive. And, yes, Codex, I enjoyed Sword Coast Legends *for what it was. Revel in my decline.*

Finally, many heartfelt thanks and a lusty "kill that rat!" to the King Rat himself, Matt Barton, for allowing me to journey with him on this quest to make a great (and important) book even better.

From Matt

I'd like to dedicate this book to my dearly departed grandfather, or "Papa," Edward E. Barton (1932–2018). Papa served in the United States Army in the Korean War receiving the Army of Occupation Medal, Combat Infantry Badge, Purple Heart Medal and Korean Service Medal with Four Bronze Service Stars. He was also my grandpa. He never let me give him a free copy of any of my books—no, he insisted on going to his local bookstore and demanding they order him a copy of my latest "bestseller." Well, were I to sell a million and a million more, the ones I sold to you paid the highest royalties.

We co-authors would both like to extend a shoutout to the staff at Milky Way Ink, Inc. You are all passionate for your projects, and may your respective efforts prove successful.

Contents

Acknowledgments

Special thanks to Brian Fargo, Richard Garriott, Tim Lang, David Wesely, CRPG Addict, Lazy Game Reviews, Robbie Sambat, Griffith Archduke, Nathaniel Tolbert, Adam Dayton, Mike and Sam Witwer, and David Swofford.

Chris Avellone's Preface

FIGURE i.1 Chris Avellone is one of the world's greatest CRPG designers, best known for his critically acclaimed work on *Planescape: Torment* and *Fallout: New Vegas*.

I've been an RPG fan ever since I was nine years old. I remember the exact moment, in fact. I was tossing a baseball around in my backyard with Michael, one of my friends from the neighborhood, and he brought up a game called *Dungeons & Dragons*.

I had never heard of *D&D*, so he explained it to me—it was like living out an adventure in *Lord of the Rings*, similar to playing a game of make-believe, but there were *rules* to it, and randomness determined by rolling dice to determine outcomes. The way he explained the "rules" is what grabbed me most—the adventure wasn't a static construct, it wasn't a fantasy story of the kind I'd read and loved—it was something that went beyond that, where you could *be* the protagonist, but rather than being an unstoppable hero, you would experience challenges and setbacks, even fail at them. That was amazing, and even more important to me at the time, it felt *fair*.

Getting a group (gathering a party) to actually *play* the game, however, was a pain in the ass.

D&D was a game meant to be played with others, and if you don't have a car (I wasn't able to drive when I started playing), and you don't live close to your friends, it turns out getting together and finding a group is a challenge. Even when I finally got a driver's license, another problem presented itself—even if you had a group, you had to find someone to be the "Dungeon Master," who was the one who "ran" the adventure, made the rule calls, controlled the monsters in the dungeon, and gave quests to the players around the table. They were the ones who did most of the work. And it was a LOT of work.

Still, because I'd rather be a Dungeon Master than not play at all, I often took on the role—and over time, found myself enjoying it quite a bit, even though I was rarely able to play as a player, which had sort of been the point of the whole thing.

So, in the wake of those challenges, I stumbled across *Bard's Tale II* playing on a friend's Commodore 64, and I suddenly realized this was a version of *D&D* I could play on my own when I couldn't get a gaming group together—it was a digital Dungeon Master, and I could go on an adventure the game developers had scripted by myself. That revelation started me playing an avalanche of games ... *Bard's Tale I, II, and III; Pool of Radiance* and all the Gold Box games; the *Ultimas; Might and Magic; Eternal Dagger; Wasteland;* and more. Whenever I wasn't doing homework or running a game of my own, it was time to boot up the CRPGs and start playing. My mom put up with it, because she's cool like that (it helped that I kept up my grades).

Over the years, this passion ebbed somewhat, mostly due to college and other constraints. I didn't stop enjoying role-playing games, though, but it wasn't until I started writing pen-and-paper adventures for publication that a true opportunity opened up, and I suddenly had the chance to contribute to the CRPG genre I enjoyed so much. Over the next twenty-plus years I worked on: *Planescape: Torment, Fallout 2, Icewind Dale 1* and *2, Star Wars: Knights of the Old Republic II, Neverwinter Nights 2, Alpha Protocol, Baldur's Gate: Dark Alliance,* and even back to the *Fallout* franchise with *Fallout: New Vegas* and a chance to contribute to further iterations of games I'd loved in my youth—*Wasteland 2, Wasteland 3,* and new ones *Divinity, Pathfinder: Kingmaker,* and more. It's been a fantastic experience to be able to participate and give back to a genre I love so much—the only drawback being that it means I have less time to play the same games, but it's a small price to pay.

You also get involved with the community that enjoys CRPGs, which brings me to Matt and Shane.

I've known Matt and Shane for a long time. I've spoken to them at length, in interviews and outside of interviews. If there's anything I can tell you, it's that both of them *love* computer RPGs, and this book you're holding, downloaded, or are reading in the future through scrolling cybernetic retinal displays is proof positive of their passion for RPGs.

This isn't the first edition—the fact there's a second edition is also proof of the growing market and growing interest in RPGs. RPG mechanics of skill progression, experience points, character customization, item inventories, and giving the player's avatar more freedom to make decisions and see different outcomes is making itself into *all* gaming genres, even making itself felt in global hits as *God of War.* It's an experience players want: more "voice" and progression in the world they are exploring.

Looking back from this, RPGs have come a long way. Back in the 1980s, if you played *D&D*, you weren't exactly in the cool kids' club, so nothing has been more gratifying to me than seeing *D&D* become appreciated, and something that almost everyone is willing to at least give a try … and rarely looked down upon. Seeing shows like *Critical Role* and others draw a following from showing their gaming sessions has even been more welcome.

Books like the one you're holding now let people get a closer look at the history of CRPGs and what makes them tick. Matt and Shane have put together something special—even if you're a CRPG veteran (some might say lich) like me, you're likely to learn a lot about your craft or your passion; it stems from every page.

So, welcome. Grab a tankard, pull up a chair, and join us—this book's about to take you on an incredible adventure.

And thanks to my neighborhood friend Michael for that game of catch so many years ago. It changed my life.

Chris Avellone, Lich

Authors' Preface

FIGURE i.2   Your humble authors, Shane Stacks and Matt Barton.

Welcome back, brave adventurers! Or, if this is your first foray into the world of computer role-playing games, greetings! Infinite quests, glory, and epic amounts of lost sleep await!

But before we set out once again to slay those pesky dragons, let's deal with the one in the room: Why a new edition? History is history, right? Unfortunately—or fortunately as far as hungry historians are concerned—while the facts of history don't change, our ability to find and present those facts changes frequently. To put it simply, in the decade following the publication of the original *Dungeons and Desktops,* your authors have gained enough experience points to level up once, if not a few times. We simply know much more than we did, not only about the genre this book covers, but about book writing and publishing in general.

To cut to the chase, here are four good reasons to justify a new *Dungeons and Desktops*: full-color screenshots, behind-the-scenes stories from developers and designers, a complete reorganization, and, of course, a general update to cover the startling developments in CRPGs since

2008—including the unanticipated shot in the arm the genre received from crowdfunding platforms like Kickstarter.

Let's start with what was clearly the most justified criticism of the first edition: the quality of the screenshots. In the previous edition, these were small grayscale images that didn't convey the artistry of the games they showed. CRPGs have always been a highly visual medium, where colorful artwork and animation play a crucial role. Thankfully, unlike the first edition, this tome features full-color, high-resolution images of hundreds of games.

Another solid improvement to this edition is the incorporation of Matt and Shane's interviews with professional game designers, publishers, artists, musicians, and coders. Broadcast weekly on YouTube, Matt's *Matt Chat* series is an invaluable resource for anyone interested in game history and design. Likewise, co-author Shane Stacks has his own podcast and terrestrial radio show called *Shane Plays Geek Talk,* which regularly features CRPG as well as tabletop role-playing designers and experts. Matt and Shane have thoroughly harvested these interviews for quotations and insights into the design, reception, and influence of hundreds of key games. These luminaries include Richard "Lord British" Garriott, Brian Fargo, Jon Van "JVC" Caneghem, Chris "MCA" Avellone, Josh Sawyer, Tim Cain, and Leonard Boyarsky, just to name a few, plus new talents like Whalenought Studios and Almost Human. Their personal accounts give us unique insights into the how's and why's of our favorite CRPGs.

One of the problems with writing about so many different games is how easy it is to lose the narrative thread. To that end, we've created an appendix for this edition called "The CRPG Bestiary" and relegated games there that, while certainly worthy of coverage, aren't influential or significant enough to warrant distracting readers from the broader story. If you see a game title in **bold**, that means it's in the bestiary, but you'll also find many games there that aren't mentioned elsewhere.

Finally, much has changed in the world of CRPGs since *Dungeons and Desktops* was first published in 2008, and not just a wealth of new games such as *Pillars of Eternity, Divinity Original Sin,* and *Torment: Tides of Numenera.* However, more significant than any of these new games is the introduction of crowdfunding. Back in 2007, when Matt was finishing up the first edition, he feared that the CRPG was in its death throes. Major studios and publishers simply weren't interested in single-player games with turn-based combat or isometric points of view, much less dusty old franchises such as *Baldur's Gate* or *Wasteland.* Instead, the only games in town were those based on first-person shooter engines, such as *Skyrim*, or massively multiplayer online games like *World of Warcraft*.

Matt was happy to be wrong—and Shane was happy to make note that he was wrong for later sick burn ammunition! Far from dying, the CRPG is in a Renaissance thanks to Kickstarter, Indiegogo, and Fig. These new publishing platforms have led to a rise in indie and niche titles as well as the resurgence of franchises thought long dead and commercially unviable. Back in 2007, who could've possibly predicted *Wasteland 2* (2014) or *Bard's Tale IV* (2017)? Certainly not Brian Fargo, founder of Interplay, who said this in 2011, a few years before Kickstarter's first major funding breakthrough with Double Fine Adventure:

> I think the biggest issue is really the cost of making games. If you go to the mid-90s, you have a game like *Descent* that was made by a couple of guys. I think the budget on that was three hundred thousand dollars. You could reasonably expect two or three guys to forgo their salaries, put together a pretty good sample, and put something out for six figures.... You could do some really innovative stuff. As [the cost of] games started going up higher and higher, that breed of person disappeared. There was nowhere for them to go except to get a job. Now you're just at a job, working on big projects, just pulling tasks off the wall. There was no commerce—no opportunity to sell.... No publisher is going to give you the five million dollars to make a new game.

At the time, Fargo, like many, found hope in the burgeoning mobile and social games industry, where cheaper games by smaller teams were the norm. How could he have known that the very next year he'd use Kickstarter to raise nearly $3 million for *Wasteland 2*? Or that Obsidian would raise $4 million for *Pillars of Eternity* in 2012? If the classic CRPG was dying back in 2011, crowdfunding was just what the cleric ordered!

By the way, with some exceptions, we use first-person or the "royal we" in the text unless otherwise indicated.

We sincerely hope you're as excited about this new edition as we are. As you can see, there's quite a lot to cover, so now, without further ado, here is *Dungeons and Desktops 2.0. Let the hybrid, mutant mad science that is MattShane begin!*

CHAPTER 1

Introduction to Computer Role-Playing Games

"Beware, foolish mortal, you trespass in *Akalabeth,* world of doom!" These foreboding words, printed in a suitably gothic typeface, graced the card insert of Richard "Lord British" Garriott's initial foray into computer role-playing games: *Akalabeth,* "a game of fantasy, cunning, and danger." Inside the humble Ziploc bag lay the ultimate loot—a 5¼″ Apple II floppy diskette containing "10 different Hi-Res Monsters combined with perfect perspective and infinite dungeon levels." For obsessed *Dungeons & Dragons* fans, this was the Holy Grail: unlimited fantasy role-playing at the touch of a button!

First published in 1979, *Akalabeth: World of Doom* (Figure 1.1) is one of the earliest computer role-playing games (CRPGs). CRPGs are a genre of video games as well as a subcategory of role-playing games, a broader category that covers everything from *Dungeons & Dragons* (*D&D*) to some forms of therapy and training exercises. *Akalabeth* and later CRPGs were and continue to be greatly inspired by *D&D* and other tabletop RPGs such as *Shadowrun* and *The Dark Eye,* but they are much more than their computerized equivalents. By combining elements of tabletop RPGs and computer games, Garriott, his peers, and millions of players realized that computer RPGs were more than the sum of their parts.

BEWARE,
FOOLISH
MORTAL,
YOU
TRESPASS
IN

AKALABETH!
WORLD OF
DOOM!!

BY
LORD
BRITISH

FIGURE 1.1   Richard "Lord British" Garriott's first commercially released CRPG established many conventions still in use today. Note the rather excellent rat in the lower left corner.

A diehard fan of Halloween, haunted houses, Renaissance fairs, and *Dungeons & Dragons*, Garriott lacked neither the imagination nor the ambition to turn his dreams into reality. Perhaps

> *Akalabeth*, like many early computer games, was packaged in a humble plastic bag instead of a custom printed box.

he inherited such traits from his father, Owen K. Garriott, whose own role in history is secured as an astronaut. Richard's father made his living exploring space, spending months aboard the Skylab space station. His son would also experience the wonders of space travel as a tourist on a Russian spacecraft. For now, though, the young Garriott's mission was not to leave this world, but to bring us to his: Akalabeth.

As he described in the game's manual, Akalabeth was a paradise where "man and beast lived in peace," enjoying abundant food and opulence. This Golden Age came to an abrupt end when Mondain, the second brother of the great King Wolfgang, coveted his elder brother's inheritance and embraced evil. He created vast dungeons, protected above by thieves and skeletons and guarded below by demons and balrogs (Figure 1.2). This once prosperous land was ravaged by sickness,

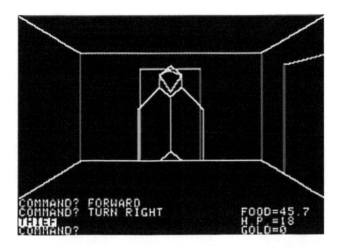

FIGURE 1.2 *Akalabeth*'s dungeons are drawn with wireframe graphics to simulate a 3D environment. Shown here is a thief, one of many vile threats you'll find roaming the dungeons.

pestilence, and war. In this age of darkness, "Man and beast lived in constant fear."

Rising to face this challenge, Lord British, Champion of the White Light, defeated and banished Mondain. Now Protector of Akalabeth, Lord British must leave it to adventurers like us to finish the job, ridding Akalabeth once and for all of Mondain's evil creatures still lurking in those dank, dark dungeons.

As an experienced *D&D* Dungeon Master, the Society of Creative Anachronisms, and Renaissance Fairs (Figure 1.3), Garriott had no trouble coming up with epic stories, settings, and lore for fantasy role-playing campaigns. But how would any of this work as a computer game? As far as he knew, he was going where no one had gone before. There were no commercially successful CRPGs he could imitate or even a proven market for such a product, and he certainly didn't see anything like it in the arcades.

It's one thing to have a great idea for a computer game. It's quite another to put in the many long hours of hard work required to make one. Even today, with so many do-it-yourself game-making tools at our disposal like Unity, Unreal Engine, or RPG Maker, making a CRPG is a serious commitment. Garriott had to make do with books like the *Apple II Basic Programming Manual* and simple trial and error. He taught himself BASIC, designed and programmed the game, and even published it himself. In short, like his fictional counterpart Lord British, Garriott had

FIGURE 1.3 There's not much that Lord British loves more than a good Renaissance fair. As a game designer, he strives to capture some of the magic of these events, whether in single-player games or his later massively multiplayer online games.

cleared the way for ordinary adventurers—folks who'd rather fight with rats in dungeons than errors in syntax.

There were plenty of desktop heroes ready to answer his call. Later teaming up with California Pacific Computer Company, Garriott sold tens of thousands of copies, providing himself with a lordly income during his years at college. One wonders how many of his classmates neglected their literature to battle monsters in those infinite dungeons. As he himself once said to Steven Levy, "I can't spell, have no grammar techniques, and have read less than twenty-five books in my life."

While much has changed since Garriott (shown in Figure 1.4) sold his first copy of *Akalabeth,* much remains the same. CRPG fans are still obsessed with leveling up characters, acquiring the best arms and armor, and vanquishing ever more powerful foes. They're out there now, stomping around one proving ground or another, searching for their next grand adventure. There are many other genres of computer game, but none offers its cocktail of thrilling combat, tactics and strategy, character

FIGURE 1.4   The creator of *Ultima* and founder of Origin, Richard "Lord British" Garriott is a key figure in both the CRPG and MMORPG genres. Photo courtesy of Conley Swofford Media.

development, branching storylines, fantastic worlds to explore, and personal enrichment. It just doesn't get any better than a quality CRPG.

> *Shane:* Go to fantastical places, meet new and interesting exotic peoples, and waste them with your crossbow ... all from the comfort of your own chair, baby.
> *Matt:* That's enough out of you.
> *Shane:* What if the new and interesting exotic peoples are rats?
> *Matt:* Now you're talking!

Bethesda's *The Elder Scrolls V: Skyrim* (2011) and *Fallout 4* (2015); Larian Studios' *Divinity: Original Sin 2* (2017); CD Projeckt Red's *The Witcher 3: Wild Hunt* (2015); and Warhorse Studios' *Kingdom Come: Deliverance* (2018) are currently five of the most popular CRPGs, but there's a plethora of respectable titles from independent studios such as Whalenought Studios' *Serpent in the Staglands* (2015), Iron Tower Studio's *The Age of Decadence* (2015), and Harebrained Schemes' *Shadowrun: Dragonfall* (2014), just to name a few. This vibrant independent movement is fueled not only by access to affordable, yet powerful development tools like Unity, but also by crowdfunding apps such as Kickstarter and Fig, which let developers bypass publishers—the game industry's traditional gatekeepers. Crowdfunding has

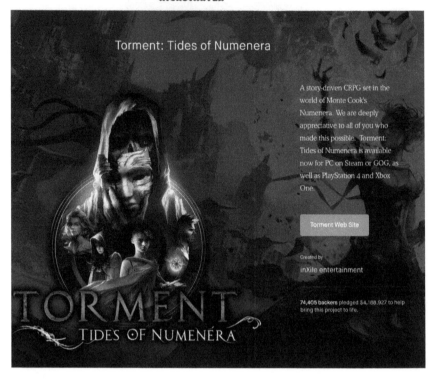

FIGURE 1.5   Kickstarter and other crowdfunding platforms have led to an explosion of CRPGs. InXile's *Torment: Tides of Numenera*, a spiritual successor of the classic *Planescape: Torment* from 1999, raised over $4 million.

paved the way for more of what we might call "alternative" CRPGs, such as inXile's *Torment: Tides of Numenera* (2016) (Figure 1.5) and, indirectly, Obsidian's *Tyranny* (2016). While these games arguably lack mainstream appeal, they are bold experiments that push the boundaries of CRPGs.

The best CRPGs require a diverse set of skills, such as long-term planning, problem solving, teamwork, and resource management. Some demand advanced navigation and even cartography; inept players would end up hopelessly lost in a maze or dungeon. Others are loaded with puzzles and riddles. Several punish players for winning in an unethical way. CRPGs are not a matter of agility with a gamepad or mouse clicks-per-minute. Rather, they demand that players weigh risks, make decisions, manage, and lead. They delay gratification and teach the value not only of perseverance, but of experimentation and adaptation in the face of progress. Many challenge players to create or assemble a whole crew of characters, each with a diverse skill set and specific strengths and weaknesses; success in these games takes effective team management.

CRPGs AS A GENRE OF VIDEO GAMES

Before we advance further into the amazing history of our favorite genre, let's define it—or at least narrow it down. CRPGs frequently blend into other genres, and it's hard to isolate features that are mutually exclusive. Dozens of successful games span multiple genres and are best described as hybrids, such as Infocom's *Zork Zero* (1987), a fusion of text adventures and CRPGs, and Ion Storm's *Deus Ex* (2000), a first-person shooter/CRPG.

> *Shane:* Oh man, there's not much more of a ravenous sucking abyssal maw of a debate topic among gamers than "what is a CRPG?" I once almost lost control of an entire hour's radio show topic by bringing this up.
>
> *Matt:* I feareth not and have tread these paths before. Keep me in sight!

Even among games commonly regarded as CRPGs, there can be enough variation to make you wonder if they really belong in the same category. Take FTL's *Dungeon Master* and Masterplay's *Star Saga*, both published in 1987. Whereas *Dungeon Master* is a real-time, colorful three-dimensional game depicted in first-person perspective and based on a fantasy setting, *Star Saga* (Figure 1.6) is a science fiction CRPG with a text-only display, physical booklets, and a printed game board (shown here) upon which players move small tokens.

We can put these two together because, in this book, what primarily distinguishes CRPGs from other genres is their statistical-based role-playing systems. CRPG designers rely on statistical calculation rather than physical manipulation for the bulk of their gameplay mechanics. In other words, they are more about statistical reasoning than facility with a mouse, joystick, or game controller.

The other crucial factor, which we'll get into later, is that players control a single character or small group rather than an army. Identifying with an *avatar* allows you to experience a virtual world in a more intimate fashion than is possible with the more abstract relationship between, say, the player and a battalion or fleet. In the tabletop realm, this is the key difference between role-playing and wargaming.

It's helpful to consider how CRPG designers think differently than most other game designers. Let's say you were making an archery game. What

FIGURE 1.6 *Star Saga* is a hybrid tabletop/CRPG game that includes this colorful map and small tokens to track movement. Photo courtesy of CRPG Addict.

would it look like? How would players control it? How closely would it approximate the real thing? Most importantly, how could you make it fun?

In action games, such as *Track & Field* (1983) for the Nintendo Entertainment System, players hold down a button and release it at just the right moment to hit a moving target (Figure 1.7). The game also factors in wind speed and direction. In *The Elder Scrolls V: Skyrim* (2011), a hybrid CRPG/first-person shooter (FPS), players aim a bow using on-screen crosshairs, compensating for longer distances by aiming above the target. In the archery activity on *Wii Sports Resort,* the designers implemented the Wii Motion Plus and Nunchuck to introduce some truly remarkable physicality. This game goes so far as to simulate the pulling of the string and the positioning of the bow. Virtual reality (VR) technologies such as Oculus Rift and HTC Vive already offer several archery games. The "Longbow" portion of Valve's *The Lab* is essentially a VR-enhanced version of the abovementioned *Wii Sports Resort* game, albeit with cartoonish violence.

As these examples show, there are countless ways game designers have attempted to answer the questions we posed earlier. Each of these games looks and feels entirely different, and all of them are fun. Yet they have as

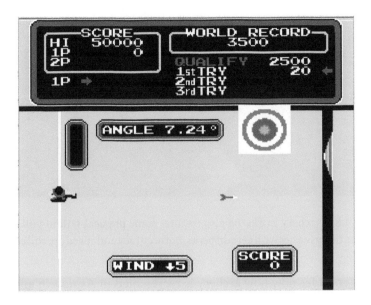

FIGURE 1.7   *Track & Field* tries to mimic the sport of archery with gameplay mechanics based on precision and timing. You might get lucky occasionally, but it takes practice and skill to reliably hit the moving target.

much in common with shooting a bow as reading this book has with playing a CRPG. Nevertheless, there is undeniably some physical skill required to reliably hit the target in these games. They all attempt to mimic the physicality of archery in some fashion, whether it's a simple timing mechanism or an elaborate system of accelerometers and motion sensors.

By contrast, in a pure CRPG there is no attempt whatsoever to match what's happening on the screen with what's happening with the keyboard, mouse, or controller. Most, if not all, of the physicality called for in these games is to move the characters, navigate menus, and, above all else, constantly save the game. Otherwise, only the character's skill matters. In such a CRPG, the outcome is not determined by manipulation (a word that derives from the Latin word for "hand"), but calculation. For this reason, it is possible to play a CRPG without ever touching a keyboard or mouse; you could simply direct someone else to do it for you. This often happens when multiple players huddle around the same PC to play games like *Wizardry* or *Pool of Radiance* together. In these cases, the player at the keyboard simply asks the others what they'd like their character to do (attack, cast a spell, etc.) and executes it for them. Imagine, by contrast, how awkward and boring this would be with a game like *Track & Field*!

FIGURE 1.8 Archery in *Skyrim* also requires some physical skill to pull off. You can make things easier with certain perks, but accuracy and speed are still essential.

Let's consider now how archery is represented in *Akalabeth* and a few later CRPGs such as *Skyrim* (Figure 1.8). The first important thing to know about bows in *Akalabeth* is that magis can't use them (sorry, Gandalf). The second is that their maximum damage score is 4 (whereas a rapier's is 10). Third, the bow is a ranged weapon, meaning it can hit enemies that are up to five steps ahead of where the character is facing. Otherwise, the weapon is treated like the others; it either hits or misses depending on the character's dexterity attribute as well as the level of the monster and dungeon. The amount of damage it does is determined by the weapon's damage range (1–4) and the character's strength attribute. Firing the bow is done by pressing the letter *a* for attack followed by *b* for bow. Quite a lot is left to the player's imagination; we don't hear the twang of the bowstring or see arrows flying toward monsters.

Later CRPGs such as *Pool of Radiance* (1988) take several more factors into consideration, such as the type and quality of the bow (short, long, composite, etc.); range; dexterity; a score called THAC0, or To Hit Armor Class Zero; and the armor class of the target. We don't need to get into the math of any of this here; the point is that this model, which is based on TSR's *Advanced Dungeons & Dragons* rules, strives for complexity and realism by bringing more variables into the equation. Keep in mind, however, that as a system devised for tabletop play, it still strives to keep these calculations manageable with a handful of dice and some scratch paper. The computer just makes this process more accurate and efficient. Incidentally, one nice difference from both *Akalabeth* and *AD&D* is that in *Pool of Radiance* we do get to hear the twanging string and see an arrow fly across the screen.

Naturally, not every CRPG designer feels obligated to stick with the limitations imposed by tabletop games. Indeed, some games factor in so many elements that it would be all but impossible to calculate them by hand. Tim Lang, a veteran of New World Computing (makers of the *Might & Magic* series), recalls a conversation he had with Jon Van Caneghem, the company's founder. Lang asked him why the combat system of *Might & Magic* is so complex compared to *Dungeons & Dragons'*. Caneghem responded, "It's more complicated because it can be, and it makes for a better game. We don't have to worry about teaching all this stuff to players because it's all handled behind the scenes for them." It's a valid point, but I argue that even if the computer can easily handle far more calculations than a poor human, it doesn't necessarily make for a better game. As we'll see, to be effective as a role-playing system, it must be simple and intuitive enough for humans to handle in their head.

Later games became quite good at not only handling all the math for the player, but also in effect hiding the fact that there was math there at all. For instance, in BioWare's classic *Star Wars: Knights of the Old Republic* CRPG, a player can easily play all the way through and never realize it was actually using the *Dungeons & Dragons,* 3rd Edition–based "d20 System" for its core game mechanics.

But let's get back on target with the archery example: Regardless of whether an individual CRPG is based on a tabletop RPG, the player's first crucial task is to learn how ranged combat is modeled in the game (if at all!), and then what aspects of it he or she can manipulate to improve the odds for an archer character. This could include improving an archery skill, raising a dexterity attribute, or acquiring a better bow. The point is that in a pure CRPG, the player's own speed, timing, or accuracy with the keyboard, mouse, or game controller makes no difference (outside of accidentally hitting the wrong button or issuing the wrong commands). As soon as these things begin to matter, we've crossed over into action RPGs.

Shane: See! Look there! The definition of a CRPG's already going wonky, not straight as an arrow one might say. And there are some gamers who say an action RPG **is** a—

Matt: Keep quiet! How can I knock that apple off your head if you keep talking? Twang!

If the sales of games like *The Elder Scrolls V: Skyrim* and other action RPGs are any indication, mainstream gamers desire more physicality than we find in games like *Akalabeth*. As we'll see, much of CRPG history amounts to how (and how well) individual designers balance physicality or action with statistical reasoning or tactics in their games. Nevertheless, for us, a pure CRPG requires only trivial physical ability on the part of the player.

CRPGs AS A GENRE OF ROLE-PLAYING GAMES

Though CRPGs have much in common with their tabletop ancestors, they are in crucial ways fundamentally different. Whereas the tabletop games benefit enormously from the players and the Game Master's (GM's) ability to improvise story and dramatic elements on-the-fly, the CRPG's underlying hardware lets it perform millions if not billions of operations per second. This makes CRPGs better at following and enforcing complicated systems of rules, but this power comes at a price when it comes to improvising.

For tabletop GMs, in-depth knowledge and enforcement of the rules are not only unnecessary, but in many cases undesirable. Many great GMs never bother to learn all the rules of the systems they play; their priority is an imaginative gameplay experience, not slavish fidelity to a rule system. This point was nicely illustrated at PAX Prime in 2014, where GM Chris Perkins (who wrote the rules for multiple editions of *Dungeons & Dragons*) ran into a situation he didn't know how to handle: the players wanted to impale a dragon with a zeppelin. After admitting he didn't know how the rules would apply in this situation—and perhaps none would apply—Perkins simply concluded, to great applause from the audience: "You just do it. You just run this thing right through!" RPG players will constantly try creative new approaches to the same set of problems, or at least say different things than they said during previous sessions. Otherwise, they would not be playing a game at all, but rather performing one.

It's practically a law of the universe that tabletop RPG players will do things and tear off in directions the GM never considered. It may drive some GMs nuts, but it's a huge part of the fun. While this ability to improvise solutions to unanticipated problems is routine in a tabletop RPG, it's cumbersome in a CRPG. This is because computers can do nothing *but* follow rules. If the option to impale a dragon with a zeppelin was not implemented into the program, it simply can't happen. For fans of tabletop RPGs, this is a serious limitation, as it was for Garriott:

> What's interesting about the early days of *Dungeons & Dragons* was that rules were irrelevant. The rules were insufficient and nobody cared. Instead, it was a group of people sitting around

the people having an interactive narrative. When the gamemaster described a scenario, as long as the rest of the participants came up with something that sounded clever, sure, it worked. Since there were no rules, the only things that mattered was whether you had a good storyteller at the helm and highly participative players.

My *D&D* campaigns were laid out very logically, but they had another part that we've still never mastered in computer gaming. There were lots of very custom portals and gateways to get past, such as a big door with a pentagram on the front and lots of spots for colored gems. You had to go find the gems and put them in the right spots to open the door. It's very easy to describe all this verbally, but in a computer game, that's a custom piece of code for just one moment in the entire scenario. My *D&D* campaigns were moment after moment of these little puzzles that were very difficult to execute cost-effectively in a computer game.

However, the same hardware that makes CRPGs limited in some ways can make them unlimited in others. In fact, the entire gameworld of a CRPG can be generated on-the-fly by algorithms. *Akalabeth* creates its own "infinite" dungeons in just this way. While the quests are simplistic compared to the tabletop RPGs of the era—you do little more than slay monsters for Lord British—the game's procedurally generated maps let you play it over and over again without getting bored. Unless the player inputs the same "lucky number" asked for at the beginning of each game, the dungeons will be laid out in a fresh pattern, making any of the players' maps from previous sessions obsolete. Thus, even Garriott himself wouldn't know his way around *Akalabeth*'s dungeons!

A case can be made that *Akalabeth* and other procedurally generated games are the best sort of CRPGs, turning their most severe limitation into their most powerful asset. Rather than strive to imitate the social and creative dynamics of tabletop RPGs—something CRPGs are generally terrible at—they take the opposite approach, leveraging the computer's strengths to create procedurally generated content, which computers are great at.

To put it another way, what the tabletop RPG is to custom manufacturing, the CRPG is to mass production. What is trivial for a custom auto shop—such as letting buyers choose what color paint to use—is cost-prohibitive for the other. As Henry Ford quipped, "Yes, any color so long as it's black!" As Garriott describes above, it's trivial for a GM to describe a door surrounded by sockets for gems and the actions involved in opening it. In a computer game, of course, all of this would be implemented with custom code and a number of assets (e.g., animations of the gems going into their sockets, sound effects, code to track the state of the sockets, etc.). Needless to say, computer game developers have to weigh the costs involved with every idea. Perhaps it's critical to the plot, or the game has several such doors, meaning these elements could be recycled. Otherwise, this element would likely be scrapped. It's a safe estimate that for every good idea that makes it into a finished game, there were a dozen better ones that didn't.

Of course, more sophisticated procedurally generated CRPGs, such as *Diablo* or *The Elder Scrolls II: Daggerfall* (Figure 1.9), go far beyond *Akalabeth*'s capabilities—indeed, their complexity can lead to "emergent gameplay," or outcomes that even the designers didn't realize were possible. Even an outright bug can end up as a celebrated feature. One of the best examples of this phenomenon is called "the abyss" or "the void," and it comes from *The Elder Scrolls II: Daggerfall*. Whether by accident or intention, players can find themselves outside the game's intended boundaries, yet still able to move about otherwise inaccessible areas and attack enemies who can't strike back. A video on YouTube by David Caldarola

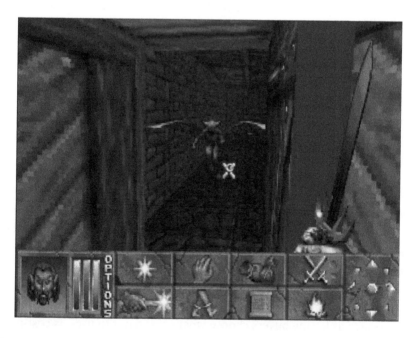

FIGURE 1.9 *The Elder Scrolls II: Daggerfall* is one of the most ambitious procedurally generated games to date. Here, Matt's about to fight a particularly vicious little imp.

demonstrates this phenomenon, and a comment there by Karen Elizabeth says it all: "I'd like to think that going into the void is magic or botched inter-dimensional travel, since this universe has some precedent for this."

Such fun oddities aside, most CRPG fans seem to prefer games with as much custom-made content as possible. With a few notable exceptions such as the games already mentioned, few hit CRPGs are primarily procedural. Instead, they balance computation with craft, fleshing out the trappings of a procedurally generated system with predefined characters, stories, lore, and events. As we'll see, over the decades designers have tried different approaches to finding the right balance. For example, in *Diablo,* Tristram Village is always the same, whereas its dungeons are different for each playthrough. Other games have little to no procedurally generated content, relying instead on the players themselves to expand their games (user-generated content). We'll return to these and related topics throughout this book.

EDUCATIONAL BENEFITS OF CRPGs

It may come as a revelation to some readers to learn that CRPGs can be educational as well as entertaining. Indeed, they hone the four basic skills that Robert Reich, author of *The Work of Nations,* argues are absolutely critical for the workplace of the future: "abstraction, system thinking, experimentation, and collaboration." Like literacy scholar James Paul Gee, author of *What Video Games Have to Teach Us About Learning and Literacy,* we want to avoid the "video games = waste of time" model and "say some positive things about them," because there is so much more going on here than the violence and sex that dominate the media's coverage of the subject. Indeed, CRPGs are not only the most fun and addictive type of computer game, but also an excellent way to learn the crucial skills identified by Reich—even if their creators aren't necessarily experts in grammar or literature.

To clarify this point, let us return to one of those twenty-five books Garriott did manage to read at college, namely Jef Raskin's *Apple II Basic Programming Manual.* Raskin, who later conceived the Apple Macintosh, insists that no amount of study was sufficient to learn programming. As he writes in the book's introduction, "Be warned that programming, though not difficult, can only be learned by *doing.* This is a book to be used, not merely perused." For aspiring game designers like Garriott, this wasn't a turn-off, but a turn-on. Indeed, Garriott adapted this "applied" or "experiential" approach to learning, as we'd call it today, to *Akalabeth.* Indeed, in all CRPGs, any sort of rote memorization or out-of-context learning is an aberration. Compare Raskin's statement with these from Garriott's five-page manual for *Akalabeth*:

> Though doest now know the basics of the game, experiment with the commands. There is much left unsaid for thee to discover in the future.... Go forth unto Akalabeth and seek adventure where thou wilst!!!

Indeed, the only explicit instruction Garriott provides is to "be sure to buy enough food so as not to starve to death." Incidentally, this is still great advice for any aspiring game designer.

Shane: Didn't you say that if enough people bought this book **we** wouldn't starve to death?
Matt: Actually, I said **I** wouldn't starve.

What could possibly be educational about slaying monsters in a dungeon? According to Gee, "Video games situate meaning in a multimodal space through embodied experiences to solve problems and reflect on the intricacies of the design of imagined worlds and the design of both real and imagined social relationships and identities in the modern world." In other words, the actual *content* of a game, such as its story, characters, lore, and so on, is less important than the roles and skills it nurtures. A gamer playing a new CRPG must act like a scientist, exploring and probing the gameworld, devising theories based on observations, re-probing, and finally reflecting and rethinking those hypotheses in light of what amounts to experiment. Here we see two of Reich's skills being developed—system thinking and experimentation.

Imagine playing *Akalabeth* for the first time. Some of the most important decisions are made at the start. After the game rolls some virtual dice to compute hit points, strength, dexterity, stamina, wisdom, and gold, the game asks, "Shalt thou play with these qualities?" Even if you read the in-game instructions and the manual, there's little useful advice for determining whether you should indeed play with these qualities or reroll. Wisdom, for instance, is described as being "used in special (quest) routines." Gee's point is that much of our educational system is like this explanation; we may read and memorize such facts, but outside of context or "embodied experience," they mean nothing. You really learn about wisdom in *Akalabeth* only by repeatedly playing the game, adjusting the score, observing the results, and reflecting on the playthrough. Eventually, an understanding of the wisdom score's effect on the system emerges, but by that time the manual's definition is valuable only as a reminder of what you learned by doing.

Gee is not saying that knowing how wisdom works in *Akalabeth* is useful in the real world. Rather, his argument is that the mental habits such games demand and reward end up being far more useful than much of the disembodied learning we get in traditional schools. In the same way that playing *Akalabeth* is more fulfilling than reading its manual, playing a CRPG is closer to doing science than memorizing definitions out of a science textbook, even if its gameworld is entirely fictional. Once a child (of any age) has thoroughly internalized this critical thinking process, he or she can apply it anywhere, even, perhaps, to that boring science class. The ability to abstract knowledge from one realm and apply it to another is, of course, another of Reich's key skills for success, yet criminally undervalued in schools.

Lincoln E. Moses, a pioneer in the field of statistics, defines his field as "a body of methods for learning from experience." This definition applies equally well to CRPGs, which as we've discussed are themselves elaborate statistical models of experience. CRPG designers use statistics to model their systems, working out formulas for computing a myriad of probabilities—what are the odds that the character will spot a rat or be surprised by it? Will the rat hit or miss when it swipes at him? If its claws connect, how much damage is absorbed by the character's armor—plate, chain, or leather? These formulas can get complex as armor durability, the character's dexterity, and even magical effects are factored in. Yet players are able to learn from their experience just as their characters do, gradually getting a feel for how all of these intertwining mechanics function together as a system. They may be unable to write out the formulas for any of it, but they've learned by doing it.

Compare this type of learning to what happens in schools, which, as Gee points out, privilege the retention of facts (such as formulas), spoon-fed without any sort of context, with few opportunities to question, experiment, or innovate upon any of it. Students are not expected to figure out their own solutions, but merely to follow a narrowly prescribed path. No wonder so many students find school boring and video games like CRPGs so engrossing!

Reich's final skill for success in the careers of the future is collaboration, and here is where we can best distinguish CRPGs from wargames in terms of benefits. Both Reich and Gee (and countless other education experts) stress the importance of collaborative learning; students learn as much (if not more) by discussing topics with each other as they do by quietly listening to a teacher. This social dimension of education is all but absent in many schools, where often the greatest challenge is just staying awake.

> *Shane:* I once stayed up all night in high school reading *Dragonlance* and fell asleep during the last class of school the next day. Great nap but the teacher let me sleep through the final bell and told the students not to wake me up on the way out. I bolted awake with slobber all over the desk and sort of lurched around the room like a dazed zombie trying to get oriented while the teacher just watched.
>
> *Matt:* Wake up, Shane!

Arguably, this is the area where CRPGs have less to offer than either tabletop games or massively multiplayer online role-playing games (MMORPGs). In both of these game types, players must frequently work together to learn and play the game. Kids can learn a great deal about collaboration from tabletop RPGs. Just having an opportunity to talk to each other face-to-face seems worthwhile, and shy people are more likely to open up when acting out a role rather than "just being yourself." This said, access to a group of friends willing to play these games is not guaranteed, especially in rural areas. Even if such a group exists, it can be next to impossible to get everyone together for weekly or even monthly sessions. Thus, these groups tend to be quite small, dedicated, and not necessarily open to casual players dropping in and out of their campaigns.

For these and other reasons, MMORPGs seem like a better option. However, here we have the opposite problems—a massive player base, but one that's anonymous. Sure, it's easier to find people to play with, but they may be less than ideal. Beyond dealing with the "toxicity" of degenerate player communities or scammers, new players may find themselves harassed or excluded by veteran players who have no wish to mingle with "n00bs." Indeed, far from teaching effective collaboration skills, these games may well end up teaching players how to be hermits or elitist jerks! Even if an MMORPG community seems perfectly benign, parents might not like the idea of their children playing with strangers (Figure 1.10).

For this and related reasons, even if CRPGs tend to be single-player, they may teach effective collaboration better than MMORPGs. Many CRPGs let players control more than a single character. Some games allow players to create and control an entire crew or party of adventurers, as in *Wizardry,* or directly or indirectly control predefined characters, as in the

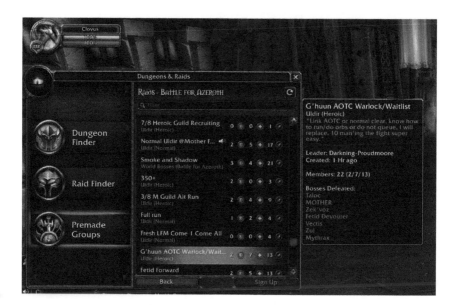

FIGURE 1.10 While you can find plenty of friendly people in games like *World of Warcraft*, you'll also find players with no tolerance for novices. Getting booted out of a group for making a simple mistake can be discouraging, so avoid groups like this one if you're new to the raid—and maybe even if you're not.

later *Ultima* games, *Baldur's Gate,* or *Dragon Age: Origins.* Winning these games requires that these characters successfully leverage each other's strengths and weaknesses. While it's a stretch to call this "collaboration" from an educator's perspective, players are clearly managing a (mostly) idealized form of collaboration, and designers like Garriott take pains to use this opportunity to promote good ethics (see our discussion of *Ultima IV* in Chapter 7). To the extent that these characters are realistically autonomous and capable of arguing with or even turning on the player, successful players must learn to collaborate with people unlike themselves. Abusing or neglecting them can result in their leaving the party, possibly causing the players to lose the game. Thus, as paradoxical as it may seem, CRPGs can be more effective at teaching people skills than communities of other human players in MMORPGs!

Hopefully, I've shown the educational benefits that CRPGs have to offer, which are precisely the skills that Reich and Gee have identified as crucial for thriving in the workplaces of the future. Tireless reformers like Gee have made some progress innovating our schools with lessons gleaned from good game designers—a movement awkwardly labeled "gamification"—but there's still plenty of room for growth.

THE EVOLUTION AND TAXONOMY OF CRPGs

CRPG development has not taken a linear path, and, as we'll see, the most successful games of any given era are not necessarily the most technologically sophisticated or innovative. Indeed, time and time again, we'll see good design and attention to detail trump advanced graphics or interfaces. We can see this advantage clearly in the late 1980s and early 1990s, when turn-based two-dimensional games sat comfortably alongside the new real-time 3D games on the shelves.

Nevertheless, we'll need some way to keep our bearings, and what seems most logical is to proceed more or less chronologically. For the sake of the narrative, in these chapters we will focus on the most influential games, many of which spawned new subgenres as others rushed in to imitate and innovate upon them. For instance, *Rogue* and *Diablo* popularized the *Rogue*-like and *Diablo*-like subgenres, respectively. Meanwhile, Garriott's *Ultima* series introduced new innovations with each iteration. Some of them were more successful than others, but they always sent ripples across the entire computer games industry. More obscure but still notable games are listed in the appendix, where we provide basic information and brief reviews and commentary on what makes them notable.

Before we get into all these games, though, we'll discuss the Dark Age, so named because many of these games are lost to history. Comparatively little is known about these progenitors apart from the recollections of those few lucky enough to have played them. The Dark Age begins in 1974, when the first CRPGs were being developed for mainframe computers such as DEC's PDP-10, and ends in 1979 with the publication of the first two CRPGs for personal computers, Garriott's *Akalabeth: World of Doom* and Epyx's *Dunjonquest: Temple of Apshai*. These two games mark the beginning of the commercial era and the beginning of the CRPG as we know it.

We'll start, however, not with the first CRPGs, but rather with the games that inspired them: pen-and-paper strategy games like *Strat-O-Matic*, wargames like *Chainmail*, the fantasy role-playing game *Dungeons & Dragons*, and finally, *Colossal Cave Adventure*, the first adventure game. Each of these games exerted a profound influence on the CRPG.

Shane: Hey, what kind of switcharoo are we pulling here? They want to read about computer RPG games, not some flippin' sportsball paper-based game simulators.

Matt: Have patience, grasshopper, it all comes together.

CHAPTER 2

Origins

When pondering the origins and inspirations of CRPGs, most writers begin with Gary Gygax and Dave Arneson's *Dungeons & Dragons* fantasy role-playing game. *Dungeons & Dragons*, or *D&D* for short, was published in 1974 and quickly swept across the country. It's still actively played today—indeed, Wizards of the Coast (the company that purchased *D&D* from TSR) reported that 2017 was the biggest year of sales for the game, ever.

There's no doubt that *D&D* played a vital role in the development of the first CRPG. Richard Garriott, creator of *Akalabeth* and *Ultima*, is a dedicated fan of the game. *Pool of Radiance, Baldur's Gate, Neverwinter Nights*, and *Icewind Dale* are just some of the *Dungeons & Dragons* CRPGs licensed by TSR and later Wizards of the Coast, publishers of the popular tabletop role-playing game (Figure 2.1).

However, if we look a bit further into the issue, we can identify four other influences that are at least as important as *D&D*, if not more: sports simulation games, tabletop wargames, the writings of J.R.R. Tolkien, and Will Crowther's *Colossal Cave Adventure*, the first true computer adventure game. Each of these made a unique and significant contribution to the genre.

BASEBALL SIMULATION GAMES

Although you might assume that fantasy football and other "fantasy" sports are a recent phenomenon, tabletop sports simulation games were popular in the 1960s and 1970s. There were dozens of spinoffs and competitors, but the most popular games were *Strat-O-Matic* (1961), *APBA* (1951), and *All Star Baseball* (1941). The first two of these games attempt to recreate the excitement of baseball using a combination of cards and dice; *All Star*

FIGURE 2.1 Countless players all over the world continue to enjoy tabletop role-playing games. Not all such games require miniatures as shown here, but they're still fun to collect—and paint, if you're so inclined.

Baseball uses spinners instead and is intended for younger players. Real statistics from current professional baseball players are used in these games, thus necessitating annual updates and creating a steady revenue stream for the game makers. It isn't just a marketing ploy; players value the accuracy of these statistics and their ability to predict actual seasons. Steven Johnson, author of *Everything Bad Is Good for You,* sums them up as "games of dice and data." *Strat-O-Matic* and *APBA* have been and remain quite popular and boast celebrity players such as Spike Lee (moviemaker), Trip Hawkins (founder of Electronic Arts), and both President Bushes.

> *Shane:* I guess you could say these games hit a home run?
> *Matt:* You're out!

Although the games are not identical, both *Strat-O-Matic* and *APBA* put players in the role of team managers. Players make decisions about batting order, starting lineups, and pitchers, then use the dice and tables to simulate the ballgame. In the case of *Strat-O-Matic,* gameplay involves cards for every baseball player and five different dice: three six-sided dice (one white, two colored), and, notably, a twenty-sided die. Players roll the six-sided dice to determine the outcome of the batting (the numbers correspond to tables on the cards). There are a fair number of rules to learn, and the more advanced versions of the game even take into consideration the weather and differences among ballparks. In any case, the game can be quite complex, and expert players learn the minutest details of professional baseball. The baseball-themed games were the most successful, but there were also versions for football, hockey, boxing, and other sports (Figure 2.2).

It's easy to see how much these games have in common with *D&D* and CRPGs. First, dice and statistics are used to realistically model fantasies, though here it's imaginary sporting events instead of battles with fantastic creatures. Rather than just watching sports and discussing them with friends, *Strat-O-Matic* and *APBA* players feel more actively involved in the sport, even if it is from the comfort of their bedrooms. Later on, we'll see the same sort of trend among *D&D* players, when Tolkien-obsessed fans wanted to do more than simply read about fantastic battles with orcs and dangerous treks into dank, dark places.

FIGURE 2.2 Baseball and other sports simulation games were a key influence on, among others, Brian Fargo and Joel Billings of Interplay and SSI, respectively. *Strat-O-Matic* is still played today, though now there are online and mobile options in addition to the board game.

All of this involvement comes from what some would see as a very unlikely source: the mathematical science of statistics. While this subject seems hopelessly dry and abstract to many people, it nevertheless drove some of the most compelling and addictive games ever designed.

> *Shane:* Speaking of statistics, isn't it statistically improbable they would be so important to pursuits of imagination and fancy?
>
> *Matt:* Never tell me the odds!

While we're on the subject, it's worth asking a few questions about why these statistical games emerged when and where they did. The formal study of statistics is a relatively new field, becoming important only after World War I, when the United States and other nations emerged as industrial leaders. Leaders of both government and industry needed more accurate ways to measure increasing populations and the effects of policies. Of particular interest to the government, of course, were better ways to conduct the census and collect taxes. These needs fueled the launch of the nascent computer industry—companies like IBM were called upon to help the government manage the massive amount of occupational data needed to comply with the Social Security Act of 1935.

Avid players of games like *APBA* and *Strat-O-Matic* found themselves well prepared for new careers that required familiarity with statistics. Incidentally, one of many such gamers-turned-professionals was Trip Hawkins, founder of Electronic Arts, who credited *Strat-O-Matic* and *D&D* with helping him make "invaluable social connections" and making his brain "more active."[1]

These games are still going today but have been eclipsed by the rise of fantasy sports, hugely popular games based on many of the same principles—but typically involving a computer to handle the statistics. Some other key differences are that players draft their own teams and follow their statistics through the real-time season (rather than the previous one). Several prominent commercial sports hubs offer fantasy sports for free on their websites to stoke interest in their team as well as professional sports in general.

TABLETOP WARGAMES

Wargames have a much longer pedigree than the sports simulation games mentioned above. The first such game probably arose among Prussian officers in the early 19th century, where it was used as a training exercise.

The game, called *Kriegspiel* ("war play"), involved both dice and an experienced officer who could referee the game based on his own combat experience (much like the DM in *D&D*). This practice spread to other countries and other branches of the military, such as the U.S. Naval Academy, where it continues to serve as a useful tool for training officers and analyzing actual tactical situations. Although the professional activity and the hobby have much in common, we're concerned with the hobbyist game.

In the early 20th century, H. G. Wells, one of the godfathers of science fiction, wrote two books outlining rules for games involving toy soldiers and spring-loaded miniature cannons. There were also naval wargames available, such as *Naval War Game*, developed by Fletcher Pratt in 1940. This game involved small wooden ships, complicated mathematical formulas, and a tape measure to mark off distances to scale. In each case, the key factor was a random element (usually dice) to make the outcome of any battle realistically unpredictable. This random factor is what differentiates wargames from games like chess (Figure 2.3).

"Miniature wargames," whether involving toy soldiers or ships, could be expensive hobbies, owing to the large number of materials they required. Nevertheless, gaming clubs arose throughout the 20th century, and by 1952, Charles S. Roberts had published the first mass-market wargame, *Tactics*.

FIGURE 2.3   Wargaming with miniatures is a fun hobby enjoyed by players all over the world. Shown here is a game from the 2015 Festival del Gioci in Italy. It uses miniatures made from paper. Photo by Moroboshi.

This game included maps and cardboard counters rather than miniature soldiers. It was played on a square grid and factored in the effects of the terrain on troop movement. Roberts went on to found Avalon Hill, which soon

> Gary Gygax was an avid wargamer and tried to shop *Dungeons & Dragons* to a baffled and bemused Avalon Hill before publishing it himself.

dominated the war and strategic board games market. Later wargames from Avalon Hill introduced many features now common in CRPGs, such as hexagonal movement and zones of control. Avalon Hill went on to publish several highly successful wargames based on specific historical battles, such as *Panzerblitz* (1970), *Midway* (1964), and *Blitzkrieg* (1965).

Miniature wargaming made a return in the 1970s, when economies of scale placed them at last within reach of the average teenager. In ways similar to train modeling, fans of miniature wargaming lavish time and energy on painting miniatures and reproducing scenery to look as realistic (or as fantastic) as possible. These games are much more tactile and visual than other wargames, allowing gamers to think in three dimensions well before the rise of advanced computer graphics.

Of particular interest for our purposes is a 1971 miniatures wargame named *Chainmail*, designed by Gary Gygax and Jeff Perren. *Chainmail*, as the name implies, is a medieval-based wargame, and it introduced several conventions that would become standard in later fantasy role-playing games and CRPGs. The famous "fantasy supplement" adds fantasy creatures made popular by J.R.R. Tolkien, including hobbits, balrogs, and ents. It also has wizards who can cast powerful spells to produce fireballs and lightning. Some of the game's miniatures represent individual heroes rather than corps of troops, an important step away from traditional strategy games and toward what would soon become proper role-playing.

Indeed, it is this game that led most directly to *D&D*, and the first edition of *D&D*'s rules even suggest players own a copy of *Chainmail*. Both Gygax and Dave Arneson (co-creators of *D&D*) were avid wargamers, and *Chainmail* is a clear precursor to what would soon evolve into fantasy role-playing as we know it today. There are other connections between wargaming and CRPGs. Strategic Simulations, Inc. (SSI), one of the most influential CRPG developers, first made its mark publishing computer-based wargames. There has also been a persistent tension between the more wargaming aspects of CRPGs (e.g., the strategy and tactics component) and the role-playing aspects (i.e., stories, characters, and dialog).

Throughout this history, we'll see that developers have experimented quite often to find the perfect ratio of math to make-believe.

> *Shane:* A lot of gamers call that "roll" playing versus "role" playing. Many heated and prolonged debates have occurred since the dawn of tabletop RPGs over which is "better," and they still continue today. I've considered selling tickets.
>
> *Matt:* Roll up! Roll up! See the fight of the century!

J.R.R. TOLKIEN AND FANTASY ROLE-PLAYING

In some ways, games like *Strat-O-Matic* are the most socially acceptable of the games we've identified as precursors to the CRPG. The reason for this acceptance is the close association with professional sports, a traditionally manly activity and thus an appropriate interest for men and boys of all ages (indeed, *Strat-O-Matic* was frequently played by fathers with their sons). Wargaming, particularly of the historical variety, can also seem acceptable. Famous men throughout the centuries have been interested in famous battles and brilliant tactics, and, if nothing else, few parents have a problem with their teenagers learning history.

However, to outsiders, fantasy role-playing may seem juvenile, alien, or both. It's one thing to walk past a group of boys passionately discussing the stats of their favorite pitchers and batters, or to saunter past wargamers in a heated discussion of the Battle of Gettysburg—even if the sight of grown men "playing with toys" strikes some as childish.

It's quite another matter, however, when people are displaying the same sort of passion for sorcery and dragons, much less for demons and priests of darkness. Indeed, many parents and concerned citizens considered fantasy role-playing games a serious threat—both to the people who play them and to society at large. A variety of memes show that this tension still exists today. A typical one shows a man in a football jersey watching a game; the text reads, "Knows statistics of every player on his fantasy football team. 'Wow, you play role-playing games? Nerd!'" However, before we get into the social and cultural aspects of this topic, let's take a look at the history of fantasy role-playing and try to determine the scope of its influence on CRPGs.

> *Shane:* I like the meme that says: "*D&D*: Nerdiest game ever. Requires friends". Gimme a hug, you lovable rat-killing galoot!
>
> *Matt:* Nerd!

Perhaps the best place to start is with the English novelist J.R.R. Tolkien, specifically his *The Lord of the Rings* novel (Tolkien intended for the work to constitute one massive tome, but it was broken into multiple volumes and first published during 1954 and 1955). However, it wasn't until the ready availability of the authorized mass-market paperback editions by Ballantine Books in the 1960s that the Tolkien phenomenon really kicked off. Of course, nowadays it's hard to find anyone who hasn't read Tolkien or at least seen the movies. It's even more difficult to find a *D&D* or CRPG fan who hasn't read and watched them all at least twice. For instance, Garriott's game, *Akalabeth,* which we discussed in the previous chapter, derives its name from *Akallabêth,* a reference to *The Silmarillion,* one of the more obscure works from the Tolkien canon (it's also evident that Garriott wasn't lying about his trouble with spelling).

Tolkien's work influenced much of what later became staples of the fantasy genre, such as our conceptions of magic, elves, dwarves, orcs, and so on, and plenty of role-playing games (computerized or otherwise) borrow directly from his stories. What's more critical, though, is his obsessive attention to detail. He didn't just write novels; he spent the better part of his life creating a vivid fictional world.[2] Unlike the typical "swords and sorcery" novels and stories that appeared in pulp magazines, Tolkien's works are much deeper and more complex, involving epic struggles rather than the antics of a single swashbuckling hero.

Tolkien's key academic interests were language and philology, and he created artificial languages for the various peoples in his book. Finally, he studied ancient mythologies, particularly those of the Celts, Scandinavians, and Germans, assimilating this diverse information into a coherent whole. These interests were, of course, shared by Garriott, who also created his own rune system and a rich lore for his *Ultima* games.

Tolkien's grand achievement was Middle-earth, a fantastic setting so vivid and detailed that it seemed to many readers to be a real place, an alternate reality they longed to visit. Passing references and allusions in the books hinted at vast, untold stories and mysteries. Adoring fans pored over the many appendices, references, and other materials devised by Tolkien or others. In short, the Tolkien phenomenon paved the way for a new type of game, one that would allow fans to go beyond reading and actually enter exciting worlds of fantasy to play a role in their own adventures.

Two diehard wargamers offered them that chance. In 1974, Gary Gygax (Figure 2.4) and Dave Arneson created *Dungeons & Dragons*, published by Gygax's company, Tactical Studies Rules (TSR). Arneson had been

FIGURE 2.4 Gary Gygax is often credited as the father of *Dungeons & Dragons*, though he had plenty of help from Dave Arneson and others. He did, however, do more to popularize it than anyone else, and was a frequent fixture at gaming conventions. He passed away in 2008. Photo by Moroboshi.

experimenting with fantasy-based miniature wargames with *Blackmoor*, a medieval barony of his own creation. Instead of corps or armies, *Blackmoor* lets players control a single character who gains increased strength and new abilities as he or she wins battles. Arneson's players were pleased with the game, but unhappy with the rather arbitrary way Arneson handled combat. Fortunately, he was in contact with Gygax, who sent him a copy of *Chainmail* to provide a more coherent structure to the fighting portions of the game. When Gygax himself sat down with Arneson to play the new game, he knew they had a hit on their hands. The new rules worked up by Gygax and Arneson became *Dungeons & Dragons*.

However, we must note that the history of *D&D* is more complex and controversial than this casual summary implies. Though Gygax and Arneson rightly receive much of the credit, there were many others involved, including David Wesely, an avid wargamer who also helped revitalize wargaming as a training exercise for the U.S. Army. According to Wesely, it was he who took the crucial step when he created a scenario in which players did not control armies, but rather individuals such as a mayor or tavern owner. However, Wesely left for Vietnam soon after this innovation, leaving the nascent game in Arneson's hands.

Since this is a book about *computer* role-playing games, we'll refer readers interested in these matters to Shannon Appleline's three-volume series *Designers & Dragons* (2015), Jon Peterson's *Playing at the World* (2012), and Michael Witwer's *Empire of Imagination* (2015). Your plucky co-authors have also had the pleasure of discussing these topics with the experts on their respective interview shows: Refer to *Matt Chat* episodes 344–347 (with Michael Witwer), 369 (with David Wesely), and *Shane Plays Geek Talk* episodes 61 (with Michael Witwer), 65 (with Jon Peterson), and 112 (with Witwer and Peterson).

In any case, the combination of *Chainmail* and Arneson's *Blackmoor* was the special sauce. *Dungeons & Dragons* offers several key innovations to the well-established wargaming model. Playing a character rather than commanding a large force feels fundamentally different; the emphasis shifts from abstract tactical considerations to something more like improvisational theater. Players love creating and acting out characters such as a noble elf wizard, a cunning hobbit thief, or a gruff dwarf warrior. The game also shifts the role of the Game (Dungeon) Master from a referee into a full-fledged narrator, who keeps the story going in addition to enforcing the rules and arbitrating disputes among the players.

In a typical game of *D&D*, players go on an adventure, or story-based quest, either designed by the Dungeon Master or derived from a published module. A series of interconnected adventures is called a campaign, and the shared setting of these campaigns is called a campaign setting. TSR is still widely regarded today for its detailed and imaginative campaign settings, such as Forgotten Realms and Dragonlance, which are also used in some of the most successful CRPGs. Most are fantasy based, though there are others with science fiction and horror themes such as Spelljammer and Ravenloft. Of course, TSR was not the only publisher of role-playing games. Following in the wake of *Dungeons & Dragons* came a number of competitors with a wide variety of genres, such as Flying Buffalo's fantasy RPG *Tunnels and Trolls* (1975), Game Designers' Workshop's "hard" science fiction RPG *Traveller* [sic] (1977), Fantasy Games Unlimited's superhero-themed RPG *Villains and Vigilantes* (1979), and the *Generic Universal RolePlaying System* (GURPS), published in 1986 by Steve Jackson Games. The advantage of *GURPS* is that it can be applied to any setting whatsoever, fictional or historical.

Fallout, one of the best-known and most influential CRPGs, actually started life as an adaptation of the *GURPS* tabletop RPG.

Between 1977 and 1979, TSR published *Advanced Dungeons & Dragons* (*AD&D*), a better-organized and expanded version of the original that many consider less a sequel than an entirely new game (a reasonable view, considering "Basic" *Dungeons & Dragons* and *Advanced Dungeons & Dragons* were published simultaneously with new books and resources each for several years). Volumes like the *Monster Manual* provide rich detail to the game, making it seem nearly as vivid as Tolkien's Middle-earth. For our purposes, the most significant later editions are *Advanced Dungeons & Dragons,* 2nd Edition (1989) and *Dungeons & Dragons,* 3rd Edition (2000) (which was updated to "3.5" in 2003). These games make significant and sometimes controversial innovations and are used in several important CRPGs that we'll discuss in later chapters.

> *Shane:* Although mentioned in the first edition, *AD&D,* 2nd Edition is when the (in) famous THAC0 system became a widely used game mechanic. It stands for "To Hit Armor Class Zero (0)" and helped streamline the combat attack rules. OUCH! What the heck?
>
> *Matt:* What? I was just testing my THAC0.

Early *D&D* players often used miniatures imported from *Chainmail* or other wargames, though this feature was soon pushed to the fringes of fantasy role-playing. Since combat and other matters could be handled verbally, the miniatures seemed unnecessary or even a hindrance to some, even if they did help players visualize combat. Significantly, there have been very few purely text-based CRPGs, and even the earliest CRPGs were quite graphically advanced for their time. This difference makes sense when we consider that it is the verbal nature of *D&D* that makes it so appealing; a great part of the fun is the playacting. Specifically, players are asked to speak in character and to use first-person to describe their actions (e.g., "I cast a lightning bolt at the minotaur!"), preferably with an appropriate accent.

The most realized form of such play is called live-action role-playing, or LARPing, which can be described as improvisational theater with rules. LARP players dress up in costumes, wield (harmless) weapons, and address each other strictly as characters within the setting (Figure 2.5). In some ways, LARP

Playing through encounters and combats in a tabletop RPG without the use of a battle map and miniatures is called "theater of the mind" by most players.

FIGURE 2.5 Live-action role-playing, or LARPing, often involves elaborate props and costumes. Shown here is the Hardenstein Adventurers Group: (left to right) Anja Arenz, Chris Kunz, Dossmo, Niamh, Paolo Tratzky, and Svenja Schoenmackers. Photo by Ralfhuels.

is comparable to the activities of the Society for Creative Anachronism. Founded in 1966, the SCA is a historical reenactment group focused primarily on the Middle Ages and the Renaissance. SCA events typically include jousting, fencing, and archery, as well as non-combat-related skills like cooking, dancing, and even embroidery. A related activity is Renaissance fairs, though these are much more audience-oriented—visitors aren't expected to dress up or act in character, though doing so may be strongly encouraged (not to mention fun!). The SCA and Renaissance fairs are much less rule-oriented than LARP, but they're worth keeping in mind as part of the cultural milieu that led to (and continues to fuel) the CRPG. Garriott is just one of many CRPG designers active in the SCA, and he begins his masterpiece *Ultima IV* with a virtual visit to one of these "RenFairs." If you would like to learn more about the SCA, refer to *Shane Plays Geek Talk* episode 103 for a full discussion with a longtime member as well as the president of the SCA himself (who once wrestled a bear, no foolin').

If playacting is so vital to fantasy role-playing, you might wonder where the statistics come in. During the typical role-playing game, much of the number crunching is provided by the Game Master, who has a bevy of tables and charts at his or her disposal. Players are asked to roll their dice at certain intervals to determine the outcome of various events (such as who will strike first in combat, whether a trap is successfully spotted or disarmed, and so on). One of the key questions in all such gaming is whether the math should be the focus of the gameplay or transparent, handled mostly behind the scenes by the Game Master.

For example, a warrior might be described in the game as a level 3, but it's ridiculous to think that warriors themselves would actually use this kind of terminology. Parodies make this point quite humorously, usually involving some arrogant wizard warning his enemies, "Back off—I'm a level 20." Other wits have poked fun at the idea of experience points. Several role-playing games introduce alternative systems, such as the skills-based system introduced in the 1977 science fiction game *Traveller*. The key difference there is a character creation system that factors in education and background. Basically, players can opt to have their characters begin with more education and better skills, but then face penalties incurred by age. Rather than striving to gain levels, characters follow a chosen career path, rising in rank to acquire wealth, titles, and political power (we'll see this model adapted for several CRPGs). In *Traveller*, player characters can suffer injuries or even die during character creation before the game actually begins! The 1978 game *RuneQuest* further refines the skills-based system, abandoning the class system and focusing entirely on skills (comparable to the role-playing system in Ion Storm's *Deus Ex*). Combat is considered just another branch of skills, and gamers can easily adapt the system to cover other genres. *D&D* itself has adapted its rules in modern editions to allow players to either roll their characters randomly with dice or use a point-based buy system.

Nuances aside, all fantasy role-playing games require a statistics-based rule system to provide structure for the playacting and make-believe; without them, the game would seem hopelessly arbitrary and, assuming you're not in it totally for the improv, probably not much fun to play. What we'll see over the course of this history of CRPGs is this tension between math and narrative, with some games hiding most of the math from the player, whereas others foreground it.

In 2000, Wizards of the Coast (who had acquired TSR in 1997) published the aforementioned *Dungeons & Dragons*, 3rd Edition, introducing a "skills and feat" system and fewer class restrictions. These changes allow players significantly more options for personalizing their characters. The 3rd Edition also simplifies some of the more complicated calculations such as altering THAC0 to the "AC 10" mechanic, while at the same time adding crunchier tactical combat mechanics like attacks of opportunity. Not everyone is happy with these changes, naturally, arguing that in some cases they simply dumb down the game so that younger or less-dedicated players can understand the gameplay (the old anti-"n00b" elitism we noted in the preceding chapter) and in other cases change the game simply for the sake of selling more books. We'll see a similar sort of complaint when we discuss the action role-playing games like Blizzard's *Diablo* (1996), which some old-school CRPG fans argue are too simplistic and designed purely for the masses.

As noted previously, it is all-too-easy to get carried away and assume that CRPGs are little more than computerized adaptations of *D&D*. This claim disregards one of the most critical aspects of conventional *D&D*—namely, the playacting. As Daniel Mackay, author of *The Fantasy Role-Playing Game*, puts it, "In the role-playing game the rules are but a framework that facilitates the performance of the players and the game master." Though it's certainly possible for a CRPG fan to pretend to be a character, even going so far as to dress the part, it is doubtful that the computer appreciates these antics. Furthermore, the scope of possible actions is greatly reduced when a gamer is playing with a program rather than a creative and deft Game Master, who can always find ways to deal with unexpected developments and even reward such behavior. This limitation is particularly felt during dialog sequences in CRPGs, where the player is often presented with only a small menu of preprogrammed choices instead, of, well, the whole range of human language.

Of course, one place where we see this distinction wearing away is in online role-playing games, first in MUDs (multiuser dungeons) and now in MMORPGs (massively multiplayer online role-playing games). With now-ubiquitous equipment such as headset microphones and ever more realistic graphics, it is possible that the performance aspects of traditional fantasy role-playing will reemerge. However, let us table this discussion for now (pun intended).

COLOSSAL CAVE ADVENTURE

So far, we've identified sports simulation games, wargaming, and fantasy role-playing games as the progenitors of the CRPG. The technical correlations are easy to see. Each of these games relied on statistics and random numbers (dice) to model imaginary events, be they baseball games, Civil War battles, or wizard duels. More important, however, is their cultural impact. Although people have played games in every society, it's still common to hear them described primarily as activities for children, with the few exceptions (board, card, and dice games) viewed either as frivolous amusements or opportunities to win money.

Games like *Strat-O-Matic, Chainmail,* and *D&D* helped form a subculture of gamers, particularly among teenagers and young adults. The more hardcore of these gamers spend a great deal of time not only playing but thinking about and discussing these games with others. Many create their own variations or even entirely new games to share with friends. For a small but increasing number of people, gaming is no longer "just a hobby" or something to be grown out of, but a lifestyle—one that demands active engagement. It's not, however, entertainment for the masses. According to one large manufacturer, "It's not a mainstream hobby; it requires too much active participation from the participants to ever capture a significant part of our society who have been spoon fed passive entertainment all their lives." Of course, these gamers have long been viewed with suspicion or disdain by many around them. Undoubtedly, the game that caught the most flak was *D&D*, which was the subject of all manner of wild and unfounded accusations that we need not rehearse here. Fortunately, it would take more than a few naysayers to quash gaming culture.

One man who contributed greatly to that gaming culture is Will Crowther, known to history as the author of the famous *Colossal Cave Adventure* and the founder of the interactive fiction or adventure game genre. Also known as *Adventure* or simply *Advent, Colossal Cave Adventure* immerses players into a virtual world full of puzzles and perils (Figure 2.6). Although graphical games had existed at least since 1962, Crowther's game is composed entirely of text, a fact that hastily led to its label as "interactive fiction." Gameplay consists of reading brief passages of text (describing the character's location or visible objects) and responding with simple, two-word commands (e.g., "GET TORCH," "GO NORTH"). Although certainly primitive by the standards of later text-based adventure games, *Colossal Cave Adventure* nevertheless established a new gaming paradigm.

Crowther, a professional programmer, designed his game sometime in 1975 and distributed it on the ARPANET, the progenitor of today's Internet. Since it was available only on large and expensive mainframe computers, its audience was limited, but word got around. While many *Colossal Cave* fans were content just to play the game, others wanted to improve it. In 1976, a twenty-two-year-old Stanford graduate student named Don Woods

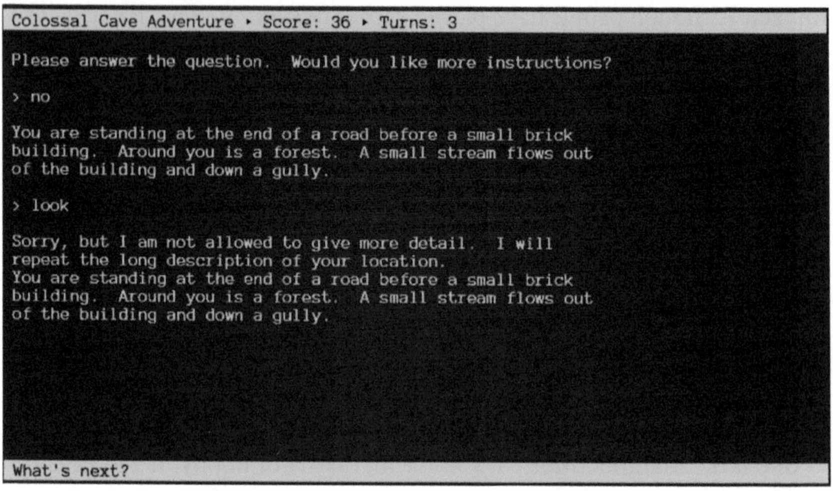

```
Colossal Cave Adventure ▸ Score: 36 ▸ Turns: 3

Please answer the question. Would you like more instructions?

> no

You are standing at the end of a road before a small brick
building. Around you is a forest. A small stream flows out
of the building and down a gully.

> look

Sorry, but I am not allowed to give more detail. I will
repeat the long description of your location.
You are standing at the end of a road before a small brick
building. Around you is a forest. A small stream flows out
of the building and down a gully.

What's next?
```

FIGURE 2.6   Text adventure games like *Colossal Cave,* shown here, rely entirely on textual descriptions and inputs for immersion. They're not as popular today as they were in the early 1980s, but new ones are still being made and enjoyed by fans of the genre.

acquired Crowther's permission to improve and expand his game, adding several fantasy elements (though Woods officially denies using Tolkien's works or *D&D* as inspirations for his work). Later adventure games like Infocom's *Zork* (c. 1977) and Sierra On-Line's *King's Quest* (1984) descend from Crowther and Woods' groundbreaking game.

Although many people acknowledge the link between *Colossal Cave Adventure* and the first CRPGs, the relationship is not obvious. *Colossal Cave Adventure* is not a CRPG, though it introduces several key innovations that paved the way to that genre. To help us better understand the relationship between this early adventure game and CRPGs, it's worthwhile to compare Crowther's original game with Woods' revised version.

Crowther was an avid caver, and he and his wife Pat had spent a great deal of time exploring Mammoth Cave in Kentucky. The cave, with its spectacular caverns with wonderful names like "Hall of the Mountain King," made a lasting impression on Crowther. Crowther wanted to create a game for his daughters that would combine the pleasures of caving with that of his other hobby, fantasy role-playing. The end result was mostly a caving simulation, albeit with a few fantasy elements, treasures, and puzzles thrown in for fun. Woods' contribution was to make these "fun" elements much more central to the gameplay.

In effect, by focusing the player on puzzles, Woods pushed the game away from role-playing and further toward what would eventually become the adventure game as we know it today. The text-based version of this genre would peak in the 1980s with the many hits of Infocom, but it is survived by independent developers and even limited commercial operations. Sierra On-Line introduced the first graphical adventure game, *Mystery House*, in 1980, but it really wasn't until its *King's Quest* series (1983) that the industry moved away from text. Later, companies like LucasArts and Cyan innovated or refined the genre. As immersive as these games may be, their lack of a statistical-based combat or skills system means we shouldn't conflate them with CRPGs.

Indeed, the brilliance of *D&D* is precisely this statistical system for determining the outcome of combat and other unpredictable events (whether characters spot a trap, detect an illusion, and so on). Rolling some dice and looking up the outcome on a standardized table seems much fairer than, say, a Game Master declaring a character dead because the player swiped the last Mountain Dew. As Lawrence Schick, the "Lore Master" of *The Elder Scrolls* series puts it, "The rules hold the group creation together and keep it from becoming mere chaos by committee." In short, what's really clever about *D&D* is the way it's able to combine the illusion of "anything goes" with this practical and formalized set of rules that make it seem fair for all involved.

It's revealing to consider how adventure games handle the same issue. Although adventure games *Colossal Cave Adventure* and *Zork* may provide the illusion of total freedom, in actuality the player is limited by the relatively small set of commands recognized by the parser. Indeed, one of the most common invectives hurled against any adventure game (textual or graphical) is that only one solution to a problem has been implemented, when the player can easily imagine several very plausible alternatives. Espen Aarseth, a key figure in the academic study of video games, goes so far as to call these games "autistic." In any case, their linearity allows even the brightest players to get hopelessly stumped on a puzzle and unable to continue.

As we'll see, CRPGs ease this problem by channeling the players' energies into a much smaller set of activities, particularly combat. Players fight wave after wave of monsters, usually in pursuit of some quest or mission. However, the trade-off here is that even though these battles may be difficult, there's always a chance the player will succeed if he or she is persistent (eventually those dice rolls will work out to the player's advantage).

Shane: Let's be honest, a longtime "advantage" of many CRPGs over their tabletop cousins is that you can save your game right before a battle and then embark on a "save scumming" spree, reloading over and over until you win the battle either through sheer random luck, better tactics, or trial and error. Most people look down their nose in public at this practice, but still do it when no one's looking. Prove me wrong, baby!

Matt: Reload that comment and try again.

On the other hand, if an adventure gamer gets stuck on a puzzle, the game comes to a grinding halt. Furthermore, even though a CRPG might seem linear because players have no choice but to engage in so many battles, they can usually take these opportunities to improvise new strategies. Indeed, in all but the most uninspired dungeon crawls, players are offered a wealth of options for dispatching their foes (i.e., combinations of spells, melee or ranged combat, party configurations). Particularly difficult battles can require substantial trial and error before players stumble upon a viable means of achieving victory.

Furthermore, the randomness of CRPGs makes them fun to play over and over, even after the last dragon is defeated. By contrast, with games like *Colossal Cave Adventure,* once players have figured out all the puzzles, there is little reason to replay the game. One approach for dealing with this issue is simply to make the games longer and longer, adding more puzzles and rooms, or ratcheting up the difficulty level to force players to spend more time getting through the puzzles (this tactic usually leads more to frustration than satisfaction, however). Modern adventure game developers still wrestle with these issues.

Other programmers who played Crowther's game took it in a much different direction than Woods and Infocom. These programmers, whom we'll discuss later, took the concept of text-based exploration pioneered in *Colossal Cave Adventure* and wedded it to the statistical combat system made popular by TSR's fantasy role-playing games. Who did what first is controversial, but in any case, one of the earliest and most influential games is Roy Trubshaw and Richard Bartle's *MUD,* created in 1978. *MUD* (*Multi-User Dungeon*) allows many players to explore the virtual world together, teaming up to fight monsters, and the word *MUD* is now commonly used to describe any game that matches this description. We'll discuss MUDs and other early mainframe CRPGs much more later.

In short, Crowther and Woods' *Colossal Cave Adventure* performed a number of feats that proved essential to modern CRPGs. The most important of these is the creation of a virtual world and the means to explore it. The game also contains magic and monsters to overcome, even if the combat is not based on a statistical system. For instance, players must periodically throw an axe at dwarves to kill them. However, the character doesn't level up no matter how many dwarves are slain. Furthermore, when the player encounters a dragon, the solution is simple (spoiler alert!)—the player just kills it with his or her bare hands. This battle seems more like a spoof of *D&D* than anything else, since players expect a battle with a dragon to be a serious undertaking. The way such encounters are lampooned here suggests a line in the sand between the two genres.

In the next chapter, we'll turn to the first true CRPGs, which emerged as early as the late 1970s. Unfortunately, many of these games are not extant, and a great deal of critical information (release dates, names of programmers, and so on) is lost to history—thus warranting the name Dark Age for this obscure but historically vital period.

NOTES

1. See J. Fleming's "We See Farther—A History of Electronic Arts" at https://tinyurl.com/ybvmw75n.
2. For religious reasons, Tolkien preferred to call himself a "subcreator" rather than a "creator," which to him sounded blasphemous.

CHAPTER 3

The Dark Age

"Let's have fun with rules and statistics!" Saying this to a group of young people will garner more groans than gratitude. However, rules and statistics are what make games such as *Strat-O-Matic, Chainmail,* and *Dungeons & Dragons* possible. Take them out, and these games are no more than make-believe. While there's nothing wrong with kids pretending to be knights and orcs, a real game needs more formal structure—rules or guidelines that players can refer to in times of disagreement ("Whoa— you're a wizard! You can't wear plate mail!"). Without such rules, these games would be arbitrary; some kid would always be making up whatever rules were needed to win the game.

However, the rules need to be flexible enough to accommodate the unpredictable and the unexpected. In real life, we seldom know precisely what will happen as a result of even our best-informed decisions, and a realistic game should take the whims of fortune into account. On the other hand, if the game is too random, it can quickly get absurd. Sure, it's possible that a tiny kobold might kill a giant ogre with a well-aimed stone from his sling, but it'd take a miracle. What's needed is a careful balance, with just enough randomness to make the game exciting. One of the many reasons *Dungeons & Dragons* became so popular was the rational and sophisticated way it handled so many unpredictable phenomena, requiring just the right ratio of dumb luck to smart planning.

Shane: Most RPG systems, tabletop and otherwise, will use game mechanics such as the critical hit (i.e., rolling a "natural 20" on a twenty-sided dice) and critical fumble (i.e., rolling

> a "natural 1") to allow for rare but spectacular successes (such as that kobold and ogre scenario) and failures while still maintaining carefully crafted game balance.

Matt: I'm still trying to decide which one of those I rolled the first time I met you.

However, working with so many complex calculations gets cumbersome, and it's easy to make mistakes. Furthermore, the rules are often ambiguous, leading to conflicts among players and Game Masters more reminiscent of courtrooms than Camelot. Today, of course, the solution is obvious—let a computer handle the math and objectively enforce all those rules. However, affordable personal computers were still out of reach in the late 1970s, and players had to make do with oddly shaped dice, pocket calculators, and a set of thick volumes to help resolve disputes. Many of the rules and conventions were borrowed from the world of wargaming, in which an obsession with accuracy and meticulous calculation was the norm. For many players, though, these features of the game were but necessary evils. A computer could shoulder some of this burden and allow players to focus on the activities they found much more appealing.

Thankfully for the future of CRPGs, at least one group of gamers did enjoy at least intermittent access to computers—college students. By the early 1970s, it was rare to find a major college campus that didn't have at least a few mainframes, such as DEC's PDP-10. The earliest CRPGs and MUDs emerged during the 1970s on these powerful but expensive machines. Of course, many university administrators, faculty members, and no doubt a few boards of regents didn't want to see these machines being "wasted" on gaming. On most campuses, computer gaming was strictly forbidden, and when games were noticed by the wrong people, they were promptly and unceremoniously deleted. Sadly, until programmers learned to print out their source code as a backup measure, many historically critical CRPGs were lost to history.

PLATO AND THE MAINFRAME ERA

Many students had access to a powerful and flexible learning system called PLATO, an advanced time-sharing system that supported many simultaneous users on one mainframe. Unlike today, when many of us have our own dedicated machines, back then the typical model was to connect a giant mainframe computer to several "dumb" terminals. Although PLATO had been designed and promoted as a way for students to work on lessons, users quickly discovered the joys of chatting and gaming; it led to the first online communities. It also let users make new programs or "lessons" using a programming language called TUTOR.

It didn't take long for enterprising students to put together the first CRPGs. We know little about these early efforts—they were, after all, often forbidden by campus policy, and few people had the foresight to realize that history was being made. All they saw were some unruly students breaking the rules. The result is that we have only the sketchiest details of these early CRPGs—they truly existed in a Dark Age, with few credible sources to verify what people at the time so fondly remember. In any case, it is certainly irresponsible to declare any of these early games the first CRPG until more reliable information becomes available. Indeed, at least a few websites claim that one or another CRPG was created before Gygax and Arneson published *Dungeons & Dragons* in 1974! Such a feat seems unlikely at best, though not impossible—after all, Gygax and Arneson had been developing and play-testing the system before 1974, and it's possible that word leaked out to programmers.

The best we can do here is discuss a few of these early efforts to create CRPGs and try to give some impression of what playing these games was like. One such game was *pedit5*, authored by Rusty Rutherford for PLATO. Rutherford, a PLATO programmer for the Population and Energy Group, had been playing *D&D* since 1975 and heard that a computer game called *DND* was already in development, but he still decided to try his hand at it. According to Rutherford,

> I had to compromise a lot. First of all, the multiplayer feature was often promised but never implemented, so I wrote a solitaire game. The available storage space only allowed for a single-level dungeon with 40–50 rooms. The dungeon design was the same for every user, but the monsters and reassures were random—created at the same time as a new character, and stored with the character record. Only about 20 characters could be stored; when the game became popular, this turned out to be a real hassle.
>
> I used the basic features of *D&D* as much as possible: hit points, monster levels, experience and treasure awards, and so on; the character was a combined fighter/magic user/cleric; in a monster encounter, the character had a choice of fight (F), cast a spell (S) or run (R); after that, if the monster was not defeated or avoided, it was a fight to the finish run entirely by the computer.

It should be apparent that this was a very primitive game, but the visuals (the PLATO plasma panel) made it quite tense and surprisingly addictive. I wrote it all in about 4–6 weeks in the fall and winter of 1975.

Another game that might lay claim to being the first CRPG is Don Daglow's *Dungeon,* written sometime between 1975 and 1976 for the PDP-10 mainframe. Daglow's game offered multiple players the chance to band together to explore a dungeon, earning experience points and leveling up as they progressed. Though represented entirely in textual characters, it features a line-of-sight display, realistically depicting what the characters could and couldn't see. The game was distributed by DECUS, a user group composed of DEC programmers. DECUS also played a role in distributing and popularizing other important games of the era, such as the mainframe versions of *Colossal Cave Adventure* and *Zork.*

We know more about *dnd,* a graphical CRPG for the PLATO platform programmed by Gary Whisenhunt and Ray Wood in the mid-1970s. The game contains most of the genre's staples, such as the ability to create a custom character, a leveling system based on experience points, a general store, and monsters that get tougher the deeper a player descends into the dungeon. The game also has a plot: enter the Whisenwood Dungeon, kill a dragon, and retrieve his orb. This orb-fetching quest will show up again and again in later CRPGs. The game was in continuous development until 1985 and influenced many pioneering CRPG developers.

Incidentally, around this time Daniel Lawrence created a game named *DND,* not to be confused with Whisenhunt and Wood's game, *dnd.* Lawrence's game was written for the TOPS-10 operating system, which ran on DEC's PDP-10 mainframe. The game was a hit at Purdue, where Lawrence was a student. Lawrence later ported it to the TOPS-20 system, and it circulated among DEC's employees. The game would later cause a legal headache when Lawrence used *DND*'s code in his *Telengard* game, a commercial product published by Avalon Hill for home computers. In September 1983, DEC officially ordered the game purged from all of its computers to avoid litigation. Further legal issues over *DND* arose in 1984, when a company named R.O. Software ported the game to MS-DOS under a $25 shareware license—without bothering to get Avalon Hill's or Lawrence's permission.

There are several other CRPGs written for PLATO between 1976 and 1979, such as *Oubliette* (1977), *Moria* (1978), *Avatar* (c. 1979), and *Orthanc*

(1978). These games are largely based on *dnd*, though they offer innovations. For example, they all allow simultaneous multiplayer romps through their dungeons. Except for *Orthanc*, they also have a first-person, 3D view of the dungeons, which crops up later in Sir-Tech's *Wizardry* games.

Moria, Avatar, Orthanc, and *Oubliette* are all currently available for play at https://www.cyber1.org, a modern reincarnation of PLATO. The version of *Moria* was updated in some fashion in 1984, though the earliest copyright notice was 1978. The authors credited are Kevet Duncombe and Jim Battin, and they did some impressive work. The in-game user guide and help options are highly detailed and well written, in stark contrast to most of the early CRPGs for personal computers, which were forced by memory restrictions to print such material in a manual. Like *Oubliette*, *Moria* has a tiny first-person, 3D view of wireframe dungeons and allows for multiple players (indeed, many of the more interesting aspects of the game require players to group up with other adventurers). There are many intriguing innovations here that aren't seen in other games, such as a magical string that players can tie in a room and then follow back if they get lost (the manual warns that monsters will occasionally chew through the string). The screen also displays other useful information, such as the player's condition and inventory (Figures 3.1 and 3.2).

> *Shane:* Perhaps the first time someone speculated it was a monster that had eaten through his or her string, players referred to it as "early CRPG string theory."
>
> *Matt:* I theorize your string was chewed through years ago.

There are only four player stats in *Moria*: cunning, piety, valor, and wizardry, which link up nicely with the four guilds advanced players may join: the Thieves' Guild, the Brotherhood, the Union of Knights, and the Circle of Wizards. Members of these guilds gain special powers that affect the entire group the player is traveling with—for instance, a wizard can teleport the party to a new location. There is also a skill system here that tracks the players' actions and awards skill boosts depending on their frequency. Instead of hit points, characters have vitality, which is used up by engaging in combat or other actions. Vitality will recharge automatically if the player has food and water on hand. All in all, *Moria* is an enjoyable and sophisticated game.

Avatar is in many respects comparable to *Moria*, though perhaps less inviting to novices. One version lists 1979 as the earliest release date, but

FIGURE 3.1 Shown here is the title screen of *Moria,* a multiplayer CRPG running on the PLATO system.

several later versions were produced (up to 1984). Though it's not clear who did what or when, the six authors credited on the menu screen are Bruce Maggs, Andrew Shapira, David Sides, Tom Kirchman, Greg Janusz, and Mark Eastom. *Avatar* is a good example of a game that was freely modified and built up over time—what we now call the open-source or free-software model of development.

The screen setup is almost identical to *Moria*'s, though the small first-person view of the dungeon is located in the top center of the screen rather than on the left. *Avatar* offers ten races (including uncommon ones such as "cirillian" and "morloch") and a more traditional stat system with hit points and standard attributes (strength, intelligence, wisdom, constitution, etc.) One of the game's strengths is its extensive inventory of items that range in quality—such as bronze, iron, or steel swords. Combat is very similar to *Moria*'s; the player simply exchanges

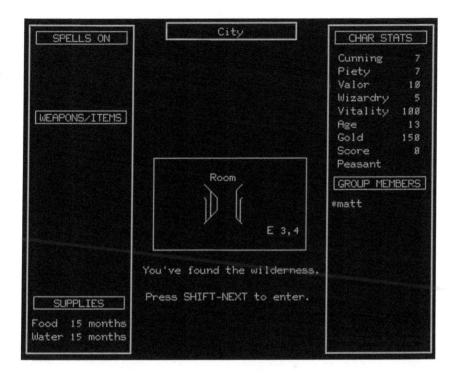

FIGURE 3.2   Another screen showing *Moria's* gameplay.

blows in the random encounters until one combatant prevails. The game is quite challenging; you may create and equip a character only to have him or her die a few minutes after leaving the safety of the city. Clearly this game would be easier (not to mention more fun) with a group of friends (Figure 3.3).

Oubliette is yet another first-person, 3D game, again with plenty of options for creating rather diverse characters. Of the lot, it's probably the one most closely based on TSR's official rules and J.R.R. Tolkien's writings. There are fifteen races with various stat bonuses and penalties, as well as fifteen available classes, each with a preferred type of armor, shield, helm, and weapon. Although single characters can wander the dungeons, it's advisable to travel in parties (the manual recommends at least four companions), who can be found in the various taverns in the city. There are also guilds for players to join and "charmees," or animal companions. Combat is also loaded with options, including the option to seduce, which can only be performed by females. A failed seduction can result in instant death, whereas success will force the opponent to become a loyal and dedicated companion. All in all, it's another highly sophisticated game. In 1984

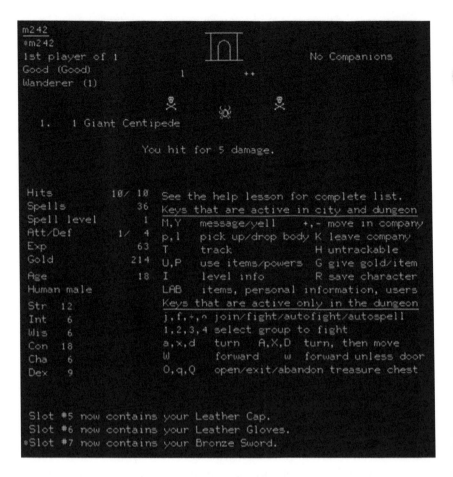

FIGURE 3.3 *Avatar,* shown here, puts a lot of emphasis on groups and clans, rather like the guilds of modern MMORPGs.

it was ported for personal computers by the main author, Jim Schwaiger. It was also a direct influence on Robert J. Woodhead, one of the creators of the commercial hit *Wizardry.*

Unlike the previous three games, *Orthanc* (Figure 3.4) offers a top-down perspective and a wonderful automapper tool in the lower right corner. It's quite helpful while exploring the game's twenty levels (based on 24 × 20 cell grids). It seems largely based on *pedit5* and is still undergoing development.

Though PLATO is not so well known today, it served these pioneering CRPG developers well, and no doubt many successful CRPG developers cut their teeth on these early programs. However, we should of course bear in mind that only a select few had access to these powerful systems; many,

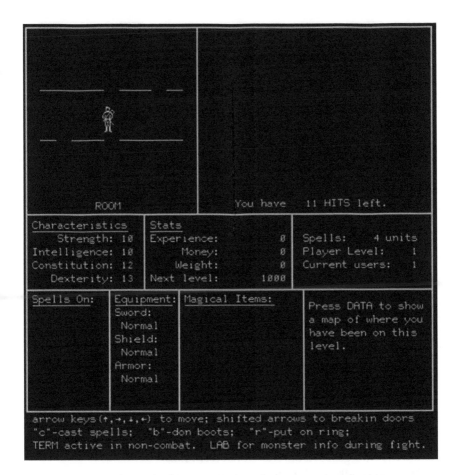

FIGURE 3.4 *Orthanc,* shown here, has a top-down view and a handy automapper.

if not most, CRPG fans would have to wait for the personal computer revolution before getting hands-on experience with one of these fascinating games.

ROGUES IN THE COMPUTER LABS

The most famous of all the mainframe CRPGs is *Rogue* (Figure 3.5). This game was created in the early 1980s by Michael Toy and Glenn Wichman for the UNIX operating system. Unlike PLATO, which as we've seen allowed for rather sophisticated graphical displays, the more common terminals of the era were limited to ASCII, a set of numerals, letters, punctuation marks, and other characters for displaying information. Furthermore, the way each terminal handled text and cursors varied from brand to brand, another major obstacle for anyone attempting graphics.

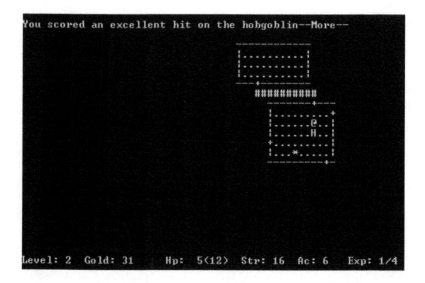

FIGURE 3.5 This early version of *Rogue* may not look like much, but its innovative procedurally generated dungeons spawned a whole subgenre of CRPGs that are still being made today.

The missing ingredient was Curses, a "cursor optimization library" developed by Ken Arnold. Toy and Wichman used Curses to control the display and arrangement of the ASCII characters on the screen to form dungeon walls. It also let the player move the "cursor," or in this case his or her character, within these dungeons. Finally, it ensured compatibility across the smorgasbord of rival UNIX terminals.

The game really gained a boost when it was included with BSD UNIX, a very popular version of the operating system developed at the University of California at Berkeley (where Toy was a student). This meant that the game was now available at university campuses all over the world. Later on, the *Rogue* team signed a deal with Epyx to distribute the game for home computers, but, sadly, their commercial efforts failed miserably. However, the game was wildly popular on the public domain and shareware scenes and has been ported to hundreds of different platforms.

There are three features that set *Rogue* apart from most CRPGs. Perhaps the most obvious is the graphics, which are entirely composed of the character set available on any particular platform; numbers, letters, and symbols are mixed together to depict the scene. For example, the player's character is usually represented with the @ sign; monsters are depicted by letters of the alphabet (*a* for aquator through *z* for zombie). A more fundamental characteristic of *Rogue* is that the dungeons are randomized each time a player starts a new game with a procedural content generation system—thus, there are always new areas to explore. Though we've seen this in plenty of other games, *Rogue*'s greater availability and accessibility gave it significant advantages over the PLATO games.

The mission is simply to descend into the Dungeons of Doom and fetch the Amulet of Yendor (it's easy to see the similarity to Whisenhunt and Wood's earlier *dnd*). A less typical aspect of the game is that it doesn't offer a General Store where the player can buy new equipment. Instead, all arms, armor, and magic items must be found in the dungeons, either on the floor or on corpses. Finally, the game implements the "fog of war," which means that instead of showing the entire map, players uncover it gradually as they explore. Monsters roam freely in these dungeons, but players can only see the ones in the room they're currently exploring.

Wichman was rightly proud of *Rogue,* which quickly became the most popular game on college campuses. "It was interesting to see the surge of adrenaline you'd get when you'd see a *T* on the screen," recalled Wichman. "That *T* was a troll, the first really threatening monster you'd see if you were doing well. You could watch people hitting the keys harder, thinking it would help them beat it. We'd hear screams."

Rogue inspired hundreds of other games that are usually categorized as "Roguelikes." These include *Hack* (1982), *Larn* (1986), *Moria* (1983),[1] *Ancient Domains of Mystery* (1994), and *Angband* (1990), to name just a few. *Hack* adds stores and pets, which follow the player's character and serve as sidekicks, fighting and even leveling up along with the character. *Nethack* (Figure 3.6), released in 1987, is a later version of *Hack*, whose development was facilitated by the Internet (one of the earlier projects to benefit from it in terms of development as well as distribution). *Angband* is based on Tolkien's works and has also spawned many derivatives. *Ancient Domains of Mystery* (also known as *ADOM*) is the most hardcore of the bunch. It offers a myriad of options for character development and is celebrated for its die-and-learn gameplay—players are not allowed to have multiple saved versions of their character, so there is no way to restore a dead character.

In 1984, Toy joined with Jon Lane to form Artificial Intelligence Design, a company that published the first commercial version of *Rogue* for the IBM PC and Apple Macintosh platforms. We'll have more to say about these efforts in Chapter 6.

For some CRPG fans, *Rogue* or one of the many Roguelikes are the best games the genre has to offer despite their humble graphics. Indeed, efforts to update these games with a graphical interface, such as Hansjörg

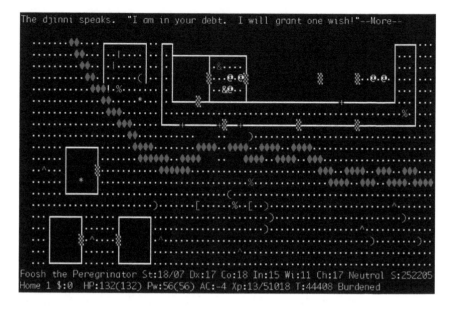

FIGURE 3.6 *Nethack* is one of the best of the Roguelikes with near infinite replay value. Here, the player has stumbled upon a djinni.

Malthaner's *Iso-Angbad*, have failed to impress many fans of the originals. Indeed, Malthaner claimed that "some people were openly hostile towards the idea of a graphical front-end." To date, most Roguelikes are still based on character set-graphics.

Shane: Reinforcing the popular maxim in game development of gameplay first, graphics second. Which as a longtime gamer I fully, unwaveringly, and unequivocally support until my dying breath without exception. Unless, y'know, there's a quick buck to be made!

Matt: You're reinforcing my popular maxim that you're an unwavering and unequivocal knucklehead.

WALLOWING IN THE MUD

We've already mentioned a few games that cater to groups of players rather than solo adventurers. These games typically focus more on social interaction among players than on tactical combat and earning experience points. They were well suited for mainframes, where users were already connected via a series of terminals. Since users were already networked together, making a multiplayer CRPG was a relatively straightforward endeavor.

By contrast, the majority of home computer users were limited to stand-alone games. The Internet as we think of it today did not exist. Instead, proprietary online services such as America Online and CompuServe granted fee-based access to multiplayer online games (at a price that was compounded if the gamer had to dial long-distance). Furthermore, slow modem speeds and lack of graphics support made anything beyond ASCII-based graphics infeasible. Since playing these games could get quite expensive, it wasn't until the rise of the Internet in the 1990s that graphical MUDs (multiuser dungeons, precursors to modern MMORPGs) hit the mainstream.

In short, when we study the history of the MUD (Figure 3.7), we see a lag between the dawn of personal computing and the rise of the Internet. Although plenty of single-player CRPGs were released for machines like the Apple II and Commodore 64, online multiplayer games were mostly limited to gamers with access to a mainframe. As noted above, the bulk of these were noncommercial, free-to-play games that had few graphics beyond what could be done with text or ASCII characters. Nevertheless, thousands of gamers would come to love these games, and it's understandable why many of them would scorn the humble offerings on personal computers, which didn't allow any of the social elements that made MUDs so addictive and compelling.

```
This is a pleasant dale, hugging the slopes of a huge forest-covered
escarpment which rises to the south. East is more forest, but the dale curves
southeastwards behind it. West is a slope of scrubland, which rolls down to
the sea beyond. North is a railway line, which runs from east to west,
standard gauge.
A nanny goat is tethered here.
*examine goat
You can examine 'til your heart's content, you won't find anything special.
Heavens, if I let folk examine things they'd spend the whole game doing it!
*slap goat
You'll have to try something else, I don't understand the first word
(which should be an action).
*kill goat
*The force of a forehand by the goat sends you staggering.
Yet courageously you pull through, and hurl yourself into the fight.
*Your follow-through blow sends the goat backwards!
*You are wounded by the weight of a lunge from the goat!
Summoning strength you concentrate, and start into the slaughter.
*Your retributive whack sends the goat staggering!
```

FIGURE 3.7 Early versions of MUDs closely resembled text adventure games, but looks can be deceiving. These are multiplayer games with persistent worlds and plenty of combat.

The original MUD was created in 1979 by Roy Trubshaw and later expanded and improved by Richard Bartle. Both men were students at the University of Essex in the UK. Written for the DEC PDP-10 with the TOPS-10 operating system, the game is simply titled *MUD*, an acronym for *Multi-User Dungeon*. The name pays homage to an adventure game named *Dungeon*, which would later be published as the *Zork* trilogy by Infocom (both Trubshaw and Bartle had played both *Zork* and *Colossal Cave Adventure*). When Trubshaw was introduced to *Dungeons & Dragons*, he "got to thinking about writing my own version of *ADVENT* but based on *D&D* type character generation."[2] When Trubshaw serendipitously uncovered the source code for *Colossal Cave Adventure*, he was finally inspired enough to begin work on *MUD*, incorporating a database to make the system more efficient to program. When Bartle joined the project, he began creating a dungeon and requested that Trubshaw extend the parser to enable more creative gameplay—including the all-important randomized combat system. After Trubshaw left the project, he handed Bartle roughly a quarter of the code that Bartle expanded into *MUD*.

MUD became wildly popular—so popular, in fact, that administrators worried the game was wasting too much of their computers' resources. However, the officials allowed gamers to play—so long as they logged on only in the wee hours of the morning, with a bit more flexibility for weekends. Even with these restrictions, the game had no shortage of players. Several derivatives were soon underway, including *MIST*, *BLUD*, and *Rock*, a game based on the TV show *Fraggle Rock*. *MUD* was eventually hosted by the commercial CompuServe network under the name *British Legends*, where it attracted a large American following. Once he realized that the game had commercial potential, Bartle officially placed the name *MUD* into the public domain so that it could be used as a generic term rather than a trademark. Besides, according to Bartle, CompuServe found the name unattractive.

The influence of the early text adventures is easy to see in *MUD*, where the main goal is simply to gain enough points to "make wiz." The *Zork*-tradition of finding treasures and depositing them in the right location (in this case the swamp) is preserved, as well as the tongue-in-cheek descriptions of rooms. Furthermore, players earn points by performing various actions (e.g., shaking a baby rattle) in addition to combat. Combat is a relatively simple affair—players simply tell the parser what to kill and what weapon to use. Success boils down to three variables—the character's strength, dexterity, and stamina. As players accumulate points, their characters gain levels, a process that boosts their stats. Furthermore, characters at higher levels have a better percentage of success when trying to cast spells. However, it seems safe to say that the appeal of the game is more about interacting with other players than roaming about the countryside killing things.

Another early MUD was *Milieu*, a program written by Alan E. Kleitz in 1978. *Milieu* was written in a language called Multi-Pascal and ran on a CDC Cyber mainframe. It was originally intended only for educational purposes, but Kleitz rewrote the game in C and ported it to the IBM XT in 1983, renaming it *Scepter of Goth*. Kleitz ran the system on a pay-to-play system, supporting up to sixteen simultaneous users who connected via modem. The system was franchised, with rates running somewhere between $2 and $4 per hour (in addition, of course, to relevant long-distance charges).

Later MUDs, such as *M.U.D. II* (Figure 3.8), *Mirrorworld*, *AberMUD*, *Gods*, and *Shades*, added loads of new features and improvements to the design. Some of these were free, but others charged for access and

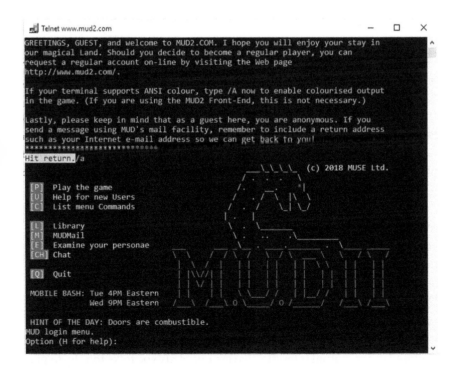

FIGURE 3.8 Later MUDs integrated color text and more sophisticated ANSI graphics and even simple animation. Shown here is *M.U.D. II*, still in operation.

were located on commercial rather than public networks. For instance, Simutronics' *GemStone* series ran on the commercial network GEnie. The game was first demonstrated in 1987 (*GemStone*), playtested in 1988 (*GemStone II*), and finally officially launched in 1990 (*GemStone III*). By the third iteration, the game was stable and attracting a healthy following. GEnie used an interesting gambit to promote the game: some players who found gems in the game would receive real gems as prizes. The game was based on Iron Crown Enterprises' *Shadow World* campaign setting, a competitor with TSR's *Dungeons & Dragons* franchise. Unfortunately, the relationship faltered, and the developers removed all references to the setting from *GemStone*, a move that also entailed substantial changes to the gameplay mechanics. Shortly afterward, the game became available on CompuServe and Prodigy, generating another large surge of players. The latest version of the game, *GemStone IV*, is available at https://www.play.net/gs4/.

Flying Buffalo, the role-playing game publisher of *Tunnels and Trolls*, took a different approach to commercial online role-playing. In 1982, it converted its popular play-by-mail game *Heroic Fantasy* for use on an early commercial network called TheSource. When the costs are tallied, this was quite an expensive game to play, even though gameplay consisted of only one to two turns per week. It cost $100 to register and $10 per hour to access TheSource, and each turn on *Heroic Fantasy* cost $2.50 (these figures are all in 1982 dollars; adjusting for inflation more than doubles these numbers). The system was no doubt more popular in its play-by-mail pen-and-paper version, in which such costs could be kept within the budgets of more gamers. The high costs of most commercial online games kept them out of the hands of most gamers until well in the 1980s.

Of course, there was nothing stopping groups of *D&D* fans from forming their own groups to play with over commercial networks. Special interest groups (SIGs) like the GameSIG on CompuServe were popular hubs for this type of grassroots gameplay. Players and Game Masters simply typed out the things they would ordinarily have said in a tabletop game, such as the results of dice rolls and room descriptions. Participants were often avid gamers who couldn't find fellow gamers in their local area, and again the members of these impromptu groups often became good friends who explored other mutual interests. Players might also be folks too shy to participate in face-to-face sessions; one magazine describes how a "five-foot tall teenager with a poor complexion can become a courageous fighter" or an "overweight housewife with a sink full of dishes may be transformed into a sylph-like minstrel or a cunning sorceress." Despite these advantages, however, the games came at a high price: two hours of gaming per week cost up to $50 on CompuServe.

In 1989, an American named James Aspnes authored *TinyMUD*, based largely on an older MUD named *Monster*, an ambitious but poorly written program. *TinyMUD* lets players work together to create and extend virtual worlds. Aspnes envisioned it as a "vehicle for user-generated *Adventure*-style puzzles" but soon realized that the "social aspect seemed to be much more important." Though many users found the creativity liberating and fulfilling, at least a few critics complained about the haphazard construction of the worlds. Furthermore, players spent more time creating new areas than exploring the ones already there. Bartle quipped, "TinyMUDs are indeed limited only by the imagination of the builder—with heavy emphasis on the word 'limited.'"

As just one example of the kind of creativity allowed in world building by continuing iterations of MUD-like software, in the 1990s, a MUSH (described below) called *DarkMetal* (Figure 3.9) launched that allows the

FIGURE 3.9 DarkMetal, a MUSH first created in the early 1990s, is still accepting telnet connections.

vampires and werewolves of White Wolf's *World of Darkness* RPG setting to coexist (often in conflict) with a dystopian cyberpunk setting and its cyber-enhanced denizens. Your humble co-author Shane may or may not have spent entirely too much time telnetting into this amazing text-based world in the early days of widespread dial-up Internet access. He played a cyberpunk character named Slider with stylized lightning bolts on his pupils and who would make cyberspace runs with an electric blue mongoose as his avatar. Slider may have never burned Chrome, but Shane definitely burned precious hours at the keyboard more than once when he should have been sleeping!

TinyMUD became one of the most popular MUDs available on the Internet. Aspnes eventually made the source code publicly available, and derivative projects such as *TinyMUCK*, *TinyMUSH*, and *TinyMOO* quickly followed. One revealing aspect of these derivatives is their new acronyms (for example, MUSH was most often described as multiuser shared hallucination, and MOO as MUD object oriented); the multiuser dungeons were evolving away from their roots in fantasy role-playing and toward more general uses as online social environments, in essence becoming little more than sophisticated chat programs.

What's interesting about the history of MUDs is how they slowly evolve (or, as some might say, "devolve") from gaming to socializing. Even in MUDs that place more priority on combat and leveling up, there is still a strong emphasis on conversing with other players; indeed, MUD weddings are commonplace, and many people have found their real-life spouses on MUDs. In our own extensive experiences playing MUDs throughout the mid-1990s, we saw the pattern repeated many times. First, players are obsessed with finding the best equipment, fighting monsters, gaining levels, and rising in rank. Eventually, though, they are drawn into parties of other adventurers, where they not only pool their resources to fight bigger battles but also make friends. Inevitably, the player will spend more time socializing with these friends than going on quests or earning experience points. After a certain point, actually playing the game is worthwhile only when a player's friends are not online. Bartle describes this phenomenon as the main sequence, borrowing the term from the entropy of the life of stars (Figures 3.10 and 3.11).

It's for this reason that we insist on maintaining a distinction between MUDs (and their descendants, MMORPGs) and CRPGs. Although the two are related and have much in common, the socializing impulse of MUD players makes them into much different animals. We'll come back

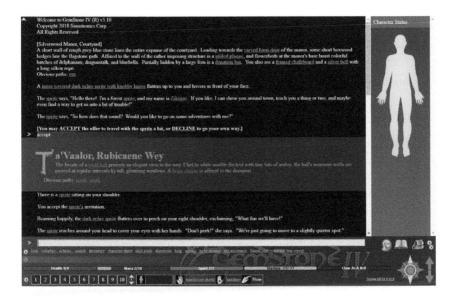

FIGURE 3.10 Many people still play MUDs, though graphical interfaces have evolved to make them easier to play and navigate. Shown here is *Gemstone IV*.

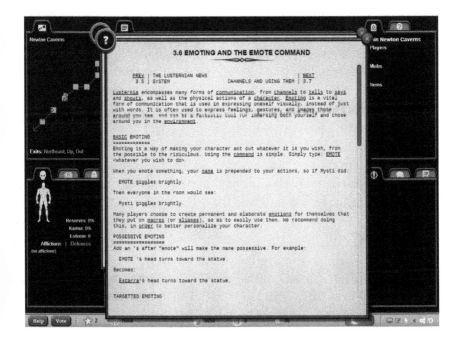

FIGURE 3.11 *Lusternia: Age of Ascension* is a popular MUD with a constantly evolving world, extensive crafting system, and a vibrant community.

to this topic in later chapters that explore the rise of MMORPGs, so let's end our analysis of MUDs for the moment.

> *Shane:* You might even say we're going to get our feet out of the mud for now, eh?
> *Matt:* Here's mud in your eye!

THE END OF THE DARK AGE

As we've seen, the early history of both CRPGs and MUDs is often obscure. Since so many of these early yet pivotal games were intentionally deleted, poorly documented, or simply forgotten, reliable facts are hard to come by. There's no shortage of folks claiming to remember "for sure" about this or that, even if they frequently contradict each other's accounts on key details. This makes identifying the first CRPG a risky business. Indeed, as we'll soon see in the next chapter, it's just as difficult to name the first CRPG available for home computers, since publishers had a bad habit of postdating their copyright notices, and few had an adequate understanding of copyright law (a dire situation that led to countless court cases throughout the 1980s and well into the 1990s).

Nevertheless, with the arrival of the first commercial games for home computers, history becomes easier to document. For one thing, it's much easier to acquire these games and run them on a modern computer, whereas we must rely on secondhand accounts of games such as *pedit5* and *Orthanc*. Emulating a PLATO system, while certainly possible, is not an endeavor to be undertaken casually, particularly by people who aren't already familiar with the platform. Also, once game developers began releasing their games commercially, they had a greater stake in asserting authorship and protecting their code. In the next chapter, we'll explore the earliest CRPGs available for home computers. They debuted during a period of bold but often crude experimentation we've termed the Bronze Age.

NOTES

1. Not to be confused with the earlier *Moria* for PLATO.
2. See http://archive.gamespy.com/articles/january01/muds1/index5.shtm. Also, remember that *ADVENT* and *ADVENTURE* are other common names for Crowther and Woods' *Colossal Cave Adventure*.

CHAPTER 4

The Bronze Age

America got its first taste of the personal computer revolution in the late 1970s. 1977 was the vital year, witnessing the birth of three magnificent machines: the Apple II, Tandy TRS-80, and Commodore PET. Though astonishing for their time, these "home" computers were a pale imitation of IBM's or DEC's mainframes. Nevertheless, the personal computer (PC) opened up a world of possibilities for game programmers, who at last had the potential to earn real profits and turn their hobby into a career. This trend increased dramatically as hardware dropped in price while simultaneously skyrocketing in performance. These early PCs were a long way from the user-friendly devices we know today, but at least you could get your hands on one.

Since the topic of this book is *computer* role-playing games, it's important to keep in mind what they were competing with. In the Bronze Age, it was primarily arcade games. Throughout the late 1970s and well into the 1980s, any serious video gamer haunted the neon-lit arcades, pumping quarters into the likes of *Space Invaders, Pac-Man, Defender,* and *Donkey Kong.* Check out our *Vintage Games* books if you want to read about the history of these games, but the point here is that you just couldn't get anything close to the graphics and audio quality of these dedicated machines at home.

CRPGs also faced competition from another quarter: consoles. Then as now, many gamers just want to play games and have no interest in computers per se—and even if they did, the difference between, say, an Atari 2600 ($199.99) and an Apple II ($1,298.00) meant that only rich or very lucky kids could afford a ticket to *Akalabeth.* Keep in mind that when adjusted for inflation, these machines were over $700 and $5,000, respectively;

you were privileged just to own a console! These prices fell dramatically over the next few years as competition heated up, but it's important to remember that a home computer was a major investment for the average American family.

Yet there was at least one good reason for some gamers to want a home computer: They could use them to make their own video games. True, most of these homebrew titles were garbage, but a few were good enough to share or even sell at a local computer club or by mail. For the first time, it was becoming possible to actually earn a decent living making computer games—and you didn't need a college degree or a job at Atari to make it happen.

The older computer culture operated mostly on what we'd today call an open-source or free-software model, in which programmers freely share their programs and source code. The personal computer culture operated on vastly different assumptions from the start.[1]

Before the advent of the PC, the computer industry consisted of a few hundred mainframes sprinkled across the country and were used, officially, at least, by a privileged few for serious applications. The money and prestige was thought to be in hardware. If you wanted to make a living "merely" doing software, you took a job at a corporation like IBM or DEC, a research institution, or a high-tech government agency.

Now Apple and other manufacturers were putting computers in front of thousands of regular folks—people with the leisure time, disposable income, and nerdiness to appreciate software written purely for entertainment. Furthermore, although some computer makers, such as Texas Instruments, prohibited third-party software development, most did whatever they could to encourage it. This was a new frontier, and there was gold in these hills.

The 49ers of the "PC Revolution" had a new perspective on software. Now it was a product to be sold and protected by both legal copyrights and technological copy protection. Rather than see themselves as part of a programming commune or member of a bland corporation, commercial game developers were entrepreneurs who thrived on fierce economic competition.

The old generation freely shared software and source code because the rewards they sought, if any at all beyond a paycheck, were recognition for their skill, dedication, and value to the community. As long as no one else falsely claimed credit for their work, they were usually happy when their programs and underlying source code spread far and wide. Indeed, what is better way to impress your fellow programmers than to let them see and admire your code? Furthermore, as long as you gave proper credit to those who had come before, you were usually free to debug, improve, or modify programs as you saw fit.

By contrast, the PC whippersnappers didn't want other programmers to see their code. Indeed, Apple II programmers like Richard Garriott longed to get away from BASIC, a language that was usually interpreted rather than compiled. This meant that a competitor could see exactly how he'd programmed *Akalabeth* or *Ultima* simply by telling the computer to print the code. By contrast, the more powerful assembly languages were compiled into executable files that only machines could read. This allowed for a more business-friendly model that allowed source code to remain a trade secret.

In addition to these cultural differences, there were also more practical reasons to shift to proprietary software. The great majority of early PCs were not connected to networks. Instead, PC owners relied purely on removable storage media, such as data cassettes, floppy disks, and ROM cartridges. Relatively few personal computers were equipped with modems, which suffered from miserably slow transfer rates over copper phone lines—not to mention the steep fees incurred by long-distance charges and commercial telecom networks. PC software was purchased from a store in a package, just like any other widget. This model made sense to consumers, but it was a paradigm shift in software development— now they were products to be purchased, not resources to be shared.

Naturally, not all PC owners were happy with all this. Many made their own illegal copies of games and wantonly distributed them to family and friends. Eventually, groups of these individuals organized into global networks of "crackers" and "traders," exchanging bootleg copies by mail and eventually high-speed modems. The industry's fight against pirates plays out all throughout the rest of this book. Many failed game developers blame piracy for their downfall, though, just between us, it's possible that other factors such as poor quality were responsible. Indeed, a common argument in support of piracy is that it supplies word-of-mouth advertising or an opportunity to try-before-you-buy. Finally, treating code as a trade secret also has its negatives for developers, who constantly have to reinvent the wheel. If you like what you see in another person's game, you either have to figure out how he or she did it on your own or find another way.

The budding industry also grappled with its own legal issues over trademarks and copyrights. As with the early mainframe programmers, many makers of commercial software for home computers borrowed blatantly from tabletop role-playing games such as TSR's *D&D* as well as literary sources such as J. R. R. Tolkien or the TV show *Star Trek*. Although these borrowings went unnoticed for a brief while, when the publishers and copyright holders caught on they wanted the infringing games off the shelf. They were wise to do so. Later, TSR and other publishers of tabletop games forged lucrative licensing agreements with computer game developers, proving that these trademarks and copyrights were well worth protecting.

As we might expect, the first CRPGs for home computers are simplistic and crude. Programmers had to work with extremely low memory, small display resolutions, and miserable color palettes. This is, of course, relative; PC developers unfamiliar with mainframes certainly didn't feel this pinch the same way. In any case, it is all too easy to scoff at these games, with no respect for the individual achievements they represent. The truth is that aspiring home computer developers overcame great odds to make these games. What they churned out demonstrated the true potential of the CRPG and laid the foundation for everything else that followed.

THE FIRST CRPGs FOR PERSONAL COMPUTERS

So what was the first CRPG ever to grace a home computer? We have no idea. There could have been any number of hobby programmers who made CRPGs purely for their own enjoyment (or perhaps for a group of close friends) and never released them to the public. During the early days of home computing, one of the main reasons to buy a machine was to learn how to program. How many students set themselves the task of building a CRPG? How many succeeded? Richard Garriott, for instance, wrote twenty-seven CRPGs before *Akalabeth*. These earlier games were text-based, but other programmers may well have integrated graphics. We suspect there were also many programs for assisting with the tabletop version of *D&D*, taking over the burdensome task of calculating and maybe even dice rolling for technically inclined Game Masters.

Even when dealing strictly with commercially published games, we find inconsistencies regarding copyright notices. The game might indicate one year on its title screen, while the box or printed materials give another. In any case, just knowing the year doesn't help much, since we'd need more specific dates to make an accurate judgment. Furthermore, developers then and now have an interest in being first with a new concept, and not just for the prestige—no one wants to risk being sued for copyright infringement or accused of ripping off a competitor. A logical course of action might be to contact the publishers themselves and ask to see their official records, but many of them are long defunct, their records lost, destroyed, or locked in the vaults of a holding company. Software catalogs are helpful, but they give us only a rough idea of when a game was available to a certain company, not when it first appeared on shelves. Finally, promotional materials are untrustworthy, since it was then (and still is) a common practice to assert that a new game was to be released on a certain date, only to have it show up much later—or never. Computer magazines of this era are lousy with ads for vaporware.

Perhaps we should adapt an observation of Francis Darwin, son of the famous scientist,[2] to suit our own ends: "In science the credit goes to the man who convinces the world, not the man to whom the idea first occurs." Even if Garriott's games weren't the first CRPGs to hit home computers, they were certainly the most influential. However, it's worthwhile to look at what else a *D&D*–obsessed computer owner could find on the shelf in the late 1970s.

These include Joseph Power's *The Wizard's Castle*; Donald Brown's *Eamon*; Edu-Ware's *Space*; Highland Computer Services' *The Tarturian*; Synergistic Software's *Dungeon Campaign, Wilderness Campaign*; and Automated Simulations' *Dunjonquest: Temple of Apshai* and *Dragon's Eye*. Though they all came out about the same time, they are about as identical as a warbler and a vegetarian finch (just ask Francis' dad).

The Wizard's Castle and *Eamon*

These first two games are great examples of how the early computer gaming industry was so much different from what we find later on. *The Wizard's Castle*, for instance, wasn't published on disk or cassette, but printed in a magazine. This practice, virtually unheard of today, was common in the days when removable storage media (e.g., cassettes and disks) were prohibitively expensive. Furthermore, since most computers had such limited supplies of memory, games were by necessity written in as few lines of code as possible. The upshot was that fully playable games could be inputted in a few hours even by a certified hunt-and-pecker. Besides, many people bought computers specifically to learn programming, and typing in games seemed like an easy way to pursue that goal. *The Wizard's Castle*, then, was just one of many of these games that were fun to play and helpful to aspiring CRPG developers (Figure 4.1).

Originally written by Joseph R. Power for Exidy's Sorcerer computer, *The Wizard's Castle* was ported to a variety of systems, a relatively easy feat since it was programmed in BASIC. It's a simple game, with no graphics and only a meager story. The player's character ("a bold youth") must

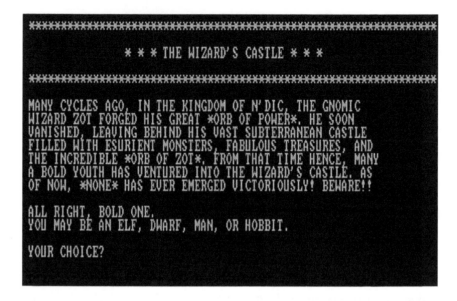

```
****************************************************************
              * * * THE WIZARD'S CASTLE * * *
****************************************************************
MANY CYCLES AGO, IN THE KINGDOM OF N'DIC, THE GNOMIC
WIZARD ZOT FORGED HIS GREAT *ORB OF POWER*. HE SOON
VANISHED, LEAVING BEHIND HIS VAST SUBTERRANEAN CASTLE
FILLED WITH ESURIENT MONSTERS, FABULOUS TREASURES, AND
THE INCREDIBLE *ORB OF ZOT*. FROM THAT TIME HENCE, MANY
A BOLD YOUTH HAS VENTURED INTO THE WIZARD'S CASTLE. AS
OF NOW, *NONE* HAS EVER EMERGED VICTORIOUSLY! BEWARE!!

ALL RIGHT, BOLD ONE.
YOU MAY BE AN ELF, DWARF, MAN, OR HOBBIT.

YOUR CHOICE?
```

FIGURE 4.1 *The Wizard's Castle* is one of the earliest CRPGs for home computers. If you wanted to play it, you had to carefully transcribe it, line by line, from a computing magazine.

descend into the subterranean castle of the gnomic wizard Zot to fetch the all-powerful Orb of Zot. Players choose a race (elf, dwarf, man, or hobbit) and gender, then allocate attribute points into three stats: strength, intelligence, and dexterity. They can then purchase armor, weapons, lamps, and flares. There are also magical items, such as a green gem that prevents memory loss, an opal eye that cures blindness, or manuals that permanently boost stats. Again, what's so impressive about this game is that all of this was crammed into 5,000 lines of code! The game is survived today by a freeware version with sprite-based graphics, programmed by a man calling himself "Derelict" who also hosts the source code to the original game.

In an email exchange with us concerning his game, Power remarked that his first encounter with a CRPG was at a science fiction convention held in 1975. Power was presented with an obscure mainframe game named *HOBBIT*, which featured "minimal character creation" and a "messy" stat-based combat system. Power remembers playing the game via a printer terminal (there was no monitor display). Nevertheless, Power enjoyed the game and decided he wanted to make his own, though improving on the areas he found deficient.

Donald Brown's *Eamon* (Figure 4.2), also known as *The Wonderful World of Eamon*, was never released commercially. Instead, it was distributed

FIGURE 4.2 The splash screen from *Eamon*. Its modular design was a great innovation that let users make their own adventures.

as part of the Apple II's public domain library, which was itself disseminated by groups of local Apple enthusiasts called "user groups." The game is mostly text-based and resembles a text adventure, but is focused on "defeating horrible monsters and finding glorious treasures." The CRPG elements are fairly simple, such as a three-attribute system based on hardiness, agility, and charisma. There are five types of weapons and three types of armor, and characters slowly gain proficiency with them with time and experience (e.g., the more hits a player lands with an axe, the greater the player's likelihood of doing so again; luck becomes skill). There is also a rudimentary magic system based on four spells. The system was later expanded by John Nelson and Tom Zuchowski after Brown left to focus on *Sword Thrust*, a commercial project (Figure 4.3).

What was so great about *Eamon* is how easy it was for other people to create their own modules or expansions for it. The distribution included a Dungeon Designer Diskette that lets players make their own adventures for *Eamon*, and these didn't have to be fantasy-based. Over 250 games were developed for this system, with dozens of writers contributing their talents to the project. It was eventually ported to other platforms, including MS-DOS, and developers are still making modules and improving the code to this day! This emphasis on user-generated content will crop up again later, most noticeably after the rise of the Internet, which greatly facilitated this type of grassroots development. BioWare's *Neverwinter Nights* (2002) is a more recent example of this phenomenon.

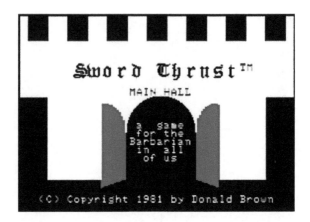

FIGURE 4.3 The Splash screen from *Sword Thrust,* "a game for the barbarian in all of us." Essentially a commercial version of *Eamon*, it was never as successful as its predecessor.

Brown's commercial project *Sword Thrust*, published in 1981 by CE Software, is similar to the public domain version, though with some upgrades such as save game capability, the ability to wield a weapon in the left hand, new spells, a fatigue system, and a separate window for the room description and the player's status. A new complication is the vulnerability of weapons and armor, which, like the real things, eventually wear out and break. Like the earlier *Eamon*, *Sword Thrust* is a modular system, and seven expansions were published—six by Brown himself, and the last, "The Hall of Alchemie," by Peter Wityk. The series fared well, and contemporary reviewers praise it by comparing it to the popular skills-based fantasy role-playing game *RuneQuest*. However, unlike *Eamon*, *Sword Thrust* is rarely played today.

Edu-Ware's *Space* and *Empire*

Edu-Ware's *Space* was developed by Steven Pederson and Sherwin Steffin, and probably released in 1979 (though some sources posit 1978). As the name suggests, Edu-Ware published educational software, though it also produced a few CRPGs it called "interactive fantasies." *Space*, a science fiction CRPG, is set in a futuristic society and based on the *Traveller* tabletop role-playing game developed by Game Designers' Workshop (GDW). Like *Traveller*, *Space* avoids the common practice of starting the player off with a weak, unprepared character. Instead, players specify how long and what kind of training their characters have already received, as well as a career path (Army, Navy, Scouts, Merchant Marines, or other services)—or they

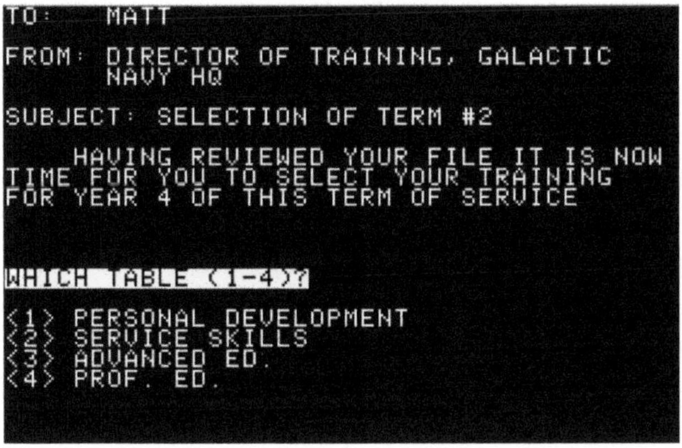

```
TO:   MATT
FROM: DIRECTOR OF TRAINING, GALACTIC
      NAVY HQ
SUBJECT: SELECTION OF TERM #2
      HAVING REVIEWED YOUR FILE IT IS NOW
TIME FOR YOU TO SELECT YOUR TRAINING
FOR YEAR 4 OF THIS TERM OF SERVICE


WHICH TABLE (1-4)?
<1> PERSONAL DEVELOPMENT
<2> SERVICE SKILLS
<3> ADVANCED ED.
<4> PROF. ED.
```

FIGURE 4.4 *Space* essentially makes a game out of character creation. Unfortunately, once you answer the seemingly endless questions, there's not much else to do!

can just get drafted (Figure 4.4). After this selection, the character is run through a series of physical and psychological tests to determine his or her suitability. I had to create several characters before finding one who wasn't too "out of touch with reality," and the game advised me to create a new character rather than play as a "defective product"! Likewise, the poor recruit struggled with all sorts of health issues that rendered him unfit for combat, such as thirty decibels of hearing loss and cardiovascular problems. The level of detail here is staggering.

Players also made numerous choices about how their character is trained, though much depends on the results of the initial exams. For instance, a character with little education may focus on learning, whereas other characters may choose skills such as using bribery or operating all-terrain vehicles. These four-year training cycles are repeated throughout the character's life. Between these training periods, the player can embark on six different (and utterly underwhelming) scenarios, which range from defending a planet from aliens to engaging in the stock market. All in all, *Space* is an ambitious game, but don't confuse that with being fun—it's more like taking the ASVAB test than playing a game!

In 1979, Edu-Ware published *Space II*, an expansion containing two additional scenarios, one of which was "Psychodelia." This scenario puts the player on "the Zintarian colony, homeworld of the Galaxy's supply of recreational drugs." Characters can explore these drugs at their own discretion, though doing so can have either positive or highly negative effects: "It is up to the player to determine the exact nature of a drug through experimentation, knowledge of the character, and clues provided by the program." The other scenario was hardly less controversial—this time the player was out to recruit followers into a cult.

GDC, the maker of *Traveller*, was not pleased when it discovered *Space*. The game clearly infringed on its copyrights, and neither Pederson nor Steffin had asked for permission. Furthermore, GDC planned to release its own computerized version of *Traveller*, and *Space* was just unfair competition. The game was hauled to dry dock, where David Mullich worked on removing the infringing material and salvaging what was left for a new game. That project became a trilogy named *Empire*, which was published exclusively for the Apple II between 1981 and 1984. It offered better graphics and sound than its predecessors, and it won several awards before it passed beyond the solar system.

The Tarturian

Another curious game from this era is *The Tarturian* (Figure 4.5), a graphical Apple II game released in 1980 (some sources claim 1981). The game looks similar to Sierra On-Line's classic *Mystery House* (1980), the first known graphical adventure game. *The Tarturian* depends heavily on its printed manual to guide the player—which literally stops players at the gate if they don't know the right command to start the game. Much of the gameplay consists of exploring the 160 rooms, "gathering

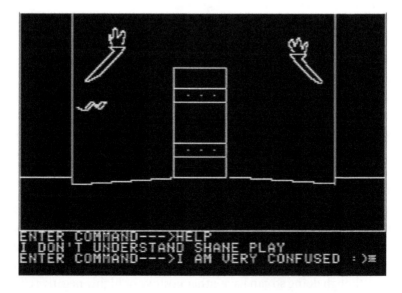

FIGURE 4.5 *The Tarturian* is bad enough to make your teeth ache.

weapons and treasure that will prepare you for the final battle against the TARTURIAN," though there are plenty of adventure game elements such as deciphering the "YUMMY YAKKY's" secret code and navigating mazes. The simplistic combat system doesn't impress, and the text parser is crude even by 1980 standards.

This isn't to say that the TARTURIAN doesn't have class. Indeed, it's remarkable for precisely the way it handles character classes. Rather than control a single character of a given class, the player is put in charge of a large team (ten each) of various classes. The classes (cleric, thief, gladiator, strongman, magician, elf, or wizard) have unique powers that are needed at various points in the game. For instance, only the thief can pick locks, and only the strongman can move or smash things. However, only the character leading the party can perform actions, so the player must change to another character to find the right way to solve a puzzle. To further complicate matters, slave traders roam the dungeons and will randomly capture a number of the party (say, three clerics, four thieves, two gladiators, and so on). Creatures can also randomly attack and kill the leader. There's no need to panic, though; the player has forty morticians in the party to promptly and properly dispose of fallen teammates.

The game is virtually unknown today, and I certainly don't recommend it. However, at least one well-known modern developer, John Romero of *Doom* and *Quake* fame, liked it enough to contribute a description of it for the website Mobygames (mobygames.com).

Odyssey: The Compleat Apventure

Sometime between 1979 and 1980, a programmer and entrepreneur named Robert Clardy formed Synergistic Software, which he used to publish his game *Dungeon Campaign, Wilderness Campaign* for the Apple II. As the name implies, this is a game consisting of two scenarios, though both are similar in terms of gameplay. Featuring an overhead map view combined with text, the game puts you in control of an army of nameless adventurers—and the numbers can swell to well over ninety. The group roams either a dungeon or the countryside looking for treasure to claim and monsters to fight. Combat is a simple affair that depends mostly on the size of the combatants' armies and the quality of their equipment, though other elements such as a luck roll are factored in.

This luck roll business is an interesting twist. Random numbers rapidly flash on the screen, and the player can try to hit the spacebar at just the right moment to load the dice. The player then rolls again for the enemy—this time going for a low roll, naturally. It all happens too quickly for an ordinary human to reliably strike the best numbers, but it does an admirable job of recreating the visceral thrill of rolling the dice across a tabletop.

There is also an innovative haggling system based on the character's charisma, which is randomly assigned at the start of the game. Players can attempt to wheedle down merchants, but they run the risk of offending them—in which case the merchant will permanently withdraw the item.

Winning victories calls for a large party, but this comes at a price—the player must feed all these hungry mouths, and the men can carry only so much weight (which must also include any treasure you manage to find). Managing such a large group is challenging, but also makes the game seem more like a strategy game than a true CRPG.

After *Dungeon Campaign, Wilderness Campaign*, Clardy produced *Odyssey: The Compleat Apventure* (Figure 4.6). It features better graphics than his first game, but borrows heavily from his previous effort. However, rather than two distinct campaigns, this game strings three scenarios together into a single epic. The resulting product felt like a much larger game than many gamers had experienced before.

The first chapter takes place on a dangerous, monster-infested island. The party must explore it, searching for treasure and items necessary to proceed to the next level. Specifically, the party must procure a ship and

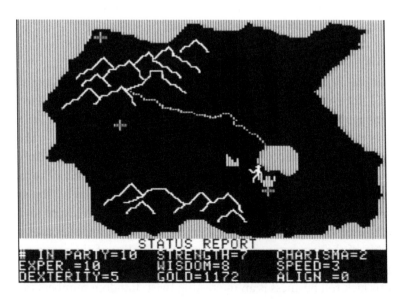

FIGURE 4.6 Clardy's *Odyssey: The Compleat Apventure* is a marvelous game with some intriguing gameplay mechanics.

sails, but also a variety of apparently useless things (such as a monkey) that turn out to be necessary to, er, *compleat* the game. The second chapter is solved when the player finds a magical weapon and arrives at the island of an evil wizard, who must be vanquished in the third chapter after the party overcomes some obstacles. *Odyssey* was a surprisingly ambitious project that received praise from critics and was popular among Apple II gamers. Clardy published a sequel called *Apventure to Atlantis*, which also sold well. Clardy adapted many of the innovative elements of these games for his later strategy games, including *J.R.R. Tolkien's War in Middle Earth* (1989) and *Spirit of Excalibur* (1990). More recently, Logic Artists' *Expeditions: Conquistador* (2013) and *Expeditions: Viking* (2017) hearken back to this style.

The unusual spelling of the game, by the way, was Clardy's effort to "sound medieval" in the case of "compleat," and to appeal to members of Apple II user groups, who he thought would parse "apventure" as "Apple Adventure." "More often than not, however," says Clardy, "I got angry letters from grammar nazis correcting me and accusing me of corrupting their kids' education."

Dunjonquest: The Birth of *Apshai*

Automated Simulations' *Dunjonquest: Temple of Apshai* (c. 1979) is better known than the other games discussed in this chapter. It owes much of that success to the exposure it received by being ported to so many different platforms—it originated on the TRS-80, but was soon ported to the Commodore PET. Later ports include the Apple II (1980), Atari computer (1981), DOS (1982), and the Commodore VIC-20 and 64 (1983) (Figures 4.7 and 4.8). If you didn't have an Apple II, the *Apshai* games may well have been the first (if not only) commercial CRPGs available for your system. Automated Simulations later changed its name to Epyx and produced several other top-selling games throughout the 1980s only to go bankrupt in 1989.

The *Apshai* games were great for their time, but perhaps their most enduring aspect is their wonderful manuals. The *Dunjonquest* manual is a lavishly illustrated, colorful overview of fantasy role-playing games and their unique appeal. The following excerpt provides a good sample of their style and tone:

Did you grow up in the company of the Brothers Grimm, Snow White, the Red Fairy Book, Flash Gordon serials, The Three

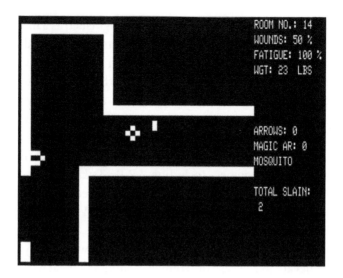

FIGURE 4.7   The original TRS-80 version of *Apshai*.

Musketeers, the knights of the Round Table, or any of the three versions of The Thief of Bagdad? Have you read the Lord of the Rings, the Worm Ouroboros, The Incomplete Enchanter, or Conan the Conqueror? Have you ever wished you could cross

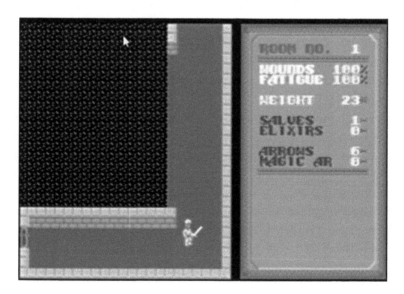

FIGURE 4.8   A later Commodore 64 version of *Apshai*. To conserve precious memory, both versions require you to consult the printed manual for descriptions of the rooms, treasures, and so on.

swords—just for fun—with Cyrano or D'Artagnan, or stand by their sides in the chill light of dawn, awaiting the arrival of the Cardinal's Guard? Ever wondered how you'd have done against the Gorgon, the hydra, the bane of Heorot Hall, or the bull that walks like a man? […] If any or all of your answers are "yes," you're a player of role-playing games—or you ought to be.

The manual goes on at some length in this fashion, arguing that "RPGs allow you a chance to step outside a world grown too prosaic for magic and monsters." Games like *Dunjonquest* allow nerds and other social outcasts to test their mettle and "can and often do become, for both you and your character, a way of life."

Even more intriguing is how the manual argues that CRPGs are simply a more convenient way to engage in fantasy role-playing, portraying the tabletop version as tedious and time-consuming: "Ordinary role-playing games require a group of reasonably experienced players, an imaginative dunjonmaster [*sic*] willing to put in the tremendous amount of time necessary to construct a functioning fantasy world, and large chunks of playing time." Indeed, the manual insists that "twenty-four hour marathons are not unheard of." This unbiased account goes on to contrast this hellish toil with the pure bliss of CRPGs, which offer preconstructed worlds and fast, error-free calculation of all those headache-inducing math problems.

However, anyone familiar with the tabletop game realized that there was a lot more to it than math—there are also the elements of role-playing and making important decisions that directly affect the narrative. The manual acknowledges the "greater practical limits to your actions" imposed by computerized role-playing, but argues that there are still "a large number of options to choose from." Indeed, many of the more intriguing features of the game are its attempts to bridge this gap between RPGs and CRPGs. As with *Odyssey*, players can haggle with the storekeeper. Furthermore, as with Garriott's *Akalabeth*, much of the in-game text is in character, with medieval dialectical markers such as *ye* for *you* and *thy* for *your*.

The manual also includes textual descriptions of each room of the dungeon—a necessary concession to the limited memory of early home computers. However, these brief prose passages are also reminiscent of the way a real game master would describe a room. Here is the description of Room 15:

Room Fifteen is an irregular cave of native rock. The walls and floor are covered with a heavy matting of multi-hued moss. The walls are brilliant reds, greens, and blues, while the floor is a pastel yellow. A wooden box lies topless in the middle of the cavern floor. Inside lies a well-made cloak. The material of the cloak seems to shimmer in the torchlight.

As you can imagine, these descriptions add a great deal of context and flavor to the game, making the manual a critical part of gameplay. The same feature shows up in many later games, such as Interplay's *Wasteland* and SSI's *Pool of Radiance* (both 1988). However, by then it was less a technical necessity and more a means of stymieing piracy, since making and shipping photocopies of all these documents could get quite costly.

Another important aspect of the *Apshai* games is the combat system. The manual claims that the developers were inspired by "historical research, a knowledge of various martial arts, and practical experience in the Society for Creative Anachronisms." In any case, there is a fatigue system that limits how often the character can attack and how far he can run (the character's wounds and the weight of his equipment also influence the fatigue rate). The character can also "hearken," or listen for the presence of a monster in an adjoining room, and even try to talk monsters out of combat. If a character dies, he suffers one of four fates—consumption by a roaming monster, or rescue by a dwarf, mage, or cleric. If the dwarf or mage performs the rescue, the character loses equipment; the pious cleric asks for nothing. The game also allows for ranged combat (bow and arrow), which is an effective way to dispatch monsters without risking damage. Unlike most games of the era, the *Apshai* series is set in real time. Even if you're away from the keyboard, the monsters will continue to roam about the dungeons, so don't take too long reading those room descriptions!

While the player's goals are typical of CRPGs of this era—explore ruins, loot as much as possible, and kill anything that gets in your way—critics still found much to praise. In a 1979 review of the game published in the very first issue of *Compute!* magazine, Len Lindsay describes it as "a game for anyone who is tired of simple 'video games,'" no doubt with his lip well curled in the general direction of an arcade. It was named "Computer Game of the Year" by the Academy of Adventure Gaming Arts & Design.[3]

Temple of Apshai was followed by *Datestones of Ryn* (1979), *Morloc's Tower* (1979), and *Curse of Ra* (1982). Related games and expansions include *Hellfire Warrior* (1980), *The Keys of Acheron* (1981), *Upper Reaches of Apshai* (1981), and *Gateway to Apshai* (1983). Epyx released the *Trilogy* compilation for a variety of platforms in 1983, but perhaps the best of these was the Commodore Amiga version released in 1986. *Trilogy* combined all of the sequels and add-ons and offered enhanced graphics and sound to boot. Anyone seriously desiring to play the series today should try this version, even if purists still prefer the older ones. In any case, the *Trilogy* sold very well and was the first time many players had experienced this wonderful series—making it both a Bronze Age as well as a Silver Age phenomenon.

A final game to mention here is *Dragon's Eye* (Figure 4.9), also published by Automated Simulations and released in 1981 for the Apple II and the Commodore PET (and later for Atari's 400 and 800). Developed by Southern Software, *Dragon's Eye* is one of many games that integrate the "twitch" or action gameplay mechanics found in most arcade games with the more refined pleasures of the CRPG.

After choosing a name, title, and preferred type of sword, the player is presented with a complex map (almost a schematic diagram) that offers a view of the land. Movement is essentially a matter of traveling between

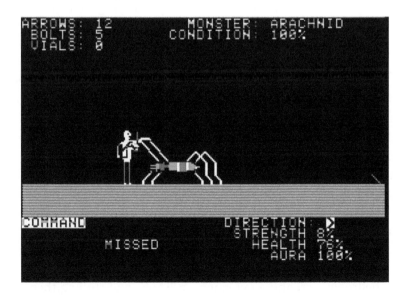

FIGURE 4.9 *Dragon's Eye* is an early effort to mix arcade-style gameplay with RPG mechanics. It wasn't a great success, but you can't fault the developer for trying. Image courtesy of CRPG Addict.

interconnected nodes on this map. It doesn't take long, however, before the character randomly encounters a monster. During these combat sequences, the perspective shifts to third-person, and we see the character standing to the left and the monster on the right of the screen. A real-time battle commences, and players must select and properly time their attacks if they wish to win. For instance, hitting "F" fires an arrow; this must be done quickly, before the monster gets too near the character. After that, players can hit "C" to chop, "S" to smash, and so on, depending on what type of sword their character is wielding. Complex strategies are possible, such as leaping forward several steps, stabbing, and withdrawing before the monster can react. The ultimate goal of *Dragon's Eye* is to find the titular amulet and return to Fel City before twenty-one days have gone by (we find similar "fetch" quests in many games of the era). It's not a great game by any means, but it shows how even at this early time CRPG developers were already trying to woo the "twitch" crowd.

THE END OF THE BRONZE AGE

The first batch of CRPGs for personal computers were ambitious, eccentric, and as awkward for modern gamers as a penny farthing at the Tour de France. It's not hard to see why. The programmers worked virtually without precedent, save for those few lucky enough to have played mainframe CRPGs. Slow processor speeds and terrible memory restrictions on the early PCs were severe obstacles, but a bigger problem was that programmers simply hadn't had enough time to optimize their coding practices. Many were programming in BASIC, which is an easy but inefficient language compared to assembly languages. As we'll see in the next chapter, early home computers were capable of much more.

There are certainly those who continue to play Bronze Age games today, especially if they grew up with them and enjoy the nostalgia. However, when we enter the Silver Age in the next chapter, we'll encounter games that are much better known, such as the first *Ultima* and *Wizardry* games. As CRPGs became more sophisticated, fans grew more selective. The days were numbered for those lone teenagers in their bedrooms, cranking out games in BASIC and stuffing them into Ziploc bags for sale at the local Computer Mart. All their hunting and pecking into the wee hours had at last woken the dragon, and it was flexing its wings.

NOTES

1. Early hardware manufacturers (particularly IBM) assumed the money was in the hardware and made little effort to protect their software, and usually benefited only from improvements implemented by others outside the company. Most software was made in-house and was of little use outside the company or institute that created it.

2. Charles Darwin faced a comparable problem regarding his theory of evolution by natural selection, but was lucky enough to get his theory published before being scooped by a fellow scientist, Alfred Russel Wallace.

3. This academy still exists, even though it has snubbed computer games since the 1990s.

CHAPTER 5

The Silver Age

In 1981, the personal or "home" computers were new kids on the block. Most of the marketing for this nascent industry focused on education; buy an Apple II and give your kid an edge. No less an authority than William Shatner was asking parents why they'd buy "just a video game" when they could improve their kids' grades *and* plan their finances with a Commodore VIC-20.

The truth was that if all you wanted to do was play games, you could play better ones at the arcade. Indeed, one of the key selling points of both consoles and computers was how well they mimicked the arcade experience at home. The arcade was where all the excitement was, and no one's ever paid a quarter for ninety seconds of *Dungeons & Dragons*.

But our bold young CRPG developers were undeterred. Along with other computer game makers, they were learning assembly language and tapping into the true capabilities of personal computers. Standards were emerging, interfaces were improving, and doubts were receding.

The CRPGs we've talked about so far were intended for hardcore role-playing fans; folks who were already intimately familiar with tabletop role-playing games. They were already hooked on the concept and well versed in the basics. But even these insiders didn't relish the idea of learning a whole new role-playing system every time a new game came out. If the CRPG was to survive, it needed series of games, which it got with *Ultima, Apshai,* and *Wizardry.* These franchises had great benefits for developers and gamers, and they mark an important turning point in the history of the CRPG.

Unlike the previous era, when you never knew what to expect, these games offered consistency and reassurance—once you learned one, you could move on to the next without having to learn a whole new set of rules and tomes of lore. Furthermore, these games were moving away from their tabletop origins, providing a different, more computer-centric, experience. Prior to this, CRPG players and designers both seemed to assume that CRPGs were just lame substitutes; something to do in your downtime between *D&D* or *Traveller* with friends. Silver Age CRPGs, however, had broader appeal and greater ambitions, and they won over computer types who'd never cracked open a *Player's Handbook*.

These all-important games of the Silver Age were *Ultima I: The First Age of Darkness* and *Wizardry: Proving Grounds of the Mad Overlord* (both 1981). Both launched successful and influential series that lasted into the 2000s, but it was *Ultima* that hoisted the genre into the mainstream. Indeed, its influence was worldwide, inspiring the Japanese console RPGs, or JRPGs like *Final Fantasy* and *Dragon Quest*.

Wizardry, meanwhile, earned a reputation for challenging, hardcore gameplay that appealed to gamers all over the globe. It demonstrates the power—and also the liability—of "engine recycling," or reusing the bulk of a game's code in subsequent games. On the plus side, this technique allows developers to create games faster for less cost. It also lets designers focus more on content, such as graphics and stories, than programming. On the negative side, many gamers expect sequels to be better or at least different than what came before, while others resent nearly every change (#notmyultima). We'll see this tension brought out nicely by comparing the *Ultima* and *Wizardry* series.

The Silver Age also saw several other important and influential games, such as *Telengard*, *Sword of Fargoal*, *Dungeons of Daggorath*, *Tunnels of Doom*, and *Universe*. Each of these games introduced or refined gameplay concepts that showed up in countless later games, and each vividly demonstrates the diversity of the genre in the early 1980s. Many are still beloved and played by hundreds of nostalgic gamers all over the world.

THE BIRTH OF *ULTIMA*

After his rousing success with *Akalabeth*, Garriott was ashamed of himself. Yea, verily, the game sold well. It impressed his publisher, and he had a tall stack of fan mail addressed to Lord British. But to Garriott, this was premature glorification. As he put it, he was just a hobbyist who'd stumbled into the commercial sector by accident: "I had been working for my own enjoyment and edification, not my dinner."[1] Now the *Akalabeth* hour was over, and it was time to put *Ultima* on the table.

There would be nothing even vaguely noobish about his next production. This was a commercial endeavor from the start, targeted at a larger, discriminating audience who'd appreciate the difference. There was no mention of his earlier game anywhere on the box; and, by the way, this time there would be a *box*, not a *bag*, thank you very much.

Rising to his self-imposed higher standard, Garriott teamed up with his friend and coworker Ken Arnold, whom he promptly dubbed "Sir Kenneth." Arnold earned his knighthood by writing an assembly code routine for tile-based graphics; a system reminiscent of a miniatures tabletop game. His technique had a crucial advantage: it required much less storage space but allowed for large, colorful environments, since the tiles could be reused again and again to create different scenes. It made all the difference in, and to, the world Garriott was building.

Garriott took full advantage of Arnold's system to depict a vast countryside, but he also incorporated the wireframe, first-person perspective of *Akalabeth* for his dungeons. Switching between these perspectives gave an impression of vastness: Explore the vast overland area, then delve down into bottomless dungeons. *Ultima* was as expansive as it was immense.

When California Pacific published it in 1981, there was no shortage of praise for its epic size and scope. Indeed, rather than limit himself to one time period, *Ultima* takes gamers from the Middle Ages to the Space Age. Critics just couldn't believe that characters who started off with maces ended the game with "phazors" and full-fledged space combat sequences. There were many smaller innovations, too, such as monsters (gelatinous cubes) that destroy armor and others that steal from the character's food supply (Figure 5.1).

The game handles hit points in a similar way to *Akalabeth*: instead of regenerating by resting or healing, the character must either buy hit points from the king or receive them upon leaving a dungeon. If the hit points run out, he dies and must be resurrected. Unfortunately, this resurrection system doesn't always work: There's a chance of respawning in the middle of a lake.

As before, Garriott did not plagiarize *D&D*'s rules for character creation. Instead, he refined his system from *Akalabeth*. Now instead of just rolling and rerolling randomly hoping for decent stats, the player is given 90 points to distribute across six categories: strength, agility, stamina, charisma, wisdom, and intelligence. Of course, a sensible distribution depends on the choice of type, or class: fighter, cleric, wizard, or thief. There are four races to choose from, one being hobbits—no doubt a nod to Tolkien.

FIGURE 5.1 Garriott's *Ultima* may very well be the most important and influential CRPG ever designed.

We'll see this point distribution system in many later games, and it raises an interesting question of how much control players should have over this aspect of a CRPG. Is it more fun to play with random stats, embracing the challenge of a poorly endowed character? Should players at least have to roll and reroll repeatedly to achieve high stats, which at least gives some impression of how improbable and rare such people are in real life? In my opinion, Garriott had the right idea: just let players decide this on their own.

The storyline builds on *Akalabeth*'s. The evil wizard Mondain has enslaved the lands of Sosaria using a gem of power that makes him completely unstoppable. It's the player's mission to travel back in time and kill him before he can use the gem and take over the world. Solving the game means traveling across vast distances, fighting random encounters along the way.

Garriott programmed his parts in BASIC while Arnold did his tile-based system in assembly. Initially, it was available only for Apple IIs equipped with at least 64K of memory (a stock machine could have as little as 4K!). Here, we see an early glimpse of Garriott's unwillingness to compromise when it came to his creative vision (Figure 5.2).

Despite his rampant perfectionism, as a lifelong Apple II snob, Garriott left it to others to reprogram his games for other systems. In 1983 Doug Ferguson reprogrammed *Ultima* for Atari's 8-bit computers. In 1986, it was reprogrammed again, this time by Dave Holle and others into assembly language, who updated the graphics and made a few other small changes.

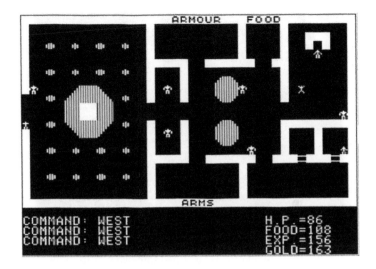

FIGURE 5.2 Richard Garriott has a habit of inserting his alter ego into his games. In this image, he's the stick figure in the upper right corner, in front of the throne. Hail to thee, Lord British!

This version was ported to the Commodore 64, MS-DOS, and MSX platforms and is probably more familiar to most gamers than the original.

The Revenge of the Enchantress

Ultima was an unqualified success, and Garriott wasted no time producing the sequel. *Ultima II: The Revenge of the Enchantress* (August 1982) (Figures 5.3 and 5.4) was published by Sierra On-Line rather than California Pacific, which had somehow managed to go bankrupt in the interval. Garriott had several offers from major publishers, but chose Sierra because they agreed to include a cloth map with the game. This unusual pack-in became a venerable tradition and a hot item with collectors. It was inspired by Terry Gilliam's 1981 film *Time Bandits,* where such a map figures prominently.

The second game made several improvements, such as the ability to talk to nonplayer characters and more routines written in assembly language that increased the game's speed. It also doubled the number of tiles used for the graphics, a noticeable and desirable improvement.

Like the first *Ultima, The Revenge of the Enchantress* mixes fantasy and sci-fi elements. This time it's not Mondain, but rather his apprentice and lover, Minax, who aims to eradicate the human race. Her weapon of choice? Nuclear war. Again the player has to track down a magical item,

FIGURE 5.3   *Ultima II's* reputation is tarnished somewhat by its many bugs.

a quest that involves traveling to several villages, time periods, and even different planets. It's an enormous game whose impressive scope is comparable only to Sierra's other big game of 1982, *Time Zone*, a sprawling $100 graphical adventure game by Roberta Williams. However, *Ultima II*

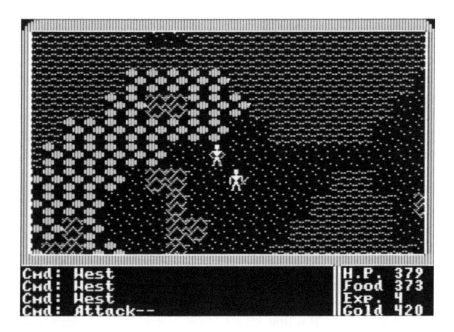

FIGURE 5.4   *Ultima II* doubles the number of tiles used for representing the gameworld.

has several bugs, and some critics complained that the game has a rushed, unpolished feel. Nevertheless, it sold even better than the previous one.

When it was time for *Ultima III,* Garriott decided to break from Sierra and publish the game under his own company, Origin—primarily a family affair consisting of his brother and their parents. Garriott did not leave Sierra on good terms, however. According to a 1986 interview published in *Computer Gaming World,* he felt that Sierra "did not seem very author friendly," and that "I never really knew if I was getting a fair shake."

What exactly did Garriott have in mind when he made these comments? Some sources claim that the comments refer to an argument about the royalties for the IBM PC port of *Ultima II.* When Garriott had signed his contract with Sierra, the IBM PC didn't exist, and thus was not factored into the royalty agreement. According to Garriott, Sierra offered him a "take it or leave it" arrangement with lower royalties than he felt he deserved. This is the explanation offered by Shay Addams in his *The Official Book of Ultima* and suggested by *Wikipedia.*

A persistent rumor is that it had something to do with a game called *Ultima: Escape from Mt. Drash,* published in 1983 exclusively for the Commodore VIC-20. It was programmed by Garriott's friend Keith Zabalaoui, who'd helped him out with both *Akalabeth* and *Ultima II.* The rumor claims that it was done behind his back, exploiting the *Ultima* brand for a quick buck. However, Jimmy Mayer of *The Digital Antiquarian* argues that Garriott knew all about the game and gave his permission. After all, he owed his friend a favor, and at this point his *Ultima* brand wasn't nearly as valuable as it became later.

In any case, *Ultima: Escape from Mt. Drash* was a poor seller and is so rare today that it has become a Holy Grail for collectors of vintage software. In 2003, the loose data cassette alone fetched $865 in an online auction! The game itself is a straightforward dungeon crawl, albeit one featuring a three-sectioned interface and 3D dungeons. A review in the July/ August issue of *Computer Gaming World* praises its "unique graphics and marvelous musical score," but its collectability owes more to controversy than quality. Addams doesn't even mention it in his *Official* book.

Ultima III: Exodus

As impressive as the first two *Ultima* games are for their time, *Ultima III: Exodus* is impressive for all time. First published in 1983 by Origin, the third *Ultima* was an instant success, firmly establishing Garriott as a master of the genre: a "veritable J.R.R. Tolkien of the keyboard," as one

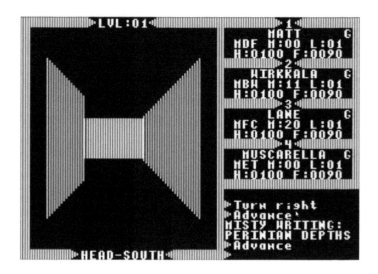

FIGURE 5.5 *Ultima III* sports an improved interface and audiovisuals, but the biggest innovation is that you now control an entire party of adventurers rather than a single avatar.

earnest reviewer put it. The game inspired and influenced not only countless other CRPGs, but also inspired Japan's console RPGs (JRPGs) such as *Dragon Quest* and *Final Fantasy*. It's certainly no exaggeration to call it one of the most important games ever made and the absolute pinnacle of the Silver Age.

Several innovations make *Exodus* stand out from the earlier *Ultima* games. First, now players control a party of four adventurers rather than just a single hero (Figure 5.5). Not coincidentally, by this time another CRPG series called *Wizardry* was making its presence felt. As Garriott himself put it, "Since *Wizardry* had multiple characters, I needed them too."[2] The characters could be one of five different races and eleven different classes. Unfortunately for Tolkien fans, "hobbits" are no longer an option, though perhaps this game's "bobbits" aren't too far removed. As always, these manuals are written in-character, with a style and tone suited to the theme. Following is the description of "Sominae," which amounts to a simple light spell:

> Thine enlightenment hath expanded and will continue to unfold like the star-filled heavens above.

> The first light which thy Truth created for thee was wondrous indeed, and luminance of this sort will continue to be of great service to thee.

Yet in order to fulfill some greater needs, more enduring illumination is required.

If thou dost now meditate on this enchantment, thine entire self will radiate from the light of Truth. Know that even this light cannot be sustained indefinitely, for it doth draw from thine own inner force.

This poetic style is maintained throughout; even when explaining the banalities of the interface, Garriott can't help but slip in the occasional "thy" and "thou." It's wonderfully nerdy stuff, and a good reason to seek out a complete copy.

A second major innovation is a new combat mode (Figure 5.6). Although the party is depicted as a single character on the map, once combat is initiated, the game separates the party into individuals and shows them on a new screen. This is a tactical, turn-based combat system with time limits (if a player takes too long to move a character, the game automatically skips to the next character or monster's turn). Now players have to consider more fully the implications of distance and direction of attacks. Furthermore, while the player's characters can attack only in the cardinal directions, the

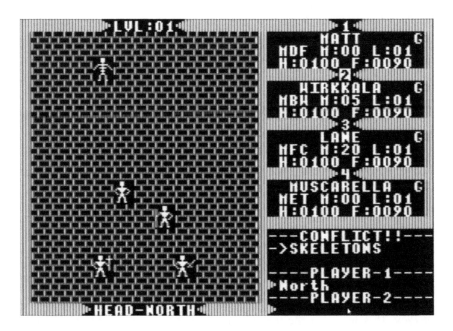

FIGURE 5.6 Combat in *Ultima III* is a good deal more tactical than before. Hopefully, this lone skeleton won't stand much of a chance against my hardy band.

monsters are free to attack diagonally—which makes it all too easy to get surrounded. There are sixteen hand-to-hand and ranged weapons, eight armor types, and thirty-two magic spells with names inspired by Latin. This system proved remarkably durable, and we'll see something similar in SSI's *Wizard Crown* and *Pool of Radiance*.

One unusual and somewhat frustrating aspect of the combat system is that only the character striking the deathblow gets any experience points for the battle. This can lead to a severely unbalanced party, so it's important to let characters take turns finishing off enemies. Once characters have enough points, they can ask Lord British to raise their hit points.

Garriott also reworked the scenes involving sea travel, introducing a ship-to-shore combat system and wind navigation. To top it all off, Garriott added a dynamic musical score that changes with various settings, though Apple II owners needed the optional Mockingboard expansion card to hear it. Yet again, Garriott was more concerned with achieving his creative vision than whether gamers could afford such options—a Mockingboard cost $99, or nearly $300 in today's currency.

Yet another important innovation is the fixed dungeons. Rather than random and mostly irrelevant dungeons, *Ultima III* integrated a series of stable dungeons directly into the gameplay, perhaps as a response to the frequent complaint that the dungeons in the previous games were practically superfluous. Furthermore, the dungeons in *Ultima III* aren't wireframe, but solid color and reminiscent of later CRPGs such as *The Bard's Tale* (1985), though predated by Texas Instruments' *Tunnels of Doom* (1982).

The storyline avoids the sci-fi elements that played such an important role in the first two games. Simply put, the player must seek out and kill an evil overlord, this time one named Exodus. Exodus is the offspring of Mondain and Minax and has been terrorizing the land of Sosaria with no regard for diplomacy. Solving the game requires seeking out the mysterious Time Lord and working out the secrets of the Moon Gates. It isn't enough just to build up a strong party, though—players must talk to townspeople to gather enough clues to solve a series of puzzles.

Once again, Garriott spared no expenses on the game's packaging and materials. In addition to another lovely cloth map, he included three booklets: *The Ancient Liturgy of Truth*, *The Book of Amber Runes*, and *The Book of Play*. This was also the first *Ultima* with an official clue book: *Secrets of Sosaria*, a forty-eight-page collection of maps and tips. It was authored by "Lord Robert," aka Richard Garriott's brother, Robert. A great collectible today, this booklet is much more than just a cheat sheet. Indeed, it's filled with vivid descriptions and quotations from Lord British and other beloved *Ultima* characters such as Iolo the Bard: "Here the jesters sing hoho/but why they do/I'll never know." Though often overlooked even in books like this one, official and unofficial clue books are an important part of the industry.

Ultima III was a smash hit, selling some 120,000 copies and cementing Lord British's reputation as the foremost maker of CRPGs. It was ported to most of the available platforms of the day and later even to the Nintendo Entertainment System (NES).

WIZARDRY: THE PROVING GROUNDS

Although Garriott's *Ultima* is the best-known CRPG series of the 1980s, it was certainly not the only one. As early as 1981, a worthy competitor threw down the gauntlet: Sir-Tech. Founded by Robert Woodhead and Norman Sirotek, Sir-Tech's CRPGs are known for their excellent designs and extraordinarily challenge. Its *Wizardry* series did much to standardize the genre, and would remain vital throughout the 1980s and early 1990s.

The first of these is *Wizardry: Proving Grounds of the Mad Overlord* (Figure 5.7), published in 1981 for the Apple II (and in 1987 for other platforms). Unlike *Ultima*, *Wizardry* allows players to create their own parties from the start: up to six, who can be almost any mix of five different races (humans, elves, dwarves, gnomes, hobbits), four starting classes (fighter,

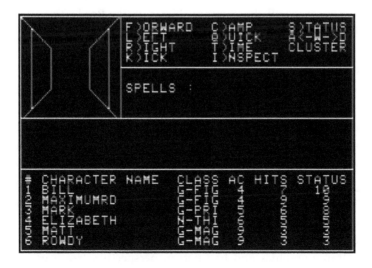

FIGURE 5.7 *Wizardry's* clean interface and immense wireframe dungeons proved a hit with gamers. Just keep the graph paper handy!

mage, priest, thief), and three alignments (good, neutral, evil). (I say almost because good and evil characters can't join the same party.) After these selections, the player distributes a random number of bonus points among six stats (strength, I.Q., piety, vitality, agility, and luck). Needless to say, going through this cycle six times can take a while, particularly if you're determined to create the best possible party. The manual puts it well: "Playing *Wizardry* for the first time is like kissing for the first time— you want to do it right, and you're not quite sure exactly what you are supposed to do."

Creating a group rather a single character leads to a much different gameplay dynamic. Players must carefully balance their parties to get the right combination of skills necessary to complete the ten-level dungeon. In other words, players are required to make many important decisions before gameplay commences; the character creation process is long, involved, and of paramount importance. A few poor selections can easily make the game extremely difficult, if not unwinnable.

Further complicating the party issue are four elite classes, which are more or less hybrids of the four basic classes: bishop (priest/mage), samurai (fighter/mage), lord (fighter/priest), and ninja (fighter/thief). The ninja is similar to what many later games would call the monk, a fighter that shuns weapons and armor and excels at critical strikes. There are some alignment restrictions as well: Bishops can't be neutral, samurai can't be evil, lords must be good, and ninjas must be evil. The elite or prestige class is something that will show up again later in *The Bard's Tale* (1985) and many later CRPGs.

The magic system is also fairly elaborate, with some fifty total spells for priests and mages. Perhaps as a tactic to ensure that players purchased a legal copy of the game, spells can only be cast by entering their names— which are only revealed in the manual, of course. Although most of the spells are combat-related, a few are useful in other ways. For example, the mage spell "DUMAPIC" reveals the player's current position in the maze relative to the stairs leading out of the maze, and "MALOR," if cast in camp, will teleport the party to a precise location. The magic system uses a special spell point system involving slots for each level of spell. These points can be replenished only by resting in The Castle.

Like *Akalabeth*, *Wizardry* portrays the dungeons (called The Maze) in 3D wireframe graphics and first-person perspective. However, one nice innovation is that when battle is joined, the dungeon graphic is replaced by a color portrait of one of the attacking monsters (up to four groups of them

FIGURE 5.8 Combat in *Wizardry* is turn-based and requires not only luck but also good resource management.

can attack) (Figure 5.8). It's a great opportunity for art, and we'll see it in countless later games such *The Bard's Tale* and *The Pool of Radiance* (1988).

The dungeons are arranged on a 20 × 20 grid, which makes them ideal for mapping onto graph paper. Since the dungeons are fixed rather than procedurally generated, players really benefit from a good map. The manual offers detailed instructions on making such a map and lets player know that "mapping is indeed one of the most important skills that successful *Wizardry* players possess." Whereas some gamers find the task irksome, others enjoy it almost as much as playing the game. I find the cartography fascinating, especially when I consider how CRPGs evolved from *Colossal Cave* and other exploration games. Mapmaking remained a critical skill for many years, at least until CRPGs began including automapping tools. It's always a delight to come across a boxed copy of one of these earlier games and find it filled with the previous owners' hand-drawn maps.

The storyline of *Wizardry* is standard fare. The Evil Wizard Werdna has stolen a magical amulet from Trebor *(Robert* spelled backward), the Mad Overlord. Furthermore, Werdna has used the amulet to create a ten-level fortress maze beneath Trebor's castle. Trebor has declared this maze the proving grounds for his bodyguards, and of course it's up to the party to descend into it, battling whatever monsters stand between them and the amulet. It's easy to see the connections to the older mainframe games, many of which offer the same quest for an all-powerful magical amulet.

Wizardry was created by Andrew C. Greenberg and Robert Woodhead, then students at Cornell University. They spent some two and a half years developing it. The reason for the delay was that the game had originally been programmed in BASIC, but that language had proven too inefficient for the game to run smoothly on an Apple II. They converted the game to Pascal, a decision that it made it much easier to port the game to other platforms later on. Unfortunately, Pascal programs required 48K of RAM to operate, and Apple II needed an optional RAM expansion called a Language Card to run them. It wasn't until 1979 that Apple introduced the Apple II+, which shipped with the required 48KB of RAM. In short, Greenberg and Woodhead were at least a year ahead of the technology and had to wait for gamers and the computer industry to catch up with them.

It's no coincidence that *Wizardry* looks and plays a lot like the *Oubliette* game we discussed earlier. Woodhead was obsessed with PLATO and certainly played his share of *Oubliette* with his friends. On one hand, the games are fundamentally different—*Wizardry* has no network capability and is usually played by one person. *Oubliette,* by contrast, is more like an MMORPG. However, Jim Schwaiger, the author of *Oubliette*, claims that he "could not find any meaningful difference" between his game and *Wizardry*. Even the spell names are clearly derived from it. Indeed, Schwaiger suggests that even the multiplayer functionality would have been copied if that had been feasible at the time. In any case, even though Schwaiger's own adaptation of his game for home computers was much less successful than *Wizardry,* he seems to bear it no grudge.

Fighting for Your Right to Party

Wizardry brings us to an interesting question about CRPGs. Is it more fun to control a party or a single adventurer? One way to get at this question is to pose another: Which is more like tabletop role-playing games? On one hand, almost all conventional *D&D* games involve groups of players and their characters. Usually, Game Masters will encourage the players to select characters who complement one another, ideally having at least one of each basic type (fighter, thief, cleric, and mage). This way, the characters can work together to devise strategies and overcome obstacles—for instance, a sorceress might be extremely vulnerable in hand-to-hand combat, but devastatingly effective at range; it becomes the fighters' job to occupy the monsters so that she can cast her spells. Thus, it would seem that party-based games like *Wizardry* and *Ultima III* are closer to the *D&D* model.

On the other hand, *D&D* players control only one character at a time and are asked to assume the role of only that character during the session. Looked at from this perspective, single-hero games like *Ultima* and *Rogue* are closer to the model, since it's much easier (theoretically, at least) to identify with a single character than a whole group of them. This problem has yet to be solved, and CRPG fans and developers have long been divided on the issue. Currently, most popular CRPGs are either single-character games or a compromise (the player creates and entirely controls one character, but can add predefined and semiautonomous characters later on). Games like *Wizardry* that require you to create an entire party from scratch are quite rare.

The Knight of Diamonds and Legacy of Llylgamyn

The next two *Wizardry* games are *The Knight of Diamonds* (1982) and *Legacy of Llylgamyn* (1983). Unlike Garriott's strategy to reinvent the engine with each new game, Sir-Tech seems to have followed the old adage "If it ain't broke, don't fix it" (Figure 5.9). On a technical level, these games are practically identical to *Proving Grounds,* though of course they offer new stories and areas to explore.

The Knight of Diamonds involves another fetch quest, this time to find the staff of Gnilda, a powerful magical item that formerly protected the City of Llylgamyn from attack. Unfortunately, the evil Davalpus was immune to the staff's power by virtue of being born in the city (the staff's

FIGURE 5.9 Unlike Garriott's *Ultima* series, *Wizardry's* designers followed the old adage "If it ain't broke, don't fix it."

fatal flaw). Davalpus slew the royal family except for Princess Margda and Prince Alavik, who used the staff and the armor of the Knight of Diamonds to battle the usurper. Alavik was not successful, however, and after the battle all that was left was a "smoking hole in the ground." It's the player's mission, of course, to get back the staff, but that will mean first procuring all five pieces of the fabled armor. To complicate matters, each of these pieces is a living being that must be defeated in combat. As expected, solving the game means plunging into a dungeon (this time one with only six levels) and battling whatever beasts stand in the way.

Originally, *The Knight of Diamonds* required that players previously complete the first game, the idea being to carry over their characters into the new scenario—an early example of an expansion pack. However, this plan didn't prove financially sound, and later versions allowed players either to load a pre-generated party or to create new characters. Of course, since the dungeons are calibrated for characters of level 13 or more, new characters are very unlikely to survive their first battle.

The final game of the original trilogy is *Legacy of Llylgamyn.* The goal this time is to find a dragon named L'Kbreth, whose mystical orb can save the city of Llylgamyn from a recent surge of earthquakes and volcanic eruptions. Characters can again be imported from previous games, but are stripped of their experience (they are supposed to be a new generation of adventurers). However, there is an elaborate rite of passage ceremony by which the new characters can receive a blessing from their ancestors (a boost in stats and skills). Furthermore, they can choose a new moral alignment, which determines what parts of the world they can visit. Perhaps the most intriguing innovation is that the typical dungeon crawler setup is reversed: Rather than start at the top and work their way down, the party begins at the bottom of a volcano and must work its way back up.

Certain traditions carry across all three games, such as Boltac's Trading Post, the Temple of Cant, and odd monsters such as Creeping Coins. Connections such as these add coherence to the series and are quite memorable for those who played the games.

A minor controversy surrounding this game concerns *Wizplus,* a $40 program developed by a company named Datamost and released in 1982. *Wizplus* is one of the earliest commercial utility programs that lets players to freely edit their characters as they see fit, including making them invulnerable. Sir-Tech came out against the product, arguing that such "cheat programs" interfered with the "subtle balance" they had achieved over "four years of careful adjustment."[3] It seems more of a testament to the game's difficulty, though, that such a product received so much attention in the first place. Sir-Tech went so far as to refuse to honor their warranty on *Wizardry* disks that had been tampered with using *Wizplus*.

The Return of Werdna: Turning the Tables

Although the next game in the series, *Wizardry IV: The Return of Werdna,* was not published until 1987, it's similar enough to the first three to merit discussion here. Four years had passed since *Legacy of Llylgamyn,* and when the game finally arrived, it no doubt took most fans of the series by surprise—this time, you get to be the evil wizard hell-bent on getting your revenge. The plot is perhaps the only one of its type in the history of CRPGs. In this game's narrative, Werdna (the wizard defeated in the first *Wizardry)* has awakened, but he's now without his powers and trapped in the bottom of his ten-level dungeon. Furthermore, all of the monsters and traps that existed to keep out wily adventurers now serve the opposite purpose—to keep Werdna imprisoned. Getting Werdna out of the dungeon will take time and patience, but the revenge will be sweet. Thankfully, Werdna is able to summon monsters to help him out, though the players are unable to control them directly.

The Return of Werdna is widely considered to be the most difficult CRPG ever created, and it's definitely a game suited only for veterans of the first three games. The dungeon is resistant to mapping, and there are several brain-stumping puzzles sprinkled throughout. To make matters worse, the ghost of one of Werdna's slain enemies, Trebor, haunts the dungeon and will instantly kill you if you stumbles upon him. Finally, every save of the game resurrects all the monsters on the current level. Rumors of this game's difficulty have not been exaggerated!

There's also a nice bit of history here that's not often discussed in modern reviews of this game: Sir-Tech used some of the characters from disks it had received from gamers, who either wanted them repaired or sent them to show they had indeed solved the game. The company used some of these purloined characters as do-gooder enemies for Werdna. The game also features three separate endings, the most difficult of which entitles players to the hallowed rank of Wizardry Grand Master.

The first three *Wizardry* games were quite successful and were eventually ported to the Commodore 64, DOS, and even the NES platform (which has the best graphics). Sir-Tech published them in various compilations, starting with the *Wizardry Trilogy* in 1987 for DOS. The latest publication is *The Ultimate Wizardry Archives* (1998) for DOS and Windows, which includes the first seven games in the series. The fourth game is perhaps the least known, since its graphics and audiovisuals were hardly competitive for its release date, and its difficulty level ensured that no one but hardcore fans of the original games could complete it.

Though we'll have opportunities to discuss *Wizardry* in later chapters, what's important to note here is that *Ultima* wasn't the only game in town. The *Wizardry* series was a worthy rival. Furthermore, *Wizardry* has been highly influential, even for Garriott (who, as you'll remember, acknowledged that his decision to make *Ultima III* a party-based game was in response to the popularity of *Wizardry*). Finally, it's a useful game to have in mind when discussing issues still pertinent to modern CRPGs, such as whether it's better for sequels to allow players to import their characters from previous games or to require players to start from scratch.

OTHER HIGHLIGHTS OF THE SILVER AGE

Although *Ultima* and *Wizardry* are by far the most popular and well-known CRPGs of this era, there are at least six other games that are either influential or innovative enough to deserve mention here. These are *Telengard, The Sword of Fargoal, Dungeons of Daggorath, Tunnels of Doom, Ali Baba and the Forty Thieves,* and *Universe.*

Telengard and DND

Perhaps the most historically interesting of these games is Daniel Lawrence's *Telengard,* published by Avalon Hill in 1982 for the Commodore PET (ports for other systems, including the Commodore 64, quickly followed). If nothing else, it's an enlightening study of how commercial considerations were undermining the older mainframe policies of openness and free distribution. In the case of *Telengard,* this shift resulted in a legal mess.

Telengard was based on a 1976 game titled *DND*[4] that Lawrence had programmed in BASIC on a PDP-10 mainframe. *DND* was quite a success at Purdue University, where Lawrence was a student. Later, Lawrence was invited by the engineers at DEC's factory in Maynard, Massachusetts, to port the game to the new DECSYSTEM-20. The engineers were big fans of the game and distributed it widely.

At some point in 1978, Lawrence ported the game to the Commodore PET, implementing a clever procedure to generate dungeons on the fly. This was necessary because of the PET's extreme memory limitations (8K of RAM!). He shopped the game around at conventions, finally impressing the famous tabletop wargaming publisher, Avalon Hill, enough to secure a contract. By this time, the game had become known as *Telengard,* no doubt to avoid possible litigation with TSR over its trademarks and copyrights.

The publication of *Telengard* meant that Lawrence no longer wanted the engineers at DEC to freely distribute *DND.* After a brief period of legal wrangling, DEC had the game purged from its servers. It's not entirely clear if the pressure to do so was coming from Lawrence, Avalon Hill, or TSR, but likely it was simply a commonsense decision to avoid litigation. Unfortunately for Lawrence, DEC didn't move fast enough to keep his code from ending up in the hands of "Bill," a programmer who formed R.O. Software to distribute a $25 shareware version of *DND* that he released in 1984. The game was successful enough to attract Lawrence's attention; he saw it as unfair competition and did what he could to prevent its distribution. For his part, Bill claimed that he had done enough work cleaning up the "spaghetti code" of the original game [ouch!] for his game to be considered a new product. In any case, Bill updated the game and rereleased it as *Dungeon of the Necromancer's Domain* in 1988, which he staunchly claimed was a "ground-up rewrite" to avoid future conflict with Lawrence.[5]

Like *Akalabeth, Telengard* offered procedurally generated dungeons (Figure 5.10), though rather than promote its "infinite dungeons," the publisher made a humbler claim: "50 levels with 2 million rooms." *Telengard* is set in real time, so that gamers taking a bathroom break might very well find their character dead upon their return! It features twenty different monster types and thirty-six spells, as well as fountains, thrones,

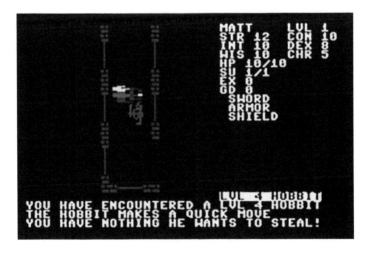

FIGURE 5.10 *Telengard* uses procedural generation to spawn a massive set of dungeons despite tight memory limitations.

altars, and teleportation cubes that produce random effects on the character. However, the game lacks a storyline; it's a pure dungeon crawler with "hack 'n slash" style gameplay. If you want to play the game today, check out Travis Baldree's *Telengard* remake for Windows.[6] Daniel Lawrence also made the IBM PC version freely available from his own website before his untimely death in 2010.[7]

Sword of Fargoal

Another early game similar to the mainframe classics is Jeff McCord's *Sword of Fargoal* (Figure 5.11), published by Epyx in 1982 for the Commodore VIC-20 (a significantly enhanced version followed in 1983 for the Commodore 64.) Though McCord denies having played *Telengard*, his game shares many of its features, such as randomized dungeons, but differs by incorporating the quest motif: descend into the dungeon, fetch the eponymous blade, and escape. One if its best innovations is a fog of war effect, which obscures parts of the overhead map until the character has explored them; it amounts to an auto-mapping tool. However, it's really the sound effects that set this game apart. Besides the catchy ditties that play between levels, an ominous chord progression plays whenever the monsters move in the dungeon. Players can hear the monsters before they see them, a technique that greatly ratchets up the tension. McCord acknowledges Steven Spielberg's 1975 blockbuster *Jaws* as inspiration for this innovation.

Sword of Fargoal has a fairly severe time limit (2,000 seconds) and is difficult to win. However, the relative simplicity of the interface makes it

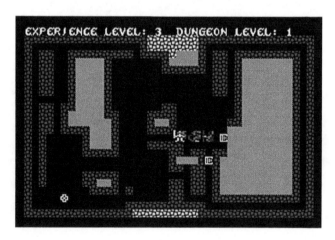

FIGURE 5.11 *Sword of Fargoal* is a fun, highly accessible CRPG by McCord. Incidentally, McCord was my first-ever guest on *Matt Chat*.

one of the more playable and accessible of the early CRPGs, and it was popular among gamers and critics—indeed, it ranked on *Computer Gaming World*'s "150 Best Games of All Time," published in 1996, and remains a fan favorite among Commodore fans. It's recently been remade for Windows by Paul Pridham and Elias Pschernig.[8] Jeff McCord worked with Pridham and Pschernig on an updated version of the game for Apple's iPhone.

McCord wrote *Sword of Fargoal* on a Commodore PET owned by his high school in Lexington, Kentucky. It's primarily based on his own *Gammaquest II,* an unpublished dungeon crawler with randomly generated dungeons that McCord designed to show off to publishers. McCord's computer science teacher, a Mr. Syler, was fond of admonishing his class that there were to be "no games in the computer room." Nonetheless, the acerbic teacher recognized McCord's gift and loaned him a key to the lab, which he used during off-hours to program and playtest the game. The finished project weighed in at a compact 14 kilobytes, an impressive feat given the depth of gameplay. McCord, the son of a computer science professor and an avid *D&D* Dungeon Master, was only nineteen years old at the time. Incidentally, the title was originally to be *Sword of Fargaol,* based on the old spelling of *jail.* However, Epyx felt that few gamers would appreciate the archaic spelling.

McCord earned roughly $40,000 in royalties during its publication run. Though it isn't as ambitious as *Ultima* or *Wizardry*, its simple interface and charming sound effects made *Sword of Fargoal* much more accessible to *D&D* novices and casual gamers. Unfortunately, McCord's next project, *Tesseract Strategy,* was never completed, though its intended publisher, Electronic Arts, had shown enough interest to fly McCord to San Francisco for a photo shoot.

Dungeons of Daggorath

The next two games we'll discuss, *Dungeons of Daggorath* and *Tunnels of Doom,* were released only on a single, relatively minor platform (the Tandy CoCo and Texas Instruments' TI-99/4A, respectively). Thus, we have an intriguing question of whether their success is owed more to their intrinsic qualities or to the lack of direct competition. In any case, they are highly innovative games that are certainly worth our attention.

Dungeons of Daggorath, developed by DynaMicro and published by Tandy in 1982, offers a 3D, first-person perspective in wireframe of the dungeons quite similar to that seen in *Akalabeth* and *Wizardry*. The storyline is the standard "kill the evil wizard buried deep in a monster-infested

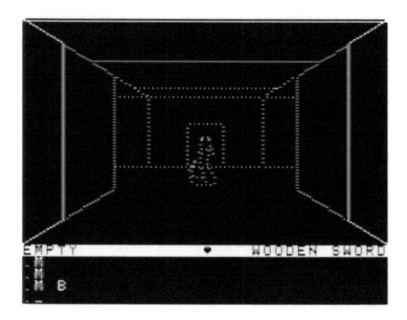

FIGURE 5.12 *Dungeons of Daggorath* is one of the best CRPGs for the Tandy CoCo computer. Its heartbeat sound effects and real-time gameplay ratchet up the tension quite effectively.

dungeon." There are only five levels, a dozen creature types, four rings, and of course the usual shields, swords, scrolls, and torches (like many games of the era, you need a lit torch to see in the dungeons).

However, what makes *Dungeons of Daggorath* stand out is its real-time fatigue system (Figure 5.12). The system is represented by a pulsating heart at the bottom of the screen; it beats faster or slower depending on the level of stress the player is experiencing. Taking damage or moving too quickly will cause the heart to pulse rapidly. If the heart beats too furiously, the character will faint (and likely become monster meat). This fatigue system does away with the numerical hit point or vitality systems so prevalent in other games. Instead, players must listen to the beating heart, a sound well known for its unsettling effect in horror films. This sound effect makes for a more visceral, arcade-like experience than most CRPGs, then or now. The game was recently remade for Windows and freely available from the Microsoft Store.

Tunnels of Doom

If *Dungeons of Daggorath* was the big CRPG for the Tandy CoCo, *Tunnels of Doom* was most certainly the best CRPG going on Texas Instruments' TI-99/4A. Texas Instruments is one of the few personal computer

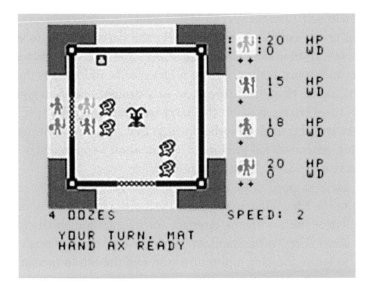

FIGURE 5.13 Kevin Kenney's *Tunnels of Doom* is one of the best (and only) CRPGs for the TI-99/4A computer. Once you complete the premade adventures, you can make your own scenarios and share them with friends.

manufacturers that actively discouraged third-party development, preferring to publish all the software for its systems itself. Rather than generate a collection of must-have exclusives that would help sell the platform, though, it only managed to disenfranchise developers. The inevitable result is that the TI-99/4A had one of the smallest game libraries in the industry; only forty or so games were ever published for it, the bulk being remakes of popular arcade games.

Nevertheless, at least one gem really stands out. Programmed by Kevin Kenney in 1982, *Tunnels of Doom* (Figure 5.13) contains many of the features that show up in later games such as SSI's Gold Box games, which debut in 1988 with *The Pool of Radiance*. Perhaps the best way to describe the game is as a combination of themes from *Telengard* and *Wizardry*. Like *Telengard*, *Tunnels of Doom* features fountains, altars, and thrones that have random effects on players willing to experiment with them. However, the game imitates *Wizardry* by allowing the player to control a party of adventurers (four, to be precise) rather than a single character. It also predates *Ultima III* in offering different screens for combat and exploration, as well as in using solid colors for the first-person, 3D dungeons rather than monochrome wireframe graphics. It even has an auto-mapper!

Like *Ultima III* and the later Gold Box games, *Tunnels of Doom* switches to a top-down, tactical screen whenever the party engages in combat. Combat is turn-based and offers ranged as well as hand-to-hand weapons. Another nice touch is the ability to target specific monsters with ranged weapons, rather than just firing them in a straight line. Although there are only three classes available (fighter, wizard, and rogue), a special hero class was available to players who opted to lead a single adventurer in the randomly generated, ten-level maze. All in all, it's an intelligent system that is relatively easy to learn and quite flexible.

The game shipped with two adventures: "Pennies and Prizes" and "Quest for the King." The first of these was more or less a tutorial designed to familiarize users with the interface (or to entertain small children). "Quest of the King" is the standard "fetch the orb" quest, though players must also locate the king and return him and the orb to the surface. A strict time limit adds to the challenge.

However, what most people remember about *Tunnels of Doom* are the many third-party modules created with Asgard Software's *Tunnels of Doom Editor,* created by a Chicago police officer named John Behnke. Fans of the game designed their own scenarios and distributed them at conventions and club meetings, and a few were even available commercially in compilations sold by Asgard. One of the more unusual of these is a game where the dungeon is a KMart store. Another was based on the popular TV show *Star Trek,* though I doubt seriously whether this scenario was authorized by Paramount.

Although the game was one of the most successful for the TI-99/4A, Texas Instruments laid off Kenney shortly after its release. Kenney speculated in a 2002 interview that the company was unhappy with his "liberal political bent." The company later contracted him to do some additional databases for the game, but sadly never released them.

Ali Baba and the Forty Players

Many of the games we've talked about so far have been assigned to one player, and the few exceptions were online games. Most party-based CRPGs can be played with a group simply by assigning each player a character; the person behind the keyboard takes the players' orders and acts accordingly (in theory). Indeed, some early manuals encourage this kind of gameplay. However, two early CRPGs written by Stuart Smith for Quality Software integrate cooperative multiplayer options directly into the interface.

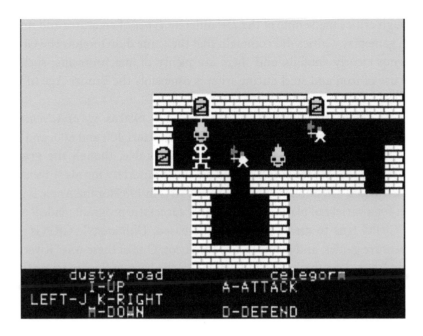

FIGURE 5.14 *Ali Baba and the Forty Thieves* trades the traditional European fantasy setting for an Arabic theme.

The first of these was *Ali Baba and the Forty Thieves,* published in 1982 for the Atari 400 and 800 and the Apple II (Figure 5.14). As the title suggests, the game is loosely based on the old Arabic stories from *The Book of One Thousand and One Nights,* which makes a pleasant departure from the conventional high fantasy motif, though a quest to rescue a Sultan's kidnapped daughter is hardly extraordinary. While relatively simplistic compared to *Ultima* and *Wizardry,* the game stands out because of its dynamic multiplayer options. New players can be added at any point during the adventure, and they are allowed to roam about the dungeons independently of the main character, Ali Baba. Co-op gameplay is of the "hot seat" method, where players either take turns behind the keyboard or simply hand their joystick or paddle off to the next player.

The game was reasonably successful, and Smith soon created a very similar game called *Return of Heracles* (sometimes *Herakles),* based on the famous Greek stories as retold by Robert Graves. This time, gameplay is structured around the fulfillment of twelve tasks, mostly involving slaying beasts, fetching items, or rescuing damsels in distress. Again, the most innovative aspect of the game is the cooperative multiplayer options, though critics made note of the 250 different types of creatures and intuitive gameplay. Critics did complain that the game didn't follow the Greek legends closely enough, and there are plenty of anachronisms, such as the use of iron and steel during what is ostensibly the Bronze Age (if not earlier).

Both games were updated and repackaged in 1986 as *Age of Adventure,* published by Electronic Arts for the Apple II, Atari 400 and 800, and the Commodore 64. Reviews were generally favorable, though the graphics were dated. Stuart Smith gained far more notoriety for his *Adventure Construction Set,* published by Electronic Arts in 1985 for the Apple II and later for a variety of platforms. The highly successful program made it easy for CRPG fans to create their own tile-based, *Ultima*-style CRPGs and adventure games, and included two scenarios. One of these was "Rivers of Light," based on the legend of Gilgamesh, the hero of Sumerian mythology. Again we see Smith's preference for ancient mythology over the standard swords and sorcery theme.

Omnitrend's *Universe*

William Leslie and Thomas Carbone's *Universe* game, published in 1983 for the Atari 400/800 and later for the Apple II, is reminiscent of EduWare's *Space* and *Empire* series that we discussed in the previous chapter. It's a very interesting game for a number of reasons, not the least of which is the rather shocking retail price of $89.96, which adjusts to over $200 in current dollars. The game shipped with a seventy-five-page manual encased in a three-ring binder, as well as four floppy disks (a record at the time).

Like *Space* and *Empire, Universe* is a futuristic CRPG that has players flying spaceships rather than slaying dragons (Figure 5.15). The game is set in the Local Cluster, a galaxy colonized by Earth but now apparently abandoned by the motherworld. Chaos is beginning to take hold in the outlying sectors, and piracy is threatening to disrupt trade and fling the galaxy into barbarism. In the midst of the crisis, rumors surface of a Hyperspace Booster, which, if found, could reunite the Local Cluster with the Milky Way. However, players are given considerable leeway in achieving this goal. For instance, they may opt to become merchant traders, shipping cargo back and forth among the twenty-one star systems of the Local Cluster. Or they may take to mining, touching down on mineral-rich planets in a search for the mother lode. Finally, they can become pirates themselves, earning rich rewards at the expense of civilization.

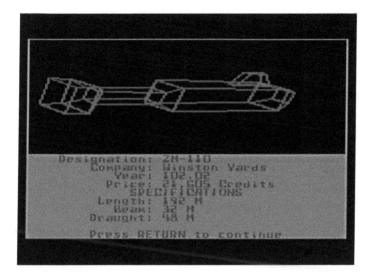

FIGURE 5.15   *Universe* is more space simulator than CRPG, but saving up to upgrade your ship doesn't feel all that different than outfitting a party of heroes with better arms and armor.

Technically speaking, it might be a stretch to define this game as a CRPG, since there is little in the way of character development. Although players must hire a crew, they are represented almost entirely by numbers and do not benefit from experience. However, players can turn their earnings into upgrades for their ship, making it more efficient or effective in combat. During this history, we'll encounter several of these space simulator/CRPG hybrids that resist easy classification. Typically, they are characterized as open-ended games and usually feature action-based combat in the style of a flight simulator, albeit with zero-G physics. Certainly, games such as Accolade's *SunDog: Frozen Legacy* (1984), Firebird's *Elite* (1985), and Origin's *Wing Commander: Privateer* (1993) spring to mind. However, we'll be discussing such games only if the CRPG element, such as a class/level system for the captain or crew members, is featured more prominently than the simulator-style action sequences.

Universe II, released in 1985, introduces precisely such role-playing elements. Now, the crew has individual names, grades, and skill types: astrogator, pilot, marine, miner, and gunner. The combat that takes place when a crew boards another ship is now more tactical and closer to combat in contemporary CRPGs. Unfortunately, the game seems to have been striving to be a jack of all trades; it incorporates a lengthy text adventure sequence with a very limited parser. This segment was panned in reviews, and that, in addition to the again-hefty price (this time $69.95) may explain its almost total obscurity today. Nevertheless, Omnitrend published yet another sequel, *Universe III,* in 1989, though it truly was an adventure game rather than a CRPG. Omnitrend had better luck in the 1990s for its *Breach* line of futuristic, turn-based strategy games, some of which contain minor role-playing elements.

SUMMING UP THE SILVER AGE

Although there were certainly some ambitious and exemplary games produced between 1980 and 1983, everyone knew the best was yet to come. Computer hardware was leaping forward and programmers continued to refine their skills. On the other hand, we can also say that, by 1983, almost all of the conventions we'll see in later CRPGs were established or at least demonstrated. From this point forward, we'll be able to describe most CRPGs as combinations of elements from Silver Age games. What is *The Pool of Radiance* but *Tunnels of Doom* meets *Wizardry?* What is *Diablo* but *Telengard* with better audiovisuals? For that matter, how far have we really come from *pedit5, dnd,* and *Moria?* It's impossible to truly appreciate later games without at least some knowledge of the groundbreaking CRPGs that came before them.

Nevertheless, there's a reason I chose to call this the Silver and not the Golden Age of CRPGs. I say this knowing that some of the games we've discussed in this chapter (particularly *Ultima III)* remain fan favorites and, at least in fans' opinions, have never been equaled, much less surpassed. While I certainly agree that these games are innovative, I still view them more as prototypes: experimental CRPGs designed at a time when developers were still finding their way. The genre simply needed time to mature.

Hopefully, you'll agree when we begin our discussion of classics like *Phantasie, The Bard's Tale, Might and Magic, Dungeon Master,* and *Wasteland,* as well as SSI's celebrated Gold Box and Black Box games. What we'll see happening between 1985 and 1993 is an explosion of innovation and diversity, with hundreds of titles and a great deal of experimentation. Although many of the triumphs will be in the realm of graphics and sound, others have more to do with the art of storytelling, world building, and character development. We'll also see developers struggling to stay ahead of the latest advances in hardware. As we'll see, for many gamers then and now, superior audiovisuals trump all else.

NOTES

1. See "Lord British Kisses and Tells All" in *Computer Gaming World* (July 1988).
2. As quoted by Shay Addams in his *The Official Book of Ultima* (ISBN 0-87455-228-1).
3. The source of these quotes is a brief review in the June/July 1983 issue of *Computer Gaming World*. The product is reviewed again in more detail in the July/August issue of the same year.
4. Not to be confused with the aforementioned *dnd* for the PLATO platform.
5. See http://dnd.lunaticsworld.com/ for more information about the history of *DND* and *Telengard*, as well as links to download the source code and binaries of many of the games in question.
6. See http://buildingworlds.com/telengard/.
7. See http://www.aquest.com/telen.htm.
8. See http://www.fargoal.com/.

CHAPTER 6

The Birth of the Golden Age

If nothing else, the unparalleled success of the *Wizardry* and *Ultima* series proved that the CRPG was a lucrative genre with a long future ahead of it. Although Greenberg and Woodhead were content with only minor innovations between their *Wizardry* games, Richard Garriott reinvented *Ultima* with each iteration. *Ultima IV: Quest of the Avatar* was an even bolder experiment, not just for CRPGs, but for games as a whole. Meanwhile, new developers were hard at work translating their own creative visions into code, and large publishers such as Electronic Arts were stepping up to help get their work before the public. Avid CRPG fans snatched up every CRPG they could find and clamored for more. Developers slaved away at their keyboards, fueled by Mountain Dew and extraordinary constitutions.

TRANSITION TO THE GOLDEN AGE

The year 1985 was a boom year for CRPGs, but the years immediately preceding it were quiet. This slowdown could be attributed to the Video Game Crash of 1983–1984, which all but destroyed the console games market. Although this media-sensationalized crash affected consoles far more than computers, computer game developers had their own problems to worry about. Commodore, led by Jack Tramiel, was engaged in a ferocious price war, and its vertical integration with a chip manufacturer (MOS Technology) gave it tremendous leverage against rivals like Texas Instruments and Tandy. Tramiel's strategy, championed by his spokesperson, William Shatner, was to question the logic of purchasing a console when a computer could be had for the same price. These tactics may well have spared the computer games industry the worst of the crash—but likely contributed to it, as well. In any case, the Commodore 64 soon reigned supreme, but it was destined to lose its crown to the onslaught of cheap "IBM compatibles" that rode in behind the powerful but expensive IBM PC.

However, most of the CRPG developers we'll discuss in this chapter clung to the exceptionally long-lived Apple II platform, which benefited from a magnificently robust programming environment and a rich community of enthusiasts. Even in the 1990s, more than a few prominent developers were reluctant to switch to the MS-DOS platform, even though it dominated the industry at that point. The upshot of all this is that porting, or adapting games for other platforms, was often farmed out to third parties. These developers were expected to enhance (or scale down) the audiovisual elements to accommodate the new platform. In other words, the goal was usually not simply to recreate them, but to improve them, particularly their interfaces and audiovisuals. This is especially true in cases where an Apple II game was ported to the Atari ST or Commodore Amiga; early DOS games were almost always inferior even to the Apple II in terms of graphics and sound. For historical reasons, we focus here on the developer's versions, but you may well prefer the enhanced ports.

MAINFRAME GAMES REVISITED

Of the relatively few CRPGs released during the Video Game Crash, perhaps the most interesting are ports of old mainframe mainstays. Personal computers were becoming more powerful, with more memory and faster processors, and it was easier now to make faithful or even enhanced conversions of beloved "hack 'n slash" games like *Moria* (see Chapter 5). The best known of these is *Rogue: The Adventure Game,* published in all its ASCII glory in 1983 for the IBM PC (Figure 6.1). Michael Toy, one of the original developers, teamed up with Jon Lane to program the port and launch their own company, Artificial Intelligence Design. Later, Epyx (formerly known as Automated Simulations, publisher of the *Apshai* games) took over marketing, and enhanced ports were released in 1986 for most of the prominent computer platforms of the day, including the Commodore Amiga, Atari ST, and Tandy's CoCo. Finally, in 1988 the rights passed to Mastertronic, a budget computer software publisher who ported the game to still more platforms, including the Commodore 64 and British computers.

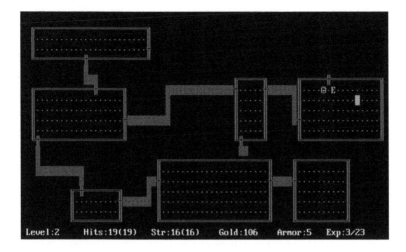

FIGURE 6.1   The commercial version of *Rogue* is charming and quite fun to play, but the simple visuals failed to impress most gamers of the era.

Although *Rogue* was a huge hit with mainframe gamers, it never gained traction in the commercial sector. Co-creator Glenn Wichman asserts that Epyx wanted a serious game that avoided the "whimsical and a little off-the-wall" character of the original game. However, he claims piracy was the primary culprit.[1] While these might certainly have been factors, we'd also point out that perhaps non-nostalgic gamers simply weren't drawn to the character set graphics. Meanwhile, former mainframe users who could have appreciated them preferred public domain or cheap shareware versions of the game over the $40 (over $80 in modern dollars) Epyx version. Some of these public domain games, such as *Hack,* were even more advanced than the commercial release! One contemporary reviewer wrote, "I found the Amiga versions of *Hack* and *Rogue* to be remarkably similar in appearance."[2] Even these versions, with their enhanced graphics, weren't impressive when compared to other games of the era, and the lack of sound certainly didn't help. In short, the commercial version of *Rogue* was simply too little, too late.

Rogue wasn't the only mainframe classic to be commercialized for personal computers. Jim Schwaiger, author of the original *Oubliette,* formed a company named Bear Systems to release it for the Commodore 64 and MS-DOS platforms in 1983.

The DOS version has some nice innovations, such as the ability to switch between textual and graphical modes while exploring dungeons. The graphical mode features a first-person, monochrome 3D wireframe display that is much larger than the type usually seen in PLATO CRPGs. The Commodore 64 version is actually quite different, with an odd and off-putting gray and blue color scheme and crude graphics. *Oubliette* offers eight races, ten classes, and a guild-based advancement system. The player can select an appropriate guild for each character's apprenticeship, which range in quality and duration as well as danger to the student: "to short-lived races such as orcs and ogres, becoming a professional student can be a fatal mistake."[3] Players can also elect to spend some time as dungeon-wandering peasants before joining a guild, but older students don't tend to fare as well. *Oubliette* also has some rare combat options, such as seduce. It's also one of the most monster-rich games, with over 150 different types.

Unlike the PLATO version, the port allows players to control up to six other characters (ten others can be created and left in the tavern between dungeon romps). Considering the impressive array of options for each character, it's easy to see how gameplay can quickly get complicated.

THE DAWN OF THE GOLDEN AGE

The year 1985 was one of the most important years in the history of the CRPG. Never before had such a torrent of high-quality commercial titles appeared simultaneously on the shelf. The most significant of these was Interplay's *Tales of the Unknown Vol. 1: The Bard's Tale*, which introduced gamers to the highly successful *Bard's Tale* trilogy. Although there were certainly excellent CRPGs before it, *The Bard's Tale* was intuitive and addictive enough to attract a mainstream audience—and also benefited from the marketing might of its publisher, Electronic Arts. That year also saw the debut of SSI's *Phantasie* series, as well as its game *Wizard's Crown.*[4] Although SSI wouldn't reach its zenith until it acquired the venerable TSR license and began marketing official *AD&D* games, these early games are far from shabby.

Other important games of 1985 include Origin's groundbreaking *Ultima IV: Quest of the Avatar* and Chuck "Chuckles" Bueche's *Autoduel*. We'll also discuss *The Magic Candle* series, *Starflight,* and the first *Might and Magic*.

Down and Out in Skara Brae

Although the *Ultima* and *Wizardry* series established the CRPG's conventions, it was Interplay that really refined the genre and showed that it wasn't just for hardcore gamers raised on wargaming and tabletop *D&D*. Michael Cranford's *Tales of the Unknown Vol. 1: The Bard's Tale,* released

FIGURE 6.2 Cranford's *The Bard's Tale's* iconic opening has the titular bard quaffing ale and singing a song that sets the stage for the game. The original plan was for each game in the series to star a different character (*The Warrior's Tale*, etc.), but the bard proved so popular that this idea was scrapped.

in 1985 for the Commodore 64 and Apple II (ports for other platforms would follow until 1990), is probably the first CRPG that readers of our generation will recognize from their youth (and no doubt a few still play it) (Figure 6.2). Indeed, *The Bard's Tale's* undeniable mass appeal was probably not matched by another game until Blizzard's *Diablo* in 1997. The game was so successful, in fact, that Baen Books launched a series of eight novels based on them, some penned by such well-known fantasy authors as Mercedes Lackey! Although the final *Bard's Tale* game was released in 1991, in 2004 Brian Fargo and inXile Entertainment revived the franchise with a "spiritual sequel" for the PlayStation 2, Xbox, and Windows. More recently, Fargo successfully launched a $1.5 million crowdfunding campaign for *Bard's Tale IV*, which is still in development at the time of this writing.

What made *The Bard's Tale* so extraordinarily successful? Why did it enjoy such broad appeal? After all, it is certainly not an easy game and can be quite challenging even for experienced CRPG gamers. The difficulty is felt particularly during the crucial initial stage of the game, when the player's characters (up to six) are weak, poorly equipped, and inexperienced. I lost track of the times I created an entire party of adventurers, only to have them all perish in a random encounter before I could make it to Garth's weapon shop! The game's story elements are also quite Spartan—it's a humble dungeon crawler with an emphasis on fighting random encounters with monsters, building up character stats and inventories, and mapping out the many dungeons. In many ways, the game is merely an updated *Wizardry* with better graphics and sound (indeed, some versions of the game even let players import their *Wizardry* or *Ultima* characters). The main quest—to find and depose an evil wizard named Mangar the Dark, who is threatening the town of Skara Brae—is hardly novel. Even the name of the town, Skara Brae, is also found in *Ultima* (both are named after a Neolithic settlement in Scotland).

Perhaps the game's most striking innovation is the emphasis on the bard class type, a sort of jack-of-all-trades character who could perform party-boosting songs during combat and dungeon exploration.[5] The game took every opportunity to endear the class to players. Indeed, one of the best-known catchphrases of the game is "When the going gets tough, the bard goes drinking." The bard became a popular antihero, a jovial rogue who clashed with the stereotypical Conan-style warriors and Gandalf-inspired wizards that dominate the genre. Ironically, though, creator Michael Cranford admits that "the bard was just an afterthought."[6] What an afterthought!

Although most of the other character types were fairly standard, the classes available to magic-users were richly nuanced: magic-users start off as simple conjurers or magicians but eventually upgrade to sorcerers and wizards. Truly ambitious magic-users could master all the schools of magic and become fearsome archmages. Although earlier games (*Wizardry*) offer prestige classes, this is the first game in which characters could combine *four* different classes to become a fifth and more powerful class—most games penalize characters for multiclassing. It is still a great innovation that is not seen enough in later games.

Anyone who has played *The Bard's Tale* for any length of time discovers that it is much greater than the sum of its parts. Even the artwork on the cover of the box is significant. Instead of the usual illustration of an armored knight and a dragon, we see a group of men (some with pointy ears) in a darkened tavern, all clustered around a bard plucking a medieval instrument and apparently singing songs of legendary adventures. Around this image we see a top-down view of a maze, cornered by arcane symbols. The rest of the series continued this tradition, always depicting a string-plucking bard somewhere on the cover. While it's easy enough to overlook such a detail, I think these cover designs show how Interplay was trying to generate a different, more lighthearted atmosphere than was typical of CRPGs. I heartily agree with what Cranford told me in my interview with him: the game simply had soul (Figure 6.3).

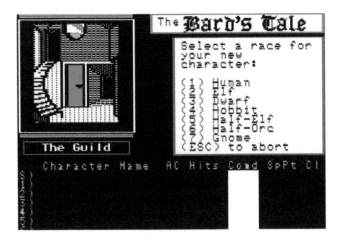

FIGURE 6.3 *The Bard's Tale* isn't all that different from *Wizardry* in terms of gameplay, but its audiovisuals, polish, and even its slick packaging were a considerable leap forward.

There are other subtle qualities that hold the game together. No doubt, the game's playability owes much to the clean interface and striking color graphics (many of which are animated). Even novice players can learn the game's rules in a few sessions, and if the characters survive to reach the higher levels, the game eases up considerably—and it's quite rewarding for players to go about slaughtering monsters that made a meal out of their former parties. Furthermore, the ability to travel outdoors as well as indoors lends coherence to the gameworld. Unlike other CRPGs, in which cities and towns are little more than menus for buying equipment, Skara Brae feels like a real place. Again, this coherence is almost surely an effect of the game's rich graphics. Even if the graphics look primitive today, in 1985 they were stunning. Each building in Skara Brae looks like it belongs there. No doubt, much of the sleekness of the game is owed to Cranford, whose proficiency with assembly language gave him a decisive edge at a time when many CRPGs were still programmed in BASIC.

The Destiny Knight

Interplay followed up its success with two sequels, *The Destiny Knight* (1986) and *The Thief of Fate* (1991). *The Destiny Knight* was essentially a rehash of the first game, using the same engine but expanding the gameworld to include five other cities (the first game occurred entirely in Skara Brae) and a wilderness area. It also adds banks and casinos to the services available in the towns, special spells for archmages, timed puzzles, and ranged combat. Though players can import their characters from the first game, the difficulty level is better balanced for new parties: Players have a much better chance of making it to Garth's store to buy equipment before dying, and a beginner's dungeon helps players level up their characters in a safer environment. The graphics are also improved, and now the important buildings each have a distinctive look.

Although the characters dispatched the evil Mangar the Dark in the first game, another evil mage named Lagoth Zanta shattered the Destiny Wand into seven pieces, scattering them across the land. Since the wand has protected the world for some 700 years, things don't bode well unless the characters can restore the wand and use it to slay Lagoth Zanta (one wonders what the wand was doing during the first game, but so it goes).

Solving the game will require gaining insights from a Sage, a process that utilizes a rather crude and frustrating text parser. One contemporary reviewer quips that the parser is merely a "comparator," a routine that simply compares the player's input with the "correct" response. For instance, typing "TOMBS" to learn the party's whereabouts does nothing—the player must type "THE TOMBS." Yet the use of the definite article was not consistent, and compounding the issue was the problem that the Sage took the party's gold whether or not their inputs matched up. No doubt, many players scurried to purchase clue books to help them bypass such inanities. Critics also complained about the tedious death snare segments, which required backtracking through dungeons.

The Thief of Fate

The Thief of Fate is probably the overall best designed game of the series, since it incorporates helpful new features such as automapping and the ability to use items to solve puzzles, which opens up many interesting opportunities for thoughtful gameplay (Figure 6.4). It also has the most ambitious gameworld: now the players must explore entirely different universes, including Nazi Berlin! In all, there are 84 dungeon levels and 500 types of monsters, including several varieties of spell casters. Finally, now players can save anywhere (previously, they could save only in the adventurers' guilds).

The Bard's Tale Construction Set

Electronic Arts also published Interplay's *The Bard's Tale Construction Set* for Commodore's Amiga and the MS-DOS platforms (Figure 6.5). This construction set included an updated version of the first game in the series

FIGURE 6.4 *The Thief of Fate* is a truly impressive entry in the series, with a massive gameworld, improved graphics, and handy features including an automapper.

(rechristened *Star Light Festival*). However, more importantly, the set allowed CRPG fans to construct their own games based on the enhanced *Thief of Fate* engine. The construction kit was popular on both platforms, but the most useful version available for MS-DOS, which had support for hard drives, VGA, mouse, and a slew of sound cards. Strangely, while music was played through the sound card, all sound effects were delegated to the PC's inadequate internal speaker. Probably the most well-known

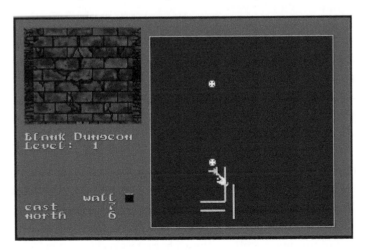

FIGURE 6.5 *The Bard's Tale Construction Set* is surprisingly fun and easy to use. Put your level design skills to the test!

game created with the set is *The Bard's Lore: The Warrior and the Dragon*, by John H. Wigforss. Of course, there are undoubtedly many hundreds if not thousands of good homebrew titles created by other fans.

Interplay continued to produce some of the finest CRPGs of all time, including *Wasteland* in 1988, which we'll discuss in Chapter 9. In 1996, Interplay created a special CRPG division named Black Isle Studios, which published the *Baldur's Gate* games and developed *Planescape: Torment* and the *Icewind Dale* series, about which we'll have more to say later. In short, Interplay ranks with Origin, Sir-Tech, and SSI as one of the greatest CRPG developers and publishers.

While Michael Cranford and Electronic Arts played a pivotal role in founding the Golden Age of CRPGs, they were certainly not alone. Another company that was beginning to flex its muscles was SSI, an old publisher of wargames that now set its sights on the budding CRPG market.

The Infant Phantasies of Strategic Simulations, Inc.: Any Questrons?

Today, Strategic Simulations, Inc. (SSI) is best known for its fabulous "Gold Box" and "Black Box" games, series of CRPGs that bore the official seal of TSR, holder of the sacred *Dungeons & Dragons* copyrights and trademarks. This invaluable license was sought after by nearly every other CRPG developer, but SSI emerged victorious from the struggle. It's likely that TSR's decision was swayed by SSI's legacy as an eminent developer and publisher of computer-based wargames (as you remember, *D&D* emerged from tabletop wargames). SSI's first game was *Computer Bismarck*, published in 1979 for the Apple II. SSI quickly became the market leader in this niche, even with the premier wargames publisher Avalon Hill competing against it. However, by the time SSI acquired the license, it had already established itself as a respectable CRPG publisher with games such as *Questron, Phantasie,* and *The Wizard's Crown*. Although these early games aren't as well known as SSI's licensed titles, they are full of innovations and are more than worthy of our attention.

SSI's first two CRPGs were published in 1984: *50 Mission Crush* and *Questron*. *50 Mission Crush* is more like a conventional wargame than most CRPGs and is probably better described as a turn-based strategy game. The game consists of fifty B-17 bomber missions flown during World War II. The player assigns each position in the plane to his or her characters (i.e., tail-gunner, bomber). These characters receive experience points each time they survive a mission, eventually gaining competence and winning promotions. The magazine *Computer Gaming World* published a fascinating review of the game written by an actual B-24 bombardier named Leroy W. Newby, who found it realistic enough to evoke dozens of wartime memories, which he duly juxtaposes alongside his gameplay narrative.[7] Newby also served as SSI's consultant on the game, which may account for some of its depth and realism. In any case, *50 Mission Crush* is the only CRPG I am aware of that is set during World War II.

The Dougherty Brothers: Questron *and* Legacy of the Ancients
Whereas *50 Mission Crush* is a highly innovative and even unique game, *Questron* (Figure 6.6) is an unabashed clone of Garriott's *Ultima*. To their credit, SSI took the precaution of securing a license from Garriott for the game's "structure and style." Critics recommended the game as a "perfect warm-up" for *Ultima III*, arguing that the game's relative simplicity and low difficulty made it well suited for novices.[8] One good example of the game's relative ease is the lack of a character creation stage; all players begin with a default character with all stats set at 15. Instead of gaining levels and experience points, players complete specific quests to rise in the ranks. The goal of the game is standard fantasy fare. Beginning as a humble serf, you must take the Book of Evil Magic away from an evil wizard named Mantor, destroying his many minions (100 types) as you builds up your character's stats. The game's three dungeons are rendered in wireframe 3D but look more realistic than those in *Ultima,* with curvy rather than straight lines to make the walls look more like roughly carved stone.

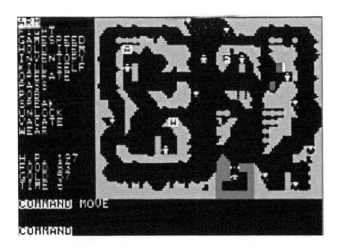

FIGURE 6.6 *Questron* plays a lot like *Ultima,* but it has its share of innovations and is arguably more accessible for novice players.

Questron did have some promising features, such as a series of action minigames that can boost the character's stats; for example, there's a skeet-shoot game to improve dexterity. There are also casinos where players gamble for gold. Finally, *Questron* is one of the earliest games in which certain monsters can be killed only by special weapons. Hit points are purchased either from the occasional wanderer or from the priests stationed at cathedrals. Perhaps the most questionable feature of the game is the option to "kill self," displayed prominently on the menu—certainly not a good idea at a time when fantasy role-playing was already controversial. Fortunately for SSI, neither critics nor concerned parents seem to have paid it much notice. Indeed, contemporary reviews for the game were quite positive.

Charles "Chuck" Dougherty, *Questron*'s designer and programmer, would go on to write another popular CRPG named *Legacy of the Ancients* (Figure 6.7) with his brother, John. After a falling out with SSI, the brothers submitted the game to Electronic Arts, which published it in 1987. Based largely on *Questron*'s core engine, *Legacy of the Ancients* is more epic in scope, with gameplay focused on a mysterious museum built long ago by a forgotten race of aliens (the Ancients). The player must explore each exhibit in this museum, which requires finding lots of special coins. The ultimate goal is to destroy an evil scroll that contains fearfully powerful magic. *Legacy of the Ancients* shares many of *Questron*'s features, such as the arcade-style minigames, premade characters, and a quest-based rank system.

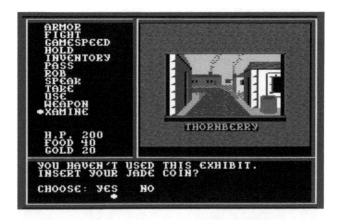

FIGURE 6.7 *Legacy of the Ancients* is a great game that'll keep you busy for weeks. If you find a used copy, be sure it includes the code wheel you'll need to bypass the copy protection.

Apparently, business arrangements didn't work out with Electronic Arts either; Chuck and John Dougherty submitted their next game, *The Legend of Blacksilver,* to Epyx for publication in 1988. The game recycles the *Questron* engine yet again, though updating the graphics and targeting the Commodore 64 platform. The player's mission this time is to rescue a king captured by an evil baron who is striving to create a weapon of mass destruction using the titular blacksilver artifact. Apparently, the game was not successful enough to keep Chuck and John in business; their company, Quest Software, closed its doors shortly afterward, and the brothers seem to have been relegated to the "Where are they now?" file.

Meanwhile, SSI retained its rights to the *Questron* trademark but didn't develop its own sequel. Instead, it solicited Westwood Associates for the task—the Dougherty brothers were not involved. Westwood persevered, and *Questron II* was published in 1988. This game is based largely on the first, though set in an earlier time period. The mission is to depose six insane sorcerers and prevent the creation of the Book of Magic. It features an automapper and 3D dungeons in color, but it's essentially the same game in a new costume. Still, it's certainly the better known of the two, and you'll hear more about Westwood later.

The Phantasies *of Winston Douglas Wood*

Better known than *Questron* is SSI's 1985 classic, *Phantasie* (Figure 6.8), programmed by Winston Douglas Wood. *Phantasie* was a tremendously

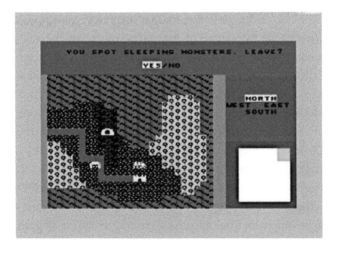

FIGURE 6.8 *Phantasie* doesn't get much love today, but it was a popular game in its time. Shown here is the Commodore 64 version.

successful game that won over many gamers and critics. The games offer just the right balance of story, puzzle, and combat elements; and critics raved about the intuitive and addicting gameplay. The game employs a well-organized, split-screen interface and separate menus for purchasing equipment, exploring dungeons, roaming the world map, and engaging in combat. It features 80 monsters, 50 spells, 100 pieces of equipment, and plenty of areas to explore. Furthermore, the game tracks where the party has been, obviating the need for mapmaking. One particularly enthusiastic contemporary reviewer remarks that *Phantasie* "may be the best fantasy role-playing game to come down the silicon pike since Sir-Tech conjured up *Wizardry*" and, "at the risk of sounding blasphemous," even finds it superior in some aspects.[9] Building well on the success of this series, SSI was soon a dominant player in the CRPG market.

Phantasie allows players to control up to six adventurers from a pool of thirty-seven, the rest of which can be left in the various town guilds between missions. Character creation has an interesting twist. Besides the standard races (human, dwarf, elf, gnome, and halfling), players can also select "random," which may result in a gnoll, goblin, kobold, lizard man, minotaur, ogre, orc, pixie, sprite, or troll—truly an impressive list, and each race has its advantages and disadvantages. In the first game, for instance, only a party with a minotaur can enter a certain dungeon. There is also some racism: certain races have charisma penalties and will find their training fees steeply raised on account of their poor reputations. A final racial consideration is that the characters age over the course of the game, and some of the more short-lived races may begin to suffer attribute penalties before the game is over.

In addition to the usual stats (dexterity, strength, and so on), each character also has points in the following skills: attack, parry, swim, listen, spot trap, disarm trap, pick lock, and find item. Points in these skills are distributed according to the character's race and class. The classes include the usual fighters, priests, thieves, and wizards, but also monks (fighter/mage/thief) and rangers (fighter/priest). One unusual feature of character creation is that any class can use any weapon or armor; limitations are imposed only by low stats (especially low strength scores). Thus, many players prioritize strength and dexterity when creating characters of any type. The class and level system is based on the character's current level of experience points (won after each battle) and possession of gold, since the trainers must be paid for their services. The amount they must have on hand rises with every new level, so there is always a need to raise money by finding treasure and selling off items.

Phantasie also features an innovative turn-based combat system imitated in several later games, particularly in console RPGs. The characters are shown in a line along the bottom of the screen, with their foes arranged in ranks above them. During a turn, the player selects attack options for each character, which are then initiated in a random sequence after the turn is completed. One nice innovation is that characters aren't limited to a single type of attack but can select among several options: attack (two normal swings), thrust (one hard swing), slash (three or four quick swings), and lunge (one swing at the rear rank of monsters). The thief and wizard can target any row of monsters, but melee is usually limited to the frontline. Once battle ensues, the attacking character or monster is briefly animated, perhaps shown raising his sword or casting a spell. The characters perform a brief victory dance if they win—a feature seen in countless Japanese console RPGs (Figure 6.9).

Phantasie's story is standard fare and is derived rather blatantly from Tolkien. Besides obvious nods such as a character named "J. R. Trolkin," many elements seem straight from the pages of *Lord of the Rings*. The player must kill the Black Knights and their master, the evil sorcerer Nikademus, who supplies them with powerful but soul-stealing magic rings. To accomplish this task, the characters must gather twenty scrolls, each of which contains a vital clue. Furthermore, the story is woven more closely into the gameplay than was seen in other games, and players are given more opportunities to make decisions that have a direct effect on the gameplay. For instance, they can avoid set encounters by using secret passages or by attempting to bribe or plead with monsters rather than fight them.

FIGURE 6.9 *Phantasie*'s combat screen as seen in the MS-DOS version. The characters perform a joyful dance if they manage to win.

SSI followed up the first game with *Phantasie II* in 1986. The plot this time is even less original than the first—Nikademus is back, and this time he's used a magical orb to enslave an island and its population. Naturally, the party must find and destroy the orb. Other than the new story, there is little difference between this game and its prequel, save the ability of characters to hurl rocks at enemies during combat. Players of the first game can import their old characters, though doing so confers only minor benefits (equipment and most of their gold and experience do not transfer).

The final *Phantasie* was released in 1987 for the Apple II and given the subtitle *The Wrath of Nikademus*. Wood coded the Apple II version; Westwood handled the enhanced ports for other systems. Nikademus has returned yet again, and after two defeats (and apparent deaths!) his ambition has only grown—this time he's out to control the world.

The third game offers better graphics and more sophisticated combat, such as the ability to target specific body regions, a wound system, and better tactics. For instance, now the player can easily see which monsters and characters are hit in combat and how badly they are injured. Characters can also move forward to get a better shot, and it's possible to strategically place weaker characters in the rear. Another nice addition is the "fire bow" skill, which allows all characters to wield bows. Bows are perhaps the most powerful weapons in the game, since they are the best for achieving the head shot, an extremely damaging attack that can bring down almost any monster—and there are no penalties for firing a bow point-blank at monsters in the frontline. The skill system is refined, and now players are given a few skill points to distribute in the various skill areas each time the character levels up. Finally, the third game introduces social class, which is randomly assigned to each character (peasant, laborer, craftsman, noble). Characters with a higher social class start off with more money and receive more each time they level up, and of course characters of less reputable races are far less likely to come out on top.

Phantasie III is widely regarded as the best game in the series, even though it is noticeably shorter than the first two games. Indeed, one contemporary reviewer remarked that it "was so close to perfect, I have to dig really deep to find any fault."[10] In 1990, a company named WizardWorks released the first games in a retro-styled package called *Phantasie Bonus Edition* for the DOS and Commodore Amiga platforms. Unfortunately, despite its initial popularity and many innovations, the *Phantasie* series has not managed to attain the enduring legacy it deserves and has been long overshadowed by SSI's later Gold Box CRPGs.

The Wizard's Crown

Another classic SSI game released in 1985 is Paul Murray and Keith Brors' *The Wizard's Crown*, a CRPG with an overtly complex tactical combat system (Figure 6.10). Probably the most hardcore CRPG of its time, *The Wizard's Crown* lets players control up to eight characters, multiclassing them however they see fit (e.g., a character could be a thief/fighter/sorcerer/priest, though such hybridization slows advancement). Instead of the conventional level and class system, characters improve their stats and skills, such as hunting, haggling, alchemy, and swimming (a system very similar to that seen in much later games such as *Fallout* and *Neverwinter Nights*). Experience points are won in battle and must be traded in to raise skill points. How many experience points translate into skill points depends on the current score of that skill; inflation occurs at higher levels. Murray and Brors were big fans of the tabletop games *RuneQuest* and *Traveller*, which no doubt helped inspire this skill system.

Likewise, the combat system is more dynamic than most other games. Brors and Murray had an extensive background in miniatures wargaming and wanted to create a CRPG that similarly emphasized tactical combat and military science. Their game contains more than twenty combat commands, including unusual ones like Fall Prone, which makes a character harder to hit with arrows but easier to hit with melee weapons. As in *Questron* and *Phantasie*, different situations call for different weapons. However, *The Wizard's Crown* goes a step beyond with added realism—shields work only if the character is facing the right direction, for instance; and characters are still vulnerable to axes and flails, which can destroy or circumvent, respectively, a shield. There are also ranged weapons, which

FIGURE 6.10 If tactical turn-based combat is your thing, you'll find much to appreciate about *The Wizard's Crown*.

of course can play an important role in tactical combat. Another nice touch is that spears have extended reach; they can attack monsters two squares away, whereas other melee weapons (swords) are limited to one. Characters can even be wounded in two different ways—injuries, which result in temporary stat penalties, or bleeding, which continuously drains the character of life points. Both injuries and bleeding can be normal or serious, with results you can easily imagine. To make matters even more complicated, there's a morale system that takes fatigue and nervous strain into consideration. Morale is recovered either by resting or, ideally, by drinking ale in a tavern. Perhaps the only glitch in an otherwise realistic combat system is that the monsters never flee or surrender but always fight to the death.

The magic system is also fairly complex, based on a mathematical formula. Each spell costs a certain amount of spell points (the "power" of the spell), but just having enough points doesn't guarantee success. Instead, the chance of casting the spell correctly depends on the difficulty level of the spell and the magic-user's "cast spell" skill. For instance, the spell Life Blast costs 4 power points and has a difficulty level of 80. The difficulty level is subtracted from the caster's cast spell stat, the remainder being the chance of a successful cast. Thus, a sorcerer with a cast spell score of 90 has only a 10 percent chance of avoiding a miscast. Spell points are regained by resting in the inn. The maximum score for any skill is 250.

The only real flaw in the game concerns movement in the dungeons. Each of the characters is shown on-screen while the party is in the dungeon, though only one character is active (the rest are programmed either to follow him or to stand still). Unfortunately, the artificial intelligence is rather lacking, and it's all too easy for characters to get mired behind an obstacle, necessitating a tedious series of commands to get everyone lined up again.

Although a major battle can last up to forty minutes, players can also choose quick combat, which automatically resolves the combat in seconds. The catch is that the results of a quick combat are seldom satisfactory, with party members taking more damage than they would under the direct control of an able tactician. Nevertheless, it's a massive timesaver when the party is substantially more powerful than the enemy. This useful and desirable feature will show up in later SSI games but is sorely missing in many other turn-based CRPGs.

While the storyline is typical (find a wizard, kill him, and take back the titular crown), the extraordinary attention to character development and strategic combat make up for it. *The Wizard's Crown* remains one of the most sophisticated tactical CRPGs ever designed: a rich blend of wargaming and fantasy role-playing.

SSI released a sequel called *The Eternal Dagger* in 1987. Thanks to an evil Necromancer (is there any other kind?), demons from another dimension are invading the world, and the only item that can seal the portal is the titular dagger. Other than the new storyline, the sequel is virtually identical to the first game, though some elements, such as the Fall Prone option mentioned above, are omitted; and players can trade experience for skill bonuses anywhere (as opposed to only in the tavern). Players can import their old party from the previous game, though they'll arrive without their equipment.

One welcome improvement is the revamping of the dungeon movement system. Now the entire party is represented by a single character, thus avoiding the aforementioned issue with clunky artificial intelligence. The game also takes the seasons into account, distributing daylight hours accordingly (summer months have extra-long days). Since the party cannot travel at night, players are advised to plan a year or so ahead for extended forays into the wilderness. To make matters worse, if the party is attacked at night, only the party members posted on guard will be wearing any armor! It's truly staggering to think of this level of detail in such an early game. However, not all critics were pleased. One contemporary reviewer remarks, "It may be realistic, but there is a point where realism begins to have negative effects on playability and game enjoyment" and recommends the game for "patient players only."[11] Fortunately, the developers were able to learn from their experience and chose carefully which elements to include and which to omit in their game *Pool of Radiance,* which we'll discuss at length in the next chapter.

The Shard of Spring *and* Demon's Winter

The Shard of Spring is a 1986 game written for the Apple II by Craig Roth and David Stark, and ported to MS-DOS by D. R. Gilman, Leslie Hill, and Martin deCastongrene—who did the whole game in Microsoft QuickBasic (Figure 6.11). It's a bit crude compared to the other SSI games of the era and falls somewhere in between *The Wizard's Crown* and *Phantasie* in terms of complexity. The story is that an evil sorceress has stolen the Shard of Spring, a magical item that brings eternal springtime to the land. Now that it's gone, the world has fallen into chaos, and the solution is hardly unexpected.

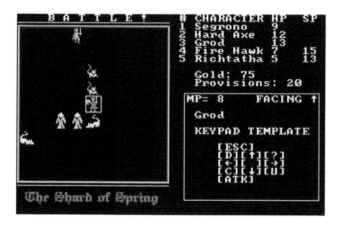

FIGURE 6.11 *The Shard of Spring* is inspired by Steve Jackson's *The Fantasy Trip* role-playing game.

The player is allowed to create a party of up to five characters of five races (human, troll, dwarf, elf, gnome) but gets a choice of only two classes (warrior and wizard). Unsurprisingly, some races are excluded from one race or another—no troll wizards allowed. This game also has a fairly interesting skill system based on a character's intellect—the higher that score, the more skills he or she can learn. Skills are divided between warrior (sword, axe, mace, karate, armored skin) and wizard skills, which are based on the five elements of nature: fire, metal, wind, ice, and spirit runes. Some of the more interesting and useful noncombat skills are monster lore, which gives crucial information in combat, and dark vision, which allows the party to see in dark dungeons. Another notable aspect is the training system. To gain a level, a character must find a suitable guild (fighter or wizard), whose members are willing to perform the training for free, provided the character has sufficient experience points. Characters receive three random trait bonuses each time they reach a new level. Craig Roth cites Steve Jackson's pen-and-paper *The Fantasy Trip* role-playing game as his inspiration for this innovative system.[12]

Roth and Stark wrote a sequel called *Demon's Winter*, which was published by SSI in 1988. While very similar to the first game, *Demon's Winter* features an exponentially larger gameworld and a greatly expanded set of character classes: ranger, paladin, berserker, monk, cleric, thief, wizard, sorcerer, visionary, and scholar. Visionaries have some unusual abilities, mostly dealing with reconnaissance—for instance, they can view a room to check for monsters without being seen. Furthermore, any class can learn any skill, though there are point penalties for crossing the wizard/fighter boundary. For example, a wizard trying to learn to wield an axe must spend 9 points, whereas the skill is available to the barbarian for a single point. Since total points are limited by the character's Intellect, it is much more efficient to stick with traditional skills for each class. Furthermore, the concept of the training guild has been extended here to cover skills; now, characters must seek out special colleges to learn new skills, and the training isn't free.

Two of the new skills are priesthood and shaman, which tie in to the game's religious system. A character with these skills can choose one of ten shaman or priest gods to worship, each of whom has some benefit to bestow upon those who call upon him—though too much calling can annoy the god, who must be appeased by a visit to one of his or her temples. The various towns may also have a patron deity. In general, the shaman gods are considered barbaric, more suited for barbarians than paladins (who favor the priestly gods). Roth felt that these touches added "an extra level of depth" and give the character's alignment more concrete consequences. They also offer a nice last resort, since calling upon a god might indeed work miracles.

The game also has more puzzle elements than its predecessor, most of which hinge on a new ability to manipulate objects. For instance, at one point a character must use a mallet to break open a glass case and use two vials of serum to awaken a man from a trance—he manages to utter a vital clue before drifting off back to dreamland. Such puzzles were likely added in response to some of the criticism of the first game's overemphasis on combat. Nevertheless, the story is still rather conventional—the land of Ymros is faced with eternal winter unless the characters can find and destroy the evil demon god Malifon.

Unfortunately, neither *The Shard of Spring* nor *Demon's Winter* has advanced graphics or quality sound (even on the Amiga platform), factors that no doubt led to lackluster reviews in most game magazines. Even Roth admits that they "were a tad behind the stage-of-the-art." That said, Roth still feels the game would have been more successful if SSI hadn't focused so closely on its promoting its officially licensed *AD&D* games.

Rings of Zilfin

Ali Atabek's *Rings of Zilfin*, released in 1986, is a game intended for novices—and thus focuses more on story and atmosphere than tactics and stats (Figure 6.12). It features amusing cut scenes that establish and

FIGURE 6.12 *Rings of Zilfin* is a charming game that's more about story than combat.

maintain the Tolkien-inspired storyline, which amounts to keeping an evil necromancer named Lord Dragos from finding both of the rings of power and using them to take over the world. *Rings of Zilfin* puts the player in the role of Reis (whose name can be changed), a budding magic-user who must develop his abilities and take on Dragos and his minions. It's probably more accurate to describe the game as an adventure/CRPG hybrid, since there are many inventory-based puzzles. If you've ever wanted a CRPG that lets you feed a cookie to a water dragon, look no further.

Players are spared the bother of creating a character and rolling for stats, and the combat sequences are more like mini–arcade games than the tactical affairs seen in *The Wizard's Crown* or *The Shard of Spring*. Most of the game is spent traveling between towns, and along the way the character can collect plants—such as mushrooms and herbs that boost stats or cure poison. There are also pools that have random effects. The world is composed of some 100 villages, and the player needs to talk to many villagers to gather clues. Naturally, the character gets fatigued from traveling and must rest to restore his vitality. The fatigue score decreases in proportion to the character's walking speed—and if it reaches zero, the game is over. Other actions, such as climbing, fighting, and casting spells, also deplete this all-important attribute.

Overall, it's an interesting game and quite different from most of SSI's other offerings. Although *Phantasie* has its share of humor, *Rings of Zilfin* almost seems to indulge in self-parody. For instance, passing monks have lines such as "SSI forever!" and "Have you eaten your Yurpin today?" In short, it's a far cry from the grim, no-nonsense *Wizard's Crown.* Contemporary reviewers seem divided about its quality, though. One calls the game "extraordinarily playable," while another bemoans its "clumsy user interface" and "primitive graphics." Atabek went on to create a trilogy of very popular *Ultima*-like games called *The Magic Candle,* a fan favorite we'll discuss in a moment.

ORIGIN AND *ULTIMA:* THE GREAT ENLIGHTENMENT

When last we spoke of *Ultima,* Garriott had just formed Origin and published *Ultima III: Exodus,* which was regarded at the time as the best CRPG ever made. However, Garriott was just getting started. In 1985, Origin published the next great installment in the series, *Ultima IV: Quest of the Avatar,* an instant classic that is still played by thousands of fans all over the world. Indeed, in 1996 *Computer Gaming World* named it the #2 Best Game of All Time for the PC, and Garriott himself cites it as one of his favorite games of the series. It is also one of the most widely ported of the *Ultima* games, with versions available for almost every major platform of the era, including the NES and Sega Master System game consoles.

Quest of the Avatar marks an important turning point in the *Ultima* series. It's the first game set in what Garriott calls the "Age of Enlightenment" trilogy, and it emphasizes social and cultural conflict over "hack 'n slash." The game is almost philosophical, encouraging gamers to think about the good life and ponder age old questions of good and evil. The new shift is made visible even by the box art: *Quest of the Avatar* sports an image more reminiscent of Jesus than Gandalf. Garriott insists that the game is "more philosophical than religious," but the many allusions to Christianity and other religions are hard to miss. Origin even included a small metal ankh (an Egyptian holy symbol) in every box![13]

Just how different *Quest of the Avatar* is from other CRPGs is evident as soon as the player tries to create a character. Instead of rolling dice and generating stats, players answer a series of difficult questions about moral dilemmas (Figure 6.13). Each of the questions is designed to test the player's own moral center, or at least to determine which of the game's eight virtues he or she most holds most dear. Once this virtue is determined, the player's character (the Avatar) will be assigned one of the eight possible classes: shepherd (humility), tinker (sacrifice), bard (compassion), druid (justice), fighter (valor), ranger (spirituality), paladin (honor), or

FIGURE 6.13 Rather than let you simply roll or input your own stats or attributes, *Ultima IV* asks you a series of ethical questions.

mage (honesty). Furthermore, the Avatar's initial power is greater if the player's answers strictly adhere to a single virtue (e.g., always choosing the honorable thing to do rather than what might be more compassionate or just). Instead of offering up the usual generic warrior and wizard types, Garriott's system lets players create characters that reflect their own personalities and interests (Figure 6.14).

Garriott thought his games might have a real-life impact on players, a fact the manual makes clear: "The Quest for the Avatar is the search for

FIGURE 6.14 In *Ultima IV*, you don't want to wantonly kill every enemy that attacks you. However, we daresay this rogue has it coming.

a new standard, a new vision of life for which our people may strive. We seek the person who can become a shining example for our nation and guide us from the Age of Darkness into the Age of Light." After forming his own company, Garriott had begun receiving mail from fans and critics, some of whom accused him of intentionally corrupting youth. Though unfounded, these accusations bothered Garriott deeply. He decided that if players were going to invest so much time playing his games, he might as well try to do some good by encouraging ethical behavior rather than the mindless pillaging and looting that dominated the genre. Extremist groups were preaching that RPGs were satanic and immoral; Garriott wanted to show how they could in fact teach moral virtue. Much was made of the new moral and philosophical element of the game, and contemporary reviewers praised Origin for bringing new vitality to the genre.

Another interesting innovation is the magic system, which requires that mages find reagents (ingredients like ginseng and garlic) to cast spells. This reagent business is an integral part of many tabletop *AD&D* campaigns but is omitted from most CRPGs, including SSI's Gold Box games. The system was inspired by Garriott's research into medieval alchemy, an esoteric protoscience that combines magical rites and mysticism with rigorous experimentation. For instance, ginseng has long been thought to have restorative effects. In the game, ginseng combined with the right incantation and a dash of spider silk can heal wounds. The manual puts it well: "All magic is accomplished by use of means both human and of nature, for true magic is but the melding of human will and natural force." This quotation should also give some suggestion of its overall tone, which sounds more like a venerable medieval tome than a computer game manual!

Quest of the Avatar also depends heavily on conversations with nonplayer characters, some of whom can even join the Avatar on his quest (up to eight, or one of each character class). In some ways, the game reinforced the now infamous tradition of requiring players to talk to every single character in the game, exhausting every possible topic. Dialog is facilitated by a mini-parser, a simple text input that matches keywords (i.e., "job," "name") against a database. The player finds new keywords in the characters' responses. All of this dialog soon leads to a glut of information, and players must take copious notes if they hope to progress very far into the game—and it's a huge game, taking an estimated 150 to 200 hours to finish. Thankfully, players have many ways to get about in the world—horses, ships, and moon gates, to name just a few modes of transportation.

We should also add that game included a cloth map and a small metal ankh in addition to two manuals, and you could also spring for *The Way of the Avatar*, a forty-page clue book with detailed maps, tips, and plenty of flavor text. Both the manuals and clue books for each of the *Enlightenment* games are lengthy and loaded with information that establishes the context for the games. For instance, besides lengthy discussions of virtues, ethics, combat, and magic, *Ultima V*'s manual includes lyrics to a song called "Stones," penned by Gwenllian Gwalch'gaeaf, wife of the famous folk musician Iolo Fitzowen. In short, if you don't have the printed materials that were included with these games, you're missing out on a big chunk of the *Ultima* experience.

Modern gamers may want to check out xu4, a remake of the game engine that runs on Windows, GNU/Linux, OS X, and even the Sega Dreamcast game console.[14] There are also user-made modules for *Neverwinter Nights* based on the game.[15] However, the original has officially been relicensed as freeware and is available for download on many websites.

Ultima Trilogy

Origin released the *Ultima Trilogy* in 1987. Although often thought of as merely a compilation of the first three games, we shouldn't overlook the substantial amount of revision that went into them. Nor should we overlook that it was published by Origin, after some negotiation with Sierra. The earlier games were rewritten in assembly language and offer enhanced graphics, compared to the originals. The collection was yet another financial windfall for Origin, and no doubt legions of *Ultima* fans were introduced to the first three games via this series. It was first released for MS-DOS, with ports for Commodore 64 and Apple II following in 1989. Already, we see Origin moving away from the Apple II platform and focusing on the IBM-compatible base, which was already swelling in numbers far exceeding Apple's.

Ultima Meets Death Race: Autoduel

The second of Origin's 1985 breakthroughs is the classic masterpiece *Autoduel,* one of the earliest CRPGs set in a postapocalyptic wasteland. This genre had been popularized by several cult classic films of the era, including *Death Race 2000* (1975), *Damnation Alley* (1977), and *Mad Max* (1979), just to name a few. The advantage of this setting for CRPGs is that it provides a plausible scenario for combat and random encounters with thugs and mutated beasts; it can soon become just as fantastic as

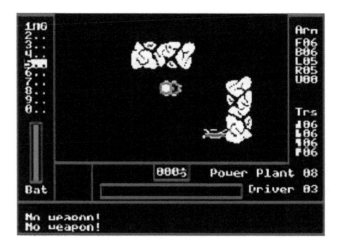

FIGURE 6.15   Vroom! Chuckles' epic game is a hybrid racing CRPG with tons of fun vehicular combat.

any conventional swords and sorcery setting. *Autoduel* was programmed by Richard Garriott and his friend and longtime collaborator Chuck "Chuckles" Bueche (Figure 6.15).

Autoduel is based on Steve Jackson's influential tabletop role-playing game *Car Wars* (c. 1980), in which players strive not to slay dragons but to build the most deadly vehicles on the road. Accomplishing this goal requires forethought, luck, and quick reflexes; in some ways we might describe *Autoduel* as a combination of *Ultima* and racing/shooter hybrids such as Exidy's controversial *Death Race* (1976)[16] and Bally Midway's arcade hit *Spy Hunter* (1983), a popular top-down driving and shooting game. In short, it's a game requiring not only effective planning and sound strategy but also dexterity with the joystick. As in most CRPGs, the player's first priority is simply to stay alive in a dangerous and hostile world. The player's long-term goal is to make a name for himself or herself as a successful autodueler, building his or her own custom-made hellion on wheels. However, the manual hints at another goal: to defeat "Mr. Big," the big boss of all the gangs—though the player's character must earn an outstanding reputation before learning more about this special mission.

The game is also noteworthy for being one of the earliest open-ended CRPGs. Instead of being railed into a linear plot or forced to "hack 'n slash" through wave after wave of enemies, players are given a choice of activities: fighting in the arena, hauling cargo between cities, or roaming the highways in search of renegades and gangs.

Each character starts off with 50 points to distribute among three skills: driving, marksmanship, and mechanic. Later on, these skills can be refined by paying for training or earning experience. The final stat is prestige, which is slowly accumulated during the game. Instead of hit points, players have to worry first about the condition of their characters and then about the damage to their cars. Although most of the action takes place in a vehicle, the character can also jump out of the car (usually to make a run for it after a breakdown), but body armor can also protect the driver if his or her car explodes a mine. Players can even buy a clone to take over if they die!

Without a doubt, the most fun part of the game is building a custom car. Building a vehicle is a sophisticated process involving seven crucial decisions: body type, chassis, suspension, power plants, tires, weapons, and armor. The manual includes a "theory of car design" with recommendations to build anything from a heavily armored and slow-moving "turtle" to the light and speedy "rabbit." Obviously, the choice of car will depend strongly on the player's strengths; those going the courier route will want the better armor, whereas those good at combat may want a sleeker, deadlier model. The degree to which players can customize the car is staggering; they can even select where they want their weapons placed (front, rear, and side), though only one weapon can be fired at the time. Players are allowed to own up to eight different cars, allowing them to explore the options at their leisure.

Critics raved about the game, and it soon became one of Origin's most popular titles. Even its motto "Drive offensively! The life you save may be your own" became a familiar catchphrase. As usual, Origin loaded up the packaging with plenty of nicely printed manuals and a "feelie," this time a set of miniature tools. SSI noted *Autoduel*'s success and developed *Roadwar 2000* in 1987 and the sequel *Roadwar Europa* in 1987, turn-based strategy games based on many of the same concepts. More recently, *Car Battler Joe,* a game published for the Game Boy Advance in 2003, almost certainly derives much of its gameplay from the Origin classic. Unfortunately, the original game is no longer published, and according to *Wikipedia,* Steve Jackson Games has forbidden that this wonderful and historically vital game be freely distributed on the web. When I asked the company to explain its decision, the response was that it does not want to be associated with "an old, buggy game."[17] These are harsh words indeed for this beloved old classic.

The Magic Candle

Atabek's *The Magic Candle*, published in 1989 by Mindcraft, is one of the more popular and enduring games inspired by the early *Ultima* games. It's noted for its excellent writing, colorful graphics, and sophisticated gameplay. Like *Ultima*, it offers top-down perspective and tile graphics. The game also borrows the *Ultima* convention of putting the player in the role of a single character who can later enlist up to five other pregenerated characters to aid in the quest. Although there are two clear sequels and one spinoff, most fans recognize this game as the best of them.

One interesting aspect of the game is the ability to split the six-character party into groups, which can then explore dungeons independently—a feature we've seen in very few earlier games (Figure 6.16). This ability is taken much further in this game, though, and the possibilities are really intriguing. For instance, some of the available companions practice professions such as carpentry and tailoring. The player can choose to temporarily leave these characters behind in a town, earning money for the party as the rest venture onward. The game tracks the location of the split parties, so it's easy enough to rejoin later.

There's also a rudimentary skill system based on four skills (sword, box, hunter, learn). The skills are improved when players using them or when

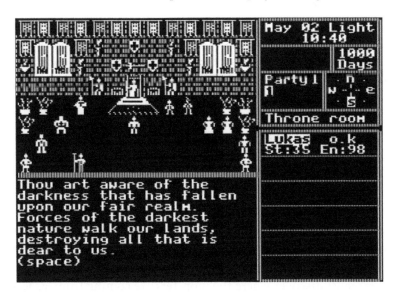

FIGURE 6.16 *The Magic Candle* is a great game in the *Ultima* style. One neat feature is that you can split up your party and let them moonlight for you.

they seek out special trainers (there are no experience points and levels per se). The magic system is interesting as well. Mages learn spells in camp, and then can ready (or recall) them for use in combat or exploration. The mages come equipped with some spells, but new ones are learned from spell books. Casting spells (as well as any other activity) requires energy, which must be replenished by sleeping. The spell system here seems to be an effort to blend the *AD&D* system with the more familiar point-based systems of games like *The Bard's Tale*.

The game's story concerns a demon named Dreax, who will soon be released to wreak havoc upon the world if the Magic Candle in which he is trapped is allowed to burn itself out. The candle's custodians have inexplicably gone missing. It's up to the hero ("Lukas" by default) to restore the candle, a quest that will take him and his companions all over the game-world, exploring and interacting with other characters.

All in all, *The Magic Candle* is an excellent game that received praise from critics and established Atabek's reputation as a master crafter of CRPGs. It won *Computer Gaming World*'s prestigious Fantasy Role-Playing Game of the Year award in 1989 and remains a favorite of many veterans of the genre.

The Keys to Maramon

Rather than make a straightforward sequel to *The Magic Candle*, Mindcraft developed *The Keys to Maramon*, a real-time action CRPG published in 1990 by Mindscape (Atabek doesn't appear to have been involved). This time the player controls only one character, chosen from a set of four premade heroes (huntsman, courier, blacksmith, and scholar). While the CRPG elements have been boiled down to their essentials, the player still needs to plan the character's development carefully, particularly in building up the right skills and saving up for the best arms and armor—as well as for herbs and potions for healing and combat boosts.

Although not as popular as the other *Magic Candle* games, this one does offer an appealing plot. The hero accepts a commission to deal with a small island city's monster problem. Of course, the hero must do more than simply bash heads: he (or she, if the player chooses the courier) must discover where the monsters are coming from, as well as the purpose of the mysterious towers located in the town. Eventually the hero will descend into the dungeons beneath the town, where the real dangers await.

The Four and Forty

Atabek did get involved for the first official *Magic Candle* sequel, *The Four and Forty,* published in 1991 by Electronic Arts for the DOS platform. It's based mostly on the original *Magic Candle,* though with some important changes. Besides featuring 256-color VGA graphics, the game also added a notebook feature to track quest information, a better automapper, and a more comprehensive save system with eight slots.

The second game also tweaked the party formation and division capabilities that made the first game so noteworthy. Although the player can no longer divvy up the party into multiple units, it is still possible to assign characters to jobs in towns and substitute new members in their place (there are some thirty characters available to join the party). Players can also import characters from the original game or from *The Keys to Maramon.*

The story has the party searching for the forty-four guardians of the original candle, who, in an ironic twist, have become trapped in magic candles themselves. The quest will take the party all over the world of Gurtex, where, again, they'll need to interact with a great many characters in a well-contrived plot.

Though *Four and Forty* offers some major improvements to the original model, fans of the series are somewhat divided about its overall quality. Some were miffed about not being able to properly split the party, and others complained that the game lacks depth and overemphasizes combat (Figure 6.17).

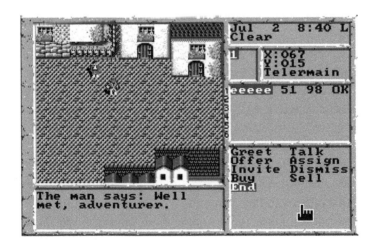

FIGURE 6.17 Not everyone liked the changes made for the second *Magic Candle* game, but it's still a quality adventure.

Magic Candle III

The third game in the series also failed to surpass the brilliance of the original—at least for most long-term fans. Published by Electronic Arts for DOS in 1992, this game still offers the familiar top-down perspective of the original, but the party management system has been tweaked yet again. This time, the player selects and customizes three characters to join the hero but can recruit pregenerated "companions" (faithful followers) and "hirelings" (mercenaries) later on in the game. Party members can again be assigned to work at various jobs, but this time the player can also tell them to wait or go to a stronghold. The hero can communicate with distant members via magical items called mindstones. Characters assigned to work jobs won't always stick with it, though—they may decide to move on if they feel they're being abused, particularly if their loyalty attribute is low.

The hero sets out to determine the source of a mysterious blight, which is ruining crops and spreading plague, and is probably linked to the appearance of monsters in the hills and forests. The hero and the party must travel to all sorts of interesting locations in the course of the game, including the respective homelands of the orcs, dwarves, elves, and goblins.

Critics didn't respond well to the game. Many complained that it was simply more of the same, which perhaps wouldn't have been a criticism had not *Four and Forty* made a better impression. While still mandatory playing for *Magic Candle* fans, the third game simply wasn't strong enough to extend the life of the franchise, which sadly worn down to a stub.

Bloodstone

Mindcraft attempted to recycle the *Magic Candle III* engine with *Bloodstone: An Epic Dwarven Tale,* developed and published for DOS in 1993. It's a very large game, with an extensive plot (with multiple endings) and myriad characters. Atabek described it thus: "[There are] no technological marvels, no startling new features. It's the gameplay and intriguing story that make *Bloodstone*."[18] Indeed, interface-wise, there are few changes to the *Magic Candle III* engine. The graphics look quite primitive compared to other 1993 games, a fact that no doubt led many gamers to dismiss this rather excellent game.

As the subtitle implies, this is a game about dwarves—specifically those of the lands of Tarq (Figure 6.18). The dwarves are divided into warring factions, and much of the game's plot depends on which side the player chooses to help out most. Meanwhile, a new enemy named the Taldor

FIGURE 6.18 If you can appreciate a good story about dwarves and plenty of turn-based combat, give *Bloodstone* a chance.

has been raiding the dwarves—soon becoming a grave threat—but the dwarves can't settle their differences long enough to fight them off. It's up to the player's character to unite the dwarves and defeat the Taldor. The game is indeed epic in scope, with plenty of intrigue and plot twists to keep players invested until the end.

Despite the similarities to the third *Magic Candle*, *Bloodstone* seems to have fared better. It's still highly playable, with a low learning curve and fun turn-based combat. In our opinion, it's a great game for novices as well as more advanced fans wanting to try something different.

MIGHT AND MAGIC: A BRAVE NEW WORLD

Although there have been many successful CRPG series over the decades, the most long-lived are *Ultima*, *Wizardry*, and New World Computing's *Might and Magic*. Indeed, each of these series received installments into the 2000s. Of the three, however, *Might and Magic* seems at times to be hidden in the shadow of the other luminaries. Nevertheless, it's an interesting series that made several key developments to the genre. We'll introduce the series here and talk more about it in the next chapter.

The first *Might and Magic*, subtitled *Book I: The Secret of the Inner Sanctum*, debuted in 1986 for the Apple II and ported a year later to the Commodore 64, MS-DOS, and Macintosh (Figure 6.19). It is a labor of love by developer Jon Van Caneghem and his wife Michaela. Caneghem did the bulk of the coding and design himself and then co-founded New

FIGURE 6.19   Jon Van Caneghem's epic *Might and Magic* series debuted in 1986. Shown here is the DOS version.

World Computing with Michaela and Mark Caldwell. Contemporary reviewers praise the game highly, comparing it very favorably with the competition at a time when *The Bard's Tale* was winning over huge audiences for the genre. The biggest draw was the immense size of Varn, the gameworld: there are over 4,000 locations and 55 areas to explore, with environments ranging from glaciers to deserts. Furthermore, the game is much more liberal than most in allowing players to explore the map however they wanted, in contrast to the more linear setups of many games of the era. It offers first-person perspective and colorful but static graphics (no animation).

Might and Magic made several refinements that show up in later games, such as having the characters' race and gender exert a strong effect on the gameplay. As in *Phantasie,* there are some areas of the gameworld that cannot be explored without the right party members, such as an anti-male kingdom where an all-male party is unwelcome. Alignment (good, neutral, or evil) also plays a role in which locations the party can visit. Finally, the game's difficulty level was lower than most other games on the shelf and was thus quite popular with gamers not yet ready to tackle *The Wizard's Crown* or *The Bard's Tale.* (We should note that the early releases of the game started the characters off with no money and no weapons but clubs; versions were quickly released with a stronger starting party.) Combat is a simple text-driven affair, with the strengths of the monsters balanced to avoid overwhelming the party. Even if the party dies, players can easily restore the game at the most recently visited inn.

The plot focuses on six adventurers in a quest to discover the secret of the Inner Sanctum, though little information is offered up front about this quest or its object. Indeed, the ultimate quest is kept intentionally vague and left for players to gradually piece together as they explore Varn. Like the early *Ultima* games, *Might and Magic* contains a mixture of fantasy and sci-fi elements. It also has one of the best manuals of any of the early CRPGs, a spiral-bound affair with a fold-out map of Varn. In short, the first *Might and Magic* game made a great impression on critics and gamers, a considerable feat when one considers the stiff competition.

Starflight and the Space Sim CRPG

So far, we've discussed three series that belong to what we might call the space CRPG: Edu-Ware's *Space, Empire,* and Omnitrend's *Universe.* These games evolved alongside more conventional CRPGs and offer an alternative to swords and sorcery, though the amount of roleplaying varies from game to game. Now we come to what might be the most successful of such hybrids, Binary Systems' *Starflight,* published in 1986 by Electronic Arts (Figure 6.20). Although *Starflight* is primarily a space exploration game, it does feature CRPG elements, most notably a crew that can be trained as the gameplay progresses, as well as a ship that can be outfitted with better weapons and equipment.

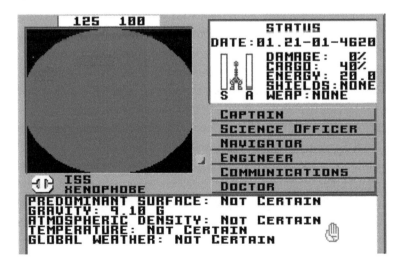

FIGURE 6.20 *Starflight* is another ambitious space game that reportedly took over fifteen years to make. Shown here is the Amiga version.

I like to think of *Starflight* as a *Star Trek* CRPG, albeit without any official endorsement from Paramount. The gameplay is quite reminiscent of many episodes of the popular sci-fi series and seems to be structured around the concept of away missions. There's a captain, navigation officer, and so on, and the manual and in-game text are full of obvious allusions such as "Boldly go where no man has gone before!" Indeed, some reviewers quipped that it was the best *Star Trek* game ever made.

The story behind *Starflight* is similar in some ways to the one found in the earlier *Universe*. The central theme is again that of a distant colony that has been cut off from the motherworld (or, to be more precise, mother galaxy) and must fend for itself. However, this time the period of isolation is much longer (1,000 years), and takes place after a devastating catastrophe that reduced the colony to a state of barbarism. Thankfully, enough time has passed for the colonists to reclaim civilization and rediscover science and technology. The game begins shortly after they rediscover spaceflight and start to realize that the old myths of originating as an Earth colony are, according to recent archaeological evidence, not myths at all. Furthermore, the people of Arth seem to be threatened by the same warlike race that wiped out their ancestors. The story is actually quite rich and full of interesting twists and turns, but these are revealed only as the player advances in the game.

Players begin by buying a ship, hiring a crew, and paying for whatever training they can afford. The crew members can be any of five races (human, Elowan, Thrynn, Velox, and android), each with its own affinities and limitations. They are also classed into six professions: captain, science officer, navigator, engineer, communications specialist, and doctor. The races also vary by how much damage they can take (durability) and how fast they learn (learning rate). Once the ship is outfitted and manned, it's time to start gathering information and generating revenue.

Like other games in this genre, *Starflight* offers different modes of gameplay, such as mining for minerals, selling artifacts, capturing and selling exotic alien species, finding a viable planet for colonization, and, for those lacking scruples, practicing piracy (but only in self-defense, of course). In any case, the player will spend a great deal of time exploring space as well as roaming the surface of planets in the all-terrain vehicle. Successful players will eventually attain enough capital to buy better equipment, which passes through five stages of technological development as the game progresses.

The combat portions of the game are no doubt the weakest; it's a boring affair involving a small window with icons of the battling ships. Players essentially spend their time dodging enemy fire and hoping their lasers or missiles will wear down their enemy's defenses. What ultimately matters is who has the best-equipped ship. Indeed, many players strive to avoid combat whenever possible, preferring instead to communicate with aliens, learning enough about their culture and language to make meaningful contact possible.

Starflight allegedly took over fifteen years to make, and, if you're to believe the box and other promotional materials, the delays were caused by the developers' extreme perfectionism. At any rate, the game was a success, winning critical acclaim and routinely showing up on lists of the best games ever made. It was first released for DOS and Tandy, with support for EGA graphics. Later it was ported to most available platforms, including the Sega Genesis.

Trade Routes of the Cloud Nebula

Binary Systems followed up in 1989 with *Starflight 2: Trade Routes of the Cloud Nebula.* This game is very similar to the first, though with a new storyline, aliens, technologies, and the ability to trade with alien races as well as the home base. The graphics were touched up, but overall, it's more of the same—certainly not a bad thing given the quality of the first one.

Electronic Arts had forged a contract with Tsunami Media to develop a third game for the series, but because of "various business reasons,"[19] the agreement fell through and Tsunami was forced to publish the game itself, removing all references to the original series. Nevertheless, its game *Protostar: War on the Frontier,* released in 1993, was a modest success for the company—though not even all *Starflight* fans are aware of its existence. A fan-made *Starflight III* is currently in production, and the fans working on it have received formal approval from Binary Systems to use the trademark title.[20]

Starflight's influence is obvious in many later games, such as 1992's *Star Control 2: The Ur-Quan Masters,* as well as many sci-fi themed CRPGs we'll discuss in later chapters. Although the series shares much in common with Omnitrend's older *Universe* game, it still represents plenty of innovation and, if nothing else, a keen sense of audience and a masterful design.

THE END OF THE EARLY GOLDEN AGE

In this chapter, we've stuck mostly with the mid-1980s. These were bountiful years for CRPG fans, but much more was on the way. In the next chapter, we'll cover SSI's famous Gold Box games, the officially licensed *AD&D*

titles that established a long and fruitful franchise. We'll also cover the rise of real-time, first-person 3D games such as FTL's *Dungeon Master* and SSI's *Eye of the Beholder,* and catch up with Sir-Tech as it begins its next big wave of *Wizardry* titles.

However, it's during the early Golden Age that the CRPG really established itself as a viable, permanent genre of computer game. Critics no longer had to explain what a CRPG was during every review or compare each new game to *Ultima,* hitherto practically the only touchstone with which they could trust gamers were familiar. Furthermore, CRPGs were diversifying, moving away from the *Ultima* and *Wizardry* models and exploring new horizons. Finally, computer hardware was fast approaching the 16-bit standard, and the IBM PC was gradually replacing Commodore and Apple as the dominant computing platform. Developers finally had more memory, storage space, and graphics power to work with, and they never looked back.

NOTES

1. See http://home.arcor.de/cybergoth/gamesc/rogueinterview.html.
2. See Roy Wagner's "Amiga Preferences" column in the August 1986 issue of *Computer Gaming World.*
3. From the game's manual.
4. CRPG Addict notes that it's unclear if *Wizard's Crown* was published in 1985 or 1986.
5. *Ultima III* has a "lark" class, shown in the manual as an elf with a harp. In practice, they are simply magic-users who could wield weapons.
6. These quotations from Cranford are from personal email correspondence with the author.
7. See "A 50 Mission Recall" in the March 1987 issue of *Computer Gaming World.*
8. See "Adventure Trends" by Michael Ciraolo in the November 1984 issue of *Antic* magazine.
9. See James V. Trunzo's review of the game in the December 1985 issue of *Compute!* magazine.
10. See Steve Panak's review in the August 1988 issue of *ST-Log* magazine.
11. See Scorpia's review of the game in the October 1987 issue of *Computer Gaming World.*
12. The quotations and references from Roth are from personal email correspondence with the author.
13. Garriott claims his interest in this symbol comes from the cult classic science fiction film *Logan's Run,* in which it is prominently featured.
14. To learn more about xu4, visit http://xu4.sourceforge.net/index.php.
15. See http://nwvault.ign.com/View.php?view=Modules.Detail&id=2693.

16. The controversy concerned the violent nature of the game, which appeared to consist of running down pedestrians with a vehicle. Exidy claimed the figures were actually evil "gremlins," but few were convinced. The game made headlines and was soon widely banned, leading to some of the first protests over game censorship.
17. This quotation is from a personal email sent to me by Fade Manley, webmaster for Steve Jackson Games.
18. See Shay Addams' "Virtual Unreality" article in the October 1993 issue of *Compute!* magazine.
19. See http://www.mobygames.com/game/dos/protostar-war-on-the-frontier/trivia for some excerpts of an interview with the game's designer. The interview was originally available on the CD version of *Protostar.*
20. See http://www.starflightcentral.com for information about this project.

CHAPTER 7

SSI's Golden Age

The five years between 1987 and 1993 were exciting but uneven for CRPG fans. Groundbreaking hits such as FTL's *Dungeon Master* (1987) for the Atari ST were so far ahead of their time that it's hard to imagine their competing for shelf space with Origin's *2400 A.D.* or SSI's *Rings of Zilfin* for the Apple II. The budding genre was a hydra, sprouting new heads in every direction—and gobbling up legions of new gamers. The CRPG burst out from a small niche of hardcore *D&D* fans to the mainstream gaming community—now there was something for everybody.

One unfortunate trend, however, was a widening gap between the haves and the have-nots of graphics and sound technology. On one side of the chasm were venerable old platforms such as the Apple II and Commodore 64, which had penetrated deeply into America and represented an over-whelming base of loyal, dedicated users. The beloved machines were showing their age, but it was foolish to ignore their massive user bases. Furthermore, critics were quick to bash hastily done ports that failed to live up to these older machines' full potential. Many developers continued to develop on them, and they outsourced the task of creating enhanced versions for newer machines. This practice proved quite significant for companies such as Westwood, who earned a reputation for fine ports that were often superior to the original games.

On the other side of the chasm were the newer, more powerful machines such as the Commodore Amiga, Atari ST, and Apple Macintosh, which not only had better graphics but, more importantly, more user-friendly interfaces. We can't overlook something as seemingly trivial as the mouse, or the windowed graphical interfaces that made such efficient use of it.

These advances represented an intriguing paradox for the personal computer revolution. On the one hand, they were much easier and less intimidating to operate than the older machines, thus appealing to a wider demographic. On the other hand, they were much more expensive (particularly the Macintosh), a fact that kept them out of the hands of budget-minded computer enthusiasts for years.[1] The price wars of the early 1980s had taught consumers to think of computers in terms of hundreds of dollars; now they cost thousands. Needless to say, only committed enthusiasts or wealthy casual users were willing to cross this digital divide.

All of this changed in the 1990s, when, slowly but surely, the IBM PC and a massive army of cheaper "IBM Compatibles" saturated the market. From a gamer's point of view, these machines were stymied by pathetic graphics and sound capabilities, especially compared to the Macintosh, Amiga, or Atari ST. Nevertheless, the IBM PC had a few key advantages, particularly in memory, processor speed, and storage media (especially the large hard drives). However, the decisive advantage was its modular, eminently expandable design. Unlike its rivals, the IBM PC was based on an open architecture, which made it easy for other companies to manufacture components—including graphics and sound cards specifically for gamers. Furthermore, the IBM PC was built from off-the-shelf components, and Microsoft's nonexclusive license with IBM meant that it could sell the MS-DOS operating system to any other computer manufacturer, igniting the vicious "clone wars." In short, there was competition at every level, from the system itself to each and every peripheral, component, and application. With these powerful economic forces at play, it was all but inevitable that the IBM PC would become the dominant computer.

Unfortunately, game developers targeting the IBM PC were hindered by late adopters, who were slow to upgrade to the latest CGA, EGA, and then VGA standards, to say nothing of the smorgasbord of sound cards. They were mired in a morass of incompatible standards across the various expansion cards, and it would take years for industry standards to emerge from this pandemonium. To the casual gamer, the typical off-the-shelf IBM PC—with its monochrome or four-color CGA graphics, inept internal speaker, and text-based operating system—seemed decades behind multimedia powerhouses such as the Amiga or Atari ST, whose users had long been wielding mice and clicking windows. The PC eventually won the war, but not without a long and bitter struggle.[2]

The last piece of this story is the rebirth of game consoles, which rose from the ashes after the great crash in 1984. As the major computer manufacturers shifted their attention to more expensive machines, an opening was left for cheap Japanese game machines. The Nintendo Entertainment System (NES) swept across America, followed by its major rival, Sega. Until this time, CRPGs were overwhelmingly made exclusively for personal computers, but Japanese game developers exported *Ultima* and *Wizardry* inspired titles such as *Dragon Warrior* (1986), *The Legend of Zelda* (1986), *Final Fantasy* (1987), and *Phantasy Star* (1988). These more advanced games made the role-playing games of earlier consoles, such as Mattel Electronics' **Advanced Dungeons & Dragons Cartridge** (1982) for the Intellivision, look primitive. As game consoles became more powerful in subsequent generations, the quality gap between console and computer games narrowed, practically disappearing in the 2000s. Although this book is focused primarily on computer role-playing games, we'll discuss console role-playing games in the next chapter, paying special attention to the dynamic influence they exerted on the genre.

We will begin, however, with SSI's celebrated Gold Box games, well-wrought products that benefited immensely from a lucrative and exclusive licensing agreement with TSR. We'll then catch up with Origin, Sir-Tech, and New World Computing, who were vigorously pumping out some of the best games of their career. We've got a lot of great CRPGs to cover in this chapter, so let's ready our trusty Longsword +3 (+4 vs. Rats) and charge into the fray!

UNFORGETTABLE REALMS: SSI'S GOLD BOX GAMES

Pool of Radiance. Curse of the Azure Bonds (Figure 7.1). For many—merely titles of obsolete games. For others, sacred words, hallowed words, words never spoken without that telltale sigh of longing brought by years of

FIGURE 7.1 SSI's *AD&D*–licensed games came in shiny gold boxes sporting terrific cover art by Clyde Caldwell and other great fantasy artists.

insatiable, incurable nostalgia. Of all the games we've discussed, the only ones that might rival their long-lasting fame and popularity are *Ultima IV* and, just possibly, *The Bard's Tale*. Indeed, it is hard to convey the sort of raw enthusiasm, nostalgia, and even ecstasy that SSI's Gold Box games still arouse in the hearts of many who played them in the late 1980s, but I will be so bold as to make the attempt:

These games kick ass.

Pool of Radiance and the Forgotten Realms Series

I remember the day I first laid hands on *Pool of Radiance*. Although I had played *The Bard's Tale* and a few other CRPGs, it wasn't until I planted my foot on the corpse of the evil dragon Tyranthraxus that I knew what it meant to love a computer game. Never before had a game held me so deeply in its power. My humble Commodore 64 had become a portal to another world, one so compelling that I happily endured hunger and exhaustion rather than look away! After *Pool of Radiance*, I knew I would play computer role-playing games until the day I died.

But what makes *Pool of Radiance* so special? After all, it's hardly original or unique, since it contains virtually no element that cannot be found in earlier games, such as a tactical combat system lifted straight from SSI's own *The Wizard's Crown*. The interface and windowed display are seen in the earlier *Wizardry* and *Might and Magic* games. The graphics, though pleasant enough, are only marginally more impressive than those seen in *The Bard's Tale*, released three years earlier. Finally, no one would accuse this game of being easy to learn. Death comes surely and swiftly to inexperienced players, and even grizzled old CRPG veterans often find the fate of their party resting on a single roll of the dice. As if all this wasn't enough, a single battle can often last up to forty-five minutes or even an hour; this is definitely not bite-sized entertainment.

Yet all masterpieces are greater than the sum of their parts, and *Pool of Radiance* is no exception. Let's start with the box, which sports magnificent artwork by the celebrated fantasy illustrator Clyde Caldwell, one of TSR's regular artists (Caldwell also created the cover for *Curse of the Azure Bonds*). Caldwell's magnificent cover speaks to the legions of tabletop *AD&D* gamers: this is the real thing. Of course, having the words "Official Advanced Dungeons & Dragons Computer Product" displayed prominently above the image helps as well. In the age of Steam and digital downloads, it's easy to forget the impact that effective packaging had on gamers; Garriott realized this early on and fought hard to ensure that his own products were attractive and eye-catching. A large part of the aesthetic experience is opening a box for the first time, poring over the contents, and even whiffing the faint, lingering scents of the factory where the floppy disks were magnetized.

Pool of Radiance was written for the Commodore 64 in 1988 and ported to MS-DOS and Atari ST. Other ports were soon available for most major platforms, including the NES. It was an instant best seller, and not just because it was the first officially licensed *AD&D* computer game. Awash in strong competition, SSI took the sensible approach—take the very best elements of its own and rival CRPGs and pool them together. Indeed, the Gold Box engine is essentially a medley of *The Bard's Tale* and *The Wizard's Crown*, which can trace their own ancestry back to *Ultima III* and *Wizardry*. Rather than go back to the drawing board, the approach seemingly favored by Origin, SSI took a more pragmatic approach, building on the strengths of past accomplishments. The result was one of the best (if not the very best) CRPG engines ever designed. Later Gold Box games would refine the engine and address some irritating flaws in the interface, but all the qualities that make the Gold Box games so legendary are fully present in *Pool of Radiance*.

The game's key strengths are its gameworld, story, combat system, and overall game structure. Since the gameworld and story are so closely related, let's discuss those first. The player's task is to help rebuild Phlan, a once-proud city that has long lain in ruins (Figure 7.2). The characters arrive at New Phlan, the part of the city that has already been restored.

FIGURE 7.2 *Pool of Radiance* opens with a guided tour of Phlan and the game's mechanics.

There the party can accept commissions from the City Council to perform various quests, such as clearing the slums of monsters and recovering legendary artifacts. The characters are more than just hired thugs—they are also archaeologists, digging into Phlan's ancient past to learn more about its history. The quests vary widely and all make sense in the context of the story. Eventually, the player learns that an evil dragon named Tyranthraxus is at the root of Phlan's problems, but defeating him will take time, effort, and luck. Unlike later CRPGs, which are lauded for their byzantine stories with multiple arcs and complex characters, this story is one that any player can wrap his or her head around without getting distracted from the action—more J.R.R. than G.R.R., if you will.

Like *The Bard's Tale*, *Pool of Radiance* features a coherent gameworld that feels like a real place. No doubt much of this realism is generated by the 3D, first-person perspective players see in exploration mode. The interface has a generously sized window on the top left that shows the direction in which the characters are currently facing, and the rest of the screen is neatly divided to display pertinent information. Whereas most games were lucky to have fifteen or so different type of walls to look at, *Pool of Radiance* has eighty. This variety made it easier for the game's artists to make each area look unique, rather than using the drab, lookalike corridors of so many other CRPGs. The city and dungeons are laid out on 15 x 15 square grids; the wilderness gets a rectangular 15 × 35. The areas were easy to map onto graph paper, but many players (including me) sprang for SSI's official cluebooks, finely produced manuals with maps and tips. The engine's built-in area function, which presented a portion of the overhead map, shows only the outline of walls and is certainly no substitute for a good map.

However, no interface can make a dull and repetitive game fun to play. SSI was luckily able to draw upon the rich body of literature TSR had created for its Forgotten Realms universe of tabletop *AD&D* games. The Forgotten Realms world is nearly as well developed as J.R.R. Tolkien's Middle-earth, and possibilities for new stories are virtually unlimited— indeed, novels set in this fictional universe are still being published, most notably those by R. A. Salvatore. The Forgotten Realms world is an ideal environment for CRPGs and adds great depth to *Pool of Radiance* and its sequels. Later games in the series draw even more from the story elements and characters from the Forgotten Realms campaign setting.

Pool of Radiance places a great deal of emphasis on tactical combat (Figure 7.3). When the characters engage in battle, the screen changes to

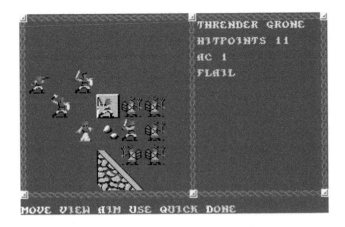

THRENDER GRONE
HITPOINTS 11
AC 1
FLAIL

MOVE VIEW AIM USE QUICK DONE

FIGURE 7.3   Combat in the Gold Box games is turn-based and tactical. While some battles do drag on, smarter enemies will flee or surrender rather than fight to the death.

a top-down mode very similar to the one found in *The Wizard's Crown* or *Ultima III*. The battle is divided into rounds and turns. During each round, the player decides what action his or her characters will undertake, though these actions are taken immediately rather than after all the commands have been issued (as in *Phantasie* or *Wizardry*). When all characters and monsters have moved, the turn is over. A large and intense battle can easily last an hour, and even simple battles can quickly turn disastrous if the player rushes through them (or, worse, puts his or her characters in computer-controlled "quick" mode).

The reason combat can be so prolonged is the difficulty of actually connecting with a weapon in combat. The likelihood of a successful strike is based on a score called the THAC0, or To Hit Armor Class Zero, and the armor class of the target. Each attempt is based on a random number between 1 and 20; if this random number is greater than the attacker's THAC0, he makes a successful strike. The end result is that misses are more common than strikes, a fact that can significantly increase the duration of a battle. The manual does not spell out how THAC0 is calculated, but it is likely based on a complex formula that factors in the character's strength, dexterity, and the stats associated with the readied weapon. Of course, logically it makes little sense that a figure decked out in full plate mail would be harder to hit than one wearing only leather, but the system did help maintain balance and prevent any attacker from becoming too powerful. After all, even a professional archer misses occasionally.

There are plenty of options available to each character depending on his or her class. For instance, fighters can wield melee or ranged weapons, and magic-users function like artillery or sharpshooters, depending on the spell (fireball versus magic missile, for instance). Thieves also have the option to backstab an opponent, a devastating move that requires careful positioning. Furthermore, retreating characters (or enemies) are penalized by giving all surrounding enemies a free swipe at their backsides (an attack of opportunity). If a character's hit points fall below zero, he or she is wounded and must be bandaged by another character to avoid death. Thankfully, not every battle is to the death—intelligent monsters will usually surrender when they realize they're outmatched. This simple mechanic spares time and tedium and ought to be part of every CRPG.

It's also possible to simply talk monsters out of combat. Rather than present players with a dialog tree, the parley menu consists of five options: haughty, sly, nice, meek, and abusive. If the player selects the appropriate option, the monsters may flee or even provide tips and information rather than fight. It helps if players know enough about Forgotten Realms lore to know something about the cultures they encounter; a kobold, for instance, is not likely to respond well to the nice approach. Admittedly, the game doesn't do as much with this parley system as we might like, but at least it does make the attempt to reinforce the role-playing element without literally putting words in the player's mouth. We greatly prefer this system to countless later games, which present players with an extensive menu of prewritten dialog options—which, more often than not, the game ignores anyway and has the character say something completely different. Leaving these details to the player's imagination promotes better role-play.

Players can level up when they reach a preset level of experience points, but they must journey to a training hall and pay a master for the service. This inconvenience is mitigated by the infrequency of the leveling process; the maximum level for each character is low, and it takes many experience points to reach the next step. The highest level possible is for the thief, who can advance to level 9—fighters are capped at 8, and magic-users and clerics at 6. The training hall is also a place to recruit mercenaries, who fight for the party in exchange for a share of the loot. Players have to think hard about the best way to spend their loot: should they pay for training, better equipment, or a mercenary? The currency system, by the way, is more complex than in most games. Instead of just gold coins, the characters find everything from copper to platinum. The cheap copper coins will soon weigh the party down; platinum is preferable.

There are only four classes available: fighter, cleric, magic-user, and thief. Humans can be only one class, but the other races (dwarf, elf, gnome, half-elf, halfling) can take on more than one, though they are penalized with even more restrictive caps on their maximum level. However, multiclassed characters have a huge advantage over humans: they can wear whatever armor and wield whatever weapons they want, provided that one of their classes allows them. For example, an elven fighter/magic-user can cast spells while wearing armor. Both race and gender affect certain stats. For instance, female halflings are limited to 14 strength points, but male halflings can reach 17. The other stats aren't affected by gender, but racial restrictions and bonuses apply to most of them. Even the stupidest elf has an 8 intelligence score, whereas even the clumsiest halfling scores an 8 in dexterity. The gender restrictions and some of the racial penalties would be quietly dropped in later Gold Box games, no doubt in response to pressure from socially conscious gamers. Since the system is based on rolling three six-sided dice, the lowest any score can possibly be is 3.

Critics made much of the fact that players can customize the portraits and icons of their characters. The system for the portraits reminds me of playing with paper dolls; it's basically a collection of heads and torsos that are interchangeable. The icons are a bit more dynamic, with lots of options for colors and parts, such as the weapon, head, cap, and so on (later Gold Box games facilitate this process with customizable templates.) These icons can be altered during the course of the game, such as when a character starts using a new weapon or acquires new armor. Though we might look at this system today and chuckle, it was nothing short of remarkable in an age when every other CRPG offered non-customizable icons and, if they had them at all, standardized portraits. Whether it was done intentionally or not, the *Pool of Radiance* system allows you to match female heads onto masculine bodies and vice versa.

Much of what makes *Pool of Radiance* special is its faithful adherence to official *AD&D* rules. For instance, instead of magic points, magic-users are given a set number of spells to memorize. How many spells they get per slot depends on their level of experience and intelligence (or wisdom, in the case of clerics). Although mages receive one new spell per level, they will learn most of them by scribing them from scrolls found in the unsettled areas. Once a spell is cast, it erases itself from the magic-user's memory and must be relearned. Memorizing spells (and restoring hit points) takes several hours of inactivity, which means setting up camp. Although there are many safe spots where the characters can rest unmolested, many of the more dangerous areas make camping a risky endeavor. Thus, a player can't just focus on one battle at the time; she must always plan ahead. For instance, wasting all of a mage's fireball spells to quickly dispatch a group of kobolds might leave the party totally vulnerable to a troll attack. This magic system helps balance the party—the problem in so many other CRPGs is that eventually the mages become so powerful as to render the fighters superfluous. Some critics saw these rules as an annoyance, but others praised them. One contemporary reviewer writes, "It seems to us like a logical extension of the kind of resource management which is necessary to any sophisticated strategy game."[3]

The gameworld has many intriguing areas to explore, such as a mysterious pyramid and a haunted library—or you can choose to fight duels in the local arena (Figure 7.4). But eventually you'll want to go across country in wilderness mode, which anyone familiar with older SSI games like *Questron, Phantasie,* or *Ultima* will instantly recognize. Later SSI games experiment with different wilderness modes, such as showing players a large map and having them click on different regions. In any case, the wilderness mode makes *Pool of Radiance* seem even larger and gives gamers something to do after they've completed the game (e.g., slaughtering groups of wandering monsters).

The game includes a printed journal, which contains a numbered list of text passages that the player is to read at certain points of the game. We've seen the same setup in the much earlier *Apshai* games, but it's also seen in *Wasteland* and taken to the extreme in *Star Saga,* which we'll discuss later.

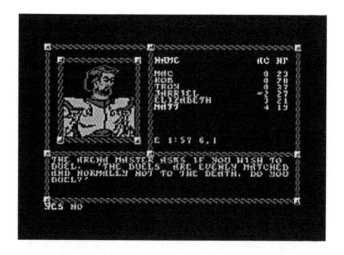

FIGURE 7.4 The arena is a convenient place to test your mettle.

The journal for *Pool of Radiance* contains maps and other illustrations, as well as a collection of Tavern Tales. Of course, one of the problems with a printed journal is that players can cheat by reading all the passages at once, thereby prematurely learning many of the game's secrets. However, the journal warns players that some entries "contain false information that can lead them astray." Besides providing additional context for the game, the journal was intended as a means of thwarting illegal distribution. To that end, SSI included a code wheel, without which the game could not be started. Today, these methods may seem crude, but they were at least less bothersome than the disk-based copy protection schemes then in existence, which could be difficult on the delicate floppy disks and drives of the era.

Pool of Radiance was a critically acclaimed, undisputed success. TSR even commissioned a novel based on the game, as well as a campaign for the tabletop version. However, it also marked an important change in the way CRPGs would be developed ever afterward. I had the pleasure of talking to Craig Roth, author of SSI's *The Shard of Spring*, about the matter. Roth visited SSI's offices in Sunnyvale, California, while programmers were working on *Pool of Radiance*. Roth's vivid description of the scene is worth quoting here:

> There was a big room with no overhead lighting where what must have been a dozen artists were working full time just drawing the pictures in the game. Then I was shown a cube with two assembly language coders. There was a full-time writer for the manual, and more. And here I was—just me and a friend of mine doing everything! I saw that this was the direction the market was heading, and if I wanted to continue to play along it would take a big bet and becoming a big business. For me, creating CRPGs was a labor of love—I enjoyed it the whole time I was doing it. I'm sure I still would have enjoyed it in a big-business environment, but it just wasn't the same.

SSI's game had raised the bar on CRPG development, and other developers and publishers had to accept that it was no longer a cottage industry of teenagers hacking away in their bedrooms. Now it needed a corporate hierarchy and a specialized division of labor. The ramifications of this shift were powerful and permanent, and soon the only refuge for solitary developers was the public domain and shareware markets.

Curse of the Azure Bonds

After achieving such success with *Pool of Radiance,* it's hardly surprising that SSI would want to get a sequel onto the shelves as soon as possible. The next game, *Curse of the Azure Bonds,* appeared in 1989. While the game engine was virtually identical to the previous game, it does offer some very desirable enhancements, such as a fix command. One of the most repetitive and laborious aspects of *Pool of Radiance* is healing the party after a battle. It requires having the clerics cast all their healing spells, click through a menu to have them re-memorize the spells, then sleep and repeat the tedious process. The fix command reduces the operation to a single click.

The designers also removed the individual character portraits, but they kept the icons. No doubt this move was a concession to free up room for more data, but it also sped up the character creation process. Furthermore, the portraits took time to load, causing a delay each time the player viewed the character's status screen. *Pool of Radiance* has an option to turn off the portraits to alleviate this, which I suspect many players did. *Curse of the Azure Bonds* simply does away with them. It also reduced some towns to a menu (store, inn, temple, and so on). Again, this change seems to have been a concession both to memory and loading speed.

One undisputed improvement is the addition of two new and exciting character classes: the ranger and the paladin. Rangers are fighters with a few druid spells who receive bonuses when attacking giant creatures. Paladins, the quintessential good guys, get some clerical spells and a bonus against any evil combatants. However, they cannot travel in a party that includes any evil characters. Another big change is the ability for humans to "dual class," which amounts to a permanent career change. The character does not gain any new hit points or abilities until reaching the level of proficiency in the new class that was acquired in the old class, and no dual-classed characters can cast spells while wearing armor. Even with these caveats, there's just something cool about a magic-user who can also swing a sword or draw a bow. As before, nonhumans can multiclass as they see fit. Players can import previously made characters from either *Pool of Radiance* or *Hillsfar,* an early action CRPG we'll discuss later. However, characters lose their equipment in the transfer, though they are given enough platinum to buy new gear.

Curse of the Azure Bonds is perhaps best known for its storyline, which is based on TSR's previously published novel *Azure Bonds,* by Kate Novak and Jeff Grubb (Figure 7.5). The player's characters awaken with five azure

FIGURE 7.5 *Curse of the Azure Bonds* has a more tightly integrated story than the first game. It's based on a novel by Kate Novak and Jeff Grubb.

tattoos (or "sigils") on their arms, each one controlled by an evil force. The tattoos enslave the party, forcing them to perform certain deeds. Of course, it's up to the player to track down the various groups responsible for the sigils, eliminating them one by one. Tyranthraxus, the party's nemesis in the first game, is back, resurrected in the form of a storm giant. The storyline is competently integrated into the game. For instance, the various towns will respond differently to characters depending on which sigils they still carry, charging higher prices and so on. Although some critics complain about the focus on "hack 'n slash" gameplay, the story is at least set in a more intriguing context than most other CRPGs.

Secret of the Silver Blades

The third game in the original Gold Box series is *Secret of the Silver Blades*, released in 1990. By this time SSI had launched a few spinoffs, which we'll discuss later, but it's worth noting here that this game borrowed some innovations from *Champions of Krynn*, released a few months earlier. Perhaps the most important of these is a difficulty selector, which players can adjust at any time to reduce the power of their enemies. It's useful for getting through particularly nasty encounters, but the trade-off is fewer experience points. The game is also touted for having the largest game-world yet seen in a Gold Box game and cut scenes that illustrate the story.

A few other nice features include a town vault where the party can store its unused equipment and wealth and a teleportation network that shortens travel time. It also adds a series of riddles, though it's debatable to what extent these move the game from away the "hack 'n slash" reputation of the Gold Box games, which several prominent critics bashed them for (one wonders why they weren't playing adventure games instead). Indeed, *Secret of the Silver Blades* is one of the most combat-intensive of any of the Gold Box games and takes a great deal of time to complete.

The storyline is that a small mining village is being threatened by a horde of monsters, unleashed from their glacial prison. The monsters were placed there along with their master, Eldamar, but the miners are tricked by an evil group called the "Black Circle" that misleads them into releasing Eldamar and his minions. Long ago, Eldamar's brother Oswulf and his group of mighty "Silver Blades" defeated him, and now it's the player's turn to take him on.

Although it's not my favorite Gold Box game, other critics rave about it. One particularly ludicrous review in *Compute!* magazine argues that players might even want to make a video recording of the game to "show as background video for parties and gatherings." Now that sounds like my kind of party![4]

Pools of Darkness

The last game of the original series is *Pools of Darkness,* which was released for DOS in 1991 and for the Amiga and Macintosh a year later. Unfortunately, critics have mixed feelings over this last entry in the grand-old series. It is a difficult slog, and though parties can be imported from *Secret of the Silver Blades,* the only race that really has a chance is human. All other races suffer from stringent caps on their maximum levels, and since some of the best abilities (multiple attacks for fighters, awesome spells) are available only at the highest level, nonhumans just hold the party back. A further irritant is a cumbersome equipment loss when traveling through portals; few players enjoy losing or doing without their hard-earned equipment just when they're up against the most powerful foes in the game.

Nevertheless, this is the biggest game in the series, with a huge world to explore (and even other dimensions), and the engine was updated to take advantage of VGA's 256 colors. It also features music by the fabulous Dave "The Fat Man" Govett. Unfortunately, the game was never released for the Commodore 64, so gamers who had played the series on that platform were forced to upgrade to one of the newer platforms and start over with new characters.

Pools of Darkness begins with a trip back to Phlan, which has grown quite large and prosperous since the first game. However, the party soon encounters trouble when the evil god Bane begins wreaking havoc all across the land, plunging it into darkness. It's up to the party to hunt down Bane's lieutenants, eliminate them, and finally gain enough power and artifacts to take on the balor Gothmenes. However, many critics complain that the ending is rather anticlimactic. I won't spoil it here, but let's just say it would be forgettable if not so disappointing. Perhaps as restitution, victorious players are given the chance to play "Dave's Challenge," an incredibly difficult dungeon.

Champions of Krynn *and the* Dragonlance *Series*

The first of SSI's Gold Box spinoffs is *Champions of Krynn* (Figure 7.6), released in 1990 for Amiga, Apple II, Commodore 64, and of course, DOS. Chronologically, it was the third Gold Box game and employs some innovations that show up in later games, especially the level difficulty selector we discussed earlier. These games are based on TSR's best-selling *Dragonlance* universe, which includes a set of fine novels by Margaret Weiss and Tracy Hickman. The stories are based mostly on the exploits of a group called the Heroes of the Lance, a group of eight adventurers whose racial and professional makeup is suspiciously close to the typical *AD&D* party (including a representative from each class). These characters make guest appearances in SSI's *Dragonlance* games, though players never control them directly as they did in SSI's action game, *Heroes of the Lance* (which we'll discuss shortly). The games are based more or less on the novels.

FIGURE 7.6 *Champions of Krynn* is set in the *Dragonlance* universe instead of the *Forgotten Realms*. Get ready to fight some Draconians!

In *Champions of Krynn,* the players team up with the Knights of Solamnia to defeat the evil draconians, a collection of five dragon-like humanoid species who were thought to be extinct after the War of the Lance. It was an easy sell to fans of the novels and modules who longed to test their mettle against the Baaz, Kapak, and the ever-popular Bozak, whose bones explode upon death. SSI went out all in promoting the new spinoff, going so far as to include a large poster of the cover art in every box. As with all the other Gold Box games, much of the game's story and plot development is contained in the printed journal.

From a gameplay perspective, the most interesting differences introduced in this series are the new races, classes, and moon-based magic system. The race options now include two types of elves (Qualinesti and Silvanesti) and dwarves (hill and mountain), as well as the "kender," a diminutive and highly playful race that resembles Tolkien's hobbit. Kender are the only race that can taunt enemies, driving them into a rage, lowering their THAC0, and forcing them to focus their attacks on the fast-moving kender.

The new class, Knight of Solamnia, replaces the paladin. Knights are organized into three orders (Crown, Sword, and Rose) and begin the game equipped with plate mail, a longsword, and a shield. However, they must take a vow of poverty, which means that they must give up a portion of their gold each time they enter a city. In the case of the Knights of the Sword or Rose, this entails giving up everything but a mere twenty steel coins. A knight of one order can petition to join a higher one, but only if he has the requisite ability scores. The higher-order knights get some added powers, such as the ability to cast some clerical spells. Since some quests require that a knight be in the party, they are essential characters. Knights can be male or female, but only humans, half elves, and hill dwarves need apply. The manual suggests human.

The magic system is revised to include the four phases of three moons, each corresponding to a different order of mages (basically, good, evil, and neutral). It's a somewhat complicated system, but the result is that some spells can be cast only by certain orders, and the phase of the order's moon determines certain benefits or penalties. The current phase of the moons is shown on-screen. Another change is that clerics now have their choice of deities, a system that brings to mind SSI's older game *Demon's Winter.* The gods are also organized into good, neutral, and evil, and confer bonuses. For instance, clerics who worship Majere get an extra spell (Silence 15′ radius) and can turn undead as if they were two levels higher. No characters can be evil.

All in all, there are enough differences here to distinguish the game from the other series, but many contemporary critics seem to have overlooked these changes. To be fair, the games look virtually identical, and players have to be intimate with both series to really appreciate what makes them unique.

Death Knights of Krynn

The next game in the series, *Death Knights of Krynn,* was released in 1991 for DOS, the Commodore 64, and the Amiga. It is set a year after the events in the first game and is virtually identical in terms of interface and gameplay, though this time the party spends more time fighting undead creatures than draconians. The game allows players to import characters from *Champions of Krynn,* with most of their gold and possessions intact. There is also a premade party available for those who do not wish to roll their own. It also features higher level caps and some additional spells. Thankfully, this time the player's previous spell choices are preselected, thus eliminating a lot of unnecessary pointing and clicking.

Perhaps the most interesting aspect of the game is the storyline, which pits the party against Sir Karl, reincarnated as a death knight, a powerful undead warrior who was formerly a Knight of Solamnia. Though certainly an enjoyable game for anyone who loved the first one, it is, as one contemporary reviewer put it, "pretty much standard Gold Box fare." However, as with *Pools of Darkness,* there are a few bonus areas to explore after completing the main quest, including another "Dave's Challenge."

The Dark Queen of Krynn

The last of the *Dragonlance*-inspired Gold Box games is *The Dark Queen of Krynn,* published in 1992 for the DOS, Amiga, and Macintosh platforms. The most noticeable change here is an upgrade to the 256 color VGA, which allows better animation and more detailed graphics. However, the underlying engine is left intact, albeit with a few new monsters and abilities. This game is set two years after the party's victory in *Death Knights of Krynn.* The party is summoned to the city of Caergoth to investigate rumors that monsters are gathering there. The player soon learns that the Dark Queen herself is preparing to send the accumulated forces of evil in a last bid to conquer Krynn.

The Dark Queen of Krynn was not developed internally but outsourced to MicroMagic, who had earlier gained recognition by porting Origin's *Moebius: The Orb of Celestial Harmony* from the Apple II to the other important computer platforms of the day. MicroMagic later made *Unlimited Adventures,* a construction kit based on the Gold Box engine. We'll talk more about it later.

All in all, the Gold Box games set in *Krynn* served their purpose. They expanded SSI's line and allowed it to exploit more of TSR's valuable campaign settings, all without having to substantially modify the engine. While they are perhaps not as famous as the original series, they were popular and are mandatory for anyone who enjoys the other games. However, SSI wasn't done milking the Gold Box engine or its TSR license.

The Savage Frontier

The last of SSI's TSR-licensed fantasy series are the two *Savage Frontier* games: *Gateway to the Savage Frontier* (1991) and *Treasures of the Savage Frontier* (1992), both developed externally by Beyond Software, Don Daglow's company that changed its name to Stormfront Studios in 1993. We'll have more to say about Beyond Software when we discuss *Neverwinter Nights,* the first graphical online role-playing game, which is also based on the Gold Box engine.

The two games are set in the Savage Frontier, an area to the extreme west of the setting for the older games set in TSR's *Forgotten Realms.* The plot is concerned mostly with preventing the tyrannical Zhentarim from conquering the land. The armies of Zhentil Keep have hitherto been blocked by the sands of the impassable and monster-infested Great Desert of Anauroch, but the Zhentarim hope to use four ancient magical statues to clear the desert and guarantee the success of their invasion. The player's party has celebrated the night before in a tavern in Yartar and wakes up to find all their equipment stolen. They're left with no choice but to search for work, and it doesn't take them long to learn of the Zhentarim's plot. The party must find a way to stop the advancing hordes and defeat their leader, Vaalgamon.

The only noticeable innovation to the engine is an emphasis on wilderness travel, which makes the world feel larger. Overland travel is fraught with peril, of course, particularly for parties who wander off the beaten paths. A similar mode is present in *Pool of Radiance,* but this game makes much more use of it.

Treasures of the Savage Frontier

The next game, *Treasures of the Savage Frontier,* was released only for the Commodore Amiga and DOS platforms. It takes place only a few weeks

FIGURE 7.7 *Treasures of the Savage Frontier* was made by Stormfront Studios. Its biggest innovation was a new romance mechanic, but some critics lament that the game is just more of the same. Disregard them—this is a great game.

after the events in the first game. The players are now hailed as the Heroes of Ascore and are summoned by the wizard Aminitas to eliminate a few last bastions of Zhentarim troops from Llorkh, a dwarven city. After failing to properly protect some ambassadors, the party is accused of treachery. Naturally, they must clear their names and expose the Zhentarim's plot.

Treasures of the Savage Frontier (Figure 7.7) introduces a few innovations to the admittedly aging engine, such as weather and romances between party members and other characters. The weather system incorporates the effects of rain and snow on movement, slowing down travel and making it harder to maneuver in combat. Of course, the longer the party stays in the wilderness, the more likely they are to encounter roaming monsters, so the snow and rain mean more combat.

The romance system is more interesting. Essentially, it boils down to two nonplayer characters, or characters that are controlled by the computer rather than the player. These characters are a female named Siulajia and a male named Jabarkas, one of whom may fall in love with the active character at a certain point in the game (the choice of Siulajia or Jabarkas depends on the active character's gender; only heterosexual relationships are possible). However, love is not ensured—romance will bloom only if the lead character has conducted himself or herself so as to attract a partner, helping out the weak and standing bravely in battle. Assuming that all goes well and love does flourish, the loved one can join the party, and the two lovers will receive combat bonuses. However, if the lover is injured, the partner will fly into a berserker rage, charging recklessly into the fray. If the lover dies or is dropped from the party, the partner will become depressed and suffer penalties. At some point the lovers will admit their feelings to the rest of the party, who will then be asked to approve or condemn it. If the other members disapprove, the nonplayer character leaves the party, and the forlorn lover will thereafter fight with much less zeal and effectiveness. It's an innovative system that opens up some interesting role-playing opportunities. Romances are fairly common in later CRPGs, including appropriate options for LGBT players.

Despite these innovations, the *Savage Frontier* series was never as popular as the previous two. Nevertheless, they are highly playable and a good introduction for modern gamers who aren't familiar with the Gold Box canon.

Buck Rogers

The only non-fantasy-based Gold Box games are two based on the pulp sci-fi hero Buck Rogers. The first of these, *Countdown to Doomsday*, appeared in 1990 and is set in the year 2456 (Figure 7.8). Earth is in ruins after centuries of industrial exploitation, and a single megacorporation, RAM, runs the show. Your party, however, is working for NEO, an extremist group out to smash RAM and liberate Earth. They are led by Buck Rogers, a legendary hero who has been in cryogenic sleep since the dawn of the 21st century and thus remembers what Earth was like before the fall.

Both *Countdown to Doomsday* and its sequel, *Matrix Cubed*, are based on the TSR-owned *Buck Rogers XXVc (Buck Rogers in the 25th Century)*

FIGURE 7.8 *Buck Rogers* are Gold Box games with a sci-fi setting.

franchise rolled out in 1988. The setting extended up to 1995, and, like TSR's other campaign settings, was supported by a variety of novels, comic books, role-playing games, and other materials. Unfortunately for TSR and sci-fi fans, *Buck Rogers XXVc* never performed as well as the fantasy settings; and, at least according to Keith Brors, former technical director of SSI, the company was pressured by TSR into developing its Buck Rogers computer game against its better judgment. In any case, these games are noteworthy for making the most sweeping changes to the Gold Box engine.

Naturally, since *Countdown to Doomsday* is based on pulp sci-fi magazines and serials instead of Tolkien-inspired fantasy, SSI had to make several important modifications to the Gold Box engine. One of the key problems that has always faced sci-fi role-playing games is that, realistically, the typical level zero character with no experience and skills would simply never make it in a technological world, where a great deal of formal education is assumed from the outset. The most common answer to this problem (as seen in games such as *Traveller*) is to introduce a technical skills system and allow players to select which skills their characters learned in school. *Countdown to Doomsday*'s skill system is divided into career skills, which are based on a character's class or career choice, and general skills, which can be learned by anyone. While it's possible for a character to learn any skills regardless of career choice, doing so incurs a penalty and can be quite wasteful.

The game features six races (Terrans, Martians, Venusians, Mercurians, Desert Runners, and Tinkers) and five careers (warrior, medic, rogue, rocketjock, and engineer). As you might expect, certain races are a better fit for certain careers. For instance, Desert Runners, a genetically engineered species with retractable claws, make the best warriors. Likewise, each class has a small bevy of career skills that can be learned at reduced cost in skill points, which are distributed at character creation and each time the character levels up. Some skills have prerequisites and can be learned only once the character has enough points invested in certain other skills. Most skills are affected by one of the seven randomly generated attributes (strength, dexterity, constitution, intelligence, wisdom, charisma, and tech). The only unusual attribute here is tech, which affects the character's affinity with machinery and skills such as jury rigging and repair electrical. All in all, it's an impressive system, and it's a pity SSI didn't try to implement it in other Gold Box games.

Another big difference from the other Gold Box games concerns combat, where futuristic ray-guns and plasma grenades replace swords and

FIGURE 7.9 Combat in the *Buck Rogers* games is still turn-based, but with futuristic weapons and grenades.

bows. Of crucial importance here is a weapon's range, damage, and rate of fire, which determine how many attacks a character doles out per round. For instance, the needle gun can be fired six times per round but is quite limited in range and deals only up to 3 points of damage per hit. The powerful laser rifle, on the other hand, deals up to 12 points of damage at very long range but gets only two attacks per round. These types of considerations play a large role in the overall tactics and gameplay (Figure 7.9).

Unfortunately, the one innovation that might have proven most decisive for this series—ship-to-ship combat—falls short of its full potential. Obviously, battles between ships is a huge part of the *Buck Rogers* mythos, and SSI wisely introduced just such a mode into its game. During space combat, the characters assume various roles on the ship. The crucial role is the pilot, who has a different set of options than the crew—most importantly, firing the ship's main weapons, closing the distance to the enemy ship, and withdrawing, ramming, and boarding. The crew can fire lasers, reload the ship's weapons, boost its engines, aid other characters, probe the enemy ship, jury rig a damaged system, or take command if the pilot is hurt. You also have the option to fire at will or target specific systems on the enemy's ship.

This all looks great on paper, but in practice is less than fulfilling. The main problem is that the rewards, particularly for boarding a ship, simply aren't worth the risk and hassle. Your characters win more experience points from regular combat, and benefits from salvaging defeated ships are minimal at best. Simply fleeing from combat is nearly always the best option, though successfully boarding and defeating the toughest enemy crews is the only way to get the best equipment in the game. In any case, it's interesting to see how SSI tried to incorporate such a crucial element from the space sim subgenre.

The second and last entry in this series is *Matrix Cubed,* published in 1992 only for the DOS platform. It is set after the action in the first game, and players can import their old characters, weapons and all. The plot is concerned primarily with the Matrix Device, an invention that can transmute matter into energy. The party is recruited to track down the scientists capable of building the device and convince them to work for NEO. The fact that SSI failed to port the game to other platforms suggests that it was not a best seller. Overall, SSI's Buck Rogers games represent some desirable enhancements to the Gold Box engine, but their influence was marginal.

Neverwinter Nights: The Gold Box MMORPG

We've already mentioned Beyond Software, the development team responsible for SSI's *Savage Frontier* games. However, perhaps its most historically important game is *Neverwinter Nights,* a very early online role-playing game hosted by the commercial network America Online (AOL) from 1991 to 1997 (Figure 7.10). Based on the Gold Box engine, *Neverwinter Nights* is likely the first massively multiplayer online role-playing game (MMORPG), usually distinguished from the MUD by the incorporation of advanced, sprite-based graphics. *Neverwinter Nights* offered real-time multiplayer gameplay and soon became one of AOL's key attractions.

FIGURE 7.10   Not to be confused with BioWare's CRPG, this *Neverwinter Nights* game ran on America Online.

Players long accustomed to solitary gameplay found themselves chatting, fighting, and collaborating with up to 500 simultaneous players from all over the country.

As with the MUDs and other multiplayer online games we discussed previously, the main appeal of *Neverwinter Nights* was fraternizing with like-minded players. Most famously, *Neverwinter Nights* saw the rise of dozens of guilds, or loose affiliations of gamers who united for their common good. A few dozen of these guilds were officially sanctioned by AOL, which granted them their own private and public message boards on the commercial network. The most successful of these guilds held regular events to keep players coming back, such as the Guild of Heroes' joke and story-telling contests. Fans also made their own newsletters and distributed them on the network.

AOL originally charged an hourly rate to play *Neverwinter Nights,* which led many players to spend hundreds (if not thousands) of dollars every month on the game. In 1996, AOL changed to a flat-fee rate of $20 per month, a move that spelled doom for the popular game. The problem was that as long AOL was charging by the hour, programs like *Neverwinter Nights* and the aforementioned *GemStone III* were highly lucrative, since they lured new subscribers and kept them online as long as possible. After the switch to a flat fee, these highly addictive games became albatrosses for the company. AOL's ideal customer was now someone who logged in only intermittently but still paid the monthly fee. *Neverwinter Nights* was yanked from the network on July 1997, and the last Gold Box game was laid to rest. Many fans felt betrayed by the decision and circulated petitions and launched letter-writing campaigns. In the end, though, the resistance was futile.

However, there are at least two efforts underway to bring back the game. One is a project called *Neverwinter Nights: Resurrection,* which uses BioWare's *Neverwinter Nights* editor and server to recreate the original setting in a 3D environment. Another option is *Neverwinter Nights Offline,* a somewhat buggy attempt to reproduce much of the game's features in a single-player, non-networked version. There are also several active fan and community sites dedicated to the game, such as the *Neverwinter Nights Archive.*[5]

Concluding Thoughts on the Gold Box Games

There is no question that SSI's Gold Box games were influential and played a vital role in shaping the future of the genre. For the most part, SSI seems to have been content to follow Sir-Tech's example with the early *Wizardry* games, offering essentially the same game engine with only minor improvements. Although some critics deride the practice as "engine recycling," we must also see it as an essential strategy for driving down costs and ensuring that fans of the previous games will be comfortable with the new ones. Of course, even under ideal conditions, such a tactic can sustain interest for only so long—eventually gamers begin demanding a game that isn't merely the old one in new clothing. The major problem was that the Gold Box engine was built on and for the Commodore 64, which was already nearing the end of its dominance by the time *Pool of Radiance* hit the scenes in 1988. Even when SSI finally abandoned support for the platform with *Pools of Darkness* in 1991, it kept most of the old engine intact, warts and all.

On the other hand, what's really surprising about the Gold Box engine is just how versatile and long-lived it turned out to be, even serving as the basis for one of the most successful of the early MMORPGs. For many CRPG fans, it still represents the perfect blend of story and strategy. As for us, we'd be more than happy to play any of these games today, which you can easily do by downloading the *Forgotten Realms: The Archives* collections from GOG.com.

SSI's Action CRPGs: *Heroes of the Lance* and *Hillsfar*

From virtually the beginning of CRPG history, there have been efforts to wed what some see as a placid, contemplative genre to the more tactile and frenetic world of arcade and console gaming. These include SSI's previous CRPG/shooter hybrids, **Gemstone Warrior** and **Gemstone Healer.** Such games are usually referred to as action CRPGs, an unwieldy but useful conglomeration. Unfortunately for aspiring developers, action CRPGs didn't fare well alongside pure CRPGs during the Golden Age, though Blizzard's Platinum Age hit *Diablo* demonstrated conclusively that this subgenre did indeed have far more appeal than the conventional CRPG. It's enlightening to see why earlier action CRPGs failed, repeatedly disappointing gamers and convincing many CRPG fans that action and role-playing mixed like oil and water.

Heroes of the Lance

Let's turn our attention, then, to SSI's TSR-licensed *Dragonlance* action CRPGs. The earliest of these is *Heroes of the Lance* (Figure 7.11), released in 1988 for a large number of computing platforms, including

FIGURE 7.11 *Heroes of the Lance* is a steaming pile of Draconian dung best enjoyed with a sharp blow to the back of the head.

the Commodore Amiga and Atari ST as well as the British Amstrad and ZX Spectrum machines. Two years later it was ported to the NES, where it soon acquired a reputation for its wretched gameplay. The game was developed not by SSI but by U.S. Gold, a British developer and publisher later acquired by Eidos Interactive. As its name suggests, it specialized in importing popular American titles and porting (or having them ported) for the European computer market.

Heroes of the Lance is based on TSR's first *Dragonlance* campaign module, called *Dragons of Despair,* as well as the tie-in novel *Dragons of Autumn Twilight* by Margaret Weiss and Tracy Hickman. The goal of the game is to guide the eight Heroes of the Lance into the ruins of Xak Tsaroth, a deadly place crawling with monsters, mercenaries, and a black dragon named Khisanth. The party's quest is a desperate attempt to recover the Disks of Mishakal, upon which are inscribed the teaching of the True Gods. The game assumes intimate familiarity with the novels, which are excellent works highly regarded by many *AD&D* and fantasy fans. U.S. Gold's game hasn't fared as well—particularly the NES version, which some critics consider one of the worst games ever released for the platform. YouTube has plenty of hilarious video reviews demonstrating the poor controls and incoherent gameplay. Contemporary reviewers of the computer versions are more forgiving.

The basic setup of the game is the horizontal fighting style of arcade games like *Street Fighter* or the older *Karateka*. In many ways, it seems to be an attempt to update Origin's **Moebius: The Orb of Celestial Harmony** (1985), an older but more effective fighter/CRPG hybrid. In *Heroes of the Lance,* the player can switch among the eight heroes, though only one can be on-screen and active (the first four can use magic but also take some of the damage during combat). Although a large part of the gameplay calls for agility with the joystick or gamepad, there are also tactical considerations—particularly concerning magic. Raistlin and Goldmoon, the party's mage and cleric, respectively, have powerful magic but are extremely vulnerable in physical combat.

I should point out that while the game awards experience points for overcoming monsters, there is no leveling up system—a surprising omission that for many critics, including this one, challenges its identity as an CRPG, action or otherwise. In effect, the eight party members serve more as extra lives for the player than a well-balanced party. Although most of the negative criticism leveled against the game concerns its slow speed and bad collision detection, a well-thought out leveling system may have atoned for its other sins. Despite these criticisms, SSI and U.S. Gold produced a sequel called **Dragons of Flame** in 1989.

Shadow Sorcerer

A modern gamer struggling through *Heroes of the Lance* and *Dragons of Flame* would be astounded that yet a *third* game would appear in this lamentable series. Yet SSI published U.S. Gold's *Shadow Sorcerer* in 1991, though only for the Commodore Amiga, Atari ST, and DOS platforms. *Shadow Sorcerer,* however, is a much different game than the previous two and deserves some discussion (Figure 7.12).

The most obvious changes concern the graphics and the interface. The perspective is a combination of overhead view and 3D isometric, and now the player can see and control four characters simultaneously. The interface is icon-driven and well suited for mouse control. Critics were pleased with the graphics and especially the sound of the DOS version, which takes advantage of the AdLib sound card. However, feeble AI routines (the characters have a hard time dealing with obstacles in tactical mode) and a very stiff time limit to complete the game marred the fun. Like the other games in this series, the gameplay is set in real time, though saving is allowed at any point. However, we should note that the manual discourages saving the game, instructing players to "take your losses like a man." I've yet to find such candid prose in other SSI manuals.

FIGURE 7.12 *Shadow Sorcerer* is better than you'd think, but its association with the previous debacles clung to it like a kender to his hoopak.

The story is based on two *Dragonlance* modules called "Dragons of Hope" and "Dragons of Desolation," and involves escorting a huge group of refugees through the wilds while evading the forces of the evil Dragon army. One of the more interesting (infuriating?) aspects of the game is that these refugees won't always comply with the party's requests. Their leaders might decide to head back to Pax Tharkas, where certain death awaits at the hands of the evil Verminaard. While it might be possible that the refugees would entertain a serious death wish, some critics chastised the developers for this implausibility. The manual insists that "no matter how irritating [the refugees] become, it is your job to keep them healthy," but no doubt some frustrated players prefer to see them slaughtered.

Unlike the previous games, *Shadow Sorcerer* at last incorporates a simple level system. As characters gain levels, they receive a larger maximum hit point score and refine their class skills. The levels are also important for magic-users, who receive more powerful spells as they progress. Although this class and level system is simplistic compared to some of the later action CRPGs we'll discuss, at least it fully qualifies *Shadow Sorcerer* as a true CRPG and one of the true precursors of Blizzard's *Diablo*.

One final note about *Shadow Sorcerer* is that it adopts the Gold Box convention of putting important material into a printed journal. The printed journal is no doubt a move to discourage illegal distribution, since portable storage media had by this time become more than capable of storing large amounts of text. Nevertheless, the entries are well written and add value to the game.

The Summoning

While we're on the subject of *Shadow Sorcerer*, it is only fair to mention *The Summoning*, another real-time isometric CRPG published by SSI. This 1992 game was developed by Event Horizon Software, the company that was later renamed DreamForge. We'll take a moment here to explore Event Horizon's early impact on the genre, briefly looking at *The Summoning, Darkspyre, Dusk of the Gods,* and *Veil of Darkness.*

The Summoning is a woefully obscure game today, but it has at least one fascinating innovation: a magic system based on hand gestures (Figure 7.13). The system requires the character to memorize spells, just as in the Gold Box games, but now this process is instantaneous and requires no period of rest. In fact, the character can even memorize spells in the din of battle! However, the spells are memorized only after the player is able to enter the correct sequence of hand gestures, which are found on scrolls or learned from other characters encountered in the game (actually casting a spell requires a quantity of spell points as well). *Dragonlance* and other fantasy novels often describe arcane hand gestures as part of the spell-casting process, but *The Summoning* actually incorporates them into the gameplay. It makes a great deal of sense to

FIGURE 7.13   *The Summoning* uses an intriguing system of hand gestures to cast spells. It isn't easy to master, but neither is magic—right?

have the magic process be a highly complex and precise affair, since if it were really as easy as most games make it out to be, everyone would be doing it! Unfortunately, previous attempts to complicate the magic system have resulted in less-than-stellar gameplay, and developers are still searching for ways to make magic both plausible and fun.

The Summoning's combat system is fairly detailed, involving proficiencies for each type of weapon. Weapons wear out and eventually shatter, so there's a strong incentive to get experience with all of them. However, most of the emphasis is on solving puzzles, which mainly involve pressure plates and traps. Still, the game's awkward controls and simplistic storyline seem to have banished it to obscurity.

Darkspyre

The Summoning is actually a sequel to an earlier Event Horizons game called *Darkspyre,* which was published by Electronic Zoo in 1990 for DOS and a year later for the Commodore Amiga. This real-time game features a top-down view reminiscent of Atari's 1985 arcade classic *Gauntlet. Darkspyre* is most notable for its innovative character creation system. The player reads a story, making critical decisions at key junctures (think about the *Choose Your Own Adventure* books). The answers determine the character's abilities as well as his or her strengths and weaknesses. The game even takes into consideration whether the character is left- or right-handed! The magic system is a tiered system in which basic spells evolve into more powerful versions as the mage gains experience. The advantage of such a system is that it eliminates the problem of spell inflation, that is, the mage's early spells becoming useless later in the game. For instance, hardly anyone bothers with the first-level clerical spell "cure light wounds" in the later stages of a Gold Box game; by that point, "cure serious" or "cure critical" is more useful.

Dusk of the Gods

The game engine of *The Summoning* is based on Event Horizon's 1991 game *Dusk of the Gods,* published by Interstel. *Dusk of the Gods* is a real-time, isometric CRPG based on Norse legend. It's sometimes casually referred to as an educational game because of emphasis on Norse mythology, though the manual warns that it is not intended to be a "historically accurate depiction of the Viking era." The manual goes on to say, "If we remained absolutely true to everything in the mythological lays, there would be no reason to play the game. You could, simply put, 'read the book.'" Indeed, according to the game's bibliography (a rather rare section to find in any game manual!), players find no fewer than eleven scholarly sources that were consulted during the game's design stages. The designer's note section of the manual goes on to complain about the overemphasis on graphics in most games and reviews, and correctly states that "it is the design that makes a game fun." Chris Straka, Event Horizon's creative designer, would return to this theme in the designer's notes to *The Summoning*, where he bemoans the fact that not many manuals are bothering with designer's note sections. The graphics versus gameplay debate will crop up again and again, though perhaps more strikingly later on, as game development further migrates from the teenager's bedroom to the corporate cubicle.

Veil of Darkness

The last of Event Horizon's games based on *The Summoning* game engine is *Veil of Darkness,* published by SSI in 1993 (Figure 7.14). This game is set in a vampire-infested valley in Romania, where an isolated village is threatened by a vampire lord named Kairn. The character arrives in the valley by crashing his cargo plane there, coinciding nicely with a local prophecy. Naturally, you can't escape the valley until you've tracked down Kairn and put a stop to the menace.

FIGURE 7.14 *Veil of Darkness* is an early vampire-themed adventure/CRPG hybrid.

Although the game is not terribly well known today, it was noted at the time for the nice twists in the plotline and a cast of intriguing characters. The atmosphere is quite dark and appropriate for the Gothic vampire theme and provides wonderful tension. There's even a splash of romance. However, it's really more of an adventure game than a CRPG (there are plenty of fights but no class or level system).

Hillsfar

SSI's *Hillsfar,* developed by Westwood Associates and published in 1989, represents a much different approach to action CRPGs than we see in *Heroes of the Lance* (Figure 7.15). It's a much closer cousin to the Gold Box games, and it's even possible to import characters from *Pool of Radiance* or *Curse of the Azure Bonds,* though only the latter accepts an exported *Hillsfar* character. The game is also set in the *Forgotten Realms* campaign setting and shares most of its rules and conventions.

However, *Hillsfar* departs from the Gold Box formula in major ways. For one thing, the player is allowed to create and control only one character, but the differences don't stop there. The most striking alteration is a number of minigames, such as a side-scrolling horse-riding game in which the player must buck the joystick to jump over obstacles (or lower it to duck). The gameplay here is reminiscent of the 1983 arcade classic *Moon*

FIGURE 7.15 *Hillsfar* is more or less a compilation of minigames. I really like the exploration interface, shown here. You get a first-person view in the top left and a nice large top-down map view on the right.

Patrol. Other minigames include an archery range, a lock tumbler puzzle, timed mazes, and, of course, an arena. Each of these minigames has its own screen mode and control scheme.

The screen changes when the character is traveling in *Hillsfar.* At the top left is the familiar 3D view of the Gold Box games, but on the right is a large, top-down view of the town. The status window lists character's stats and condition, as well as his or her supply of "knock rings," which are used to open locks. At the lower left is the current time, which is important to know since the various shops and other buildings are available only during certain hours. There are plenty of quests for players who join one of the town's various guilds.

Critical reactions to the game are rather mixed, with some critics praising the same elements that others condemned. For instance, some reviewers feel that the minigames are fun and offer much-needed variety, whereas others find them distracting and repetitive. Regardless, there is little question that some areas needed improvement, such as the arena combat sequence that does not let mage or clerics cast spells during the fight. Many argue that the horse-riding sequence is overused—it's fun once or twice, perhaps, but certainly not called for each time the character needs to travel overland. Some critics complain about the lack of story arcs or even an ultimate quest. Instead, the player merely performs a few quests for the chosen guild (fighter, cleric, thief, and mage). Nevertheless, the game certainly fared better than *Heroes of the Lance.* It was ported to the NES in 1991 by Pony Canyon. Unfortunately, the port is lackluster and toned down compared to the original. For instance, players seeking a pint in the tavern are offered pink lemonade and root beer instead of ale or wine. Hell, no!

Unlimited Adventures: The Gold Box Construction Set

The final SSI product we want to mention in this chapter is *Unlimited Adventures,* developed by MicroMagic and published in 1993 for Macintosh and DOS. For the first time, Gold Box fans were able to easily construct their own CRPGs, using SSI's celebrated if somewhat dated engine. *Unlimited Adventures* also included a mini-adventure called *The Heirs to Skull Crag,* which users were also encouraged to modify (and its poor design practically begged for it). Along with *The Heirs to Skull Crag,* SSI tossed in many of its Gold Box assets; the box mentions 112 monsters and 200 "classic art images" from the Gold Box series. However, *Unlimited Adventures* is limited to a certain extent—users cannot, for instance, modify the walls, combat backdrops, and title screens of their games. Nevertheless, the program became quite popular; and fan communities took it upon themselves to hack the code, removing these limitations and introducing many new features.

You might be surprised to learn that a strong community still thrives around this product, and dozens of new modules are released each year on the web.[6] There is also *Dungeon Craft*, a GNU-licensed version that emulates *Unlimited Adventures* but adds many innovations. The program is freely available for download from the Sourceforge website.[7] As of this writing, this project is actively maintained with regular updates.

It's easy to compare SSI's *Unlimited Adventures* with Electronic Arts' *The Bard's Tale Construction Set,* which we discussed in a previous chapter. These programs are focused on user-generated content, the idea being that some gamers enjoy designing games as much as (if not more than) playing them. We can compare these construction kits to the Dungeon Master's role in tabletop role-playing games. Although some Dungeon Masters simply purchase official campaign modules and stick closely to them during gameplay, others take a more creative approach, creating their own scenarios, settings, and sometimes even their own role-playing systems. Of course, the quality of these do-it-yourself games varies widely, but the point we want to make here is that at least some players of both tabletop RPGs and CRPGs share a desire not only to play, but also to design their own scenarios. As the CRPG evolves, we'll see an increasing trend toward such user-generated content, particularly when we discuss BioWare's *Neverwinter Nights,* which, unlike *Unlimited Adventures* and *The Bard's Tale Construction Set,* could at last take full advantage of the Internet to help distribute modules and assets.

We'll return to SSI in the next chapter, when we discuss the *Eye of the Beholder* games. For now, though, let's turn to some of the other big games of the late 1980s and see what Origin was up to during the Golden Age.

NOTES

1. In modern dollars, a new Macintosh bought in 1984 would have cost well over $5,000, and the Commodore Amiga 1000, debuted in 1985, would've cost nearly $3,000. The IBM PC XT, introduced in 1983, was the most expensive, running well over $10,000—no doubt a bargain for a machine running at 4.77 MHz with 128KB of RAM and a 10MB hard drive (a "cheap clone" was half that price). Meanwhile, a new Commodore 64 could be had for around $500 at retail.

2. Ironically, IBM itself would lose terribly. After the company realized that it was competing with an armada of clone-makers running Microsoft's operating system, it started from scratch and introduced the PS/2, which had an exclusive, proprietary operating system. Unfortunately for IBM, though its IBM PC was an unprecedented success, the new platform failed to catch on despite its brand recognition.

3. See Johnny L. Wilson's review of the game published in the July 1988 issue of *Computer Gaming World*.

4. See Russ Ceccola's review of the game in the November 1990 issue of *Compute!* magazine.

5. See http://www.bladekeep.com/nwn/main.shtml.

6. See http://frua.rosedragon.org/index.htm.

7. See http://uaf.sourceforge.net/index.html.

CHAPTER 8

Origin's Golden Age

THE *ULTIMA* SERIES

When last we spoke of Origin's *Ultima* series, we saw Richard Garriott sailing his flagship CRPG series into uncharted waters—most notably into the turbulent seas of morality and ethics. Critics praised these efforts as a move toward more substantial role-playing, that is, moving the genre past its simplistic "hack 'n slash" origins. *Ultima IV: Quest of the Avatar* introduced a bold new dynamic: a quest for spiritual fulfillment rather than yet another dungeon romp.

Ultima V: Warriors of Destiny, published in 1988, took this theme in a new direction (Figure 8.1). What happens when morality and correct living are not personal choices, but requirements enforced by law? The storyline is set after the action in *Quest of the Avatar.* Lord British, benevolent protector of the land, has disappeared into the Underworld, and a fundamentalist despot named Blackthorn has taken the throne. Blackthorn is terrorizing the people by enforcing a draconian moral code based on the eight virtues of the previous game (e.g., "Thou shalt donate half of thy income to charity, or thou shalt have no income.") Although most of the core elements are identical to the earlier game, the writing is more polished and professional, and while there are fewer nonplayer characters, interaction with them is more substantial. You need to be very careful to write down any potential keywords that might trigger a crucial response from a nonplayer character. Making matters even more difficult is a running clock that determines whether it's night or day on Britannia. Many events take place only if the Avatar is in the right place at the right time, a fact that makes a hint book nearly indispensable.

FIGURE 8.1 The fifth *Ultima* game makes some changes to the formula, but it still has some great battles with giant rats. My favorite!

There are some other important differences between the two games. The number of classes is reduced from eight to three (fighter, bard, and mage). This limitation is particularly felt when importing characters from the previous game; the specialized classes lose their magical abilities. The magic system is also revamped; now reagents can be purchased in stores, and the spell system is structured around eight circles and strings of Latinate syllables. As with FTL's *Dungeon Master* (1987), you can fine-tune spells by combining different sequences of magical incantations. The combat system is more realistic and complex, taking friendly fire into consideration. All classes can wear whatever armor and wield whatever weapon they wish, provided they have the requisite strength score.

Warriors of Destiny also marks a few important turning points. For one, it is the last of the series to originate on the Apple II and the last game for which Garriott did most of the coding. It was also during this time that the series began thriving in Japan. *Ultima II* had been available there since the early 1980s, but in an English-only form. Nevertheless, it had inspired several clones, including the famous *Dragon Quest*. One particularly brazen clone-maker approached Origin for the rights to translate *Ultima IV* into Japanese, but their earlier unauthorized clone, *Xanadu*, was such a blatant copyright infringer that Garriott refused, receiving a large settlement instead.[1] Eventually, the *Ultima Trilogy* and *Ultima IV* finally made it to Japan, where they sold exceedingly well and won major awards. More importantly, these games exerted an incalculable influence on the Japanese console RPG, an influence that is still easily perceived in modern games. We'll have more to say on this topic when we discuss Japanese console RPGs.

The False Prophet

Ultima VI: The False Prophet was released in 1990 for MS-DOS and marks the end of the "Age of Enlightenment" trilogy begun with *Quest of the Avatar* (Figure 8.2). By 1990, the Apple II was really showing its age, and Origin was convinced that the Apple IIGS didn't have enough users to warrant its attention. *The False Prophet* takes advantage of the PC's new VGA cards, which Origin correctly determined would become the new standard for MS-DOS gamers. The game has 2,048 different tiles in 256 colors. Garriott even went a step further and added support for the new Roland and AdLib sound cards, one of the first major developers to do so.

However, though the game features enhanced graphics compared to its predecessors, in some ways it's actually more limited—the dungeons, for instance, are rendered entirely in 2D, a step back from the 2D/3D switching that occurred in earlier games. The lack of 3D dungeons was a consequence of the dramatically stepped-up physics of the gameworld. Chairs and other objects have weight and size and can be moved around, and walls and doors have hit points and can be destroyed. A player so inclined

FIGURE 8.2 *Ultima VI*'s opening is quite intriguing from a meta-perspective. Are you ready to once again leave the mundane world behind to save Britannia? The painting in the left corner is based on a print by an airbrush artist named Keith Berdak.

can even grind wheat into flour and bake bread! However, including 3D dungeons would have meant implementing two routines for functional objects such as torches, which would of course look and behave differently depending on the perspective. In any case, dropping the 3D mode did make the world feel more coherent. The immense size of the world is impressive, and it's always displayed on the screen along with the characters. The interface was also cleaned up, and the old alphabetical list of twenty-six commands was swapped for a streamlined menu of only ten icons. The reduction is due mostly to conflation; *jimmy, ignite,* and similar verbs are now *use.*

Interaction is enhanced with small portraits of the interlocutors, and keywords are marked in red for easy recognition. An abundance of cinematics add to the narrative. The towns and villages are better populated and seem more realistic; in addition to the usual assortment of taverns and blacksmiths, there are now weavers and bakers plying their trades. Finally, random monsters are now mostly extinct, and there are sensible limits concerning when and where the party can be attacked. The most dangerous and exotic beasts are tucked away in the dungeons, not roaming the town a few feet from the pub.

The moral imperative in this game is based on racism and xenophobia—you must learn about an alien culture and explore issues of cultural relativism. At first, you know only that a race of gargoyles has attacked Britannia, and it's up to the Avatar to stop them. However, eventually you learn that the gargoyles aren't simply evil; they have their own problems and justifications. Instead of the brute force approach, the Avatar must learn about their culture, including their language. It's a brilliant setup, and certainly stands out against the all-too-common black-and-white CRPGs in which the enemy is clearly defined and unambiguously in need of a mace to the skull. However, some critics feel the story is unfocused and criticize the gameplay for being too heavily invested in menial sidequests.

Still, the game is cherished by many fans, although the next *Ultima* game—the first in the "Age of Armageddon" games—tends to make the accomplishments of *The False Prophet* pale in comparison (Figure 8.3).

The Black Gate

Ultima VII: The Black Gate, released in 1992, is, for many critics and gamers, the crowning achievement of the *Ultima* series. When we consider the many achievements and innovations represented by the earlier games,

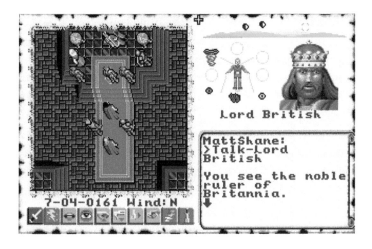

FIGURE 8.3   Here we see Lord British, looking quite regal in his crown and royal robes.

though, we might wonder what it would take to justify such a bold claim. After all, every *Ultima* we've discussed so far is touted as revolutionary by at least some critics, and even the worst of the lot is better than countless other CRPGs, then or now. Richard Garriott himself hails it as "the most masterfully executed of the *Ultima* series."[2]

But what could possibly make *The Black Gate* stand out so boldly against so many previous triumphs?

You might assume that it must be the graphics, since they are what tend to get the most attention from modern critics and gamers. However, although *The Black Gate* features much more advanced graphics than *The False Prophet,* it still relies on the familiar top-down perspective of its predecessors. This fact is even more surprising, perhaps, when we consider that Origin released the revolutionary *The Stygian Abyss* the same year, a first-person 3D game.

Indeed, the most significant change to the interface is a switch to real-time gameplay, which drastically alters the way combat and exploration are handled. Attacking an enemy is as simple as entering combat mode and clicking with the mouse—or the player can opt to have the computer control everything. The Avatar's companions aren't under the player's direct control, but they can be assigned one of nine attack modes, such as "attack weakest" or "flank." The game can be controlled entirely by the mouse, which the manual claims is "highly recommended by Lord British." We might not think much of this issue today, but this was at a time when many PC owners didn't even own mice, much less consider them as a gaming device. Most players found it advisable, however, to have their finger near the *c* key, which instantly enters combat mode.

Still, the innovations to the interface and combat aren't enough to explain the game's enduring appeal. Far more important are the gripping plot, well-developed characters, and painstakingly detailed environments. Critics *still* gush about the game's unprecedented level of interactivity. How many CRPGs do you know that will let you milk cows and change a baby's diapers just for the heck of it? *The Black Gate* is an unforgettable experience to those who take the sixty or so hours required to complete it, and it retains a loyal and dedicated fan base.

The Black Gate's plot is also quite sophisticated compared to most games of the era. As the game opens, the Avatar is taunted by a mysterious and infuriating being called the Guardian (Figure 8.4). Afterward, the Avatar is whisked away to the land of Britannia, some 200 years after his previous visit. Enough time has gone by that he's been mostly forgotten, his valiant deeds chalked up to myth. He arrives just after a gory, ritualistic murder that serves to introduce the plot and the new but certainly not improved Britannia, which has withered in his absence. A new Fellowship cult has arisen to give people something more concrete to believe in. The Fellowship claim to be a force for good, yet they hold that the Avatar's eight virtues are irrelevant and standing in the way of progress. It's obvious that something sinister is going on.

Perhaps more endearing than the plot are the characters, who are far better developed here than in almost any other CRPG. Instead of merely

FIGURE 8.4 The Guardian taunts you throughout the game and can really get under your skin.

standing in one place for all eternity just to offer a thinly disguised hint or geographical tidbit, the characters are shown walking about, engaging in their daily activities—they even go to bed at night. Furthermore, the Avatar's nemesis, the Guardian, is always watching your progress and occasionally mocks you, especially when you do something less than virtuous. Most CRPGs pit the player against an evil nemesis, but that nemesis is generally merely a shallow pretext for hack 'n slash gameplay. When you finally confront him, it's just another boss fight with little emotional investment. This is not the case with the Guardian, who is with players every step of the way, antagonizing them in a thoroughly despicable way. It's hard not to take his affronts personally.

The game is often praised for its open-ended gameplay. There are very few guard rails in *The Black Gate*, a fact that can either thrill or intimidate inexperienced players. It's easy for players to end up wandering about the game without the faintest clue of what they're supposed to do. Obviously, this lack of clear direction wouldn't bother players raised on *Rogue* and other sandbox style games, but players more accustomed to linear "connect the dots" type games may find themselves disoriented. Though the Avatar certainly has an important role to play in the plot, *The Black Gate* takes a decidedly hands-off approach, letting you make decisions that are typically reserved for designers (Figure 8.5).

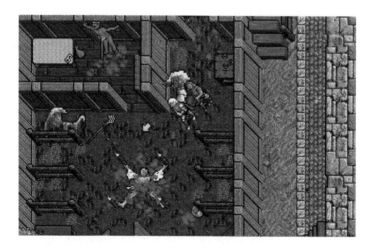

FIGURE 8.5 *Ultima VII* features an unprecedented level of interactivity with its gameworld. There's very little here that's just for decoration; you can pick up, move, open, or manipulate just about everything you come across.

Just to give you some idea of how intriguing the world of *The Black Gate* can be, we'll quote a bit from Oleg Roschin's detailed review of the game at MobyGames. At one point in the game, Roschin's party meets up with a unicorn, who, as legend has it, communicates only with virgins. The first time around, Roschin's Avatar is, in fact, a virgin and admits as much to the unicorn, who then speaks to him. On a later visit, however, Roschin's Avatar has slept with a harlot at Buccaneer's Den, and the Unicorn refuses to utter a syllable. As usual, we see Garriott's subtlety: Sure, you *can* do sinful things, but you won't always get away with it. Later on, Bethesda and others capitalized on this high level of choice and consequences in the *Elder Scrolls* and other series.

No doubt, many modern gamers playing *The Black Gate* for the first time will be unimpressed with the jerky animation and glitches in the AI (particularly with pathfinding). Nevertheless, a patient player will be rewarded with a rich and meaningful experience. It's available in digital format from GOG.com, though serious fans should scour eBay for a complete boxed copy.

Serpent Isle

Origin released an expansion for *The Black Gate* titled *The Forge of Virtue* later in 1992, but it wasn't until 1993 that *Serpent Isle* appeared. Instead of calling this game *Ultima VIII*, Origin chose to label it as *Ultima VII: Part Two*. This odd naming convention is owed to Garriott's principle that no two *Ultima* games should share the same game engine.

Serpent Isle may have shared *The Black Gate*'s game engine, but it's much more linear and story-based than *The Black Gate*. The story begins eighteen months after the first part and involves traveling to Serpent Isle to restore the balance destroyed there by the Guardian.

Apparently, the game was rushed through production by Origin's new owner, Electronic Arts, a popular claim lent weight by the game's many dead ends (players who find themselves in one have to restore an earlier saved game). Origin's struggle with Electronic Arts bears an uncanny resemblance to Garriott's earlier conflict with Sierra On-Line. That conflict also led to a lackluster entry in the series, *Ultima II*. In any case, Origin did release an expansion to the game called *Silver Seed* later that year.

In 1997 Electronic Arts released the *Ultima Collection* for DOS and Windows, which includes the first nine games (including a PC port of *Akalabeth*) and both expansions. Nowadays, you can just buy them from GOG.com.

Worlds of Ultima

Origin released two games based on the *Ultima VI* engine as part of a spinoff series named *Worlds of Ultima,* mostly as an effort to capitalize further on the engine. While these games have a suggested connection to the rest of the series and star the Avatar, they take place far from Britannia.

The first of these, *The Savage Empire* (1990), is set in Eodon, a time-lost land where dinosaurs roamed—a place reminiscent of many a jungle adventure B-movie and Arthur Conan Doyle's *The Lost World,* complete with safari hats and hunting rifles (Figure 8.6). It's more focused on dialog and puzzle solving than the main *Ultima* line and has a simpler spell system. Like Origin's other titles, the documentation is extensive—with a full novelette to provide context for the action. The story has the Avatar saving the land from insectoid creatures named Myrmidex, a task that necessitates getting Eodon's thirteen tribes to work together.

The next and final *Worlds of Ultima* game is *Martian Dreams,* released in 1991. It's based on Jules Verne's classic *From the Earth to the Moon,* an 1865 story in which members of a gun club blast off to the moon in a hollow shell shot from a giant cannon. In Origin's game, the shell is accidentally launched to Mars with several celebrities trapped inside; you are part of a rescue operation. Like Paragon's *Space 1889* (a 1990 game we'll discuss

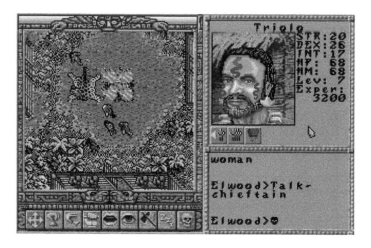

FIGURE 8.6 The *Worlds of Ultima* spinoffs got creative with their themes and settings. The one shown here, *The Savage Empire*, is set in a fierce jungle with dinosaurs and Stone Age warriors.

in the next chapter), the physics are based on a "what if" scenario—what if the Victorian science writers had been correct about things such as the Martian canals and radium-powered mechanical men? Several famous historical personalities are among the cast of characters, including Mark Twain and Sigmund Freud—who psychoanalyzes players in the character creation process. As with the previous game, the emphasis is on interaction and puzzle solving rather than combat.

Though the *Worlds of Ultima* series is touted by many critics, Origin never completed *Arthurian Legends,* a planned third installment based on the tales of King Arthur.

Times of Lore

In 1988, Origin published Chris Roberts' *Times of Lore,* an action CRPG set in real time with top-down perspective (Figure 8.7). The game was eventually ported to almost every capable platform, including the NES and the British ZX Spectrum and Amstrad CPC computers. In an interview published in the February 1990 issue of *Computer Gaming World,* Roberts admits that the game was "affected by the video game market," particularly Nintendo's extremely popular NES game console and *The Legend of Zelda.* It's no doubt that the unparalleled success of the NES and *The Legend of Zelda* is partially, if not mostly, responsible for the surge of action-oriented CRPGs we find in the late 1980s. We'll return to this point later on.

FIGURE 8.7 *Times of Lore* is a much-loved game by Chris Roberts. Its game-world has over 13,000 screens worth of area to explore.

Times of Lore is a fantasy game in which the player controls one of three archetypal characters: a muscle-bound barbarian, a svelte valkyrie, or an armor-clad knight. High King Valwyn has gone missing, and the kingdom of Albareth has fallen into disorder. It's up to you to seek out the king, find some artifacts, and restore the kingdom to peace and harmony.

Times of Lore doesn't offer a leveling system, and with a single exception, the player's character is stuck with the same arms and armor. This is most decidedly an action adventure game, with more emphasis on hand-eye coordination than stats or character development. Indeed, the system trades hit points for an image system: a candle at the bottom right of the screen burns high or low depending on the character's condition. The candle is restored either by resting, waiting, or quaffing potions. The game pleased most critics, who consider it a fine game for introducing newcomers to the CRPG. A brief but superb musical score by Martin Galway certainly doesn't hurt.

Bad Blood

Roberts next project for Origin was *Bad Blood,* a game set in a postapocalyptic wasteland. It is based on the same game engine employed in *Times of Lore,* with mostly cosmetic changes. For instance, instead of a burning candle to show the character's condition, it has a green bottle with varying amounts of soda. The player's task is to prevent Lord Dominix from launching a genocidal war against mutants, which he believes are polluted with bad blood. The game has obvious parallels to the 1988 game *Wasteland,* a more famous postapocalyptic game we'll discuss later.

Critics complain about the game's repetitive gameplay but also about its violence and lack of ethics. One contemporary reviewer wrote, *"Bad Blood* encourages players to act in reprehensible ways," citing the abundance of murder, theft, and general mayhem required to win the game.[3] For instance, one effective way to restore lost hit points is to chow down on fresh hearts ripped still beating from "turkels," mutant turtles that really just want to be left alone. I find this criticism quite significant, especially since we are talking about Origin, a company built on the principle that games should take ethics seriously. In any case, *Bad Blood* was certainly less successful than *Ultima* or some of Origin's other titles and seems all but forgotten today.

Knights of Legend

One of Origin's lesser-known masterpieces is Todd Mitchell Porter's *Knights of Legend* (1989), a turn-based CRPG with an extraordinarily detailed combat and character creation system. It seems to be an attempt to combine *Pool of Radiance* with the earlier *Ultima* games. It has the top-down perspective familiar to *Ultima* fans, but a turn-based tactical combat more akin to *Pool of Radiance* and *The Wizard's Crown*. This game goes a step further, though, introducing stats for fatigue and foresight, which let the character anticipate the next attack. It also has customizable icons for the characters, a convention we saw in *Pool of Radiance,* but this one lets you draw your own icons. There's a total of thirty-three character classes to choose from—quite a variety. If you've ever wanted to play a Lintle Plainswoman or a winged Rock Ranger, this game will accommodate you (Figure 8.8).

Combat requires making far more tactical decisions than required in most CRPGs. Like the *Phantasie* series, attacking characters choose between different maneuvers—hack, thrust, and slash. However, *Knights of Legend* expands the concept, with special attacks for unarmed styles and ranged attacks. There's also a body part–specific wound system that lets you target the most vulnerable regions of enemies. If a character's foresight score is high enough, he or she might be able to select a suitable defensive strategy as well, such as ducking or jumping to avoid a blow. Foresight is also necessary for ranged attacks, since the archer needs to predict how the target will move during the round. Every action brings

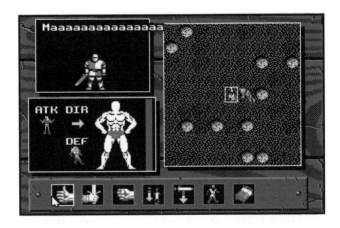

FIGURE 8.8 *Knights of Legend* never has received the attention it deserves. It's an ambitious, polished, and sophisticated game—but you'll definitely need the manual.

the character closer to fatigue, and it may become necessary to rest up between strikes. How effective the respite will be depends on the character's condition. If characters earn enough gold and adventure points to hire a weapons master, they can also take time to train and hone their skills with a particular weapon. Overall, it's a remarkably sophisticated and realistic system.

The magic system is no less complex, involving five or six syllables strung together to form a "word of power." These syllables are organized into the categories race, stat, severity, range (+ duration), and subclass. Each time magic-users cast a spell, they must consider the race being targeted and the stat they wish to affect (strength, intelligence, and so on). You can fine-tune each spell. One such spell is "VORYORWYRAMI," which "greatly decrease the intelligence of a skeleton at long range for minimal duration." Such precision!

Critics also marvel at the game's twenty-four quests, which are long and intensive. In short, there's hardly anything about *Knights of Legend* that was done halfway. Even the manual is over 145 pages long, with the bulk of it in small print. This is certainly a hardcore game on the opposite pole from Origin's *Times of Lore*. Unfortunately, despite the game's overwhelming ambition and attention to detail, it was never followed up with the expansions promised in the marketing materials.

Concluding Thoughts on Origin's Golden Age

Without question, these years saw Origin at its zenith. Lord British's *Ultima* series in particular made a huge impact, not just on the CRPG genre but on computer games in general. His persistent drive to innovate and embrace the latest audiovisual technology helped move the industry forward. But let's not forget that Origin was also a great publisher, launching the careers of Chris Roberts and many others. Even John Romero, one of the co-creators of *Wolfenstein 3D* and *Doom,* did an eight-year stint programming games for Origin.

If we had to pick one game that epitomized the Golden Age, it'd most certainly be *Ultima VII: The Black Gate.* With this game, Lord British brought together all of the skill and knowledge he'd accumulated in a lifetime of designing and producing great games. It raised the bar on what gamers could expect from a virtual world. Adam Smith of *Rock Paper Shotgun* put it nicely in a valentine he wrote to the game back in 2011: "*Ultima VII* was the game that first made me realize I preferred worlds that moved around me rather than worlds that I simply moved through."

It used to be tricky to get the game up and running on modern PCs, but now it's a cinch. Just go to GOG and look for *Ultima 7: The Complete Edition,* which includes the expansions and PDFs of the manuals, guides, cluebooks, maps, and even a bunch of design documents. It's a fantastic value for any CRPG fan.

NOTES

1. See Shay Addams' *The Official Book of Ultima* (ISBN 0-87455-228-1).
2. See http://www.gamespot.com/pc/rpg/tabularasa/news.html?sid=6143760.
3. See Charles Ardai's review of the game in the September 1990 issue of *Computer Gaming World.*

CHAPTER 9

Sir-Tech, New World Computing, and Sierra

GOLDEN-AGE *WIZARDRY*

Let's turn back now to Sir-Tech's *Wizardry* series, which was *Ultima*'s only serious rival during the Silver Age. Unfortunately for Sir-Tech, *Wizardry* had grown rather stale since the glorious *Proving Grounds of the Mad Overlord,* and the fifth game, *Heart of the Maelstrom* (1988), seems like just another attempt to squeeze a few more drops of blood from a well-worn engine. Although the box boasts of new mazes, abilities, spells, monster encounters, and combat system, the screenshots certainly don't look new. The dungeon corridors are still depicted in monochrome wireframe. Furthermore, the larger and more realistic mazes are even more difficult to map than before; they no longer fit neatly on 20 x 20 grids. "Such a significant change in *Wizardry*'s mapping design is especially curious at a time when many maze games are trying to *de-emphasize* paper and pencil mapping," writes one contemporary.[1] Although many critics are forgiving and still recommend the game, it is rarely discussed today beyond hardcore fans of the series. It's notable for being the first game in the series designed by David W. Bradley; Robert Woodhead and Andrew Greenberg had moved on to other projects.

Bane of the Cosmic Forge

The *Wizardry* series got a long-overdue overhaul in 1990 with the publication of the sixth game, *Bane of the Cosmic Forge* (Figure 9.1). The game sets off a great new trilogy by Bradley and introduces an enigmatic character

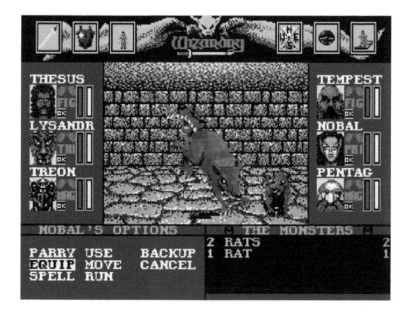

FIGURE 9.1 Bring on the rats! David W. Bradley's *Bane of the Cosmic Forge* is a terrific Golden Age CRPG that gave the aging *Wizardry* series just the boost it needed to bring attention and critical acclaim back to the franchise.

called the Dark Savant. The new engine sports much better graphics and a sleek, mouse-driven interface designed for the EGA era. Furthermore, it's four times larger than any previous *Wizardry* game and makes a decisive break from the previous games. To that end, it's one of the few games in the series that doesn't let you import characters from a prequel.

Both the combat and character development systems are enhanced. The characters can now be one of eleven different races and fourteen professions, each with options for prestige classes. Characters also learn dozens of skills, divided into three main categories (Weaponry, Physical, Academic) and subdivided into Sword, Oratory, Mythology, and many others. Characters also gradually accrue bonuses for using the same weapon type. Combat is similarly complex; there are now eight different styles of attack, each with pros and cons. The manual is 130 pages, and it's well advised for anyone serious about the game to read it cover to cover in order to learn the subtleties of this new system.

Bane of the Cosmic Forge's storyline concerns a magical pen whose scribbled words become reality—a conceit similar to the Cyan's *Myst* adventure games. Bradley's game also contains more puzzles than most CRPGs and is decidedly more focused on story and plot than the previous

Wizardry games. The manual emphasizes the role-playing aspect: "just like professional actors and actresses, you pretend to be a character, acting and reacting to situations as he or she would." Although the box's claim that the game would "make all other attempts obsolete" is not borne out by the gameplay, it's still an excellent game worthy of the Golden Age.

Crusaders of the Dark Savant

The seventh *Wizardry* game, *Crusaders of the Dark Savant* (Figure 9.2), debuted in 1992 for DOS. It finally brought the series up to 256-color VGA graphics and is generally considered one of the best entries in the series.

Taking a page from the *Ultima* and *Might and Magic* series, *Crusaders of the Dark Savant* is a blend of fantasy and sci-fi. The powerful pen introduced in the last game was captured by a cyborg named Aletheides. The disappearance of the pen has revealed the secret it was guarding—the lost planet of Guardia. Somewhere on Guardia is the secret to incredible power, and several groups (including the player's party and the Dark Savant) set out to find it. This idea of competing with other groups for the same prize is quite innovative and opens up several new gameplay possibilities—should players join one of these other groups or slaughter them? Another nice development is four multiple beginnings, a twist on the multiple endings introduced in the prequel.

Like its predecessors, *Crusaders of the Dark Savant* is a difficult, complicated game that is intimidating to beginners, even if it does feature automapping and a mouse-driven interface. The combat engine even factors

Aboard the ship of the Dark Savant is a young girl, by name of Vi Domina...

FIGURE 9.2 As you can see, *Crusaders of the Dark Savant* is less *Conan* than *Krull*, freely mixing sci-fi with fantasy tropes. The "young girl" shown here, Vi Domina, returns as an NPC companion in *Wizardry 8*.

in the characters' mental and physical fatigue, which steadily grows during the many protracted battles. Picking locks is likewise no easy task but requires quick reflexes (players must hit the button at just the right moment as the tumblers roll). Nevertheless, *Crusaders of the Dark Savant* is praised by critics and was not eclipsed until the release of *Wizardry 8* in 2001.

NEW WORLD COMPUTING IN THE GOLDEN AGE

When last we spoke of New World Computing's *Might and Magic* series, Jon Van Caneghem (JVC) had just released his 1986 *Book I: The Secret of the Inner Sanctum,* an ambitious labor of love and a very promising debut for a bold new series. Several high-quality games indeed followed, each with technical and creative innovations to the interface and game engine.

Gates to Another World

In 1988, New World produced *Might and Magic II: Gates to Another World* (Figure 9.3). Although the engine was left mostly intact, the graphics are updated for the PC's EGA standard, and the already vast gameworld is expanded even further. The biggest changes are automapping, two new character classes, more spells, and the ability to add two nonplayer characters called hirelings to the party. Again, we find abundant examples of JVC's nerdy humor: the party can add such worthies as "Mr. Wizard" to its ranks. Most of these mercenaries can be added only after the party rescues them or completes an appropriate quest.

FIGURE 9.3 Not one, but six massive sewer rats in dire need of a good solid thwacking. Pure bliss!

Another change is the introduction of a skills system. In addition to the usual sorts of skills associated with the various professions (e.g., thieves pick locks, fighters wield swords), characters can learn two of fifteen secondary skills. Most of these boost a statistic; for instance, Gambler increases luck, and Gladiator boosts might. Other skills are more interesting. For instance, Cartographer enables the game's automapping tool, and Pathfinder allows the party to pass through a forested area as long as two different members have it as part of their skill set.

Perhaps the most unusual feature of the game is an algorithmic process for leveling up and enchanting weapons. Most games have a cap on how many levels the characters can reach, but *Gates to Another World* lets the inflation run rampant, countering high-level characters with increasingly difficult random encounters. The result is stat inflation. For instance, later in the game players might find themselves in a battle with 255 Time Lords—though hopefully the character's Flaming Sword +57 would be enough to dispatch them. This inflation problem has plagued many CRPGs as well as tabletop RPGs; eventually, the designers simply run out of names and resort to tacking on numbers to distinguish items.

Like its predecessor, *Gates to Another World* is a flexible game that offers players considerable freedom to move about the gameworld (this time, CRON). Eventually, though, players learn that Sheltem, the villain from the first game, is set to destroy CRON by forcing it into the sun. Beating the game requires not only thoroughly traversing CRON, but also traveling through four elemental planes and even through time. There are plenty of surprises in store for the player, including devices that change the characters' genders. Like SSI's earlier *Phantasie* games, the characters age and die soon after reaching seventy-five, though there are places in the game to restore their youth. The game was ported to all major platforms of the day, including the Sega Genesis and SNES game consoles.

An interesting bit of history about this game occurs in the pages of *Computer Gaming World*. Scorpia, the magazine's chief contributor of adventure and CRPG reviews, wrote a rather lukewarm review of the game, bemoaning the lack of innovation and overemphasis on combat. Caneghem was incensed by the review and wrote a lengthy response, which the magazine published in its letters column. There, Caneghem takes the critic to task for a number of reasons, but perhaps the most humorous is a squabble over the game's surprise ending. Unlike most CRPGs then and now, the endgame does not consist of a difficult battle with an overpowering foe (or boss), but rather a cryptogram. Players have precisely fifteen minutes to complete the puzzle. Scorpia blasts it as pointless and disappointing, whereas Caneghem holds it up as a prime example of originality. In any event, Caneghem had his revenge in the next game, where he introduced the "Scorpia monster" as one of many vile new foes to be vanquished by the heroes.

Isles of Terra

Might and Magic III: Isles of Terra was released in 1991 and was the first game in the series to utilize the PC's new VGA graphic card and sound cards. It's also the first *Might and Magic* to support the mouse. These were significant improvements, of course, but they're not what makes *Isles of Terra* stand out in a sea of other high-quality releases (Figure 9.4).

The other key innovation is that now the on-screen character portraits change to reflect the status and mood of each character. One of the biggest problems with first-person perspective is that players cannot see their characters' facial expressions—which, as anyone who has ever watched a film knows, play a very important role in helping audiences identify emotionally with the characters. Now the player can look down to see

FIGURE 9.4 The third *Might and Magic* game introduces several pertinent innovations to the interface as well as the audiovisuals. In particular, the substantially larger view screen makes it feel much more immersive than before.

if his or her characters are happy, sad, asleep, crazed, or stoned (that is, turned to stone). However, some gamers feel that first-person is inherently more immersive than third, even with this limitation. The beauty of New World's system is that players can have it both ways: first-person on top, and third-person on bottom. New World used this system throughout the rest of the series.

Another visual cue is the characters' "life stones." The life stones simplify the traditional hit point system with a color code—green for good, yellow for not so good, and red for critical. Monster labels use the same system. Other visual cues include little gargoyles on the border of the first-person window. One of them will signal with his arm when the party passes by a secret door, provided that one of the party members has the skill Detect Secret Passages. The game also makes excellent use of sound effects, with different sounds for each type of weapon.

Other enhancements include two new classes (druid and ranger), a high-quality automapper, ranged combat, a more liberal save-game scheme, and a checklist of incomplete quests. A last nod to novices is a button that, when pressed, instantly transports the party back to an inn. However, this panic button has a cost—each character loses a level of experience.

Finally, we should consider the addition of "secondary" skills and hidden trainers for them, a feature that shows up in later *Might and Magic* as well as *The Elder Scrolls* series. There are eighteen of these. Some, like Body Builder and Arms Master, are directly tied to combat, granting extra hit points or hit chance per level respectively. Others deal with quality of life or interface enhancements, such as Direction Sense, required to use a compass. A third category concerns accessing certain terrains, such as Swimming, Pathfinder, and Mountaineer. Some skills are easier for certain classes or races; Sorcerers, for example, start off with Cartographer (an all-important skill that enables the automapper mentioned above). Robbers and ninjas receive a base rating bonus for thievery. Gnomes start off with Spot Secret Doors. The masters who can train your party in these skills are sprinkled across the map, and they certainly don't work for free. In *Might and Magic III*, a skill isn't improved once learned; you either have it or you don't. As we've come to expect in CRPGs with skills, some are more useful than others and one, Tracker, is altogether useless. We'll see this system further refined in *Might and Magic VI* as well as in the *Elder Scrolls* series. In short, *Isles of Terra* is an impressive and substantial sequel that secured the *Might and Magic* franchise a place in a rather crowded market.

World of Xeen

With the fourth game, *Clouds of Xeen* (1992), New World quietly dropped support for other platforms and focused solely on MS-DOS (though a special 1994 combo called *World of Xeen* was ported to Macintosh). *Clouds of Xeen* and *Darkside of Xeen* (1993) are really one large quest broken into two chunks—the ultimate goal is the destruction of Sheltem. Indeed, both games can be combined into a single game called *World of Xeen,* which grants access to areas unavailable in either standalone game (adding up to about one fourth the size of the game). Both games offer only slight enhancements to the core engine used in *Isles of Terra,* but New World made good use of the new CD-ROM storage medium by adding quality soundtracks.

Clouds of Xeen's story has the party venturing into the netherworld to put down the tyrannical Lord Xeen, a demon impersonating King Burlock's long-lost brother. The demon is wreaking havoc, and the party is summoned by Crodo, the king's advisor, to set matters right. Doing so entails quite a bit of slaughter over a gargantuan world, or, to be more precise, multiple worlds. Like the previous *Might and Magic* games, *Clouds of Xeen* features dozens of optional sidequests in addition to the big mission; indeed, New World was a pioneer in this area. Of course, the significance of miniquests is that players feel they have more freedom and flexibility, but it also increases a game's replay value, since players may opt to complete different miniquests on the second play. *Clouds of Xeen* also features two initial play modes, Adventurer and Warrior. This choice will affect the intensity of the combat and is a nice concession to novice gamers. The next game, *Darkside of Xeen,* has the same gameplay and mechanics. This time, the story has the characters traveling to another planet to revive the mysterious Corak and defeat the tyrannical Sheltem, an intergalactic despot.

While *Clouds of Xeen* and *Darkside of Xeen* are worthwhile games, it's when the two are combined to form *World of Xeen* that they really seem impressive (Figure 9.5). This giant adventure was certainly one of the most epic in scope yet seen in the genre, even in modern games. Unfortunately, developers have seemed reluctant to follow the example, preferring instead to release full-blown sequels or expansion packs.

The rarest *Might and Magic* game is *Swords of Xeen,* a fan-made game that was included as part of *Might and Magic Trilogy,* a 1995 compilation of *Isles of Terra, Clouds of Xeen,* and *Darkside of Xeen. Swords of Xeen* is based on the same game engine as the latter two *Xeen* games and picks up after the party defeats Lord Xeen. The party must enter the new world

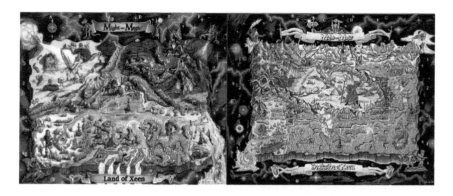

FIGURE 9.5 If you were trapped on an island and could bring only one game with you, *World of Xeen* is an excellent choice. It's fairly certain you would die of thirst, starvation, or perhaps old age before you managed to explore its every nook and cranny.

of Havec and fight hordes of new creatures. The company that designed the game, Catware, went on in 1999 to create *Shattered Light*, an isometric Windows CRPG that includes a construction kit. It was published by Simon & Schuster Interactive.

In 1996, New World Computing was bought by 3D0 and continued to publish new *Might and Magic* CRPGs (of steeply varying quality) as late as 2002. However, in 2003 the rights passed to Ubisoft. We'll discuss these games later.

Tunnels & Trolls

New World Computing is better known for its *Might and Magic* and *Heroes of Might and Magic* turn-based strategy games than any of its other products, though it did experiment with other franchises during the Golden Age. One of the best and most interesting of these side projects is Neal Hallford's *Tunnels & Trolls: Crusaders of Khazan*, a 1990 publication based on Ken St. Andre's popular tabletop fantasy RPG, which presented respectable competition to TSR's role-playing games during the early 1980s (Figure 9.6). Although few people seem to remember the computer version, it is still being published by Flying Buffalo, makers of the tabletop game.

Crusaders of Khazan allows players to control up to four characters in a party. Players can either roll their own or use pregenerated characters; the party can be modified later, substituting pregenerated for personalized characters and vice versa. Character creation is a fairly conventional affair, with four races—human, elf, dwarf, and "hobb," a diminutive and

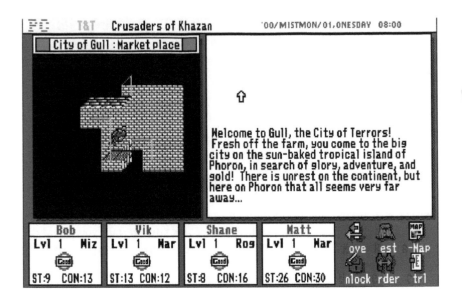

FIGURE 9.6 *Tunnels & Trolls: Crusaders of Khazan* is based on Ken St. Andre's alternative to *Dungeons & Dragons*. It was designed by Neal Hallford, author of *Swords & Circuitry,* an essential guide to CRPG design.

dexterous race that sounds suspiciously like Tolkien's hobbit. The stats are intelligence, luck, constitution, dexterity, charisma, speed, and strength, though here strength serves as a prime requisite for warriors and wizards. In the case of wizards, strength determines the potency of spells, whereas with warriors it determines the amount of physical damage they cause with weapons. The three classes are warrior, wizard, and rogue. Of the three, the rogue is the most flexible, having the ability to wield all weapons, learn spells, and, of course, pick locks and disarm traps. The final stage in character creation is selecting a portrait; there are two for each class and sex.

The combat system is similar to the Gold Box engine. It's turn-based and presented in top-down perspective. Initiative (who strikes first) is determined by the speed score. One nice innovation here is the push command, which allows a warrior of great strength to attempt to hurl an opponent into water or other hostile squares, causing damage. The magic system also bears mention, if for no other reason than the hilarious names for spells offered in the manual, such as "Oh Go Away!," "Take That You Fiend!," and "Poor Baby." This is the kind of humor and directness that runs through this unpretentious game by Neal Hallford, better known for his masterpiece *Betrayal at Krondor* and excellent books on RPG design. The magic system is also boosted by the option to pump more power into basic spells, strengthening them or making them last longer. Gameplay occurs mostly in top-down perspective, with two different screens for exploration and combat.

Crusaders of Khazan has other desirable features, such as the ability to purchase mounts to reduce travel time, a good automapper, loads of sidequests, and well-polished prose in the manual and in-game texts. All in all, it's a quality game for both novices and advanced CRPG fans, and one wonders why it hasn't attracted more attention. Some critics complain about the cumbersome interface and lackluster graphics, but other games with similar problems have been more successful. My guess is that it simply got lost in the shuffle; there were many outstanding games on the shelf in 1990, and perhaps New World wanted to focus on its *Might and Magic* franchise. At any rate, anyone wanting to play the game today should purchase the *30th Anniversary Edition* of *Tunnels & Trolls* from Flying Buffalo, which includes the game and documentation on a CD-ROM.

Planet's Edge

In 1991, New World Computing published another game designed by Hallford, this time a sci-fi CRPG named *Planet's Edge*, a hybrid game similar to the *Starflight* and *Sentinel Worlds* games (Figure 9.7). The game is usually described as a "space opera," and, given its larger-than-life characters and an epic-sized plot, the epithet seems warranted. Although mostly overlooked by modern CRPG fans, the game is noteworthy in several respects and, like *Crusaders of Khazan,* deserves more attention than it has received.

The plot is essentially a find-the-object type, though instead of a sword or orb, the planet Earth itself has gone missing—or, to be more precise, its mass has disappeared, leaving behind little more than the orbiting moon (one wonders: How the moon could sustain an orbit?). The player controls a group of four pregenerated characters who must figure out how to restore the planet and save humanity.

The game boasts over 500 planets to explore, with plenty of cryptograms, logic games, and inventory-based puzzles in place to challenge all but the most resourceful players. Combat is in real time and shown in top-down perspective, reminiscent of the combat mode seen in *Star Control.* As with most other New World games, there are many optional sidequests, though this time they are more reminiscent of *Star Trek* episodes than of *Conan* or Camelot stories.

Perhaps the most intriguing innovation is that players build their own space ships, weapons, armor, and hand weapons using raw materials,

FIGURE 9.7 *Planet's Edge* is an ambitious science fiction CRPG with real-time combat and a construction mode that lets you build your own ships, weapons, and armor.

which are acquired either by mining or trading with aliens. There are dozens of these elements, which range from humble organics and inert gases to hybrid solids and alien isotopes. The elements are ranked according to their rarity; naturally, the rarer elements are more valuable and useful.

Another innovation is the ability to clone fallen crew members. Although the game's four characters are pregenerated with their own stats and skills, players can modify them during the cloning process, reshuffling them as they see fit. In any case, characters have four attributes (body, intelligence, agility, and luck) and three basic skills (the number of secondary skills they can learn depends on their intelligence score). The sixteen skills are what you might expect from a game of this type, such as astrogation, which allows you to pilot a ship, and first aid.

Unfortunately, the game lacks a coherent leveling system, though the strength of the party does increase as it harvests raw materials and builds more powerful weapons and equipment. Some critics complain that the game's role-playing elements are too meager and object to the inability to create new characters from scratch. Others view these limitations as necessary in order to create a more coherent plot and dramatic structure. Critics also complain about some rather infuriating bugs and the abundance of typographical and grammatical errors in the game text. In short, this game had great promise, but its lack of polish and a good leveling system may well justify its obscurity today.

INTERPLAY IN THE GOLDEN AGE: *WASTELAND* AND *THE LORD OF THE RINGS*

By this point, it should be obvious that 1988 was a watershed year for CRPGs. SSI was at its peak, and Origin was rolling out masterpiece after masterpiece. New World Computing wasn't resting on its laurels, either. Needless to say, Interplay was up against some pretty serious competition, but its 1988 release of *The Bard's Tale III* had no problem finding buyers. In this chapter, however, we should discuss two other important Interplay games of 1988: *Wasteland* and *J.R.R. Tolkien's The Lord of the Rings, Vol. I.*

Wasteland

Fallout, probably the most famous of all post-apocalyptic CRPGs, can trace its roots back to Interplay's *Wasteland,* released for the Commodore 64, MS-DOS, and Apple II, and published by Electronic Arts (Figure 9.8).

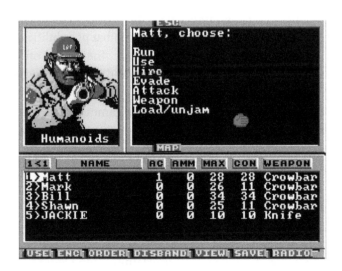

FIGURE 9.8 Interplay's *Wasteland* is a cult classic set after an apocalypse. It plays like a mashup of *The Bard's Tale* and *Ultima,* with the first-person turn-based combat mode of the former and the top-down, tile-based exploration mode of the latter.

Wasteland is set in the devastating aftermath of World War III. Players start out with a party of four Desert Rangers, though up to three more characters can be recruited later on. However, these additional members cannot be controlled directly and have their own goals that play an influential role in how the game unfolds. Two of the developers, Ken St. Andre and Michael Stackpole, had designed their own tabletop role-playing games *(Tunnels & Trolls* and *Mercenaries, Spies, and Private Eyes,* respectively), and many of their sharply innovative ideas are found in *Wasteland.*

As in SSI's *The Wizard's Crown,* character development is based not only on stats but also on skills—twenty-seven of them, to be precise. These abilities range from combat skills to sleight-of-hand and metallurgy. Obviously, sensible players will want to ensure that their party has a diverse array of talents, since there's no telling what they'll be up against—though the game is flexible enough to let players overcome obstacles in a variety of ways, such as picking a lock vs. climbing a gate. Likewise, the game has several situations in which an individual character must go it alone, thus further helping players form coherent identities for their party. This terrific role-playing system complements the game's story and ambience.

Wasteland's game engine can be described as a blend of *The Bard's Tale* (for combat and character info screens) and top-down games like *Ultima* (for travel and exploration). It's a nice setup that works well, even if it doesn't allow players quite the tactical combat possibilities of *Pool of Radiance* or *The Wizard's Crown.* At any rate, the appeal of *Wasteland* stems more from its fascinating gameworld and character customization than from combat stratagems.

Like *Pool of Radiance* and several other games of the era, much of the context for the action is provided in a printed manual with numbered paragraphs. The game refers the player to these passages at pivotal moments. The manual warns against reading ahead, but notes that once the game is finished "you can kick back in your best lounge chair under a shady cactus and read the rest of the fictional vignettes." Indeed, players who did so found some funny paragraphs designed to catch cheaters, including the first one. After several torrid descriptions of an impending sex scene, a would-be seductress proclaims, "Stop reading paragraphs you're not supposed to read, creeps. Next time I'm going to demand they put me in a Bard's Tale game, this Wasteland duty is dangerous." This is a good example of the wit and charm that characterize the manual and the game itself. As with many other games of this era, the manual also serves as a form of copy protection, since making photocopies would add greatly to the costs of illegal distribution.

Wasteland remains the favorite CRPG of many gamers who played it back in the late 1980s, and for good reason—it's a captivating and highly innovative game that deserves its place beside *The Bard's Tale*. It's a testament to the game's enduring legacy that the best-selling *Fallout,* released in 1997, is in many ways a spiritual successor to this game.

Electronic Arts released an alleged sequel to the game called *Fountain of Dreams* in 1990, but none of *Wasteland*'s developers were involved. The publisher made an uncharacteristic decision to downplay the sequel aspect as much as possible, and the game (which, by all accounts, is a lemon) made very little impression on the market and warrants no more than passing mention here. There's also a game named *Escape from Hell* based on the engine, also released in 1990 by Electronic Arts. This satirical game was designed by Richard Seaborne and Alan Murphy and is one of the few attempts at parody in what is often a highly pretentious genre.

Wasteland is also notable for inspiring one of the first major crowd-funded projects by legacy developers. Brian Fargo led this project to create a long-awaited sequel, and he raised nearly $3 million. The result was *Wasteland 2,* first published in 2014 and followed by a Director's Cut in 2015. We'll talk more about it later.

Dragon Wars

While Interplay was making the third *Bard's Tale* game, one of the developers, Becky Heineman, was thinking of some improvements she'd like to see made to the engine. However, since Interplay felt that its relationship with publisher Electronic Arts was wearing thin, they elected to keep these innovations for a new game they would publish themselves. That project became *Dragon Wars,* released by Interplay in 1989 (Figure 9.9).

Dragon Wars bears a close resemblance to *Bard's Tale,* but there are some important differences. From a gameplay perspective, the most significant changes are in character creation and development. Instead of generating characters based on random numbers, *Dragon Wars* allots the player 50 character points to distribute among stats and skills. Many of the skills are combat-related, such as fist-fighting and weapon skills, which allow characters to specialize with a weapon type. Others are useful for thieving, such as pickpocket and lockpick. There are also several lore skills that provide the party with relevant information in each of these subjects: caves, forests, the arcane, mountains, and towns. Finally, there are movement-based

FIGURE 9.9 Becky "Burger" Heineman's *Dragon Wars* doesn't have *The Bard's Tale* branding, but there's no mistaking the gameplay style and mechanics. That said, it's a great game in its own right, even if the game's title was a last-minute alteration that necessitated a rather hasty addition of said creature.

skills such as swimming and climbing. Thankfully, not every character needs every skill; as with *Wasteland,* a large part of the game's challenge is constructing a well-balanced party. Perhaps to make things easier, the player can create only four party members, though three others can be recruited later on. "Character creation is an art," states the manual. "You'll have to experiment if you want to arrive at the 'perfect' design."

Another big change in *Dragon Wars* concerns leveling up. Although characters gain new levels, doing so grants no automatic benefit to stats or skills. Instead, players receive two character points to distribute as they see fit. This system forces players to think long term and to make frequent decisions about how to best benefit their party. Although most skills require only one character point to be effective, others require more. Combat is more complicated here than in *The Bard's Tale.* In addition to hit points, each character has a measure of stun points. Each time the character is hit in battle, he or she loses a number of hit points but also twice that number in stun points. When characters run out of stun points, they lose consciousness, though they will recover eventually—hopefully well after their enemies have moved on to tougher marks. Another nice touch here is a quick fighting mode that expedites less pressing encounters, though the regular fight mode gives more options and finer control over the battle.

The setting of *Dragon Wars* is eerily familiar to those with good memories of the Cold War era. The young world of Oceana is a collection of large islands, each with its own city-state and captive dragon. These dragons help maintain the balance of power by threatening mutually assured destruction. The characters are recent, and, as it turns out, quite naïve immigrants to the fabled island of Dilmun, the world's oldest empire and finest culture. Unfortunately for the party, Dilmun isn't quite the land of opportunity they hoped it'd be. Indeed, they are stripped naked and tossed into the slum city of Purgatory. Apparently, Dilmun's power-mad ruler, Namtar (alias "Beast from the Pit"), is bent on uniting the city-states of Oceana into a new world order under his rule. To that end, Namtar has declared all magic illegal and is confiscating everything in sight that might assist him in his quest to conquer the world. Naturally, it's up to the party to escape Purgatory and knock Namtar from his throne—preferably before he loses his dragon and puts doomsday on the calendar.

Like *Wasteland*, *Dragon Wars* relies on a printed manual with numbered paragraphs to provide context and notes during gameplay. As usual in these cases, the manual warns against reading the entries out of order, though with a bit of humor: "Ultimately, you put down your hard-earned cash for this game, and you can of course do what you damn well please with the paragraphs. However, should you use the paragraphs as a free 'cheat book,' beware the wrath of Namtar." It also warns that some paragraphs are "pure ya-ya" and that "acting on ill-gotten information can prove hazardous to your health." At any rate, a quick glance through the paragraphs reveals quite a few allusions to the Sumerian *Epic of Gilgamesh*, a rich bit of ancient mythology seldom explored in CRPGs.

All in all, *Dragon Wars* is a rich game with plenty to offer fans of *The Bard's Tale*, but Interplay wasn't able to market the game as effectively as Electronic Arts did with the older series. A telling characteristic is the box art, which sports two scantily clad barbarians (one male and one female) poised to hack at a demonic-looking monster, a rather generic image that suggests little more than a by-the-numbers "hack 'n slash" game.

Neuromancer

Perhaps the most unusual of Interplay's 1988 games is *Neuromancer*, based on William Gibson's famous cyberpunk novel (Figure 9.10). Although usually described as a graphical adventure rather than a CRPG, the game has a strong enough CRPG component to blur the boundaries. Specifically, it features a skills system and, in a unique fashion, randomized combat.

The storyline here resists summary and would take considerable prose to do justice. The gist, however, is that computer hackers are disappearing

FIGURE 9.10 If you've ever tried reading Gibson's *Neuromancer,* then you can appreciate the challenge of adapting the author's densely layered prose into a playable CRPG. The designers ended up taking a lighthearted, zany approach that bears little resemblance to the novel, but it's still a fun game.

from cyberspace, which the game represents as an abstract, virtual environment in three dimensions. The player is a cowboy, someone with the technical expertise to bypass security measures and tap into government, military, and corporate bases. The bigger story here is about a race of artificial intelligences (AIs) who are kept under strict control, but who find a way to pool their resources and take over the government. Given the sorry state of things in Chiba City, Japan, one wonders if that fate would truly be so terrible.

The player doesn't create a character, but the one provided gains new skills as the game moves on. The player also gets acquires better software and hardware, items here roughly analogous to the skills, arms, and armor found in fantasy-based CRPGs. The chief enemy is ICE, or Intrusion Countermeasure Electronics, which must be brought down with software viruses. The character can sell body parts for instant cash, though the plastic replacements are cheaply built and will make survival less likely in the more dangerous regions of cyberspace. Skills are purchased as chips that are inserted in a slot on the character's skull. They range from coptalk, which allows the characters to effect an Irish brogue associated with police officers, to musicianship, which grants proficiency with musical instruments. Of course, there is also ice hacking, which helps get the character past ICE, and plenty of other skill that the character must discover later in the game. The bulk of the gameplay consists of interacting with other characters and building up a collection of facts, notes, and clues needed to win.

Neuromancer also features a soundtrack by DEVO, the zany band responsible for "Whip It." DEVO's involvement might strike fans of the novel as rather out of place, yet the game is actually quite humorous and satirical throughout. For instance, the electronics ship is named "Crazy Edo's," a not-so-subtle reference to the Crazy Eddie line of electronics stores that were popular when the game was released. The game begins with the character waking up after a "night sleeping face-down in a plate of synth-spaghetti," and the *Night City News* is full of headlines such as "Farm Animals Kidnap UFO" and "Man Eats His Own Head." In short, there is no effort here to capture the grim and unsettling world of Gibson's book; instead, we get a tongue-in-cheek game full of geeky jokes and puns rather reminiscent of a LucasArts adventure game.

Interplay's *Neuromancer,* then, is a highly innovative game that blurs the boundaries between CRPGs and graphical adventure games, much like Sierra's *Quest for Glory* series, which we'll discuss later. Although it is not as well known today as *The Bard's Tale* and the much later *Deus Ex,* it remains a favorite of many CRPG aficionados. *Gamespot* recognizes it as one of its "Greatest Games of All Time," and it's quite likely to have influenced later games in the genre. It certainly demonstrates Interplay's willingness to venture beyond the sword and spell.

The Lord of the Rings

To say that the works of J. R. R. Tolkien have influenced the CRPG is akin to saying that the Big Bang influenced the universe. The influence is deep, profound, and fundamental. It's easy enough to find allusions to (if not downright plagiarism of) Tolkien throughout CRPG history, especially when games deal with magic and races. Indeed, many early CRPGs feature a race type blatantly named *hobbit*, though more conscientious authors try to mask the borrowing by using names like "bobbit," "halfling," or "kender" instead. Likewise, we've lost track of the games based on the idea of a powerful being searching for magical artifacts to cement his power.

It was inevitable that a major developer would secure the rights to create an official *Lord of the Rings* CRPG, but it took much longer than we might have expected. Indeed, it wasn't until 1990 that Interplay finally rolled out *J.R.R. Tolkien's The Lord of the Rings, Vol. I,* a game many still consider the best Tolkien game ever made (Figure 9.11). As the title suggests, the game is based on the first of Tolkien's novels, *The Fellowship of*

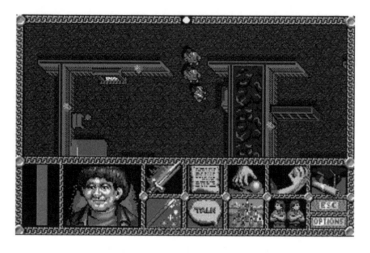

FIGURE 9.11 There are many games based on Tolkien's works, but Interplay's *J.R.R. Tolkien's The Lord of the Rings, Vol. I* is still one of the best.

the Ring. Of course, it's hard to miss that Interplay's long and unwieldy title carefully avoids the word *fellowship.* Interplay was trying hard to avoid association with an earlier illustrated text adventure game with that title, published by two book publishers in 1986. It wanted to ensure that gamers knew their game was a fresh approach to the subject matter.

The primary goal of Interplay's game is for Frodo to take the One Ring to Don Guldur and kill the Witch King, all without being slaughtered by the Nine Riders, or, for Tolkien buffs, the Nazgûl. However, the game is well known for its nonlinear gameplay and many sidequests; this is no slavish adaptation, and plenty of things happen that Tolkien never penned. This is particularly true in the player's choice of companions. Although Sam, Gandalf, Aragorn, and other characters are labeled "permanent player characters," the player can dismiss them—and, if they die, the game goes on. However, the manual assures us that they will never abandon the quest. Temporary characters, on the other hand, will join the party (or the "Fellowship") only as long as it serves their own ends. Likewise, only permanent characters can be exported to the sequel. Players can recruit and dismiss characters as they see fit, though the developers have ensured that getting through the game without the original crew (e.g., Gimli) is especially challenging, if not impossible.

Character creation and development are based on stats and skills. The skill system is quite elaborate and is broken into three categories: active, combat, and lore. Combat and lore skills are always on and need not be activated by the player; active skills must be selected. They include skills such as boats, which allows the character to navigate watercraft, and jump, which permits leaping chasms. Perhaps more unusual are the active skills charisma and bravado, which are used to sway the opinions of others (the manual warns that bravado is useless in the first game). Combat skills are focused on particular weapons, such as axes or bows. Lore skills provide the player with extra information at relevant points in the game. For instance, studying Numenorean lore can come in handy should the party explore Numenorean ruins. Skills are either learned by paying an expert for training or are added automatically after certain events in the game.

The magic system is quite interesting and unusual, possibly even unique. It is divided into two main types, white and black, though of course only white need concern us here. To cast a spell, a player must either be a Valar-approved wizard or an elf; ordinary people are denied such power. That's probably for the best, since each spell drains the caster's life points (hit points). The manual warns that "magic is weak, unreliable, and danger-ous" and should be employed only in emergencies. If the player is willing to risk it, there are plenty of useful spells available, such as animal-speak, which allows communion with birds and other animals, and counter-magic, which can dispel enchantments.

The interface is icon and mouse-driven, though conversing with char-acters requires input from the keyboard. Dialog is again based on a simple keyword system, though most important words are capitalized to make identifying them easier. Much of the game hinges on talking with char-acters, giving them items, and responding to their requests for assistance. The game features top-down perspective throughout. Combat is turn-based, though not nearly as complex as that seen in the Gold Box games. One of the less desirable features is that many objects aren't shown on the screen; instead, they are identified by name in a pop-up window shaped like a scroll. It's a rather clumsy system. The colorful graphics are lacking in other ways; the hobbits tend to look the same—you can't even tell Frodo apart from Sam or Pippin.

Interplay again resorted to printing valuable material in the manual, to which players are referred at various points in the game. This method was by this time quite well established, though critics were beginning to call negative attention to it in their reviews, seeing it quite rightly as a nuisance. It's impossible to tell whether this scheme thwarted illegal dis-tribution more than it irritated rightful owners. As for me, I prefer reading lengthy passages in printed form rather than on screen.

The Two Towers

As promised, Interplay followed up with *J.R.R. Tolkien's The Lord of the Rings, Vol. II: The Two Towers* in 1991, carrying the storyline into the second *Rings* novel. This game features some significant enhancements over the previous game, such as an automapper and more efficient access to the characters' skills, spells, and inventories. The graphics and animation are also more detailed, and combat is extended with new commands (aim, block, swing, and dodge). There is also forty-five minutes of original medieval-style music, a respectable achievement for the time.

Another gameplay device allows switching among the characters at certain points of the narrative. This ability is also present to a lesser extent in the previous game, where the player briefly played as Aragorn, but in this game it's much more central. To make the transitions more exciting, Interplay was sure to end each segment with a cliffhanger, though some critics found this practice disorienting. Overall, though, Interplay's second game seems the more promising of the two, or at least the most playable by modern gamers.

Unfortunately for Interplay, sales for the second installment were insufficient to warrant completing the trilogy. We must remember, however, that Tolkien's epic work had not yet received the powerful boost from Peter Jackson's critically acclaimed film adaptations. The contemporary reviewers seem most concerned that true Tolkien fans would reject the games because of the minor variations from the printed works, but more likely, these games were simply overshadowed by the powerful competition. Nonetheless, Interplay released a special CD-ROM version of the games in 1993, which, among other things, feature several snippets of Ralph Bakshi's 1978 animated film.

SIERRA AND THE GLORIOUS REVOLUTION

No discussion of the late 1980s era of CRPG history is complete without mention of Sierra On-Line's well-known and critically acclaimed series *Quest for Glory*. Although we've already discussed some games that grafted CRPGs with adventure game elements, this series seems to have born the most fruit. Indeed, many CRPG aficionados consider Lori Ann Cole's *Quest for Glory* series among the best CRPGs ever made.

Sierra had earned a great reputation for its adventure game line, which includes such well-known classics as *King's Quest*, *Space Quest*, and *Leisure Suit Larry*. While these games were highly successful and remain on many gamers' favorites list, some critics sound the familiar complaint: once players have beaten the game, there's little reason to continue playing. Furthermore, adventure games tend to be rather linear and limited; difficult puzzles often have a single, counterintuitive solution. If players can't figure it out, they must either cheat or give up. Cole's idea was to take Sierra's highly successful adventure game engine and modify it, incorporating CRPG elements to alleviate these problems. The result was highly playable (and replayable) games that, for many gamers, offer the best of both genres.

Hero's Quest

The first *Quest for Glory* game was originally titled *Hero's Quest: So You Want to be a Hero* and released for MS-DOS in 1989 (ports for Amiga and Atari ST followed) (Figure 9.12). Sierra later found itself in a quandary with board game maker Milton Bradley, which also had a game named *Hero's Quest*. Rather than dispute the matter in court, Sierra decided to enhance and rerelease the game in 1992 as *Quest for Glory*.

The game looks very much like a typical Sierra GAG (i.e., *King's Quest*, *Space Quest*), but offers CRPG elements such as the ability to select a character class (fighter, mage, thief) and to improve his skills. However, class selection plays a stronger role in the narrative than it does in most CRPGs. Its influence is most clearly seen in the puzzles, which offer solutions unique to each class. For instance, fighters and thieves can climb a tree to

FIGURE 9.12 *Quest for Glory* was built on Sierra's adventure game engine and shares much of the humor and wit of its well-established *King's Quest* series.

FIGURE 9.13   The real-time combat of *Quest for Glory* is quite intense.

fetch a ring in a bird's nest, but magic-users must cast a spell. Of course, combat strategies differ by class as well. Mages and thieves should avoid close combat (melee), whereas fighters are encouraged to jump right in. In any case, combat is a timed, arcade-like affair that involves choosing appropriate moves and countermoves (e.g., strike when the monster isn't blocking). Since gameplay changes considerably depending on the character's class, the replay value of this game is much higher than in most graphical adventure games or CRPGs (Figure 9.13).

The tone of the game is decidedly satirical and often downright silly. For instance, the town, named Spielburg, is ruled by Baron Stefan Von Spielburg, and thieves can attempt to practice their pick-lock skill by typing "pick nose." It's definitely not a game that takes itself seriously or puts on literary airs. This tongue-in-cheek humor runs throughout the game and the manual, which is titled *Famous Adventurer's Correspondence School*. The humor and shallow learning curve make the game ideal for novice CRPG fans, as well as those put off by repetitive "hack 'n slash" gameplay.

Hero's Quest originally implemented a simple text parser to carry on dialogues or perform actions—for instance, "ask about the brigands" and "climb tree." The rerelease replaces the text parser with an icon-based, mouse-controlled interface. Of course, some fans of the original version are outraged by this "enhancement," arguing that it severely limits their ability to interact with the world. Sierra responded by releasing both versions in its *Quest for Glory Anthology* in 1996. I suspect most modern gamers will prefer the later version.

The story and setting are culled from various fairytale sources, but the main objective is to fight the evil ogress Baba Yaga, who has put a curse on the land and seized the Baron's children. Monsters and bandits ravage the countryside. In addition to addressing these major concerns, the player also enters into optional sidequests.

Trial by Fire

The next game in the series is *Trial by Fire*, released in 1990. This time, the inspiration for the story and setting are pulled from various Middle Eastern myths and stories, particularly those of the Arabian Nights. After succeeding in Spielburg, the hero is now beckoned to Shapeir, a desert city threatened by four elementals. Shapeir's sister city, Raseir, is missing its emir. Of course, it's up to the player to set things right. If the player succeeds, Shapeir's sultan adopts him or her into the royal family. On that note, the townspeople are also cognizant of the hero's progress and heap on praise after each achievement.

Trial by Fire allows players to import their old character, but it's also easy to create a new one. There are still sidequests available for each class and opportunities for special distinctions. Each class does get a different final scene, which improves the game's replay value.

Like the first game, *Trial by Fire* is saturated with humor, puns, satire, and allusions to popular culture. There are a Cookie Monster doll, references to *The Maltese Falcon,* and a pair of X-Ray Specs. Although the X-Ray Specs are useless during most of the game, if the character dons them at a crucial moment, he can view a woman changing behind a curtain. Of course, the low-resolution graphics still leave much to the imagination, but it's an early example of the sort of pornographic Easter egg or hidden feature that would later arouse so much publicity in the *Grand Theft Auto: San Andreas* "Hot Coffee" controversy (Figure 9.14).

Perhaps a less welcome change is a time limit: the player must solve the game within the allotted thirty days. Furthermore, certain puzzles can be solved only on a given day; some critics felt this system was rather arbitrary and forced the game into a rigidly linear frame. Many CRPG developers have struggled with ways to integrate time and a calendar into their games; we've already touched on the issue a bit in our discussion of the later *Ultima* games, in which important nonplayer characters were available only at certain times. Most gamers seem to want to explore games at their leisure, without having to worry about a time limit or perform an

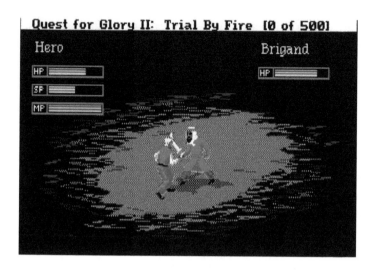

FIGURE 9.14 The second *Quest for Glory* game alters the combat mode significantly by moving the camera back and away from the action.

arbitrary sequence of activities before advancing to the next "day" or step in the plot. There's a fine line between realism and aggravation.

Wages of War

The third *Quest for Glory, Wages of War* (1992), is the first to make the transition into 256-color graphics, digitized sound effects, and an icon-based interface (Figure 9.15). In addition, an overworld map was added that simulates travel across great distances, during which the character is subject to random encounters. The game is based on Sierra's SCI1 (Sierra Creative Interpreter, Version 1), which is also used in several other Sierra adventure games of the era. Not surprisingly, all of these changes met with mixed reactions among fans, some calling the game the best and others the worst of the series. The criticisms are many but mostly emphasize the unchallenging puzzles and repetitive combat.

This game is set in the Kingdom of Tarna, an Africa-like environment. Two tribes are threatening to go to war with each other, and the hero is brought in as a peacemaker. After he's proven himself and gained membership in both tribes, they band together to fight the evil Demon Wizard.

Shadows of Darkness

The Coles seem to have recaptured some of their momentum with the fourth installment, *Shadows of Darkness*, released in 1993. One of the

FIGURE 9.15 *Wages of War* has superior audiovisuals to its prequels, but some felt it was a step backward in other departments.

most noticeable changes here is a new combat system. The perspective shifts to a side view during battles, making the experience even more arcade-like, though it's important to note that there is an option to let the computer fight the battles instead. The game was released on floppy disk and CD-ROM, the latter of which features voice acting (most notably John Rhys-Davies and Bill Farmer). Unfortunately, the game was plagued with bugs, though some were later patched and others can be worked around.

As the title implies, this is a much darker game than the rest in the series. The story takes place in Mordavia, a setting clearly derived from the much-storied Transylvania. Vampires and other monsters are plaguing the locals, and the hero must find a way to fend off the darkness threatening the land.

Dragon Fire

In 1998, Sierra released the fifth and final *Quest for Glory* game, *Dragon Fire* (Figure 9.16). Although the previous game had failed to generate good sales, fans pleaded with Sierra to let Lori Ann Cole put an end to the much-loved series. Unlike the previous games, *Dragon Fire* puts much more emphasis on conventional CRPG elements (such as a wider variety

"So, dear boy, the reason Fenris and I brought you here is this -- you are a Hero. And so, in the grand tradition of all Heroes, you need to go where you are most needed. That happens to be Silmaria at this moment."

Erasmus

Health
Stamina

FIGURE 9.16 The fifth and final game in the series, *Dragon Fire,* introduces a 3D engine, but fans and critics alike found much to complain about.

of arms, armor, and magic items). Critics tend to be kind to the game despite its dated graphics, bugs, uneven voice acting, and awkward combat interface. Much was made of Chance Thomas' musical score, which lasts over three hours.

The game is set in the island Kingdom of Silmaria. The king has been assassinated, and the wizard Erasmus has declared a contest to determine the next ruler. The hero is brought in as a contestant, the idea being that he will ferret out the assassin. The bigger picture involves the lost Kingdom of Atlantis and a captive dragon. The dragon has hitherto been prevented from savaging the countryside by some enchanted pillars. Surely, only a madman would try to free the beast, and, naturally, it's precisely such a madman the hero must outwit to win the game.

Despite the series' initial success and continued popularity, few other CRPG developers have followed the example set by *Quest for Glory.* More recent adventure games such as *Myst V: End of Ages* and *Dreamfall: The Longest Journey* offer no conventional CRPG elements, such as the all-important class and level system or experience points. Meanwhile, recent CRPGs still contain only the occasional puzzle or riddle, and JRPGs tend to prefer story and character development over combat and tactics. Perhaps the relative lack of successful adventure/CRPG hybrids today is a testament to the unique qualities of the *Quest for Glory* developers, who triumphed where so many others had failed.

The Coles are one of now several old-school developers who've crowd-funded a spiritual successor to their earlier classics. In their case it was *Hero-U: Rogue to Redemption,* which was finally released in 2018 after a tumultuous five-year development cycle. Although not technically part of the *Quest for Glory* series, nostalgic fans will find much to enjoy.

IN THE NEXT CHAPTER

In the past few chapters we've covered some of the finest CRPGs ever created. We saw an explosion of creativity and innovation between 1986 and 1988, and anyone remotely serious about the genre will recognize the landmark titles and famous series that succeeded during this period. However, as any student of history knows well, progress is neither linear nor orderly. Indeed, as we'll see in the next chapter, CRPGs with real-time 3D graphics were available as early as 1987, though they would remain on the cutting edge for several more years before reaching the masses. We'll also discuss some intriguing but nevertheless failed experiments, such as *Star Saga,* a unique attempt to merge tabletop with computer role-playing. And we'll discuss the rise of the Japanese RPG, made possible by Nintendo's and Sega's new game consoles, which were far more powerful than the humble units of the previous generation.

NOTE

1. See Dennis Owens' review of the game in the February 1989 issue of *Computer Gaming World.*

CHAPTER 10

Early Japanese Role-Playing Games

In the past few chapters we covered most of the major CRPG developers of the Golden Age, but there's more to the story than what was happening at SSI, Origin, Interplay, and New World Computing. Indeed, a little-known Californian studio named FTL Games was revolutionizing the genre with its acclaimed *Dungeon Master*, which we'll cover along with the subgenre it spawned in the next chapter. Here, however, we'll turn to Nintendo and Sega, whose new game consoles introduced millions of American gamers to the best-selling Japanese role-playing games, or JRPGs, of all time.

NINTENDO AND THE RISE OF JRPGs

Although this book is focused on the computer RPG, we can't ignore its younger brother, the console, who, as it turns out, grew up to be a much bigger boy. RPGs made specifically for consoles, such as the ***Advanced Dungeons & Dragons Cartridge*** for Mattel's Intellivision, appeared as early as 1982. Simple as it was, it was still much better received than SSI and U.S. Gold's *Advanced Dungeons & Dragons: Heroes of the Lance* (1988), an unmitigated disaster and one of the worst games for the NES. Fortunately, by the early 1990s ports of *Ultima III, Wizardry*, and *The Bard's Tale* were available for the Nintendo Entertainment System (NES), where they flourished in Japan and heavily influenced the first generation of JRPGs (Figure 10.1).

FIGURE 10.1   The NES version of *Ultima III* looks, feels, and sounds quite different than Origin's versions, but it was still warmly received.

For technical as well as marketing and cultural reasons, these console
ports are much different than the originals. In each case, they were ported
and localized by Japanese developers, as you can tell from their anime or
manga-style artwork. Some differences are subtler than others, but there
was also the need to adapt the interface for a controller. They also tend
to feature different soundtracks, often by well-regarded composers. The
music for the Japanese port of *Ultima III,* for example, was released as a
standard music CD, complete with lyrics. Here are some of them translated from the game's main theme, "Hitomi no Naifu":

ULTIMA love is

The knife of the eye

If it stares at me

I cannot move

However, by far the best JRPGs were not ports of established CRPGs, but
new franchises designed specifically for Japanese computers and consoles.
One of the earliest and most influential, *The Black Onyx,* was published
in 1984 for the NEC PC-8801, a Japanese computer. It was not made by a
Japanese developer, but rather Henk Rogers, a Dutch game designer more
famous for his role in bringing *Tetris* to the masses. Rogers didn't speak

Japanese, but he was familiar enough with the Japanese gaming scene to realize there was an opening for a good *Wizardry* clone in the language. Even though the resulting game doesn't compare favorably to the game it's based on, it's still a fun game and, more importantly, is one of the first RPGs in Japanese—and it soon spread to other computers and consoles in Japan. It sold well and undoubtedly spurred a demand for more (and better) games like it.

In the rest of this chapter, we'll focus on the first few waves of influential JRPGs that were translated and exported to America, including *The Legend of Zelda, Final Fantasy*, and *Dragon Warrior*, as well as a few later games for the Super NES (SNES) and Sega systems.

The first point to note is that the audience for JRPGs was and is orders of magnitude larger than that for CRPGs. There are at least two good reasons for their overwhelming numbers. First, the NES was powerful, accessible, relatively cheap, and had a massive library of spectacular games. It emerged from the ashes of the Video Game Crash to become an international cultural phenomenon, with the largest user base of any previous system. Even modest hits sold well over a million copies, whereas *Ultima III* for home computers was considered a runaway best seller with a mere 120,000!

Unfortunately, gamers who were raised exclusively on JRPGs tend to have a myopic view of the genre, possessing a fanatical zeal for *Final Fantasy* or *Zelda* but little knowledge of or appreciation for CRPGs. We can't tell you how many times we've come across a so-called games journalist breathlessly proclaiming *The Legend of Zelda* as not only the first but the best-ever RPG—and it's not even an RPG!

On the other side, it's all too common to hear a curmudgeonly CRPG fan dismissing JRPGs as simplistic or juvenile, with none of the depth or mental challenge of the real thing. Their most common complaint is that JRPGs are too linear, prodding the player from plot point to plot point; the player's ability to affect the narrative is tightly constrained. JRPG fans often counter by claiming that such constraints are necessary for proper character development and narrative structure, and the best JRPGs are celebrated for precisely these reasons. Of course, we can find endless counterexamples for each of these claims, but browse any RPG forum and you'll encounter these discussions.

Another often noted characteristic of JRPGs is their cartoonish aesthetics and humor. JRPGs often contain mature and even erotic themes, but these elements are intermixed with cute, comic-relief characters. Although common in Japanese popular culture, these intrusions of cuteness or *kawaisa*

FIGURE 10.2   Most JRPGs combine dark themes with painfully cute elements. Here we see one of the most iconic of these, the cheerfully smiling slime monsters from the *Dragon Warrior/Quest* series.

may strike Americans as bizarre. Others may glance at these cutesy aesthetics and conclude that JRPGs are games for children, though this is in many cases a grave misconception—Nintendo enforced a strict censorship policy that sanitized many adult elements prevalent in the Japanese versions. In any case, while it's true that many JRPGs avoid the artistic realism of *D&D*, preferring instead a heavily stylized look and feel, many are quite sophisticated and certainly not intended for children (Figures 10.2 and 10.3).

A true analysis of the difference between CRPGs and JRPGs would require an in-depth analysis of Japanese culture and language. We'd also need to familiarize ourselves with Japan's complex economic and political relationship with the United States. First and foremost, we'd want to play them in their original language, thus avoiding all the issues associated with poor translations and localization. As fascinating as this would be, it's well beyond the scope of this book and its authors. What we'll do instead is discuss the most well-known of the JRPGs that were translated into English and exported to North America.

The Legend of Zelda

There are few video game characters as internationally famous as Link, the boyish avatar of Nintendo's best-selling *The Legend of Zelda* (Figure 10.4). Designed by the celebrated developer Shigeru Miyamoto, *The Legend*

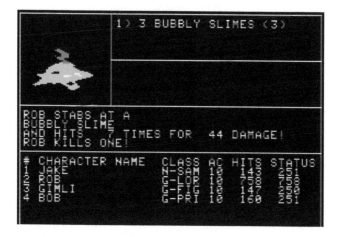

FIGURE 10.3 Here's the "bubbly slime" monster from *Wizardry* that likely inspired the smiling slime monsters of the *Dragon Warrior/Quest* series. I can't help but wonder if a translator misunderstood the way "bubbly" is being used here and sent the wrong description to the Japanese artists. In addition to being taken literally (having bubbles), it can also mean being full of cheerful high spirits. Hmm…

of Zelda sold tens of millions of copies and remains one of Nintendo's most lucrative and enduring franchises. This game and its sequels routinely show up in respectable lists of the best games ever made, and fans are happy to buy Nintendo's latest console just to play the next *Zelda*

FIGURE 10.4 This iconic screen from *The Legend of Zelda* is one of the most famous scenes in all of gaming. If you stare at it long enough, you may even hear the music.

installment. Link's image has been licensed for use on everything from sheet sets to breakfast cereal, and he's even starred in his own Saturday morning cartoon.

But *The Legend of Zelda* is not an RPG, at least according to our definition. Link doesn't gain experience points or level up, and success in combat depends more on the player's manual dexterity with the controller than tactics or strategy. Although Link can find items and weapons with magical properties, these function more like the power-up items in arcade games than the magical items in conventional CRPGs. For instance, when Link finds a boomerang, he can instantly use it as well as he ever will; success depends on the player's skill with a gamepad, not Link's mastery of ranged weapons.

On the other hand, *Zelda* shares several elements with CRPGs. The most obvious is the graphical layout, which is reminiscent of the top-down tile-based graphics of the early *Ultima* titles. There are also plenty of monster-infested dungeons for Link to explore—a defining characteristic of most CRPGs. Finally, the game's narrative is based on a classic fantasy quest to rescue the titular princess. As in most CRPGs (as well as adventure games), the player must complete a series of smaller, interconnected quests before the game can be won.

One important innovation introduced in *The Legend of Zelda* is an internal battery for saving the player's progress. Formerly, console gamers either had to start from scratch each time they played a game or deal with a cumbersome algorithmic password system. Since the typical RPG needs to track quite a few variables, these passwords (often numerical, but occasionally alphanumeric) could become quite long and difficult to manage, particularly when the codes had to be entered with a simple gamepad. The battery system eliminated the need for such codes and smoothed the way for longer and more complicated console games that could rival CRPGs.

The story behind *The Legend of Zelda* is its most clichéd aspect. As with Miyamoto's other classic, *Super Mario Bros.*, the mission is simply to rescue a helpless princess. Link must accomplish this task by finding the eight missing pieces of the Triforce of Wisdom, which he needs to enter the evil Ganon's headquarters in Death Mountain.

The Adventure of Link

The second *Zelda* game was released in the United States in 1987 and also earned Nintendo a fortune in sales (Figure 10.5). This game is a true JRPG, since Link now gains experience points, which the player can use to

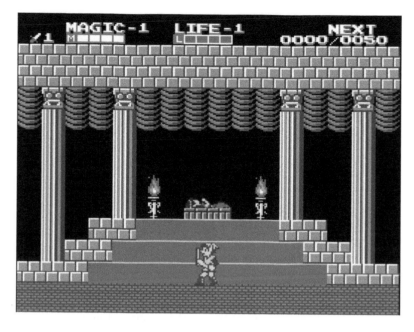

FIGURE 10.5 The second *Zelda* game sold well, but it isn't as fondly remembered as later games in the series. As you can see, some scenes switch to a side-scrolling mode that feels out of place to some fans of the original.

enhance Link's attack, magic, or life levels. The game features two graphical modes: a top-down perspective for overland travel and a side-scrolling perspective during combat and other scenes. The game also adds roaming nonplayer characters and random encounters, another borrowing from popular CRPGs of the time. Later *Zelda* games abandoned much of the RPG and side-scrolling elements, earning *The Adventure of Link* a reputation as a unique entry in the series. Again, the quest is to rescue the hapless Princess Zelda, who has been cursed with a sleeping spell.

A Link to the Past

The last *Zelda* game we'll discuss in this chapter is *A Link to the Past,* the third installment, released in 1991 for the SNES. Of course, the SNES has significantly enhanced graphics and memory capabilities compared to the NES, and *A Link to the Past* is one of the first games that really demonstrated this advantage (Figure 10.6). Nevertheless, the gameplay is more reminiscent of the first *Zelda* game than the second, abandoning the side-scrolling segments and class/level system. It does offer a far more sophisticated plot and storyline than the previous games, though Link is saddled

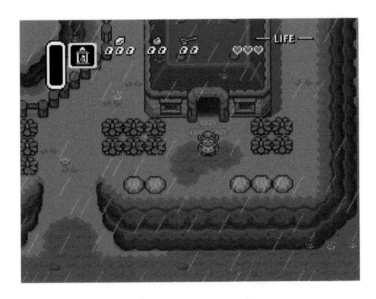

FIGURE 10.6   The *Zelda* series debuted on the SNES in a triumphant return to form in *A Link to the Past*. The game leveraged the improved audiovisual technology of the new console in many ways, including darkening effects to emphasize the seriousness of this storm.

yet again with the onerous task of getting Zelda out of trouble. This quest is less straightforward than before, however, with plenty of twists and turns to keep things interesting.

Most of the gameplay focuses on acquiring the quest items necessary to enter new areas, such as a hammer that can demolish otherwise impassable boulders. Although the game doesn't allow Link to gain levels, he can find special heart-shaped icons that boost his maximum hit points (also represented as hearts). There is also a basic magic system. If Link has the requisite magical item and enough magical energy (amassed by collecting green magic pots), he can cast spells. Like items, magic is primarily used to bypass obstacles. For instance, Link can use magical ether to stop the rain falling in the Swamp of Evil, thereby revealing the entrance to a dungeon.

Even if *The Legend of Zelda* games are often disqualified as true JRPGs, they have certainly influenced the genre. Indeed, as we'll see in later chapters, many Western developers and fans played these games extensively, and their views of what a CRPG should be were in large part determined by the sweaty-palmed gameplay of *Zelda*. As I'll argue in later chapters, the rise of action CRPGs is largely a response to this influence. However, unlike the *Final Fantasy* series, *Zelda* has remained exclusive to Nintendo's consoles; none have ever been legally ported to American computer platforms.

On a side note, relatively few *Zelda* fans are aware of three poorly conceived *Zelda* games made exclusively for Philips' short-lived CD-i platform. Nintendo licensed the *Zelda* franchise to Philips as part of a deal to develop a CD-ROM for its Super Famicom system, but later dropped the idea. Philips, however, took advantage of the licensing agreement to develop and release *Link: The Faces of Evil, Zelda: The Wand of Gamelon* (both 1993), and *Zelda's Adventure* (1994). These games have full-motion video sequences created by Russian animators, but they suffer from wretched voice acting, bad writing, and unpolished gameplay. They are wonderfully obscure today, though they're still great fodder for YouTube videos and command high prices on eBay.

The *Dragon Warrior* Series

Enix Corporation's *Dragon Warrior* was originally released in 1986 as *Dragon Quest* for the MSX computer platform, which was popular only in Japan (Figure 10.7). It wasn't until 1989 that the game finally arrived in America, having been translated and ported to the Famicom/NES. The name was then changed to *Dragon Warrior* to avoid legal problems with an unrelated American tabletop RPG also named *Dragon Quest*. Although phenomenally successful in Japan, the series hasn't fared as spectacularly here, though it's far from obscure. Unlike the *Zelda* series, the *Dragon Warrior/Quest* series is most definitely an RPG, with an experience point-based level system, a spell point-based magic system, and fairly standard *D&D*–style weapons and armor. *Dragon Warrior* seems to have laid the foundation for most other JRPGs, not surprising given its monumental sales record in its home country.

Dragon Warrior was clearly inspired by the early *Ultima* games. Much of the gameplay occurs from a top-down perspective and features colorful tile-based graphics. Combat, however, is turn-based and reminiscent of *Wizardry* or *The Bard's Tale,* with the attacking enemies shown in first-person. The player controls a single, predefined character, although this character can be assigned a new name.

This character is the descendant of the legendary Erdrick, a brave warrior who once used the Balls of Light to vanquish evil. Erdrick gave the Balls to King Lorick of Alefgard, who used them to protect the kingdom. The Balls were handed down to Lorick's heirs until they were stolen by the evil Dragonlord, who used them to sow chaos across the land. Of course,

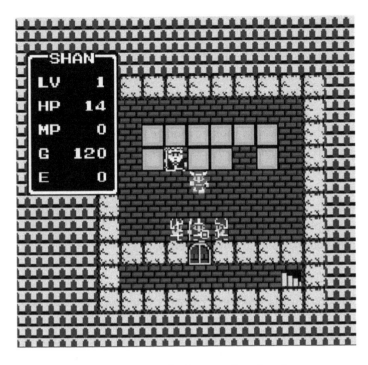

FIGURE 10.7 The *Dragon Warrior* (or *Dragon Quest*) series was more popular in Japan than the United States. Though it looks a bit like *The Legend of Zelda*, it plays quite differently, and is much closer in spirit to a CRPG.

it's up to the player to confront the Dragonlord and seize his Balls. If you've been chuckling as you read this summary, you may have some idea of the difficulties involved in translating a game intended for Japanese players to American audiences. No doubt, many of the game's subtleties are lost on the typical American gamer, and there's plenty of accidental humor.

There are other oddities that can perhaps be summed up by the word *kawaisa*, a term used by Chris Kohler (author of *Power Up!: How Japanese Video Games Gave the World an Extra Life*) to describe a marked Japanese tendency toward cuteness. For instance, one of the most characteristic aspects of the *Dragon Quest* series is a cheerful smiling slime, which looks about as threatening as Hello Kitty. For American gamers accustomed to serious CRPGs like *Pool of Radiance*, this style can be disconcerting. Such jarring juxtapositions of light and dark elements are common in Japanese popular culture; no doubt their absence would be sorely missed by Japanese gamers. In spite of these differences, plenty of American gamers fell in love with the style and came to prefer it.

FIGURE 10.8 The second *Dragon Warrior* game opens with a dramatic attack on the king and his daughter.

Dragon Warrior II

The second *Dragon Warrior* game for the NES arrived in 1990 (Figure 10.8). This time, the main character is not alone but can recruit up to two other adventurers: a princess who wields magic and a prince with fighting and magical abilities. Combat is also more complex: up to six enemies can attack at once (all the battles in the former game are one-on-one). The mission is of the "kill the evil wizard" variety. The game also features a battery backup system like the one seen in *The Legend of Zelda*.

Dragon Warrior III

The third installment, released in 1992, offered even more innovations to the original model (Figure 10.9). This time, the player can name the main character and select a gender. Better yet, now it's possible to recruit up to three other characters from six possible classes to form a party. These recruits can be swapped in and out as necessary. While most of the available classes are conventional, there are a few novelties: merchants, who can appraise items; goof-offs, who enjoy tremendous luck; and sages, a prestige class with skills in fighting and magic. The goof-off is the greatest challenge; the manual warns that he will only become more useless as the game progresses! Who could resist that?

This game is set before the action in the first game and amounts to another quest to "kill the fiend," this time a demonic being named Zoma.

FIGURE 10.9   If you really want to goof off in style, try the third *Dragon Warrior* installment for the NES. There's a big world to explore and no shortage of combat.

Solving the game requires fetching keys as well as six magical orbs. The gameworld is quite large and varied, with everything from Egyptian-style pyramids to arctic lands.

Dragon Warrior IV

The final *Dragon Warrior* game for the NES is the fourth installment, developed by Chunsoft and released in 1992 (Figure 10.10). It's probably the most epic in scope, with five distinct chapters. The player plays a different role in each of the first four chapters, switching among characters who unite in the fifth chapter, tying the seemingly disparate stories together. Other innovations include an artificial intelligence system for guiding the characters in battle, and a horse-drawn wagon that allows the player to choose which party members participate in battle. The wagon allows the player to have up to nine characters in the party, though only four can engage in combat. This wagon system seems to be the first of its type; at least, we don't know of anything similar in earlier JRPGs or CRPGs. Although the formal classes are gone, the characters still seem to more or less fit neatly into traditional categories (soldier, wizard, and so on).

The storyline and plot of the game are more sophisticated than in the previous *Dragon Warrior* games, and the characters are far better developed, with their own motivations that change over time. Nevertheless,

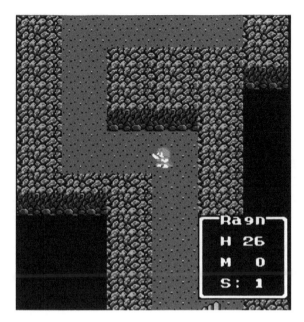

FIGURE 10.10   Exploring a dungeon in *Dragon Warrior IV*, a classic JRPG for the NES.

there's quite a bit of hack 'n slash gameplay, since the party will need to gain high levels to keep up with their enemies—who quickly increase in power as the game progresses.

The fourth game is often considered the best of the NES *Dragon Warrior* titles, even if it failed to win over audiences in the United States as well as it did in Japan. Apparently, sales were so below expectations here that Enix failed to release the fifth or sixth installments in America; these shores didn't see another *Dragon Warrior* game until 2001's *Dragon Warrior VII* for the Sony PlayStation. Even so, the influence of this series on the genre is powerful, though indirect. If nothing else, other Japanese developers were surely intimately familiar with the series, since it posed such substantial competition for them in the Japanese market. Furthermore, the series established many of the conventions that became standard in other JRPGs, particularly the simple (yet intuitive) gameplay and focus on linear storytelling with well-developed characters.

The Perennial *Final Fantasy*

Another groundbreaking JRPG is *Final Fantasy,* a game developed by Hironobu Sakaguchi of Square (later Square Enix) in 1987, though it didn't

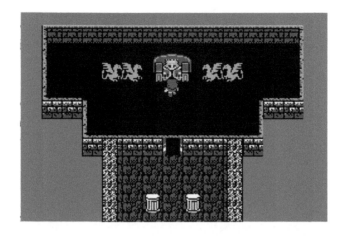

FIGURE 10.11 The first *Final Fantasy* game for the NES appears to be a straightforward rescue-the-princess story at first, but the plot soon thickens. Shown here is the party (represented by a single lead character) interacting with the king. Any similarities to a certain Lord British are purely coincidental.

debut in North America until 1990 (Figure 10.11). Unlike the *Dragon Warrior/Quest* series, *Final Fantasy* was a smash hit in the United States, where it remains one of the most highly regarded JRPG series. Indeed, it's hard to exaggerate the adulation heaped on the series by its legions of staunchly loyal fans. Like *The Legend of Zelda*, it spawned a lucrative franchise of licensed merchandise and spinoffs. It even served as the basis for an ambitious but unsuccessful feature film—*Final Fantasy: The Spirits Within* (2001). Despite this hiccup, the franchise is still alive and strong today.

The first *Final Fantasy* is a fairly straightforward hack 'n slash game with a heavy emphasis on battles with random encounters and exploring a large overland gameworld. The player controls a party called the Light Warriors, composed of four adventurers. There are six classes available: fighter, thief, black belt (monk), and three types of mage (red, black, and white). Each class can also be upgraded to a prestige class and gain new abilities. For instance, the warrior can become a knight, who can cast low-level White Magic spells. Most of the game is shown from a top-down perspective, using tile-based graphics similar to those seen in the *Ultima* series.

Combat is turn-based and offers an unusual screen mode, with the player's four characters lined up vertically on the right and the enemies in a larger window on the left. During each turn, the player selects an appropriate action for each character and a target. One nuisance in this combat system is that if the selected monster is killed before the round is over, any other characters directed to attack it will lose their turns. The order of attack is random.

The game's plot seems to poke fun at the typical fantasy game. At first, the game seems to be yet another "rescue the princess" quest, but that mission is completed very early. The bulk of the game is actually spent hunting down four magical orbs needed to restore order and defeat Chaos himself. As Kohler puts it, "*Final Fantasy* is about much more than saving the princess. Compared to the adventure that is about to take place, saving a princess is merely child's play and prologue." Like some of the *Ultima* and *Might and Magic* games, the fantasy soon gives way to sci-fi elements, with robots, airships, and time travel. To succeed, the party must solve dozens of smaller quests, and, as in most JRPGs, it's absolutely necessary to talk to every character in the game and take careful notes in addition to surviving combat (Figure 10.12).

The first *Final Fantasy* is usually considered the weakest in terms of gameplay. The main problem is an inordinately high frequency of repetitive and tedious random encounters, which make the game unwinnable by all but the most persistent players. Despite this flaw, it spawned a massively influential franchise.

An often told story is that the game was called *Final Fantasy* because the developer assumed it was the company's last project; it was facing bankruptcy. Another story is that it was the designer himself, Sakaguchi,

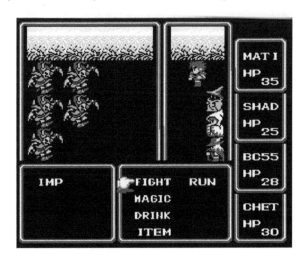

FIGURE 10.12 Shown here is one of the many—and we do mean many—random encounters you'll face in your struggle to complete *Final Fantasy*.

who was ready to quit the industry and go back to college; this would be his final game. Sakaguchi claims that both these stories are false; the developer simply liked the way the name sounded and wanted something that could be abbreviated *FF,* which also has a nice ring to it in Japanese. Indeed, the original plan was to call it *Fighting Fantasy,* but Sakaguchi learned that name had already been claimed and needed to change it. Other developers associated with the series have said other things, but I'll take Sakaguchi's word for it.

Final Fantasy II

Here's where things get a bit confusing. Technically, *Final Fantasy II,* released in the United States in 1991 for the SNES, is not the second but the fourth game in the series (Figure 10.13). However, the second and third games were released only in Japan, and Square apparently thought it better to represent the next international release as a direct sequel to the first game. Later releases reverted to the Japanese numbering, adding further to the confusion. For our purposes, we'll use the original American titles and ignore the Japanese-only releases unless otherwise noted.

Final Fantasy II offers quite a few enhancements to the original engine, the most obvious being the improved audiovisuals made possible by the

FIGURE 10.13 *Final Fantasy II* on the SNES doesn't take long to get into murky ethical territory.

16-bit SNES platform. Other key changes include a five- rather than a four-character party, and the Active Time Battle (ATB). ATB blurs the boundaries between real-time and turn-based combat in an interesting way. Simply put, the characters and monsters need time to recover after each action, but after this period of recovery, they can immediately perform another action. Thus, the player must think quickly during combat, rapidly selecting options as soon as a party member is ready, rather than sitting back waiting for the next turn. The system proved quite popular with gamers and has been widely used in other JRPGs (Figure 10.14).

The second game is much more character- and plot-driven than the first and carefully balanced. There are twelve characters available, each with a preset class, personality, and role to play in the carefully contrived and rather impressive plot. The story follows the actions of a brave young captain named Cecil, who has lately begun questioning the motives of his king, who seems to have traded virtue for megalomania. Like the previous game, *Final Fantasy II* contains a mixture of fantasy and sci-fi elements— such as dwarves piloting tanks and a race of moon men.

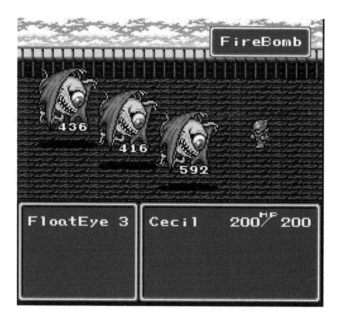

FIGURE 10.14 The opening sequence demonstrates a battle. The audiovisuals are quite a leap forward from the previous game. Though the setup might look similar to the combat system from the first game, the Active Time Battle mechanic gives it a much different feel.

Final Fantasy II was a rousing success, ensuring the series a solid foothold in America. Critics seemed to find no fault, heaping on the accolades and awards. The title regularly shows up on "Best Ever" lists, despite some glaring problems with the English translation.

Final Fantasy III

The last *Final Fantasy* game we'll cover in this chapter is the third game, which is actually the sixth in Japan. *Final Fantasy III* was released in 1994 for the SNES. The game engine retains most of the conventions established by *Final Fantasy II* but has a more flexible character development system. Although the characters are pregenerated with their own personalities and fixed classes, you can alter them later. Furthermore, you can choose which spells the magic-users will learn rather than have them automatically assigned.

The game's story is even more sophisticated and nuanced than in the previous game, with a long list of main quests as well as a dozen or so optional missions. The game is set a millennium after the War of the Magi, a magical war of apocalyptic proportions that destroyed much of the world and purged magic from the land. Now, technology reigns, though a power-hungry emperor seeks to revive magic, certainly not for virtuous purposes. The players soon find themselves entangled in a web of dangerous intrigue, with many unpredictable twists and turns.

Final Fantasy III is often considered one of the finest (if not *the* finest) of the series, most notably for the intricate storyline and sharply developed characters. It's certainly an impressive feat in terms of polish and attention to detail; even the soundtrack is classic, having been rearranged for a professional orchestra and released as an album, *Final Fantasy VI Grand Finale,* composed by Nobuo Uematsu and arranged by Shiro Sagisu and Tsuneyoshi Saito.

Secret of Mana

Another popular JRPG by Square is *Secret of Mana,* released for the SNES in 1993 (Figure 10.15). It has real-time, action-style combat sequences instead of a turn-based or ATB system. It also allows up to three simultaneous players, though the third player needs a special "Super Multitap" accessory. A final noteworthy innovation is an icon-based ring, or radial menu, that appears around the character during combat. A similar contrivance shows up in later games, including Troika's CRPG *The Temple of Elemental Evil* (2003).

MATT:Whoa! What's a
Rabite doing in a place
like this?

50/50

FIGURE 10.15 The *Secret of Mana* is another much-loved classic JRPG for the SNES. It's often lighthearted, but it has a serious, well-developed story, great characters, and fantastic music.

Combat in *Secret of Mana* is arcade-style, comparable to *The Legend of Zelda* games. A stamina bar located at the bottom of the screen shows the character's hit points. Characters gain levels in weapons and magical powers depending on how much they use them. Characters also gain more powerful spells or weapon attacks as they gain experience, though the efficacy of these powers is counterbalanced by mandatory recovery periods (the more powerful the special attack, the longer the charge-up period).

In *Secret of Mana*, the player controls a young village boy who finds a sword mired in a river bottom. Unfortunately for the boy, the sword summons a horde of vile monsters, and the villagers expel the boy from the village. He is then assisted by a knight named Jema, who sends him on a quest to repair the sword and take control of the eight Seeds of Mana. Of course, solving the game will require exploring and gathering clues from the many characters roaming the Land of Mana.

Some critics complain about the poor quality of the English translation. It also has more kawaisa, or cute, elements than Square's other games, such as a mission to rescue Santa Claus. There are also problems with the AI engine, particularly with pathfinding (the computer-controlled characters have a hard time navigating around obstacles), and the hit detection is poor, especially for a game with so much focus on action. These issues aren't trivial, but there's much more to like than dislike about this game. In any case, one thing that everyone agrees on is the high quality of the soundtrack. It was composed by Hiroki Kikuta and routinely shows up in compilations of the greatest video game soundtracks.

Chrono Trigger

Chrono Trigger, a game released by Square for the SNES in 1995, isn't part of the official *Final Fantasy* series, though it is based on the same game engine and gameplay (Figure 10.16). It's worth mentioning simply because of its outstanding quality; it's one of the most carefully polished JRPGs in existence, and that's saying something. It was designed by a dream team of experienced JRPG developers, some from *Final Fantasy,* and others from *Dragon Warrior/Quest.* It offers multiple endings, sidequests that relate

FIGURE 10.16   Ah, *Chrono Trigger.* It's by far my favorite of the SNES-era JRPGs, with charming characters, a rich story, great audiovisuals, and superb music. What else could you ask for?

directly to the plot, and a captivating soundtrack. It's still one of the most popular JRPGs of all time.

One slight but notable innovation in the ATB combat system is that the battles occur directly on the exploration screen, and characters can team up for special cooperative attacks. Since the player will likely be adventuring with several different combinations of characters, the possibilities for coordinated attacks are vast. Another nice touch is that the player sees enemies at a distance rather than stumble upon random encounters. These innovations create a highly intuitive and compelling battle system.

However, the main appeal of this game is the superbly developed characters and intricate narrative based on a trek through time. The player's character, aptly named Chrono, must travel through the past, present, and future, fulfilling quests and eventually confronting a terrifically powerful foe who seeks to destroy time itself. The game also boasts excellent graphics and a superb score. In short, it's a masterpiece of design and is as playable today as it was in 1995. If you haven't played it, I strongly suggest you correct that error as soon as possible. Square released a sequel called *Chrono Cross* in 2000, a PlayStation game that dazzled critics and gamers with its charm and highly addictive gameplay.

Super Mario RPG

One of the most unusual of the 16-bit era JRPGs is *Super Mario RPG: Legend of the Seven Stars,* a game developed by Square and published by Nintendo in 1996 (Figure 10.17). As the title suggests, the game is based on the internationally famous characters popularized in the *Super Mario Bros.* games, but it differs tremendously in terms of gameplay. It sports some of the best graphics ever seen on the SNES, but its late release date allowed Sony's PlayStation (released a year earlier) to steal much of its thunder.

Super Mario RPG is an interesting hybrid of action and tactical combat. Much of the gameplay is familiar to fans of the other *Mario* games, such as precision jumping sequences. However, the game also incorporates a turn-based combat system reminiscent of Square's *Final Fantasy* or *Chrono Trigger* games. The combat sequences include action elements, such as rapidly tapping a button to increase the damage of an attack. Square did a fine job integrating the two types of gameplay, and the polished graphics and smooth controls make *Super Mario RPG* a great deal of fun.

However, we should take a moment to consider just how alien a game such as *Super Mario RPG* appears when placed alongside nearly any of

FIGURE 10.17 A JRPG based on Nintendo's *Super Mario* franchise still seems improbable, but the production values are among the best the SNES has to offer.

the CRPGs we've discussed in this book. Even if we stick strictly to action CRPGs, such as *Diablo* and *Dungeon Siege,* the differences are profound. For the most part, CRPGs tend to be dark, gritty, and serious, with realistic aesthetics and over-the-top violence. By contrast, games like *Super Mario RPG* enjoy broader appeal, yet demonstrate that many of the addictive and compelling qualities of CRPGs, such as tactical combat and point-based leveling systems, are universal, and needn't be confined to traditional swords and sorcery or sci-fi settings. Indeed, we see this tendency taken even further in Square's later *Kingdom Hearts* (2002) and *Kingdom Hearts 2* (2005), games that juxtapose *Final Fantasy* and Walt Disney characters in a manner that is downright surreal.

Sega's JRPG: *Phantasy Star*

After spending so long discussing JRPGs for the NES and SNES, it's only fair to consider *Phantasy Star,* a long-lived JRPG designed for Sega's line of game consoles. The first of these debuted in 1988 for the Sega Master System.

Phantasy Star has much in common with the *Ultima* series. For instance, overland travel is shown in top-down perspective and utilizes colorful tile-based graphics, whereas dungeons are rendered in first-person with monochrome graphics. Combat and conversation segments are shown in first-person, with pop-up windows for displaying text. The game also follows *Ultima*'s example of blending sci-fi with fantasy elements. It's also notable for being one of the few JRPGs (or CRPGs, for that matter) to put the player in the role of a female—a fifteen-year-old named Alis.

Phantasy Star has its share of kawaisa. Alis' first companion is a talking yellow cat named Myau. She can fight with her claws, cast healing spells, and disarm traps. Instead of quaffing healing potions, characters wolf down burgers and colas. However, the storyline veers into darker territory. When the game begins, Alis comes upon Nero, her dying brother, who has just been brutally attacked by robotcops. The robotcops are the storm troopers of a tyrannical and warped king named Lassic, who was once a fine ruler but succumbed to hubris in his mad quest for immortality. Alis' brother tells her to seek out a strong warrior named Odin, who apparently has some means of helping Alis avenge her brother and restore prosperity to the solar system.

Despite its unusually high price ($69, or $125.34 in 2008 dollars), the game is one of the better-known entries in the Sega Master System's game library. Along with *The Legend of Zelda,* it was one of the earliest cartridge games to feature a battery backup system to record saved games.

Phantasy Star II

The second *Phantasy Star* was released in 1989 for Sega's new Genesis platform, the 16-bit descendant of the older Master System (Figure 10.18). Besides updated graphics and audio, the designers made some important changes to the interface and gameplay. It again retailed for a staggering $69, but it was quite popular among Genesis gamers, and critics gushed with praise. As with most critically acclaimed JRPGs, the main draw is a worthwhile plot and multifaceted characters. It also steers bravely into more mature themes than most JRPGs, incorporating the death of beloved characters and raising issues about the future of technological societies. With *Phantasy Star II,* we've moved well beyond the trite rescue the princess or fetch the orb storylines and into compelling dramatic territory. These features help explain why *Phantasy Star II* is so often hailed as the best JRPG for the Genesis.

One noticeable change from the first game is the lack of first-person, 3D dungeons and a revamping of the combat screen. During a battle, the camera is stationed behind the party, who appears in a horizontal line facing the enemy. The backdrop is a simple grid shown in perspective.

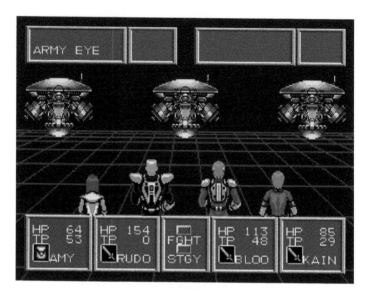

FIGURE 10.18   Behold *Phantasy Star II*, the finest JRPG for the Sega Genesis.

Though we can't see the characters' faces, it still feels more intimate than the abstract vantage points of *Final Fantasy* or *Phantasie*.

Like many other JRPGs, the player must assemble a party from a cast of premade characters, though these can be swapped in and out of the party as desired. Another innovation is a technique system based on technique points. Techniques are *Phantasy Star II*'s magic system, though there seems to be an effort here to supply at least a suggested scientific rationale for their effects. For instance, Zan Magics creates an atmospheric vacuum, sucking the air out of an enemy and crushing it.

The game is set a full millennium after the first game. This time, the player takes on the role of Rolf, an agent sent to investigate an accident at the Bio-Systems Lab. The accident seems to be responsible for the sudden appearance of Biomonsters, which now threaten the planet. Of course, there's much more to do here than squash a few monsters, and it takes time and substantial skill to solve the game.

Generations of Doom

The third game was published in 1992, but critical reactions were (and remain) mixed. The problem is that *Generations of Doom* differs strikingly from the first two games, being set primarily in a medieval world and lacking the solid character development of the second game. On the other hand, it's a highly ambitious game with a unique plot device. Instead of controlling a single character or group, the player is put in charge of subsequent generations of heroes. In each case, the player is allowed to choose one of two spouses for his character, and the choice will affect which characters appear in the next generation.

If nothing else, this setup should have ensured a high replay value, but, alas, the huge cast comes at the cost of character development. Instead of the sharply defined and multifaceted characters we saw in *Phantasy Star II,* we get generic personalities with little enduring appeal.

Some critics disliked the pronounced Westernized style of the art and graphics, which seem to have abandoned the more heavily stylized anime art and kawaisa elements of the previous games. Only the character portraits maintain the original style, aesthetically clashing with the rest of the game. Another upset for some fans is the lackluster combat screen, which abandons the waist-up rear view of the party, opting instead for a rather plain window with text and a few small icons. For these reasons the game is often considered the black sheep of the series, though it doesn't lack defenders.

The basic gist of the game involves two feuding peoples, the Orakians and the Layans. The Orakians are a nonmagical race with physical strength, whereas the Layans are weaker but more proficient with techniques (the *Phantasy Star* equivalent of magic). The feud lends itself well to the generational setup of the narrative, since the player can decide whether to allow interracial marriages. There are several multiple endings that depend on which character the player ends up with in the last iteration.

The End of the Millennium

The last *Phantasy Star* game released for the Genesis is *The End of the Millennium,* published in 1994 (Figures 10.19 and 10.20). The game was originally intended for Sega's new CD-ROM add-on and was a very ambitious project that planned to offer first-person dungeons and full motion video cut scenes. However, poor sales of the Sega CD peripheral convinced Sega to scrap that idea, salvaging the rest of the design for a regular Genesis game.

Phantasy Star IV returns to the unique battle mode of the second game, showing the backs of the party members from the waist up as they faced their opponents. The game goes a bit further, though, by adding colorful backgrounds rather than relying on the gridlike environment seen during battles in the second game. The colorful backgrounds add greatly to the realism. Combat is further enhanced with a macro system, which involves

FIGURE 10.19 *Phantasy Star IV: The End of the Millennium* started off as an ambitious game for the Sega CD, but that idea was canceled. However, the "salvaged" game is still a hell of a game. It uses a dramatic comic book–style format for cut scenes.

special coordinated attacks involving multiple characters. We saw a similar system used in Square's *Chrono Trigger* (1995).

The game is set 1,000 years after the events in *Phantasy Star II* and follows the adventures of a young bounty hunter named Chaz. Chaz and his companions must find a way to save Algo, a solar system threatened by a malfunctioning computer network. The plot thickens as the story progresses, eventually culminating in a fantastic confrontation

FIGURE 10.20 A combat screen. Note the "MACR" option; the game engine is sophisticated enough to let you create macros to optimize your play style.

with a seemingly immortal being of great evil. The fourth game has better developed characters than the third; the generational system, while interesting, simply hasn't fared well among fans of the series. This game takes players back to great drama with characters gamers can care about.

The End of the Millennium is widely hailed as the best game of the series. Unfortunately, it appeared rather late in Genesis' career, and Sony unveiled its Sony PlayStation a year later, devouring its market share. There's little doubt that it would have been much more successful had it been released a year earlier, or if the original plans for the ambitious Sega CD version had come to pass. Nevertheless, it's a great JRPG and a must-play for Sega Genesis fans.

Concluding Thoughts on Golden Age JRPGs

For millions upon millions of gamers, JRPGs such as *Final Fantasy* and *Phantasy Star* are what come to mind when someone mentions role-playing games. Younger generations had better access to Nintendo's and Sega's game consoles than home computers, which were more expensive and difficult to operate. For these legions of gamers, heavily stylized art and linear, character-driven stories continue to define the genre. For these gamers, kids with spiky blue hair, talking kitties, and smiling blobs of slime are what fantasy role-playing is all about.

As gamers who admittedly prefer CRPGs, we're happy playing both. That said, it's doubtful that we'll ever experience a JRPG the way Japanese gamers might. Even with a superb Japanese-to-English translation, we're still missing out on some of the cultural references and subtleties of the dialog. Nevertheless, I appreciate a fine game when I see it. *Chrono Trigger, Final Fantasy III,* and *Phantasy Star IV* are exquisitely crafted games that deserve their reputations for excellence.

The staggering success of JRPGs in the United States moved several prominent CRPG developers, including Richard Garriott, to incorporate more action mechanics into their games. As we'll see, their results were often mixed. Meanwhile, although they borrowed heavily from CRPGs to get the die rolling, as it were, JRPG designers soon went their own way, leaving these models behind and boldly experimenting.

Indeed, the only Western series that seemed to have any staying power in Japan was *Wizardry*. Various Japanese developers acquired the rights to make several different spinoff series and even an MMORPG called *Wizardry Online*. The majority of these games are only in Japanese, though a few, such as *Wizardry Chronicles,* have been translated into English and unofficially released by fans.

For the most part, Japanese gamers have tended to prefer Japanese-made games, and they certainly have no shortage of great JRPGs to choose from. That said, however, *The Elder Scrolls V: Skyrim* was granted a perfect score by *Famitsu,* a prominent Japanese video game magazine—the first Western game to earn this coveted distinction. Whether this was an anomaly or a sign of change is hard to say, but it's certainly encouraging.

CHAPTER 11

Dungeon Master and the Rise of Real-Time 3D

You might find it difficult to imagine a time when real-time 3D games were far and few between. With a few notable exceptions such as *Dungeons of Daggorath* (1982) and **Alternate Reality: The City** (1985), the great majority of early first-person CRPGs were turn-based. If your character or party doesn't move, neither does anything else in the gameworld. A few, such as *The Bard's Tale,* did generate random encounters even if the player was away from the keyboard, giving the impression that the monsters weren't just sitting on their thumbs waiting for adventurers to stumble across them. However, such tricks are no substitute for a truly persistent gameworld in which monsters and other characters are always moving around independently of the player.

Unfortunately, persistent gameworlds posed quite a challenge for early developers, since most personal computers lacked the requisite memory and processor speed. Real-time 3D graphics were certainly possible on these machines, but they came at the expense of colors and textures, leaving a great deal of the gameworld to the imagination. However, by the late 1980s, a growing percentage of computer gamers had replaced their 8-bit machines with Atari ST and Commodore Amiga computers. These machines offered better graphics, sound, memory, and storage options—assets not lost on game developers, who saw the growing demand for games that showed off the impressive new capabilities of these new systems.

REAL-TIME 3D GAMES

Dungeon Master

FTL Games responded early and decisively to the challenge, releasing its classic hit *Dungeon Master* in 1987 (Figure 11.1). *Dungeon Master* spread like wildfire on the Atari ST, and it remains the most successful game ever released for that platform. The game struck gold a second time after it was ported to the rival Commodore Amiga platform in 1988, again dropping jaws and sending hordes of gamers scrambling to their local game shop. Contemporary reviews sound like overhyped ad copy. One reads, "This has to be the most amazing game of all time, anywhere, ever—the best game we've ever seen."[1] Even today, some twenty years after its initial release, *Dungeon Master* is still enjoyed by thousands of fans, many of whom flock to online message boards to compare notes and swap stories about their favorite CRPG.

But what was it about *Dungeon Master* that explains its enviable success? Though it was hailed for its innovative use of sound and a storyline by a professional novelist (Nancy Holder), for our purposes the most significant feature is the game's interface and real-time gameplay. The bulk of the screen is composed of a first-person view of the party's current

FIGURE 11.1   FTL Games' *Dungeon Master* blew away Amiga and Atari ST owners with an incredibly immersive new style. The developers recommend wearing stereo headphones to experience the full benefit of its directional sound.

perspective. This screen is updated in real time as the player explores the dungeon, much like a modern first-person shooter game but with grid-based movement; the camera snaps rather than pans from vantage point to vantage point as you turn or move. On the top of the main window are four boxes showing the current status of the four characters, the items they're holding, and their relative position (e.g., who is in front and back). The rest of the screen is dedicated to the magic system, attack mode, and directional buttons. Although the directional keys are a bit cumbersome on the ST version (players must click on them with the mouse), later versions allow all movement (including rotating) to be executed from the keyboard.

We should note that as impressive as *Dungeon Master* is for its time, it's not truly 3D. Rather, it relies on an old trick called pseudo-3D or 2.5D. Simply put, this means that the game uses flat or 2D sprites and tiles rather than true 3D objects. True 3D CRPGs with a dedicated Z-axis wouldn't come along until much later.

What *Dungeon Master* does offer is real-time combat. When the party is attacked, you have to work frantically to issue orders (i.e., attack, cast a spell, quaff a potion), always considering how long it will take each character to perform and recover (we could compare this system to Square's later Active Time Battle system). Since very few of these actions can be automated or prepared beforehand, you need rapid reflexes and considerable endurance to complete the game. Many gamers suffering from carpal tunnel syndrome today may well have *Dungeon Master* to blame!

Rather than let you build your own characters, *Dungeon Master* lets you resurrect heroes who died on their earlier excursions. The available classes are male and female ninjas, priests, wizards, fighters; the characters are either dedicated to one profession (in which case they are "journeymen"), or multiclassed. As usual, the more a classes a character takes on, the less proficient they are in each—but the tradeoff is greater versatility. Iaido Ruyito, for example, is a male ninja with fighting and priest skills. As you can see in Figure 11.2, each character also comes equipped with appropriate gear. Ruyito gets a karategi uniform and a samurai sword.

Despite its action-based combat, *Dungeon Master* is far from a simple clickfest. Most noticeably, the game's magic system is complex and arguably more logical than simple point-based systems (*The Bard's Tale*) or slot systems (*Pool of Radiance, Wizardry*). In *Dungeon Master,* players cast spells by stringing together runes. Although only certain predetermined sequences actually have effects, you can determine the potency of any spell

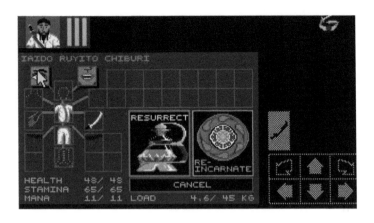

FIGURE 11.2 Let's hope our new friend Chiburi has learned from his past mistakes!

(or potion) and subsequently how much magical energy to expend in the process. Furthermore, although any character can try to cast a spell, only practiced mages and priests can pull off really effective feats of magic. However, the manual doesn't include a magical recipe book, so you have to either find recipes sprinkled throughout the vast dungeon, experiment in a trial-and-error fashion, or consult a hint book. In any case, it's a versatile if somewhat daunting spell system for novices. A comparable system shows up in Event Horizon's *The Summoning* (1992) and Dynamix's *Betrayal at Krondor* (1993).

Adding to the real-time aspect is the need to provide food and water for the characters—a gameplay element seen in many earlier games, including *Ultima* and *Might and Magic*. Thankfully, the need for sustenance in *Dungeon Master* is infrequent enough to avoid being a nuisance. As in *Rogue*, hungry characters can gobble down the carcasses of many of the slain monsters, though it's best to collect the turkey legs and other foods conveniently left lying about the dungeon corridors (one wonders about the sanitation, though). Navigating those many corridors is itself quite challenging. Particularly infamous are the rotating traps that spin the party and bewilder the player. It's well worth hunting down the compass, a rather essential item secreted away in the dungeon.

Chaos Strikes Back

Considering the success of the first *Dungeon Master*, one wonders why FTL took a full two years to follow up with *Chaos Strikes Back*. Although details are hard to come by, there seems to have been substantial production delays. One contemporary reviewer quipped, "The game has been due out 'in two weeks' for over a year and half."[2]

When *Chaos Strikes Back* was at last released, it was marketed as "expansion set #1," though no further expansions were ever offered. Usually, expansion sets require the original program to run, but this was not the case with *Chaos Strikes Back*—though the difficulty level is enough to stop all but the most determined new players at the gate. Indeed, even veterans find the game exceptionally challenging. FTL seems to have anticipated a negative reaction to the game's difficulty and included a Hint Oracle, which offers hints based on the party's position in the dungeon.

Chaos Strikes Back uses the same game engine as the first game, though with some new graphics and monsters. There's a greater emphasis on puzzle solving and navigation; in general, the game makes what was already hard about the first game even harder. Players can either create new characters or import their old ones, editing their portraits and names using the included Utility Disk. In any case, the party begins the game without equipment or supplies. Their mission is to find and destroy four pieces of a magical ore called corbum, which Lord Chaos needs to draw power. Naturally, the corbum was hidden deep within a booby-trapped and monster-infested dungeon and can be disposed of only in the magical Forge of Fulya.

Considering the unprecedented success of the first game, it's no surprise that *Chaos Strikes Back* sold well initially. However, the game's extraordinary difficulty and long production delay probably explain why it's not as well loved as its predecessor.

The Legend of Skullkeep

The last of the *Dungeon Master* games, *Dungeon Master II: The Legend of Skullkeep,* appeared in 1994 for the Sega CD, and a year later for DOS and Macintosh. Although FTL was an American company, it decided to first release the game in Japan, targeting the PC-9821, FM Towns, and Sega CD platforms. Again, FTL seems to have been stymied by production delays, and by the game's release date had still barely managed to enhance the aged game engine with an automapping system and shops for buying equipment. The game met with harsh criticism, especially of its graphics and gameplay. Although the first *Dungeon Master* is a fine game, it was really the wow factor of the graphics that catapulted it into the mainstream. Lacking impressive graphics and the enthusiastic support of the Atari ST community, *The Legend of Skullkeep* was doomed from the start.

Eye of the Beholder

SSI was one of the first publishers to follow in the wake of FTL's *Dungeon Master,* releasing Westwood Associates' *Eye of the Beholder* in 1991 for the Commodore Amiga and DOS platforms (Figure 11.3). *Eye of the Beholder* is the first in what would become a trilogy of Black Box games, so named after their distinctive black packaging that otherwise resembled the highly successful Gold Box CRPGs.

We've already encountered Westwood in previous chapters: It was responsible for porting several popular Apple II CRPGs to other platforms and thus was exposed to a wide variety of design strategies. In 1988 it released its first original CRPG, a sci-fi game called *Mars Saga* for the Commodore 64, enhanced and rereleased as *Mines of Titan* for DOS. These games are much in the vein of the Gold Box series, with first-person exploration and turn-based, top-down combat. The year 1988 also saw the release of one of Westwood's most popular CRPGs, *Battletech: The Crescent Hawk's Inception,* a game based on the well-known *Battletech* wargaming franchise. We'll talk more about this game later.

Westwood's *Eye of the Beholder* games are set in TSR's Forgotten Realms, the same popular universe used in *Pool of Radiance* and its sequels. As in *Dungeon Master,* the player controls a party of four characters—however,

FIGURE 11.3 Westwood's fantastic *Eye of the Beholder* game applies the *Dungeons & Dragons* ruleset to *Dungeon Master*–style gameplay, and the results are glorious.

in *Eye of the Beholder,* two nonplayer characters can also join the party. Another key difference is that players create their own characters rather than select them from a Hall of Heroes, as in *Dungeon Master.* Further differences are a built-in compass and a slot-style spell system with over forty spells. Players select which spells they wish their mages to memorize or clerics to pray for, then camp until the characters are done completing the task; it's basically the same system seen in the Gold Box games.

The story in the first game concerns a mysterious evil presence underneath the city of Waterdeep. Little is known about the nature of this evil, but the name Xanathar seems relevant. Naturally, the characters are instructed to investigate, but a sudden cave-in leaves them stranded in the sewers beneath the city. The only way out of the sewers is through the dungeon, which, of course, is crawling with monsters and loaded with booby-traps.

The Legend of Darkmoon

The second *Eye of the Beholder* game, *The Legend of Darkmoon* (1991), adds outdoor areas and focuses more on plot and dialog with other characters. It also has a better system for saving the game: Instead of replacing a single saved game with each save, players choose among six different slots.

The story starts off as vaguely as the first—players must explore a mysterious evil in the Tower of Darkmoon. People have been inexplicably disappearing from villages to the north and west of Waterdeep, and it's suspected that a powerful artifact might be involved. Perhaps as a nod to the classic Gold Box games, the manual includes a sampling of numbered journal entries that provide additional context, though (thankfully) these are meant to be read all at once rather than at appointed times during the game.

Most fans of the series consider *The Legend of Darkmoon* the best of the series. While it sports impressive graphics and sound for its time, it's probably the meticulously crafted gameplay and fascinating setting that endears it to so many gamers.

Assault on Myth Drannor

The third and final *Eye of the Beholder* game is *Assault on Myth Drannor,* released in 1993 and almost universally regarded as a disappointing and lackluster finale to the series (Figure 11.4). One possible reason for the game's poor performance is that it was not developed by Westwood, but rather by SSI's own internal development team. It does add some nice

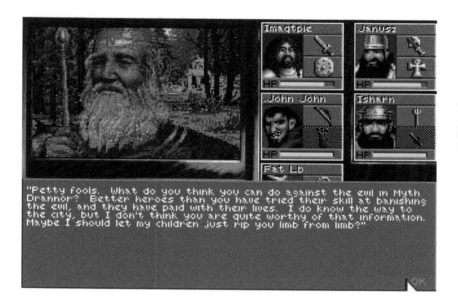

FIGURE 11.4 The final *Eye of the Beholder, Assault on Myth Drannor,* is a disappointing game that doesn't live up to the standard set by the previous installments. That said, it's still more fun than many games out there today. You can pick up the collection complete with digitized manuals and more from GOG.com.

features, such as an ALL ATTACK button that commands the entire party to attack with a single mouse click. Another nice innovation concerns pole-arms, or weapons with long shafts. Now, a character wielding a spear or halberd can attack from the rear, taking advantage of the extended reach of the weapon. It also offers more cinematic intermissions than the previous game. Even the manual tries to surpass the previous installments, featuring a twenty-six-page novelette by Ed Greenwood, creator of the *Forgotten Realms* campaign setting. However, these touches aren't enough to salvage the dull, repetitive, and frustrating gameplay.

Like the other *Eye of the Beholder* games, the party's ultimate goal is kept shrouded in mystery. Ostensibly, their quest is to enter the haunted ruins of Myth Drannor in search of an artifact held by a lich, a powerful undead being. Unfortunately, neither Greenwood's novelette nor the storylines of the previous two games are integrated into *Assault on Myth Drannor.* Instead, we get a drab and unimaginative hack 'n slash.

Dungeon Hack
Although not technically part of the *Eye of the Beholder* series, *Dungeon Hack* shares much of the underlying graphics technology. However, as

the name suggests, *Dungeon Hack* is an attempt to update the old random dungeons of games such as *Rogue* with a first-person, 3D interface. Developed by Dream-Forge and published by SSI in 1993, *Dungeon Hack* is a straightforward dungeon crawl with an emphasis on hack 'n slash–style gameplay. As with *Rogue* and *Nethack,* the player creates and controls a single adventurer.

Indeed, even the plot is reminiscent of many an old mainframe CRPG: players must descend into a dungeon to recover an orb. Still, while simplistic, the random but customizable dungeons and *AD&D* game rules make for a compelling, if brief, experience. It's a great game for gamers who don't wish to invest the hundreds of hours necessary to complete an *Eye of the Beholder* game; it's a quick fix, much like the mainframe games it's based on. The only real complaint from critics (then and now) is the difficulty of finding enough food to keep the adventurer alive.

Crystals of Arborea and the *Ishar* Trilogy

Crystals of Arborea is the prequel to the well-regarded *Ishar* trilogy, a series of games developed and published in 1990 by Silmarils, a French company founded by brothers Louis-Marie and Andre Rocques (Figures 11.5 and 11.6). *Crystals of Arborea* quickly faded into obscurity, though it does offer an interesting innovation to the *Dungeon Master* model: The six-member party can be split up into smaller, autonomous groups as in *Hired Guns,*

FIGURE 11.5 The Ishar games feature great graphics and fun *Dungeon Master*–style gameplay. Just look at this magnificent pixel art! Image courtesy of GOG.

FIGURE 11.6 Visit GOG.com to purchase the Ishar Compilation, which contains all three games in a ready-to-run format. Shown here is a battle with three rather moldy skeleton warriors. Image courtesy of GOG.

which we'll discuss in a moment. Another change from the *Dungeon Master* model is a special tactical screen for combat—a simple grid with only the heads of characters and monsters shown.

Crystals of Arborea puts players in the role of Prince Jarel of Arborea. The evil Lord of Chaos and Death, Morgoth, has been so vile of late that the gods send a great flood, which leaves all but the land of Arborea underwater. To appease the gods, Jarel must recover the four crystals stolen by Morgoth and replace them in their shrines. The game had promise but was not a hit with critics, who dislike its steep difficulty level and overemphasis on combat.

Ishar: Legend of the Fortress

Ishar: Legend of the Fortress, released by Silmarils in 1992, was the first of what would become a modestly successful series of CRPGs based on the *Dungeon Master* model. Critics were impressed with the high-quality graphics, vast gameworld, and nonlinear gameplay.

Legend of the Fortress does away with the autonomous parties and special combat mode of *Crystals of Arborea*. Instead, it uses an interface that resembles *Might and Magic III: Isles of Terra,* with a row of character portraits at the bottom of the screen and a large, 3D view of the scenery. Perhaps the most original aspect of the game concerns the party, which must be recruited from a cast of predefined characters encountered during the game. Each character has a unique personality, and some are treacherous and less than polite. Party management is a key part of the game, since the companions can form friendships with each other. If the player wants to dismiss a companion, the decision will be put to a vote by the party, who may choose not to honor the request. The storyline is rather vague but amounts to entering the titular fortress and liberating Arborea from the evil overlord Krogh.

Perhaps the least popular innovation in *Legend of the Fortress* is a save game system that costs the player gold. This is especially problematic at the start of the game, when gold is scarce and probably better spent on other needs.

Messengers of Doom

The next *Ishar* game is *Messengers of Doom,* released in 1993. *Messengers of Doom* is based largely on the previous game engine, though the gameworld is greatly expanded, with over 40,000 locations. The party members can now recruit pets for allies (a feature common to several roguelikes) and have the ability to create potions. Players can create new characters or import their old ones. The story this time concerns an evil wizard named Shandar, who is trying to conquer Arborea with a powerful hallucinogenic drug. Reviewers were again impressed with the overall quality of the game, granting it high scores and recommending it strongly to fans of the genre.

The Seven Gates of Infinity

The third and final game of the trilogy is *The Seven Gates of Infinity,* released in 1994. Widely considered the best of the series, the final episode boasts photorealistic graphics, puzzles, and sidequests, as well as an exceptionally large gameworld.

The party defeated Shandar in the previous game, but he's determined to make a comeback—by transferring his spirit into the body of a black dragon! Of course, it's up to the party to stop him, a task that will take them all over the world and even through time.

Although reviewers are generally approving of the game's photorealism, they do poke fun at the discrepancies in the characters' costumes. As one put it, "Leather-clad fetishists rub shoulders with cider-swilling country bumpkins—the effect is ludicrously laughable rather than atmospheric."[3] Many of these characters are part of the background and cannot be interacted with, which annoys some reviewers—though others find them handy references for navigation. We'll talk about other experiments with photo and cinematic realism (full motion video) when we discuss *Guardians of Destiny* and *Prophecy of the Shadow*.

All in all, the games of the *Ishar* series are impressive at times but seem to have been more popular in Europe than North America. Though the games were available for Atari ST and DOS, the Amiga versions were the most successful. This fact might explain why the series fared better in Europe, since the Amiga remained a well-supported platform there for many years after it had ceased to be supported in the United States.

Realms of Arkania

In 1993, Sir-Tech jumped on the *Dungeon Master* craze by publishing Attic's *Realms of Arkania: Blade of Destiny* (Figures 11.7 and 11.8). It's the first of what would become a trilogy of games based on the tabletop RPG *Das Schwarze Auge,* or *The Dark Eye,* a strong competitor for *D&D* in Germany. One of the innovations of this role-playing system is that

FIGURE 11.7 *The Realms of Arkania* games were designed by the affable Guido Henkel, a German-born American designer.

FIGURE 11.8 The isometric, turn-based combat mode of these games feels fundamentally different than *Dungeon Master*.

the characters have seven negative qualities (superstition, acrophobia, claustrophobia, avarice, necrophobia, curiosity, violent temper) as well as the seven positive qualities (courage, wisdom, charisma, dexterity, agility, strength, intuition), all with direct effects on the gameplay. Although these qualities are selected randomly by rolling for each statistic, the player has the option to tweak them with the change attributes tool. However, every positive trait raised in this fashion is counterbalanced by a mandatory 2-point change to a negative attribute. It's a brilliantly balanced and intuitive system but seems to have spawned few imitators.

In addition to the fourteen attributes, each character also has training in skills, which are broken up into seven basic categories: combat, body, social, nature, lore, craftsmanship, and intuition. Each time a character levels up, he or she gets a certain number of points to distribute among these skills, though the points are not allocated equally. For example, a character leveling up will get only 1 point to put toward a combat skill, as opposed to 2 points for body skills and 3 for lore. A check is made against the characters' skill level whenever they attempt a relevant action. As if this weren't complex enough, some of the checks also take various attributes into consideration. For instance, if a character wants to earn a few extra crowns playing music in a tavern, a check is made against his or her instrument skill, which factors in wisdom, intelligence, and dexterity. Likewise, the attributes can be affected by the character's condition—drink too much ale, and charisma plummets (completely unrealistic, in my experience).

Another major deviation from the *Dungeon Master* model is a separate interface for combat, which utilizes a tile-based isometric perspective. Furthermore, combat is turn-based rather than real time, allowing for more emphasis on tactics and strategy. The game is also noted for its realism, which takes into consideration the party's hunger and thirst as well as the effects of weather and terrain on movement. Careful study of the seventy-six-page manual is essential for successful gameplay.

Like *Legend of the Fortress*, *Blade of Destiny* penalizes players for saving the game, this time costing them experience points rather than gold. Players who save the game frequently see their party steadily weaken. The rationale behind these design decisions is that conventional save-game systems lower the stakes too much, reducing the vital element of risk that makes a game fun to play. We'll see plenty of other attempts to deal with this "problem," which seems to bother developers more than players.

As the title suggests, *Blade of Destiny* is a quest for a magical sword. The six-member party must first seek out the map, which has been torn into nine pieces and scattered across the land. Attic went to great pains to flesh out the gameworld with details from the tabletop RPG, much as SSI did with its TSR-licensed games. The result is a richly nuanced game with plenty to offer those willing to dedicate the time and attention needed to learn it.

The next two entries in the series, *Star Trail* and *Shadows Over Riva*, shift from the *Dungeon Master* mold to the smooth-scrolling technology of *Ultima Underworld*, which we'll discuss in Chapter 14.

Lands of Lore

After completing *The Legend of Darkmoon*, the second game in the famed *Eye of the Beholder* series, Westwood set to work on *Lands of Lore: The Throne of Chaos*, the first of what would become a three-game series (Figure 11.9). However, only the first game employs the *Dungeon Master* model of discrete rather than fluid movement through the 3D environment. Despite this supposed limitation, fans usually consider it the best game in the series.

FIGURE 11.9 The first *Lands of Lore* game is a charming, accessible, and highly polished *Dungeon Master* style.

The Throne of Chaos was published in 1993 by Virgin and quickly won over gamers and critics with its intuitive interface, polished graphics, quality soundtrack, and intelligent story. It is an exceptionally accessible game, with enough wit and charm not only to please existing CRPG fans but to make new ones as well. Westwood even managed to recruit the voice talent of Patrick Stewart, the famed Captain Picard of *Star Trek: The Next Generation*. What really makes this game stand out, though, is the almost alarming ease with which a new player can master the interface and become emotionally invested in the outcome.

Much of the game's brilliance lies in its simple yet effective interface. The commands and statistics are deliberately kept to a minimum—each player has only two ability scores, might and protection—the higher the number, the better. The three classes (fighter, rogue, and mage) are not predefined but are treated as skills that increase with practice. A simple bar graph shows how much more practice is needed to advance to the next level in each skill. Players are also spared the need to create a character from scratch, instead choosing one of four premade characters at the beginning of the game. Other characters are recruited later on.

The interface also follows the precedent established in *Might and Magic: Clouds of Xeen* by showing the characters' faces along the bottom of the screen; damaged characters appear swollen and bruised. Such visual cues are much more emotionally engaging than a simple number or line graph. Another good example of superior design concerns the shops: Rather than select items from a text menu, the player simply clicks on the items he or she wishes to purchase. Westwood seems to have taken every opportunity to replace text and numbers with self-explanatory visuals. Even the automapper is a cut above, showing not only where the party has been, but also the location of doors and the names of special rooms.

The magic system is quite intuitive, consisting of a short list of spells that can be cast at different levels of power. Pumping more power into a spell deals more damage but costs more magic points. We saw a similar system in *Dungeon Master,* though in that game casting spells is greatly complicated by the need to memorize and quickly arrange runes.

The game's storyline concerns an evil witch named Scotia, leader of a Dark Army and wielder of a powerful artifact that allows her to assume the form of any creature. The player is commissioned by King Richard to fetch a mystical ruby, but the party arrives too late, and the king has been poisoned in the interval. It's up the party to save King Richard as well as defeat Scotia.

If *Realms of Arkania* extends the *Dungeon Master* model to add complexity and nuance, *Lands of Lore* compresses it, making a game that's much easier to learn. The result is a thoroughly captivating game that is as fun to play today as it was in 1993. Westwood followed up with two sequels, which we'll discuss in Chapter 14.

Anvil of Dawn

One of the last *Dungeon Master*-style games is *Anvil of Dawn,* developed by DreamForge and published by New World Computing in 1995 (Figure 11.10). *Anvil of Dawn* is often compared to *Lands of Lore* because it offers a good balance of combat, story, and puzzle solving. The interface is quite intuitive, with a great automapper, a journal (to keep track of the story and quests), and a sensible inventory system.

The player starts off by selecting one of five avatars, three males and two females (including a black female). The characters come with preset attributes, though the player can modify them as desired. The choice of character also affects the narrative, especially the ending (each character has a unique ending). The story concerns a terrible Warlord whose might seems unassailable. The player's character is among five volunteers who pledge their lives to defeat the Warlord, though it'll be awhile before the player learns how to achieve this goal.

Combat is superbly handled—the left mouse button attacks with the weapon in the character's left hand, and the right mouse button swings with the right. It's a simple and straightforward technique that enhances

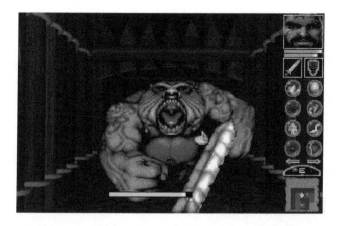

FIGURE 11.10 *Anvil of Dawn* arrived a little late to the *Dungeon Master* party, but it's one of the best of the bunch. Image courtesy of GOG.com.

the player's identification with the hero. The magic system is also quite clever. Instead of casting spells from a book, the character traces out a magical pattern with his or her finger. Doing so uses up spell points but also takes time, depending on the symbol; there may not be enough time to cast a long spell before a monster is near enough to attack.

All in all, *Anvil of Dawn* is one of the best of the *Dungeon Master*–inspired games and remains quite playable today. Although it lacks the real-time rendering of later games such as *Ultima Underworld,* careful pacing, splendid music, and a superior interface more than make up for this disadvantage.

Stonekeep

Interplay released *Stonekeep* in 1995, touting it as an "epic production" with "Hollywood special effects" (Figure 11.11). What's interesting here is that the "snapping" camera of *Dungeon Master*–style engines was actually quite dated by 1995, some three years after *Ultima Underworld* and DOOM established a new standard for first-person perspective gameplay. The relative obsolescence of the engine is likely explained by its painful production cycle; it spent nearly seven hectic years in development. However, the game does feature some of the best cinematic elements of 1995, making good use of the new CD-ROM storage format. It's noted for its full-screen gameplay, which is kept free of informational windows.

Stonekeep is comparable in many ways to *Anvil of Dawn,* particularly regarding combat. Again, the left and right mouse buttons correspond to

FIGURE 11.11 *Stonekeep* was designed by Peter Oliphant, a former child actor. Shown here is Wahooka, easily one of the most memorable of all CRPG characters. I interviewed Oliphant back in 2012 for *Matt Chat* 136.

the left and right hands of the hero. However, in this game the player has no say in the generation of the main character (or the other characters who join him later). There's also a good journaling and automapping system that tracks the hero's activities, and players can add their own notes.

The character's development is based on a simple skills system: the more the hero uses a particular weapon (hammer, dagger, etc.), the more skilled he'll become in its use. The "magick" system is rudimentary but intriguing in concept. To use magic, the hero must first find runes, which can be scribed onto wooden sticks called rune casters. The rune casters must be regularly recharged via Mana Circles. Many of the spells are offensive, though there are also defensive, preparatory, and teleportation spells.

The point of the game is to free the goddess Thera by recovering nine receptacles. Only then can the evil god Khull-Khumm be defeated and Stonekeep restored to its former glory. Of course, finding the receptacles will entail quite a bit of combat as well as puzzle solving.

The critics who praise this game do so because of the immersive atmosphere created by the music, sound effects, voice acting, cinematics, and packaging–the game box features a hologram on the cover and includes a paperback novel named *Thera Awakening*, penned by Steve Jackson and

David Pulver. Unfortunately, critics also lament the many bugs, including several that cause the game to crash.

Other *Dungeon Master*–Inspired Games

If we judge CRPGs according to their influence—as measured by the number of clones and imitators that follow in their wake—then *Dungeon Master* certainly deserves a revered place in the canon. Although SSI's *Eye of the Beholder* series is probably the most famous to follow FTL's footsteps, others followed all throughout the 1990s, slowing down only when computer technology finally made it feasible to offer fluid rather than discrete movement.

Some *Dungeon Master* clones, such as Pandora's 1988 release *Death Bringer* (released in Europe as *Galdregon's Domain*), are quite rough, unimaginative, and unplayable by modern standards. Others are of much higher quality, with promising innovations to the original *Dungeon Master* model: *Captive, Liberation,* and *Hired Guns.* If you still can't get enough *Dungeon Master*–style games, see the appendix for entries on **Abandoned Places, Black Crypt,** and **Bloodwych.**

Captive

Captive, by Antony and Chris Crowther of Mindscape, is an imaginative and well-regarded game, released in 1990 for the Atari ST and the Commodore Amiga, and two years later for DOS (Figure 11.12). Perhaps the best way to describe the game is as an amalgamation of *Dungeon Master* and Infocom's classic text adventure *Suspended* (1982), with a hint of Interplay's *Neuromancer* tossed in for spice.

In brief, *Captive* casts players in the role of an imprisoned amnesiac, whose only means of interacting with the outside world is a briefcase computer. The computer is networked to four droids, who must explore a series of bases (sci-fi-themed dungeons) located on different planets, gathering information and battling vicious alien creatures and robots. Once the droids have explored all the bases, they can free the player and end the game—or the player can opt to be recaptured, restarting the game with a fresh mission. Like *Telengard, Captive* generates dungeons using an algorithm, allowing up to 5,957 different missions on some versions (the DOS version is limited to 257).

The droids gain experience points that can be used to increase their skills. Most of these deal with proficiency with certain weapon types (i.e., rifles, swords, automatics). The robotics skill is more generalized; if it's

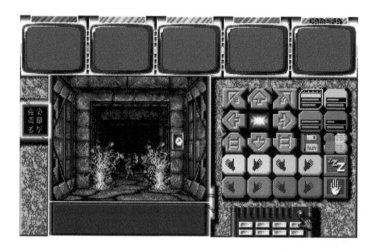

FIGURE 11.12 Here we have *Captive* running on an Amiga. Image courtesy of CRPG Addict, who, by the way, is no fan of the game: "It rubs me wrong in just about every way, from the goofy framing story to the pseudo-sci-fi setting to the unnecessary reliance on the mouse and the furious clicking that has to accompany every combat." Ouch!

too low, the droid won't be able to use advanced gadgets and accessories. The droids also have scores in dexterity (ability to hit), vitality (ability to dodge), and wisdom (percentage of experience points gained). The droids' various parts can be upgraded and accessorized with all sorts of useful gear, such as radar and an automapper, as well as a diversity of weapons. As in *Dungeon Master*, the droids are arranged in a front and rear rank; the ones in front do the bulk of the heavy fighting, while the rear droids are limited to projectile weapons. The most damaging weapon in the game is the dreaded spaygun, a rather humorous compositor's error for *spraygun*.

Captive won many awards but fared better in Britain and France than North America, perhaps not surprising since Mindscape is based in Europe. On a side note, it's this company that purchased SSI in 1994, becoming part of Ubisoft in 2001.

Liberation

Mindscape published Antony Crowther's sequel to *Captive* in 1994, a game titled *Liberation* for the short-lived Commodore Amiga CD32 game system and later for the stock Amiga platform. The game picks up after the conclusion of the first game, though this time the setting is a cyberpunk world. The story concerns a powerful corporation named BioCorp that has infiltrated the political system to cover up a deadly defect in the droids it is manufacturing for the police. It's up to the player—and his four trusty droids—to expose the plot and convince the emperor to address the situation.

Liberation is most often noted for its exceptional graphics, which began with an extensive and well-crafted introductory cinematic that established the context for the game. The characters and creatures roaming the city are composed of solid-color polygons, appropriate considering that they're being viewed through robotic eyes. As before, the player can upgrade the droids with new weapons, parts, and accessories. Combat is fast and furious, though there are also plenty of opportunities for dialog.

Liberation was critically acclaimed by contemporary reviewers, but it's not very well known today. The main problem is that it was intended for the CD32 platform, which became defunct rather quickly. Although Mindscape later offered a stripped-down floppy disk version for the stock Amiga platform, it wasn't nearly as impressive. Finally, the game has a fairly steep learning curve, with a complex interface that requires a thorough reading of the manual to understand. Nevertheless, *Captive* and *Liberation* are certainly two of the most intriguing and unusual of the *Dungeon Master*–style games.

Hired Guns

Another company that made bold innovations to the *Dungeon Master* model is DMA Design, whose *Hired Guns* was published in 1993 by Psygnosis for the Amiga and DOS platforms (Figure 11.13). *Hired Guns* expanded on the multiplayer model of **Bloodwych** by allowing up to four simultaneous players. The screen is broken up into four rectangular windows, one for each of the characters. Characters can move independently or be commanded to follow others (quite useful in single-player mode).

Like *Liberation*, *Hired Guns* is set in a dystopian cyberpunk future of 2712. A party of mercenaries is sent to Graveyard, a planet whose terraforming project has gone horribly awry, churning out deadly mutants. A nice twist is that the party has been told they're only there to rescue some hostages but then is marooned on the planet to kill or be killed. The game includes a novella titled *Countdown to Graveyard,* which establishes the context and biographies of the twelve playable characters.

Hired Guns was sensationally popular on the Amiga platform, though mostly unnoticed by DOS gamers. If nothing else, it raises interesting questions about the role of cooperative gameplay in CRPGs; obviously,

FIGURE 11.13 Scott Johnston's *Hired Guns* has an amazingly ambitious interface with a separate screen for each of its four characters.

such teamwork is essential in tabletop RPGs. Carving up the screen into multiple windows is certainly one way to bridge the gap, though DMA's example was not followed by others. The problem is that such divisions greatly reduce the viewing area of each window. Later CRPG developers would solve the problem by using local area networks (LANs) and, still later, Internet servers, which allow players to coexist in the same game-world without having to share the same monitor.

Modern Grid-Based Dungeon Crawlers

It might come as a surprise to some that grid-based dungeon crawlers have returned in recent years, much to the delight of *Dungeon Master* and *Eye of the Beholder* fans around the world. The most prominent modern game is *Legend of Grimrock* from Almost Human, a Finnish indie developer who published it for Windows, Mac, and Linux in 2012 (Figure 11.14). It's a great return to the format, with lovely graphics, clever puzzles, and plenty of monsters who want to make you their breakfast. The team returned in 2014 with the first sequel, *Legend of Grimrock II*.

FIGURE 11.14   Almost Human's *Legend of Grimrock* series are some of my favorite CRPGs ever. If you're a fan of the *Dungeon Master* style—or even if you're not—I highly recommend you give these games a try.

The unexpected success of *Legend of Grimrock* inspired several similar efforts, including Fatbot's *Vaporum* (2017), a steampunk dungeon crawler; *Arakion: Book One* (2018), which brings in world building and crafting; and Two Bits Kid's *Aeon of Sands* (2018). We'd also consider Ubisoft's *Might & Magic X—Legacy* (2014) a good fit for this category.

NOTES

1. See the review of the game in the April 1989 issue of *Zzap!*
2. See Heidi Brumbaugh's review of the game in the June 1990 issue of *START*.
3. See Steve McGill's review of the game in the September 1994 issue of *Amiga Format*.

CHAPTER 12

Other Games of the Golden Age

Although *Dungeon Master*–style games seem to dominate the cutting-edge platforms of the early to mid-1990s, there are plenty of other worthy contenders. Some of these, like Infocom's *Beyond Zork* and Masterplay's *Star Saga,* are eccentric, one-of-a-kind games whose design strategies have not been reattempted by major developers. In this chapter, we'll look at some other gems that didn't spawn subgenres, but are still worth playing today.

OTHER POPULAR GAMES

Battletech: The Crescent Hawk's Inception

We've already talked a great deal about Westwood Associates, the talent behind the *Eye of the Beholder* games and *Lands of Lore.* Now we turn our attention to *Battletech: The Crescent Hawk's Inception,* a popular game published in 1988 by Infocom (Figures 12.1 and 12.2). *The Crescent Hawk's Inception* is based on the FASA Corporation's *Battletech* wargaming franchise, a highly developed fictional universe comparable in scope to TSR's various campaign settings. However, in *Battletech* the battles are between giant, highly advanced "Mechs" rather than orcs and dragons. Mechs come in many different sizes and shapes, and serve different purposes, but they're usually large fighting vehicles with legs for movement—somewhat like the two-legged AT-ST walking artillery in *Star Wars: Return of the Jedi.*

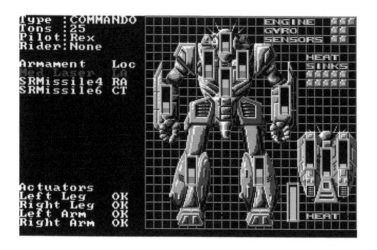

FIGURE 12.1 *Battletech: The Crescent Hawk's Inception* has you fighting in giant walking vehicles called mechs. Shown here is the loadout screen where you can arm and equip your mech as well as check its condition. Screen courtesy of CRPG Addict.

Westwood could have taken many different approaches to adapting *Battletech* as a computer game, and most subsequent developers chose strategy or first-person shooter styles. Westwood's game, on the other hand, is a top-down CRPG with turn-based tactical combat and manga-style graphics. The plot focuses on Jason Youngblood, eighteen-year-old son of a fallen war hero, who is just learning how to pilot Battlemechs.

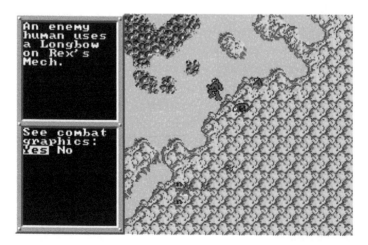

FIGURE 12.2 *Battletech: The Crescent Hawk's Inception* uses a tile-based mode for overland travel. Screen courtesy of CRPG Addict.

However, soon after the game begins, Jason's base is overrun by an attacking army. Narrowly escaping from the enemy, Jason must team up with the "Crescent Hawks" special forces and attempt to restore order.

One unusual aspect of the gameplay is the need to invest in the stock market. Money (called c-bills) is very important in the game, since Jason needs it to buy equipment, upgrade, and repair his Mechs. Although many CRPGs offer banks or casinos as a way to earn money, few have gone as far as *The Crescent Hawk's Inception*.

The game was generally well received, though some gamers complain about the graphics and sound, which are quite weak by 1988 standards. Most praise the dialog and story, which are well developed and relevant to the gameplay. Infocom followed its tradition of including some "feelies" in the box, this time a poster and a lapel pin. Westwood and Infocom followed up in 1989 with *The Crescent Hawk's Revenge* for the DOS platform. However, despite the similarity of the name, it's a real-time strategy game and not a true sequel.

There are certainly those who intensely dislike like the game, including CRPG Addict, who says it is "completely linear, non-replayable, too easy, too short, and it ends with the worst puzzle inclusion I've ever seen in a CRPG." I'll concede much of my love for the game is probably due more to nostalgia—as a kid obsessed with giant robots, it's easy to see how I might have overlooked the game's shortcomings.

In any case, in 2018 Jordan Weisman and his company, Hare Brained Schemes, released *BATTLETECH*, a project funded on Kickstarter. This ambitious game updates the gameplay of *The Crescent Hawk's Inception* and is certainly worth consideration by fans of that game or the broader *Battletech* universe.

B.A.T.

B.A.T. is a cyberpunk CRPG, developed by a French team named Computer's Dream and published by Ubisoft in 1990 (Figure 12.3). It's a very unusual game set in an environment reminiscent of the movie *Blade Runner*, with an odd point-and-click interface and a rapid combat mode that gives players mere seconds to respond. Instead of moving by selecting a direction as in most CRPGs, the player sweeps the mouse over the screen until the pointer indicates a possible exit or action (e.g., talk to a character). This system is very common in most graphical adventure games of the era. The player's mission is to find Vrangor, a criminal mastermind who has just escaped from prison. Vrangor is out to conquer the entire city of Selenia.

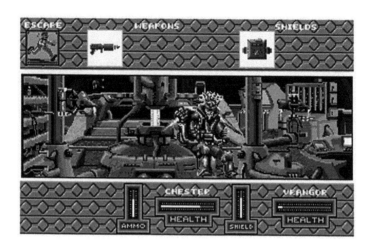

FIGURE 12.3 *B.A.T.* is a cyberpunk-themed adventure/CRPG hybrid game. Image courtesy of CRPG Addict.

The most intriguing aspect of the game is the B.O.B., a "biodirectional organic bioputer." B.O.B. is a computer that's embedded in the character's arm. B.O.B. monitors the character's condition and translates the language of the many robots and aliens he'll encounter. The player can also program B.O.B. using a primitive form of *BASIC*. Doing so automates many procedures, such as switching between the alien and robot settings when translating dialog, or alerting the player if the character is hungry or thirsty. It's a brilliant innovation that opens up a great many possibilities. There's also a minigame based on a 3D flight simulator.

The character creation system includes fixed attributes as well as selectable competencies and aptitudes, which are similar to the skills systems we've discussed earlier. For instance, there's the Evaluate aptitude, which is checked whenever the character tries to make a purchase. If it's high enough, he'll instantly recognize forgeries; otherwise, he'll be tricked. There are a total of twelve competencies covering a broad spectrum of activities.

Unfortunately, despite *B.A.T.*'s originality, its cumbersome interface kept it out of the spotlight. The second game, *B.A.T. 2: Koshan Conspiracy* (1992), improves the interface and is usually considered the better of the two. In the sequel, players must stop terrorists and restore the economy, which has been wrecked by the titular conspiracy. The game is considerably larger than the first, and includes racing and arcade as well as flight simulator minigames.

Both *B.A.T.* games are respectable achievements, with unique gameplay and sophisticated (but not overly complex) character development. Why they didn't fare better in the marketplace is a mystery; the most likely explanation is that they simply got lost in the shuffle. Another possibility is that the point-and-click interface, while so familiar to adventure gamers, simply doesn't work well for CRPGs.

Beyond Zork

Infocom is far better known for its classic text adventures than its occasional foray into other genres, though after its acquisition by Activision in 1986, it seemed more willing to experiment. One such experiment was Brian Moriarty's *Beyond Zork: The Coconut of Quendor* (1987), a zany game that introduces CRPG elements into the classic and much-loved series. Although mostly text-based, it does offer a graphical automapper and an endurance bar for combat, as well as limited support for the mouse.

The CRPG elements are concerned mostly with character creation and combat. The main character now has six attributes: endurance, strength, dexterity, intelligence, compassion, and luck. The attributes improve as the player progresses through the story, and some puzzles can be solved only if the requisite score is high enough.

The story has the player seeking the titular coconut, which somehow will ensure the continued existence of magic. Naturally, there's much more to the plot, with plenty of characters and conundrums along the way. Critics were generally pleased with the game, though by 1987 text-based games had long retreated to the fringes of the commercial game industry. As usual with hybrid games, fans of one or the other contributing genres offered contrasting complaints. CRPG fans didn't feel there was enough focus on combat and character development, whereas text adventure fans thought there was too much. In any case, no other major developers have been willing to revisit the design.

Star Saga

Another of Masterplay's forays into CRPGs is *Star Saga*, a highly innovative game from the co-creator of *Wizardry*, Andrew C. Greenberg. Published by Electronic Arts in 1987, *Star Saga* was intended to be a trilogy, but only two games were ever made—a sad but common fate in the annals of CRPG history. *Star Saga* is unique because of its determined effort to more closely emulate tabletop role-playing games (it's allegedly based on a tabletop game called *Rekon*). The approach was to heavily integrate extra-game materials, such as a hefty collection of printed texts ("textlets") and even a game board and pieces.

The idea was that players could enrich their computer game experience by referring to these materials during game sessions, for example, moving the tokens around on the map. All that appears on the screen is text describing the current situation and the effects of the players' actions. *Star Saga* is intended to be played by more than one player (up to six), and each player has a unique role and set of tasks. In so many ways, the game functions as a robotic Dungeon Master, and the real action takes place on the tabletop. Obviously, the game can't be properly played via an emulator, so anyone interested in learning more should find an original copy with all the included printed material (nearly three pounds' worth). By all accounts, the writing is quite excellent.

The sequel, *Star Saga Two: The Clathran Menace,* appeared in 1989. Unfortunately, despite hyperbolic praise from critics, the games turned out to be an evolutionary dead end. Indeed, nowadays it's rare for developers to include a printed manual and even rarer to find in the box the type of fancy and costly accessories included with *Star Saga*.

MegaTraveller

GDW's *MegaTraveller 1: The Zhodani Conspiracy* was not the first attempt to adapt GDW's classic *Traveller* tabletop RPG for the desktop (Figure 12.4). That honor goes to Edu-Ware's *Space,* a 1979 game we discussed in Chapter 4. However, Edu-Ware had failed to license or even ask permission before it marketed the game, and GDW was not pleased. GDW announced then that it would license another game based on the franchise, but it took eleven years for GDW to honor its promise. It selected Paragon to publish and co-develop the game, a company that at the time had published only one other CRPG, the surreal **Alien Fires: 2199 A.D.**

The Zhodani Conspiracy is certainly an ambitious CRPG, with inordinately sophisticated character creation and development, a massive gameworld, and real-time tactical combat. As we might expect, much of the gameplay is similar to what we saw in *Space. The Zhodani Conspiracy* offers a five-member party, and each member can develop fifty-four different skills. The game shipped with a 144-page instruction manual—quite a lengthy read for the casual gamer. Needless to say, this game had little appeal beyond the hardcore CRPG community and is better suited to those who already on intimate terms with the *Traveller* RPG. Although contemporary critics are

FIGURE 12.4   *MegaTraveller* is a sci-fi game based on the *Traveller* tabletop RPG.

genuinely well-disposed toward the game, noting its varied and open-ended gameplay and almost obsessively compulsive attention to detail, they are quick to alert novices to its steep learning curve and complain about the unwieldy combat mode.

The game is set in the distant future, long after humankind has colonized the stars. The story concerns a particularly aggressive alien race named the Zhodani, which is plotting to ignite a war against the Imperium (the good guys). Treachery and duplicity abound.

After *The Zhodani Conspiracy,* many of Paragon's developers defected and formed their own company, Event Horizon, whose SSI-published games we discussed in Chapter 7.

Quest for the Ancients

The next *MegaTraveller* game is *Quest for the Ancients,* released in 1991—an impressive achievement, considering that most of the original team had left the company. Critics were immediately impressed with the better graphics and improved interface, though the combat mode still poses a few problems, and a serious bug prevents some lines of text from disappearing.

The story concerns an ancient alien artifact that has inexplicably begun to produce a poisonous slime. It's up to the player to find a way to shut it down before it destroys a planet. Again, the game's inordinate complexity ensured that novices had a great deal to learn before playing the game, and again sales were limited mostly to hardcore gamers and fans of the tabletop RPG; the planned third game never appeared.

Space 1889 *and* Twilight 2000

Paragon also developed two other CRPGs based on GDW tabletop games: *Space 1889* (1990) and *Twilight 2000* (1991).

Space 1889 is a steampunk game set in an alternate universe based on the futuristic writings of early science fiction authors (Verne, Wells, Doyle, and others). The player can create up to twenty characters, each with six attributes and twenty-four skills, and swap them in and out of the five-character party as desired. The game boasts over 500 distinct nonplayer characters and a large arsenal of unusual weapons, such as "Dr. Gattling's machine gun." Unlike most of Paragon's other offerings, this game is more focused on exploration and puzzle solving than on tactics. Space travel is a matter of sailing through the "ether," navigating by the constellations.

The story concerns time travel, which in this universe has been invented by Thomas Edison. The characters set off to find King Tutankhamen's fabulous treasure but can easily get lost in the countless subplots and nonlinear gameplay. Though the game is something of a cult classic today, it seems to have slipped under the radar of most CRPG fans at the time. No doubt this obscurity is mostly owed to the game's overwhelming complexity.

Twilight 2000 is set in the postapocalyptic aftermath of World War III. Players control only one character, though they're in command of twenty soldiers, each of whom has a unique personality and motivations. As in the *MegaTraveller* games, players must grapple with intricate character development, with five attributes and forty-nine skills, and three career types broken into sixty specific occupations. It's really amazing how detailed character creation can become. The manual outlines a typical scenario: "A character becomes a Farmer for his first four years. After being a Farmer for four years, he may join a military branch or go to school." The manual also warns that not all of the skills and stats will have a direct bearing on the gameplay, but they may be useful for gamers who wish to transfer their characters to the tabletop game.

The game also features a sophisticated simulation mode for vehicle operation, but ground operations are turn-based. The game is just as complex as the other Paragon/GDW games and takes players about as far from instant gratification as they can get without joining a monastery.

Paragon's games raise an interesting question about the degree of complexity that goes into a successful CRPG. More complexity makes for more realistic and nuanced gameplay, which appeals strongly to a certain type of gamer. However, most gamers don't want to read a 100-page rule book just to get started. On the other hand, it's easy to get carried away in the other direction, creating games that can be mastered quickly but subsequently become tedious. It would take developers several more years to master the art of gradually (and painlessly) teaching novices how to play their games using in-game tutorials.

Whale's Voyage

Whale's Voyage is a 1993 game released for the Commodore Amiga and DOS platforms. It's probably best described as an attempt to blend *Starflight* and *MegaTraveller*. The most interesting aspect of the game is the character creation process, which begins by selecting parents for each of the four characters in the party. The next step is choosing a name (gender is assigned randomly), then mutating the DNA of the baby. However, too much mutation will weaken the baby's genetic structure, theoretically making him or her more susceptible to diseases. I say theoretically here because, although the manual includes this warning, there do not appear to be any such diseases in the game. To my knowledge, this is the only CRPG to introduce such a scheme, though we saw something similar in the JRPG *Phantasy Star II*. Finally, the player must select a school and a college for each character. There are six possible careers, which are determined by the choice of school and college.

While some of the game takes place on a spaceship, the CRPG elements kick in when the player beams down to a planet. Then, the interface changes to the classic *Dungeon Master* model but with a nice automapping tool. The game's storyline amounts to defeating General North, a powerful commander in charge of a fleet of warships, though most of the game is concerned with acquiring wealth and fame, usually by buying and selling goods. The biggest problem (at least at the start of the game) is the party's lack of funds and the rather sorry state of *Rustbucket,* their scrapheap of a ship. The graphics are primitive, but the soundtrack is very pleasant.

Unfortunately, *Whale's Voyage* suffers from a downright unbearable interface. Attacking an enemy requires clicking through several menus. Since the battles are in real time, the party might die before the player can wade through all the menus and select an attack. Critics are united in their disdain for the interface, but the developers (NEO Software) didn't bother to address these issues when it released an enhanced version for the Commodore Amiga 1200 and CD32. The save-game system is also poor, allowing only one save per game. Curiously, the game does offer codes at certain points. If the party dies, the player can use these codes to restart the game at a later point, with a predetermined party and inventory. Obviously, such a scheme isn't likely to appeal to gamers who grow attached to their original characters. Despite its initial promise, *Whale's Voyage* was far from successful, even on the CD32, a platform on which it had very little competition.

Darklands: A Historical CRPG

Darklands, published by MicroProse in 1992, is a meticulous historical CRPG set in medieval Germany (Figure 12.5). It is undeservedly obscure, despite its mindboggling attention to detail. For instance, not only does the game include historically accurate arms and armor, but even the weight and relative effectiveness of weaponry are incorporated into the gameplay. Even the old German calendar and currency are preserved. The game also boasts a huge gameworld with over ninety German cities and towns, all with historically accurate place names. The manual crams historical information as well as detailed instructions for gameplay into 115 pages.

The character creation process bears an uncanny resemblance to the one seen in the *MegaTraveller* games, beginning with the birth of the

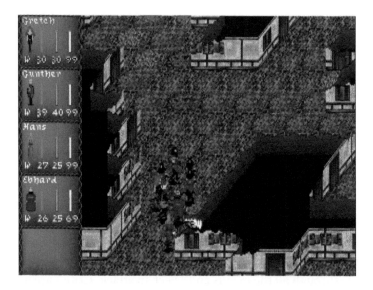

FIGURE 12.5 Arnold J. Hendrick's *Darklands* CRPG is probably the most historically accurate CRPG ever produced. It's also one of the earliest, if not first, CRPG with real time with pause combat.

character. After selecting a name and gender, players select one of six family backgrounds, which affect the stats and skills and restrict the choice of occupation. The next step is choosing from a list of a dozen or so available occupations, which the character will engage in for five years. The player can then decide whether to spend another five years in an occupation or begin adventuring. As with *MegaTraveller,* there's a trade-off. Spending more years at various careers builds up skill and experience, but aging decreases agility and other attributes. The player controls a party of four adventurers, so the creation stage can be lengthy—however, the game includes a quick start option that automates much of the process.

The goal of the game is simply to win fame and fortune; the game is quite open-ended and avoids many of the stale *D&D* clichés. There's not even a defined ending. However, there are countless quests to keep the player busy and a rather pertinent mission to save the world from total destruction.

Magic is based on the ancient art of alchemy and is quite intricate. First, the would-be alchemist needs a formula, which states the difficulty of the potion and list of ingredients. The alchemist can mix only a single batch per day but can vary its size (at a proportionate risk of failure). A big goof can damage the party and its equipment; a catastrophe can make an inn or campsite uninhabitable. Any character can use the finished potions. Clerical magic is also more complicated than in the typical CRPG. Clerics can discover and call on 130 different saints, each with a unique personality. However, calling on a saint uses up divine favor points, which must then be regained by performing various deeds. The cleric can also find relics (sacred artifacts) that can boost stats and decrease the cost of calling on saints; maintaining high virtue is always important for clerics.

Overland travel is shown on a map, but battles are shown from a top-down perspective in real-time. As in the later game *Baldur's Gate,* the player can stop the battle at any time to issue orders, such as aiming at a new target or quaffing a potion.

As far as I can tell, *Darklands* is the first CRPG with Real-Time with Pause or RTwP combat, though two relatively obscure JRPGs, *First Queen* (1988) and *Knights of Xentar* (1991), were earlier. Arnold Hendrick, whom I had the pleasure of interviewing back in *Matt Chat* 78 (2010), claims he'd never seen RTwP previous to his own design. Here's how it's described in the manual: "Battles have two states: orders pause and real-time action. During the orders pause, action is frozen, allowing you to examine the situation and select orders for your characters. During real-time action, you watch the characters act out your orders, fight the enemy, etc." Combat starts out in orders paused mode, but you could toggle between the modes at any time by hitting the spacebar. On paper, RTwP looks ideal, but in practice it was often chaotic, requiring constant micromanagement as multiple characters suddenly decide to disobey orders—and the crude graphics of the era certainly don't make it easy to see what's going on.

The game's code is riddled with show-stopping bugs, and the save-game system is irritating at best. Despite these problems, *Darklands* is now a cult classic, and Hendrick has announced plans for a modern remake.

The Four Crystals of Trazere

Another exotic game of the Golden Age is Mindscape's *The Four Crystals of Trazere* (1992), released in other countries simply as *Legend*. It's worth mentioning just because of its forward-thinking interface, which involves (among other things) a real-time isometric perspective with independent control of four characters—in other words, an early form of the interface seen in *Baldur's Gate* and *Diablo*.

The Four Crystals of Trazere (Figure 12.6) also features one of the most interesting magic systems of any CRPG, comparable in some ways to the component-based systems of the Golden Age *Ultima* games. Preparing a spell requires both spell ingredients and magical runes. There are sixteen of these runes broken into two categories: Effecter runes determine

FIGURE 12.6   Visiting a tavern in *The Four Crystals of Trazere*.

the spell's effect, whereas Director runes control the area to be affected. However, these runes are useless without the necessary ingredients. There are eight of these in the game—the stereotypical arcane substances such as wing of bat and phoenix claw. The spells require at least one component from each of the two types of runes. For instance, making a simple magic missile spell requires first applying the Director rune to a batwing, then the Effecter rune to a piece of brimstone. These two components are then mixed to form a spell. A handy remix button lets the player prepare a number of these spells at once, though doing so uses up ingredients.

The starting runemaster has very few runes and can get more only by buying them from The Ancient, a mountain-dwelling master mage. Ingredients can be bought in shops or found in dungeons; found reagents have disguised names, such as "bag of ugly teeth" for dragon teeth. There are hundreds of possible spell combinations, many of which have multiple effects and can be quite powerful. In short, it's a highly flexible and dynamic system, but quite easy to master once the player understands the basic principles. Although many spells are used for combat purposes, others are used to solve puzzles, mostly involving floor tile activators. For instance, the magic missile spell must be cast on a marked floor tile to open a door in the first dungeon.

Like many other games of the post–*Dungeon Master* era, the player doesn't create characters but selects them from a roster of predefined adventurers. However, the player can tweak their stats by adjusting the "four elements," which raise some stats and deplete others. The player can also rename the characters to further customize them. The party consists of four adventurers, one from each class: berserker, runemaster, troubadour, and assassin. These are basically equivalent to the standard fighter, mage, bard, and thief classes of *D&D*. The game is carefully balanced to take advantage of each of the companion's special abilities.

The story assigns the party the unenviable task of saving the citizens of Trazere, who have mutated and are rampaging across the countryside. It's up to the player to put a stop to the mutations, which will require gathering up the titular crystals and figuring out how they work. The task will take the player all over and under the land of Trazere. Overland travel shows the party and their enemies and allies as moving flags on a map, whereas dungeons utilize the real-time isometric view.

This game had great promise, but failed to win much of a following in the United States. It's hard to say why. Some critics complain about the rather sparse manual, which doesn't go into much detail about the spell system and leaves out some rather important caveats that can easily frustrate would-be runemasters.

Mindscape followed up later in 1992 with *Worlds of Legend: Son of the Empire,* which is very similar to the first game except for a change in setting (the Far East). Though critics grumble about the simplistic graphics, they applaud the spell system and the intensity of the real-time combat sequences.

Legend of the Red Dragon and BBS Door Games

Here we'd like to mention a special category of CRPGs called BBS Door Games. These games are similar to the MUDs we discussed in Chapter 3. However, these games were not run on mainframes but on personal computers equipped with modems and BBS (bulletin board system) software. In most cases, private enthusiasts would dial up their local BBS to exchange messages or software. Smaller BBSs might have a single line, though more sophisticated and commercially oriented services could offer dozens of lines and allow visitors to interact in real time. BBSs thrived throughout the 1980s and 1990s, though the rise of the Internet (and especially the World Wide Web) eventually rendered them obsolete.

Many BBSs offered "door games" as a means of attracting and entertaining visitors.[1] These games are often quite simple compared to MUDs and standalone CRPGs. Graphics are either nonexistent or little more than an ANSI or ASCII title screen. Gameplay often consists of selecting options from a text menu. Nevertheless, many door games were quite popular and are the source of no small amount of nostalgia today.

The most important CRPG door game is Seth Robinson's *Legend of the Red Dragon,* released in 1989 for the Commodore Amiga and MS-DOS platforms (Figure 12.7). A dragon is plaguing a small town, and it's up to the player to gain enough experience and power to dispatch the beast. This quest requires dealing with random encounters in the forest, where the character slays monsters for experience points and gold.

Although *Legend of the Red Dragon* may not sound thrilling to gamers raised on *Dungeon Master,* it manages to compensate for its simplicity with charm and wit—it's not a game that takes itself seriously. There are also many random events that can occur, such as meeting fairies or a talking severed head in the forest—it's even possible to get a proposal of marriage from Violet the barmaid and have children. The game limits players to a mere ten to twenty minutes daily, a limitation that helped free up the line and keep players from growing bored. For most fans, *Legend of the*

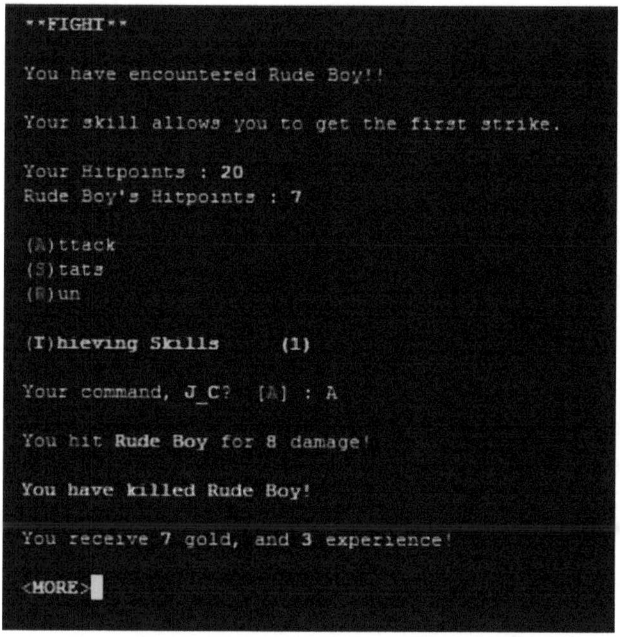

```
**FIGHT**

You have encountered Rude Boy!!

Your skill allows you to get the first strike.

Your Hitpoints : 20
Rude Boy's Hitpoints : 7

(A)ttack
(S)tats
(R)un

(T)hieving Skills      (1)

Your command, J_C?  [A] : A

You hit Rude Boy for 8 damage!

You have killed Rude Boy!

You receive 7 gold, and 3 experience!

<MORE>
```

FIGURE 12.7 *Legend of the Red Dragon* may not be much to look at, but it was a big hit in the pre-Internet days of online gaming.

Red Dragon is enjoyed the same way you enjoy a daily crossword puzzle—a pleasant way to occupy a few idle moments, but certainly not the sort of hobby that eats weekends for breakfast.

Legend of the Red Dragon was successful enough to warrant a sequel, *New World,* released in 1992 for MS-DOS. This game is a significant departure from its predecessor, offering top-down ANSI graphics and real-time gameplay. It's probably best described as a Roguelike, though with more quests and opportunities for interaction with other players. We'll have a chance to talk more about Robinson in Chapter 15, when we discuss his *Dink Smallwood* action CRPG.

Today, gamers can play *Legend of the Red Dragon* in their browsers by visiting http://lord.nuklear.org, which offers a JAVA version of the program. There is also a PHP version available at http://lord.lordlegacy.com.

SUMMING UP THE GOLDEN AGE

Although we still have plenty of groundbreaking CRPGs to cover, the late 1980s and early 1990s were by far the most prolific and diverse period in CRPG history. Imagine the diversity, with games like *Star Saga* and

Beyond Zork sitting alongside *Dungeon Master* and *Quest for Glory* on the same game rack. Meanwhile, countless games were flooding in from Europe, and console owners were getting a steady diet of Japanese hits like *Final Fantasy* and *Phantasy Star.*

We also see in this age plenty of games obviously designed with the hardcore gamer in mind, the type of person who knows the rules of complex RPGs like *Traveller* inside and out. Imagine opening a game box to find a textbook of 100 pages or more of is mandatory reading just to get past the character creation process, much less survive the first hostile encounter. Games requiring this much preparation are virtually unheard of today, when gamers expect to be up and running with even the most sophisticated new game in minutes.

On the other hand, we also see the opposite trend, particularly with the JRPGs flooding into North America via Nintendo and Sega's game consoles. These highly successful and well-crafted games captivated gamers with thoughtful (if linear) narratives and deeply developed characters.

As the Golden Age draws to a close in the mid-1990s, we see a rising concentration of power in the hands of a few mega-sized publishers who cater exclusively to the mainstream. Now a billion-dollar industry, game development will become increasingly specialized and professionalized. No longer will lone programmers or even a single team of designers be responsible for an entire game. Instead, large and often unwieldy groups of diverse specialists will collaborate on games, though the lack of effective team programming tools and techniques (as well as a myriad of incompatible hardware and software standards) will lead to many bugs and glitches in their products.

Furthermore, publishers (and thus developers) will become more focused on interfaces and graphics than on bold but financially risky experiments in game design. In short, we'll see less invention and innovation, but more craft and sophistication as CRPG developers consolidate their gains.

NOTE

1. These programs were called "door games" because they were launched externally by the BBS software. For more information, see http://en.wikipedia.org/wiki/BBS_door.

CHAPTER 13

The Epic Fails

The bigger they come, the harder they fall. It's one thing for a small indie studio to produce a poor game, but only a major studio, with a long track record of outstanding achievements behind it, can fail so spectacularly as to threaten the future of an entire genre.

At least, that's one way we can account for the spectacular disasters we're about to see as we head into the 1990s. SSI, Origin, and Interplay—the three biggest names in the industry—went from making the best CRPGs to the worst. It was a time when even diehard fans turned their backs on their hobby, fed up with the stinking, bug-infested games piling up in the local bargain bins. The very words *role-playing game* were enough to trigger critics, who never tired of proclaiming the death of CRPGs.

To really tell this bit of the story, we need to step back for a moment and discuss the computers games industry at large. Two industry-wide paradigm shifts occurred in the early 1990s: 3D graphics and CD-ROM. As exciting as these developments were, they represented a daunting challenge for developers accustomed to 2D graphics and floppy disks.

The 3D graphics revolution began when id Software, a tiny shareware developer based in Shreveport, Louisiana, released *Doom*. It wasn't the first true first-person shooter (FPS) game; id earned that distinction with their previous game, *Wolfenstein 3D* (1992). However, it was *Doom* that shook up the industry; critics and gamers were totally hooked on its immersive gameplay and incredibly fast 3D graphics. For our purposes, what's important to note is that with all the international hype around *Doom*, 2D games now had a very hard time getting noticed. For example, Corey Cole, part of the husband and wife team responsible for the *Quest for Glory* series, confessed that one of the reasons *Quest for Glory V: Dragon Fire* was such a disaster was that they were "pushed into 3D too early," and several promised features that titillated fans were left out of the finished product.

This sudden, urgent need to go 3D had many other developers quaking in their boots. Id Software may have been a small team, but they were a small team of geniuses. For ordinary mortals, building a 3D game engine was a massive undertaking, and there wasn't yet an option to simply license an existing engine such as *Unreal* or *Unity*. Programmers with well-earned reputations for 2D work found themselves totally unprepared. Team sizes expanded to fill the gap, but without the benefit of today's collaborative frameworks, chaos was the inevitable result. It was one overhyped glitchfest after another.

The other innovation of concern here is the CD-ROM. As a portable storage media, CD-ROMs were hard to beat, offering enormous gains in data storage at a fraction of the cost of floppy disks. Just one disc could hold all the data on over 400 floppies! In 1993, two adventure games from upstart developers showed off the potential of these devices—Trilobyte's *The 7th Guest* and Cyan's *Myst*. These games leveraged the CD-ROM with spectacular prerendered graphics, full-motion video clips, and digitized audio. Neither of these games holds up all that well today, but they were breathlessly reported on in the media—not just game magazines, mind you, but in mainstream magazines and television news. They breathed new life into what had become a moribund computer games market.

As with 3D graphics, CD-ROMs caught many of the old guard flat-footed, particularly other adventure game makers like Sierra and Lucasfilm. These companies had mastered the art of doing a lot with a little. Now they had the opposite problem—what to do with all that extra space. The countless throngs who'd shelled out for CD-ROM drives certainly weren't going to settle for anything less. Oh, and it had to be in 3D, too?

Finally, don't forget that consoles had dwarfed the computer games industry. Though it'd be a while before the above developments caught up with consoles, the sheer numbers involved made many developers (or, more likely, their publishers) think that CRPGs needed to be more like console games: action, action, and more action. Action RPGs (or ARPGs) are common today, but in the pre-*Diablo* world, almost of these games were flops. Nevertheless, much like Metallica, companies like Origin and Sierra kept trying to broaden their appeal to the masses regardless of how their fans felt about it.

As we'll see, the CRPG was far from dead—indeed, in a few short years, gamers would be treated to the best CRPGs ever made, ambitious new projects from bold new developers raised on and respectful of the grand-old games of better years. Indeed, the best of these weren't even in 3D!

But this chapter isn't about the mammals who adapted. It's about the dinosaurs who didn't.

SSI's UTTERLY FORGETTABLE REALMS

We'll start with SSI's fall from grace, which began in 1992. The old computer wargames publisher earned respect with early classics such as *Wizard's Crown* and *Phantasie*, then international recognition in 1988 with its *AD&D*–licensed title *Pool of Radiance*. After the company milked the Gold Box engine for all it was worth, it turned to Westwood Associates, who produced the *Eye of the Beholder* Black Box engine for SSI in 1991. That game and Westwood's sequel were rousing successes, but SSI decided to go it alone with the third installment: the disappointing *Assault on Myth Drannor*, released in 1993.

Any company with SSI's glowing reputation can afford a few mistakes, and, indeed, most publishers rely on a few smash hits to compensate them for their larger bulk of average sellers or outright flops. But, as all too often happens, a few became one too many.

Spelljammer

One of SSI's biggest shipwrecks came in 1992 with Cybertech's *Spelljammer: Pirates of Realmspace*, a game based on TSR's steampunk campaign setting (Figure 13.1). As with *Space 1889*, which we discussed in the previous chapter, we're presented with an alternative reality based loosely on the works of novelist Jules Verne and ancient astronomy. In short, the alternate physics makes it possible to "sail" from planet to planet in magical ships called "spelljammers." The unusual campaign setting is an interesting blend of sailing ships, steampunk, and high fantasy. The setting was unique, but many of the *Forgotten Realms* conventions, such as the spell system and racial profiles, were carried over.

Pirates of Realmspace offers a variety of gameplay modes, including real-time, first-person 3D flight simulation (for space travel), turn-based tactical "boarding combat," and a menu-driven planet interface (for buying and selling cargo). It's a sophisticated game, though not as nuanced or detailed as *Space 1889*.

FIGURE 13.1 *Spelljammer* was a successful tabletop game, but Cybertech didn't have much luck with its DOS game.

Although the setting was moderately successful with tabletop RPG fans, Cybertech's effort to adapt it for DOS failed miserably. Besides lackluster graphics and a pedestrian plot, the game wasn't properly beta tested and frustrated gamers with bugs and misspellings. It was Cybertech's first and last game, and it brought bad publicity for SSI. Nevertheless, SSI developed two other steampunk games, which we'll discuss in a moment.

One recurring theme I've encountered in interviews with CRPG designers over the years is a deep aversion to standard fantasy settings. It's just not much fun for these creative individuals to sail in well-charted waters, working with the standard tropes that trace back to J.R.R. Tolkien and Robert E. Howard. Designers are almost always more interested in less explored settings such as *Spelljammer,* or, more recently, Monte Cook's *Numenera.* Steampunk, cyberpunk, postapocalyptic settings, Westerns, Civil War—almost anything seems preferable to them than good-old swords and sorcery. I suspect that since many CRPG designers are also heavily into tabletop RPGs, they simply get burned out on traditional settings.

However, what I've found over the years is that what gets designers excited about a new story or setting might fall flat with gamers, especially those who aren't also burned out by playing too many fantasy tabletop

RPGs. Although designers and critics alike enjoy unusual settings and twists on convention, I'm certainly not alone in my affection for more traditional fare. Yes, I'm as guilty as anyone of lambasting games with "kill the evil wizard/dragon/witch" style stories, but, when I'm really honest with myself, I still prefer the comforts these games offer over the overwrought plots and unfamiliar settings common in modern games. After all, there's a reason why these tropes and traditions got to be, well, tropes and traditions—they're battle tested and proven to work.

Prophecy of the Shadow

Let's return to SSI's story fall from grace with *Prophecy of the Shadow*, an original game aimed at novices. The player creates and controls a single character, using a simple question-and-answer process reminiscent of the *Ultima* series. It has real-time combat and a fairly intuitive icon- and mouse-based interface. The graphics are typical for the era except for the keyword-based dialog mode, which features briefly animated digital images of live actors (usually turning their faces toward you or blinking).

There are no character classes, but the character does advance by mastering certain skills (e.g., attacking with a dirk or casting spells). Magic is based on a simple points system, though the player has to find "catalysts" and magic books to learn new spells. Your choice of catalyst determines the strength as well as the type of spells the character can cast.

Overall, *Prophecy of the Shadow* isn't a bad game, at least for beginners. It seemed well poised to earn SSI a decent profit, but it suffers from a plebian plot and terrible combat segments. The storyline concerns the titular prophecy, which foretells of a Shadow Lord who will destroy civilization (starting with the magic-users). The player's character is a young apprentice, whose master (Larkin of Bannerwick) is killed by an unknown assailant. There's little character development, and the old "it's in the prophecy" gimmick had long gone the way of cliché. Furthermore, the combat and magic systems are too simplistic, and the dialog doesn't allow the player to make meaningful choices. Plus, just getting around can be a chore because of jerky animation and unbalanced speed. Players can slow or speed up the character's gait, but this change exponentially increases the speed of opponents. Since combat is real time, this effectively makes it essential to play in slow or normal mode.

In short, *Prophecy of the Shadow* isn't terrible, but it certainly was not good enough to compete with the many excellent titles sitting by it on the shelf.

Dark Sun: Shattered Lands

In 1993, SSI published *Dark Sun: Shattered Lands*, a top-down CRPG based on TSR's postapocalyptic Dark Sun campaign setting, a harsh, arid water and metal-deprived world where only the strong survive (Figure 13.2).

Shattered Lands was SSI's effort to revamp the old Gold Box engine. Gone are the separate screens for exploration, combat, and dialog—now everything occurs on the same screen, shown in top-down isometric perspective. The player controls a four-member party, which, as in *Ultima III*, is represented by a single character during exploration but by multiple characters during the turn-based combat sequences. The magic system is also streamlined, omitting the memorization routine altogether in favor of a simple slot-style system.

Despite an intuitive interface and intriguing setting, the game's mediocre graphics, jerky animation, typos, and buggy code kept it out of the limelight. Nevertheless, SSI released a sequel called *Wake of the Ravager* in 1994. Even though the graphics are improved, the bugs are even worse than before. One particularly nasty one was simply dubbed "The Bug." The Bug prevents monsters from attacking the avatar, making the game a cakewalk rather than the intensely challenging experience it's supposed to be.

FIGURE 13.2 *Dark Sun: Shattered Lands* is a gritty, brutal alternative to the *Forgotten Realms,* but was never quite as popular.

Although such bugs can be easily enough addressed today by downloadable patches, that practice wasn't common in the early 1990s. Players unlucky enough to buy an early version of the game just had to live with The Bug or demand a refund.

Ravenloft: Strahd's Possession

SSI also published games based on TSR's horror-themed Ravenloft campaign setting. The first of these, *Ravenloft: Strahd's Possession*, was developed by DreamForge and published in 1994 (Figure 13.3). Like Origin's *Ultima Underworld* (which we'll discuss later), *Strahd's Possession* is a first-person perspective, 3D game with smooth scrolling, but a "step" mode is available. A sequel named *Stone Prophet* appeared in 1995, offering enhanced graphics and some new abilities such as flying and levitating. Both of these games are based on neo-Gothic themes and seemed poised to take advantage of the vampire fad spurred by Anne Rice's vampire novels and Neil Jordan's film adaptation *Interview with the Vampire*, which descended into packed theaters in November 1994.

   Why these games didn't receive more recognition is hard to determine. Perhaps they were damned by faint praise from critics, who couldn't find

FIGURE 13.3 The two games in the brief-lived *Ravenloft* series didn't save SSI, but they have their share of fans. Many of the bugs that tainted their initial release have long been patched. Image courtesy of GOG.com.

anything notably good *or* bad about the series. Some critics complained that DreamForge just didn't understand what makes the Ravenloft setting appealing, and that their game lacked the ambience generated by the tabletop version. In any case, these games are surely better than Take 2 Interactive's *Iron & Blood: Warriors of Ravenloft*, a rotten fighting game published by Acclaim in 1996 for DOS and Sony's PlayStation.

Al-Qadim: The Genie's Curse

Al-Qadim: The Genie's Curse is, as the title suggests, based on a TSR campaign setting reminiscent of tales from the *Arabian Nights* (anything but standard fantasy!) (Figure 13.4). It uses a similar engine to the one seen in *Dark Sun*, but this game is far more action-oriented—the player can't even upgrade the single character's armor or weapon. Instead, you must be dexterous with the keyboard or joystick, deftly dodging fireballs and striking opponents with the scimitar. Although there are plenty of monsters to dispatch, the emphasis here is on evading traps and solving puzzles.

The story puts the player in the role of the youngest son of the al-Hazrad family. The character has just completed training as a Corsair and is ready

FIGURE 13.4 *Al-Qadim: The Genie's Curse* is set in an *Arabian Nights*–inspired gameworld. Its game engine is a stripped-down version of the Gold Box style, ideal for novices, perhaps, but not as engaging for veterans. Image courtesy of GOG.com.

for the final test. After the test, he must negotiate a peace between the al-Hazrads and the Wassabs, a rival family. Unfortunately, the family genie is accused of attacking a Wassab, claiming to have acted under the orders of the character's father. This leads to their banishment and the player's main quest—to piece together the real story.

The game was developed by Cyberlore and published by SSI in 1994. Although the game had favorable reviews (including one in *Dragon* magazine, the world's leading magazine for tabletop and miniatures role-playing), it wasn't enough to halt SSI's spiral into obscurity. One contemporary reviewer quipped, "Through some cosmic alignment of planets or other miracle, [SSI] has managed to produce a worthwhile game." This comment shows just how far SSI's reputation had fallen since the days of *Pool of Radiance* and *Eye of the Beholder*.

Menzoberranzan

The last TSR-licensed game SSI published is the infamously wretched (and hard to spell) *Menzoberranzan*, which appeared in 1994 for DOS. Another first-person, 3D game in the style of the *Ravenloft* games, *Menzoberranzan* had all the ingredients necessary for a hit. It features one of TSR's most famous characters, Drizzt Do'Urden, a dark elf of the Underdark popularized by the novelist R. A. Salvatore. Furthermore, to its great credit, the developer (DreamForge) had listened to earlier criticism and worked hard to improve the game engine.

Nevertheless, gamers quickly complained about the endless number of boring battles that drag out the game and ruin its pacing. This is particularly noticeable in the crucial first stages of the game; it takes a long time for anything interesting to happen. The lack of strong sales of these games and of SSI's two dismal console action titles *Slayer* (1994) and *Deathkeep* (1995) are no doubt what led TSR to sever its exclusive licensing agreement with SSI. I won't go into detail about these, but to give you some hint about their reception, here's a rebuke from a contemporary reviewer: "[*Deathkeep*] has groundbreaking graphics. Unfortunately, they would only be groundbreaking if the game had been released in 1980."

TSR decided to reverse its policy of exclusive licensing and extended its franchises to several rival companies, most notably Interplay, who, along with Black Isle Studios, published BioWare's *Baldur's Gate* in 1998. We'll discuss that game in the next chapter.

World of Aden

After losing its licensing agreement with TSR, SSI decided to invent its own gameworlds and campaign settings. In 1995, SSI developed *World of Aden: Thunderscape* and, with Cyberlore Studios, *Entomorph: Plague of the Darkfall*, both published by Mindscape (who bought SSI in 1994). These games are based on a world similar to the one found later in Sierra's *Arcanum* and in the earlier *Space 1889* and *Spelljammer*; swords and sorcery meets steampunk. Magic is based on "mechamagic," which the box describes as a "crude marriage of steam-age technology and powerful sorcery."

Thunderscape (Figure 13.5) takes place during the Darkfall, a mysterious blight that is spawning hordes of bestial "nocturnals." The nobler races are at war with these nocturnals, and it's up to the player to become the one leader capable of dispatching the threat. Combat in *Thunderscape* is turn-based, quite unusual for this type of game. The player controls a four-member party (fighter, healer, wizard, and thief), though nonplayer

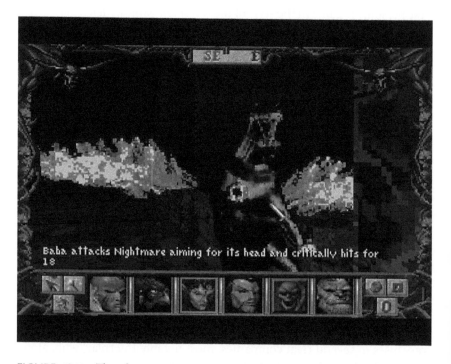

FIGURE 13.5 *Thunderscape* is a steampunkish dungeon crawler with tons of turn-based combat, traps, and puzzles. It's not great, but it does offer some interesting race and class options.

characters may later offer to join the party (but their true motives might not be clear until later).

The first game had first-person perspective similar to that in *Ultima Underworld*, but the second reverted to isometric perspective. *Entomorph* puts the player in the shoes of a young squire slowly falling victim to the Darkfall and becoming a giant insect. The squire must discover what's causing the Darkfall and stop it. One nice twist here is that the squire can take advantage of his new insect-like abilities to gain an edge in combat, though doing so speeds up the transformation. The box promises a "skin-crawling experience," which will no doubt be the case for anyone who dislikes bugs.

Sadly for SSI, these well-crafted and highly playable games attracted little interest. Perhaps if SSI hadn't ruined its reputation, it would have fared better, despite the many bugs. As it was, most gamers were fed up with SSI. The company's last gasp was the dreadful **Legends of Valour**, touted loudly as "better than Ultima Underworld." You can read about it in the appendix; for now, I can simply say that it was nothing of the sort.

To be fair, though, even the best of SSI's post–Black Box era games were mediocre at best, certainly nothing that could compete squarely with the truly magnificent titles we'll discuss in the next few chapters. SSI, once ranked among the world's best CRPG developers and publishers, had lost its way. After trading hands a few times, the brand ended up at Ubisoft and was laid to rest in the early 2000s.

AD&D GETS DUMBER AND DUMBERER

Although TSR was probably correct in the assumption that SSI was no longer the best company to represent its interests, it didn't exactly strike gold with its next few licensees. Many of these games were action or strategy titles, but there were a few CRPGs in the mix, such as Sierra's *Birthright: The Gorgon's Alliance* (1996) and Interplay's *Descent to Undermountain* (1998).

Birthright was developed by Synergistic Software and is a mix of adventure and strategy as well as more conventional CRPG elements. It's based on TSR's highly successful *Birthright* game and has a great story about a menace named The Gorgon, who is hellbent on killing and extracting the divine blood of kings to secure his power. The game promised plenty of political intrigue and many multifaceted characters, with players controlling not just single heroes but entire kingdoms. Finally, *Birthright* had Sierra's formidable name recognition behind it, which included their stunningly successful and highly innovative *Quest for Glory* series we talked about in the previous chapter.

Unfortunately, *Birthright: The Gorgon's Alliance* didn't live up to the hype. Yet again, a promising game was stymied with game-crashing bugs that irritated even the most forgiving players, but the real problem was that it was a jack-of-all-trades, master of none. It tried to be a strategy, CRPG, and an adventure game all-in-one. There's a reason genres exist; they stabilize around proven formulas and reliable fanbases. Successful hybrid games such as *Quest for Glory* are the rare exceptions to the rule. In *Birthright*'s case, all these different modes resulted in a steep learning curve, and the adventure mode felt tacked-on feel and poorly integrated with the rest of the game. Although it had its moments, this *Birthright* amounted to little more than a few freckles and a mole.

Descent to Undermountain

Interplay's *Descent to Undermountain* (Figure 13.6) is an even less satisfying game than *Birthright*; indeed, with the possible exception *Pool of Radiance: Ruins of Myth Drannor* (2001), it's the worst CRPG ever produced by a major developer. *Descent to Undermountain* attempted to ride

FIGURE 13.6 *Descent to Undermountain* is a game whose color palette is as brown as the excrement it reminds one of. Screenshot courtesy of Lazy Game Reviews.

some of the hype surrounding its immensely popular *Descent* (1995) by modifying its marvelous 3D engine. As you may recall, in that game you fly a ship through twisting mines in a zero-gravity environment. It was incredibly fun and spectacular, but nothing at all like playing a CRPG.

Interplay must have envisioned that transforming Parallax Software's brilliant engine would result in something like Blue Sky Productions' *Ultima Underworld* (1992) or *The Elder Scrolls: Arena* (1994). We'll talk about these games later, but the key point is that they are first-person CRPGs with continuous movement and 3D effects. Critics and fans alike gushed about their graphical realism and incredible immersion—suddenly, games with grid-based movement, like Interplay's *Stonekeep* (1995), seemed hopelessly antiquated.

If immersive 3D graphics were what gamers demanded, then the *Descent* engine seemed like Interplay's ace-in-the-hole. Its graphic engine was incredibly efficient, offering fully 3D polygon meshes and textured environments, noticeable improvements over the other first-person shooters of the day. It even ran decently on lower-end machines, which is certainly something the CRPGs mentioned earlier couldn't say. In short, it was a terrific engine, and no one saw any reason why it couldn't be easily modified and used to create the best-looking CRPG to date.

To top it all off, Chris Avellone, who went on to design some of the best CRPGs of the Platinum Age, and Steve Perrin, creator of the popular *RuneQuest* RPG, were just two of the designers Interplay assigned to the project. Finally, let's not forget Interplay's stellar reputation as a CRPG developer (*The Bard's Tale, Dragon Wars, Wasteland*). Couple all this talent with a well-established *D&D* campaign setting and cover art by celebrated fantasy artist Clyde Caldwell, and who wouldn't bet on its success?

The biggest problem was that no one had anticipated just how difficult it'd be to convert *Descent*'s engine for use in a CRPG. Massive parts of the code had to be scrapped and redone from scratch. Feargus Urquhart, then the division director at Interplay, claimed that his "lead programmer told me that there's about 5% of the *Descent* code left in there." Furthermore, Interplay was going through a major internal shakeup at the time. By the end of it, *Descent to Undermountain* had gone through "three producers, two division heads, a couple of lead artists, and two lead programmers."

Obviously, with a development environment like that, you'd expect more bugs than the Florida Everglades, and that is perhaps the only way in which *Descent to Undermountain* doesn't disappoint. Game-crashing bugs alone aren't usually enough to turn away gamers from an otherwise solid production, but the lack of polish is immediately apparent. The levels are muddy, dreary, and look too much alike, and the confusing, maze-like arrangement that worked so well for the original *Descent* is just frustrating here. The trite story—yet another quest—is so uninspired that it might well have been thought up by the game's own terrible artificial intelligence. Once word got out, the game promptly descended from the shelf to the landfill.

The blurb on the game's box was apropos: "In the end, you'll trust no one but yourself." TSR must indeed have been wondering whom it could trust with its venerable franchises and campaign settings! Fortunately, events would soon take a major turn for the better with the publication of *Baldur's Gate*, the game that finally returned TSR-licensed CRPGs to the public eye. I'll return to that game in the next chapter.

ORIGIN AND THE DEMISE OF *ULTIMA*

Origin's story during the mid to late 1990s is one of peaks and valleys. Richard Garriott had shown remarkable foresight by publishing Chris Roberts' *Wing Commander* in 1990 and Blue Sky Productions' *Ultima Underworld: The Stygian Abyss* in 1992. I'll have more to say later about the latter game in the next chapter, but the point here is that these games prove that Garriott recognized the promise of 3D gaming early on. We also see Origin embracing the CD-ROM, with *Wing Commander III: Heart of the Tiger* in 1994, which stars Mark Hamill, Malcolm McDowell, and John Rhys-Davies in numerous full-motion video segments. Clearly, Lord British knew a good thing when he saw it.

Sadly, though, it's to Origin's flagship series, *Ultima*, that we must now return. Would Garriott stay faithful to his own gut instincts as a designer, or would he lose that faith, trusting instead to the heretics of market analysis? I'll let the title of his next game give you a clue.

Ultima VIII: Pagan

Origin published *Ultima VIII: Pagan* in 1994 for DOS (Figure 13.7). It immediately provoked controversy among long-term fans of the series. Garriott was well known for returning to the drawing board to reinvent the series, but this time he deduced that more action would appeal to the console crowd. Thus, in *Pagan* the avatar can run, jump, and climb across moving platforms, just like Mario. Some wit was quick to dub it "Super Mario Avatar," and the name stuck.

FIGURE 13.7 *Ultima VIII: Pagan* introduces some action mechanics to cater to the console crowd, but many fans thought it was a move in the wrong direction. Image from GOG.com.

Combat is reduced to a series of rapid-fire mouse clicks. For lovers of the older games, this is nothing short of an abomination. Many of the key innovations that made *The Black Gate* so successful, such as depicting night and day, are inexplicably abridged or omitted. It's not even set in Britannia! As if these faults aren't enough to justify burning *Pagan* at the stake, a multitude of bugs surfaced, turning even hardcore *Ultima* fanatics against it. Garriott blamed all these problems on Electronic Arts, whom he'd sold out to in 1992 for a fast $35 million. Interested more in profits than quality, and eager to cash in on the *Ultima* brand, Electronic Arts rushed the production and released it before it was ready.

However, the worst and final *Ultima* was yet to come.

Ultima IX: Ascension

The last and worst of the single-player *Ultima* games, *Ultima IX: Ascension*, was published in 1999, and fans were even more incensed than they'd been with *Pagan* (Figure 13.8). The problem this time was a bait-and-switch game played by Garriott, who promised a product more in line with the classic *Ultima* games and went to fans for advice. They provided it, diligently, pointing out all the flaws in *Pagan* and reminding him about what

FIGURE 13.8 The last single-player *Ultima* is an unmitigated disaster and a tragic way to end the beloved series.

was really great about the older games. This conversation went a long way toward rebuilding his fans' trust and goodwill after the *Pagan* debacle.

Unfortunately, the production cycle hit gravel early on, and the code went through at least four different versions and twice as much drama. *Ultima Online* was also in production at this time and consuming nearly all of Garriott's attention (I'll have more to say about that game later). The end product is a buggy and even more reflex-oriented game than *Pagan*. It abandons the by then conventional isometric perspective for a fully 3D world in third-person perspective. It was a complete betrayal; an ignominious end for the legions of *Ultima* faithful who'd really believed that Lord British would restore the series to glory.

Most *Ultima* critics bitterly dismissed *Ascension* out of hand, but the game did manage to attract a small but dedicated community of iconoclasts. The complaints and defenses are many. One of the most often heard is that it's really more of an action adventure than a true CRPG, a claim based on *Ascension*'s limited leveling up capabilities and linear plot structure. Fans of *The Black Gate* were appalled by the rigidity of many of the game's events, such as a love story that some felt is "shoved down their throats."

On the other hand, no one complained about the game's lush graphics or excellent music. The day/night cycle returns, and there's also a high level of interactivity with objects. Sadly, a combination of poor voice acting, lackluster dialog, and banal characters didn't win back deluded *Ultima* fans, much less appeal to the mainstream. Indeed, even a special Dragon Edition large-box version of the game with several trinkets—a nod toward older and more revered *Ultima* games—failed to impress.

If we can learn anything from the *Ultima* story, it's that any long-running series has to be careful to preserve enough consistency across games to please the fans. We know that Garriott and Origin thought deeply about what elements really made the older games successful, but nevertheless miscalculated. Some of *Ultima*'s many fans are derisive of "twitch" games such as *The Legend of Zelda*, which were selling tens of millions more copies than even the best-selling *Ultima* ever had. The fact that *Ultima* games aren't for everyone only adds to their appeal for these folks.

I can see the logic behind Origin's decision to graft action elements onto the series, but the result was not what it'd hoped. Instead of attracting millions of new gamers to the franchise, it only angered the shrinking pool of loyal fans. My guess is that Origin would have fared much better by simply giving fans more of what they wanted rather than catering to the fickle mainstream. On the other hand, as we'll see when we discuss the last of the *Might & Magic* series, it's also important to freshen up a series with a constant flow of useful innovations and modest experiments.

Transcending *Ascension*: The Gothic Series

Ascension flopped, but German developer Piranha Bytes was able to follow more successfully in its footsteps, proving that action and adventure could mix well with more traditional CRPG mechanics. Its *Gothic* series debuted in November 2001, featuring a real-time, 3D world set in third-person perspective (Figure 13.9). Gameplay focuses on inventory-based puzzles as well as a challenging arcade-style combat system. The game is most noted for its dark, realistic ambience, open-ended gameplay, and rich character interaction. Despite some interface problems and bugs, the game attracted a loyal and dedicated following that remains strong today. Piranha Bytes followed up with *Gothic 2* in 2003 and released *Gothic 3* in 2006. Both sequels were well received, offering considerable graphical and interface enhancements over their predecessors.

Much like earlier German imports, such as the *Realms of Arkania* series, the *Gothic* series has never received the attention it deserves. While the

FIGURE 13.9 Pirahna Bytes' *Gothic* series seems to be what *Ultima IX* was aspiring to be—a fun, 3D action RPG with more than enough meat for old-school CRPG fans to sink their teeth into. I highly recommend them.

strong competition has undoubtedly been a factor, there are other rationales for *Gothic*'s mediocre ratings. The second game suffers from occasionally bad voice acting and translations, and the third game was glitchy. As one sharp tongued reviewer put it, "When the scenery looks like a postcard, but the Hero wears his shield inside of his humerus, there are some major quality control issues going on." Some criticized the combat system, which is pretty far removed from the turn-based style of other CRPGs.

However, I've come to really enjoy the series after revisiting the first *Gothic* in 2012 for *Matt Chat*. Although the combat system can be frustrating at first, you soon develop a feel and rhythm for it, and it's great fun learning the best way to defeat different types of monsters. I also love the quirky humor of the game, such as a village of swampweed merchants who must be bribed with beer. The second game is even better, with a more ambitious story and huge areas to explore. Official and fan-made patches have long since resolved the worst of the bugs, and it's easy to find fans who consider it among the best CRPG series of all time. One commenter put it this way: "What *Witcher* is for the Polish, *Gothic* is for the German."

After falling out with *Gothic*'s publisher, Jowood, Piranha Bytes created the *Risen* series, which debuted in 2002. That series certainly had its ups and downs, but I had a blast with the first one when I played it back in 2016 for *Matt Chat* 325. It's a worthy spiritual successor to *Gothic*, and that's saying something.

IN THE NEXT CHAPTER

Some might readers might assume that with so many disappointing games, the 1990s must have been a terrible decade for CRPGs. However, nothing could be further from the truth—for, although Origin and SSI seemed to have lost their edge, other CRPG developers were emerging to take up the slack. In the next chapter, we'll talk about some truly revolutionary games that reestablished the genre and propelled it to new heights.

CHAPTER 14

The Platinum Age

In the previous chapter we covered the nadir of the 1990s, which included the pathetic collapse of SSI and Origin. It was widely believed that the CRPG had joined the adventure game in the dustbin of gaming history. From now on, PC gaming would be dominated by intense 3D action games, especially first-person shooter games like *Doom, Quake,* and *Half-Life.*

However, in the latter half of the decade we find the best CRPGs ever made—the magnificent *Baldur's Gate, Elder Scrolls,* and *Diablo* games, as well as *Might and Magic: Mandate of Heaven* and *For Blood and Honor.* We left Interplay smarting after the disgraceful *Descent to Undermountain,* but it triumphantly returns with *Fallout* and *Planescape: Torment,* among the best CRPGs ever to grace a desktop. It's for this reason I call this the Platinum Age of CRPG—the best and most influential games that have stood the test of time.

But let's be clear. The developers of the Platinum Age stood on the shoulders of giants. Bethesda, Blizzard, and BioWare didn't start from scratch— they, like the makers of *The Bard's Tale* and *Pool of Radiance,* had excellent precedents to follow, and, more importantly, the enlightening results of failed experiments like *Ultima IX.* Furthermore, propelled by the intense requirements of 3D gaming, computer technology surged ahead, and the bewildering array of incompatible graphics and sound cards for the PC coalesced into a few recognized industry standards. Microsoft Windows 95 operating system consolidated and expanded the games industry, even if it did mean the end of powerful rivals like the Commodore Amiga, Atari ST, and even Microsoft's own MS-DOS platform.[1]

Microsoft lured game developers to its Windows operating system with its DirectX application programmer interface (API), which made integrating advanced graphics, sounds, and game controllers easier to implement and less prone to failure. Now game developers could focus their resources on a single platform instead of struggling to accommodate a smorgasbord of incompatible operating systems, graphics, and sound cards. Furthermore, new collaborative frameworks, coding practices, broadband Internet, and the licensing of third-party graphics engines helped CRPG developers speed up production, reduce game-crashing bugs, and release patches and updates.

Nevertheless, the cost of producing games was never greater, with budgets that rivaled or exceeded Hollywood blockbusters. The tombstones of bankrupt developers littered Silicon Valley, grim warnings to those whose aspirations outweighed their resources. Years of overhyped sludge had jaded even many hardcore fans of the genre, and who could say if even a superb new CRPG could compete with first-person shooters. PC gamers were just now discovering the joys of LAN parties, a movement that would eventually morph into the massively multiplayer online (MMO) games that now dominate the industry. No doubt many hardworking marketing analysts concluded, based on very sound evidence, that the classic single-player CRPG as we knew it had moved on to the underworld.

And, lo and behold, for once they were right.

ULTIMA UNDERWORLD: THE FIRST DUNGEON SIMULATOR

Origin's *Ultima Underworld: The Stygian Abyss,* published in 1992, deserves a special place in any book on CRPGs—or computer games in general, for that matter (Figure 14.1). It's one of the earliest games to offer fluid movement through a 3D world of fully textured polygons, rendered on the fly in first-person perspective. This was quite a feat at a time when similar games offer only wireframe or solid-color polygons; achieving anything greater meant prerendering the scenery and snapping rather than panning smoothly to new vantage points like you would in a flight simulator. Indeed, one way to distinguish *Ultima Underworld* and the subgenre from the older *Dungeon Master* style is to think of them as "dungeon simulators" rather than "dungeon crawlers."

Clearly, *The Stygian Abyss* represents a remarkable technological achievement, and let's not forget it debuted months before id's *Wolfenstein 3D,* the direct precursor of *Doom.* Indeed, John Carmack, one of id's key developers, saw a demo of *The Stygian Abyss* a year before

FIGURE 14.1 *Ultima Underworld* is to *Dungeon Master* what *Dungeon Master* was to *Wizardry*: that is, a great technological leap that dramatically increases immersion.

his company released its celebrated FPS.[2] Furthermore, *The Stygian Abyss* is more technically advanced than either *Wolfenstein 3D* or *Doom*, neither of which boasts the detailed realism of *Ultima Underworld*.

The Stygian Abyss was not developed by Origin, but rather a small group named Blue Sky Productions (later called Looking Glass Technologies) founded by Paul Neurath and Ned Lerner. Blue Sky showed Origin the prototype of their engine, and they decided it should become a spinoff of their *Ultima* series. However, this game would focus more on physical reflexes than on mental acumen. It was produced by Warren Spector.

Beneath the surface, *Ultima Underworld* seems like a brazen attempt to plagiarize *Dungeon Master*. Like *Dungeon Master*, *The Stygian Abyss* is set in a dank, dark dungeon, and the Avatar needs to continuously look for food and light sources (in this case, torches). Even the magic system is similar: Spells are cast by arranging sequences of rune stones found sprinkled throughout the dungeon.

However, unlike *Dungeon Master*, *Ultima Underworld* features fluid 3D movement in 360 degrees (by contrast, *Wolfenstein 3D* only let you look left and right). You can even take a swim! You also have more control over combat: The type of attack (slash, stab, hack) is determined by the position of the mouse pointer, and the power by how long you hold down the mouse button. Many critics agree these innovations make the game realistic and more immersive, as though you're actually in the game rather than controlling a character from a distance. Another nice feature is a powerful automapper, which not only tracks movement but lets you input your own notes. Finally, shown on the screen at all times are two large glass bottles, one red (for hit points) and one blue (for magic power). These bottles empty out as the character suffers damage or expends magical energy. It's an eminently intuitive system that shows up in plenty of later games, most notably Blizzard's *Diablo*.

The story is more or less of the "damsel in distress" type; this time a baron's daughter has been kidnapped by a mysterious creature. The Avatar happens to materialize during the abduction and is held as a suspect. The Avatar tries to explain the odd circumstance, but the baron decides to put his word to the test by sealing him into the titular abyss, with the mission to recover the princess or die in the attempt. However, the abyss isn't just crawling with monsters. Indeed, part of the fun here is interacting with the many intelligent denizens wandering the corridors.

Another important aspect of *Ultima Underworld* to consider is that the player controls only one character, the Avatar. What's the big deal? Well, one of the most frequent complaints I hear from novice CRPG players is that class systems are too rigid. Why would anyone living in a world with magic not want to take advantage of it, even if that person happened to be a knight? What sensible adventurers wouldn't want some clerical training, so they could heal themselves if the need arose? Why should rogues be the only folks capable of picking locks or spotting traps? Old-fashioned pen-and-paper RPGs, as well as most party-based CRPGs, depend on class restrictions for balance; characters who can do it all might sound like fun, but they'd soon get incredibly dull—not to mention irritating to other players who'd suddenly feel redundant: Who needs a rogue when everyone else can also pick locks and disarm traps? However, in CRPGs where you only control a single character—who is nonetheless expected to perform all the roles of a traditional *D&D* party—rigid class restrictions just don't work.

Ultima Underworld and several of the games it inspired tries to get around this potential issue with class options like the shepherd (a jack-of-all-trades) and a separate skills system. For example, there are skills for picking locks and disabling traps, which get their bonus from dexterity and aren't restricted to a single class. Some classes require certain skills, but you can also choose some optional ones. However, several of the skills turn out to be useless in the game, probably as a concession to the fact that you can't learn all of them. These useless skills include the thievery-related ones mentioned above; there are not nearly enough traps or lockpicks in the game to make them worthwhile. In short, rather than require players to build versatile characters that could take on all the traditional roles of a *D&D* party (fighter, mage, cleric, and thief) they just avoid situations that any one class couldn't handle.

You don't have to be a games historian to see how this game paved the way for the *Elder Scrolls* series and countless other games. It was immediately recognized as an important breakthrough in the genre, and *Computer Gaming World* named it the best role-playing game of the year. Indeed, the only folks who weren't excited was Origin; despite all the hoopla, it was only a mediocre seller.

Labyrinth of Worlds

Despite middling sales of the first game, Origin published Blue Sky's sequel, *Labyrinth of Worlds,* the following year. The sequel makes a few technical innovations, including digital sound effects and an expanded viewing area. The storyline is more sophisticated as well, and it's better tied in to the main *Ultima* series. A magical crystal of blackrock has formed over Lord British's castle, isolating the land of Britannia from its foremost defenders. Fortunately, the Avatar can use a smaller crystal to travel to eight different dimensions in search of a solution. It's a massive game, and the alternate dimensions allow for many intriguing scenarios, such as a fortress floating in the sky, an icy wasteland, and a surreal Ethereal Void. Critics raved—but, once again, sales were average at best.

Why wasn't *Ultima Underworld* the smash hit it clearly deserved to be?

There's been much speculation on this question over the years. One likely reason is that Blue Sky's games demanded more computing power than most PC gamers had at their disposal in the early 1990s. The games themselves were a whopping $79.95 each, well over $130 in today's money. By contrast, id's products were much cheaper and partly distributed freely as shareware. Meanwhile, the minimum specs for *The Stygian Abyss* call for an Intel 80386-equipped PC with a full two megabytes of RAM. According to a 1993 survey published in *PC Week*, only 46 percent of PC users had a i386 or better at the time (and most of those machines were on the low end). Compare that to *Wolfenstein 3D's* specs, which required a i286 processor with only 640 kilobytes of RAM. To put it simply, you needed a very expensive PC just to run *The Stygian Abyss*, much less at a decent framerate.

This explanation doesn't satisfy everyone, however, including Paul Neurath. He claims that Origin failed to properly support his games, perhaps unwilling to see a spinoff eclipse Lord British's signature series: "The Underworlds never got the level of marketing that some of the other top Origin games received," said Neurath.[3] When he approached Origin with ideas for a third game, he was turned down.

Perhaps if Origin had waited until the latter part of 1993 to release *The Stygian Abyss*, it might have ridden the wave made by *Myst* and *Doom*, which also benefited from cutting-edge machines. However, those games enjoyed a tremendous burst of media publicity and word-of-mouth advertising, which were enough to convince countless PC gamers to ante up for the new standards despite the cost.

Then again, Origin published Blue Sky's *System Shock* in 1994, a 3D action-adventure sci-fi game with many similarities to the *Underworld* series. It too sold badly. The sequel, *System Shock 2,* was developed in conjunction with Irrational Games and published by Electronic Arts in 1999. It's an absolutely exquisite fusion of FPS, CRPG, and survival horror, and widely regarded as a masterpiece. Inexplicably, *System Shock 2* also sold below expectations. In a 2008 interview with Kieron Gillen of *Rock Paper Shotgun*, Ken Levine (*System Shock 2*'s lead designer) admitted that whenever he mentioned it, only "the intelligentsia of the intelligentsia of the game industry" had ever heard of it! Thankfully, *System Shock*'s reputation has improved substantially, and meanwhile, Looking Glass enjoyed much better commercial success with *Thief: The Dark Project,* a stealth-action series that debuted in 1998. Warren Spector went on to produce *Deus Ex* for *Ion Storm* in 2000, another sci-fi first-person action RPG. Happily for Spector, this game sold much better than his previous efforts and secured his reputation as a brilliant game maker.

Ultima Underworld and the Rise of Fluid First-Person 3D

Although Blue Sky's *Ultima Underworld* games weren't exactly hits, other CRPG developers and publishers saw their potential and jumped on the 3D, texture-mapping bandwagon. Two of the earliest are Synthetic Dimension's **Legends of Valour** (1992) and Psygnosis' **Hexx: Heresy of the Wizard** (1994), but there were also better-known series such as *Realms of Arkania, Lands of Lore,* the later *Might and Magic*s, and, of course, the *Elder Scrolls,* which we'll get to in a moment.

For now, though, let's consider why none of these 3D CRPGs ever really competed with the likes of *Doom* or *Quake*. Are FPS games simply more fun than CRPGs, regardless of whether they're 2D or 3D?

To answer this, it's critical to keep in mind that the success of *Doom* and later FPS games had as much to do with clever marketing as brilliant coding, graphics, and level design. Id's publisher, Scott Miller's Apogee, adapted a software marketing strategy called shareware. Previously, games and other software were either sold commercially at retail, with whatever copyright protection a publisher could muster, or simply released into the public domain for free—obviously not a viable option for people hoping to earn a living (Figure 14.2). Shareware was an innovative third option that amounted to try-before-you-buy.

Games released as shareware were usually just demos, which let you see a game in action, but not let you play it. It sounds crummy, but this was quite a step up from simply staring at screenshots on the back of a box or reading about a game in magazines. Other shareware games let you play the game in question, but only for a limited time. Others pester you for donations, either politely at the beginning or end or, more annoyingly, intermittently during gameplay. All of these methods have their flaws. Many gamers didn't like paying for disk magazines

FIGURE 14.2 *Doom* is, without question, one of the greatest video games of all time, but don't overlook the role that Miller played with his clever marketing and distribution strategy.

or wasting precious bandwidth just to watch a short demo or play a stripped-down version of a game.

Miller's innovation was to freely release a fully playable game as a loss leader for extra levels or episodes that he sold by mail. Miller guessed correctly that if you liked a game enough to play through an entire episode, you'd be strongly tempted to buy the additional content. We still see vestiges of Miller's methods in the form of paid "downloadable content" or DLC, as well as episodic games like Telltale's *The Walking Dead* series. Indeed, whenever I see Telltale release the first episode of one of its adventure games for free, I think of Miller and Apogee.

For id, though, the crucial breakthrough was that the free version of *Doom* included its networked multiplayer mode. This allowed *Doom*-obsessed gamers to give the game to their friends, who could then lug their PCs over and network them together for the ultimate deathmatch—and the LAN (local area network) party was born. All the word-of-mouth advertising this movement generated led countless gamers to pay for the full commercial versions. This strategy was tremendously successful, and the tiny company was soon among the top computer game developers in the world. By contrast, most CRPGs were only sold commercially and limited to solo play, and it took some time before developers (most notably Blizzard's *Diablo* series) accommodated LAN parties or created Internet-powered MMORPGs.

Finally, both *Wolfenstein 3D* and *Doom* were purposefully built for high-speed action. This is a point that John Romero emphasizes in my interviews with him. *Wolfenstein 3D*, as the title suggests, was inspired by Silas Warner's *Castle Wolfenstein* (1981), a pioneering stealth action game that required a great deal of cunning and patience. Id started off trying to replicate these mechanics, but abruptly decided to strip out the stealth mechanics for the sake of fast run-and-gun action. It was certainly the right call; often enough, a fun game is simply a boring game with one less mechanic. For gamers playing *Doom,* just the experience of fast 3D graphics in first-person perspective was exciting enough; role-playing or stealth mechanics would've been too much too soon. Later, of course, when gamers had grown accustomed to or even bored with standard first-person shooters (FPSs), more sophisticated games like *Thief* and *Deus Ex* finally had their chance.

For these and other reasons, even as 3D CRPGs overcame their growing pains and emerged as wonderful games in their own right, they still languished behind FPSs in terms of sales and popularity. Then as now, many PC gamers would much rather frag their friends in explosive, trash-talking deathmatches than sit quietly for hours crawling through dungeons. However, just as golf and tennis coexist with football and basketball in the world of sports, there's still plenty of room in the games industry for great CRPGs.

Realms of Arkania: Star Trail

In Chapter 11 we discussed Attic's *Realms of Arkania*, a series of German CRPGs that brought *The Dark Eye* tabletop game to a *Dungeon Master*–style interface (Figures 14.3 and 14.4). The next entry in the series, published by Sir-Tech in 1994, is *Star Trail*, upgraded the series with smooth-scrolling 3D movement *and* animated isometric 3D combat. It's often considered the best of the trilogy despite—or perhaps because of—its steep learning curve and daunting complexity, a characteristic of German CRPGs. It also boasts superior graphics and digitized sound, made possible by CD-ROM.

Finally, there are quality-of-life enhancements, such as a more powerful automapper with zoom. This aspect of CRPGs tends to get overlooked, but in my experience, they're absolutely crucial, and a developer's time spent on them is never wasted. Once the razzle-dazzle of the graphics and animation wears off—which happens all too quickly—seemingly minor

FIGURE 14.3 *Realms of Arkania: Star Trail* has smooth-scrolling movement for exploration instead of the grid-based movement of its predecessor.

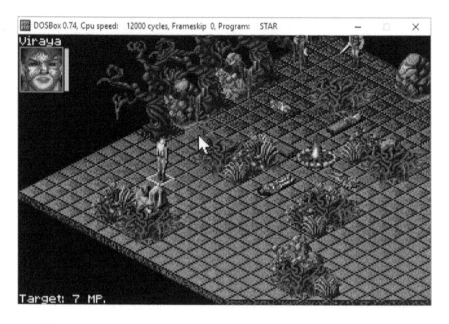

FIGURE 14.4 *Realms of Arkania: Star Trail* keeps the turn-based isometric combat. For many fans of this series, it's the best of both worlds—immersive exploration *and* tactical combat.

annoyances, such as a cumbersome inventory system, long loading times, or a confusing automap, become unbearable.

Star Trail starts off with a seemingly straightforward quest for the ancient Salamander Stone, though two different parties ask for it, and the player can't please both. The party is also asked to retrieve a throwing axe called Star Trail, though the motives behind these requests are vague and ambiguous. Meanwhile, the orcs are terrorizing the land in force, and the dwarves and elves can't seem to settle their differences long enough to fend them off. In short, there's plenty to do and lots to explore, and it's well worth playing today.

Shadows Over Riva

Shadows Over Riva, published in 1996, is the last of the *Realms of Arkania* games. Like its predecessors, *Shadows Over Riva* has a real-time, first-person exploration mode and turn-based isometric combat. While critics are generally impressed with the former, the combat mode seems (to them!) a bit cramped and dated, but no one complains about the high level of detail and options for character customization. What other game allows a character to learn dancing or become a jester? There's also an interesting option to split the party, temporarily leaving a member behind if he or she needs time to recuperate.

The story concerns the titular town of Riva, which is under siege by orcs. There's evil magic involved, and it's up to the player's sextet to discover its source and save the town. The plot quickly thickens, and the many intriguing characters earn the game much praise in the storytelling category. Most fans of the series, though, focus on the game's extraordinarily character development options.

Overall, the *Realms of Arkania* games are well worth playing today. The mechanics take time to master, and there's potential for endless party management and character options. Furthermore, the amount of content is extremely impressive, especially when you consider that you can carry over your characters (and their equipment!) from one game to the next. As noted before, the German pen-and-paper game these games are based on, *Das Schwarze Auge* or "The Dark Eye," isn't nearly as well known here as in Germany, but don't let that stop you. Indeed, it's not hard to find American CRPG fans who prefer it to *Dungeons & Dragons*.

Lands of Lore: Guardians of Destiny

Let's turn back now to Westwood, a studio that rightfully comes up often in this book. As you'll recall, it made its mark with a bevy of enhanced ports for Amiga, Atari ST, and other systems, but it also developed *BattleTech: The Crescent Hawk's Revenge* (1990) and SSI's *Eye of the Beholder* (1991) series. In 1992, it launched an original franchise called *Lands of Lore,* the first of which (*The Throne of Chaos*) is a *Dungeon Master*–style game with grid-based movement.

It's the next game in this series, *Guardians of Destiny,* that concerns us here (Figure 14.5). First published in 1997, it has an enhanced graphics engine that allows for fluid 3D movement, but goes a step further by introducing hours of full-motion video (FMV) and live action sequences. It also incorporates many action sequences, including some timed sequences and lots of running and jumping, to the point where some critics deride it as an action adventure rather than a true CRPG.

The CRPG elements are limited because the player controls only a single character, Luther, who comes to the game with a predefined personality and purpose in life. Luther is the son of the villainess in the first *Lands of Lore* and has inherited his mother's poor reputation as well as a powerful (but uncontrollable) ability to morph into different forms (human,

FIGURE 14.5 The second *Lands of Lore* game makes copious use of full-motion video, live action, and voice acting. Shown here is an early battle with a lamp-carrying warrior.

lizard, beast). Luther's task is to clean up after his mother, stopping Belial from coming back to wreak havoc. There are five possible endings that hinge on whether Luther succeeds in his quest and whether he's been good or evil.

As before, the game limits the CRPG elements to gradual increases in magic and combat, and the quality of armor and weapons is shown abstractly as lines on a graph. The interface is relegated to the lower right corner, dedicating the rest of the screen to the gameworld. Luther's animated face is shown in photo-realistic detail at the lower right corner of the screen, blinking, shifting his eyebrows, and changing to reflect his condition. The superb soundtrack is by Frank Klepacki and David Arkenstone.

Fans of the series have long been divided over whether *Guardians of Destiny* is the best or the worst of the series. The popularity of FMV plummeted in the late 1990s, when it became seen as a cheesy gimmick rather than a technological marvel. Furthermore, the 3D graphics look more like *Ultima Underworld* than *Quake 2,* the smoothest and best-looking FPS anyone had ever seen (and with which *Guardians of Destiny* had to compete with for shelf space). I think it's well worth trying out for yourself, especially if you're a fan of the *Might and Magic* games we discuss later in this chapter.

Lands of Lore III

The last game in Westwood's series, *Lands of Lore III*, wisely ditched the live action for motion-captured animation and voice acting, but it's still the weakest of the three (Figure 14.6). There are many flaws, including repetitive gameplay, poor artificial intelligence, unbalanced graphics, the tiresome mechanic of having to constantly find food, and, of course, plenty of bugs—the telltale sign of a harried production.

This time the player assumes the role of Copper LeGré, the illegitimate son of the king's brother. While on a hunting trip, Copper and the family are ambushed by rift hounds, who pop in from another dimension and slaughter everyone but Copper (though they steal his soul). Everyone suspects that Copper killed his companions to secure the throne for himself, so he must prove them wrong and recapture his soul in the process. That will entail traveling to over six worlds and battling plenty of monsters, as well as solving puzzles and navigating tricky action sequences.

Westwood responded to the limited character development in *Guardians of Destiny* by revamping the leveling system. *Lands of Lore III* offers four guilds for the character to join, each with its own skill sets, quests, and familiars. The familiars serve to complement the player's strengths and weaknesses, but they also have their own personalities. You can join any combination of the four guilds (warrior, mage, cleric,

FIGURE 14.6 *Lands of Lore III* opens with an impressive cinematic, but even that wasn't as impressive as the in-game graphics in other 3D games of the era.

and thief) and recruit any familiar. In most games of this type, too much hybridization results in a useless character, but here the difficulty level is low enough that it pays to gain skills in each guild.

Once again, the graphics look dated compared to other 3D games sitting beside it on the shelf. Furthermore, although the game has several deceptively expansive outside areas, you're constrained to narrow paths through them. One user reviewer of the game on GOG.com, Ikalx, puts it memorably: "The forest—almost the main hub of the game, suffers most from this, and I would trade Copper's right foot for a small section of *Oblivion's* forests."

The game was immediately smeared with scathing reviews, as a quick glance at their titles makes clear: "Strike Three!," "Criminal!," etc. Its reputation has not improved since. In Westwood's defense, I should point out that Electronic Arts gobbled it up back in 1998, the same crew that often gets blamed for ruining Origin's *Ultima* series. In Electronics Arts' defense, it's not hard to see why they would be more interested in Westwood's real-time strategy cash cow, *Command & Conquer,* than a charming but modestly selling labor of love.

BETHESDA, *THE ELDER SCROLLS,* AND PROCEDURAL GENERATION REVISITED

Perhaps the most successful of all games inspired by *Ultima Underworld* are the *Elder Scrolls* series, a line of first-person, 3D CRPGs developed by Bethesda Softworks. Indeed, it's the longest-running CRPG series still in active development and rightfully so. In addition to their immense size and scope, these "sandbox" games are celebrated for their open-ended and unpredictable gameplay, which heightens replay value while providing tremendous room for customization and character development. The games are also praised for their cutting-edge graphics and sound effects— a well-earned reputation that proves decisive as we delve deeper into the 1990s. In short, these are games that are well worth the hundreds if not thousands of hours that so many of us have sunk into them.

The two games we'll cover in this section rely heavily on procedurally generated content, similar to what we saw in *Rogue* or *Nethack*. There's always a trade-off with this method: Eventually it becomes apparent that the dungeons, quests, loot, or the monsters you encounter were put there by a machine, not the hand of an experienced storyteller. Many things just don't make sense at all, and you'll eventually start to see the strings, or the code behind the curtain, if you will.

There's a reason why good storytellers are so highly valued in every culture—we all savor the coherence of a well-crafted tale, where every detail serves some meaningful purpose. As playwright Anton Chekhov famously put it, "If you say in the first chapter that there is a rifle hanging on the wall, in the second or third chapter it absolutely must go off. If it's not going to be fired, it shouldn't be hanging there." The idea is that anyone reading the story will know the rifle is a significant detail and remember it, then wait expectantly for its narrative purpose to be revealed. When, sure enough, the hunter uses it to shoot the bear menacing the cabin at the story's climax, we feel satisfied; everything has come together.

Of course, in a procedurally generated story, there's no way of knowing whether that rifle will serve a purpose or not. The player might not even look at it, or they could just leave it behind and never come back. Thus, authorial intention is a moot point when it comes to purely procedurally generated content. By contrast, no matter how many narrative branches or sidequests a conventional CRPG offers you, you're always being guided or led down paths laid there by the designer who can, by hook or by crook, ensure the rifle mentioned in the first act will indeed go off by the third. Only procedurally generated content frees you entirely from the narrator's hooks and crooks, but usually at the cost of narrative coherence or, for that matter, any coherence whatsoever. We'll return to this theme in a moment.

The Elder Scrolls: Arena

The first *Elder Scrolls* game, *Arena,* was published by U.S. Gold in 1994 for DOS. Like its many sequels, *Arena* has real-time 3D graphics in first-person perspective (Figure 14.7). It has a huge gameworld with over 400 cities, towns, and villages, all of which can be explored. Although it's not as well known today as *Morrowind* or *Daggerfall,* some fans still rank it as not only the best game in the series, but as the best CRPG, period. I wouldn't go that far, but *Arena* clearly deserves a respected place in the annals of CRPG history.

One way to think about *Arena* is as a combination of *The Stygian Abyss* and *The Black Gate.* While *Arena* offers a real-time, 3D, first-person perspective like that of *The Stygian Abyss,* it also has a realistic and persistent gameworld like *The Black Gate*'s. Not only do players observe the passing of time from night and day, but it even rains and snows according to the season. It's really the sophistication of this virtual world that makes it so

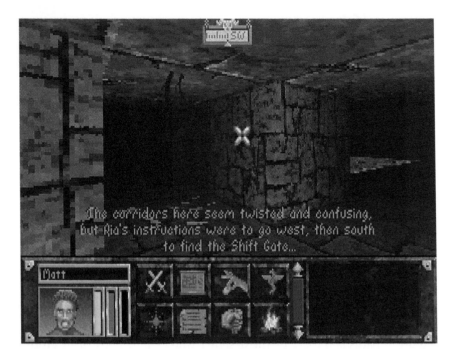

The corridors here seem twisted and confusing, but Ria's instructions were to go west, then south to find the Shift Gate...

FIGURE 14.7 The first *Elder Scrolls* game, *Arena*, is an incredibly ambitious CRPG that updated and refined the *Ultima Underworld* formula. Bethesda offers it as a free download from its *Elder Scrolls* website, but you'll need an emulator to run it.

notable. The quest—find the eight missing pieces of the Staff of Chaos and rescue the Emperor from a dimensional prison—is minimal, but it does make it possible to win the game (as opposed to a true sandbox game, where there's no preestablished ending). What draws praise from critics and dollars from gamers was the incredible size of its world and the open-ended nature of the gameplay. Note, however, that although the game has considerably more freedom of action than most games of its type (particularly regarding stealing), you still need to perform a fairly linear sequence of quests in order to win.

Arena has an intriguing combat system: the position of the mouse pointer determines which of five attacks the avatar performs. We see something similar in *The Stygian Abyss*, though that game has only three attacks (bash, slash, and thrust). With *Arena* we get two diagonal slashes, horizontal cut, vertical chop, and thrust. These are accomplished by holding the down the right mouse button while moving the mouse as directed.

This method is more complex than simply clicking a button, but it arguably adds to the immersion by tying the player's mouse movements to the movements of the weapon on the screen.

As I noted in our discussion of *Ultima Underworld*, games that limit you to a single character must decide whether to make that character versatile enough to do all the things a diverse party can do, simply avoid these situations (or at least make them unnecessary), allow NPCs to perform these tasks, or provide workarounds. Like *Ultima Underworld*, *Arena* opts for a combination of workarounds and an extensive set of hybrid classes. However, it doesn't borrow its skill system.

Arena's character development system is based on eight stats and races, and eighteen classes grouped into three main categories (thief, warrior, mage) with subclasses for each. Most of these classes are hybrids of conventional *D&D* classes. For instance, Battle Mages can cast spells but also wield any weapon, wear up to leather armor, and carry a round shield. The Spellsword mage is even more skilled in weaponry and armor but takes a hit in spell points. The Bard, a subclass of Thief, is a jack-of-all-trades that can do pretty much anything. Players can either select their class from a list or answer a series of *Ultima*-style ethical questions to determine it for them.

The game also has a more sophisticated armor system than most CRPGs. Instead of just a single suit of plate mail, for instance, characters accessorize with unique helms, pauldrons (shoulder guards), cuirasses (chest and back guards), gauntlets, greaves (waist and upper-leg guards), and boots. I wish more CRPGs had these extensive options for gearing up; it certainly gives you more to look forward to as you're out pillaging and looting. Further adding to the realism (and the need for more pillaging and looting), arms and armor become damaged and broken with use. They are composed of eight different metals, including silver—the only metal that can damage certain creatures.

Although the game is still impressive, it's not perfect. Like so many other games of this period, it was riddled with bugs. The battles are also quite a bit tougher than some gamers can handle, and the game's formidable specs limited its appeal to those with cutting-edge machines. For these reasons, it had little more success than Origin's *The Stygian Abyss*. In any case, the game set a new standard for this type of CRPG, and it demonstrated how much room was left for innovation. Bethesda generously rereleased this classic as freeware and even offered it as a free download from its home page.

Daggerfall

In 1996 Bethesda followed up the modestly successful *Arena* with *Daggerfall*, a game that's still regarded as one of the most immersive and extensive CRPGs ever designed (Figure 14.8). Like *Arena*, it's set in Tamriel, which has now been expanded into one of the largest interactive worlds ever seen in a CRPG. The replay possibilities are virtually endless. It's also the first *Elder Scrolls* game to use Bethesda's XnGine 3D graphics engine, which it had developed for two *Terminator*-licensed first-person shooter games.

Most notably, the developers purposefully downplay the story. No reference to an overarching quest is made on the box, and the manual reads: "'What's the story?' It is not for us to answer. Follow your own spirit and tell your story in your own way. We hope only to help you make it *real*." To this end, the manual warns players against abusing the save-game feature. "If your character is caught pickpocketing, if a quest goes wrong, or some other mundane mishap occurs, let it play out. You may be surprised by what happens next." Personally, I reload after such "happy accidents," but I appreciate this perspective.

FIGURE 14.8 The second *Elder Scrolls* ups the ante with better audiovisuals and fewer narrative rails. Who needs a complicated story butting in when all you really want to do is kill some rats?

The manual paints a rosy picture of story-by-algorithm, but a hilarious things happened to me while doing *Matt Chat*. For episode 118, I play *Daggerfall* and have a great time. However, in one house, I casually chat with a scantily clad lady lounging beside a pipe organ. This was odd enough, but what's even stranger is that she's doing so while a sabretooth tiger is loudly ravaging downstairs! I thought I'd stumbled upon a scene from *Monty Python's Flying Circus*. Of course, it's just one of countless unintentionally absurdist moments concocted by the algorithms of *Daggerfall*.

As we'll see, in later *Elder Scrolls* games, Bethesda tones down or eliminates most of the procedurally generated content, relying more on intentional design to achieve narrative coherence and avoid incidents like the one just mentioned. This all begs the question of whether CRPGs that let you "tell you story in your own way" are superior to those with great stories already built in. This also gets at the heart of many a CRPG versus JRPG debate: Are sandbox or "open world" games more fun than linear ones? How important is it that a player make "meaningful" choices, and how much effect should these choices have on the development of the story and its outcome?

Let's face it: the stories in most CRPGs make the clumsiest swords and sorcery novel look like *The Lord of the Rings* by comparison. They are rotten with stilted dialogs, clumsy stereotypes, cringeworthy puns and inside jokes, tedious expositions, and even rampant misspellings. Now there are also plenty with well-written stories, but, subjectively speaking, I'd rather read their stories in print than have them constantly interrupting my gameplay. This is one reason I like the early CRPGs so much; memory limitations required that designers put the bulk of their story (or at least backstory) into printed manuals or novellas, which you can comfortably read in your armchair. As those memory limitations went away, designers began incorporating more and more text (and eventually, digitized speech) directly into the game, and the results have been mixed.

The problem with these story-heavy CRPGs amounts to what creative writing teachers are always going on about, namely "show, don't tell." But what does this advice actually mean? First, they're talking about the need to let readers come to realizations on their own, not tell them what to think. For example, instead of simply describing a wizard as "cowardly," you could have a scene where he soiled his robe at the sight of a kobold off in the distance. "Telling" is like spoiling the end of a mystery story; it's more fun for readers if they can put the pieces together and figure it out on their own.

Second, you should avoid interrupting the flow of a narrative with lengthy expositions such as those found so frequently in (gasp) Tolkien. Try reading The Council of Elrond scene from the first book again. Not only does Tolkien bring the action to a standstill, but he dumps a ton of information on us before we have any real reason to care about it. The problem with CRPG stories is that they tend to be one Council of Elrond after another, with lengthy expositions and dialogs between characters we barely know or care about. In the worst games, it's just assumed we should care, but we never do, and simply skip the constant cutscenes or skim the text as quickly as possible just to get on with it. In fact, it might even be a worse flaw than in written stories, where at least the exposition doesn't stop you from *reading* in the way a cutscene stops you from *playing*. To put it simply, it's not that procedurally generated games are better in any intrinsic sense; it's just that the stories told in most CRPGs are done so badly, with so much "telling" and so little "showing," that you're better off without them.

Another argument in favor of procedurally generated games is that they can be more personally meaningful. Whenever I talk to fans of *Rogue*, *Diablo*, or *Daggerfall*, they're always excited to tell a story about something unexpected or memorable that happened to them while playing, such as getting infected by a werewolf and spending the rest of the game as a lycanthrope. These events wouldn't be half as thrilling if they were part of one-size-fits-all story that everyone else experienced, no matter how epic that story was purported to be.

On the other hand, I must admit I still prefer games with a strong and conscientious storyteller. *Baldur's Gate, Betrayal at Krondor, Planescape: Torment*—these are games that really do a great job of meshing story, backstory, and action together in ways that complement rather than compete with each other. We'll get to these games in due course. Sadly, though, these games are precious precisely because they are so rare. All it takes to fail is one self-indulgent author, more in love with her words than with her readers, to ruin an otherwise fine game.

In any case, Bethesda's decision to hand over narrative control to the player paid off handsomely. Critics explicitly praise the lack of narrative guardrails, reveling in the freedom to explore Tamriel and develop their characters as they see fit. A contemporary reviewer describes the gameplay quite well: "No longer forced to play the way The Man wants, we are now free to ignore the pleadings of the princess, wander off, and get involved in other complex tales that change and evolve in response to our actions."[4]

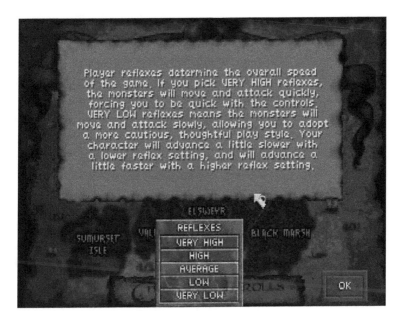

FIGURE 14.9 *Daggerfall's* developers smartly try to accommodate different kinds of players with a "reflexes" rather than a "difficulty" selector. I say "smartly" because many games represent this simply as a question of difficulty rather than play style preference: Choosing a mode called "Easy" or "Novice" affects one's dignity in ways that these options do not.

Comments like this are ubiquitous in most fans' discussions of the game and explain its broad appeal (Figure 14.9).

The leveling system is also more dynamic than the previous game, with dozens more skills to choose from. These skills are divided into primary, major, and minor depending on the character's occupation. Many skills are directly related to combat and weapon proficiencies, but others are for magic and thievery. Others, such as etiquette, mercantile, languages, and streetwise, help you get the most out of interactions with NPCs. Each skill also has a governing attribute, such as strength for jumping and climbing.

In most CRPGs, characters fight monsters to gain experience points, which eventually add up and enable them to advance to the next level and receive various bonuses. In CRPGs with skill systems, such as *Wasteland,* gaining a level also awards you a certain number of skill points to distribute. *Daggerfall* flips this system on its head; now, improving your skills is what leads to gaining a level. Skills are raised either by using them repeatedly or paying a trainer. Level gains are based on a formula that factors in increases to these skills; primary ones are weighted more heavily than major and minor. All in all, it's a logical and refined system.

Furthermore, the old rigid class structure is abandoned in favor of a much more open-ended guild system. Players now customize their character as they see fit, letting their creativity run wild. Since the statistics can be rather daunting to novices, Bethesda keeps the *Ultima*-style morality quiz option it employed in *Arena*.

Unfortunately, Bethesda's coders weren't up to the challenge, and we're again tormented by a myriad of bugs. By this point it was becoming common practice to issue bug fixes and patches for downloading from the Internet, but it was still a major annoyance. Another caveat is the lack of balance in the game's difficulty. It doesn't take experienced players long to gain enough experience to simply walk through the game, obliterating even the most powerful enemies with a light swat. Finally, there are problems with movement; players can get stuck between objects and have to restart. Nevertheless, most critics are willing to overlook these issues, and *Daggerfall* received countless well-earned awards from the most prestigious PC and gaming magazines. The game continues to enjoy a loyal fan base even today, supported by several dedicated fan sites and message boards.

Battlespire

Bethesda developed and published two spinoffs before releasing the third entry in the official *Elder Scrolls* series. These are *An Elder Scrolls Legend: Battlespire* (1997) and *The Elder Scrolls Adventures: Redguard* (1998) (Figure 14.10). Although not nearly as well known as the main series, these two games represent some of Bethesda's more radical experiments with the genre and paved the way for its later hit *Morrowind*. Both games use an enhanced version of XnGine, the 3D graphics engine used in *Daggerfall*.

Battlespire is in many ways a simplified, "hold the extras" version of *Daggerfall* and is really more of an FPS than a CRPG. The reduced learning curve is apparent from the character creation stage, which now utilizes a series of on-screen help menus to guide you through the process. More importantly, the game is much less random and open-ended than *Daggerfall,* with linear, story-driven gameplay. The story is set in the titular spire, which was once a proving ground for the Imperial Guard (one thinks of Sir-Tech's first *Wizardry* game). The spire has been overrun by the legions of Mehrunes Dagon, a vile Daedra Lord, who cares very little for our young

It looks like the Seducer would like to have a word with you.

FIGURE 14.10   *Battlespire* simplifies the RPG mechanics to place more emphasis on action and, apparently, buttocks. Image from GOG.com.

hero's safety. The gameplay emphasizes precise control and jumping, which has never been easy in first-person perspective games like this one.

If Bethesda was trying to prove that open-ended games were better than linear ones, *Battlespire* was an expensive if conclusive experiment. It was not well received by critics. However, players were also frustrated by bugs, many of them caused by the now-outdated XnGine, which was designed for DOS and ran poorly on Windows 95. The enemy's pathfinding routines are also subpar, and otherwise challenging opponents are prone to getting stuck on things—and other objects just float in midair!

Redguard

Redguard departs from the first-person perspective of the other games in favor of a third-person view, with the player's avatar visible on-screen. If *Battlespire* leans toward the FPS, *Redguard* leans toward the traditional adventure game. Completing it requires conversing with a great many characters and plenty of backtracking, but also some *Tomb Raider*–like action sequences including climbing, jumping, and swimming. For obvious reasons, being able to see your character on screen makes these sequences easier to deal with.

Although both *Battlepire* and *Redguard* have their good points, they had more gamers scratching heads than opening wallets. I think Bethesda used these games as an opportunity to experiment with different interface and gameplay techniques as they prepared for a proper sequel to *Daggerfall*.

Morrowind

One of the best of the *Elder Scrolls* games appeared in 2002: *The Elder Scrolls III: Morrowind. Morrowind* combines the first-person perspective of the earlier *Daggerfall* with the third-person of *Redguard* (Figure 14.11). For the first time, players can choose between the different perspectives as they see fit. It is just one more way to make the story theirs—to see what *they* choose to see—and players soon discover that each mode has its advantages. For instance, third-person perspective makes it easier to dodge attacks. *Morrowind* is also the first of the series to be available for consoles, namely, Microsoft's Xbox.

The leveling system is revamped and reorganized into two parts: Primary Stats (speed, personality, luck, etc.) and Secondary Abilities

FIGURE 14.11 *Morrowind* is one of the all-time best CRPGs, and there's plenty of people who still love it. Indeed, many fans of the series consider it the best *Elder Scrolls* game. Shown here is the Game of the Year Edition from GOG.com.

(combat arts, magic arts, etc.). Primary stats rise only when you gain a level, but secondary abilities improve only with each *successful* use (not with every use, as with *Daggerfall*). Trainers are also more limited, training only three skills each, and harder to find. As with the later *Might and Magic* games we discuss below, each skill has a secret master trainer who must be located and placated in order to raise it up all the way. I've always liked this idea; mastering a skill can become a quest in and of itself.

Although Bethesda made the lack of a story in *Daggerfall* a key selling point, it reverses this policy entirely with *Morrowind*. The gameworld is much smaller, but it's handcrafted. Todd Howard, the game's project leader, claims this was a huge improvement from *Daggerfall*'s "random buildings" that "got old very fast when the player realized it was just the same stuff over and over again." In another interview he refers to "tons of procedurally determined garbage," but contradicts himself by arguing that that's what makes *Daggerfall* so great. However, while he was still interested in a "free-form experience" for *Morrowind*, he felt the best way to achieve it was for content to be carefully designed by hand, even if it meant a much smaller gameworld. Given the game's success and continued high regard by fans of the series—not to mention my own personal enjoyment of the game—I think Howard was right.[5]

Despite its lack of procedurally generated content, sometimes less is more, and there are few CRPGs as complex and flexible as *Morrowind*. Even after I completed the main quest, I saw that I'd explored only 60 percent of the gameworld. Bethesda even included *The Elder Scrolls Construction Set,* a somewhat intimidating program that allows users to make their own modifications to the game. Hundreds of users have made their mods freely available online, but the quality varies. Most mods consist of powerful new items, though others add new textures or alter the interface. Some just seem plain unnecessary—like the popular "20 Books" module, which incorporates several works of H. P. Lovecraft, the brothers Grimm, and Lewis Carroll. Once the mod is installed, you can visit various booksellers in the game to buy these texts and read them verbatim on the screen. Why? Well, why not? Others, such as "A Call to Issilar," add massive quests, characters, and areas. Provided players are willing to separate the wheat from the chaff, this free content adds value to an already good game.[6]

Morrowind is not without its problems. As in *Daggerfall*, players will eventually reach a level of experience that reduces even the game's most formidable foes into pushovers. There are also many ways to exploit the game's leveling system, such as standing in one place and casting the same spell over and over again. Nevertheless, the game continues to attract gamers and is still actively played—as the many bustling fan websites and message boards attest. Bethesda produced two expansions for its third game: *Tribunal* (2002) and *Bloodmoon* (2003). Both expansions have fairly good reviews, though the latter is perhaps the better of the two. In 2017, Bethesda published *Morrowind* as a chapter for *The Elder Scrolls Online* MMORPG. It's set 700 years before the single-player game, but still features many of its locations and inspires plenty of nostalgia for fans of the original.

As mentioned above, this is the first *Elder Scrolls* game available for consoles, thanks mostly to the Xbox's internal hard drive. For gamers who'd only played JRPGs like *Final Fantasy*, it must have been quite a culture shock; here was a giant open world and a level of freedom virtually unknown in the JRPG world. It was certainly a remarkable achievement even if it did lack some of the PC version's features, most notably access to the modding community. Still, I have little doubt that the lessons learned doing *Morrowind*'s Xbox version paved the way for much of what would come.

We'll return to this series in Chapter 21.

MIGHT AND MAGIC: FROM PLATINUM TO PABULUM

New World Computing's *Might and Magic* series received a major overhaul with *Might and Magic VI: The Mandate of Heaven* in 1998. It had been a full five years since the previous installment, enough time for many fans of the series to have long ago moved on to other games. New World knew its flagship franchise needed more than a facelift if it were to compete with the massively successful CRPGs of the late 1990s, which include such classics as BioWare's *Baldur's Gate,* Blizzard's *Diablo,* Interplay's *Fallout,* and Bethesda's *Daggerfall*—in short, the games that define the Platinum Age. New World needed plenty of its own might and magic to stand up to this competition!

In 1995 New World released *Heroes of Might and Magic,* a highly successful turn-based strategy game that is still spawning sequels. Although the *Heroes* games differ fundamentally from the main *Might and Magic* series, they were competition for New World's development and marketing resources—particularly as we head into the 2000s. The *Heroes* games, which trace their ancestry back to New World's 1990 *King's Bounty,* eventually replaced *Might and Magic* as New World's premier franchise. The older series peaked with *The Mandate of Heaven* and its sequel, then nose-dived with its ninth game, precisely as Origin's *Ultima IX* had done.

Finally, bear in mind that Trip Hawkins' 3DO company had purchased New World in 1996. 3DO had just given up on its attempts to market an expensive CD-ROM–based game console, and it was hoping to leverage its marketing resources to publish games for other platforms. It started off great, but just as Richard Garriott lived to regret his decision to sell Origin to Electronic Arts, Jon Van Caneghem eventually found himself at odds with 3DO. In a 2004 interview, Caneghem complains that 3DO was "very scared of doing something new." It's worth quoting a bit more from this interview, since it sheds much light on the debacle that follows:

> [3DO] always wanted to stick with building a sequel that they knew had a built-in sales number they could achieve. The execs look at the numbers and they go, "Hey, but we got such a fan base. Can you make another one?" Nine *Might and Magic* and four *Heroes* later, it gets to the point where I go, "Come on guys, let's do something new!"

3DO probably should have listened to Caneghem, since it declared bankruptcy in 2003 and ended up as part of Ubisoft. Caneghem later joined Garriott's NCSoft company. But let's not get ahead of ourselves; there are some great games to cover here.

The Mandate of Heaven

New World's *The Mandate of Heaven* is the first in the series to feature fluid 3D motion, placing it firmly in the camp of *Ultima Underworld* or *Elder Scrolls* games (Figure 14.12). However, *The Mandate of Heaven* is much more than a clone of these masterpieces, and it's one of my personal favorites. Rather than offer up yet another single-character game, New World adapts most of the established conventions from its earlier games in the series. The most noticeable of these is the familiar row of animated character portraits along the bottom of the screen, though now they are digitized from real actors and more lifelike. As before, the characters' faces react to situations and change to reflect their mood and condition. Seeing characters wince from a blow adds greatly to the immersion, as does seeing them blink or yawn. They also speak at certain intervals, particularly when the party enters a new dungeon or after a particularly ferocious

FIGURE 14.12 *Might and Magic VI: The Mandate of Heaven* is one of my favorite CRPGs of all time. Even if the graphics look outdated, its creative level designs, role-playing mechanics, and soundtrack still hold up well—and you're going to *love* the fly spell.

attack. This cheeky banter makes you feel like you're role-playing with actual friends, not the standard cardboard characters of so many other games.

As with previous games in the series, *The Mandate of Heaven* requires you to make many important choices as you develop your characters, and it's worth taking a moment to examine this system in detail. Though a quick start option puts you into the action right away, many players (especially expert CRPG fans) should roll their own. After an initial choice of class, you must decide how to spend skill points. The skill system is much more sophisticated than the one introduced in *Might and Magic III*. Here, skills are divided into four basic areas: Weapon, Armor, Magic, and Miscellaneous. This last category includes some metaskills such as learning, which affects all the other skills by boosting the experiences points awarded after a battle. Although each character has a limited number of free skills available at creation, the rest must be secured by joining guilds and paying to learn skills.

Unlike *Daggerfall* or *Morrowind,* where skills are improved by using them, the skills in *The Mandate of Heaven* are governed mostly by level.

Each time characters gain a new level, they receive a number of skill points to distribute among the skills they had learned—or save them for later. The cost of raising a skill level increases incrementally. For example, raising a character's chainmail skill from one to two cost 2 points, whereas raising it a third time costs 3. If you have a careful eye, you can find magical horseshoes in stables, which give you a free skill point to spend however you like. The system encourages well-rounded parties whose characters employ a variety of useful skills, such as the ability to spot and disarm traps, identify mysterious items, or haggle with merchants.

Once a character has 4 points in a skill, he or she is eligible for expert training. As with *Morrowind,* these special trainers are sprinkled across the gameworld. Each skill is granted extra abilities at the expert level, such as reduced recovery time for armor or the ability to wield two daggers instead of one. Later on, the expert character can become a recognized master of the discipline, though the prerequisites vary across the different skills (many of the most important require the fulfilling of special class-related quests). Expert and master training are especially exciting for mages and clerics, whose entire spell books change with each stage. For instance, a spell that affects only a single character at the novice level may affect the entire party at the expert level, and in general all spells became more powerful and useful.

All in all, it's an intuitive and highly customizable way to handle the leveling issue. Also note that characters do not automatically gain levels; they must seek out and pay for general-purpose trainers once they have enough experience points. Since cash is relatively hard for new parties to come by, players make strategic decisions about how to spend it—does it make more sense to buy a new weapon or magic scroll, learn a new skill, or level up a character? Though training costs are negligible at first, they become much steeper at higher levels.

Combat is also handled well in *The Mandate of Heaven,* offering a real-time and a turn-based mode. During a battle, you can act in real time by attacking or casting "readied" spells, or you can hit a key to enter turn-based mode. In turn-based mode, the game pauses between each action on the battlefield and is thus very useful for major encounters. However, there's a problem with this system. All four characters are assumed to be standing in a horizontal line facing their enemies; thus, weaker characters are just as exposed and vulnerable to attack as well-armored warriors and clerics. Thankfully, mages can wear leather armor and protect themselves with magical items and spells; in general, a mage can end up with an armor class comparable to a knight. Still, I wish that weaker characters could simply stay behind the plate mailed warriors, as in *Dungeon Master*.

As with the earlier *Xeen* games, *The Mandate of Heaven* offers players a myriad of subplots and sidequests. There are so many of these that it's quite easy to get distracted from the main mission, which concerns aliens who have invaded the planet. Eventually the party confronts these aliens, but only after equipping themselves with futuristic armor and weaponry. Thus, *The Mandate of Heaven* hearkens back to the early *Ultima* games that blend conventional fantasy with sci-fi elements (laser blasters, spaceships, and so on). In true *Might and Magic* tradition, *The Mandate of Heaven* has a huge gameworld and enough gameplay to keep you busy for months. Indeed, I happily spent the summer of 1996 playing *The Mandate of Heaven* and the following summer playing the sequel! Upon completion of these games, you can print a certificate of your achievement to hang on the wall alongside your college degrees and other lesser diplomas.

The game won high praise from critics, and for good reason. Who could forget the first time their wizard cast a fly spell, sending the party soaring high above Enroth? The music is also lively and inspired, setting a great mood for many nights of gaming. Perhaps more importantly, though, *Might and Magic VI* is blissfully free of bugs. At a time when almost every other major CRPG has so many errors that manuals urge you to save the game every few minutes, this stability is remarkable.

For Blood and Honor

New World's next entry in the series, *For Blood and Honor*, is the last great *Might and Magic* CRPG (Figure 14.13). It offers a few welcome innovations to the interface over its predecessor, but it shares those qualities that worked so well. One important change is the introduction of three new playable races—elves, dwarves, goblins—each with their own benefits and weaknesses. The photorealistic portraits are replaced with CGI style faces; I liked the digitized actors better, but I seem to be alone in this. Other tweaks include a more robust note-taking system and the option to always run. This last improvement may sound minor, but in the previous game the only way to run is to hold down the shift key. Since there's no fatigue system in either game, running reduces a great deal of tedious travel time.

For Blood and Honor also hones the skill system by doing away with some of the guilds. Now characters can learn new skills at shops, such as axe and bow at the local weaponsmith. The game maintains the expert and master system described above but extends it with a grandmaster level.

FIGURE 14.13 *For Blood and Honor* trades the digitized actors' portraits for more conventional CGI characters. Most critics applaud the change, but to me the previous system is more charming.

However, each class can reach expert, master, or grandmaster rank only in certain skills. For instance, only snipers and master archers (prestige classes for the archer class) can attain grandmastery with the bow. There are also quite a few new classes, including thieves who can steal from shops.

The game's story is more involved than *The Mandate of Heaven's,* and it gives the player significant leeway in determining how the plot unfolds. You decide which one of many groups to side with, taking on quests that favor one or another. In short, you choose the light or dark path, which leads to very different quests and endings. *For Blood and Honor* also introduces a popular minigame called *Arcomage,* which is roughly based on the popular Wizard of the Coast collectible card game *Magic: The Gathering. Arcomage* shows up again in the sequel, as well as in a standalone, multiplayer game published in 1999.

For Blood and Honor was noted at the time for its excellent operatic score, composed by Paul Romero and produced by Robert King. However, some critics complain about the voice acting, which does tend to get repetitive after hearing the same utterance for the thousandth time. This is a common problem for games of the era, however, and I still encounter it from time to time even in modern games. Others criticize the game for its dated graphics. By the late 1990s, games like Epic's *Unreal Tournament* were setting much higher benchmarks for 3D graphics, and *For Blood and Honor* does look antiquated by comparison. Still, most fans of the series are more than happy to overlook these faults and enjoy what is truly another classic *Might and Magic* experience.

Day of the Destroyer

With *Day of the Destroyer,* the eighth *Might and Magic* game, the series took a turn for the worse. Released in 2000 and still using *Mandate of Heaven*'s engine, the game looked dated and even obsolete before it hit the shelf. However, poor graphics weren't the only problem.

Although the earlier games have their share of dull moments, *Day of the Destroyer* is painfully repetitive. Even the surprising decision to let you create only one character (the rest of the five-member party must be recruited later) does little to affect the monotony, since the additional characters are almost entirely devoid of personality and impact on the story (Figure 14.14). Sure, the option to add a dragon to the party sounds cool, but doing so ruins the game's balance, reducing it to an unbearably dull walkthrough. Sadder still was the unforgivably buggy code. The game made little impression on those who weren't already in love with the series—and they were disappointed.

Nevertheless, *Day of the Destroyer* does have its good points and is noted for its storyline. The main story focuses on the land of Jadame, where a giant crystal popped up out of the Earth, devastating the area and opening four elemental portals. It's up to you and your party to set the balance right again—a quest that takes many weeks in real time as you level up your characters in preparation for the big bout with Planeswalker Escaton.

The turn-based combat mode is also enhanced. After all the combatants execute their moves, the party has the opportunity to advance or withdraw a short distance. This movement phase can make a big difference in major battles, particularly if the party's strength lies in ranged attacks.

Might and Magic IX

The last game in the series, *Might and Magic IX,* was released in 2002 to very harsh reviews (Figure 14.15). Although 3DO finally took the plunge into full 3D graphics with Monolith's LithTech Talon engine, the graphics

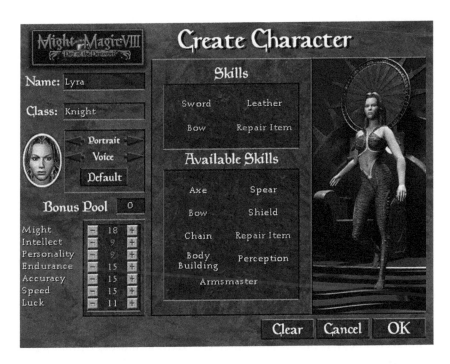

FIGURE 14.14 *Day of the Destroyer* lets you create only one character, but you can recruit more later on. Bah.

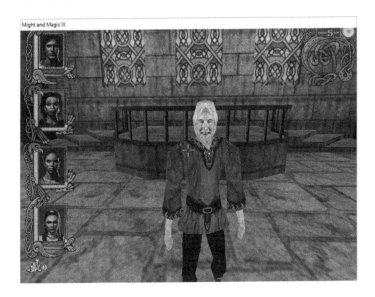

FIGURE 14.15 *Might and Magic* is yet another epic series that ends with an epic fail—in this case, *Might and Magic IX*. It doesn't even have a subtitle, so let me propose one: *The Secret of the Missing Caneghem.*

are still behind the times, and the interface is unwieldy. The game was rushed through production, with the typical result—hundreds of serious bugs and rough spots. To its credit, 3DO quickly issued a patch, but it was up to fans to address most of the issues in unofficial patches.

The LithTech Talon engine powers some successful games from the early 2000s, such as Fox Interactive's *No One Lives Forever* and *Aliens versus Predator 2*. However, even with this proven 3D engine at its disposal, New World didn't seem to have the resources or determination to put it to good use. Many settings and characters are recycled over and over, to the extent that one wonders whether the gameworld is overrun by clones. Indeed, the crude, polygonal characters and monsters look less realistic than the old 2D versions in the previous installments. Worse, the storyline is incoherent, especially during the crucial first stages of the game. Reviewers lampoon it, giving it pitifully low scores and warning everyone to stay away. One contemporary correctly prophesied that "nobody will ever wax nostalgic about *Might and Magic IX*." In short, New World and 3DO repeated the miserable failure of Origin and Electronic Arts' *Ascension*, which ended the grand-old *Ultima* series on a similarly bad note.

Nevertheless, the development team had some good ideas, even if the game overall was a flop. For one thing, it returns to the older convention of having the player select four characters, who can be half orcs, dwarves, elves, or humans (the party can later add three nonplayer characters [NPCs] to its ranks). Like *Baldur's Gate,* you customize your characters with a wide selection of portraits and voices—handily described as assertive, arrogant, happy, cowardly, dim, or angry.

New World simplified the class system substantially from previous games. Now there are only two classes available at the creation stage: fighters and initiates. These characters can specialize in different skills and join one of a dozen different classes. For instance, a fighter can become a mercenary, and from there an assassin or gladiator. The old personality and intellect stats are subsumed into a single magic stat. The skills are pretty much intact from previous games, except for magic. Now, all mage spells are learned via the elemental skill, and all clerical spells rely on the spirit skill. There are also light and dark magic skills, which concern attack spells and healing spells, respectively. It's certainly different, but not a very good improvement over the old system which, if nothing else, maintains a healthy distinction between schools of magic and a greater semblance of variety.

Some other interesting changes concern movement. Now, the party can climb, crouch, swim, and strafe (move from side to side). I might point out, though, that occasionally this mobility makes odd demands on the player's suspension of disbelief. For instance, how can a party walking side-by-side walk across a tightrope?

One welcome touch is that you could finally arrange your party members into ranks, putting the more heavily armed units in front and weaker characters in the rear. Unfortunately, this feature isn't well integrated into the game; characters in the back still get frequently attacked.

Combat is altered for the worse. Now it mostly depends on your ability to line up a pair of crosshairs on the enemy, who is often quite small and indistinguishable from the background. Attacking is done by rapidly clicking the mouse buttons. Thankfully, there is still the trusty turn-based mode for players with slower reflexes.

The game is also hamstrung by a poor automapping system, which is accessible only on a separate, slow-loading screen—and it isn't even accurate. All the old information pages (character display, spell books, and the journal) are redone in a nice style reminiscent of an ancient book, but these also take an excruciatingly long time to load. Since you'll likely want to check these screens thousands (or even tens of thousands) of times during the game, it soon gets annoying.

Apologists for the game insist that it gets better after fifteen or so hours of rather dull, repetitive gameplay, but who could be expected to endure that much tedium? What happened? Jon Van Caneghem remarks in an interview in *Computer Gaming World* that he had "little to no involvement" with the game, and that "if it had been my decision, it would have never shipped."[7] That probably says it all. In any case, it's a dismal way to end a long-lived and much-loved series. Yet again we're reminded why developers should think twice about selling out to a major publisher, who may not understand or appreciate the creativity, vision, and, most importantly, the endless fine-tuning that goes into truly great games.

Arx Fatalis

Before moving on to the isometric games of the Platinum Age, I'd be remiss not to mention another great game inspired by *Ultima Underworld*. In 2002, French developer Arkane Studios released *Arx Fatalis*, a game that started out as *Ultima Underworld III* (Figure 14.16). Unfortunately, if predictably, the developer was unable to come to an agreement with Electronic Arts over the licensing.[8] Arkane Studios went ahead with the

FIGURE 14.16 *Arx Fatalis* is *Ultima Underworld III* in all but name. It's not flawless, but it's a fun and immersive game with an unusually interactive gameworld.

project anyway, and while the final product doesn't bear the moniker, *Ultima Underworld*'s influence is unmistakable. Although not technically set underground, the gameworld's lack of a sun makes for a dark and brooding atmosphere.

There are other innovations here worth noting. One is Arkane's goal to keep the player immersed in the main game window. Whereas most CRPGs switch to a different screen and interface when players are purchasing items in a store, for instance, *Arx Fatalis* handles the transaction by having the player drag items from the merchant's chest into the character's inventory.

The game begins just after the main character is knocked on the head and tossed into a goblin prison. Predictably, he's lost his memory, and a good portion of the game involves rediscovering his identity. Although we've seen this setup in other CRPGs, it works well within the plotline, a morbid tale involving the summoning of an evil god. The plot is rather linear, though the character's ability to interact with the environment compensates for this limitation. *Arx Fatalis* is one of only a handful of CRPGs that allow item combining, a feature far more common in adventure games. For instance, combining a rope with a pole results in a fishing pole; this can be used to catch fish, which can be combined with fire to cook a good meal. We'll see this idea again in Larian Studios' *Divinity: Original Sin* series.

There are no classes, but the character does receive four primary ratings and some secondary skills (ranged attack, close combat, and so on). These skills are boosted by completing quests and gaining combat experience, and you decide which skills warrant improvement. The spell system is rune-based and comparable to *Stonekeep*. In *Arx Fatalis,* you first need to find runes, then to discover which combinations of them result in useful magic. The runes are "drawn" with the mouse, though three of them can be precast and cast instantly later on. A great part of the fun is experimenting with runes to chance upon more powerful spells.

Although critics praise the graphics and storyline, most find the combat system clunky. Besides poor collision detection and physics, the combat mode is just too simplistic and boring: click the mouse on the enemy, repeat. Critics also railed against the many game-crashing bugs, some of which caused the player to lose saved games (and possibly hours and hours of work). Thankfully, most of these bugs were fixed in subsequent official and unofficial patches.

NOTES

1. Yes, we know Windows 95 and 98 were based on MS-DOS. It wasn't until Windows XP in 2001 that this cord was finally snipped—for good or ill.
2. See Dave Kushner's excellent book *The Masters of Doom* for a detailed account of id Software.
3. See http://www.computerandvideogames.com/article.php?id=28003.
4. See Trent C. Ward's review of the game at http://www.gamespot.com/pc/rpg/daggerfall/review.html.
5. See http://www.ign.com/articles/2000/06/09/elder-scrolls-iii-morrowind-interview and https://www.imperial-library.info/content/interviews-MW-team for the source of these quotations.
6. For a list of freely available and ranked mods for *Morrowind,* see http://planetelderscrolls.gamespy.com/View.php?view=mods.HOF.
7. See the April 2004 issue of *Computer Gaming World.*
8. See http://www.gamespot.com/pc/rpg/arxfatalis/news.html?sid=2856384l.

CHAPTER 15

Diablo and the Rise of Action RPGs

So far, the Platinum Age games we've discussed are concerned primarily with massive 3D worlds that can be explored in real time in first-person perspective. The best of these, *The Stygian Abyss, Daggerfall, Morrowind,* and *Mandate of Heaven,* try to put the player directly in the boots of a single or a small group of adventurers, trading the contemplative joys of tactical combat for the adrenaline-pumping thrills of a first-person shooter. These games owe much of their inspiration to FTL Games' *Dungeon Master,* but also id's *Wolfenstein 3D* and *Doom.*

However, whether CRPGs work better in first-person or third-person perspective is still an open question. The fact is that third-person can still be impressive in 2D, particularly when it uses isometric rather than a flat top-down perspective. We've already discussed a number of isometric CRPGs, such as *Ultima VII,* as well as combinations such as *Pool of Radiance* and *Realms of Arkania.* In general, a third-person perspective has the distinct advantage of allowing you to actually see your characters in action, which is often just as appealing as seeing through the characters' eyes. It also resolves the occasional weirdness of party-based CRPGs such as *Mandate of Heaven* that use a first-person perspective to represent what the entire party sees; why can't we see each other?

A handy analogy for understanding this advantage is the miniatures version of *D&D,* which is arguably a more tactile and tactical experience than a purely verbal "theater of the mind" session. There's also something to be said for the visceral reaction many gamers have when they actually get to see their characters in a computer game getting mauled by monsters. Though they may not feel like they *are* these characters, they can and often do empathize with them.

I also like to use the example of computer chess games. All of the successful ones are either simple top-down affairs or isometric; no one seems interested in a first-person chess game. Would it make the game more immersive? Perhaps, albeit at the cost of driving you batty as you try to keep track of possible moves and the state of the match. Likewise, in many cases it's very useful to see your characters in a CRPG, if not for tactical reasons—Is something coming up behind me?—at least to better appreciate the aesthetics of your badass armor and weapons. For these reasons, I don't know anyone who consistently plays *World of Warcraft* in first-person perspective, even though that's an option. On the other hand, I tend to stick to first-person while playing *The Elder Scrolls V: Skyrim* and *Fallout 4,* mostly because the controls are better in that mode and the walking and running animations tend to look clunky. Still, it's nice to occasionally switch to third-person just to admire my gear.

In any case, with the key exceptions of *Ultima*'s *The False Prophet* and *The Black Gate,* previous efforts to incorporate real-time gameplay into 2D-isometric CRPGs were not successful. The popularity of the FPS ensured that many publishers favored CRPGs with similar interfaces; anything else would seem hopelessly outdated before it hit the shelf. Nevertheless, the most successful CRPGs of the late 1990s and early 2000s are in fact real-time, isometric games that are in every way as immersive as their first-person counterparts, if not more so. The secret of their success was not graphical wizardry, but exquisitely crafted gameplay.

DIABLO AND *DIABLO*-LIKE RPGs

Diablo

Blizzard is best known today for *World of Warcraft,* an MMORPG loosely based on the company's best-selling real-time strategy (RTS) series *Warcraft* which launched in 1994. Blizzard also made gaming history with *StarCraft* in 1998, an immensely successful RTS that became an international "e-sport." Clearly, Blizzard knows how to make great games with broad appeal. When the company entered the CRPG market with *Diablo* in 1996, it scored yet another triumph. Critics raved about it in magazines and websites, doling out awards and giving it near-perfect scores in their reviews.

At first glance, *Diablo* looks like a dumbed down CRPG for the masses, only slightly more sophisticated than the old *Gauntlet* arcade game from

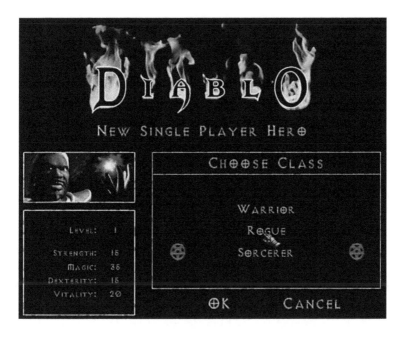

FIGURE 15.1 *Diablo* reduces the often-daunting character creation process to one simple choice: Warrior, Rogue, or Sorcerer?

1985. Indeed, it's labeled as an action RPG (ARPG) because its gameplay is focused more on reflexes than tactics. It also has a vastly simplified character development system compared to most CRPGs. The player controls only a single character of one of three basic types (Warrior, Rogue, and Sorcerer) (Figure 15.1). The differences among these types aren't rigid; warriors can cast spells and sorcerers can wear armor. However, the choice of class does determine the best strategies for surviving battles, and, as usual, it's the magic-using class that starts off weakest and ends up strongest. Each time the character gains a new level, you receive five points to distribute among four attributes: strength, magic, dexterity, and vitality. Compared to other CRPGs with manuals of hundreds of pages, this was Fisher-Price stuff. However, Blizzard's genius was doing more with less. Instead of baffling players with a complicated skill system like those in the *Elder Scrolls* or *Might and Magic* games, *Diablo* allows fewer choices but makes each of them more significant.

The interface is also simple, based almost entirely on rapid-fire mouse clicks. Left clicking on part of the screen sends the character to that location, and clicking on a monster triggers an attack. While a single blow dispatches many monsters, others require multiple strikes (and thus multiple clicks with the mouse). A right click activates the current spell or skill and is also used to quickly quaff potions or recite scrolls stored in the character's belt. A simple paper doll system lets you equip the character. Finally, two globes—one red, one blue—show the character's current hit and mana points (recall a similar convention in Blue Sky's *The Stygian Abyss*). It's an interface that even a total novice can master in minutes.

Another key aspect of the game is its frequent and abundant rewards: there's loot constantly dropping everywhere. This generosity is also noticeable in the leveling up process. Most CRPGs are quite stingy with both loot and levels, promoting characters only after hours or even days of gameplay. *Diablo* challenges this trend by greatly reducing level requirements. Indeed, especially at the crucial early stages of the game, you literally gain levels every few minutes. Likewise, powerful arms and armor can drop off anything, not just powerful bosses. The system is consciously geared toward providing a continuous stream of expectation and rewards that keep players clicking that mouse.

Diablo is also noted for its high degree of randomization. The dungeons, monster locations, and item capabilities are procedurally generated, not only ensuring surprises but also enhancing the game's replay value. Indeed, one of the most common phrases used to describe *Diablo* is "a Roguelike for the 90s," though there are plenty of *Rogue* fans who object to the comparison. For one thing, *Diablo* has a coherent storyline. The game takes its title from the Lord of Terror, an evil demon whose magical prison (a "soulstone") lies forgotten beneath the town of Tristram (Figure 15.2). The soulstone has eroded, and now Diablo is able to exert enough influence on the material plane to wreak havoc there. Of course, it's your job to put Diablo back in the soulstone.

Another aspect of *Diablo* that sets it apart from *Rogue* (as well as most CRPGs) is its support for free multiplayer, which ranges from LAN party setups to a new Internet server named Battle.net. Although not without flaws (cheating was rampant), *Diablo*'s multiplayer capability is clearly a significant factor in the game's long-lasting popularity. Battle.net was really a loss leader for Blizzard; the hope was that it would generate enough word-of-mouth advertising for the game to pay for itself. It turned out to be a smart move, and Blizzard soon became a major figure in the online gaming world—a reputation that proved most valuable when it launched *World of Warcraft* several years later.

Finally, no description of *Diablo* would be complete without reference to its masterful musical score, which is among the best ever composed for

FIGURE 15.2 The village of Tristram serves as a home base in *Diablo*. It's also where you can hear some of the best music ever composed for a CRPG.

a computer game. Matt Uelmen, the score composer, rightfully received the International Game Developer Association's award in 2001.

Yet despite strong sales and praise from many prominent reviewers, *Diablo* is not without its naysayers. Not surprisingly, the game's popularity with "virgin" CRPG gamers drew sneers from veterans of the genre. In their eyes, Blizzard had reduced CRPGs to a "clickfest." Most critics fall over themselves in bombastic praise of the game, but a few complain about the dark graphics, which are occasionally hard to make out. The on-screen automapping tool helps with navigation but frequently obscures the battle sequences (Figure 15.3). Finally, some lament the game's relatively short duration; those accustomed to the weeks or months required to slog through an *Ultima* or *Elder Scrolls* game are flabbergasted when they beat *Diablo* in mere days. In spite of these criticisms, however, *Diablo* remains a crucial game in the CRPG canon.

Hellfire

What happened next in the *Diablo* story is quite perplexing. Rather than develop its own expansion, Blizzard let Sierra On-Line publish an expansion named *Hellfire*, developed by Synergistic Software (the same

FIGURE 15.3 Rather than place the automap on a separate screen or window, *Diablo*'s designers chose to overlay it on the main screen. It takes some getting used to, but is consistent with the goal of keeping your attention focused on the action.

team responsible for the mediocre *Birthright: The Gorgon's Alliance*). This expansion, which appeared in 1997, adds two new dungeons, new creatures, spells, items, and a monk character class. Reviewers weren't enthused about *Hellfire*, seeing it as little more than a cash grab, and the lack of multiplayer support vexed many players. Some fans don't even consider it an official expansion.

Diablo II

Blizzard knew that fans had great expectations for the first official sequel to the popular *Diablo*. Four years had passed, and graphics technology was fast approaching the level of performance we expect from modern PCs. Blizzard's challenge was to update the engine without ruining the gameplay. However, a troubled production schedule delayed the game for many years, and when it finally arrived, some were underwhelmed with its graphics and layouts. Fortunately for Blizzard, *Diablo II* overcame this limitation and was overwhelmingly successful, and fast became one of the best-selling CRPGs of all time (Figure 15.4).

FIGURE 15.4 *Diablo II* wasn't a substantial improvement over its prequel in terms of audiovisuals, but there were improvements where it mattered: gameplay, story, and scope.

Diablo II is significantly larger and more sophisticated than its predecessor. Players can now explore vast outdoor areas as well as multiple dungeons. More importantly, the randomized quests are replaced with handcrafted ones, which let the developers better integrate their storyline and narrative cutscenes. These cutscenes have high production values, with good voice acting and superb animation; they add greatly to the overall coherence of the game without feeling intrusive or grafted on.

The class system was reworked, with five classes (Paladin, Barbarian, Amazon, Necromancer, Sorceress), each with unique skills and combat strategies that really make them feel different to play. The leveling system is enhanced with an oft-imitated graphical skill tree system that helps sustain your long-term interest in developing a character—there's always some amazing new ability just a few levels away (Figure 15.5). Each time a character levels up, you receive points to distribute among the character's attributes and a skill point to enhance or develop a skill. The skills are arranged so that more advanced skills, which can be learned only at high

FIGURE 15.5 *Diablo II*'s skill tree interface has influenced countless later games. It's a good example of Blizzard's talent for building intuitive and attractive interfaces. Image from *Diablo Wiki*, a great online source for all things related to *Diablo*.

levels, require specific basic skills. For instance, the necromancer's Teeth skill is a prerequisite for the sixth-level Corpse Explosion, which is itself a prerequisite for the eighteenth level Bone Spear. Furthermore, every skill takes on added importance and usefulness with more points. For example, you can add more points to the Teeth Skill to get extra teeth and have them do more damage. The beauty of this system is that even first-tier skills can remain viable throughout the game. We'll see similar systems in *Dungeon Siege II, World of Warcraft,* and *Divinity: Original Sin,* just to name a few.

The weapon and armor system is also extended with a novel socket feature on certain items. These sockets can be filled with gems and jewels found throughout the dungeons, and can greatly increase the power of an otherwise average item. Then there are the new weapon sets, collections of items that provide substantial bonuses when used in tandem. For example, the Berserker's Garb set consists of a unique helmet, hauberk, and hatchet. When all three items are equipped, you receive a hefty bonus to your defense and increased resistance to poison. Other sets are far more powerful, especially those added in the *Lord of Destruction* expansion pack. It's not hard to see how sockets and sets make gearing up more involving—and give you even more incentive to keep searching for loot.

Yet another addition is the option to recruit a hireling to assist in combat. Originally, these hirelings are quite vulnerable and stick around only for a single act. The expansion pack, which we'll discuss momentarily, increases their life expectancy and lets you gear and level them up throughout the entire game. In either case, though, they're helpful only in combat.

A persistent rumor concerns the fourth act, which alone seems to have no place to hire or recruit a hireling. The legend is that there's a secret hireling, an angel named "Evil Tyrael." As far as I know, this is all just speculation or wishful thinking, but I include it as a nod to the enormous *Diablo II* fan community, which remains active across a number of online discussion boards and social media. It's easy to forget the role that forums like these played in not only helping out players, but also spreading and maintaining interest in the game. On these forums, players give and seek advice, boast about their achievements, debate rumors, or vent their frustrations with the game or the world at large.

Anyway, back to the game. Another innovation is a fatigue system, which allows you to run for a set period. When the fatigue bar is low, you must rest or walk for a period to recover. Finally, some of the carpal tunnel-inducing mouse clicking of the first game is alleviated. Players can now simply hold down the mouse button to have their character repeatedly attack or move around. You can also hold down the ALT key to see treasures lying about dungeons—this change cut back dramatically on the need to "pixel hunt," or sweep the mouse pointer about each area to search for rings, coins, and other small items. Again, these quality of life features may seem trivial, but they make a tremendous difference when you sit down to play the game.

Multiplayer mode is better supported, and cheating was rarer. Blizzard's Battle.net server was still prone to lag, but that didn't slow the onslaught of rabid *Diablo II* fans desperate for online play. The big change from the older system is that now character information was stored entirely on

Blizzard's own servers, which curtailed cheating sharply. Millions of users logged in to Battle.net to play *Diablo II* with others from around the world.

Lord of Destruction

Blizzard wisely decided to make its own expansion for *Diablo II*, called *Lord of Destruction* in 2001. Besides many new items and quests, the expansion heightens the screen resolution (800 × 600) and adds two new character classes (Assassins and Druids). The expansion also tweaks existing features that improve the main game. For instance, characters can now store more items in their stash, and socketed items hold up to six gems. Reviewers were pleased with the improved graphics, as well as the many improvements to the Battle.net server that improved the online multiplayer experience. In short, *Lord of Destruction* is a must-have expansion that adds considerable functionality to an already excellent game.

If the only criteria we use to evaluate CRPGs are sales figures and enduring popularity, Blizzard's *Diablo* games represent two of the best (if not *the* best) CRPGs ever designed. The games brought new blood to the genre, introducing it to millions of gamers who had never played any of the classic CRPGs, much less a tabletop *AD&D* game.

It also sent hordes of badly behaved kids and teenagers (and middleaged men, no doubt) scampering to Battle.net, "pwning" each other and seeking out the latest cheats and hacks to gain an unfair advantage. This unfortunate trend continues to the present day. The *Diablo* forums are rife with complaints about the trolls, bots, and cheaters who ruin some people's experiences. As one OShogun posted on the Battle.net forums on September 14, 2018, "The online community is complete cancer, which is why I ran away from that game. Shame, really." I can certainly sympathize; I've had my share of insults and outrage.

However, as Edmund Burke one famously wrote, "It is a general popular error to suppose the loudest complainers for the public to be the most anxious for its welfare." Indeed, Burke has two more insights on this theme that are more rarely quoted: "The true cause of his drawing so shocking a picture is no more than this.... He finds himself out of power; and this condition is intolerable to him," and, "Men, in this deplorable state of mind, find a comfort in spreading the contagion of their spleen." To put it less eloquently, if we're honest with ourselves, we simply hate to lose— much less having it rubbed in by gleeful little punks. It's always easier to lambaste an entire online community for this or that intolerance than to tolerate our own injured pride.

Diablo III

The third installment is infamous for its incredibly long production, which supposedly began in 2001 but wasn't officially released until 2012 (Figure 15.6). It broke preorder and first-day sales records and eventually sold over 30 million units including its popular *Reaper of Souls* expansion. Although it arrived to some blistering controversy, which I'll get to in a moment, it seems to have aged well. I disagree with Polygon's claim that it "renders *Diablo 2* obsolete," but in it is a great game and a worthy successor to the venerable franchise.

Beyond obvious improvements such as graphics and animation, the game changes the mechanics for leveling and skills (Figure 15.7). The goal is to encourage experimentation, especially in combining them with each other. Each class has its own unique skills, as well as a class-specific resource to power them (i.e., barbarians consume fury). Rather than having to select new skills from a tree, you unlock them as you go along, and you can switch them around as long as you aren't in combat. You can also apply skill runes, which let you modify skills in various ways. For example, applying the Frostbite rune to the Barbarian's Bash skill makes each hit freeze the target enemy for a brief moment. The combinations are substantial enough that Blizzard put together a free "Skill Calculator" tool with shareable build links.

To preserve the feel of the original games, the camera rotation is fixed, though you can zoom in and out. Likewise, there's no auto-attack capability; you still have to click on enemies to attack them. Not everyone

FIGURE 15.6 *Diablo III* was a long time coming. Note the cooldowns on the abilities bar, the automap in the top right corner; the "objectives" tab…. One might think they were playing *World of Warcraft*.

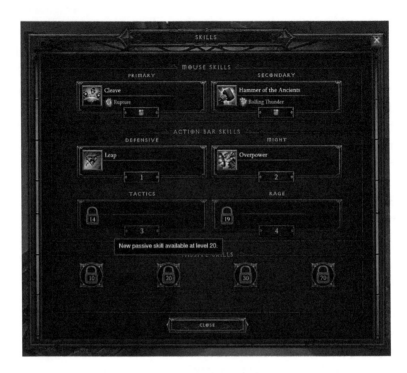

FIGURE 15.7 *Diablo III* revamps the skill system dramatically. There's no longer any need to sweat over hard, permanent choices; you can freely switch skills around out of combat. Some critics object to this alleged "dumbing down" of *Diablo II*'s system, but you can make the same complaint about the earlier *Diablo* games—which are essentially streamlined versions of far more complex CRPGs like *Ultima VII*.

appreciates these design decisions, of course, especially gamers new to the franchise—and there are quite a few of these, naturally, since Blizzard promoted the game so heavily on its *World of Warcraft* MMORPG.

One strong and, in my opinion, better-justified criticism concerns its Digital Rights Management, which requires a persistent Internet connection to play even in single-player mode. Prominent critics such as Tom Francis of *PC Gamer* magazine go so far as to call it a pathetic move on Blizzard's part: "I'm genuinely pissed off by the hostility and callousness of that decision." He isn't alone; indeed, all the furor over this DRM strategy dominates early coverage of the game. A second problem was server issues, which undoubtedly exacerbated the already tense situation. Yet another controversy arose over Blizzard's decision to remove the Auction House from the game, which it argued was promoting gold farming and other activities that aren't in the spirit of the game. None of this seems to have seriously impacted sales, however.

Diablo's Impact

Whenever we see a game attract as much attention and as many dollars as *Diablo*, it's all but inevitable to inspire a horde of imitators. Trent C. Ward of GameSpot predicted in 1997 that *Diablo* was "likely to be the clone maker for the next two years,"[1] but its influence has lasted much longer than that—indeed, *Diablo* clones are still being developed today. There's even a pen-and-paper RPG based on *Diablo II* called *Dungeons and Dragons: Diablo II Edition* (2000), by Bill Slavicsek and Jeff Grubb. While many *Diablo* clones are probably better off forgotten (*Ancient Evil, Hexplore, Blade of Darkness*), others take the model in new directions, offering many intriguing innovations. These include **Dink Smallwood, Darkstone, Clans, Nox, Throne of Darkness,** and **Heretic Kingdoms,** which you can find in the Bestiary in the appendix. Even though many prefer to call this subgenre ARPGs, I call them *Diablo*-likes in honor of the game that started it all. In this section, I'll talk about some of the most influential and interesting of these *Diablo*-likes.

Revenant

Cinematix Studios' *Revenant,* published in 1999 by Eidos, is in some ways similar to Black Isle's *Planescape: Torment,* released a month later. Like that game, which I'll discuss later, *Revenant* puts the player in the role of an undead being who has no memory of his previous life. This unfortunate soul, Locke D'Averam, has been resurrected to serve a powerful wizard—but he doesn't provide his services willingly. Indeed, Locke is quite resentful of being brought back from the dead and considers his task—rescuing Andria, a damsel in distress—beneath him. In short, what we get with *Revenant* is an antihero, a type of character common enough in literature and film but relatively rare in CRPGs.

Revenant is similar to *Diablo* in terms of graphics and gameplay, but the interface is more complex and, for beginners, even daunting. Many critics complain about the movement controls used to activate the mouse or keyboard commands. However, the game also supports gamepads, which are highly recommended. Combat is more nuanced than in *Diablo,* with more options for attacking (thrust, swing, and chop) and even combos, special sequences of attacks and blocks that result in more powerful moves. Mastering this system requires both careful timing and quick reflexes,

FIGURE 15.8 *Revenant* makes combat even more action-oriented than *Diablo*. Indeed, playing with a gamepad is recommended.

making the game far more action-oriented. There's also a fatigue system similar to *Diablo II*, though more integral—if the fatigue meter is too low, Locke does less damage and responds slowly to commands (Figure 15.8).

The leveling system is also somewhat unusual: Players determine which two attributes they would like to raise *before* leveling rather than after. This makes sense. In reality, of course, you don't suddenly get stronger, smarter, or more dexterous by fiat, but only by slowly but steadily improving the attribute in question.

The game also has an innovative magic system, based on combining twelve talismans—which are distributed throughout the gameworld. The player finds the recipes for spells on special scrolls, or cheat by relying on trial and error, thereby gaining very powerful spells quite early in the game. The spells are accompanied by impressive special effects.

On the negative side, the game suffers from poor pacing: Locke soon becomes so powerful that not even the most ferocious enemies stand a chance. The voice acting is also lamentable, unless you love yelling and screeching. It's also stymied by odd loading times, which can halt the game even at critical junctures in combat. If all this weren't bad enough, there are bugs, a point that few reviewers fail to comment on. The multiplayer capabilities are also lacking, with only a simple player versus player death-match mode.

A later game that borrows *Revenant's* combo-fighting system is Pixel Studio's *Blade & Sword,* an otherwise uninteresting *Diablo* clone set in ancient China. It was published in 2003 by Whiptail Interactive and met with lukewarm reviews from critics, although its customizable combo system (which includes thirty-six Kung Fu and twelve super attacks) is impressive. Nevertheless, repetitive levels and outdated graphics doomed it from the start.

Divine Divinity

Developed by the Belgian developer Larian Studios and published in 2002 by CDV Software, *Divine Divinity* is an oddly named *Diablo* clone on steroids, with a huge gameworld and a massive number of skills (Figure 15.9). Larian was founded by the charismatic Swen Vincke, who I interviewed in 2013 on *Matt Chat* 189 as he was promoting a Kickstarter campaign for *Divinity: Original Sin.* However, Vincke's work ethic, attention to detail, and unique personality are evident even in his earliest games.

FIGURE 15.9 *Divine Divinity* is one of the best *Diablo*-likes, with a huge world to explore, great music, and a rich set of roleplaying mechanics.

In *Divine Divinity,* each of the six character classes has up to thirty-two skills to develop during the game. As in *Diablo II,* players can either learn new skills or pump points into acquired ones, and most had prerequisites. However, one key difference is that any character can learn any skill, regardless of class. Another is that the environment is more interactive than *Diablo*'s. You can push crates to reveal hidden items or even build a bed out of bales of hay. There's more going on politically, with plenty of intrigue and important choices to make, which affects your reputation score. Characters with low reputations have to pay more at shops, and other characters may even refuse to speak to them. Although combat is in real time, you can pause the action to issue orders to the character. By this point, this Real-Time with Pause mechanic had been used in plenty of other games, including *Darklands* back in 1988 and *Baldur's Gate* a decade later.

The only real problem critics have with the game is the spotty voice acting, which is unfortunately all too common in translated games from this era. Thankfully, the musical score is superb, more than compensating for the occasional misspoken line or grammatical error. It won plenty of awards and remains a favorite among fans of *Diablo*-likes.

Beyond Divinity

Larian Studios followed up *Divine Divinity* with *Beyond Divinity,* published by Hip Interactive in 2004. Although it shares much with its predecessor, it offers one novel innovation: the main character has been "soul forged" with an evil Death Knight, and the player must work with the character to unravel the curse. It's certainly one of the more original plots in the CRPG canon and leads to plenty of opportunities for humor. We'll see a similar contrivance in *Divinity: Original Sin* over a decade later.

According to Vincke, Larian originally planned to do a turn-based combat engine for *Beyond Divinity,* and promoted it as such at E3, but it failed to interest publishers. "There was no market for a turn-based game at that time," says Vincke. It was, however, able to make some improvements to its RTwP engine, such as an option for the characters to automatically attack any enemies they encounter. This option dramatically reduces the mouse clicking required by most other *Diablo*-likes. Another interesting innovation are battlefields, or randomly generated levels. These battlefields offer pure hack 'n slash gameplay that provide a nice distraction from the main quest.

The changes Larian made to the skill system are more controversial. In *Beyond Divinity,* the characters must seek out teachers to learn new skills, and the skills offered by any individual teacher are randomized. Furthermore, the descriptions of the skills lack detail. Several critics complain about the resulting confusion and frustration. They also complain again about the miserable voice acting, particularly that of the Death Knight, whose staccato voice gets quite irritating–especially after hours and hours of gameplay.

Vincke and Larian triumphantly returned to the forefront of CRPGs with two Kickstarter-funded games, *Divinity: Original Sin* in 2014 and *Divinity: Original Sin II* in 2016. These spectacular and successful games both offer impressive graphics, turn-based combat, and highly innovative modes for cooperative gameplay. I'll have more to say about them in a later chapter.

Freedom Force

Irrational Games' *Freedom Force,* published in 2002 by Electronic Arts, introduces comic book-style superheroes to the *Diablo* formula (Figure 15.10). Many fans of the action CRPG rank it among the best of the subgenre, and I heartily agree. Although we've already seen several *Diablo*-inspired games

FIGURE 15.10 *Freedom Force* does an incredible job integrating its subject matter (Silver Age superhero comics) into its interface. Note the comic-style fonts and floating combat texts.

that depart from conventional fantasy settings, *Freedom Force* goes further and has more fun doing it.

Its style is based on the Silver Age comics of the 1960s, when camp was king. Many hardcore gamers also enjoy comic books, reveling in the stylized art and aesthetics that *Freedom Force* captures so well. The high-quality 3D graphics and (for once) sterling voice acting earn the game praise, but it's really the superb engine that makes it so fun to play.

The player takes on the role of Frank Stiles, a man who gained his superpowers (and his new alter ego) from a statue of a Minuteman. Like so many other heroes of the Silver Age of comics, Stiles decides that with great power comes great responsibility, so he dons an outlandish costume and sets out to vanquish evil. Along the way, Minuteman recruits other heroes to his cause, swapping them in and out of a four-character party.

The CRPG aspects are similar to those of many games we've discussed previously. Besides the usual stats, there's a stamina system that limits how many actions the characters can perform before resting, and a prestige stat that changes depending on the characters' ethical choices. Combat is fast, but can be paused to allow you to issue orders to the party (another instance of Real-Time with Pause, or RTwP). It's also important to note here that the 3D environment is fully interactive (and destructible), and Minuteman and the other heroes can use objects such as lampposts as weapons or projectiles. Furthermore, they can leap atop buildings and tear through walls. The characters also learn new skills and gain new abilities as they level up, keeping gameplay fresh and engaging.

The only real negative aspect is the tacked-on multiplayer capability, which is limited to deathmatches. It's a missed opportunity for some truly interesting co-op play; one thinks of all the famous crime fighting duos of comic book history like Batman and Robin or Captain America and Bucky.

Vivendi published the sequel in 2005, *Freedom Force vs. The 3rd Reich*. Unfortunately, this game didn't fare as well. According to Ken Levine, who wrote and produced it, it sold 40,000 units as opposed to its predecessor's 400,000. The main problems are the limited artificial intelligence of the enemies and a lackluster storyline that borrows too heavily from the first game. Levine argues that it's too fixated on Marvel comics from the 1960s, which might have alienated comic fans of other eras. Still, the game is not without defenders.

Superhero-themed CRPGs aren't as common as you'd think, unless you're willing to count action games with RPG-elements like the *Batman*

Arkham series. Likewise, superhero MMORPGs haven't quite lived up to their potential, either, a topic we'll get to later. All of this is surprising considering the popularity of pen-and-paper superhero games such as *Mutants & Masterminds* (*M&M*). One obvious problem with superheroes as RPG characters is that they're, well, already superpowered to begin with. How exactly does Superman get faster or stronger? *M&M* and games like it deal with this problem with a variety of checks and balances, and of course not all superheroes are as overpowered as Superman. Another possibility is that fans of superheroes are simply more drawn to action. Still, *Freedom Force* shows it can be done, and I'm hopeful that there will be even better superhero CRPGs in the future.

Sacred

Sacred is a *Diablo*-like from Ascaron Entertainment, a German company whose CRPGs share the immense size and attention to detail that characterized the older German games discussed earlier. Published by Encore in 2004, it has full 3D views and a world that takes hours to cross, even on horseback. The game is also quite open-ended, with over 500 optional sidequests. It's loaded with self-referential humor reminiscent of a *Monty Python* movie.

Each time characters gain a level, you get bonus points to boost their attributes—standard procedure in *Diablo*-likes. However, learning skills isn't automatic or a matter of training; rather, you're granted skills when you read runes received from quest rewards or loot. When you level up, you receive points you can use to increase attributes and the skills you've managed to learn. Each class has its own set of skills, though some are shared with others. The best strategy is to concentrate on the skills that best suit your playstyle rather than improve them all.

One of the boldest and most exciting innovations in the game—the ability to ride and attack from horseback—is sadly mired by a sloppy interface. Most players find it better to dismount before attack, but the horses are still convenient for faster overland travel.

Multiplayer support is offered locally and on private servers based on Blizzard's Battle.net model. Gamers can team up with three others and co-operate during the main campaign or join in massive player versus player duels. Unfortunately, the servers were constantly busy, and many gamers gave up trying to connect after hours of unsuccessful attempts. Of course, nowadays the servers aren't nearly as busy—and, indeed, the fact that they're still running is a testament to this game's quality.

FIGURE 15.11 *Sacred Gold* is another great *Diablo*-like with hours upon hours of hack 'n slash fun. Take that, goblin!

Sacred met with praise from critics, who applauded its more open-ended structure, but its many bugs weren't unnoticed. The worst would prevent you from completing the campaign. Ascaron released *Sacred Plus* in 2004, which addresses many of the worst problems and adds new functionality. In 2005 came the first expansion, *Sacred Underworld*. It has two new characters and extends the story established in the main game. *Sacred Gold,* also published in 2005, compiles the main game with both expansions and is currently available on GOG.com and Steam (Figure 15.11). *Sacred 2* was published in 2008 to mixed reviews, mostly over its bugs and glitches and lack of innovation. *Sacred 3* followed in 2014. Despite its title, it was a much different animal: an arcade brawler designed for four-person co-op play. It's notable mainly for incensing the *Sacred* fan base, who rejected the abrupt change in direction.

Dungeon Siege

One of my favorite *Diablo*-likes is Gas Powered Games' *Dungeon Siege,* published by Microsoft in 2002 (Figure 15.12). It was conceived by Chris Taylor, whose earlier *Total Annihilation* game won many awards in the real-time strategy market. Despite the success and promise of that

FIGURE 15.12 The first *Dungeon Siege* is a fantastic romp that doesn't waste time getting to the good stuff.

franchise, Taylor left Cavedog Entertainment in 1998 to found his own company called Gas Powered Games.

Taylor's *Dungeon Siege* has a large, diverse gameworld rendered in real-time 3D. The game's custom engine allows its gameworld to stream rather than preload, which makes the setting feel more like a coherent whole than a collection of discrete levels. The game's camera lets you control the angle of perspective, zooming and rotating, but not free roaming. The graphics were top notch at the time and exactingly detailed, with convincing day/night cycles and even weather effects (rain and snow).

Like most *Diablo*-likes, *Dungeon Siege* is designed with the novice gamer in mind: "We are all too busy, and have too many things going in our lives to sit and study a game manual, or be subject to long in-game tutorials," says Taylor. According to Taylor, a successful CRPG must be "way less riddled with complex rule systems, and far more forgiving to the player and just an all-around easier game to play."[2] However, even Taylor acknowledges that a CRPG must "expose enough of the guts of the game to make it compelling for those old-school gamers who like to see numbers." Thus, we're back to that old debate between "roll-play" and "role-play," and Taylor clearly understands the need to balance action with strategy to appeal to gamers.

Dungeon Siege's leveling system is determined by your actions rather than a preselected class, an innovation also seen in the *Elder Scrolls* series among others. Although you create only a single character, eight other prerendered adventurers or loot-carrying mules can be added to the party. The mules, which fight as well as carry extra equipment, became one of the franchise's signature features. Even though at later levels it probably makes more sense to swap the mule for a more powerful character, I'm probably not alone in becoming far too attached to the brave animal to even consider that.

The story pits a single, humble farmer (the player's character) against the evil hordes of Krug. The Krug have, among other foul deeds, sacked the character's farm. Naturally, he (or she) can't abide such acts and sets out for vengeance—launching a hack 'n slash campaign of epic proportions.

Combat is more hands-off than in *Diablo*; the characters can be programmed to automatically attack, though you can pause the action to issue orders as necessary. Critical reactions to this feature are varied; some gamers are grateful to avoid the relentless mouse clicking necessary to get through *Diablo,* but others feel they aren't sufficiently involved in the action—it feels to them as though the game is playing itself. I can appreciate this perspective, but, on the other hand, I'd rather spare my wrists the pain.

Like most modern CRPGs, *Dungeon Siege* has multiplayer options, including LAN and online support for up to eight players. The online option used Microsoft's Zone, a matchmaking system that helped players find and connect to like-minded gamers. Once connected, gamers can either replay the original campaign in cooperative mode or embark on a special multiplayer quest. Still, *Dungeon Siege* did not come close to matching *Diablo II* in the online arena.

Gas Powered Games released a level editor named the *Dungeon Siege Tool Kit,* which allows players to create their own campaigns (or "siegelets") for the game, and a *Fan Site Kit* to help players build fan pages without violating copyright or trademark laws.[3] An expansion called *Legends of Aranna* followed the next year, introducing a new campaign and some needed improvements, such as a global map tool.

Dungeon Siege II

The first full sequel to the series was published by Microsoft Game Studios in 2005. The game's *Diablo II* heritage is unmistakable, particularly in

FIGURE 15.13 *Dungeon Siege II* isn't as good as the first game, but it's still worth playing.

the "new" skill tree system and item sets. *Dungeon Siege II* duplicates *Diablo II*'s socketed items as well, though most players discover that the items they find or receive as rewards are superior to any they enchant themselves (Figure 15.13). Probably the most intriguing innovation is the option to feed unwanted items to pack mules and other pets. With enough food, the pet gains a level and new stats or bonuses depending on its diet. If players feed pets lots of weapons, for instance, they gain in strength. What a digestive system! Whether it makes sense or not, this system helps declutter your inventory and makes animal companions more interesting.

The multiplayer options are disappointingly basic. Games are limited to four players (with two sidekicks apiece). Furthermore, the graphics aren't as impressive as the first game's had been, and the gameplay just isn't as fresh or engaging. The voice acting and dialog range from mediocre to embarrassing. The biggest problem, though, is that the game is simply too easy. The game does score points, however, for its fine interface, much of which is based on color codes and distinctive sounds. For instance, when a special set item drops from a fallen adversary, a special sound is played, and the item's name is labeled in gold. Although seemingly trivial, such techniques reduce tedium.

Broken World, the first expansion pack for the game, was published in 2006 by 2K Games. It adds two new character classes, a new race, and several minor improvements to the interface. Many critics were unimpressed, noting sarcastically that the title was appropriate. 2K Games released the *Dungeon II: Deluxe Edition* in October 2006, which includes the original game and the expansion, as well as a "making of" DVD and other collectibles.

The worst of the *Dungeon Siege* games was excreted in 2011 to little fanfare. Developed by Obsidian Entertainment, *Dungeon Siege III* received a cool response from critics, who applauded its graphics but decried its poor multiplayer capability, tedious story, and repetitive gameplay. Gamers complained about the awkward camera controls. Not everyone hated it of course, but it was clearly a step down from the previous two games. They didn't even include the mule–unforgivable!

Titan Quest

Yet another *Diablo*-like worthy of discussion is *Titan Quest,* a game developed by Iron Lore Entertainment and published by THQ in 2006. This game has players traveling to Ancient Greece, Egypt, and Asia in pursuit of the Titans. While not especially innovative in terms of gameplay, there's a lot to like, especially the rich and very long single-player campaign—which you can also co-op with up to five friends. Some complain that it feels too much like *Diablo II,* but others might consider this its bestselling point. An expansion called *Immortal Throne* was published in 2007, and an Anniversary Edition followed in 2016 alongside a new expansion called *Ragnarok.*

The team later reformed as Crate Entertainment, licensed the engine from Iron Lore, and made *Grim Dawn* in 2016, a spiritual successor of *Titan Quest.* It's set in a dark world based on the Victorian era. The studio ran out of money, but was happily able to raise enough money from fans and CRPG websites to complete production. Again, some reviewers miss the point by criticizing it for being too much like *Diablo II,* but it still sold well and had very positive user reviews on Steam.

If the unparalleled success of *Diablo II* has taught us anything, it's that sequels don't have to be revolutionary to be exemplary. Exquisite crafting, attention to detail, and smooth gameplay will always prevail over the latest graphical wizardry or gameplay gimmicks. If you've played all the games mentioned here and still haven't satiated your lust for action RPGs, check out the CRPG Bestiary in the appendix for **Torchlight, Path of Exile, Fate, The Incredible Adventures of Van Helsing,** and **Marvel Heroes.**

NOTES

1. See Trent C. Ward's review of the game at http://www.gamespot.com/pc/rpg/diablo/review.html.
2. These comments are from a private email interview with Taylor on July 9, 2007.
3. See http://ds/heavengames.com/community/links/siegelets.html for a list of downloadable siegelets, including two based on classic *Ultima* games.

CHAPTER 16

Fallout and *Baldur's Gate*

INTERPLAY GOES PLATINUM

After *Daggerfall* and *Diablo,* the typical CRPG fan probably assumed that real-time gameplay, whether 3D or isometric, was the way of the future. However, as we saw with the publication of FTL Games' *Dungeon Master,* the evolution of CRPGs is anything but linear. Ultimately, craft trumps invention, and even though *Dungeon Master* demonstrated as early as 1987 the appeal and feasibility of first-person perspective in real time, SSI's turn-based Gold Box games sold well into the 1990s. Therefore, there's really nothing surprising about Interplay's breakthrough success with *Fallout,* a turn-based isometric game set in a postapocalyptic wasteland.

Wasteland Revisited: *Fallout*

Fallout (1997) and its sequel, *Fallout 2* (1998), are two of the finest CRPGs ever made, and if the era that produced them isn't worthy of the name Platinum Age, none will ever be (Figure 16.1). Like Interplay's previous masterpieces *The Bard's Tale* and *Wasteland, Fallout* is one of those precious games that is more than the sum of its parts. *Fallout* is another one of my favorite games of all time, and my love for it has no doubt blinded me to its flaws. However, my advice is to seek out the game on GOG.com or Steam and try it yourself. The *Fallout* games are wonderfully creative and continue to win over new players nearly a decade after they first appeared on the shelf.

FIGURE 16.1 *Fallout* does a fantastic job achieving and maintaining its unique Cold War futurism theme throughout. Check out those vacuum tubes on this dialog screen!

But what makes *Fallout* so great? Weren't there already plenty of other postapocalyptic games, such as *Wasteland, Autoduel,* and even Interstel's *Scavengers of the Mutant World*? When you really get down to it, what's so S.P.E.C.I.A.L. about its role-playing system? One of my contentions throughout this book has been that the greatest games are not necessarily the most technically innovative or original. The industry's obsession with the bleeding edge has led to some of the genre's worst disasters. Wiser developers know that a great game begins with a great vision, and the technology is only a means of achieving that vision. When the technology itself becomes the vision we get the likes of *Descent to Undermountain.*

You can sum up *Fallout*'s appeal in a single word: style. The governing aesthetic is a surreal mix of cheerfully morbid 1950s Cold War imagery and movies like *Mad Max, Planet of the Apes,* and *Dr. Strangelove.* There are even hints of *The Evil Dead* tossed in for good measure. This amalgamation makes for some of the most compelling moments in gaming history, and I bet you'll get goosebumps the first time you see the legendary opening. Furthermore, the Cold War aesthetic runs all the way through the game, including the interface.

Most games switch to boring menu screens when it comes time to level up. *Fallout* bucks this trend by presenting skills on information cards, complete with fitting illustrations to keep up the disturbing ambience. Even the game's manual stays in character, presenting itself as a "survival guide" designed to look like a government publication. Indeed, the manual refers to the game as a simulation to help long-term Vault-Dwellers prepare themselves for a return to the outside world. It even includes some survival recipes for "Mushroom Clouds" and "Desert Salad." Clearly, the development team had a blast creating *Fallout,* and their enthusiasm radiates throughout the game.

One of my favorite interviews on *Matt Chat* was with Tim Cain, the designer of *Fallout* (see episodes 66–68). According to Cain, Interplay was much too focused on *Descent to Undermountain* to mess with his *Fallout* team. This gave him considerable latitude to design the game as he wished. This level of autonomy was already rare by this point, especially for designers at a major studio like Interplay.

Perhaps if management had been more involved, they might have objected to the rather disturbing violence of the game, as did Steve Jackson. Originally, the plan had been to license Jackson's *GURPS,* or *Generic Universal Role Playing System,* but rather than try to placate Jackson by censoring the violence, the *Fallout* team created their own system— S.P.E.C.I.A.L. (Strength, Perception, Endurance, Charisma, Intelligence, Agility, and Luck). In retrospect, it turned out to be a great decision, since this meant that Interplay wouldn't have to pay steep royalties as it did with BioWare's *Baldur's Gate.*

The game's unique setting of Cold War futurism was dreamed up by Leonard Boyarsky, who is interviewed in *Matt Chat* (395–397). According to him, the initial plan was for a *Mad Max* or *Road Warrior* style setting. However, eight or so months into production, Boyarsky was driving home one night when he got the idea to set it in the future as envisioned by 1950s sci-fi films. "I'd been reading Frank Miller and Geof Darrow's *Hard Boiled,* and if you look at that, you can see the raw material for [the *Fallout*] world. But the other thing we were all into was B-movies. However, when I decided to bring in all the 50s stuff, we didn't change what was already there—the *Road Warrior* and *Alien* stuff, but it all combined. It was really organic."

Another aspect of the game is its overt social and political themes. We saw earlier how Lord British wanted his games to be morally edifying and explore complex social and cultural themes. However, perhaps since *Fallout* is set in the real world, its critique feels closer to home. According to Cain,

> We loved making social commentary. It's riddled with it. We made it quite clear that the government is lying to you, that the military needs to be answerable to citizens—because in *Fallout* the military pretty much took over. Corporations were taking over—the Vault was made by Vault-Tec, and all the products were made by this one massively invasive company that was making all this profit off fears of nuclear war and would continue to profit if there was a war. What we were trying to say is that even though this is exaggerated, a lot of it is true about our own society. It wouldn't hurt if more games would raise the consciousness of the players who played them and look at their own government and society a little more critically.

I can't speak for everyone who's played the game, but it worked on me!

Of course, great art and storytelling aren't enough to make a great CRPG; what's more crucial is the leveling and combat system—and *Fallout* excels at both. Combat is turn-based and tactical, with a wide array of melee and ranged weapons at the characters' disposal. The ranged weapons, such as the pistol, take the lighting conditions into effect, so that it's harder to hit a rat in a dim corridor than in broad daylight. It's also possible to damage your eyes, arms, and legs, which in each case dramatically reduce your combat abilities. For instance, eye damage makes it harder to hit targets in the distance (Figures 16.2 and 16.3).

The leveling system is based on eight active skills, which run the gamut of RPG activities (i.e., lock-picking, first aid, repair, disarming traps, stealing). Other skills are passive, such as "small guns," which boost your ability to hit targets with pistols, rifles, and shotguns. Characters can also have two optional traits, each with a good and bad effect (one is reminded of *Traveller*). For instance, "Chem Reliant" makes you more susceptible to chemical addiction, but you recover much faster from a chemical's side effects. "Bloody Mess" ensures that every death in the game is portrayed with maximum gore.

You also receive a "perk" every three levels. Perks are new abilities that can have drastic effects on gameplay, and some can be selected multiple times for even stronger effects. They also have prerequisites. For instance, the level 9 perk "Animal Friend" prevents animals from attacking you,

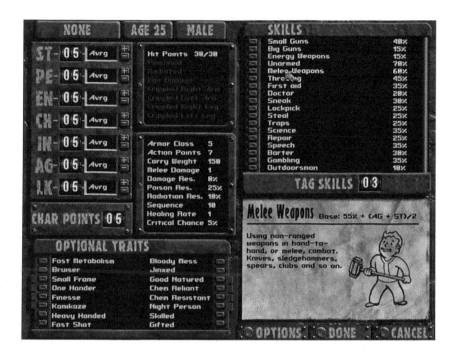

FIGURE 16.2 An example of fine interface design. Each skill has a card that shows Vault Boy cheerfully demonstrating its purpose. All these little touches add up to create a deep and powerful sense of immersion.

but requires five intelligence and an outdoorsman skill of 25 percent. The "Flower Child" perk makes you 50 percent less likely to suffer chemical addiction and reduces withdrawal times, but requires 5 endurance points and a level 9 character. There are over fifty perks available, and since you'll probably select only a dozen or so during a game, you can replay the game several times before it gets repetitive.

The story is an intriguing blend of alternate history, dystopia, and science fiction. Some eighty years ago, a nuclear holocaust wiped out most of the civilized world, but some people survived by moving into a giant underground vault, where they eventually developed their own society and culture (think *Logan's Run*). However, now the vault's water purification chip has worn out, and it's your job to find a new one before your people die of thirst. This means leaving behind everything you've ever known and entering a war-torn world full of mutants, bandits, and gangs. What seems like a fairly straightforward fetch quest soon becomes much more, and I'm not going to ruin the story here by giving away any of the twists and turns, least of all its legendary ending.

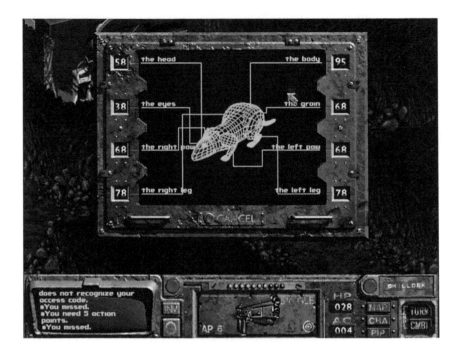

FIGURE 16.3 A combat screen showing a breakdown of your enemy's body (a rat, of course!). The numbers indicate your odds of hitting that particular part. You should probably study this carefully…but just go for the eyes, Boo!

Fallout 2

Once Interplay saw it had a true hit on its hands, it wasted no time getting a sequel in production. Unfortunately, the heightened attention meant more supervision and executive involvement, which chafed Cain. In any case, it was another excellent game and certainly a worthy follow-up.

Fallout 2 was developed by Black Isle Studios, Interplay's new division that specialized in CRPGs. It's set eighty years after the conclusion of the first game and echoes the movie *Mad Max: Beyond Thunderdome*. The avatar's tribe is on the verge of extinction and must hunt down the G.E.C.K. (Garden of Eden Creation Kit), another Vault-Tec device advertised in the first game's manual. Once again, you quickly find yourself immersed in a moving and captivating story. It culminates in one of the most heart-pounding (and difficult) climaxes of any game I've ever played and, like the original, boils over with black humor and political overtones.

Fallout 2 has more dialog options and plenty of new items and characters than its predecessor. However, the bulk of the game's engine is left intact. Perhaps the biggest change involves nonplayer characters (NPCs), who can now be trained and equipped with better weapons and armor. The box advertises a controversial option to "fall in love, get married, and then pimp your spouse for a little extra chump-change." Still, even with all these new features, some critics complain that it's really more of an expansion pack than a true sequel.

Although both *Fallout* games are critically acclaimed and cherished by many fans, Interplay did not produce a third game. *Fallout Tactics: Brotherhood of Steel (2001)* is a strategy game based on *Fallout*'s combat mode, though it does have some CRPG elements. A *Diablo* clone called *Fallout: Brotherhood of Steel* appeared for the PS2 and Xbox in 2004, but many fans of the first two games fail to acknowledge it.

After a long hiatus, Bethesda acquired the franchise and produced *Fallout 3* in 2008 and *Fallout 4* in 2015. These games maintain some elements from the first two, but they use a first-person shooter style engine. We'll talk about these games later.

ARCANUM: STEAMPUNK AND MAGICK

Black Isle wasn't the only company releasing brave new gameworlds. A new company named Troika Games, founded by former members of *Fallout*'s development team including Cain and Boyarsky, scored an early triumph with *Arcanum: Of Steamworks & Magick Obscure,* published by Sierra in 2001 (Figure 16.4). It certainly isn't the first CRPG to marry magic and technology; many of the early *Ultima* and *Might and Magic* games blend the two quite freely, but SSI's *Spelljammer: Pirates of Realmspace* and Paragon's *Space 1889* are probably more direct precursors. Nevertheless, *Arcanum* is the game many people think of when they hear the term *steampunk,*[1] and deservedly so.

Arcanum is praised for its open-ended gameplay and intriguing gameworld, which is best described as an industrial revolution taking place in a high fantasy setting. Usually, magic and technology are strange bedfellows, but when done right, the result is magical realism, in which objects that ordinarily look familiar are placed in settings that make them seem strange and exotic. It can be quite exhilarating, for instance, when a dwarf draws a flintlock pistol rather than the traditional battleaxe or warhammer. The outcome of the game depends on whether players follow the magical or the technological path.

Fallout fans will recognize many of the game's conventions, particularly the lack of classes and emphasis on skills. *Arcanum* expands the skill

Need to kill priest...Arbalah...he lives
here.He points at your map. Only
his...death will free me...

I don't know, what will you give me for doing this?
Of course...justice must prevail!
I don't think so. Goodbye.

000033

Human Bandit

036

034

FIGURE 16.4 *Arcanum* had just as much going for it as *Fallout*, with an utterly unique setting, memorable characters, and an unshakeable aesthetic. It's a great game, but a rushed production schedule and lack of resources prevented it from realizing its true potential.

set to cover three types of skills: basic, technological, and magickal, and you have tremendous freedom in selecting diverse skills for your character. Furthermore, each skill can be honed or trained, much like in the *Mandate of Heaven*. Adding skill points raises the skill level, but training confers much larger benefits—however, you must find someone willing and able to offer the training. As with *Mandate of Heaven,* it's easy enough to find basic trainers, but masters are rare and demand a high price for their services. There are sixteen colleges of magick and fifty-six technological degrees available in eight different disciplines. In fact, there are so many skills that it's unlikely you'll learn more than ten percent of them before completing the game.

There are many other reasons to recommend *Arcanum.* It has an immense gameworld that takes thirty real-time hours to travel across, and there are hundreds of sidequests if you get bored with the main plotline. There's even a scenario editor for gamers with a creative streak.

Unlike *Fallout*, there's a free multiplayer option that lets four players work through the Vormantown scenario. There was no equivalent of Blizzard's Battle.net; *Arcanum* requires at least one player to set up a server for the other players to join. However, it was obvious that the developers were more concerned with the single-player campaign; the short multiplayer campaign feels tacked on to please the marketing department.

Combat is where *Arcanum* falters, however. As we've seen countless times, no matter how puffed up and self-important a writer allows herself to be, CRPGs live or die by combat. Let the critics gush about a game's challenging story, compelling artwork, meaningful dialog, and so on—all these things are easy for them to write about—but when real gamers get their hands on a CRPG, it all boils down to how fun it is to kill a rat. *Arcanum* offers three different modes (real-time, turn-based, and fast turn-based), but none of them are perfect.

The key problem is the way experience points are doled out: you earn them only by hitting, rather than defeating, enemies. This makes strength and dexterity all-important, thus ruling out many of the more intriguing possibilities. The difficulty is also skewed toward the magickal path; technologists have difficulty finding equipment and surviving long enough to use what they do manage to find. Thankfully, there are usually alternatives to combat, but it's a bad sign when avoiding combat is something to be thankful for.

Arcanum has much in common with the *Fallout* series, no doubt due in part to sharing some key members of the development team. Both games also share the same wonderful sense of irony and humor, and the artwork is of a coherent and refreshing style that compensates for the bugs and rough edges. While not as polished as *Fallout*, *Arcanum* nevertheless stands out as a viable alternative to the standard formula, and it's become a cult classic. It used to be nearly impossible to find and get running on modern computers, but now it's available on GOG.com.

BIOWARE: THE NEW SSI

We've seen how TSR's valuable license lost credibility after SSI's last Black Box games, the *Eye of the Beholder* series created by Westwood Studios. SSI's own efforts went from bad to worse, ultimately costing the developer its exclusive license with TSR, and other companies' products flopped like dying fish despite all the *D&D* trademarks plastered on their bodies. Nevertheless, cherished *D&D* franchises like the *Forgotten Realms* were just too promising to remain unvisited for long, and many of us pined for a return to the glory days of *Pool of Radiance* and *Eye of the Beholder*.

The problem was how to update these hallowed games for the next generation. Two possible models existed in *The Elder Scrolls* and *Diablo*, but these action-oriented games had less to offer fans of tabletop *D&D* and the hardcore, tactical CRPGs of earlier years. The development team that finally succeeded in finding the right formula was not SSI, Interplay, or Sierra, but rather a trio of Canadian medical doctors-turned-game-developers: BioWare. They created what is perhaps the greatest CRPG engine ever designed: the Infinity engine. Although the Infinity engine is not 3D and lacks a free-roaming camera, these limitations are more than compensated for by an intuitive interface, detailed scenery, turn-based combat, and convincing character animation. Gone are the old tile-based graphics; now, every location could be fully rendered in exacting detail by professional artists.

Baldur's Gate

BioWare's first foray into CRPGs, *Baldur's Gate*, was an instant success, and not just among CRPG fans (Figure 16.5). Like Blizzard's *Diablo*, released two years earlier, *Baldur's Gate* won over critics and gamers by the millions, and it's still highly praised and played today, over a decade later. And what game since then has surpassed it? Indeed, were it not for the even more impressive sequel, *Baldur's Gate* would stand without equal.

First published by Interplay in 1998, *Baldur's Gate* has much in common with *Diablo*. It too features an isometric perspective and lets you create only a single character. Both have real-time gameplay, but with a key difference: *Baldur's Gate* uses Real-Time with Pause (RTwP) combat, which, while not as ideal as a true turn-based system, does allow for more tactical possibilities than *Diablo*. *Baldur's Gate* system is designed to allow most battles to be fought by a highly configurable artificial intelligence system; the player can just sit back and watch. However, if things go awry, he or she can hit the spacebar to pause the game and manually assign actions, then resume the game to see them carried out. RTwP wasn't new; we saw a similar system in *Darklands* back in 1992, and even though it's executed better here, it still isn't perfect. However, the critical thing is that it's a lot more fun than it is frustrating.

Baldur's Gate only lets you create and directly control only one member of your party, but this is so it could turn the rest of your crew into story-telling assets. You can join up with up to five other characters, each with

FIGURE 16.5 *Baldur's Gate* doesn't take long to get you into a cellar fighting rats. But is it fun? Oh, hell yes. I also love that the cat (the critter with a blue circle around it) is happy to kick back and let a rat-slaying amateur do his job for him.

a varied set of skills, unique personality, and implications for the plot. Characters of different political and ethical outlook might not get along; a few characters may actually betray you at critical junctures. Many are the *Baldur's Gate* fans who find themselves attached to Imoen, a cheerful young teenager, and Minsc, a Schwarzenegger-style ranger who provides as much muscle as comic relief. You aren't required to include either of these characters in the party; you may wish to side with evil characters, and even neutral characters will complain if the party strays too far into "goody good" territory. In short, the gameplay changes considerably depending on which characters you party with. Furthermore, although the game is divided into chapters that can be advanced only by performing predefined actions, there is still considerable room in each chapter for variation, especially in the many sidequests (Figures 16.6 and 16.7).

Many reviewers praise the game for staying so faithful to the official *AD&D* 2nd Edition rules without baffling novices with the minutiae. The math is kept mostly in the background, but there's enough of the engine exposed to satisfy players who enjoy numbers. It also introduces many

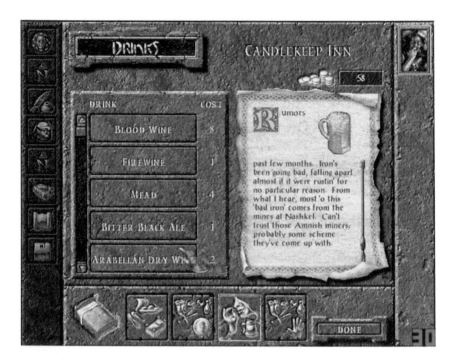

FIGURE 16.6 Shown here is the tavern menu, where you can listen for rumors over a pint of frosty ale. You can also rent a room, trade goods, or have your thief ply their trade.

rules that are sorely lacking in the Gold Box and Black Box classics, such as the effect of the party leader's charisma on character morale.

The game has a multiplayer option that lets you trade the NPCs in your party for up to five friends. While the game still revolves around the main character, the others are free to roam about, though success depends on developing cooperative combat strategies. As with tabletop *AD&D*, the multiplayer experience depends largely on the personalities and camaraderie of the actual group. Although somewhat buggy and not perfectly integrated, this option helped the game compete with *Diablo*.

Baldur's Gate features a rich, nuanced storyline that resists easy summary (and, indeed, reading such a summary would ruin much of the fun of the game; the point is to learn what's happening as you play). The basic gist is that something (or someone) has been causing a serious iron shortage, which has led to widespread banditry across the countryside. Meanwhile, two young wards of a mage named Gorion (the beautiful rogue Imoen and the player's character) have been separated from their guardian and left

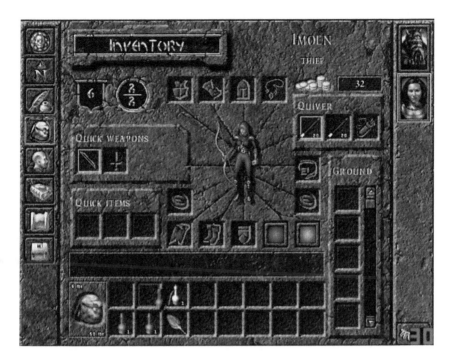

FIGURE 16.7   Imoen's inventory page. You'll probably spend more time on this screen than you think, since the game limits both the number and combined weight of the items you can carry. If necessary, you'll either have to drop items or let stronger characters shoulder some of the burden. If you're anything like me, you'll probably still have these potions at the end of the game. As they say, better to have them and not need them than to need them and not have them.

to fend for themselves. Gradually, you learn of a large conspiracy involving a secretive organization named the Iron Throne. By the end of the game, you know that your character and Imoen are more than what they seem. It's a complex but plausible story of political intrigue that's much more than the standard black and white morality tale that runs rampant through most CRPGs. The characters also benefit from solid writing and exceptional voice talent, a key factor that is the downfall of many lesser games. Who could forget Minsc's joyful battlecry, "Go for the eyes, Boo!" Even the annoying error message "You must gather your party before venturing forth" became a meme.

BioWare released the *Tales of the Sword Coast* expansion one year later. It adds new areas, spells, weapons, and makes some minor improvements to the gameplay and interface. More importantly, it adds four new quests. The consensus is that the pack offers a little more meat to chew on, but it's not to be mistaken for a sequel. At the time, some gamers resented the lack of true story developments, but others were just glad to have a little more *Baldur's Gate* to satiate their appetites while BioWare worked on the next game.

Baldur's Gate II

The first and only true sequel to BioWare's masterpiece is *Baldur's Gate II: Shadows of Amn,* published in 2000 (Figures 16.8 and 16.9). It still uses the Infinity engine, but the graphics are overhauled (800 × 600 versus 640 × 480) and now take advantage of 3D accelerators. *Shadows of Amn* adds new classes, specializations, and popular skills such as dual wielding. Several of the beloved characters are back from the first game, including Imoen, and this time personality (and even romantic) conflicts among party members are more instrumental to the gameplay. Contemporary reviews praise the game and give it the highest possible marks; it didn't take a gem of seeing to know this game was platinum.

FIGURE 16.8 Image from Beamdog's Enhanced Edition of Baldur's Gate II from 2013 showing an early fight with a Lightning Mephit.

FIGURE 16.9 Minsc's character profile. As you can see, there's quite a lot of stats represented here. Minsc is voiced by Jim Cummings, whose other credits, improbably enough, include Winnie the Pooh and Darkwing Duck. Go for the eyes, Pooh!

For what it's worth, I consider *Baldur's Gate II* the finest CRPG ever designed, and I'm not alone. The GameSpot editorial team writes that "there's little doubt that *Baldur's Gate II: Shadows of Amn* deserves to stand among the very best games of the era, or indeed the greatest games of all time."[2] It's won countless awards, and even the worst review of the game on the Metacritic website remarks that it's "just too good to pass up." Furthermore, the gameplay has stood the test of time and is still tremendous fun today. If you somehow haven't played it—which is unlikely for anyone reading this book—do yourself a favor and get a copy immediately.

The story picks up where the first *Baldur's Gate* leaves off (which is all the more reason for new players to start with the first game). It's a bit difficult to talk about the story of *Shadows of Amn* without giving away the shocking ending to the first game, so I'll just say it's mostly concerned with the magical (and sinister) blood running through your character's veins. Unfortunately, your quest for answers is rudely halted by Jon Irenicus, a wicked mage who captures the hero (and his or her friends) in an effort to tap the blood's powers for himself. The story quickly gets much more complicated and compels the characters to travel to hell and back.

One of the best aspects of *Shadows of Amn* is the degree of freedom it gives to players. Many quests are optional, and there are many different paths through the game that substantially alter events. You can either stick to the main plot and ignore these many diversions or get so involved that you lose track of the main story altogether. And, as with the original game, party dynamics play a huge role in the gameplay that goes far beyond managing combat tactics. Mixing and matching characters with differing ethics and values leads to some very interesting drama that everyone should experience at least once—particularly in a game with such good voice talent. As many reviewers point out, the experience is as close to playing tabletop *AD&D* with a group of friends as you can get in a single-player computer game. Multiplayer gameplay is also supported, though little has changed on that front since the first game.

In 2001, BioWare released an expansion for *Baldur's Gate II* called *Throne of Baal*. This important expansion is the final chapter of the saga and required playing for fans of the other games. It adds new items, spells, and even more class abilities. It features a dungeon called Watcher's Keep that can now be accessed during certain chapters in the *Shadows of Amn* game. However, perhaps the aspect most people remember was the degree of godlike power you achieved by the game's ending. For once, we have a worthy ending for a fine series.

What makes the *Baldur's Gate* games so great? Again, it's clear that it's more a matter of good craftsmanship than originality or boldness of design. With *Baldur's Gate* we get attention to what matters most to players: good stories, fun characters, meaningful quests, high-stakes combat, and even an attractive interface. The graphics, sound, and music are appealing and add much to the game's ambience. Perhaps the best testament to the game's lasting appeal is that no single element seems to rise above the others. There are no gimmicks here: just solid platinum gameplay.

Fear and Loathing in *Planescape: Torment*

If there's one thing we can say about the Platinum Age of CRPGs, it's that it has its fair share of cult classics. It's doubtful you could put together any group of CRPG players that wouldn't have a few dyed-in-the-wool fans of *Fallout* and *Planescape: Torment*. Both games are wildly different than the typical high fantasy game like *Baldur's Gate* and offered more introspective gameplay than *Diablo, Mandate of Heaven,* or *Daggerfall.* I can think of very few CRPGs that are as deep—yet, critically, still fun— as *Planescape: Torment.* The game pushes the boundaries of the genre by reclaiming the *AD&D* ruleset to serve its own ends. *Torment* wasn't as big a hit as *Baldur's Gate,* but it's a true classic and one more good reason to call this era the Platinum Age.

BioWare realized that its Infinity engine was too good to keep to itself, and it made sense to license it out to Black Isle, the elite CRPG division of Interplay that made *Fallout 2.* It was designed by Chris Avellone, whose interviews are featured in multiple episodes of *Matt Chat.* He has lots to say about designing CRPGs, but here's the part that every CRPG designer should have tattooed on the backs of their hands (so they'd have to look at it when designing!):

> First you have to be able to make meaningful choices for creating and developing your character. Then the gameworld has to react in meaningful ways to those choices. I'd even argue that having a strong storyline is absolutely secondary or even tertiary. It's the game system that's allowing players to develop; it's allowing the consequences to develop. Most RPG players will form a stronger narrative themselves based on actions that occur in the game that have nothing to do with the NPC they talked to or the big wow moment you threw at them.

Here's how I'd put it: Don't focus on writing an "epic story" that drags the player from plot point to plot point like a puppy dog on a leash. Just build a great gameworld filled with interesting places to go, things to do, and people to see, toss the player in, then get and stay out of their way. I can't tell you how many times I've rolled my eyes (mentally!) at designers waxing eloquently about their brilliant story—but then be unable to even describe the rudiments of their combat engine or what else the poor player will be able to do while they're not admiring their prose (Figure 16.10).

Avellone and Black Isle applied these principles and in November 1999 sprang *Planescape: Torment* upon the world. It's set in the *Planescape* universe, a complex setting with several interlocking planes of existence. The game's strange story and surreal ambiance lend it considerable appeal among gamers ready for a darker and more thoughtful CRPG. Indeed, several reviewers argue that it's really more of an adventure game than a CRPG, though I disagree. The truth is, *Planescape: Torment* violates so

FIGURE 16.10 Here we see Morte, one of my favorite NPCs of all time. In *Planescape: Torment,* he provides a steady stream of humor, but he's much more than what he appears.

many conventions that it's just easy to overlook the *AD&D* mechanics undergirding the gameplay.

The majority of *Torment*'s appeal stems from its unique gameworld, which lets you develop your character and react appropriately to the consequences that unfold. The game is set in a multiverse, or interconnected planes of existence. The city of Sigil serves as a portal to these other planes, but you must find the doors, which can be disguised as ordinary objects (much like the "portkeys" in *Harry Potter* stories). Furthermore, the different planes are home to beings who usually belong to the same faction, or political group, such as the Anarchists or Godsmen. You may join one of these factions, though doing so will win enemies as well as friends. There is no clear division between the good guys and the bad guys here; the point is to get you thinking deeply about morality. It's an interactive *Inferno,* and it doesn't take a Dante scholar to see the many allusions to that famous poem.

Your character is the Nameless One, a gruesome being who awakens on a slab in a giant mortuary. He's suffering from amnesia, and the plot is concerned mostly with rediscovering his identity. It's a nice, if not somewhat overdone contrivance that gives you considerable leeway in role-playing the character. However, it soon becomes obvious that the Nameless One's past deeds have earned him animosity from many of the bizarre characters he meets. Thankfully, the Nameless One can also find new and old friends, including the fabulous Morte, a floating head that becomes his wisecracking sidekick. Then there's Fall-from-Grace, a succubus who's turned from sex to philosophy, opening the "Brothel of Slaking Intellectual Lusts." There's even a robot named Nordom, a rather nerdy crossbow on legs. As you can see, *Planescape: Torment* isn't all doom and gloom; part of the game's enduring popularity was the mix of serious and comedic themes running throughout. Indeed, it reminds one of LucasArts' *Grim Fandango* (1998), a popular graphical adventure game with a comparable mix of grin and grim.

Another feature of *Torment* that sets it apart is its use of dialog not only to build the story, but to offer alternatives to combat. Many conflicts can be resolved by intelligent conversation (Figure 16.11). These conversations

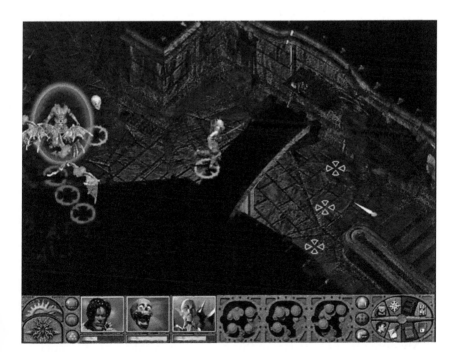

FIGURE 16.11　Just because you can occasionally talk your way out of combat in *Planescape: Torment* doesn't mean you should. Indeed, dying in this game doesn't mean you failed—sometimes it's the best option.

also help develop the other characters into much more than just henchmen. There are plenty of other innovations I could mention, such as a unique tattoo system that boosts stats as well as documents your progress, or the many ways the world reacts according to the Nameless One's decisions. It's the ideal CRPG for gamers who enjoy wit and wisdom as much as hacking and slashing.

In 2017, inXile Entertainment published a spiritual successor called *Torment: Tides of Numenera*. Avellone didn't design it, and it's set in Monte Cook's Numenera campaign setting instead of Planescape, but it's easy to see the influence of the earlier game. I'll have more to say about it later.

Fighting for Your Right to Party: *Icewind Dale*

Most of the best games of the Platinum Age let you create only a single character. Even though games such as *Baldur's Gate* and *Fallout* let you add characters to your party later on, the characters are pregenerated with their own personalities and agendas. While this setup is probably better from a narrative perspective, fans of old classics such as *Pool of Radiance* and *Eye of the Beholder* don't care about that. They still prefer the experience of creating their own party of adventurers from scratch and controlling them all directly. Black Isle met this demand in 2000 with *Icewind Dale,* another game based on BioWare's Infinity engine (Figures 16.12 and 16.13). Set in an arctic region of TSR's *Forgotten Realms, Icewind Dale* has great graphics, sound, and a score by Jeremy Soule that is still one of the finest ever composed for a video game.

Icewind Dale lets players create and control up to six characters, and since the game is so focused on combat, building a properly balanced party is of paramount importance. Furthermore, combat can be very difficult, requiring careful coordination and precise teamwork. For example, one favorite strategy is to have a stealthy thief stride ahead, attract a few enemies, and lure them back into an ambush. As usual, the magic-users' function is artillery; they dole out the most damage but are less effective in physical combat and should be protected. Major battles get quite complex and intense, with a nearly infinite number of variables, especially during the preparation stage (Which potions to give to whom? Should the mage learn enhancement or attack spells?). Complicated? Yes. Fun? Hell, yes.

My only serious criticism of this game is its pathfinding. It's tough to keep the six characters aligned in a sensible formation. You can easily slip up and have a mage stride forward to a vulnerable position, or unknowingly leave a character trapped behind an obstacle several rooms back.

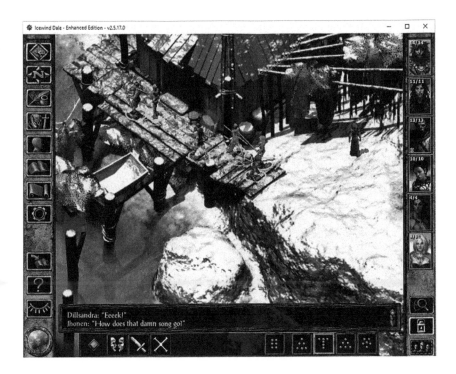

FIGURE 16.12 Creating and controlling a full party can get somewhat unwieldy in Icewind Dale, but that's just part of the challenge. Right.

Still, I doubt it'd be any easier to coordinate the movements of such a group in real life, either.

No doubt players coming from *Baldur's Gate* or *Planescape. Torment* saw *Icewind Dale* as a simple hack 'n slash game in the snow. Personally, being a resident of Minnesota, these are my least favorite settings. Indeed, this probably explains why I dislike SSI's *Secret of the Silver Blades,* my least favorite Gold Box game that is also endlessly wintery. I suppose I can see how it'd seem exotic to Silicon Valley folks, but give me the tropics any day!

On a serious note, I suspect it didn't help either that *Icewind Dale* had to compete for attention with mega-hits like *Diablo II* and *Baldur's Gate II,* both released the same year. But the game has its fans, and Black Isle developed an expansion pack for them called *Heart of Winter* the following year. It adds five new areas and plenty of new items, skills, and spells. It also has higher resolution and better artificial intelligence. If combat and party dynamics are your thing, you'll find much to enjoy about this game. Just don't forget to pack your parka!

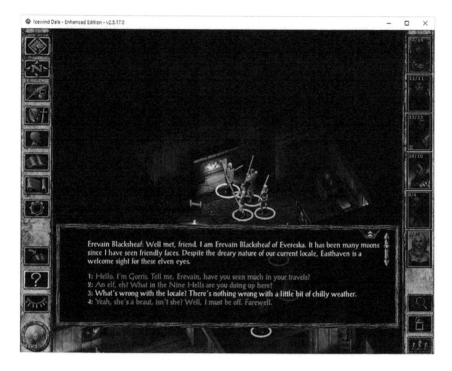

FIGURE 16.13 Early dialog with one Erevain Blacksheaf. Unlike later CRPGs, it isn't always clear which NPCs have valuable information or side quests. In general, it's a good idea to talk to anyone with an actual name; unimportant NPCs will have generic names like "Townsperson."

Icewind Dale II *and* AD&D 3rd Edition

In 2002, Interplay published *Icewind Dale II,* which differs from the original in several significant ways. First and foremost is the switch to *D&D* 3rd Edition rules, which greatly affects how characters are created and developed. Gone are the old random dice throws for stats; now you have a set number of points to distribute as you see fit. However, the catch is that pushing a stat above average requires a greater share of points. It's a smart system that makes sense and works well (Figure 16.14).

There's also a new feats system, which is a terrific innovation comparable to *Fallout*'s. Feats make leveling a more interesting and customizable process, and they add greatly to that "just one more level, then I'll stop" kind of wishful thinking that keeps you up all night. It's one thing to look forward to a boost in hit points and stats; quite another when you're about to get a cool new ability like Power Attack or Armoured Arcana. Not all the feats are worth having, but it's always fun to experiment with different combinations.

FIGURE 16.14 *Icewind Dale II* uses the 3rd Edition ruleset of *Dungeons & Dragons* and is the last of the Infinity engine games.

There's also a skill system that allows further customization and trade-offs; a thief who puts too many points into "open lock" may be rotten at disabling traps or moving stealthily. Finally, you can multiclass your characters however you wish, even to the point of giving each character a level in fighting or thieving just for kicks. Of course, again there is a trade-off; the best abilities are available only to very high-level members of a certain class. Too much hybridization results in "jack-of-all-trades, master of none" characters that are mostly worthless.

Icewind Dale II has other enhancements as well, especially interactions with nonplayer characters and more diverse settings. The voice talent is top notch, an important aspect that tends to get overlooked by reviewers (unless it's bad, in which case it becomes the focus). Although the story is more nuanced than the original, it's still primarily a hack 'n slash game more concerned with blood and sweat than tears. Tellingly, most reviewers spend far more time talking about the feat and skill system than the story arcs. In any case, *Icewind Dale II* is the last of the great Infinity engine games that brought so much joy to CRPG fans.

Of course, the other big game of 2002 was BioWare's *Neverwinter Nights,* a fully 3D game that threatened to make *Icewind Dale II* look old-fashioned before it hit the shelves. We'll talk about it in Chapter 18.

Other *D&D*–Licensed Games of the Platinum Age

Although by far the most popular TSR-licensed games of this era were based on BioWare's Infinity engine, there are other contenders: Stormfront Studios' *Pool of Radiance: Ruins of Myth Drannor* and Troika's *The Temple of Elemental Evil: A Classic Greyhawk Adventure* (2003). Neither of these games was successful, though at least the latter achieved some notoriety for being the first computer game to allow gay characters to marry.

Pool of Radiance, *Flushed*

Stormfront's *Pool of Radiance: Ruins of Myth Drannor,* published by Ubisoft in 2001, is one of the most disappointing games in CRPG history. As with *Descent to Undermountain* and *Heroes of the Lance,* the game was highly anticipated and overhyped, but immediately became the deserved target of vitriolic reviews from critics.

Indeed, its sheer wretchedness is hard to describe to the uninitiated. I'll admit that part of my own distaste is owed to the title, which to my mind was a brazen attempt to lure unwary fans of the legendary Gold Box game to this unplayable travesty. Like many other gamers, I heard about the "new *Pool*" months before it was released and counted down the days until I could reenter Phlan and challenge Tyranthraxus once again. After plunking down $70 and playing the game for several hours, I kept telling myself that eventually it would get better. Just a few more battles with these slow-mo skeletons, and surely my party would emerge from those drab, look-alike dungeons and the game would start getting interesting. Eventually I realized that it wasn't going to get any better and that I had wasted some twelve hours of my life that I would never get back.

Why was *Ruins of Myth Drannor* so terrible? After all, many gamers (me included) assumed that a return to true turn-based combat would, if nothing else, satisfy their hardcore cravings for Gold Box–style tactics. While the game looks promising on paper, Stormfront's product is shoddy, boring, and poorly executed. Besides the mind-numbing sameness of all but a tiny fraction of the gameworld, swarms of bugs (the game actually reformatted some gamers' hard drives!), and fatiguing, repetitive battles, it really is one of the slowest games ever in a literal sense. The turn-based combats become unbearable as the characters and an endless sea of skeletons lethargically plod into position, one by one. Like many others, I downloaded a hack to speed up the damn things, but I can interpret my willingness to actually complete this game as evidence of masochistic tendencies.

I hereby grant *Pool of Radiance: Ruins of Myth Drannor* the distinction of being the worst CRPG of all time. I'm not even going to do this game the honor of providing a screenshot for it (the very idea of re-installing it for this purpose makes me ill). It's a grievous insult to the legacy of its namesake, and I can only hope that any gamers unlucky enough to play this game first will do themselves a favor by playing the original. Even though the older game has much simpler graphics and interface, it has one vital advantage over *Ruins of Myth Drannor:* It's not *Ruins of Myth Drannor.*

The Temple of Elemental Evil

Troika's *The Temple of Elemental Evil* is exponentially more fun than *Ruins of Myth Drannor*, even though it's designed for hardcore CRPG fans and has its own problems. As you'll recall, Troika distinguished itself in 2001 with the steampunk masterpiece *Arcanum*, but *Temple* turned out to be too difficult for gamers raised on *Diablo* and *Baldur's Gate*. Like *Ruins of Myth Drannor, The Temple of Elemental Evil* is a party-based game set in third-person, isometric perspective and features turn-based battles. However, although it suffers from an occasionally trying interface, the pace is smooth and the combat sophisticated and challenging enough to keep players engaged.

The Temple of Elemental Evil is set in Greyhawk, one of the earliest *D&D* campaign settings, and is one of the first CRPGs to offer the new 3.5 version of the official *D&D* ruleset. Like *Icewind Dale II* and the later *Neverwinter Nights* game, it has skills and feats in addition to the usual character stats. It also has a nice radial menu that pops up around characters, though the sheer number of commands makes it somewhat unwieldy. You can create and control a party of five adventurers, a rare opportunity in an era increasingly dominated by single-character CRPGs (Figure 16.15).

Unfortunately, the game is riddled with bugs, and the lack of a good storyline and interesting characters keep it out of the spotlight. Indeed, even the surprising twist of allowing two male characters to marry failed to draw much attention to the title. Critics remain quite divided. Some praise the game for so faithfully adapting the tabletop edition rules to the computer medium. The complexity allows for some deeply compelling character development. Others complain about the lack of multiplayer options,

FIGURE 16.15   I can't help but get excited when I see all the wonderful tactical complexity the options on this dial represent. If only there was a Ready vs. Crash to Desktop.

sketchy plot, and lack of quality assurance. In short, as with *Arcanum*, it's a good game that could have been great if Troika hadn't been in such a rush to ship it. On the other hand, Troika's shortcomings highlight the importance of aspects of the industry that tend to get overlooked by gamers and critics, namely, the marketing, accounting, and sales departments. They may not have the sexy jobs, but without good people in these positions, neither will you.

The good news is that some fans have taken it upon themselves to fix bugs and expand the game. The Circle of Eight module, released in 2013, corrects many issues, improves performance, and adds or restores a great deal of content.

NOTES

1. The term *steampunk* is applied to a gameworld that blends early industrial technology (especially steam-powered machinery) with conventional fantasy or sci-fi elements.

2. See http://www.gamespot.com/features/6146695/index.html.

CHAPTER 17

Other Highlights of the Platinum Age

Many discussions of this age of CRPGs are dominated by hugely popular games such as *Diablo* and *Baldur's Gate,* but there are other, lesser-known titles that deserve our attention. The two I'd like to focus on here are *Dungeon Keeper* and the *Krondor/Antara* games.

DUNGEON KEEPER AND *KRONDOR/ANTARA*

Dungeon Keeper

Bullfrog's *Dungeon Keeper* (1997) turns the CRPG on its head by letting players assume the role of Dungeon Master. Designed by Peter Molyneux, it's a rare and startling example of a game designer making a game out of game design. Although *Dungeon Keeper* is probably closer to a strategy game than a conventional CRPG, it still offers an invigorating new perspective on the conventional dungeon crawler. How do those evil archmages manage to keep so many orcs and dragons fed and under their control? In this game, it's your job to find out (Figure 17.1).

Dungeon Keeper is the first of what became a subgenre of "dungeon management" games. The idea is to dig out rooms, furnish them with traps and doors, and populate them with creatures. Different kinds of rooms attract different monsters. For example, hatcheries attract spiders and libraries attract warlocks. These creatures work for hire and become disloyal if you don't look after them properly. On the other hand, you can slap them around if they aren't working hard enough. Each creature

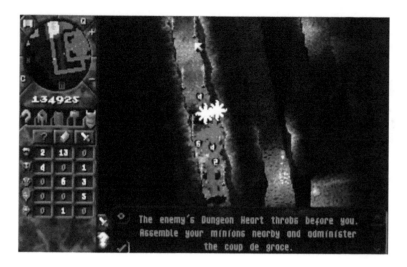

FIGURE 17.1 *Dungeon Keeper* flips the dungeon crawler on its head; now you're building and stocking the dungeons for adventurers to plunder—or hopefully die trying.

type has advantages and disadvantages, as well as unique personalities and mannerisms. The Dark Mistress likes to watch tortures and actually enjoys being slapped. The hellhounds like to cock their leg over corpses to "aid decomposition." There are six kinds of traps ranging from boulder to lava traps, and a clever player learns how to use them in conjunction with each other for maximum effect.

The "heroes" in this game are actually your enemies—adventurers who invade your lair to loot your treasure and destroy you. Like the creatures, each of the thirteen types of heroes have strengths and weaknesses to exploit. The witch, for instance, is afraid of vampires, and the archer is great at range but weak in melee. The greatest hero, appropriately enough, is the Avatar.

Like many popular strategy games, *Dungeon Keeper* uses the highly addictive research technique to keep players invested in the game. There's always some new room, spell, or creature type just a few minutes away, but of course the difficulty level increases to compensate for whatever new powers and abilities they put at your disposal. There's also a multiplayer option that lets up to four players battle it out or work together.

Molyneux claims that the publisher, Electronic Arts, was in such a hurry to rush production that he had to pay the company to keep it off his back. "They wanted to force me to finish the product a year early," says Molyneux in an extensive interview with John Walker of *Rock Paper Shotgun* in 2015.

"I said no, take the team to my house. The whole team went to my house, and we worked slavishly hard on the game and finished it."

The extra time and effort paid off. It's highly praised by critics, and Bullfrog wasted little time producing an expansion, *The Deeper Dungeons,* in 1997. *Dungeon Keeper 2,* released in 1999, borrows the bulk of its gameplay from its predecessor but was still popular with gamers and reviewers.

Today, there are dozens of dungeon management games reminiscent of *Dungeon Keeper,* including Brightrock Games' *War for the Overlord* (2015), Realmforge Studios' *Dungeons* series (2011–), and Elixir Studios' *Evil Genius* (2004). There's also Michal Brzozowski's *KeeperRL,* currently in early access on Steam, which combines dungeon management with Roguelike mechanics.

Raymond E. Feist and the *Krondor* Series

Although Sierra is much better known in CRPG circles for its *Quest for Glory* series, it also deserves recognition for the *Krondor* games, which consist of *Betrayal at Krondor, Betrayal in Antara,* and *Return to Krondor.* These games are noted mostly for their superb stories and characters, though they also offer some innovative combat and magic systems.

Betrayal at Krondor

Sierra published Dynamix's *Betrayal at Krondor* in 1993. It's most noteworthy for being based on Raymond E. Feist's world of Midkemia, made famous by the celebrated *Riftwar* saga. Feist himself even wrote a novelization of the game, but Neal Hallford wrote the game and John Cutter designed and produced it.

Betrayal at Krondor has turn-based combat, a skill-based character system (no levels), clever riddles, and a good deal of Feist-inspired text and cutscenes (Figure 17.2). It's more linear than most CRPGs, with a story broken up into nine chapters and 100 or so hours of gameplay. Much of the story is told via brief, animated cutscenes with digitized actors. Feist wrote in the instruction manual that the game "was to be the first computer game that felt like it was part of a good adventure novel," and to my mind Dynamix succeeded. The writing is probably the best of any CRPG, and even Feist himself was so impressed with the characters Hallford invented for the game that he features them in several of his later books.

The original plan was to adapt Feist's *Silverthorn* novel into a game. Hallford, however, felt that gamers wouldn't find that satisfying, especially if they'd read the book and knew how it would end. His plan, which

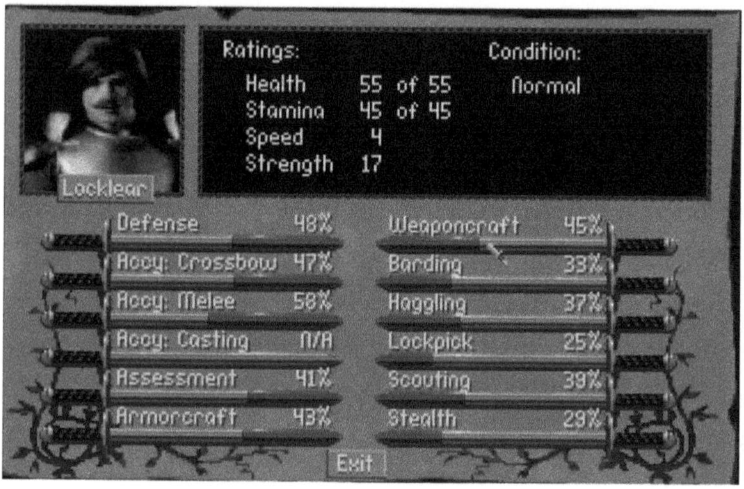

Ratings: Condition:
    Health   55 of 55   Normal
    Stamina   45 of 45
    Speed   4
    Strength   17
Locklear

Defense	48%	Weaponcraft	45%
Accy: Crossbow	47%	Barding	33%
Accy: Melee	58%	Haggling	37%
Accy: Casting	N/A	Lockpick	25%
Assessment	41%	Scouting	39%
Armorcraft	43%	Stealth	29%

Exit

FIGURE 17.2   There's a satisfying depth to the skill system in *Betrayal at Krondor*.

was ultimately accepted, was to "find a hole somewhere in Ray's universe, and we tell a story there." It was the right call: Hallford's story is both sophisticated and excellently paced. The characters are sharply drawn and convincing, and Feist's rich fantasy world lends depth to the gameworld. I suspect this had something to do with Feist's own obsession with role-playing games, which greatly inspire his fantasy novels.

The leveling system is based on twelve basic skills, which run the gamut of RPG activities (combat, stealth, barding, crafts). What's interesting in this case is that you select the skills you want the character to focus on improving, rather than doling out skill points (there's a similar system in the 1999 ARPG *Revenant* discussed back in Chapter 15). A sword diagram shows the percentage of mastery reached in each skill. Skills increase only as you use them, and the closer the skill gets to 100 percent, the harder it is to improve. Weapons and armor are also more abstract than usual. Each armor or weapon has a percentage displayed next to it, indicating the wear and tear on the item. A character with the weaponcraft skill can use a whetstone to repair damaged swords, whereas armor is fixed with a special hammer. In general, there are far fewer weapon and armor types here than in most CRPGs. Players are also regularly challenged by riddles, which are required to open many of the magical treasure chests sprinkled throughout the land (Figure 17.3).

Navigation is reminiscent of the older *Dungeon Master* game, with the party moving in discrete steps through a 3D gameworld. A nice option here is the map view, a top-down display that makes it easier to maintain

FIGURE 17.3   Combat in *Betrayal at Krondor* is turn-based and takes place in the gameworld rather than a separate combat screen.

your bearings. Conversation consists of selecting predefined options from a menu. There's also a handy "follow road" feature that keeps the party on a path, automatically rotating as needed.

Unfortunately, the graphics weren't up to many gamers' standards even in 1993, a sad fact that limited the game's success. Trees and mountains look jagged and polygonal. This is a vestige of the game engine's being adapted from a flight simulator. The characters, however, are digitized actors in cheap costumes. Even Cutter admits that "You could see the elastic bands on the fake beards. It was pretty bad." It certainly doesn't help that the digitized images clash with the abstract backgrounds. Nevertheless, it won several awards.

However, when the game first launched, it sold poorly. Hallford felt this was simply because it was such a different game than Sierra's popular *King's Quest* and other adventure games. As a result, Sierra laid off most of the team before they could complete an intended sequel, *Thief of Dreams*.

However, when the game was quietly republished on CD-ROM, sales soared. "We were one of the first games on CD-ROM," explains Hallford, and people were excited about the enhanced soundtrack. Thus, long after it had concluded it was a flop, Sierra decided to resurrect the series.

Betrayal in Antara

The second game, *Betrayal in Antara* (1997), is not based on Feist's world at all—Sierra lost its license and had to create an entirely new campaign

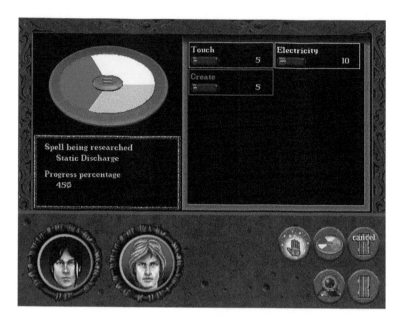

FIGURE 17.4 *Betrayal in Antara* doesn't get much respect, but I happen to like it. In particular, I appreciate the effort that went into the magic system, which is based on a clever research scheme.

setting named Ramar (Figure 17.4). If this weren't already bad news, Hallford was told he'd have a third of the budget and half the time he had to create *Betrayal at Krondor*. A board game designer named Peter Sarrett stepped up to take over design, and Steven Lee Miles, who'd never produced a CRPG, took over production from John Cutter.

For obvious reasons, *Betrayal in Antara* is smaller in scope and not as polished as its predecessor. Sierra made *Betrayal at Krondor* available for free distribution in an effort to promote it, but to no avail. Poor voice acting certainly didn't help either, and the digitized portraits of real actors are replaced with cartoonish illustrations. The game engine hasn't aged well, and ill-disposed reviewers mock the blocky scenery and limited color palette. By 1997, cutscenes with voiceovers and static portraits just didn't cut it anymore.

Nevertheless, *Betrayal in Antara* does offer some interesting features, and it says something for this inexperienced team that they were able to pull off what they did. My favorite is the spell creation system. Magic-users slowly research new spells, which they discover by combining various types of magic (touch, electricity, and create are available at the beginning). There are also two skills related to magic: spell casting and spell accuracy. Instead of the swords diagram of the first game, skill development is illustrated with a pie graph, the slices of which correspond to the various skills being refined by the character. It's a sensible and effective system that I'd love to see in more games, and it pains me that it's gone mostly ignored.

Combat is again a turn-based affair, though this time based on a hexagonal grid. The player selects among three attack modes for each character (swing, hack, and thrust) or selects the auto-combat option to resolve battles automatically. It's a suitably flexible and detailed enough to keep most gamers engaged.

In short, I think *Betrayal in Antara* warrants a lot more attention than it got then or gets now. Despite its limited production values, the designers had some great ideas that shouldn't be cast aside and forgotten.

Return to Krondor

Return to Krondor, developed by PyroTechnix and published by Sierra in 1998, brings players back to Feist's Midkemia. It also ends the disjointed saga, but not in a way that satisfies. The biggest change from the previous model is a shift to third-person, reminiscent of *Ultima IX* and *Redguard*. Like those games, *Return to Krondor* failed to rise above the competition (*Baldur's Gate, Fallout 2*) and met with lukewarm reviews.

Nevertheless, *Return to Krondor* gives us a good story concept by Hallford and well-developed and likeable characters. Although the gameplay is even more linear than in the previous games, you can still develop the characters by deciding which skills to emphasize. The combat system is similar to the turn-based procedure seen in the previous games, though, annoyingly, the handy grids are omitted.

The storyline concerns the Tear of the Gods, a sacred artifact that sank to the bottom of the sea in a shipwreck. A madman named Bear is after it, determined to raise the ship and use the powerful artifact to challenge the gods themselves. The story is told over the course of eleven chapters, with some 180 characters and plenty of high-quality voice acting and over 200 fully rendered locations. Critics make much of the graphics, though the cumbersome camera controls are limited to a selection of stationary views (Figures 17.5 and 17.6).

The game suffers from a repetitive magic system that's poorly represented on-screen. A promising alchemy system is made redundant by a plentitude of premade potions littered throughout the gameworld

FIGURE 17.5 *Return to Krondor* updates the graphics engine, but clunky camera controls and other issues limit its appeal. Image by Nathaniel Tolbert.

FIGURE 17.6 *Return to Krondor* has a great turn-based combat mode. Image by Nathaniel Tolbert.

(an all-too-common problem in many CRPGs). In short, *Return to Krondor* is a game with a great story and characters marred by a less-than-satisfying game engine. I must admit that I'm unable to get it running in Windows 10, even using GOG.com's version, so be wary before buying this game.

SUMMING UP THE PLATINUM AGE

As we've seen, the Platinum Age was a time of both innovation and refinement, but also one of increasing consolidation of interfaces and gameplay systems into a few recognizable models. *Ultima Underworld* and *Diablo* are probably the two most successful models, though Origin's *The Black Gate* and even *Ascension* have made their marks on the genre.

As we approach the modern age, we'll see the beginning of two very decisive trends in CRPGs and computer games in general. One is the shift from standalone, single-player games to massively multiplayer online games. I'll start the next chapter with a look at the history of this movement, picking up from our earlier discussion of MUDs and MOOs. The second trend concerns the console and Japanese RPGs, which by the dawn of the 21st century had truly begun to dominate the genre. Newer consoles such as Sony's PlayStation and Microsoft's Xbox were finally powerful enough to rival the PC. Furthermore, their cheaper price and lower learning curves meant that far more people had access to them, and the demand for console games overwhelmed that for PC games. Soon, most big-budget CRPGs would begin life on consoles, ported later to the Windows and only occasionally to the Macintosh.

CHAPTER 18

The Birth of the Modern Age

The first question we should answer as we move from the Platinum into the Modern Age is how to define a modern CRPG. To do that, though, we need to jump to the end of that era. The fact is, we're no longer in an era with a clear line between obsolete and modern games. A popular new CRPG for mobile might look and play like a CRPG from ten or even twenty years ago. Great old "abandonware" games from the past can be taken out of storage, touched up with a new coat of pixels, and put right back on the market. We have plenty of developers these days who deliberately create retro games such as Whalenought Studios' *Serpent in the Staglands*, something almost unthinkable at the start of the Modern Age.

What really signals the end of the modern era are three games: inXile's *Wasteland 2*, Larian Studios' *Divinity: Original Sin* (both 2014), and Obsidian Entertainment's *Pillars of Eternity* in 2015. These games show that just like people in the historical Renaissance, we're no longer scoffing at old-school games and smugly assuming they're not worth playing. Instead, we're eagerly revisiting the glories of the past and building upon their legacy. That's not to say studios like Bethesda, CD Projekt Red, and BioWare aren't still doing purely modern games, such as *Fallout 4, The Witcher 3: Wild Hunt*, and *Dragon Age: Inquisition,* but now there's a plethora of great old-school and indie alternatives to these big-budget productions.

Let us, then, define the "modern" style as a game with the highest production values, an emphasis on real-time action, advanced 3D graphics, first-person and/or third-person perspectives, and liberal cinematic cutscenes. They're also usually targeted at the console market, though PC versions are becoming increasingly relevant. In any case, they're very expensive to produce, often with massive budgets in the millions or tens of millions of dollars, with hundreds of developers, artists, animators, and other specialists. Only large, well-established studios with support from major publishers are in any position to make them. Needless to say, their desire to take risks with that kind of money on the table is low. They make games designed and market tested to reach the broadest possible audience, which means consoles come first and PCs second, if at all. That doesn't make them bad, but it's like comparing Hollywood blockbusters to Sundance films. The difference between the Modern Age and the Renaissance is that we now have our equivalent of the indie film community.

But for now, let's turn back to the late 1990s, when the trends and technologies that enabled the Modern Age are just getting underway. There's a lot to talk about, but the biggest driver of change was the Internet. Before the World Wide Web, online gaming was limited mostly to college students with access to a mainframe and private users dialing up their local bulletin board systems (BBSs). However, by the late 1980s commercial networks such as America Online, CompuServe, and GEnie were connecting millions of gamers all over the world. At first the games were limited to text or ASCII characters. Gradually developers mastered client-side architecture, which allows the bulk of a game's graphics and other data to be stored on the user's personal computer rather than transmitted via modem. We saw a striking example of this technology with the first *Neverwinter Nights,* a very early MMORPG built on SSI's Gold Box engine.

The Internet kicked this market into hyperdrive. As a free public network that anyone with a dial-up connection could access, it soon had more to offer than even the biggest commercial networks. Developers and publishers now had a more direct way to profit from online gaming, since they no longer had to share profits with a commercial network. It took some time for developers to find a successful economic model for MMORPGs, but everyone knew there were fortunes to be made in this new and rapidly expanding frontier.

The downside of this for fans of CRPGs is that MMORPGs such as *Ultima Online, Everquest,* and *World of Warcraft* seemed like the inevitable next step for both gamers and publishers. For millions of gamers, there's nothing better than exploring and interacting with like-minded people in a huge persistent gameworld. For game makers and publishers, the economics are simple: Why sell a game once for $60 or less when you can charge a monthly fee of $10 or sell in-game perks and items indefinitely? Furthermore, you didn't have to worry about used game stores ravaging your revenue. It's not hard to see why so many assumed that the CRPG was dead and that MMORPGs were the future.

The second trend that defines the Modern Age of CRPGs is the domination of game consoles. I spoke earlier about JRPGs, especially those exported to the United States for Nintendo and Sega's popular game machines. The *Zelda* and *Final Fantasy* series swept across North America, converting millions upon millions of console gamers into lifelong fanatics. For most of their history, consoles were underpowered compared even to midrange computers, particularly in terms of graphics, memory, processing, and especially networking. Furthermore, with a few exceptions, most console games were targeted at children, who were assumed (wrongly, as it turned out) to lack the comprehension and patience necessary to play complex games.

However, with the introduction of Sony's PlayStation in 1995, the paradigm begins to shift, and by the turn of the century the PlayStation 2 and Microsoft Xbox seriously blur the lines between computers and consoles in terms of both technology and audience. Now, former CRPG developers could offer their games for consoles and PCs without having to make so many changes and compromises. Since the console market was of an order of magnitude larger and more profitable than the computer game market, developers focused on the console experience first and the PC experience second, if at all. This reality angered many PC gamers, of course, especially when a PC port was poorly adapted for mice and keyboards or didn't take advantage of advanced graphics cards.

The final trend can be summed up in three words: action, action, and more action. Although some modern CRPGs often have just as many stats as the classic hardcore games, the bulk of these operations are kept out of sight, tucked under the hood. The idea is to keep you busy with a gamepad, not fussing with tables and charts. Long gone are the days when players drew painstakingly detailed maps on graph paper. These contemplative and even artistic delights are exchanged for frequent bursts of gratification. Indeed, many modern CRPGs are more like action adventures or first-person shooters than anything released by Origin or SSI, much less TSR or Wizards of the Coast.

When I wrote the first edition of this book, I assumed that I was writing a eulogy for the CRPG as I knew and loved it. I turned out to be dead wrong! But before we get there, let's see how I ended up with that idea in the first place. In the rest of this chapter, I'll focus on three great games from the early 2000s that help define the modern CRPG—*Vampire: The Masquerade, Bloodlines, Neverwinter Nights, Knights of the Old Republic,* and *Fable.*

VAMPIRE: THE MASQUERADE

As the new century dawned, we find many developers still struggling with the complexities and costs of 3D graphics versus the good-old days of 2D. CRPG gamers still expected games of epic scope and massive amounts of content of classics like *Ultima VII,* but turning out a game like that with advanced 3D graphics, cinematic cutscenes, and intense action wasn't easy, even for well-established studios. Many promising projects ended up as clunky, buggy messes that didn't come close to matching the hype.

Another perceived problem designers faced was a supposed over-saturation of high fantasy games. I say "perceived" here because there will always be room for a good fantasy adventure, no matter how trite it appears in the eyes of a designer or critic. A truly talented writer can make even the most "overdone" tropes and "clichés" exciting. After all, archetypes exist for a reason, and the devil, as they say, is in the details. Give me a reason to care–and some rats in the tavern cellar–and I'll happily rescue as many princesses, restore as many orbs, and slay as many dragons as it takes to get the job done. Nevertheless, it's understandable why designers and writers would want to make their mark by exploring radical new realms. We've already seen several games that bucked the fantasy convention, mostly with sci-fi and postapocalyptic campaigns. However, another avenue that seemed worth exploring is *Vampire: The Masquerade,* a very successful and popular tabletop RPG by Mark Rein-Hagen that debuted in 1991.

If you're old enough to recall, vampires were a huge thing in the 1990s, especially after *Interview with the Vampire* descended into theaters in 1994. That movie is based on a successful novel by Anne Rice, and it did much to renovate the stuffy old Hollywood "Dracula" vampire trope into something hipper, darker, and sexier. I could go on, but the point is that many gamers were hungry for a good vampire RPG. I should note that Rein-Hagen claimed he didn't read Rice until late in his design process; he cites the RPGs *Call of Cthulhu* and *RuneQuest* and mafia movies as his key inspirations.

We've already seen several CRPGs based on a vampire mythos, such as Sierra's *Shadows of Darkness* (1993) and SSI's *Ravenloft* games. However, the *Vampire: The Masquerade* games are much more ambitious and audacious, ratcheting up the gore and making for some truly dark and unsettling gameplay. This is largely owed, of course, to their setting in Rein-Hagen's World of Darkness (WoD), a "gothic-punk" version of our world. In the World of Darkness, vampires (known as The Kindred) and other fantastic monsters (werewolves, wraiths, and so on) secretly live among humans as part of a global conspiracy ("The Masquerade"). Each member of the kindred belongs to a clan or bloodline, and much of the game is concerned with the dramas and conflict among all these disparate groups.

White Wolf's game is most notable for its intuitive handling of the unique qualities of vampire characters. For instance, vampires have a stat called "blood pool" that corresponds to the amount of human blood ("vitae") coursing through their veins, and a "humanity" stat that measures how far the character has strayed from civilized behavior and succumbed to more bestial urges. Since much of the vampires' powers derive from drinking blood, they must regularly feed, both on humans and each other. It's a darkly compelling system, and its mature content—this was *not* a game for children—made it a hit with the Goth subculture of the 1990s.

Redemption

The first CRPG I'll talk about here is *Vampire: The Masquerade—Redemption,* developed by the aptly named Nihilistic Software and published by Activision in 2000 (Figure 18.1). It has 3D graphics, a rotatable camera, and third-person perspective (you can see your character on-screen). You're in charge of a four-member party, but only one is active at any time. You can, however, easily switch to another one by clicking on the portraits at the bottom of the screen.

Nihilistic did a good job of integrating White Wolf's vampire-centric role-playing rules to the new medium, with many skills (called "disciplines") that require blood to perform. What really sets the game apart, though, was its disturbing images and sacrilegious undertones, which even go beyond *Diablo*'s demonic themes. This is a game that delights in its wickedness. For instance, it's frequently necessary for the characters to suck each other's blood, an act that is shown in gruesome detail and accompanied by sexualized moaning. Indeed, it's hard to imagine what

FIGURE 18.1 You play *Vampire: The Masquerade—Redemption* as Christof, a twelfth-century Crusader Knight turned vampire.

commotion a game like this would have caused back in the 1980s, when so many concerned citizens were hellbent on banning *Dungeons & Dragons*! Like all action CRPGs, it has real-time combat, but poor collision detection and AI reduce its appeal.

The story is focused on a vampire named Christof, a twelfth-century warrior who falls in love with a nun, but their love is never consummated. Nevertheless, Christof takes a vow to protect her against vampires but ends up becoming one himself. Christof decides to take revenge against the Brujah, the vampires that caused his transformation. Since vampires are immortal, Christof's quest spans some 800 years and four different cities. It's a massively ambitious undertaking, and critics praise the diversity of the settings and the intimate attention to detail.

The multiplayer options require a player to be a storyteller in yet another attempt to foster user-generated content. Nihilistic's effort is hampered by a poor interface, which makes storytelling difficult and finding a good group of fellow gamers even more so. Most of the multiplayer games degenerate into simple frag fests or traps for the unwary novice, who enter a game only to be killed and robbed by a devious storyteller.

Poor multiplayer interaction isn't the game's only problem. It suffers from serious bugs and glitches that critics eagerly seized upon. The worst of these is wretched collision detection, which inadvertently causes you to miss your opponents. Another problem is an irksome save-game system, which necessitates playing large chunks of the game over and over again. Thankfully, this problem was fixed in a subsequent patch along with several other nuisances, including faulty artificial intelligence and unbalanced boss battles. Probably the worst offenders have nothing to do with coding, though—the wince-worthy voice acting and flaccid script, two letdowns that are simply inexcusable in a game that depends so heavily on drama.

In short, Nihilistic had some good ideas and no lack of ambition, but its fangs were just too short to penetrate the jugular.

Bloodlines

The next game based on White Wolf's franchise was not developed by Nihilistic. Instead, our old friends at Troika, makers of *Temple of Elemental Evil* and *Arcanum,* picked up the franchise, and Activision published its *Bloodlines* in November 2004 (Figure 18.2). The game is almost universally considered superior to its predecessor, but it's far from flawless.

Troika used Valve Corporation's well-established Source 3D graphics engine, which is put to such effective use in what is arguably the greatest first-person shooter of all time, *Half-Life 2*. Although *Bloodlines'* graphics and physics aren't as impressive as those in *Half-Life 2*, they

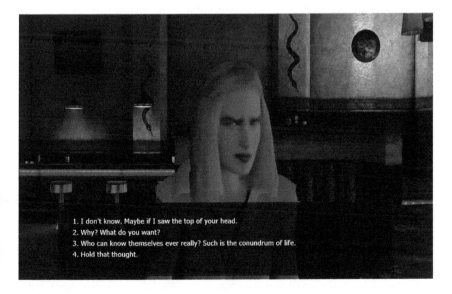

FIGURE 18.2 *Vampire: The Masquerade—Bloodlines* does a great job immersing you in White Wolf's dark universe. Role-playing opportunities abound.

were still some of the best ever seen in a CRPG. The game also boasts a soundtrack with a cut from the well-known industrial group Ministry.

However, it's really the excellent writing and top-notch voice talent that sell the game. Your character is a freshly sired vampire who is embraced against his or her will. After this rather unpromising beginning and a stay of execution, you set off to learn how to survive and thrive as one of the kindred. Naturally, it doesn't take long to get thickly involved in the complex intrigues among the rival clans.

Instead of being set in the distant past, you play in the modern city of Los Angeles. This was a great design decision, since a large part of the tabletop RPG's appeal is the idea that vampires secretly live among us. Setting it in a modern city helps capture this fun (if frightening) concept. Much like a postapocalyptic game, we see a familiar world that's suddenly very strange and frightening.

Troika made other significant changes to the model established by Nihilistic. Now you create your own character, then pledge allegiance to one of the seven available clans of kindred. Each clan has its own set of quests, so there's good potential replay value. Replay value was also enhanced with different scenarios for male and female characters, an important aspect given the prevalence of eroticism. Another enhancement is a set of feats that correspond to your character's attributes (e.g., the appearance attribute affected the seduction feat). The character development system is wonderfully nuanced, and you need to make many important choices as the game progresses (Figure 18.3).

The combat mode is also much different here than in *Redemption,* with several different moves in melee combat and a special first-person mode for firing guns. Melee and unarmed combat both use the same mechanic, which consists of holding down the attack button while pressing one of the directional buttons. You can also try a combo sequence, but success depends as much on the character's Melee Combat Feat as your own expertise with the controls.

Unfortunately, the final product didn't match expectations, particularly for those familiar with first-person shooters, where accuracy isn't affected by so many unseen variables. One reviewer calls third-person combat "sluggish and sloppy" and remarks that gun combat "never feels like a smooth, intuitive experience."[1] Others lament the lack of multiplayer options; at least the earlier game had made the effort. Still others criticize the artificial intelligence. Enemies get stuck behind objects and don't always notice the character even when in full view.

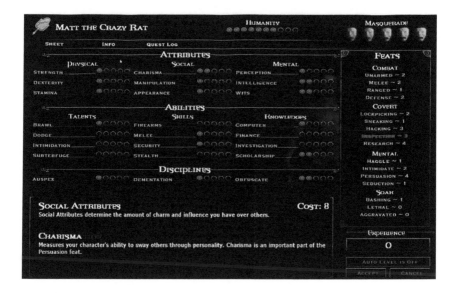

FIGURE 18.3 *Bloodlines* has a great leveling and skill system for creating and developing your character.

The biggest problem, though, is by now a familiar refrain: a myriad of bugs caused by an unforgivably rushed production schedule dictated by Activision. Troika hurriedly released patches to cover most of them, but not before critics apprised gamers of the situation. The resulting losses exacted a heavy toll on Troika, who collapsed soon after. Yet again, we have a sad story of promising game from a proven studio ruined by an inflexible publisher.

Still, the *World of Darkness* has much to offer CRPG fans, even if these early attempts ultimately failed to do it justice. I hope that a third developer will someday consolidate Nihilistic's and Troika's gains and produce something as terrifyingly fun as the tabletop game.

NEVERWINTER NIGHTS

Let's turn back to BioWare. For many CRPG aficionados, BioWare's next CRPG, *Neverwinter Nights,* published in 2002 by Infogrames, was a logical progression from its older but still highly respected *Baldur's Gate* series. The games have much in common, but *Neverwinter Nights* is powered by the Aurora engine, a fully 3D engine with more advanced graphics than the beloved old Infinity engine. Now you had a free-moving camera with zoom, and the polished graphics gave you a real incentive to take advantage of it. Even better, BioWare included a superb toolset

FIGURE 18.4 *Neverwinter Nights* is probably the best bargain in the history of CRPGs. Shown here is Beamdog's Enhanced Edition, which, among other features, lets you play it in jaw-dropping 3440 × 1440 resolution.

to let you create your own *Neverwinter Nights* modules, a crucial decision that represents a turning point for the industry. It was far from the first game to do so, but this time the stars aligned and BioWare enjoyed a flood of high-quality user-generated content that's freely shared and downloaded from the Internet. This makes *Neverwinter Nights* one of the best values in all of CRPG history (Figure 18.4).

Like *Baldur's Gate, Neverwinter Nights* lets you create and control only a single character. You can, however, add two henchmen and a familiar, and summon other creatures with magic. All of these companions are controlled by the computer, though the player can issue basic orders (such as how far to stay back or whether to use magic). *Neverwinter Nights* follows the 3rd Edition *D&D* Rules as seen in *Icewind Dale II,* with a fun and intuitive leveling system based on skills, feats, and stats. Players have a great deal of freedom in shaping their character, but again there's a danger of spreading them out too thin, resulting in a versatile but ultimately ineffectual character.

There are several significant differences between *Neverwinter Nights* and *Baldur's Gate,* and not everyone is happy with the changes. Perhaps the most important is that the player's character isn't woven so integrally into the plot. Instead, the character starts off as a blank-slate adventurer who has responded to a call by Lady Aribeth to aid the city of Neverwinter. The city is in the grips of a deadly plague, which turns out to be part of a grand conspiracy to take over the city. The roots of treachery run deep, and there are quite a few surprises in store. Though the plot is fairly linear, there is some leeway in directing the avatar's action; he or she can be a saintly type, a calculating mercenary, or a ruthless sociopath—alignment matters. These choices are mostly played out in the dialog options, but also in the sidequests the player can either accept or reject. Although the single player campaign isn't as engaging as *Baldur's Gate*'s, most critics feel that the well-crafted multiplayer and user-generated content more than compensate for it.

Official expansion packs for the highly successful game were not long in coming. The first is *Shadows of Undrentide,* developed by Floodgate Entertainment and published by Atari (Infogrames) in 2003. *Shadows of Undrentide* wasn't what most players expected; rather than extend the original campaign, it adds an entirely new one intended for new characters. It also adds five new prestige classes for advanced characters. The expansion met with generally favorable reviews.

The next expansion, *Hordes of the Underdark,* appeared only a few months later. Thankfully, this trip to the Drow homeland fared much better than Interplay's wretched *Descent to Undermountain.* Besides a few epic battles that no player will likely forget, *Hordes of the Underdark* also incorporates great new assets, including fifty new feats and forty new spells. The massive expansion is recognized as a must-have for fans and widely considered superior to the original campaign. In 2006, BioWare released *Wyvern Crown Cormyr,* 234 megabytes of downloadable content available for $11.99. Besides a new adventure and setting to explore, the module integrates "fully rideable horses," "flowing cloaks and tabards," and a new prestige class—and it's only one of six such modules.

Computer Games magazine calls *Neverwinter Nights* "the last role-playing game you'll ever desire" and the "fulfillment of a genre."[2] Such overblown praise is embarrassing, but it's hard to exaggerate BioWare's brilliance in shipping the game with the excellent Aurora Toolset (Figure 18.5). With such a powerful tool at their disposal, talented Game Masters crafted excellent campaigns and made them freely available on the Internet.[3] In short, *Neverwinter Nights* is a good game, but an even better development kit.

In 2017, Beamdog published *Neverwinter Nights: Enhanced Edition* on Steam and elsewhere. It consolidates many of the bug fixes and modules made over the years and restores the multiplayer server.

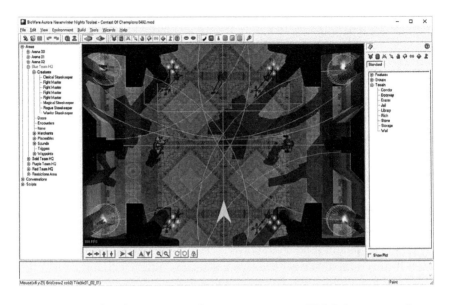

FIGURE 18.5 If you've ever wanted to create your own CRPG, I recommend trying out BioWare's Aurora Neverwinter Nights Toolset. Otherwise, it's fun to just mess around with the sample modules to get a better appreciation for how much goes into making a good CRPG.

Neverwinter Nights 2

For the sequel to its groundbreaking game, Infogrames (now known as Atari) turned to Obsidian Entertainment, a team composed of former Interplay developers. Obsidian had recently created a sequel for BioWare's other modern classic, *Knights of the Old Republic,* which I'll discuss in a moment. Released in 2006, *Neverwinter Nights 2* uses Obsidian's own Electron 3D engine, which is based on BioWare's well-established Aurora. Electron offers some graphical enhancements, such as pixel-based shading technology, but is limited strictly to the Windows platform and was sluggish on some machines (Figure 18.6).

Of course, Obsidian knew that gamers' expectations were high regarding the sequel to the mega popular *Neverwinter Nights,* and they seemed to have worked hard to address the criticisms of that game while keeping the bulk of its gameplay intact. One of the biggest changes concerns the single-player campaign, which puts the player smack in the middle of the story, more like in *Baldur's Gate* than the original *Neverwinter Nights.* The player's character begins the game as a young orphan in the tiny village of West Harbor, which is savagely attacked by the Githyanki,

FIGURE 18.6 *Neverwinter Nights 2* still looks good. Opinions are divided over whether it's better than the first one, but I say give it a try. Image by Nathaniel Tolbert.

mysterious creatures from another plane of existence that now threaten the world. The young hero barely manages to escape and is sent off to the city of Neverwinter to find answers. The plot thickens quickly, and soon enough the humble character is embroiled in all manner of intrigues, dealing with a huge variety of characters.

Much was made of the game's influence system, which responds on the fly to the player's dialog choices. Sometimes the result is instantaneous; a savage insult leads unsurprisingly to combat, but other choices take time to show their effect. For instance, disagreeing too often with a comrade may cause him or her to leave the party. It's also possible for another character to fall in love with the hero and even rashly sacrifice him or herself to prove it. A few choice words with a noble may have long and lasting consequences throughout the campaign. In short, the dialog system is more relevant than in most CRPGs, where it serves only to provide hints or context.

Although the player is again limited to creating only a single character, three others may join the quest. This time, the player can take full control of these companions, switching among them with a simple click of the mouse. This system, which bears some resemblance to Nihilistic's *Redemption,* seems a fair enhancement over the rather limited AI-driven system seen of the original. The hero's companions have their own personalities and histories, and offer optional sidequests once you earn their trust. Combat is in real time, but again you can halt the action to issue orders (up to five for each character). Another option is to let the computer handle combat, and characters can be assigned specific strategies (such as whether to cast spells).

Unfortunately, the game shipped with awful bugs, several of which crashed the game. The artificial intelligence is also inept, often letting characters get stuck behind objects or just frozen in place. Thankfully, many of these bugs were fixed in post-release patches. The item management system is also unnecessarily tedious. The biggest problem, however, is the awkward camera controls. Even with four different camera modes, you're always struggling to get a useful perspective on the action.

On a positive note, *Neverwinter Nights 2* does feature multiplayer options like its predecessor, with a new toolset to help would-be dungeon masters create and distribute their own modules. There are hundreds of such modules freely available for download, as well as tools and other resources for developers.[4]

In 2007, Obsidian released an expansion set called *Mask of the Betrayer*. Its story picks up where the last game left off, with the character embarking on a quest to remove a curse. One interesting innovation is a "spirit eating" mechanic, with which characters can restore health by devouring the spiritual force of various magical beings. The technical issues from the previous game are still unresolved, however, and some critics find the spirit eating more annoying than fun. Still, it's a must-have expansion for fans of the game, especially since it adds new races and classes that you can use in the original campaign.

KNIGHTS OF THE OLD REPUBLIC

It's hard to imagine anyone reading this book who isn't at least nominally familiar with *Star Wars*, George Lucas' extremely successful space opera franchise. However, it's possible that readers may be less familiar with Wizards of the Coast's *Star Wars Roleplaying Game*, a tabletop RPG released in 2000. It's based on a similar "d20" system as seen in the 3rd Edition of *Dungeons & Dragons*, which computer gamers encountered in *Icewind Dale II* and *Neverwinter Nights*. Although the system has its critics, most appreciate its consistency and flexibility.

In 2003, LucasArts published *Star Wars: Knights of the Old Republic*, BioWare's computerized adaptation of the Wizard of the Coast game (Figures 18.7 and 18.8). It was first released exclusively for Microsoft's

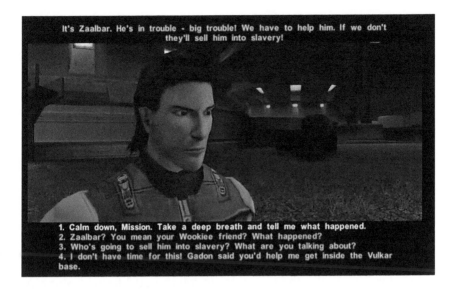

FIGURE 18.7 BioWare's *Knights of the Old Republic* is an undisputed masterpiece, with great characters and dialogs.

FIGURE 18.8 *Knights of the Old Republic* has an effective combat engine that captures the look and feel of the movies.

Xbox game console and wasn't published for Windows until two months later (a Mac version followed in September 2004). It is to my knowledge the first major Western CRPG to privilege consoles, and the start of rather distressing trend for computer gamers accustomed to preferential treatment. Let's put this issue aside for the moment, though, because *Knights of the Old Republic* is a truly wonderful game. It's easy to see how it paved the way for BioWare's *Mass Effect* and *Dragon Age* series and many others.

Knights of the Old Republic is an ambitious game based on the Odyssey engine, BioWare's effort to enhance its old Aurora engine for modern game platforms. The essential enhancements are 3D backgrounds and facial expressions. There are only ten or so facial structures for each gender, so it looks as though there's a good many clones running around. It's also rather difficult to tell aliens apart, since they tend to differ only by skin color. Thankfully, these aspects are compensated for with stunning backgrounds and interiors. It also has exceptional scripting and voice acting, critical components in any game that emphasize dialog as much as *Knights of the Old Republic*.

The game is most celebrated for its storyline, which is reminiscent of *Baldur's Gate* in that the main character turns out to be much more than the scruffy nerf herder he or she appears to be. During the course of the game, the player makes many choices regarding good and evil, and unlike most games of this type, the game has substantial rewards for both paths. Of particular note is the great surprise ending. I won't spoil it for you here, of course, but as you'll see, BioWare isn't always the best when it comes to bringing a game (much less a series) to a satisfying conclusion.

Although *Knights of the Old Republic* is intended first and foremost for consoles, BioWare chose to make the combat more like *Neverwinter Nights* than *Diablo*. What we get is a hybrid real-time and turn-based system, in which you can pause the action to issue commands. The player can also instantly take direct control of any of the hero's companions, a popular option we've seen in most games of the era (including *Dungeon Siege II*, *Neverwinter Nights 2*, and *Redemption*). The character development system has plenty of intriguing skills, feats, and Force Powers, which are essentially this game's equivalent of magical spells.

Surprisingly, *Knights of the Old Republic* doesn't offer support for multiple players, but this fact doesn't seem to bother many gamers. The low volume of complaints may be explained by the immersive story and intriguing characters, which are at least as interesting as the mobs of adolescents "pwning" each other on public servers. Critics rave about the excellent writing and dialog, which any CRPG gamer knows are quite rare and worth celebrating. The game won countless awards, including *Computer Gaming World* and *PC Gamer's* Game of the Year award, and is considered a classic by many aficionados of the genre. It's certainly the best *Star Wars* CRPG I've ever played.

The Sith Lords

BioWare turned to Obsidian Entertainment for the sequel to the highly successful *Knights of the Old Republic,* and *The Sith Lords* was published in December 2004 for Xbox and a few months later for Windows. Obsidian played it safe with the sequel, leaving the vast majority of the game engine intact. The boldest additions are thirty new Force Powers and an ambitious storyline, which picks up five years after the first game. The player is now in control of the last surviving Jedi knight, who awakens on a hospital bed with no memory of recent events (sound familiar?). From there, it's a fight across the galaxy in a forty-five-hour campaign, with plenty of memorable characters and moral dilemmas as well as tons of combat.

The Sith Lords is an easy sell to fans of the first game, though some critics complain about its lack of innovation and repetitive battles, but there are bright spots. Like the first game, *The Sith Lords* caters to both the righteous and the sociopathic.

For over a decade, rumors of a third *Knights of the Old Republic* game circulated on the Internet, but so far none has materialized. In 2011, though, *Star Wars: The Old Republic* was brought online. This MMORPG was and remains successful, but for diehard fans of the single-player games, it just wasn't the experience they were looking for. We'll talk more about it later.

FABLE

Let's turn now to another great console-based CRPG: *Fable,* an Xbox game developed by the England-based Lionhead Studios (Figure 18.9). It was first published by Microsoft in September 2004 but enhanced and rereleased a year later for both Xbox and Windows. This new version is called *Fable: The Lost Chapters,* and it's this game that I want to focus on here.

The game's title is apt, but not for the reasons you might expect. The game's designer, Peter Molyneux, made all sorts of fantastic claims about what *Fable* would offer, the most infamous being that players who planted an acorn could come back years later to find a fully grown tree. Molyneux had several impressive achievements in his portfolio,

FIGURE 18.9   Shown here is *Fable Anniversary* from 2014. It remasters the original game with HD visuals and audio and adds a Heroic difficulty mode.

such as *Dungeon Keeper* and the "god game" *Black & White,* and many critics and gamers felt if anyone could achieve visions like that, it was Molyneux. However, Molyneux had grossly overestimated the resources of his team. When the overhyped game finally appeared, critics discovered that Molyneux's proclamations were, well, more fable than fact.

In October 2004, Molyneux released a statement in which he explains *(apologizes* seems too strong a word) that the features were actually in development, but simply consumed too much of the Xbox's processor time to be viable.[5] Molyneux's bait and switch gambit might seem irrelevant to a historical understanding of the game, but it does color many of the published reviews and certainly lurks in the background of any discussion of the game or its remake, even though both are impressive in their own right.

One way to think about *Fable* is as a combination of Bethesda's *Elder Scrolls* and the more moralistic of Origin's *Ultima* games, with a dash of *Diablo* for heat. The player's avatar is a young boy who ages over the course of the game, eventually becoming an old man. Furthermore, the character's appearance changes dramatically depending on the player's choices. A player favoring melee combat sees the character becoming more muscular, for instance, and accumulating permanent battle scars. Alignment also plays a factor: evil characters sprout horns and limp, whereas good behavior leads to a saintly glow, complete with halo. There are also many types of outfits the character can don, as well as hairstyles and tattoos. The other characters react differently depending on the hero's appearance, attire, and accomplishments. Although most of these effects are purely cosmetic and do not substantially alter gameplay, they're still fun and the focus of most discussions of the game. It's even possible to get married and divorced, though, again, these features seem thrown in only for the player's own amusement; that is, they don't ultimately have much bearing on the main storyline, which is often quite shallow.

Here's a brief excerpt from an online player's guide that illustrates the point:

> Getting married isn't hard at all. It'll cost a wedding ring, but you'll gain it back. Wear your most attractive clothes in town, and try to find someone with a heart over their head. Flirt, Sexy Hero Pose, and Manly Arm Pump are the only three things you need to do to make her love you. Once her heart is huge, it will fade in and out. Give her a wedding ring and it turns golden. Buy a house and lead her there. She'll ask to get married. Say yes and a cut scene appears and you'll find that you have a dowry of several thousand. Once married, hit her. You'll be divorced almost immediately and gain 600 Dark points.
>
> You can have unlimited wives.

If this player's behavior is any indication of how morality unfolds in *Fable*, then we were surely better off with Garriott than Molyneux! Still, it's interesting that one of *Fable*'s key selling points is that characters react believably to the player's actions—if the goal is social realism, we might wonder why Lionhead didn't make an MMORPG instead, or even offer minimal support for multiplayer. Why try to fake human interaction when it's so readily available online? We'll return to this question in a discussion in Chapter 20.

The leveling system is a hybrid of *The Elder Scrolls* "practice makes perfect" system and more conventional point distribution. Frequently wielding a sword results in more points to expend on physical abilities, but most points end up in a common pool and can be spent on anything. Most players become a jack-of-all-trades, that is, a fighter/archer/wizard. Combat changes depending on what type of weapon the character is wielding. Melee battles involve repeatedly clicking the mouse, whereas ranged weapons involve holding down the mouse button, which draws back the bow and fires an arrow when released. Magic is a more cumbersome affair that requires holding down the shift key while scrolling the mouse wheel. As you can probably tell from these descriptions, *Fable* is primarily an action CRPG, which is hardly surprising given its console heritage.

Although loudly touted for its ability to respond on the fly to the player's decisions, the bulk of these features are limited to aesthetics, and the storyline turns out to be a rather linear quest to avenge the murder of the character's family. Although the player's alignment does change depending on moral choices, at any time alignment can be altered simply by dumping cash into the offering bowls of the good or evil gods. For obvious reasons, it's hard to take a game seriously that prides itself on a sophisticated morality system, then reduces the whole matter to coinage—unless, of course, the whole business is meant as satire. The game does have a habit of inserting humor at inappropriate moments, so there may be something there.

However, *Fable* does have at least one novel innovation with great potential for future games. In addition to accepting a quest, the player can opt to make a boast, such as a promise to fight without weapons or armor. If the character lives up to the hype, he or she receives extra gold as a reward. Many fans of CRPGs appreciate a good challenge, and *Fable*'s boasting system was a great way to capitalize on the desire for glory and the pride that comes with an exceptional performance.

Obviously, there was more going on in the early 2000s than the games we've discussed above. The *Diablo* phenomenon that we covered in Chapter 15 was still going strong and transitioning into full 3D with games like *Sacred* and *Dungeon Siege*. Likewise, the MMORPG scene was rapidly expanding. Next, let's turn back to consoles and catch up with the great Japanese RPGs of the age, including *Final Fantasy* and *The Legend of Zelda*.

NOTES

1. See Allen Rausch's review of the game at http://pc.gamespy.com/pc/vampire-the-masquerade-bloodlines/566646p3.html.
2. See the September 2002 issue of *Computer Games* magazine, p. 68.
3. For a huge list of high-quality and freely downloadable modules, see http://nwvault.ign.com/Files/modules/HallOfFame.shtml.
4. For a huge list of modules and other resources, see http://nwvault.ign.com/View.php?view=nwn2modulesenglish.HOF.
5. See http://web.archive.org/web/20070404110938/http://allboards.lionhead.com/showthread.php?t=83152.

CHAPTER 19

Modern JRPGs

THE MIGRATION FROM COMPUTERS TO CONSOLES

As we've seen, the closer we get to modern times, the more Western CRPG developers focus their resources on consoles rather than computers. But why would they turn their backs on the legions of loyal CRPG fans who carried them so far? In fact, there are three reasons for this shift that I ought to explain before moving on to modern JRPGs (Japanese role-playing games).

By far, the most important reason is economic. During much of the 1980s and 1990s, consoles lagged far behind personal computers in terms of graphics, sound, memory, processor speed, input devices, and storage space, and there was little to no practical support for networking. A CRPG developer would have to make many painful compromises to port a game for the Nintendo Entertainment System, and even the newer Super NES had serious limitations.

This situation begins to change with the introduction of Sony's PlayStation and Microsoft's Xbox, and with each new generation of these devices, the technological gap narrowed to a point where only high-end PC "gaming rigs" substantially outperform them. Since such machines are exponentially more expensive ($3,000–$4,000) than either a console ($350–$500) or a typical, midrange PC ($1,000–$1,500), they represent only a niche market. In short, it makes more sense for developers to target a platform such as the Xbox One, which matches or exceeds the specs of midrange PCs and represents a larger market for games. It also helps that the Xbox's internal technology is similar enough to the PCs to make porting more economical than before. Finally, these newer consoles have built-in broadband support, effectively making them "media centers" as well as gaming devices. This latter point is worth emphasizing, especially since almost everyone I know who buys one of these systems eventually uses it more for watching Netflix than gaming!

The second explanation for the shift in development is cultural. Even though many Western CRPGs did find their way onto consoles in the 1990s, they weren't nearly as successful as the JRPGs that dominate that sector of the market, which have always been controlled (at least indirectly) by the Japanese. You'll remember from our discussion in Chapter 10 that JRPGs differ markedly from their Western counterparts, and console gamers have had plenty of time to develop strong expectations of what a role-playing game ought to be like. It certainly doesn't help that so many early Western RPGs for consoles were terrible, such as SSI's dreadful *Heroes of the Lance*. Compared to contemporary Japanese games like *Zelda* or *Final Fantasy,* these games were laughable.

Microsoft's Xbox (released in 2001) and later Xbox 360 (2005) and Xbox One (2016) consoles changed this situation, offering a viable Western alternative to the Japanese-dominated console industry. We still see this East/West divide playing out today. For instance, whereas Microsoft's *Halo* series of first-person shooters practically redefined console gaming in the West, the series is virtually unknown in Japan. For our purposes, what's significant is that Microsoft's game platforms finally created an opportunity for Western CRPG developers to penetrate the American console market, as the popularity of *Knights of the Old Republic* and *Skyrim* so vividly demonstrate. Sony likewise played a role with its PlayStation platforms, whose 3D graphics abilities wooed game developers such as Core Design, whose *Tomb Raider* (1996) action adventure became one of the original PlayStation's biggest hits. Still, the PlayStation's RPG market was and remains dominated by Japanese games, particularly the *Final Fantasy* series.

The final explanation for the shift is social. Game consoles are no longer looked down on as toys for children and young teens, a view that Nintendo encouraged throughout the 1980s and 1990s with a vigorous censorship campaign. For gamers of the 1980s, the move from console to computer gaming was literally a coming of age. This all changed in the late 1990s and 2000s; Sony and Microsoft both took pains to disassociate themselves from the toy market, offering instead a vision of their consoles as a more generalized media device that an adult could own without shame. Instead of Mario and Sonic, we got Lara Croft and Master Chief, and many of us never looked back. Even Nintendo redefined its image with the Wii, marketing it not as a kid's toy but as a versatile entertainment device for the entire family. In short, there was no longer any valid reason to assume there was no market for Western RPGs on consoles.

But let's suspend this discussion for a moment to take a look at the world's most successful JRPG, *Final Fantasy*, whose reach has extended even to the PC market. We'll also catch up with Nintendo's *Zelda* series, which continues to flourish and exert a powerful influence on American CRPG developers. There are, of course, hundreds of other JRPGs I could mention—indeed, one could easily write an entire book on them. Still, limiting ourselves to just these venerated series should provide at least an overview of how this genre evolved since the late 1990s.

Final Fantasy VII

One of the best games in the *Final Fantasy* series is the seventh game, which debuted in North America in 1997 for the two-year-old Sony PlayStation. The game quickly established itself as *the* RPG for the platform and remains one of the most celebrated entries in the franchise. It introduces innovations that became standard not only in later JRPGs but also several CRPGs, and it's one of the first major JRPGs ported to Windows. It also marks an important turning point for its developer, Square, who abandoned its commitment to Nintendo over its new console, the Nintendo 64, which lacked CD-ROM technology. Square saw (correctly) that CD-ROM was the next big thing—and, indeed, its game came on *three* CD-ROMs, making it easily the largest RPG ever released for a game console (Figures 19.1 and 19.2).

Final Fantasy VII, like most JRPGs, is a linear game with an intricate storyline and several prominent, well-developed characters, whose inner and outer struggles play out over the course of the game. It's often likened to an interactive movie, since the player ultimately has little control over how the plot unfolds. The settings are diverse but consist mostly of steampunk—robots and mutants live alongside humans and dragons. The player's character is Cloud Strife, an ex-soldier turned mercenary. Strife worked for an evil corporation named Shinra Electronic Power Company, whose patented Mako Energy turns out to be the very life force of the planet. It's up to Cloud and the AVALANCHE group to put a stop to Shinra before it's too late.

You can have up to three characters in the party at one time, but there are nine that can be swapped in and out as the game progresses. Each

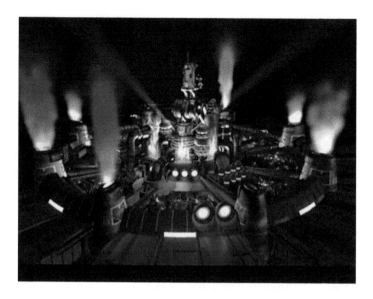

FIGURE 19.1 *Final Fantasy VII's* graphics and cinematics were some of the best gamers had ever seen, and it wasn't just technological—the artwork still holds up. Shown is the *Blade Runner*-esque city.

character has a unique personality, fighting style, and related animations. Some of the characters are secret and can be discovered only by particularly observant (or well-informed) gamers. It's even possible for Strife to date other characters, though this requires a high affection rating, which

FIGURE 19.2 *Final Fantasy VII's* impressive character modeling does a great job conveying emotion.

is determined by how you conduct yourself throughout the game. It's even possible to have a gay relationship, which was quite a progressive step for the time.

Much was made of the game's lavish graphics, which feature full 3D modes and an agile and intuitive camera control. In overland mode, the camera can rotate 360 degrees around the party, and in battle mode offers rotation, zoom, and multiple viewing angles. The character and monster models are all 3D, though the backdrops are prerendered and nicely detailed. What's even more impressive, however, are the spectacular spell animations, some of which rival the cut scenes of earlier games—even though their length can make them feel repetitive after hours of gameplay.

Combat relies on the famous Active Time Battle (ATB) system we discussed previously, which is a hybrid engine with both real-time and turn-based elements (Figure 19.3). The ATB system is expanded here with limit breaks, which build up as characters are struck in combat. When fully charged, the character can unleash a limit break attack, which does additional damage. Furthermore, the level break becomes more effective with use, though level four limit breaks require you to first find a secret item.

The magic system resists easy summary, but it is largely concerned with Materia, magical orbs that can be inserted into slots on the characters'

FIGURE 19.3　The game doesn't take long to get you into combat.

arms and armor. At first this system might seem similar to the socketed items in *Diablo II,* but it's far more sophisticated. First off, there are several types of Materia, and combining different types often leads to new and more powerful abilities. For instance, combining Restore and All Materia allows a character to cast a cure magic spell on the entire party, whereas Restore by itself will only heal one. The Materia also increases in potency, eventually becoming "mastered" and producing a new copy of itself. Materia can be traded among the characters, who instantly inherit whatever power was pumped into it by the former owner. Obviously, this is a complex system that takes time and patience to learn, a far cry from the simplistic gameplay associated with older console games.

Further separating *Final Fantasy VII* from the stereotypical console game is the abundance of expletives, which earned the game a "Teen" rating for sex and violence. Although many computer gamers may see the cute, cartoonish characters and assume it's meant for children, *Final Fantasy VII* is intended for more mature audiences. Indeed, this is a game where beloved characters are brutally murdered, and it's not hard to see the parallels between the game's storyline and contemporary social and political issues.

As if all this weren't enough to recommend this exquisite game, Square included seven minigames. The most famous of these involves the Chocobo, an animal that can be captured, trained, raced, and bred. The minigames are completely optional, yet taking the time to train and breed Chocobos can get the player into otherwise inaccessible areas of the game. The other minigames range from fighting on motorcycles to playing basketball.

Square's effort to convert the game to Windows resulted in a game of uneven quality. While the graphics and loading times is substantially improved, the music is reduced to tinny MIDI output. Perhaps this wouldn't have been so disappointing in another game, but *Final Fantasy VII* has music composed by the great Nobuo Uematsu. Fans have made efforts to address the situation, releasing special sound fonts that can dramatically improve the music quality on some PCs.

Final Fantasy VII sold nearly 10 million copies and is widely considered one of the best JRPGs ever made. Although the Windows port's lack of quality sound is upsetting, it didn't stop countless PC owners from jumping on the *Final Fantasy* bandwagon.

Final Fantasy VIII

The next game in the series was released in North America in September 1999 for the Sony PlayStation and four months later for Windows. This

FIGURE 19.4 *Final Fantasy VIII* takes a more realistic art direction. Official publicity image by Square Enix.

time, the disparity between the PlayStation and Windows versions is even more noticeable, and not in a good way. While the PlayStation version received mostly positive reviews, the PC port fared much worse.

This game makes several substantial changes to both the aesthetics and gameplay. The most obvious change is more realistic characters; gone were the "super deformed" look that lent such a cartoonish feel to the earlier games (Figure 19.4). Many critics applaud this change, noting how it makes the rich dramatic interactions among the characters more convincing. The game also introduced some rather complex innovations to the combat engine: the draw, guardian force, and junction systems. The draw system changes the way magic works; instead of using mana points to cast spells, players "draw" spells from enemies and "draw points." The guardian force is a summoned creature, without which a character cannot cast spells or use items during battles. Once a character is "junctioned" or joined to a guardian force, several important options become available. Guardian forces have their own statistics and abilities and level up along with the character. In short, they're an indispensable part of the gameplay.

In other ways, *Final Fantasy VIII* is a much simpler game than its predecessors. For instance, the characters wear no armor and wield the same weapons throughout the game. However, the weapons can be upgraded by combining them with special items at junk shops. Apologists for the series contend that this system makes a great deal of sense—after all, in practice most of the arms and armor found in other CRPGs are indistinguishable apart from their statistical value. This is painfully obvious in games that designate more powerful items only with integers (longsword +1, longsword +2). Others scoffed, seeing the lack of arms and armor merely as evidence of dumbed down gameplay. The monsters in *Final Fantasy VIII* level up along with the player's characters, gaining new skills and abilities. Fortunately for less skillful players, the characters will stay far ahead of the curve with their own abilities. Indeed, many critics complain that the game is too easy.

Besides the graphics, the best part of the game is (not surprisingly) the story and characters. The player steps into the shoes of Squall Leonhart, a young student training to become a mercenary. Leonhart isn't a very likeable character and finds himself constantly in trouble with his classmates and instructors. Leonhart's real troubles begin, however, when he's pulled into an international conflict brought by the sorceress Edea. It's up to Leonhart and his companions to save the world. All the characters are sharply drawn, and their dramatic interactions (including the much-talked about romantic involvements) are praised by critics.

Unfortunately, the story is constantly interrupted by wave after wave of random encounters, which are made almost unbearable by the lengthy animation sequences that play during battles. While these animations are stunning the first few times, incessant repetition (there's no way to turn them off or skip them) soon becomes hard to endure. Nevertheless, the game earned over $50 million after only thirteen weeks on the shelves, setting a record for the franchise.

While the PlayStation game was a masterpiece of design and engineering, the Windows port was a travesty. The graphics that looked so impressive on the television screen were uneven and flawed on the monitor, and again the soundtrack is ruined by faulty conversion. Even worse, the developer made little effort to adapt the interface to a keyboard and mouse setup, forcing PC users to wade through unnecessary menus and deal with an abysmal save game system.

Final Fantasy IX

The ninth game in the series is often described as a love letter to fans, a rather sentimental and nostalgic game that reverts to the older graphics and class system of the earlier games. The setting is distinctly medieval, the characters a group of thievish thespians. The troupe kidnaps Princess Garnet but later joins her on a mission to find out why the queen of Alexandria has succumbed to evil. The plot is still quite linear, and the narrative requires switching from one party to another—a technique used to heighten the tension. As usual, Square takes pains to make the characters more than just collections of stats and abilities. They show a full range of emotions, responding convincingly to the many dramatic situations. That the characters can act so human despite their bizarre appearance (one is literally a rat!) is impressive, and despite all the hoopla over the previous game, few critics resent the move back to the "super deformed" graphics.

The combat system is revamped yet again, and the complicated guardian force, draw, and junction systems are left out. The limit breaks are represented here as a "trance system," and the lengthy animations are greatly shortened after playing through once. Weapons and armor were restored and have a more intricate connection to the gameplay: equipping new items lets the characters learn new abilities.

The ninth game again wowed critics, many of whom assign it high scores and pinned on ribbons. It's the last of the series to be released on the original PlayStation and wasn't ported to Windows until 2016, when it was finally made available on Steam.

Final Fantasy X

By now, it shouldn't come as a surprise that the next installment in the *Final Fantasy* franchise, *Final Fantasy X* (2001), was an instant success, converting critics into ad writers and helping Sony sell a few million of its new PlayStation 2 consoles. It's also not surprising that Square again tinkered with the formula. The changes here included a switch back to purely turn-based combat and a novel level up system. While the characters in the game are more anatomically correct than in the previous game, their fashions are as bizarre as anything ever dreamed up for a 1980s MTV video. Fortunately for Square, it would take more than questionable dress to turn off fans.

Besides the better graphics made possible by the new platform, the most noticeable enhancement was the addition of digital speech and voice acting. While the voice talent was adequate for the task, the lip-syncing routines weren't designed for English, and the result is reminiscent of a kung fu movie. The only real complaint critics had about the graphics was the movement of the characters, whose exaggerated body language failed to convincingly convey their emotions (Figure 19.5).

The game's main character is Tidus, an outlandishly dressed and somewhat cocky youth whose favorite pastime is blitzball. Tidus's troubles

FIGURE 19.5 Shown here is the *Final Fantasy X/X-2 HD Remaster,* which updates the graphics to high definition. Image from Steam.

begin when his city, a futuristic place called Zanarkand, is invaded by monsters. Somehow, Tidus is transported to a different world and projected a millennium into the future. Tidus's civilization no longer exists, having been destroyed by a being named Sin. Tidus sets off with his new friend Yuna to destroy Sin.

The characters are again assigned to particular classes but can now be instantly switched into and out of the three-character party during battle. This feature is quite useful, since a character who does anything during a battle is given a full share of the experience (or action) points. This helped balance the characters and keep a single trio from gaining far more power than the rest. Although the combat is strictly turn-based, the popular limit breaks are back, though renamed the "overdrive" system. Another change is that summoned monsters behave more like full-fledged characters and stick around until they're killed.

Perhaps the most unlooked-for change is a complete revamping of the leveling system, which is here represented by a Sphere Grid. After a victory, the player receives sphere points, which allow the characters to move about the grid. The grid is composed of connected nodes, each of which offers some improvement (new skills, spells, extra hit points, and many more). Thus, characters literally advance in power as the game progresses.

The next game in the series is not a JRPG at all, but rather an MMORPG. I'll talk about it and other MMORPGs in the series later, after I conclude our coverage of other JRPG masterpieces. In addition to numerous spin-offs, there have been five more *Final Fantasy* games released since *X*, with the latest being *Final Fantasy XV* (2016). One of the most controversial moments occurred in 2006, with the publication of *Final Fantasy 12*. The controversy concerns its Gambit system, which left it up to you to program your party members' AI. Some players felt that this system was just laziness on the part of the programmers, and others said it felt like the game was playing itself, reducing your role to a spectator. Many, though, consider it one of the best innovations of the genre. Here's what Martin Robinson of *Eurogamer* says about it:

> Optimisation is a part of every RPG, but in *Final Fantasy 12* it's pushed to a brilliant new extreme—your party's a machine that must be constantly tinkered with, tweaking one variable here and tightening up another there until you've got an engine that purrs. It is glorious.

The latest game in the series, *Final Fantasy XV*, bills itself as "a Final Fantasy for fans and first-timers," and is about four friends on a road trip. The bulk of the game hinges on their evolving relationships and development as characters. The combat engine is real time, with a great deal of emphasis on cooperative attacks. It's a little early to judge its impact on the series, but so far sales and support have been strong. Indeed, Hajime Tabata, the game's director, said that it saved the series, which fell out of favor after the thirteenth and fourteenth installments suffered disappointing sales.

Ocarina of Time

Let's go back to Nintendo. In 1998, it released what millions of *Zelda* fans consider the best game ever made: *Ocarina of Time*. First released for the Nintendo 64 and subsequently ported to Nintendo's later platforms, the fifth *Zelda* game is an undisputed masterpiece, the pinnacle of Shigeru Miyamoto and Takashi Tezuka's already distinguished careers. But is it a role-playing game?

To say that *Ocarina of Time* impressed critics and gamers is a tremendous understatement. There were just thirty-nine days left in 1998 when the game was released, yet it still sold 2.5 million copies to become the best-selling game of that year.[1] It's received countless awards and earned the first perfect scores ever awarded by IGN and GameSpot, and the

"Best Game of All Time" distinction by the long-running *Nintendo Power.* Countless well-informed critics share *Nintendo Power's* opinion, and it routinely shows up near the top of the perennial "best ever" lists of games. When the game debuted, GameSpot's Jeff Gerstmann declared it to be "the masterpiece that people will still be talking about ten years down the road."[2] While this claim seemed bold at the time, it's now clear that Gertsmann should have doubled or even tripled that number!

Although critics praise the game's graphics and soundtrack, what really sets the game apart is its masterfully crafted gameplay. Although Nintendo helped pioneer 3D action gaming with its earlier *Super Mario 64* game (1996), *Ocarina of Time* offers further refinements. The most important of these is "Z Targeting," which helps Link automatically lock onto a target, allowing for circular strafing and other advanced maneuvers. The game also makes good use of the rumble pack, which vibrates the controller during certain events, such as when Link senses a hidden door. There are hundreds of clever puzzles to solve, some involving the titular ocarina (a flute-like musical instrument). Link's mission is to stop the evil Ganondorf from acquiring a powerful magical item (the Triforce), a quest that will take the young hero all across the huge world of Hyrule and even through time. It's a huge game, with an immense gameworld and tremendously varied gameplay (Figure 19.6).

But again we must ask the question: Is *Ocarina of Time* a role-playing game? Just as you saw in our discussion of the older *Zelda* games,

FIGURE 19.6 Here's a shot of Link learning a new tune for his ocarina.

this can be a contentious question. Most professional critics label the game as an action adventure, even though Link (the player's character) increases in power and gains new skills as the game progresses. As before, the story, setting, quest structure, and characters all fit nicely into a conventional CRPG. Of course, the RPG elements are simplistic compared to most action RPGs, yet this is a difference in quality, not kind. Furthermore, even if Link doesn't gain levels in a numerical sense, there's no contention that he gains in stature (literally) and increases in prestige during the game. One thing that does seem clear about *Ocarina of Time* is that the bulk of what makes the game fun (e.g., the action sequences) would not translate well (if at all) to tabletop role-playing. But the same complaint could be made about *Diablo* and *Morrowind*. In short, I see no reason to exclude *Ocarina of Time,* even though it does blur the boundaries between the action adventure and action RPG genres. In any case, it'd be a real shame for anyone not to play this masterpiece at least once.

Majora's Mask

The sixth game in the *Zelda* series is *Majora's Mask,* first released in October 2000 for the Nintendo 64. Like *Ocarina of Time,* this game also sold millions of copies, scooped up awards, and dazzled most critics, who appreciated the darker, more sophisticated storyline. As before, a good deal of critical attention was lavished on the graphics, which were sharper and detailed. Indeed, the game requires a four megabyte Expansion Pak to run on the Nintendo 64.

The story picks up after the conclusion of *Ocarina of Time* and concerns Termina, a land that is about to be destroyed by a falling moon. Link must stop the moon as well as discover the identity of a mysterious thief, who has stolen his horse and cursed him. In a conceit reminiscent of the film *Groundhog Day,* Link uses time travel to continuously relive the last three days of Termina, desperately searching for a means of preventing the catastrophe. Many of the game's puzzles concern magical masks, including the one from which the game's name is derived. Three of the masks will allow Link to change his form, not only enabling access to new areas but bestowing new abilities.

Again, more of the gameplay is focused on action and puzzle solving than conventional role-playing. Still, it's possible for Link to upgrade his sword and shield, and, as usual, Link can increase his maximum hit points by finding Heart Containers.

FIGURE 19.7 *The Wind Waker* on the Wii U, shown here, is even more impressive than the original GameCube version. Image by Nathaniel Tolbert.

The Wind Waker

The Wind Waker, the tenth installment in the *Zelda* series, was released in 2000 for Nintendo's GameCube console (Figure 19.7). Like most of the *Zelda* games, *The Wind Waker* met with high praise from critics and won numerous awards, even though the gameplay hasn't evolved much from the previous two games. I won't go into detail about the game here, except to say that the cell-shaded graphics style looks distinctly like a cartoon. Some gamers object to the new style; others embrace it. There are also complaints about the large amount of dull sailing sequences. In any case, *The Wind Waker* is considered a must-have game for any fan of the series.

Twilight Princess

Twilight Princess, released in 2006, is the first of the *Zelda* games for the Nintendo Wii, though it was initially designed for the older GameCube (Figure 19.8). The Wii version, not surprisingly, is distinguished mostly by its control scheme, which integrates the Wii's unusual Wii remote and Nunchuck devices. These controls are designed to offer more direct correspondences between the actions represented on the screen and those performed by the player. For instance, Link swings his sword when the player swings the Nunchuck. Although the scheme is imprecise, many critics find the experience intuitive and compelling. The RPG elements are extended by Link's ability to uncover hidden skills, or new sword-fighting

FIGURE 19.8 *Twilight Princess* looks even better on the Wii U. Image by Nathaniel Tolbert.

techniques. Still, with *Twilight Princess* we are far, far from the type of gameplay embodied in games such as *Neverwinter Nights* and *Oblivion*.

The game's story has Link (now a young man) out to save the Hyrule from the Twilight Realm, an alternate world that is slowly engulfing the land. When Link enters the Twilight Realm, he becomes a wolf and is joined by an imp named Midna who rides on his back and offers advice. There's a great deal for Link to do before he can save Hyrule.

This was the first game in the series to receive a "T" rating, bestowed by the Entertainment Software Rating Board (ESRB) for the animated violence. That Nintendo was willing to release a *Zelda* game with this rating may be a sign that the company realizes that many of the series' fans are no longer small children.

Naturally, Nintendo was eager to leverage the Wii's unique controller scheme, which brings us to a now-familiar question: What's a more fun way to simulate a sword fight: rolling some dice, clicking a button, or waving a Nunchuck? Of these options, the last seems to correspond best with actual swordplay, yet I could point out that although gun-style controllers have been around for some time, they haven't revolutionized the first-person shooter genre. In any case, I'd argue that the essence of a true CRPG or JRPG is the abstract nature of its combat and skill development. You win with strategy and tactics, not agility with a mouse or gamepad. Furthermore, no matter what the initial skill and knowledge of

FIGURE 19.9   Here's a combat sequence from *Breath of the Wild* on the Wii U. Image by Nathaniel Tolbert.

the player, the player's characters should themselves start off fragile and inexperienced. A character in these games learns from experience, gaining new powers and strengths. The characters in most action adventures, conversely, are only as effective as the player's own finesse.

The Latest Zelda Games

There have been many *Zelda* games since *Twilight Princess*. These include *Skyward Sword*, first published in 2011 for the Wii and Wii U, and *Breath of the Wild* in 2017 for the Wii U and Switch (Figure 19.9). Nintendo has also released high definition (HD) remakes of some earlier titles, including *The Wind Waker HD* in 2013 in 2015 and *Twilight Princess HD* in 2016. There's also *Majora's Mask 3D* and *Ocarina of Time 3D*, but these are currently exclusive to the 3DS handheld system. Rumor has it that Nintendo is planning another HD remake for the Switch, but as of this writing it's not clear which one it is.

OTHER INFLUENTIAL JRPGs

As noted earlier, there are far too many good JRPGs out there to attempt to cover them all here. That said, I'd be remiss not to mention a few more series: *Kingdom Hearts, Disgaea, Persona,* and *Xeno*. Like the JRPGs discussed above, each of these series brings something new or wonderfully weird to the table.

The *Kingdom Hearts* series is best known for mixing Disney characters (Donald Duck, Goofy, etc.) with others from *Final Fantasy*. *Kingdom Hearts II*, published in 2006 for the PS2, is generally regarded as the best game in the series, with fast-paced combat and fantastic worlds to explore. Likewise, *Disgaea 5* (2015) seems to be the most popular entry in its series. This tactical role-playing series is celebrated for its complexity, but also its humor. The *Persona* series trades the traditional high fantasy setting for a modern Japanese high school, and it is as much a social and psychological simulation as anything else. A group of students learn how to summon Personas, which are manifestations of their own personalities. The games touch on serious subjects and explore some rather deep psychological territory. There doesn't seem to be a consensus about which entry is the best, but *Persona 5*, released in 2016 for the PS3 and PS4, is a strong contender. Finally, *Xeno* is a sci-fi series with fantasy elements that also delves into psychological territory. Arguably *Xenosaga: Episode III—Also Sprach Zarathustra* (2006) is the best game in this series so far, but since it's the concluding chapter, you'd probably be better off starting with *Xenosaga: Episode I: Der Wille zur Macht* (2002).

The JRPGs in this chapter are just the tip of the iceberg, and if you're willing and able to learn Japanese, you'll find even many more series to get excited about. It's not an easy undertaking by any means, but, hey, if you're required to learn a foreign language as part of your high school or college curriculum anyway, choose Japanese so you can at least look forward to playing some great JRPGs at the end of it!

NOTES

1. See http://ign64.ign.com/articles/066/066340p1.html.
2. See http://www.gamespot.com/n64/adventure/legendofzeldaoot/review.html.

CHAPTER 20

The Rise of the MMORPG

MASSIVELY MULTIPLAYER ONLINE ROLE-PLAYING GAMES

The time has come to talk of MMORPGs—massively multiplayer online role-playing games. The fact that we still rely on this ungainly acronym is a fair indication of just how unsettled we still find this new frontier—there hasn't even been time to come up with a decent name for it!

We saw the roots of MMORPGs in Chapter 3, where we discussed PLATO, MUDs (multiuser dungeons), and MOOs (MUDs, object oriented). These games are insanely addictive, and I've met many people over the years who still log in on a daily basis to play some MUD they started back in the 1980s—or in PLATO's case, the 1970s! The games themselves are wonderful, of course, but it's really the friendships you make there that keep you coming back, long after you've explored every nook and cranny and defeated every monster in the game for the thousandth time. These are games where everybody knows your name—and just like *Cheers*, there's always something interesting going on, even if it's just the latest drama among the regulars.

In many ways, it's only a small step from these games to what we now call MMORPGs. The early progenitors are also multiplayer, allowing dozens to hundreds of players to coexist in coherent and persistent gameworlds. By "persistent," I mean that each time players revisit a MUD, they find that time has passed there. Life has gone on without them, and many important events may have occurred in their absence. Furthermore, their own activities can have a real and lasting effect on the gameworld. If they build a house, for instance, it'll still be there when they get back—assuming it hasn't been destroyed or deleted. Although most of these early games offer only text- or character-based graphics (ASCII or ANSI), others are more ambitious, particularly the games developed for PLATO. In Chapter 7 we talked about the first computer game called *Neverwinter Nights,* which was an early multiplayer CRPG based on SSI's Gold Box engine. This game ran on America Online, which at first charged by the hour but then shifted to a flat rate.

Before the Internet and the web, online gaming was a seriously expensive hobby. Besides the fees charged by the private, commercial networks, you could also incur substantial long-distance charges. Relatively few computer gamers in the early 1990s even had modems; all of their games were bought at the store and played alone at home. This situation began to change in 1993 with the introduction of the Mosaic web browser. It's difficult to exaggerate the impact this single program had on the computer and communications industry. Suddenly, it was easier than ever to access a vastly expanding network of free multimedia content and nearly as easy to build one's own website. As the web grew from a motley collection of government and academic databases to a million- and then a billion-dollar bazaar, the American public finally had a compelling reason to get connected. The commercial networks faded into insignificance as the World Wide Web was spun across the globe.

The Internet allowed game developers to offer cheap and even free multiplayer options. In Chapter 15 we talked about how Blizzard revolutionized online gaming with its free multiplayer options for *Diablo*. For uncounted legions of gamers, Blizzard's Battle.net server was their first taste of online gaming, and they were instantly hooked. Throughout the latter half of 1990s and early 2000s, almost every major CRPG featured a multiplayer mode, though, as we've seen, the quality of these experiences varied widely from game to game. Some were obviously tacked on at the last moment merely as a "value add" for marketing. Even in the case of *Diablo,* multiplayer gameplay wasn't the primary concern of the developers, and I suspect that many, if not most, players were quite content with the single-player campaign. There was another breed of online RPG, though, a new type of game designed *exclusively* for play on the Internet, and it's to this type we turn now.

Meridian 59

Although not the first such game, 3DO's *Meridian 59* is usually credited as the first modern MMORPG (Figure 20.1). We can argue about it all day long, but I limit the term *MMORPG* to Internet-based games, which disqualifies the earlier online multiplayer games designed for commercial

FIGURE 20.1 *Meridian 59* feels a lot like *Might & Magic VI*, but it was inspired by an earlier game called *Scepter of Goth*. 3DO did start work on a *Might & Magic Online*, but later canceled it.

networks. I also tend to exclude text-based or character-set games, such as MUDs and MOOs, as well as *Diablo*, BioWare's *Neverwinter Nights*, and other games for which online multiplayer is a lovely option, but not a requirement. My final test is whether the game has a massive gameworld capable of supporting thousands or even hundreds of thousands of concurrent users. *Meridian 59*, released commercially in September 1996, is to my knowledge the first game to meet all of these criteria, even though its box declares it the "first-ever internet-based 3D MUD" and it was limited to 250 concurrent players.

The game was developed by a small, unassuming company named Archetype Interactive. Graphically, it resembles *Doom*, id's ubiquitous first-person shooter. Critics consider the graphics and audio dated, but they acknowledge that the appeal of these games depends more on the caliber of the community than the eye candy. *Meridian 59* has a standard high fantasy setting and an emphasis on monster bashing, and players are limited to human characters—though they can choose among three political factions, each with their own bonuses, as well as player-created guilds. Players were charged a $10 flat fee per month.

3DO shut down the game on August 31, 2000, but it was bought and rereleased two years later by the aptly named Near Death Studios, a company co-founded by *Meridian 59* developers. In late August of 2018, the game was rereleased on Steam as an open-source, free-to-play MMORPG. And by free-to-play, we mean free-to-play; there are no in-game purchases of any sort. The only funding comes from dedicated players who make personal donations to keep the servers running. As to the *Meridian 59* community, allow me to quote from a user named urimarg's review of the game on Steam:

> There is a beautiful world waiting to be explored by people who have imagination and appreciation for great mechanics and community. You are not a faceless blob among millions. You meet real people, make real friends, and your reputation is important. Betrayals in the game often feel like a punch in real life.

If that isn't enough to convince you that this game is worth trying out, I don't know what will. Again, when it comes to MMORPGs, the decisive factor is the community. A great community can more than compensate for a mediocre game, but a bad community can ruin even the best. This is what makes it so difficult to predict whether a new MMORPG will succeed or fail; so much depends on factors beyond the developer's control. Developers must feel like one of those cat owners who turn their living room into a cat theme park—only to find ol' Whiskers prefers to play with the old milk jugs and cardboard boxes in the garage.

Even when these games do manage to attract a sustainable audience, they can leave as quickly as they came, particularly if they feel unwelcome or, worse, abused or harassed. As we'll see, the largest factor in an MMORPG's success is how it manages the worst impulses of its player base.

Ultima Online: The Grandfather of MMORPGs

It is entirely fitting that the same man who all but invented the CRPG, Richard "Lord British" Garriott, also plays a crucial role in the development of MMORPG. As with *Ultima,* he was not the first to explore this new frontier, but he did more than anyone else to settle it.

The game in question is *Ultima Online,* launched in September 1997 (Figure 20.2). Unlike *Meridian 59* and *The Realm,* this game has 3D isometric graphics in third-person perspective. It's also more sophisticated,

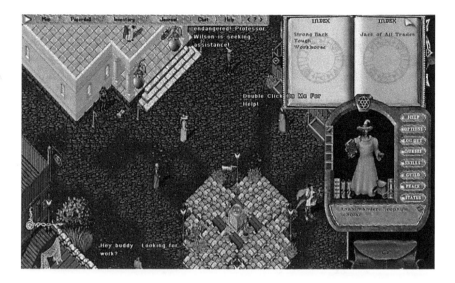

FIGURE 20.2 *Ultima Online* was the first truly successful MMORPG. There were major growing pains, but the lessons learned here benefited later MMORPGs enormously.

set in the well-known realms of *Ultima*'s Britannia. The game proved enormously successful for Origin and Electronic Arts and is the first such game to achieve 100,000 subscribers. It's still online today, but it was far more active in its early years, when it established almost all the conventions of the genre. These lessons came slowly and painfully, and later MMORPG designers are indebted to Origin for working out so many solutions to seemingly insurmountable problems. But let's not get ahead of ourselves.

In terms of gameplay mechanics, *Ultima Online* borrows a lot from *Ultima VII: The Black Gate,* particularly regarding the high level of world interaction. Just as in that game, there is so much more to do than going around killing monsters. In *Ultima Online* you can easily spend all your time peacefully, perhaps by gathering up and processing resources and contributing to the game's highly developed economy. Cooking, blacksmithing, glassblowing, basket weaving; the possibilities for crafting seem endless, even if some are more useful for social purposes than combat. You can even hire NPCs to manage your shop while you're away!

Initial interest in the game was strong. In a 1996 interview with Lord British on YouTube, he tells the story of how he secured beta testers. According to him, developers usually have to lure beta testers with raffles or even pay them directly—you're lucky to recruit a dozen. Even though playtesting might sound like fun ("You get to play games for free? Sign me up!"), it's actually genuinely hard work, since you're expected to keep careful notes and spend much of your time playing "badly"—that is, intentionally searching for bugs for programmers to fix before launch. Anyway, when British sent out a call for 1,000 volunteers, offering them nothing but the chance to play the game, he was being ambitious, if not delusional. He got 3,500.

As the publishers of the first truly successful MMORPG, the game's developers soon found themselves dealing with one crisis after another. First, the high frequency of users might have looked great for Electronic Arts' bottom line, but it caused terrible lag on the game's servers, or intermittent interruptions in the information flowing between the server and the players' computers. These can have disastrous consequences, especially if they happen during combat. A smaller problem was that the chat system placed the dialog directly above the characters' heads rather than in a separate window. This frequently resulted in one set of text overlapping another, rendering both unreadable. The leveling process was also quite slow and tedious, designed to keep players from getting too powerful too quickly (and, of course, to keep them renewing those monthly subscriptions).

Other problems were social in nature. At first the game suffered from mobs of anarchic "pkillers," homicidal maniacs and marauders who roamed the world, preying on the weak. The pkillers were paying customers who were apparently getting their own money's worth out of the game, but their behavior was annoying to many new players, and Origin feared it would lead to declining populations. They experimented with different means of handling the problem but eventually settled on a bounty system. If players engaged in notorious behavior, they would automatically receive a bounty on their heads, and all other players would be free to murder them with impunity. The system seemed to work well enough, though sometimes players accidentally broke a rule but were still gleefully persecuted by zealous bounty hunters.

Of course, for most people, an MMORPG is more fun if you enjoy interacting with your fellow players. To that end, Lord British and Origin strove valiantly to introduce novices to proper etiquette and encouraged them to get into the role-playing aspect of the game. Here's a quote from the *Ultima Online Renaissance* manual to show what I mean: "Don't name a character something foolish. People who see a character named 'Chucky D' are less likely to help that character or even associate with them." A little later: "Use proper greetings. While 'Sup' may be completely appropriate among your friends in the game, when speaking to strangers a nice 'Hello' or even a 'Hail' will go a long way to improving the opinion others have of you."

I can't help but chuckle at these admonitions, and it's doubtful that ol' Chucky D would bother to read a manual in the first place. Still, they do provide insight into the kind of experience British *wanted* to offer players: an online version of the Renaissance fairs he loves so much. Later games, such as *World of Warcraft*, honor this tradition (with about as much success) with "RP" or role-playing servers. Still, it seems that true online role-players are a rare breed, and many folks find their behavior more off-putting than welcoming. Indeed, even at a Renaissance Fair, I delight in the acting and accents of the professional staff, but not so much when the average guest attempts it. My theory is that role-playing is much more important in table games, where it plays a vital role in keeping everyone immersed in the fiction. In online games like *Ultima Online* or *World of Warcraft*, the rich graphics and animations shoulder much of this burden, freeing up players to participate in a more passive fashion, at least as far as role-playing is concerned.

Although *Ultima Online* was not without its problems, it's remained in a constant state of development, and many of the worst issues have long since been addressed. Many expansions and countless updates have been released since 1998, adding new areas to explore, classes, quests, and loads of new weapons and magical items. In June 2007, *Kingdom Reborn* was introduced, a new client with better graphics and enhanced interface. As of this writing, the latest major update was Publish 101, issued on August 31, 2018. It included a Halloween event called "Treasures of Khaldun," Caddellite crafting, puzzle chests, and rewards to celebrate the game's 21st anniversary.

Shroud of the Avatar

Garriott latest project, *Shroud of the Avatar: Forsaken Virtues*, released on March 27, 2018, might well be called a spiritual successor to *Ultima Online* as well as the many single-player *Ultima* games. It began as a Kickstarter-backed project that raised nearly $2 million in 2013. It spent over five years in production and beta testing, but the finished product was met with mixed reviews. Though many aspects of the game have met with criticism, I suspect much of it has to do with British's desire to "bring role-playing back to role-playing," as he puts it in several interviews. British was peeved by the tendency of later MMORPG players to mindlessly complete quest after quest, barely paying attention to what NPCs have to say:

> You're no longer exploring, you're no longer actually problem-solving, you're no longer actually thinking about why or how should I interact in a particular way in this particular situation.[1]

I applaud British's ambition, and perhaps the mixed reception says more about the players than the game, but that's likely unfair. Gareth Harmer of mmorpg.com ravaged the game, not just for its "dated" or inept graphics, animation, and audio, but its interface, which to his mind resembles "a jumbled collection of scout badges and POG caps.... For all we complain about the 'dumbing down' of MMOs, the quality-of-life improvements are significant."[2]

I suspect that it's a bit too early to tell whether Portalarium and Garriott will overcome its growing pains, or whether enough players will stick around to sustain it in the long term. Note, however, that it also offers a standalone client, so even if the multiplayer servers do go down eventually, you'll still be able to play. As for Garriott, he remains confident the game will run "forever. We have total confidence we'll go through all five episodes, come hell or high water."[3] I hope he's right, and that this game fares better than his *Tabula Rasa* (2007), a short-lived sci-fi MMORPG that ended in a stinking cloud of litigation.

EverQuest

In March 1999, when a game called *EverQuest* burst onto the scene. *Ultima Online* was regarded as a success, but *EverQuest* soon made its numbers look insignificant (Figure 20.3). *EverQuest* is the first MMORPG that really caught the mainstream media's attention, who were fascinated by the game's addictive power and economic impact (much was made of players selling their characters and equipment for real money.) The game soon earned the nicknames "EverCrack" and "NeverRest," and, like *Dungeons & Dragons*, was blamed for corrupting the youth, breaking up marriages, and even causing suicides. Nevertheless, the game won many awards and wowed critics, several of whom admitted to being addicted to the game themselves.

Part of *EverQuest*'s appeal was its superb graphics, which require a 3D accelerator. The gameworld has a day/night *cycle* and weather effects, and the spell animations are dazzling. The game's servers averaged some

FIGURE 20.3 *EverQuest* was an even bigger hit than *Ultima Online*, and it still commands a respectable player base.

24,000 concurrent players, but was mostly lag free—a huge advantage over *Ultima Online*. While *EverQuest*'s gameworld (Narrath) isn't as interactive, it had five continents and some 400 zones to explore.

Another aspect that distinguished *EverQuest* is a strong emphasis on cooperative rather than player-versus-player (PvP) gameplay. In fact, the code simply doesn't allow players to attack each other except under very special (and mutual) conditions. Instead, players are encouraged to join together in groups (up to six players) and "raids" (50 to 200 players), working together to overcome otherwise unbeatable foes. The strategy paid off, and soon players were collaborating as never before, forming guilds and even coining their own argot ("buffs" for spell enhancements or "twinking" for taking advantage of a flaw in the game's code). By far, the most fun aspect of any MMORPG is meeting new friends and adventuring together; this is exactly what made *Dungeons & Dragons* so successful in the first place.

In February 2003, Sony released *EverQuest Online Adventures,* which introduced the game to PlayStation 2 owners. Though it wasn't the first online multiplayer game for consoles, it is the first MMORPG—unlike, say, *Phantasy Star Online,* there are no options here for playing the game offline. Why had it taken so long for game developers to introduce the MMORPG to the bursting console market? The reason is mundane: These games derive much of their appeal from social interaction, particularly in the form of chatting, and it's hard to do that without a keyboard—and voice chat wasn't yet feasible. Sony got around this problem in two ways, first by ensuring that all other operations could be handled easily with the standard game controller, and secondly by encouraging console owners to spring for a USB keyboard (which, by 2003, were quite easy to come by). The new game also tweaks the gameplay, such as a much lighter penalty for dying. Formerly, a dead character would simply lose experience points and even levels, negating hours of hard work. The new method was a debt system, which lets the player keep the benefits of his or her current level but increases the experience needed to reach the next one.

EverQuest reigned supreme for many years, and its developers released twenty-four expansions, each of was purchased separately (in addition to the monthly fee). In November 2004, Sony published *EverQuest II,* which offered updated 3D graphics and lots of new gameplay abilities. Players can now ride horses, sail ships, and own real estate, but player versus player combat is no longer allowed.

Though *EverQuest*'s popularity has greatly waned since its heyday, it's still in operation and shows no signs of shutting down anytime soon. As of this writing, it's ranked number 33 on mmo-population.com, a site that tracks MMO popularity based on reddit subscriber information, with an estimated population of 34,158.

Phantasy Star Online

Phantasy Star Online is the heir to Sega's flagship JRPG series *Phantasy Star,* which we discussed in Chapter 10. The original games defined role-playing on the Sega Master System and Genesis, but *Phantasy Star Online,* released in January 2001, was too little, too late. Sega announced that very month that it was discontinuing the Dreamcast, whose sales had dropped sharply after Sony introduced its PlayStation 2. Fortunately for *Phantasy Star* fans, this did not end the series—later episodes were released for Nintendo's GameCube and Microsoft's Xbox, and eventually it was even available for Windows. Later entries in the series include *Phantasy Star Universe,* published in 2006 for PlayStation 2, Xbox 360, and Windows, and *Phantasy Star Online 2,* published in 2012, the latter of which is available only in Japan.

MMORPG aficionados are quick to point out that *Phantasy Star Online* is not a true MMORPG, since it can be played offline. This puts it in the same category as games such as *Diablo,* which treat online multiplayer as an option, not a requirement. Indeed, the game is often referred to as a

"*Diablo* clone in space." This *Diablo* comparison seems a bit hasty, since *Phantasy Star Online* is obviously designed for online play; the single-player mode is simply a stop-gap measure for players lacking access to the Internet. In any case, the servers allowed up to only 1,000 concurrent players, a quite humble number given the tens of thousands available in other online games.

As with most games of its type, *Phantasy Star Online* encourages players to work together, this time in teams of four (Figure 20.4). One obvious question is how players interact with each other without a keyboard, and the developers (Sonic Team) came up with an interesting solution. Firstly, there are several preset dialog strings to choose from; the advantage here is that the dialog is automatically translated into English, French, German, Spanish, and Japanese—an important and useful feature. There is also a symbol chat system that uses mostly universal symbols to help players understand one another, such as hearts and smiley faces. Probably the best option, though, was to spring for a Dreamcast keyboard, even though there's no automatic translation of user-entered text.

Another often touted feature is the MAG, a type of pet that tags along with the character. The MAG can be fed items to increase its power and abilities and ends up becoming a very valuable asset. For many

FIGURE 20.4   A combat scene from *Phantasy Star Online*. Image from Wikipedia.

Phantasy Star Online players, taking care of their MAG was one of the highlights of the game.

The game features a 3D engine set in third-person perspective. While the graphics and audio are certainly commendable, many gamers found the camera control awkward and frustrating. The game lacks the handy Z-targeting system of the later *Zelda* games, and a glitch makes it easy for the player's character to end up with his back turned to the enemy. Another problem was lack of broadband support: Broadband play was possible, but only after a great deal of trouble. Fortunately, even with the Dreamcast's built-in 56K modem, lag was barely noticeable. The Sonic Team developed *Phantasy Star Online Version 2* in September 2001, just a month before the Dreamcast went out of production.

The first non-Dreamcast version was *Phantasy Star Online Episode I & II*, released for the GameCube in October 2002 and the Xbox in April 2003. It's an interesting game for several reasons. First, up to four players can play on a single GameCube using a split screen reminiscent of the much earlier *Hired Guns*. The graphics and interface are better, but there are more similarities than differences between this and the earlier game. Unfortunately for GameCube owners, acquiring a keyboard for their console wasn't nearly as cheap and easy as it had been for the Dreamcast. The Xbox version was superior in this regard.

Phantasy Star Universe, released in August 2006, continues the tradition of offering both online and offline gameplay, and there's now more support for squad-based multiplayer action. So far, it has not been a big hit with critics, one of whom called it "one of the biggest disappointments in years."[4] The problem was that Sonic Team and Total Entertainment Software simply hadn't done enough to distinguish it from its older incarnations.

Although the official servers for *Phantasy Star Online* have long since been shut down, fans of the game maintain private servers that offer free access. Go to phantasystaronline.net to learn more.

Asheron's Call

By the time Microsoft published Turbine Entertainment's *Asheron's Call* in November 1999, the MMORPG had been around long enough for the novelty to have worn off. Turbine knew it needed to compete with the incredibly popular *EverQuest* and attempted to do so with a suite of intriguing innovations and a self-conscious desire to be different. The end result was something of a mixed bag, and most critics concluded that the innovations, while intriguing in concept, didn't live up to their expectations. The game ran until it was shuttered, along with its 2012 sequel *Asheron's Call 2: Fallen Kings,* on January 31, 2017.

Turbine distinguished its gameworld by refusing to draw (at least directly) on existing fantasy tropes. Elves were out; Olthoi (cat-creatures) and Sclavus (reptilians) were in. The race and class systems were also revamped. As with *Ultima Online,* all characters would be human, though they could choose one of three heritage groups (Aluvian, Sho, and Gharu'ndim). However, the choice of heritage affected little besides a character's starting location. Other innovations concerned experience points and combat. Character development was based on a flexible skill system, which avoided the rigid specializations of other games, such as wizards who cannot wear armor. Combat was slightly more sophisticated than in other MMORPGs; in this game, the player controls the speed and height of the attack. Unfortunately, at least in early versions, combat was mired by occasional stutters, freezing the character in place for a few moments. The magic system relies on an interesting inflation system, where any particular spell loses its effectiveness as more and more people cast it. This system encourages a constant search for new spells, as well as a desire not to share them with the rest of the magic-using population.

Perhaps the most startling innovation was the allegiance system, which was more or less a pyramid scheme for experience points. The idea here was that new players could swear fealty to a more powerful character, becoming his or her vassal. A lord received experience point bonuses from these vassals but had an incentive to reciprocate, since more powerful vassals granted better bonuses. Eventually vassals recruited other vassals, putting the original lord in an even more enviable position. Players could opt out of the system at any time, escaping the service of abusive lords. At its best, though, this system encouraged experienced players to help novices.

A final very promising aspects of *Asheron's Call* was the regular addition of new, free content on a monthly basis. These expansions weren't limited to new items; they would constitute a narrative determined by the players' own actions. In other words, the players themselves had a direct impact on the narrative as it evolved, much like what happens during tabletop RPG campaigns.

Turbine developed a sequel, *Asheron's Call 2: Fallen Kings,* which was published by Microsoft in November 2002. This game had a newer graphics engine and combat system. Now, players could choose to be one of three different races, and the skill system was reworked into the familiar branching tree system we saw in *Diablo II*. Combat now included a critical hit system, which gave characters the chance to deal extra damage at random intervals. Still, most critics wrote lukewarm reviews, and neither *Asheron's Call* nor its sequel ever rose above the competition.

Ultima Online, EverQuest, and *Asheron's Call* are referred to as the "Big Three" MMORPGs of the early era. Later MMORPG developers studied their successes and failures very closely, building on what worked and striving to find ways to improve on their models.

RuneScape

RuneScape is another early MMORPG (Figure 20.5). It's a browser-based game released in January 2001 and developed by two brothers from the UK, Andrew and Paul Gower, who call themselves Jagex. *RuneScape* is recognized for its frequent updates—there's generally new content on a weekly basis. It's been free to play from the start, though for a small monthly fee you can access extra content such as special quests, maps, and items. It's also known for how well the developers treat the vibrant player community, apprising them and soliciting their opinions on their plans.

Like many early MMORPGs, *RuneScape* was initially conceived as a graphical MUD, but in 2004 was rereleased with full 3D graphics as *RuneScape 2*—though rather than stick with that name, it renamed the original game *RuneScape Classic* and called the new one *RuneScape*. Rather than force players on old or obsolete machines to upgrade to enjoy the new graphics, Jagex reduced the game's technical requirements.

FIGURE 20.5 *RuneScape* has been online since 2001.

In 2013, *RuneScape 3* was released, which again significantly updates the graphics, but this time also the combat engine to make it more complex. The older versions used a rather casual combat system—just point and click—but now there are several combat abilities and an "adrenaline" system that determines which of these abilities can be used at any given time. Not everyone was happy with these changes, so Jagex implemented a "legacy mode" that restores the simpler combat mechanics. It's undoubtedly this sort of commitment to please its players that has kept this game going for so long.

Anarchy Online

Funcom's *Anarchy Online* was the first sci-fi-themed MMORPG on the market and had much to offer any gamer fed up with *EverQuest* and *Ultima Online* (Figure 20.6). Unfortunately, its launch in June 2001 was bungled, and gamers were soon flooding online message boards with complaints about the insecure registration procedure, faulty copy protection, and a myriad of game-crashing bugs. These grave problems were enough to turn many away, but it's held on to enough loyal players to keep the lights on for over seventeen years.

FIGURE 20.6 *Anarchy Online* is a long-lived sci-fi-themed MMORPG. It's known for its dynamic missions. Image courtesy of Funcom Productions.

Those willing to endure the bugs and glitches (which were eventually patched) were treated to an original and highly detailed campaign setting, based, apparently, on the works of Frank Herbert *(Dune)* and William Gibson *(Neuromancer)*. The game is set on a remote mining colony called Rubi-Ka, the only known source of the mysterious "notum," a mineral that plays an indispensable role in nanotechnology. Notum, like the "spice" in Herbert's novels, is so powerful that its effects seem like magic, providing a suitable justification for spell-like abilities in an otherwise realistic setting.

The gameworld is dominated by two main factions—the Omni-Tek corporation and the rebel Clans, who object to Omni-Tek's shoddy treatment of workers. You can choose among four breeds, or races, and fourteen professions, each with a set of skills to learn.

Anarchy Online's expansions have greatly expanded the gameplay of the core engine. The first of these, 2001's *Notum Wars,* added control towers and ground-based vehicles. The *Shadowlands* expansion, released in September 2003, added a perk system, which is comparable to the perks we saw in the *Fallout* games. However, in this game perks can be removed and new ones selected, a useful feature if players find they have made a bad choice. *Lost Eden,* the latest expansion (released in 2006), offers a new research system, which allows you to channel experience points into uncovering new skills and upgrades. This fascinating system is broken into two types, Personal and Global. Personal research unlocks only special abilities for the character, whereas global is a faction-wide project to unlock or upgrade vehicles. The latest "booster" was *Legacy of the Xan* (2009), which adds new areas, weapons, and equipment for high-level characters.

Like many other older MMORPGs, *Anarchy Online* eventually switched to a free-to-play model in 2004. Funcom's model was supported by advertisements on virtual billboards. It worked well enough that even though it was supposed to only last a year, the system is still in effect today. Paying customers see these ads replaced with fictitious ones in addition to other perks.

All in all, *Anarchy Online* is a surprisingly ambitious and original game with much to offer sci-fi fans.

Dark Age of Camelot

On October 9, 2001, Abandon Entertainment and Vivendi Universal launched Mythic's *Dark Age of Camelot,* a Windows MMORPG set in the days just after the death of the legendary King Arthur. "*Dark Age of Camelot* surpasses any such game to date and promises to remain the finest in its class for a long time," wrote Greg Kasavin of GameSpot. Yet despite such glowing reviews from critics and some promising innovations, *Dark Age of Camelot* didn't last long in the spotlight, and Electronic Arts shut down Mythic, who'd taken over the servers, in 2014. Thankfully, Broadsword Online Games, a company founded by former Mythic developers, ended up in control, and has kept the perpetual war running, well, perpetually.

The game is broken into three competing realms, each based on a mythology: Albion (Arthurian), Midgard (Norse), and Hibernia (Celtic). Players can either spend time in these realms, or venture into frontiers where players from different realms can battle each other. These realms also serve to differentiate character abilities. Celts, for instance, excel at magic, whereas heroes from Midgard excel at melee combat.

The game also offers interesting trade skills, such as the ability to build siege weapons (catapults and ballista). Players uninterested in combat can focus on developing these skills, playing the game as merchants or other professions. Items eventually decay and must be repaired and eventually replaced—a sensible, if perhaps annoying, technique to counter item inflation. The game also has techniques for discouraging camping, or hanging out in areas where monsters respawn after being defeated. Some players will camp out in these spots, defeating the same monster over and over to lazily build up experience points—and prevent other players from testing their mettle against the beast. *Dark Age of Camelot*'s answer to this problem is to give players additional experience if they fight a variety of monsters.

Critics were impressed that *Dark Age of Camelot* was so stable and bug free when it was released—quite an impressive feat considering it was created by a rather small studio. Other games, as we've seen, suffered horrendous growing pains, irritating gamers with lag and a host of other problems. Though the game's population has dwindled, there's still plenty of activity and a welcoming player base.

Final Fantasy XI Online

As we noted in previous chapters, the *Final Fantasy* JRPGs are really in a class of their own, practically defining console gaming in North America. Critics hail every game in the series as an undisputed masterpiece, giving them incredible scores and breathlessly demanding that players buy them immediately. Naturally, when Square Enix announced it was developing a MMORPG based on the franchise, critics and gamers took notice. Would *Final Fantasy XI Online* revolutionize MMORPGs the way the older games had JRPGs?

The game was first released in Japan in May 2002. It wasn't until October 2003 that the highly anticipated game finally made it across the Pacific, first for Windows (October 2003), then for the PlayStation 2 (March 2004) and Xbox 360 (April 2006). That the game was released first in Japan proved a boon for American gamers, since enough time had passed for most of the growing pains to ease, though critics complained about the lengthy and demanding install procedure.

The game is set in real time, and combat is (at least at first) little different than that of rival games, consisting of clicking on an enemy and standing by as the two exchange blows. Thankfully, combat gets more interesting as your character learns special moves, which can be performed whenever the tactical-point meter charges up. One nice innovation here is a claim system that inhibits other players from rushing in right before a kill and either finishing off the creature (thus reaping the experience points) or making off with the loot before the player can respond. In *Final Fantasy XI*, a monster is claimed by the character who initiates combat, and only others in the player's own party or alliance can join the battle. Originally, the game offered no mechanism for player versus player combat, though expansions included a conflict system.

The bulk of the gameplay concerns an ongoing conflict among the three nations of Vana'diel, who wrestle with each other for dominance. Players must select a home nation, from which they will receive missions. There are five available races and some eighteen jobs, though not all are available to new players. As we might expect from any game bearing the *Final Fantasy* label, there are several high-quality minigames, such as fishing, gardening, clamming, and digging with the ever-popular Chocobos (Figure 20.7). There's also a mechanism for combining items, using elemental crystals to synthesize new equipment.

Final Fantasy XI grew quickly after its release, eventually surpassing *EverQuest* in January 2004. The game's population now seems to be in decline, though it (along with every other MMORPG) has been dwarfed by *World of Warcraft*. It's a bit unclear why the game hasn't fared somewhat better, especially given the overwhelmingly positive reputation enjoyed by the franchise. However, as we saw earlier in this chapter, much of the earlier games' appeal was based on the storylines and richly developed

FIGURE 20.7 In 2006, *Final Fantasy XI* players could finally start raising and breeding Chocobos. Racing followed in 2007. Image from *Wikipedia*.

characters. The relatively open-ended, sandbox-style play of the online incarnation simply doesn't have much to offer gamers accustomed to more sophisticated online games.

Final Fantasy XIV

After released two single-player entries in the series, Square Enix returned to the MMORPG model for *Final Fantasy XIV* in 2010. This project turned out to be an unmitigated disaster for the studio due to a whole host of performance and interface-related issues. Critics warned players away from the game and plans for a PS3 version were put on hold.

It was rereleased as *Final Fantasy XIV: A Realm Reborn* in 2013, which addressed most of the issues and revamped nearly every other aspect as well. As of this writing, it boasts some 14 million registered players, and two expansions.

Beyond improved graphics and animations, *Final Fantasy XIV* is considerably different than *XI* in terms of gameplay (Figure 20.8). The biggest innovation is its class system. Instead of simply choosing your class when you create a character, you choose a discipline and a base class, then work your way up to your first "job." For example, the Disciples of War include the Archer, who can become a bard at level 30; Gladiators can work their way up to being Paladins, and so on. The nice thing is that you can easily

FIGURE 20.8 *Final Fantasy XIV: A Realm Reborn* is currently one of the top MMORPGs. Shown here is an official publicity image from Square Enix.

change classes and eventually unlock all the jobs on a single character. Otherwise, the game follows the usual Tank/Healer/DPS (damage-per-second) trinity of party roles.

It will be interesting to see where Square Enix will want to take the *Final Fantasy* franchise in the near future. Specifically, will it make another MMORPG, or choose instead to update and expand *XIV* while making more single-player JRPGs? My money is on the latter, at least for the next several years.

EVE Online

Although *Anarchy Online* was the first MMORPG out the gate with a sci-fi setting, its gameplay was not radically different than the competition. *EVE Online,* developed by the Icelandic company CCP Games, takes up the slack, offering gamers an experience more comparable to a space sim (*Starflight, Elite,* and *Privateer*). As we saw in Chapter 5, space sims are typically open-ended games that put you behind the controls of a starship, which you can use to transport goods, mine asteroids, and battle other ships for loot or bounties. It's a concept that works well in single-player games, but it's not hard to see how superbly it recommends itself to the MMORPG format, where the galaxy could be populated by other human beings rather than by computer-controlled, algorithmically generated ships and planets.

EVE Online debuted on May 6, 2003, but initial reactions were mixed. Like many new MMORPGs, it suffered from a series of mild to serious bugs and server issues. Critics complained about poor customer service as well, and most gave the game only lukewarm reviews. However, one of the main advantages of an online game is that the developers can continuously address bugs, releasing patches and updates quickly and effectively. *Eve Online* became one of the top MMORPGs, and, with over forty-two released expansions, it's still going strong today—despite a reputation as "spreadsheets in space."

EVE Online is a unique MMORPG for several reasons (Figure 20.9). Most importantly, although the player creates and works to improve a character, these characters never leave their spaceships. Instead, the bulk of the gameplay consists of piloting these vessels and navigating menus. Nevertheless, the characters can develop many skills useful in the many trades, which include mining, piracy, security, soldiering, and even corporate management. Another big difference is that the servers are not broken up into shards. Most MMORPGs don't have all the players populating the same persistent universe; instead, players are distributed among several parallel universes, each running on its own server. In *EVE Online,*

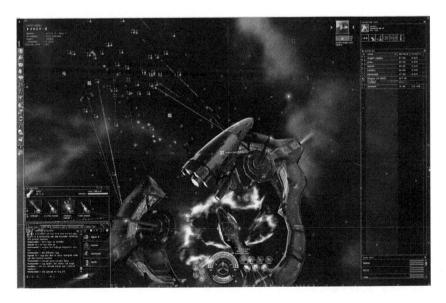

FIGURE 20.9   Back when I was playing *Elite* on my Commodore 64, I could only dream of a game like *EVE Online*. For countless fans around the world, it's the ultimate gaming experience. Image courtesy of CCP Games.

all players exist within a single shared universe. This is quite a feat, and the company boasts that it's only possible because its servers are the most advanced in the world. Another innovation concerns how experience points are handled. Rather than dole out these points as rewards for actions, they are earned over time, even if the player doesn't bother to log in for a while. This system tends to lend a powerful advantage to those gamers who've played the game the longest, though a system of diminishing returns ensures that these gains are kept in check (characters gain fewer and fewer points as they reach higher levels). Finally, there's really no story to the game beyond what the players create for themselves.

The premise of *EVE Online* is that humanity has long ago consumed all of Earth's resources and has spread out to colonize the rest of the Milky Way. Even with the entire galaxy at their disposal, humans eventually discovered themselves running out of resources yet again. Thankfully, a stable wormhole allowed the desperate humans to flee to an unknown sector of space, where there were many more solar systems (some inhabited) to exploit. Unfortunately, though, the wormhole collapsed behind them, leaving those who had fled to the other side to their own devices. These exiles eventually formed five empires. One is reminded here, of course, of *Deep Space Nine,* though such tales are common enough in science fiction. Indeed, we noticed a similar contrivance in Omnitrend's *Universe,* a 1983 game we discussed in Chapter 5.

Combat in *EVE Online* isn't much of a draw, since it consists mostly of swapping blows with an attacking ship until one or the other is destroyed. Success very much depends on the quality of one's weapons and defenses, but gamers should not expect the adrenaline-soaked space combat of games like *Elite.* The game is open to player-versus-player combat, with a bounty system in place to reduce abuses (players can receive handsome rewards for tracking down the most vicious pirates and outlaws).

EVE Online has suffered from the occasional scandal. In February 2007, news leaked that some of *EVE Online*'s developers were themselves engaged in questionable behavior, abusing their powers with an in-game spy network. While such a network is arguably necessary to ensure that players aren't breaking service agreements, these developers were using it to access confidential account information. To put it simply, they were cheating their own system and violating their own service agreements.[5] The incident hurt CCP's credibility. Since then, there have been several more scandals, mostly with player-run banks and alliances. In 2008, CCP set up a player-based Council of Stellar Management to address issues like those, but also to suggest improvements and content. As of this writing, the game has around 300,000 subscribers.

I should note in passing that *Elite: Dangerous,* developed by David Braben's Frontier Developments and released on December 16, 2014, could be thought of as a more action-based version of *EVE Online.* It's debatable whether it really counts as an MMORPG, though—you do have to be online to play it, but you can play in your private sandbox rather than the open public.

Finally, I should mention Chris Roberts' *Star Citizen,* a project that seems poised to give both *Elite: Dangerous* and *EVE Online* a run for their money. However, it's now been seven years in a controversy-riddled development cycle. It's anyone's guess whether it will ever be officially released, or to what extent it'll live up to the incredible hype that's built up around it, but enough people were interested to pledge over $50 million to its various crowdfunding campaigns. The developer is still raising money for the project by selling ships for real money—despite *Wired* magazine and other outlets declaring it "Vaporware." I'm in the "wait and see" category on this one.

Star Wars Galaxies

In June 25, 2003, LucasArts released *Star Wars Galaxies,* a MMORPG developed by Sony Online Entertainment (publishers of *EverQuest).* Given the success of BioWare's *Knights of the Old Republic* series, as well as the terrific name recognition of LucasArts' most famous franchise, *Star Wars Galaxies* was one of the most highly anticipated MMORPGs ever produced. Unfortunately, the game never managed to live up its potential and was shut down for good on December 15, 2011 (Figure 20.10).

Many of the game's most promising features turned out to be much less satisfying than gamers had hoped. The biggest disappointment concerned noncombat character professions, which allowed players to build everything from dancers to shopkeepers. However, critics complained about the boring and repetitive gameplay necessary to gain experience and hone skills. Furthermore, the massive gameworld had a desolate, unfinished feel. Finally, like most other MMORPGs, the launch suffered from serious bugs and server problems, and good customer service was hard to come by. It wasn't a very promising beginning.

Perhaps the best part of the game was the fine combat animations, which made battles much more visually exciting than the repetitive sequences in other games. Players could sign up with either the Rebel Alliance or the evil Empire, and well-known characters from the movies (Luke Skywalker,

FIGURE 20.10 This screenshot was taken by DocChewbacca, who played this wookie (Neekocha) for two and a half years.

Darth Vader) made appearances in the game. On a side note, players were not allowed to name their characters after those in the movies.

Sony Online released several patches and updates, some of which were highly controversial. One of the best new features (introduced in *Jump to Light Speed* in 2004) was new space vehicles that enabled players to fight real-time battles in space. Later expansions incorporated multi-passenger ground vehicles, a delightful addition. However, other changes were much less welcome. The most infamous of these was the Combat Upgrade Patch, which was designed to deal with the many balancing issues that had allowed players to build characters who were far too powerful. However, this patch could undo weeks if not months of tedious work, and some quit the game in protest. The final straw came in 2005 with the arrival of the New Game Enhancements (NGEs), another revamp that did more to frustrate existing players than woo new ones.

Star Wars: The Old Republic

Given the overall profitability of the *Star Wars* universe, it was only a matter of time before another MMORPG developer stepped in to try its luck. That moment finally came on December 20, 2011, when BioWare Austin

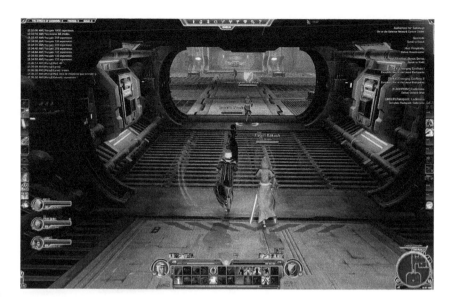

FIGURE 20.11 *Star Wars: The Old Republic* was praised for its superb cinematics and in-game graphics. Image courtesy of HiP1.

launched *Stars Wars: The Old Republic (SWTOR)*—just five days after *Star Wars Galaxies* shut down. It enjoyed a tremendous reception at launch, but eventually settled into a slow decline (Figure 20.11).

SWTOR is quite a different game than its predecessor. Indeed, many consider it more of a "co-op" or small-team multiplayer game than a true MMORPG. In any case, the developers wanted to address a common complaint about MMORPGs: Individual players often feel more like faceless visitors to a theme park rather than full-fledged characters who can make a real impact on the story. To that end, the designers spent much more time and resources developing cutscenes to provide context for quests as well as branching narratives involving a host of well-developed NPCs. However, rather than enhance the MMORPG experience, all this player-focused narrative content seemed to distract from it. Beyond the usual dungeons and raids, the game feels to some more like a half-baked *Knights of the Old Republic* than the next generation of *Star Wars Galaxies*. Tellingly, Electronic Arts/BioWare added a free-to-play option in 2012, albeit one that locked almost every feature—you couldn't even run without a microtransaction!

On a more positive note, an expansion called "Knights of the Fallen Empire" did much to address the single-player/MMORPG confusion.

Now, you can either player all the way to the level cap without grouping up with anyone, *or* you can start at the level cap and immediately start doing multiplayer content.

City of Heroes

So far we've seen MMORPGs set in fantasy, science fiction, and cyberpunk worlds. Cryptic Studios' *City of Heroes,* launched on April 28, 2004, was a fairly straightforward (though unacknowledged) effort to bring the superhero gameplay of the older *Freedom Force* games to the MMORPG format (Figure 20.12). However, *City of Heroes* wasn't just an *EverQuest* clone with dashing heroes in tights, but a worthy (if ultimately, failed) experiment in the genre.

Perhaps most importantly, *City of Heroes* was deliberately intended to be simpler and more accessible than other MMORPGs. The gameplay was based almost entirely on completing missions and engaging in battle after battle, with none of the trade skills possibilities seen in other games. The game also lacked an inventory system and thus a need for loot, though victories still yielded rewards in the form of experience points and influence,

FIGURE 20.12 *City of Heroes* was a much-loved MMORPG with a superhero theme. This image, "Rikti Raid Chaos," appears courtesy of Roxanne Ready.

which could be traded for enhancements and inspirations, or temporary enhancements ("buffs").

Perhaps the game's main appeal was the entertaining character creation process, which was flexible enough to allow players to create characters that looked virtually indistinguishable from the best of Marvel and DC—though the all-important cape accessory was mysteriously unavailable. Unfortunately for the publisher, Marvel felt that the game violated its copyrights and trademarks, and it sued in November 2004. The claims were finally settled in December 2005, without any changes being made to the character creation process.

NCSoft published Cryptic's *City of Villains* in October 2005, an expansion that, as the name suggests, put players in the role of villains rather than heroes. The expansion also allowed players to build strongholds, quintessential real estate for any aspiring master of villainy.

Although *City of Heroes* and *City of Villains* were certainly distinct from the typical swords and sorcery we see in other games, the subscriber base peaked at 194,000 and eventually shut down on November 30, 2012.

The studio went on to create *Champions Online,* another superhero-themed MMORPG that launched on September 1, 2009. It's based on the popular *Champions* tabletop RPG, and it has more emphasis on action combat than *City of Heroes* did. It started out with a subscription model, but went free-to-play on January 25, 2011. While *Champions Online* is still online all these years later, most fans of the genre still feel it's inferior to *City of Heroes.* Some object to its "borderlands" style art, which mimics a comic book with thin black lines around characters and objects, but most complaints concern the high percentage of content you're required to purchase.

Other Superhero MMORPGs: *DC Universe Online* and *Marvel Heroes*

The names "DC" and "Marvel" are practically synonymous with superhero comics, and so it was all but inevitable that we'd get officially licensed MMORPGs featuring stories and characters set in their respective universes.

DC beat Marvel to the punch with *DC Universe Online,* a free-to-play action game that went online on January 11, 2011. Developed by Daybreak Game Company and published by WB Games, *DC Universe Online* lets you create a character and join the Justice League or The Society, playing as either a hero or villain. Combat is comparable to a beat 'em up arcade game, complete with combos—it's more about your own skill than the character's, which disqualifies it as a role-playing game. In other ways, though, it's more like a standard MMORPG, with leveling, raiding, and so on. One interesting innovation is that instead of giving you hundreds of options for creating just the right costume—as in the above-mentioned superhero games—you're required to find items for your wardrobe as you play.

Marvel Heroes was developed by Gazillion Entertainment/Secret Identity Studios (helmed by David Brevik of *Diablo* fame) and released on June 4, 2013. One neat feature was that you could unlock and play as over 100 Marvel heroes such as The Punisher or Deadpool. Unfortunately, it was skewered by critics, who complained about its clunky, repetitive combat system and poor loot system in which changes to your gear aren't shown on your character. It was taken down on November 27, 2017.

World of Warcraft: The Greatest MMORPG

When it comes to MMORPGs, *World of Warcraft* stands in a class by itself (Figure 20.13). It is by far the most successful of all such games, not only soaring above other MMORPGs but many other categories of computer games as well. Though Blizzard stopped making its subscriber information public, it's undoubtedly down from its 12 million peak in October 2010—probably somewhere around 5 million. That said, it's still the most popular MMORPG, and Blizzard reports that over 100 million unique accounts have been created since the game launched.

The game's popularity is such that it even served as the basis of an uproarious episode of *South Park.* As with *EverQuest* before it, concerned

FIGURE 20.13   *World of Warcraft* has changed dramatically since 2004. Here's a shot from the latest expansion, "Battle for Azeroth."

citizens around the nation have attempted to liken its addictive gameplay to substance abuse. As usual, these dire warnings serve only as free publicity, vaulting "World of Warcrack" to even greater fame.

First released on November 23, 2004, for Windows and Macintosh, Blizzard's *World of Warcraft* had little trouble getting attention. As you'll recall, Blizzard distinguished itself in 1996 and 2000 with the *Diablo* series, which revolutionized the genre and introduced the action CRPG to millions of mainstream gamers. The company also struck gold with its *Warcraft* and *Starcraft* real-time strategy games, which are still considered among the finest such games ever made. In short, Blizzard had an absolutely stellar reputation for making outrageously successful games, and few doubted that its foray into the MMORPG market would, in so many words, not only wow the competition, but smash them into tiny bits. Furthermore, *World of Warcraft* has heavily influenced single-player, standalone CRPGs, a point we'll address later.

What makes *World of Warcraft* so damned good? The answer, it seems, brings us back to Blizzard's design strategy with *Diablo:* Take an established genre that is appealing only to hardcore gamers, isolate the elements with universal appeal, take out the rest, and make up the difference with superior graphics and polished gameplay. The result is a slimmed down but far more accessible product. In the case of *World of Warcraft,* Blizzard borrowed content from its already well-established *Diablo* and *Warcraft* games—a sensible plan given their terrific brand recognition. In short, what makes *World of Warcraft* so appealing isn't that it's different from all that came before, but that it's better.

That said, Blizzard did address many of the major problems faced by other MMORPGs, such as the often-tedious waiting associated with healing and traveling. Although gamers frequently took these delays as opportunities for socializing, Blizzard opted for a more quest-driven structure. These quests, many of which can be completed solo, feel quite natural to gamers familiar with single-player CRPGs. Fulfilling a quest is rewarded either with money, experience points, items, or some combination of the three, and many quests are strung together in linear chains. Grand narratives play out as you perform quests, culminating in the famed endgame raiding content. Of course, it's also possible to ignore most of these goings on and simply focus on player-versus-player content in battlegrounds and arenas.

One reviewer compared the experience to Disneyland, noting how "almost every location in the game's world is purpose-built, and as such, is home to a constant stream of players running around trying to fulfill some goal."[6] This isn't to say that players don't get to know one another; indeed, with *World of Warcraft* we see collaboration on a grand scale. Many players join guilds and participate in raids, either invading enemy territories or participating in dungeons or "instances." The instance is an interesting but somewhat difficult concept to explain. Essentially, the instance allows multiple groups of players to fulfill quests without fear of interfering with one another. The monsters in instances tend to be more difficult to defeat than those found elsewhere in the game, usually requiring the five-member party to work together in the familiar Tank/Healer/DPS setup. Raids are essentially giant instances, requiring up to forty players with multiple tanks and healers.

The game is set on Azeroth, a world whose constantly warring occupants are divided into the Alliance and the Horde. Each player joins one of these factions, which have their own unique races and classes (and cannot team up or communicate directly with members of the opposing faction). As with other games, characters have combat skills as well as professional or trade skills (Figure 20.14). There are many professions to choose from, such as herbalism, tailoring, and enchanting. The resources one gathers or the products one makes from them can then be traded to other players or sold on the in-game auction house.

World of Warcraft has changed greatly since its "vanilla" release, and with a game this massive, the industry tends to take notice whenever a major innovation is introduced. For instance, the mechanism for finding groups to do instances with has evolved dramatically. Initially, it was a tedious business of announcing one's intentions on the in-game chat system, but this changed on December 8, 2009, with the introduction of the "Dungeon Tool." This system, also called "Looking for Group," automatically sets you up with a party for either a specific or a random dungeon. Another major change seems trivial at first: marking quest givers with bright yellow exclamation points over their heads. Previously, players either had to find these quests on their own by finding and talking to NPCs—or, more likely, consulting a website such as Thottbot, a now-defunct site. There are many more intriguing changes I could talk about here. More recently, Blizzard introduced level scaling, which gives you more options for zones to explore while leveling. However, some players feel it also deprives them of that feeling of gradually growing stronger, since the monsters now get tougher with you.

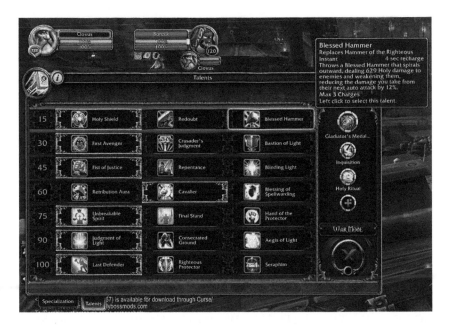

FIGURE 20.14 The game's talents and skill systems have undergone several overhauls. Long gone are the *Diablo II*–esque talent trees. Now talents are easily switched around and are more situational—that is, some are better for leveling, others for raiding, and so on.

Other changes might have angered some players, but ultimately proved their value. One such improvement eliminated a pet peeve of mine: low-level characters begging high level ones to "run them through" dungeons to quickly level up. When I first started playing back in 2007, it was commonplace to see a level 70 character running ahead of a party of low-level characters, obliterating all the monsters with an AOE, or area-of-effect ability. The others tagged along behind, safely out of harm's way, looting treasures from the slain monsters and quickly leveling up. This practice is now much rarer, since experience points are greatly reduced in parties with substantial level differentials.

Blizzard's first expansion was "The Burning Crusade," released on January 16, 2007. The expansion adds two new races, several new instances, a higher level cap, and much more. Since then there have been six more, with the latest being "Battle for Azeroth" in August 2018 (Figure 20.15). These expansions, along with free patches or updates, have added substantial content including new zones, dungeons, and raids, but also often introduced significant changes to the interface and gameplay. One of the

FIGURE 20.15 Blizzard added the Worgen playable race in its "Cataclysm" expansion back in 2010.

most critical of these concerned "talent trees." Originally, characters had to pick talents from three separate trees, similar to *Diablo II*'s system. The number of choices was compelling, but it was also easy to end up with a weak, deficient character. This system was overhauled with the "Mists of Pandaria" expansion, which greatly reduces the number of choices while ensuring that just about any combination is viable.

Naturally, not everyone is satisfied with the game in its present state, and it's not all just nostalgia. Indeed, the same features that some players applaud are decried by others as shameless dumbing down, and the cartoony "pandaren" race introduced in "Mists of Pandaria" irked players who preferred the more somber tone of previous expansions. To accommodate the jaded as well as the curious, Blizzard has been working for some years now on "vanilla" or classic *World of Warcraft* server that would recreate the original experience. Even though I personally am quite fond of the improvements made over the years, as a historian, I would very much enjoy seeing what those early days were like.

World of Warcraft's influence on single-player CRPGs has also been substantial. This is obvious for anyone who has played *Dungeon Siege II*, for instance, which not only looks very much like Blizzard's game, but often plays like its standalone version. 38 Studios and Big Huge Games'

Kingdoms of Amular: Reckoning (2012), Capcom's *Dragon's Dogma* (2012), and BioWare's *Dragon Age* series, which we'll discuss in the next chapter, also show a remarkable resemblance.

Guild Wars

Considering just how large a shadow *World of Warcraft* casts over the MMORPG scene, it can be difficult for a new MMORPG to even get noticed, much less thrive. Yet that's precisely what happened on April 26, 2005, when NCSoft published ArenaNet's *Guild Wars*. ArenaNet was originally founded as Triforge and composed of several ex-Blizzard employees. No doubt, many critics were thinking that if anyone could go toe-to-toe with Blizzard, it'd be a team that understood Blizzard's secret formula.

Guild Wars promised to be an action-oriented MMORPG with a major emphasis on player-versus-player combat. However, the game's key selling point was that there were no monthly fees. Rather than imitate the established MMORPG model, ArenaNet distributes the bandwidth costs associated with running a server across all gamers on the system. In short, everyone who plays the game helps shoulder the burden, though the process is all but transparent to them. Indeed, like *EVE Online,* all players participate in the same persistent universe rather than being segregated into shards.

ArenaNet pushed Blizzard's "nip and tuck" as far as possible, trying to reduce tedium as much as possible. For instance, a teleportation system allows players to zap instantly to areas they've previously unlocked, saving a great deal of boring travel overland. The game borrows the instance structure, which allows players to perform quests at any time without waiting for other groups to clear off. There's even an option for new players to receive a high-level character right from the start, though these characters are usable only in player-versus-player modes.

The game features six different classes, each of which has 150 unique skills. Furthermore, the characters and skills are carefully balanced for the massive campaign. Characters travel all over the world of Tyria in an adventure that culminates in a spectacular endgame.

In March 2007, ArenaNet released *Guild Wars 2* (Figure 20.16). Much was made of its dynamic storytelling system. Instead of the typical quest structure, where a quest giver stands around waiting for you to click on them and receive your next mission, *Guild Wars 2* uses "dynamic events" that are triggered as you interact and explore the world. For instance, you might come across a village being attacked by monsters. If you choose to

FIGURE 20.16 *Guild Wars 2* is one of the more popular alternatives to *World of Warcraft,* but it's much more than that. Its dynamic events system is designed to make it feel more like playing a single-player CRPG. Shown here is an official publicity image by ArenaNet.

fight them, the village might be saved; or you could simply flee the area and let them take it over. Whatever the outcome, the area will change accordingly. In short, *Guild Wars 2* feels more tailor-made than the typical one-size-fits-all experience of most MMORPGs.

The game sold over 5 million copies but became free after the "Heart of Thorns" expansion. Although players don't need to buy the core game anymore, you still need to buy the expansion to get unrestricted access to certain features and a much larger inventory.

Dungeons & Dragons Online

Turbine's *Dungeons & Dragons Online: Stormreach* was published by Atari on February 28, 2006, and it brings us back to where we started: Gary Gygax and Dave Arneson's classic tabletop game. At its core, tabletop role-playing is a social activity. With the right group of friends gathered round the table, *Dungeons & Dragons* becomes far more than just a game, a frivolous diversion for idle youths. Rather, it becomes an exhilarating opportunity for exploring not just the lairs of dragons, but the hearts and imaginations of one's closest friends. It's hard to put into words just how stimulating and beneficial these sessions can become, offering even the most frustrated and introverted person a chance to know what it feels like to be powerful and influential, successful, and accomplished. It is a game that gives mastery to the meek and glory to the geek. To say that it's "just a game" is as silly as calling *Hamlet* just a play or the *Iliad* just a poem.

Yet, as we've seen, almost every attempt to bring *Dungeons & Dragons* to the computer has ignored, either by choice or design, the eminently social aspect of the game. In most cases, these games have compensated with nonplayer characters (NPCs), who, generally in a very crude and contrived fashion, offer the player advice or some service or another. In better games, the NPCs may be as well developed as those in films or novels, though this depth usually comes at the cost of rigid linearity and predetermined conclusions. Other games, such as *The Black Gate, Fable,* or *Oblivion,* attempt to create large networks of NPCs, who are shown (as much as possible) to live their own lives according to their own agendas. Yet even in the best such cases, one needn't strain to see the wires animating these puppets.

There would seem to be at least two solutions to this problem. One is to continue developing the artificial intelligence of the NPCs. Scientists who concern themselves with such matters are generally of two opinions: convincing artificial intelligence is either (a) inevitable or (b) impossible. Although I'm far from an expert on the subject, my belief is that while simulating the real thing may be far beyond our current capacities, it seems more than plausible that we'll someday have replicants who can fake a blush response—or at least ace the Turing Test. Indeed, current research into data mining and analysis seems to be making rapid gains in this direction. If a computer can know that I want a chicken sandwich and onion rings before I do, then surely it's possible to create a genuinely entertaining NPC.

However, a much easier and immediate solution is simply to replace those NPCs with other humans, and that's precisely the draw of the MMORPG. In the best-case scenario, every player will do his or her part to create and maintain the fantasy. However, as anyone knows who has spent time with a MMORPG, the best-case scenario is rarer than dragon daycare. Even the best MMORPGs are overflowing with nincompoops, delinquents, and people whose only idea of fun is to make sure that nobody else has any. As we hinted earlier, *Dungeons & Dragons* is an intimate experience. MMORPGs, on the other hand, tend to be about as intimate as Grand Central Station.

The answer to this dilemma would seem obvious. If the official *Dungeons & Dragons* rules worked with small groups, perhaps they'd work with larger ones. We've already seen countless times how applying the official rules led to some of the best games in the CRPG canon, such as *Pool of Radiance* (1988), *Eye of the Beholder* (1991), *Baldur's Gate* (1998), and *Neverwinter Nights* (2002). Would history repeat itself?

To adapt *Dungeons & Dragons* for the MMORPG market, Wizards of the Coast and Atari turned to Turbine Entertainment. We've already seen its work with *Asheron's Call*, a promising but ultimately unsuccessful game. Sure, that game flopped, but perhaps the developer had learned from the experience. To its credit, Turbine seemed determined to preserve the hardcore nature of the game, no doubt turning away much of the riff raff from the start. The game's box boasts of "unforgiving danger in private dungeons with fiendish traps and foes that punish the foolish." Furthermore, integrated voice chat would bring the experience even closer to the tabletop ideal; why type when you can speak? Perhaps players would even mimic the high-strung tones of the elves or render their dwarf's speech in a suitably Scottish accent. It all sounded too good to be true.

And it was. The finished game was buggy and lacked polish, and many critics complained about the lackluster dungeons and poorly balanced gameplay. The sophisticated turn-based combat of the tabletop game is reduced, predictably, to a frantic real-time click-fest, and although ostensibly the engine is keeping track of rolls and critical hits, everything happens too rapidly for these sequences to be very fun or interesting. Furthermore, the game was surprisingly short—indeed, many players had already maxed out two or more characters a few months after the game's launch (Figure 20.17).

Perhaps the biggest problem, though, was the difficulty of gathering together a good group of fellow players to share in the adventure. Players lucky enough to have friends willing to join their quest had the most fun; others were left scrambling to find someone, anyone, willing to let them into a party. Even when they did gain admittance, these groups were often composed of experienced point-obsessed gamers with little interest in role-playing. Furthermore, many players were either too shy or lacked the equipment to use voice chat, and the few who did were often as annoying as they were garrulous. Reviewers spoke of shrill, overexcited kids who wouldn't have known a real d20 had one struck them in the jaw, hurled there by any number of consenting adults.

Like many MMORPGs that found themselves struggling to stay viable, *D&D Online* eventually shifted in 2009 to a free-to-play model, though

FIGURE 20.17 *Dungeons & Dragons Online* didn't exactly revolutionize the MMORPG scene, but it has its share of fans. Shown here is an official screenshot from Steam.

paying "VIP" members have exclusive access to some features. In 2016, Turbine announced it was passing the torch to Standing Stone Games, a studio composed of ex-Turbine employees. Despite these and other issues, the game proved successful enough to warrant four expansions, the latter of which is planned for early 2019.

The Lord of the Rings Online

Another major MMORPG is *The Lord of the Rings Online* (*LOTRO*), developed by Turbine/Standing Stone Games and released on April 24, 2007 (Figure 20.18). My initial impression was similar to the one for *D&D Online*: Well, it's about time! The writings of J.R.R. Tolkien are scripture for many CRPG and MMORPG fans, and the soaring success of Peter Jackson's movies have made hobbits and balrogs a household name. Beyond the name recognition, though, Middle-earth is one of the most painstakingly developed fictional worlds ever created, a feat owed mostly to Tolkien himself. As Tolkien fans are aware, many places, peoples, and events barely mentioned in the novels are developed extensively elsewhere; it's a lore-lovers dream. In short, a high-quality MMORPG based on *The Lord of the Rings* seemed like just the thing to seize the crown from Blizzard's *World of Warcraft*. Though it hasn't managed to achieve that goal, and has traded hands quite a few times, it's still quite popular and enjoyed by many players across the globe.

FIGURE 20.18 If you're obsessed with Tolkien's Middle-earth, *The Lord of the Rings Online* is the game for you. Image from Steam.

Most of the game's mechanics are similar to other MMORPGs, but there are some intriguing innovations. One is the ability to learn to play a musical instrument such as lute or cowbell, which you can use to perform melodies for nearby players using keyboard macros. Ambitious musicians have even organized their own musical festivals and concerts. Another interesting option is "monster play." Although you can't play as an evil character, you can create a monster and fight with other players in the Ettenmoors.

Of course, what draws most players to this MMORPG is the setting, and the developers have done a great job making it look and feel like the Middle-earth from the novels and movies. However, as the official *LOTRO* wiki points out, not all aspects of lore are compatible with the MMORPG format:

> Middle Earth as described by Professor Tolkien was a pretty empty place, and encounters with hostile monsters were relatively rare, except in a few places like Moria. It would not be practical to develop an MMORPG with no monsters, so Eriador has more hostile orcs than one might assume from reading the *Fellowship of the Ring*. Such is the price we pay for being able to enjoy the wonders of Middle Earth.

That said, to my mind *LOTRO* is about as close as you're going to get to traveling across Middle-earth with a fellowship of hobbits. Isengard, Brandy Hall, Minas Tirith; they're all here waiting to be explored in beautiful detail.

LOTRO went to a free-to-play model in 2010, a move that seems to have worked out well. Of course, serious players will soon be spending money, either to unlock content or subscribe as a VIP. There have been six expansions to date.

The Elder Scrolls Online

In April 2014, Bethesda published *The Elder Scrolls Online (TESO)*, a MMORPG by ZeniMax Online Studios (Figure 20.19). As we saw in Chapter 14, Bethesda's *Elder Scrolls* CRPGs are tremendously popular, with a great mix of action combat, deep role-playing mechanics, and a massive amount of lore that's built up over the course of the series. However, as much fun as it may be to explore Tamriel on your own, traveling with some friends could make it even better—or would it?

Like most MMORPGs, *TESO* had a rocky start and received mixed reviews in the press, mostly over its bugs and subscription model. However, by 2015 most of these issues had been addressed, and the subscription model was retired. The new system still requires you to purchase the game, but subscriptions are optional and grant perks such as faster leveling.

FIGURE 20.19 *The Elder Scrolls Online* is an effort to adapt the award-winning gameworld and gameplay of *The Elder Scrolls* CRPGs to the MMORPG format.

The game is set hundreds of years before the events in the single-player games. Your primary goal is to reclaim your soul from the Daedric Prince Molag Bal, but there's plenty of other possibilities for adventure. Unlike many MMORPGs, *TESO*'s zones, dungeons, and PVP areas are scaled to your character's level, so there's less need to worry about getting trounced as you explore Tamriel. Combat is comparable to the single-player games, consisting of two basic attacks (light and heavy), blocks, and dodges. Of course, to maintain game balance you're not allowed to do some of the things some people enjoy doing in Skyrim, such as wantonly slaughtering NPCs. To date ZeniMax has released two expansions or "chapters," including "Morrowind" and "Summerset."

Compared to *World of Warcraft*, *TESO* certainly has some things going for it, especially if you prefer its action-based combat to *World of Warcraft*'s cooldown system. Many players also rave about its crafting system, graphics, and high-quality storytelling.

THE CURRENT STATE OF MMORPGs

Reliable numbers are hard to come by, but as of this writing, *World of Warcraft*, *Guild Wars 2*, and *Final Fantasy XIV* seem to be the top three MMORPGs. However, there are many, many more MMORPGs out there than we've covered in this chapter. See the Bestiary in the appendix for entries on **Age of Conan, Aion, Black Desert Online, Neverwinter, Star Trek Online, Tera**, and **Wildstar**.

Back in 2007, it seemed a fair question to ask whether any MMORPG could beat *World of Warcraft*, and most reviews of new MMORPGs were framed accordingly. However, time has shown that it's mostly irrelevant; there are plenty of gamers out there willing to play and support smaller MMORPGs and thus make them sustainable, particularly if you can play it on console—Blizzard has yet to make a console client for its *World of Warcraft* game, and I doubt it ever will.

A more interesting question is how the current bevy of financial models will evolve. As we've seen, many MMORPGs begin as a retail game with a required monthly subscription, but soon end up as some version of free-to-play. This usually involves locking certain content or "quality of life" improvements behind paywalls.

However, another option exists: pay-to-win. Fans of MMORPGs typically balk at the idea, insisting that there should be a level playing field based solely on personal skill, not financial resources. For example, while it's fine to sell "cosmetic" items such as hats or pets that have no impact on stats, selling more powerful gear or armor than you can craft or find in the game is frowned upon. However, others have no problem with the idea. After all, we're well accustomed to folks lavishing large sums of money to get an edge in their favorite sport or hobby. If you don't object to your golfing buddy buying better clubs than yours, why get upset if your enemies in PVP can buy superior weapons? The analogy falls flat, of course—golfing is still primarily a game of skill; an expert golfer with a cheap set of clubs will still prevail over an amateur with the best equipment money can buy. I expect that eventually MMORPGs will achieve this same compromise—spending lots of money might give you an edge, but never guarantee success, especially against competent players.

Indeed, I think a pay-to-win model of some sort might be a boon for busy gamers, especially when it comes to endgame content like raiding. Indeed, it can be quite frustrating to return to a game after a few months and find that your guild is no longer willing to take you along on a raid—you've fallen too far behind in gear or experience, and depending on your schedule, it might take you months to catch up. By that time, they may have moved on to a new raid, and thus the cycle repeats! I imagine many gamers in this situation would gladly pay to skip the grinding and be able to raid with their friends again.

In any case, it'll be interesting to see if *World of Warcraft* will still be the dominant MMORPG when it comes time to write the third edition of this book—and, even if it is, whether it will even resemble the game in its present state.

NOTES

1. See *The Geek's Guide to the Galaxy*'s "Interview: Richard Garriott" for lightspeedmagazine.com from 2014.
2. See Harmer's "Review in Progress #1—First Steps in New Britannia" on mmorpg.com.
3. See Richard Purchese's 2018 interview with Garriott, "Is Richard Garriott's Shroud of the Avatar on the Ropes?" on eurogamer.net.
4. See http://ps2.gamespy.com/playstation-2/phantasy-star-universe/746414p1. html.
5. For details, see Joe Blancato's "Jumpgate: EVE's Devs and the Friends They Keep" at http://www.escapistmagazine.com/articles/view/editorials/ op-ed/847-Jump-gate-EVE-s-Devs-and-the-Friends-They-Keep.
6. See Allen Rausch's review at http://pc.gamespy.com/pc/world-of-warcraft/ 571585p1.html.

CHAPTER 21

The Late Modern Age

What I call the Late Modern Age begins in 2006 and is still ongoing, and it's not clear when it'll end. Perhaps a breakthrough in virtual or augmented reality might do it, but barring that or some other unforeseen breakthrough, we'll be stuck in this era for quite some time—not that that's a bad thing!

Therefore it makes more sense at this point to talk about "Late Modern" as a style rather than an era of games. It's synonymous with so-called Triple-A games, that is, games produced with the largest budgets and highest production values, rivaling or exceeding that of Hollywood blockbusters. Almost all of them are targeted primarily at consoles and intended to be played with a game controller rather than keyboard and mouse—although options for the latter are common (if not always effective) on their Windows or Mac versions. These are big games made by massive studios for the widest possible audience.

The major players we'll cover in this chapter are BioWare (*Mass Effect* and *Dragon Age*), Bethesda (*The Elder Scrolls* and *Fallout*), and CD Projekt Red (*The Witcher*). There's also a Czech company named Warhorse Studios, whose award-winning *Kingdom Come: Deliverance* (2018) shows that even games with the visuals and production values of AAA games can still be indies at heart. For many CRPG fans, these series represent the best the genre has produced, but for some they're merely dumbed-down versions of the more sophisticated games that came before. In any case, since most of these games are so recent and well known, I'll limit myself here to their most innovative, influential, or controversial aspects.

BETHESDA

Oblivion

Bethesda's *Oblivion* is the fourth in its *Elder Scrolls* series of first-person 3D CRPGs that we introduced back in Chapter 14. It was published simultaneously in March 2006 for Sony's PlayStation 3 (PS3), the Xbox 360, and Windows. As you'll recall, *Morrowind* was the first of the series available for consoles, where it performed admirably despite (or perhaps because of) its complexity compared to most big-budget Xbox games. However, *Oblivion* is the game that really brought *The Elder Scrolls* series to the mainstream. It won several awards even before it hit the shelf, and it received the "Best RPG of E3" from every major gaming magazine. *Computer Games* magazine gushed that it was "the best role-playing game ever made,"[1] though cooler heads were more reserved in their praise.

Oblivion has much in common with the earlier *Morrowind*. Again we have the open-ended gameplay across a gigantic gameworld, but here you have a clear guiding mission: find the hidden heir to the throne and close the gates of Oblivion, through which demons have been invading the world of Tamriel. However, you're free to ignore this quest, and a great part of the fun is simply exploring, soaking up the spectacular scenery and investigating every nook and cranny in search of loot. As with *Morrowind*, completing the main quest leaves the majority of the world still unexplored, so it pays to take the roads less traveled. There are countless optional sidequests and always something interesting to do; *Oblivion* nails the "just five more minutes" quality of the most addictive games.

The game world is populated by over 1,000 characters, each equipped with Bethesda's "Radiant AI" system. The characters respond to their environment and maintain convincing schedules. It's a subtle thing, but the fact that NPCs go to bed instead of standing in one spot all day and night instills a sense of realism. The characters have convincing facial animations, lip-syncing, and quality voice acting—which include the talents of Patrick Stewart as the emperor (Figure 21.1).

Unlike *Morrowind*, which originated on Windows and was ported to the Xbox later, *Oblivion* was done the other way around, and it shows. Bringing up the quest journal, for instance, requires navigating several nested menus rather than just pushing a key on the keyboard. The interface is clearly designed to accommodate game controllers, and it should've been redesigned for PC (Figure 21.2). Both console and PC versions are infested with bugs, including some that crash the game.

FIGURE 21.1 *Oblivion* was praised for its realistic facial animations and voice acting. The images shown in this section are from the Game of the Year Edition.

It might be surprising at first that *Oblivion* doesn't offer multiplayer, but this may be an asset rather than a limitation. Indeed, a key selling point of the game is that all the characters you encounter in *Oblivion* are, well, in character, behaving (at least by design) in a manner appropriate to their context. The draw here is that of entering a fictional but fully convincing world—a sort of virtual Renaissance fair. In short, you don't have to worry about other players shattering your suspension of disbelief (at the very least).

Since *Morrowind*'s construction set proved so popular, Bethesda released a similar tool for the Windows version of *Oblivion*. Hundreds of users contributed mods, a practice that continues to this day. Again, most of them consist only of a few new items, but others alter the interface or graphics or add fresh content. Anyone playing the game today will surely

FIGURE 21.2 Hitting targets with a bow takes practice and a steady hand.

want the "Unofficial Oblivion Patch," which fixes nearly 2,000 bugs, or the "Character Overhaul," which dramatically improves the character art. The site Nexus Mods even has a mod for managing *Oblivion* mods! It's truly impressive to see the variety of mods available, but also the diversity of the modders; it's truly an international phenomenon.

However, is *Oblivion* good enough to warrant the praise of "best RPG ever made"? I think it's a great candidate for best CRPG of 2006, but, honestly, there wasn't much competition at the time. Indeed, many fans of the series prefer its prequel, *Morrowind*. Almost everyone complains about the repetitiveness of the dungeons, and others object to the level scaling. Rather than risk letting players get too powerful, *Oblivion*'s designers chose to simply increase the monsters' stats and gear along with the player's. This might look good on paper, but the effect is to reduce that feeling of gradually becoming more powerful. Level scaling amounts to moving the goalposts. Not everyone agrees with that assessment, of course, and there is the idea that it makes exploring each part of the gameworld consistently challenging.

Another crucial change concerns combat. Whereas *Morrowind* still employs conventional dice-rolling mechanics for things like hitting or dodging, *Oblivion* puts the focus on the player's own timing and precision with the controller. For example, in *Morrowind,* whether you successfully block an enemy's attack with your shield is determined by your character's blocking skill. In *Oblivion,* by contrast, you block by hitting the designating button for blocking. Likewise, hitting or missing in *Oblivion* is now a matter of being in range, not a matter of the character's skill or attributes. Even lock picking takes physical skill (Figure 21.3). In short, *Oblivion* moves the series further away from the abstraction of tabletop RPGs and towards the physicality of an action game.

Skyrim

If *Oblivion* gets fainter praise today than it did then, it's mostly because the next entry in the series, *The Elder Scrolls V: Skyrim,* almost completely overshadows it (Figure 21.4). First published in 2011 for Windows, Xbox 360, and PS3, *Skyrim* was a massive hit, selling over 7 million copies just in its first week and now among the best-selling games of all time. When it was rereleased in 2016 as *The Elder Scrolls V: Skyrim Special Edition,* it again soared to the top of the charts, winning 200 game-of-the-year awards and selling nearly a million units during its opening week. As of this writing, the two editions are still performing well on Steam, at number 40 and

FIGURE 21.3 Rather than just making lock-picking a matter of a character skill, *Oblivion* makes it physical. Whether that also makes it more fun is a matter of taste.

number 38, respectively, according to *Steamcharts*. In short, *Skyrim* is still a strong seller and a dominating feature on the CRPG landscape.

Of course, the first thing that players moving from *Oblivion* to *Skyrim* note are the enhanced audiovisuals made possible by Bethesda's Creation engine. Rather than license an existing engine as it had done with *Oblivion* (which had used Havok), Bethesda relied on its own programmers. The result was a greater draw distance, better shadows, and more realistic plants and trees that moved with the wind. Since so much of the game is set in winter climates, the team implemented dynamic falling snow. There are many other aspects I could talk about, but suffice it to say that you see a clear progression from the previous games, especially for PC owners with the latest graphics hardware.

FIGURE 21.4 *Skyrim* has plenty of breathtaking vistas that make you yearn to explore.

FIGURE 21.5   Combat in *Skyrim* tends to be quick and dirty.

Underneath this shiny veneer are some major changes to the gameplay mechanics (Figure 21.5). First and foremost, the character class system was removed altogether. Instead of choosing at the outset whether to be a mage or warrior, players create whatever hybrids they want by working on a skill and modifying it with perks. For instance, repeatedly casting destruction spells gradually raises your Destruction magic skill. Once you get it high enough, you can apply a perk point (acquired by leveling your character) to gain the "Novice Destruction" perk, which halves the magick cost of novice level Destruction spells. Each skill has its requisite set of perks, which branch out and are gated by skill caps. This system really opens up a myriad of possibilities for customizing your character and enhancing your playstyle, and it even looks cool to boot (Figure 21.6). In addition to magic and physical attacks, you can also perform "Shouts," made possible by your character's status as a "Dragonborn."

Oblivion's eight attributes are reduced to a mere three for *Skyrim*: Health, Magicka, and Stamina. This might sound like a severe dumbing down, but not according to the game's director, Todd Howard:

In *Oblivion* you have your eight attributes and 21 skills. Now you have 18 skills and three attributes. What we found is that all those attributes actually did something else. A fan may say "You removed my eight attributes!," and my answer is, which ones do you want? They're all a trickle down to something else. Now when you level up you can just raise your Magicka. In *Oblivion* you have to raise your Intelligence knowing that you're Intelligence raises your Magicka.[2]

FIGURE 21.6 *Skyrim* doesn't skimp on the skill trees, or constellations as they're represented here. It's a flexible and versatile system that encourages experimentation.

Both *Oblivion* and *Morrowind* have their defenders, of course, but I have to agree with Howard on this one. These changes simply reduce some unnecessary complexity and make leveling up more straightforward.

Much was made of *Skyrim*'s "Radiant Story" system that dynamically creates quests tailored for the character. Howard describes it this way:

> You go into town, you want to make friends with somebody, we'll generate a little quest for him that seems simple and that it's ok to go through the radiant story system. For a bigger quest, we want somebody who you're enemies with. We want to use him in that quest in some way. We'll pick the closest person who hates the player. He fills in that role.[3]

It sounds good in theory, but the team quickly realized that the procedurally generated content didn't satisfy gamers. According to Bruce Nesmith, Bethesda's director of design, "Players expect from game developers that we use our creativity to create content they want to experience. If we pass the buck to a system, it's not the same."[4] To prevent the repetitive or nonsensical outcomes we've seen in other procedurally generated games, the team wisely limited them to more mundane quests. There's still some repetition with the AI system; the often-heard line "I took an arrow in the knee" even became a meme.

But all in all, there's certainly much more to like about *Skyrim* than hate, even if I roll my eyes at the idea of killing dragons so early and easily in the game. Whereas most CRPGs limit you to rats and other wimpy monsters at the early stages of the game, *Skyrim* wants to make you feel extremely powerful from the start. This is likely a matter of personal taste—or perhaps evidence of a generational divide, especially given the game's extraordinary success and enduring popularity with the "Participation Trophy" generation.

The Fallout over *Fallout*

War never changes, but war is not experienced the same way in the *Fallout* series. In between *Oblivion* and *Skyrim,* Bethesda Game Studios developed *Fallout 3* (2008) for Windows and consoles—though we'd argue it's not so much a sequel than a reimagining of the series we discussed in Chapter 16. Rather than simply update the audiovisuals and user interface of the original games, which were turn-based, isometric games, Bethesda stuck with the first-person/third-person engine it had developed for *Oblivion,* albeit with a few *Fallout*-specific modifications. The move didn't please purists, but it sold tremendously well and received a number of prestigious awards.

There's much we could talk about here, but for our purposes the focus should be on the innovations Bethesda made to capture some semblance of the original game's mechanics. By far the most significant of these is V.A.T.S., or the Vault-Tec Assisted Targeting System (Figure 21.7). The idea

FIGURE 21.7   The V.A.T.S. system is *Fallout 3*'s compromise between first-person shooter style action and turn-based combat.

behind V.A.T.S. is to offer players a turn-based alternative to the real-time combat of a standard shooter game.

The system works as follows. First, you hit V to enter V.A.T.S. mode, which pauses the game and overlays a series of tags on various body part of the selected enemy. Each tag shows the likelihood of hitting the body part in question with your ranged weapon (melee attacks can't target a specific body part) and its current condition. Successfully hitting and bringing a body part's condition down to zero cripples it and has bonus effects. For example, crippling a leg slows down the enemy's running and keeps him or her from jumping or charging. How much you can do in V.A.T.S. depends on an attribute called "Action Points." Once these are used up, you have to leave V.A.T.S. mode and wait for your action points to recharge. The number of action points you have available depends on your agility attribute as well as certain perks such as "Action Boy" and "Grim Reaper's Sprint" (Figures 21.8 and 21.9).

Using V.A.T.S. isn't required; you can play the game as a standard shooter game. However, it's a crucial innovation, since it moves the game from the action RPG category toward something much closer to the CRPG. As noted back in Chapter 1, I define a pure CRPG as a game where the character's skill is much more vital than the player's own skill at the keyboard, mouse, or game controller. *Fallout 3*'s V.A.T.S. system doesn't eliminate the need for player skill entirely, but it does

FIGURE 21.8 You can recruit some interesting companions in *Fallout 3*. Shown here is Fawkes, a super mutant with a tragic history.

FIGURE 21.9 Instead of representing the game as a computer simulation as in the original *Fallout*, in the third game you're out roaming the wasteland with your Pip-Boy on your wrist.

dramatically reduce the need for it, especially if you take the requisite perks and stat bonus to maximize it.

Rather than develop *Fallout 4* right away, Bethesda turned to Obsidian Entertainment to produce *Fallout: New Vegas* in 2010 (Figure 21.10). Designed by Josh Sawyer, *New Vegas* offers several improvements over *Fallout 3* and is an even better game. Beyond a plethora of minor but welcome improvements, the game re-introduces the reputation system employed from the early games. In short, now you can earn (or lose) reputation with eight different factions. Your goal is not to try to gain fame with each faction, however—the factions are in competition with each other, and you can't keep them all satisfied. Furthermore, none of the factions are righteous, even if they think of themselves that way. It doesn't take you long to get immersed in some really high stakes decisions, and you may well spend more time weighing your ethics than your tactics!

Bethesda took their time developing *Fallout 4,* not releasing it until November 10, 2015 (Figures 21.11 and 21.12). Besides the expected improvements in audiovisuals, it adds the ability to manage settlements and a more expansive crafting system. You don't have to deal with them at all to win the game, but they're a great way to get items and money among other benefits. Of course, you'll have to work to make sure your settlers are fed and

FIGURE 21.13 *Jade Empire* is the most action-oriented of BioWare's RPGs. It plays more like a fighting game, but there are more than enough RPG mechanics to make it more than just a brawler.

Jade Empire features real-time combat and is a far cry from the fantastic turn-based battles in *Knights of the Old Republic* (Figure 21.13). In this game, you control a character shown in third-person, who can perform maneuvers and feats of magic divided into five categories: Martial, Magic, Weapon, Transformation, and Support. These had their own styles, such as Martial's Leaping Tiger and Thousand Cuts, each with advantages and disadvantages. For instance, my favorite, Drunken Master, does impressive damage, but can be used only briefly. You also need to have Henpecked Hou as your follower so he can toss you the wine jugs that activate this style.

The combat system certainly looks impressive on paper, but not everyone was satisfied. Greg Kasavin of GameSpot writes the following in his review:

> In practice, most battles work like this: You get close to an enemy and start pushing A. When the enemy blocks (which isn't often), you press X. If the enemy attacks, you vault over him with button B ... and repeat as necessary. This same strategy works on literally every enemy in the game, from the least powerful to the most powerful.

In any case, the preponderance of action almost makes some hesitate to call it an RPG at all. It's reminiscent of Origin's **Moebius: The Orb of Celestial Harmony**, a relatively obscure beat 'em hybrid from 1985 that covered a lot of the same territory. Neither of these games really led to much. My guess is that there just aren't enough gamers out there who want to see these genres mixed.

In any case, the story and setting of *Jade Empire* are enough for me to recommend it, and it did receive several industry awards. Nevertheless, a sequel seems unlikely, and Sam Brooks of *The Spinoff* called it "the black sheep of BioWare's library." On a positive note, unlike certain other games from BioWare, this one has a great surprise ending that's well worth the effort it takes to get there.

Mass Effect

In 2007, BioWare launched *Mass Effect,* another original action RPG (Figures 21.14 and 21.15). Rather than hand-to-hand combat, though, this one integrates third-person shooter style gameplay. Originally intended as a trilogy, the franchise now has four games under its belt, but the latest one—*Andromeda*—received particularly harsh reviews and may be the last of the series. Even the critically acclaimed first game has its flaws, of course, but in my estimation it's one of the finest sci-fi action RPGs to date.

The game is set in the year 2183. Humans have invented faster-than-light travel and discovered that they are only one of several advanced

FIGURE 21.14   The first *Mass Effect* is a great synthesis of shooter, role-playing, and space sim mechanics. It's known for its great characters and dialog.

FIGURE 21.15 *Mass Effect* trades the turn-based combat of *KOTOR* for intense action sequences inspired by third-person shooters like Epic Games' *Gears of War*, which debuted a year earlier.

civilizations in the Milky Way galaxy. Your character, Commander Shepard of the Systems Alliance Military, is an elite soldier whose ultimate quest is to prevent a machine race from invading and conquering the galaxy. Fulfilling this quest will take Shepard all over the galaxy in the starship Normandy. Along the way, he (or she, if you choose the female option) meets potential allies as well as plenty of dangerous foes and even romantic partners.

The RPG mechanics are relatively straightforward. Shepard can be any one of six classes: Soldier, Engineer, Adept, Infiltrator, Vanguard, or Sentinel. The first three of these are specialized in Combat, Tech, and Biotics, respectively, with the others being combinations of these. Instead of magic, a Biotic character uses mental powers to manipulate objects or enemies in the environment. When characters level, they gain talent points to improve skills or abilities. For instance, Biotic talents include Barrier, a biotic field that protects you from weapon fire. Raising the level of a talent increases their effect, but can also unlock other talents like Stasis, which freezes enemies in place. You can also upgrade your weapons and load them with special ammo.

Shepard can take two teammates on away missions, and this is where most of the fun comes in. Each of the six characters has distinct appearances, backstories, and personalities in addition to their fighting skills. My favorite character is Garrus Vakarian, a C-Sec officer. He's a "turian," a race characterized by their disciplined military culture and metallic carapaces. If you recruit and earn Garrus' trust, he gives you a mission to track down Dr. Saleon, a geneticist who was running an illegal organ trading scheme. The friendship that develops between Shepard and Garrus throughout the game is quite effective and one of the best I've experienced in a CRPG. Another intriguingly flawed character is the beautiful Ashley Williams, a female marine who Shepard can romance. If you allow the romance to progress to its conclusion, there's a sex scene with nudity—one of several reasons the ESRB rated the game M (Mature).

In addition to the third-person shooter style gameplay, *Mass Effect* also has a six-wheeled all-terrain vehicle called the Mako. It looks neat, but the controls are clunky, especially in combat. In any case, it's fun at first to land on uncharted planets to investigate anomalies or just explore, but there's usually not much there to reward the effort.

The next game, *Mass Effect 2*, followed in 2010 and is generally regarded as the best in the series (Figure 21.16). It takes character development to a new level, giving us companions whose flaws are as meaningful as their assets. Indeed, though combat and squad management are improved for this game, it's really the relationships between and among your squadmates

FIGURE 21.16 *Mass Effect 2* is my pick for the best game in the series.

that really make it special. For example, Miranda Lawson is Shepard's second-in-command and potential love interest. She joined Cerberus, a pro-human paramilitary group, mostly as a way to escape her overbearing father, who artificially created her by doubling his X chromosome. It's hard not to get drawn into Miranda's past and conflicting loyalties. Her voice and face are provided by Yvonne Strahovski, who received the "Best Performance by a Human Female" Spike Video Game Award for her efforts.

Mass Effect 3 came two years later, and though initial reactions were positive, attention abruptly swerved to the game's ending. I won't go into the details here, but suffice it to say it is not a worthy conclusion to an otherwise great series. Plenty of lesser games might have gotten away with it, but not a series that had spent so much time expertly building up so many wonderful story arcs over the course of three long games, not to mention the impression that BioWare really valued its players' agency. BioWare eventually overhauled some of the endings in an effort to placate angry fans, but the damage had been done. At the risk of sounding flippant, though, it says a lot about the overall quality of these games that fans got so worked about the endings—if these were lesser games, nobody would've cared.

The latest installment is *Mass Effect: Andromeda* from 2017. Perhaps as a way to sidestep the controversy around the third game, this one is set in an entirely different galaxy. Unfortunately, this time there are more problems than an ineffective conclusion. In the words of Arthur Gies' review of it for Polygon, "It's a total goddamned mess." It's hard to know where to start; critics blast everything from the user interface to the poor quality writing. GameSpot's Scott Butterworth claims that after the first few hours he'd "encountered unconvincing animations, bog standard missions, clunky user interface, stilted dialogue—basically every red flag you hope to avoid when approaching a lengthy shooter-RPG." My opinion of the game isn't as harsh as some, but even I have to admit it's difficult to recall many truly meaningful moments. It's only a pale imitation of the epic *Mass Effect 2*.

So what happened? Kotaku's Jason Schreier spent some three months investigating that question and produced a lengthy expose. According to him, the production was "marred by a director change, multiple major re-scopes, an understaffed animation team, technological challenges, communication issues, office politics, a compressed timeline, and brutal crunch." In other words, pretty much everything that could've gone wrong did go wrong.

Rumors insisted that Electronic Arts and BioWare were done with *Mass Effect*, but they appear to have been unfounded. Casey Hudson, BioWare's general manager, posted on the BioWare blog that "we hear loud and clear the interest in BioWare doing more *Dragon Age* and *Mass Effect*," and claimed that secret teams were currently working on them. Let's just hope that if there any future *Mass Effect* games, they will live up to the standard set by the first two.

Dragon Age

BioWare released the first of its new line of fantasy-themed CRPGs, *Dragon Age: Origins (DA:O)*, in November 2009, just two months before *Mass Effect 2* (Figure 21.17). It's a very different game than that series, especially in terms of combat. Whereas the *Mass Effect* series employs third-person shooter mechanics, *Dragon Age: Origins* feels more like an updated form of the real time with pause combat seen in BioWare's *Baldur's Gate* series. However, as with *Mass Effect* or *Knights of the Old Republic,* the focus is on building complex relationships with a variety of well-developed characters.

DA:O has much in common with older CRPGs. You start by creating your own character, choosing a race, gender, and customizing their appearance. Classes are limited to warriors, mages, or rogues, though later you

FIGURE 21.17 *Dragon Age: Origins* employs a much different combat mode than other Late Modern CRPGs. As with *Neverwinter Nights,* you can pause the battle to assess the battlefield and issue orders.

can specialize in one of four specializations per class. For example, mages can become arcane warriors, who use conventional weapons in addition to magic, blood mages who practice forbidden magic, shapeshifters, or spirit healers. All classes have special abilities called talents or spells, broken into three categories: Activated, Passive, and Sustained. The Activated and Passive are what you'd expect, but the concept of a Sustained ability is more interesting. Those stay activated until you turn them off or run out of energy. The trade-off is that it reduces the amount of overall mana or stamina you have available. An example is the rogue and warrior talent called "Rapid Shot," which lets an archer fire with greater speed, but at the cost of critical hit opportunities. The by-now familiar action or "quickbar" runs across the bottom of the screen, where you can arrange abilities and "quick-use items" such as potions. *WoW*-esque cooldown timers are superimposed over these slots where appropriate.

Combat is probably the game's most interesting aspect. At first, it might seem straight out of the *WoW* playbook—you're essentially just selecting which enemies to attack and what abilities to use, then waiting for the cooldowns to wear off. However, in this game you can switch characters to take direct control of your party members; otherwise they are controlled by the AI, which I'll discuss in a moment. You can also pause the game to issue orders, a vital feature in our experience. You can also switch to a top-down tactical view to get a better perspective on the action.

DA:O's AI system is quite nuanced, allowing you to select or customize your companions tactics. You can issue directives as precise as "use health poultice: least powerful" when the character's health falls below 50 percent—or just select a preset such as "Archer" or "Defender." As with *Mass Effect* or *KOTOR,* you can swap characters in and out of your party as desired; the rest stay back at base camp.

It seems clear that BioWare was fed up with paying to license preexisting campaign settings such as *Forgotten Realms* and *Star Wars;* it's safe to say that *DA:O* is to *Neverwinter Nights* what *Mass Effect* was to *KOTOR.* The trick, of course, is to create something distinctive enough from these to avoid infringement, but also familiar enough to attract fans of those games.

In the case of *DA:O,* BioWare created a world called "Thedas" with a strong focus on social class. There's plenty of racism and bigotry on display, but not in ways you might expect. The familiar fantasy races are here, but the writers turn many of the stereotypes on their head. Most strikingly, elves, who are usually regarded as superior to humans in other games, are treated here as second-class citizens. The dwarves, meanwhile, seem to have missed the memo requiring them to speak with thick Scottish accents.

Magic is tightly controlled by the "Chantry," whose Templars search out those using it without their sanction. Your character is a "Grey Warden," an order dedicated to stamping out the demonic "Darkspawn," who periodically emerge from deep underground to terrorize the surface dwellers. Of course, there's plenty of political intrigue at all levels, and you'll have to make plenty of tough ethical decisions as you progress through the game (Figure 21.18).

Of course, the real draw in these games is the characters you meet and get to know during your adventures. By far, my favorite is Morrigan, a sexy, cynical shapeshifter who must have been inspired by Servalan (played by Jacqueline Pearce) from the old British sci-fi show *Blakes 7.* Raised by a reclusive evil witch named Flemeth, Morrigan is a complex character with understandable, if admittedly twisted, motives. I won't spoil the story here, but I can sincerely say that no quest has ever affected me the way "Morrigan's Ritual" did in this game.

DA:O wasn't perfect; I found myself wrestling with the camera controls, and others complained about balance or maintaining control during combat. My biggest gripe is the overuse of blood spatter. I don't know about you, but I wouldn't casually stroll back to camp after a battle, smiling and chatting, with sixteen gallons of blood on my face. Still, none of this is enough to put me off the game, which is still one of my favorites.

FIGURE 21.18 There are several possible love interests in *Dragon Age: Origins.* Shown here is Leliana, a human rogue, bard, and Chantry sister.

Dragon Age II

The inevitable sequel, *Dragon Age II,* appeared in March 2011. It's generally regarded as the weakest of the series so far, though it's not hard to find fans who prefer it to the rest (Figure 21.19). Rather than let you create your own character, you're thrust into the role of Hawke—a refugee who, over the course of three acts set three years apart, rises from misery and obscurity to become the Champion of Kirkwall. It's quite a departure from the previous game; here, you never leave the city walls. Furthermore, rather than being responsible for the game's major events, you're swept along by them. This arguably more progressive approach to a CRPG narrative proved derisive; the very features lauded by some were reviled by others. It largely comes down to a matter of taste. A more objective criticism is the drabness of the city and an overreliance on recycled assets.

According to Mike Laidlaw, the game's lead designer, the goal with combat was intended to please both action-oriented and tactically minded gamers alike: "*Dragon Age 2* can be played with the smooth responsive

FIGURE 21.19   BioWare tried to please everyone with the combat in *Dragon Age II,* but didn't quite succeed. Likewise, the carefully staged story impressed critics but disappointed gamers hoping for another open world adventure.

controls of an action RPG or more tactically, pausing and controlling your actions that way. Or of course, any combination of the two."[6] However, some claimed the first mode was little more than "button mashing," whereas the latter failed due to the way enemies always come in waves, randomly spawning in and making it difficult to position your group or plan effectively. A final criticism involves the camera—you can't zoom it out as far.

Dragon Age II brought some interesting ideas to the table, including a politically charged story and a three-act structure that gives us insights into separate periods of Hawke's life. Opinions on the game's combat vary, but it's not like it was perfect in *Origins,* either. If anything, BioWare went a little too far to please the action combat crowd at the expense of tactically minded players like me. Thankfully, the next game in the series does a better job catering to both types of gamers.

Dragon Age: Inquisition

The latest game in the series, *Dragon Age: Inquisition,* was published in 2014 and in many ways seems to be an effort, like any great sequel, to combine the best of the previous games while addressing their flaws (Figure 21.20). It's certainly one of the best Late Modern CRPGs I've seen yet, featuring a huge, beautiful world to explore, great characters, fun combat, and, well, pretty much everything we've come to expect from a BioWare flagship title.

As noted in our earlier discussion of *Fallout,* in this book a pure CRPG should privilege the character's skills over the player's. However, it seems

FIGURE 21.20 *Dragon Age: Inquisition* is a beautiful game bursting with content. You can even embrace your interior design and fashion sense. For me, though, nothing beats a good battle with … whatever the hell this thing is.

that most gamers prefer the excitement of action over tactical combat, and most Late Modern games cater to them almost exclusively. It must have been tempting for Bethesda and BioWare to follow suit, which is why I'm grateful to them for striving to integrate both styles of gameplay.

To that end, the tactical view is back in *Dragon Age: Inquisition*, and the camera zoom is improved, giving you a better view and control over the battle. Unlike the previous game with its randomized waves, here you can employ tactics to better position your troops, set traps, and plan attacks.

Furthermore, instead of shoehorning you into a well-defined character, BioWare wisely lets you create your own, choosing whatever race, appearance, class, and gender you like. In any case, your character is an "Inquisitor," charged with closing the Breach—a tear in the veil through which demons are pouring into Thedas. As always, you won't have to go it alone, recruiting plenty of well-developed and outright likeable characters to help you. As with most Late Modern games, you also have a home base (Skyhold fortress) to outfit and customize as you see fit.

One aspect of the game that was overhyped was multiplayer. I say "hyped" because instead of letting you co-op the regular campaign with a friend, the experience was limited to an entirely separate lackluster campaign. It's arguably better than no multiplayer at all, but a far cry from the immensely enjoyable co-op available in *Divinity: Original Sin,* covered in the next chapter.

Still, there's little doubt that *Dragon Age: Inquisition* is a better game than its predecessor, and even better than *Origins* in the eyes of many.

CD PROJEKT RED

The Witcher

Let's talk now about a CRPG series based on the novels of Polish author Andrzej Sapkowski: *The Witcher* (Figure 21.21). Sapkowki's novels aren't as well known in the United States as in eastern Europe, but thanks to these games, many of us are familiar with his main character, the white-haired Geralt of Rivia, and the dark fantasy world he inhabits.

In *The Witcher* mythos, a "witcher" is a professional monster hunter, specially trained, conditioned, and enhanced with supernatural powers. Although witchers are frequently called upon to deal with all manner of ferocious beasts, they're just as frequently the target of suspicion, if not outright hatred by the very people they seek to protect—often because they charge a fee for their services. The level of cultural, social, and political

FIGURE 21.21   *The Witcher* is known for its challenging action combat, but also its rich story and gameworld. Shown here is the Enhanced Edition.

depth in *The Witcher* novels and games is just as crucial to their success as their intense action-based combat and frank approaches to love and sex.

The first game, simply titled *The Witcher,* was developed by CD Projekt Red and published by Atari in 2007 (Figure 21.22). It was built with BioWare's Aurora engine, the engine used for *Neverwinter Nights,* though it supplied its own rendering module. However, the combat system, which is based on actual medieval swordplay, is much different and varies depending on whether you choose one of the two isometric views (high and low) or the over-the-shoulder (OTS) option. This choice profoundly affects the gameplay. In the isometric mode, you move by clicking on the ground wherever you want Geralt to move, whereas in OTS mode, you

FIGURE 21.22   The first *Witcher* game has an isometric mode that plays more like an older CRPG. Not many people prefer it to the OTS mode, but it is a nice alternative.

move with the WASD keys. Combat also works differently. For instance, in isometric mode, you dodge by double-clicking somewhere away from the monster, whereas in OTS mode you double-click a direction button. Much to my chagrin, the isometric option isn't available in later *Witcher* games, so you might not want to get too used to it if you intend to play through the whole series.

In either case, combat in *The Witcher* is something of a rock-paper-scissors affair, requiring different tactics for different situations. Most famously, Geralt is armed with two swords: one silver, for dealing with supernatural monsters, and one steel, for everything else. In either case, Geralt employs either a strong, fast, or group style, the effectiveness of which depends on the armor, speed, and number of enemies respectively. In addition to his swordplay, Geralt can also use magic potions, bombs, oils, and magic via "signs." There are five signs you can use, and each is quite distinctive and more useful in some situations than others. Aard, for instance, is a telekinetic blast that can knock down enemies but also clear rubble. Like the other signs, you can expand its usefulness by investing talent points into it. Fully maxed out, Aard can knockdown, stun, and disarm a whole group of opponents.

However, combat in *The Witcher* tends to feel more like a fighting game than a traditional CRPG, even if you do employ the isometric mode and take frequent advantage of the "active pause" option to change out swords or signs. The usual advice is to reduce the difficulty level if you're struggling with it, but a better option is to take better advantage of alchemy. Geralt can find ingredients to make a variety of potions, bombs, and oils, and used correctly, can greatly ease combat. The Blizzard potion, for instance, slows down time (or speeds up Geralt, if you prefer) so you have more time to parry and dodge. It can take some time to gather the appropriate materials for alchemy, but the results speak for themselves.

In other regards *The Witcher* plays a lot like an updated *Gothic*, covered in Chapter 13. Indeed, Polish friends tell me that it's often referred to as "Poland's *Gothic*" in Poland, which seems apt. As with those games, *The Witcher*'s Geralt is a lone wolf—there's no real party system as in *Dragon Age*. It's also often compared to FromSoftware's *Dark Souls* action RPG series, but I disagree; *Dark Souls* is primarily characterized for its difficult action sequences, which require far more timing and precision than I'm comfortable calling an "action RPG," much less a CRPG. However, *The Witcher* (and *Gothic*, for that matter) has plenty of action, but not to

FIGURE 21.23 *The Witcher 2.* The game has gorgeous audiovisuals and some of the most visceral combats you'll find.

the point where an old-school CRPG fan with slower reflexes need not apply (Figures 21.23 and 21.24).

Later *Witcher* games include *The Witcher 2: Assassins of Kings* from 2011 and *The Witcher 3: Wild Hunt* in 2015. Both of these are masterpieces of the action RPG genre, with great writing, exploration, and, of course, lots of great action (and we're not just talking about combat here). Even if you're not a fan of the combat system, there's still plenty of well-written dialog, story arcs, and intriguing environments to explore.

FIGURE 21.24 *The Witcher 3* is even prettier than its predecessor. Just look at those sunflowers!

WARHORSE STUDIOS
Kingdom Come: Deliverance

The final game I'd like to cover in this chapter is Warhorse Studios' *Kingdom Come: Deliverance,* published in 2018 for Windows and consoles (Figure 21.25). This game is essentially this generation's *Darklands* from Chapter 12. It's intensely focused on historical accuracy—though this time the setting is 15th-century Bohemia. Indeed, by far my favorite aspect of this game is simply exploring the world, talking to people, and feeling as though I'm participating in a carefully prepared historical reenactment. Based in Prague, Warhorse Studios really went the extra mile to achieve this level of historical authenticity, but the realism doesn't stop with the backstory. You'll have to sleep and eat, your clothing wears out, food spoils, and combat—well, let's just say it doesn't suffer fools gladly. The developers really wanted to show just how much skill it takes to really be effective with ancient weapons, going so far as to implement a physics system that takes weight and speed into consideration. To be honest, I never could quite get the hang of it, but I don't consider that more a fault of my own than with the game.

FIGURE 21.25 *Kingdom Come: Deliverance* has spectacular audiovisuals, but the real draw here is the historical realism. Like Henrick with *Darklands,* Warhorse did its research, and the results are impressive and intriguing. Forget about what you *think* you know about the period; part of the fun (and challenge) is learning the social customs, political systems, and even the clothing fashions of 15th-century Bohemia. Image from Warhorse.

The story concerns the son of a blacksmith named Henry, a peasant from Skalitz, a silver mining town. The town is invaded by a Cuman army, and though Henry manages to escape, his parents are slain. I won't spoil more of the plot than that, but suffice it to say it'll be a long time before Henry will be in any position to avenge the murder of his family. I should add, too, that the game doesn't hesitate to expose you to the gruesomeness and barbaric nature of war.

It's not the sort of game you can pick up and play casually, and it has its share of bugs and interface issues. Still, I don't know how anyone willing to give it a chance won't be at least somewhat impressed by the efforts Warhorse has gone to depict a historical era accurately, warts and all.

As noted in the introduction to this chapter, the Late Modern currently isn't so much an age as a style of game, one that I imagine the major studios will continue to churn out for years, if not decades, to come. The audiovisuals will improve, of course, and refinements will continue to be made to the interface, combat and leveling systems, and so on. However, for me the truly exciting CRPGs aren't coming out of major studios anymore, but rather the much smaller "indies," especially those inspired if not led by legacy developers from the Golden and Platinum Ages. Even if these games can't match the productions of AAA games, they can afford to take bigger risks for smaller, more discriminating audiences. Let's turn, then, to the latest age—the Kickstarted Renaissance.

NOTES

1. See the June 2006 issue of *Computer Games* magazine, p. 61.
2. See Charles Onyett's "Five Changes from Oblivion to Skyrim" on IGN from April 25, 2011.
3. Ibid.
4. See Heinrich Lenhardt's 2012 interview with Nesmith, "Bethesda's Nesmith Reflects on the Difficult Birth of Skyrim's 'Radiant Story' System" for Venturebeat.com.
5. See Hilary Goldstein's 2004 interview with Bishop, "Jade Empire Massive Interview," on IGN.com.
6. See Robert Purchese's "BioWare: PC Dragon Age 2 Is Strategic" on Eurogamer.net.

CHAPTER 22

The Renaissance, Kickstarted

When I wrote the first edition of this book over ten years ago, I was pessimistic about the future of the CRPG. At best, I thought, whatever spirit the CRPG as I knew it had left in it would find its way into MMORPGs or ARPGs. The very words "turn-based" were enough to make publishers and critics curl their lips. I had good reason to fear that CRPGs were over—cast aside in favor of action games.

This all began to change, however, when I interviewed Brian Fargo back in 2011. After some routine questions about the history of Interplay, I happened to ask Brian the fateful question: "If you had made *Wasteland 2,* what would that game have been like, and how it would it be different than *Fallout?*" The question caught him by surprise, but I will never forgot his response: "Let me think about that—I'm designing the game in my head as we speak."

Eventually this idea became *Wasteland 2,* one of the most unlikely CRPGs ever produced. In the trailers and interviews inXile produced for its Kickstarter campaign, Fargo explained that he'd been trying for years to get publishers interested in new turn-based games, but they all turned him down flat. They claimed that there simply wasn't enough demand for old-school CRPGs to make the project worthwhile.

> Hey gang, this is Shane. I'm going to break the fourth wall or whatever you want to call it and step out from behind the word processor because I feel this is an important enough point to warrant it.

Matt is actually being a bit modest here. In a 2014 interview, Brian Fargo had this to say: "I did an interview with *Matt Chat*— he does kind of hardcore gamer interviews, podcast stuff, so anyway, and this was a couple years before the Kickstarter—he said 'If you were to do another *Wasteland* game, what would it be like today?' You can actually see me spitballing in my mind, and I actually describe pretty much what we're doing here, you know tactical combat, all that stuff. He kind of forced me on camera to think about it, and it's kind of funny that that's pretty much what we're doing now."[1]

Now, I'm not claiming (and Matt's not claiming) that that one interview exchange single-handedly led to *Wasteland 2*, the success of which in turn helped fuel the CRPG explosion via crowdfunding platforms like Kickstarter. But it was important enough that His Fargoness remembered it a few years later as part of the chain of events. Which, I have to admit, is pretty cool.

OK, enough of me. The Great and Terrible OzShane will now step back behind the word processor. Mainly because I see Matt switching the safety off on his taser.

It probably would've ended there, had it not been for Kickstarter and other crowdfunding sites. The idea behind these sites is simple, yet brilliant: rather than rely on a publisher to supply the funds necessary to make a game, why not just go directly to fans? It might seem dicey to some—pledging to a campaign in hopes of receiving a game that may or may not ever see the light of day—but then Tim Schafer's Double Fine Adventure campaign (now known as *Broken Age*) raised over $3.3 million (with a much lower goal of $400,000) on Kickstarter in 2012. This opened the floodgates (not to mention the wallets), and inXile, Larian Studios, Obsidian Entertainment, Harebrained Schemes, Owlcat Games, and several others have successfully funded and delivered games that in all likelihood would've never been made otherwise. While some of these games raised more money and sold more copies than others, they prove that there is, after all, a healthy market for the kind of games we've been covering in this book. This distribution of patronage has finally left designers free to pursue the games they want to make, not what a publisher's marketing research indicates they should. As we'll see, it's all led to a flourishing of wonderful new CRPGs that I deem a Renaissance (Figure 22.1).

FIGURE 22.1   As of this writing, the highest-funded CRPG on Kickstarter is *Torment: Tides of Numenera* ($4.18 million) with *Pillars of Eternity* ($3.98 million) a close second and *Wasteland 2* ($2.93 million) third. The highest-funded MMORPG is *Ashes of Creation* ($3.27 million) (shown here) followed by *Camelot Unchained* ($2.23 million) and *Shroud of the Avatar: Forsaken Virtues* ($1.9 million) third. For comparison, the highest-funded video game to date is *Shenmue 3* ($6.33 million). The highest-funded campaign ever on Kickstarter is the Pebble Time color e-paper smartwatch at an astounding $20,338,986. Image courtesy of Intrepid Studios.

It's worth noting that not every high-profile CRPG proposed on Kickstarter makes its funding goal, even if the people or companies involved have an excellent games pedigree. A great example of this is *Seven Dragon Saga*, a proposed CRPG from Tactical Simulations Interactive (TSI), TSI itself being formed by alumni of SSI, one the highest-regarded developers of Golden Age CRPGs like *Pool of Radiance*. With a campaign goal of $450,000, the Kickstarter campaign was canceled two weeks in with a funding level of just over $100,000 achieved. In its final campaign update on Kickstarter on March 23, 2015, TSI president David Klein stated it wasn't giving up on *Seven Dragon Saga*: "We'll be coming back as soon as humanly possible, with a better, more refined Kickstarter, and some code you'll actually be able to play, along with killer videos and artwork." Sadly, to date there's been no word on *Seven Dragon Saga*.

Yet even with that caveat there are still more great games here due to the Kickstarter Renaissance than we can reasonably do justice to in a single chapter, so again we'll have to narrow our focus to the most influential, innovative, controversial, or just too much fun to pass over. In other words, it's totally subjective and at the whim of the authors; your mileage may vary.

KICKSTARTER-INSPIRED GAMES

We'll start with Larian Studios' *Divinity: Original Sin.*

Divinity: Original Sin

You'll recall the discussion back in Chapter 15 of *Divine Divinity,* a popular *Diablo*-like from 2012 (Figure 22.2). It was made by a Belgian company named Larian Studios, helmed by Swen Vincke. When I interviewed Vincke back in 2013, he told me that all along he'd wanted to make turn-based games, but publishers balked at the idea—*Diablo* was rocking the charts, and most thought it owed much of its success to its fast-paced, hack 'n slash combat. Clearly the era of turn-based games was over.

Vincke finally got the chance to prove them wrong in 2013, when Larian Studios launched a Kickstarter campaign on March 27. His goal was $400,000, but it ended up raising $944,282 by the end of the campaign. That's still a modest sum for the kind of ambitious game Vincke had in

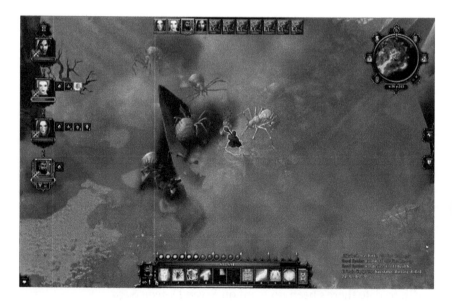

FIGURE 22.2 *Divinity: Original Sin* proves that turn-based combat is far from dead. Done well, it's every bit as exciting as real time.

mind, and the company nearly went bankrupt in the process. Fortunately for all of us, the game was a rousing success and met with critical acclaim from all the major gaming sites.

The game is set in Larian's *Divinity* universe, but the setup is quite different beyond the obvious switch to turn-based. For one, you control two heroes, a pair of "Source Hunters," though in co-op mode each player controls only one of them. Source Hunters are tasked with finding and eliminating "Source," a dangerous type of magic wielded by "Sourcerers" [*sic*]. However, the start of the game is about investigating a murder—specifically, the councilor of a port town named Cyseal. I won't spoil any more for you here, but there's plenty of twists and turns to the tale, and it all culminates in a terrific battle.

Given turn-based combat's unfair reputation as boring, much was made of Larian's combat mechanics. The system is based on "action points," which limit how many actions you can perform each round. These can be used immediately or saved for the next round, where they might be needed for extra powerful abilities. What makes all this interesting is the emphasis on combining spells and elements, which allow you to take advantage of (or be disadvantaged by!) features of the terrain and other effects. For instance, if a group of enemies is standing in water, you can try frying them with electricity by targeting the puddle. That's just for starters, though; in some situations you can spray an enemy with acid, set fire to it (causing the acid to explode), douse it with water to create water vapor, and then electrify the cloud!

Another tactic to prevent the game from getting too repetitive is to limit the number of battles while ratcheting up their stakes. In *Divinity: Original Sin*, there are no random encounters but only set battles, which can often be quite difficult. Therefore, it's important to carefully explore each area to find every opportunity to gain experience points for leveling.

Divinity: Original Sin 2

In 2015, Larian returned to Kickstarter to fund *Divinity: Original Sin 2*, and this time easily managed to raise over twice the funding ($2 million). While the first game is good, this one is truly great, surprising fans by easily rivaling if not surpassing many of the greatest CRPGs of all time. It received top scores and numerous awards and is still one of the most actively played games on Steam. This is all the more impressive given its learning curve, assuming you play it on its default difficulty. Nevertheless, if you're up for the challenge and enjoy experimenting with different tactics and strategies, you can't go wrong with this game.

> *Shane:* Kinda funny how "hard" games with learning curves that major publishers run like the wind from not only established the genre, but are delivering masterpieces in modern times.
>
> *Matt:* Kinda funny how I'm agreeing with you on this one.

There are many changes from the previous game, including more extensive character creation options and an arguably better story. Instead of switching between two characters (and some companions), you can either play as a character with an existing backstory or create your own. Later, you can either recruit other characters into your party or make new ones from scratch. In any case, co-op gameplay is great fun and this time supports up to four players. This time your characters are Sourcerers, captured and banished to an island fortress. There's so much to do and explore; you'll likely want to play it multiple times to see everything it has to offer.

After that, you might try one of the fan-made campaigns or try your own hand at Game Master mode, building new adventures for your friends. This mode, which Larian refers to as a full modding package, is evidently very robust and not just an afterthought. The developers (with Wizards of the Coast's permission) adapted the "Lost Mine of Phandelver" module from the *D&D* 5th Edition starter set, a comprehensive adventure for levels 1–5 with many environs and encounter types intended to teach new DMs and players alike the ropes of the game.

> *Shane:* I've run "Lost Mine of Phandelver" at the table with a group of players. That's no small potatoes.
>
> *Matt:* Speaking of, can you run out and get me some potatoes? And, uh, accidentally forget to come back?

When is a stretch goal not just a stretch goal? A Polygon article in 2017[2] mused that Larian was still trying to get a handle both conceptually and commercially on what it had created with the Game Master mode on top of an already fantastic game. "The game master mode was a Kickstarter stretch goal," says Vincke. "It's grown a little bit out of hand. It's become its own thing. But we're really happy with it."

It's possible this Game Master mode could propel *Divinity: Original Sin 2* from a really outstanding game to a long-remembered and honored

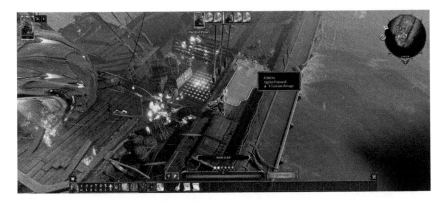

FIGURE 22.3 Even at the default difficulty, combat in *Divinity: Original Sin 2* requires careful tactics and environmental awareness. Here, The Red Prince's dragon breath can ignite this poisonous ooze on the ground, but it might be better to wait for the enemies to move closer. The image shown here is from the Definitive Edition.

classic (Figure 22.3). Many games both inside and outside of the CRPG genre owe their longevity and fan adoration to a strong modding community that developed (pun intended) due to the modding tools and open community the game developer fostered. Only time will truly tell.

Perhaps the most controversial change is the armor system. Unlike most CRPGs, you have two sorts: physical and magical, each with their own health bars that must be ground down in order to inflict that form of damage on the enemy. A monster might have weak physical armor but be strongly resistant to magic; therefore, it'll be much harder to kill it with magical attacks than conventional weapons. For these reasons, you may find it easier to focus your party's skills on a single type of damage; otherwise you'll find yourself having to wear down both kinds of armor.

All in all, I can't recommend the *Divinity: Original Sin* games highly enough, especially the second one; they really are modern classics. It's unclear at this point whether we'll see a third game in the series, but until then you can enjoy the Enhanced Editions and downloadable content.

Wasteland 2

With the possible exception of *Bard's Tale IV, Wasteland 2* must surely be one of the most long-awaited sequels in the history of CRPGs (Figure 22.4). As you'll recall from Chapter 9, *Wasteland* is a turn-based, *Bard's Tale/Ultima*–style game set in a postapocalyptic world. It was published in 1988, nearly thirty years before this epic sequel in 2014.

FIGURE 22.4 Here the team faces off against a ... honey badger? As you can see, like the first *Wasteland,* the sequel doesn't shy away from corny jokes and pop culture references, but make no mistake, this nasty beast will eat you like a snake.

The game, however, is set only fifteen years after the events in its predecessor. Now the Desert Rangers control Guardian Citadel, formerly home of the Guardians, a group of crazed monks. When the game begins, General Vargas learns that Ace, the Ranger he sent out to investigate strange reports of "man and machine becoming one," has been brutally murdered. Your task is to pick up where Ace left off and try to figure out what's going on before it's too late.

Shane: I guess you could say ol' Ace didn't exactly ace it with flying colors.

Matt: Yup. Looks like he finally got his ace kicked.

Though it shares many of the same themes and features, *Wasteland 2* is a vastly different game than its predecessor. The most obvious difference, of course, is the modern interface. Rather than the top-down view of the original, this one has 3D graphics and a rotatable camera. You can recruit up to seven characters: four of your own design, and three more NPCs. The attribute system is called CLASSIC: Coordination, Luck, Awareness, Strength, Speed, Intelligence, and Charisma. Each of these affects multiple things. For example, Awareness influences how soon you get to act in combat, your chance to evade attacks, and how far you can see. As with *Divinity: Original Sin,* Wasteland 2 incorporates an Action Points system to determine how many things you can do during each round of combat. There are also twenty-nine different skills you can work to develop, ranging from weapon-specific skills such as Shotguns to social skills like Kiss Ass and Smart Ass. Finally, there's the ever-popular Toaster Repair skill, which might seem useless at first—but sometimes you can find great loot stashed in old toasters lying in the Wasteland.

Combat is a highly tactical affair that's about as close to a miniatures RPG as you're likely to get on a PC. You can see your characters from above and turn on a visual grid to help position them—usually behind cover for protection, but you might also seek out the high ground to improve your chance to hit your targets. The distance between you and your adversaries is critical, and the ideal range varies depending on your weapon. A sniper rifle, for instance, is highly accurate at long range, but completely useless up close. While this setup makes sense from a game balancing perspective, I sure wouldn't want to be shot with a sniper rifle at point-blank range!

Wasteland 2 was warmly received by critics, especially those old enough to remember playing the original. It received *PC World*'s Game of the Year Award and earned over $12 million in sales. InXile released a "Director's Cut" version in September 2014. It's likely the version you'll want to play, since it has better graphics, "perks and quirks" for customizing your party, precision strikes, and more voiceovers.

Some reviewers have commented that *Wasteland 2* is what *Fallout 3* should've been, and I can certainly see where they're coming from. Whereas Bethesda's game is essentially a first-person shooter set in the *Fallout* universe, *Wasteland 2* feels much closer to *Fallout 1* or *2* in terms of gameplay.

> *Shane:* Are you saying there was a ... falling out among the fans over the direction *Fallout 3* took?
>
> *Matt:* You're a S.P.E.C.I.A.L. kind of annoying.

A third *Wasteland* game is currently in development, expected sometime in late 2019. Rather than use Kickstarter, though, inXile used Fig—an "equity crowdfunding" platform that includes such gaming luminaries as Brian Fargo, Tim Schafer, and Feargus Urquhart on its advisory board. The key difference is that fans can choose to invest in the game and possibly receive some return on their investment. (It's also worth noting that Fig is only for games, unlike Kickstarter and Indiegogo, and its criteria for launching a campaign is much stricter.) Fig managed to raise over $3 million for *Wasteland 3* back in November 2016.

Pillars of Eternity

Obsidian Entertainment, a studio founded by ex-Black Isle employees including Feargus Urquhart and Chris Avellone, announced "Project Eternity" and launched a Kickstarter campaign for it on September 2012. The idea was to create a new game like *Baldur's Gate,* and fans took notice. The campaign raised over $4 million—setting a new record—and was released to immediate acclaim as *Pillars of Eternity* in March 2015 (Figure 22.5).

Rather than license an existing fantasy universe, Obsidian created a new world called "Eora." It's just different enough from the typical medieval high fantasy setting to be its own thing but still seem familiar. Obsidian rolled the dice with this approach. On the one hand, it stood to benefit by creating its own intellectual property that it can build on and potentially license to others—and avoid having to pay licensing fees to anyone else. On the other hand, an original IP lacks the drawing power of a well-established world like The Forgotten Realms. Luckily for the Obsidian, its roll was good: the game won over more than enough fans to warrant a sequel.

FIGURE 22.5 *Pillars of Eternity* is sure to appeal to anyone who likes the old Infinity engine games, but it's also won over plenty of new fans.

Set in the Dyrwood, a nation where infants are mysteriously being born without souls, you play as a "Watcher," gifted (or cursed?) with the ability to see and communicate with souls. Your mission is to deal with this "hollowborn" situation. As with *Baldur's Gate,* you don't complete this mission on your own. Indeed, you can recruit up to eight companions, all with some connection to the story and their own sidequests.

Rather than let you control the camera yourself, Obsidian opts for a fixed isometric interface, with prerendered 2D backdrops. If the goal of this design decision was to make the game feel more like *Baldur's Gate,* it certainly succeeds. Likewise, combat is RTwP (real time with pause) and requires extensive micromanagement (get ready to pause the game a lot!). In yet another comparison with *Baldur's Gate,* whether you like or dislike this game will depend largely on how much you enjoy the story and interacting with your companions. The combat, while serviceable, can certainly be trying at times, and it's usually where the game gets the most flak from reviewers. On a positive note, I certainly appreciate that you can slow down combat instead of pausing it completely.

Another nice touch is the Stronghold, a sort of headquarters you can develop along with your characters. In addition to the usual aesthetic upgrades, you can send your idle companions off on their own adventures (gaining a little experience and loot in the process). Plus, there's a multilevel dungeon under the Stronghold that exists purely for the sake of dungeon crawling. Like any good dungeon, it gets tougher the deeper you descend. You can also collect taxes from the populace—but they'll expect protection in return. One reviewer referred to the Stronghold as "Kickstarter stretch-goal fluff," but it's a worthy addition. Besides, there's something at the bottom of this dungeon that's central to the plot of the sequel.

One aspect I'm less enthused about is all the souls wandering around with golden name plates. These were placed in the game as rewards for some Kickstarter pledges. I'm not sure how rewarding they are for those who funded them, but they have little to no connection to the rest of the game and can be distracting. If you're like one of your co-authors (cough, cough, Shane), it takes a few hours of gameplay before you realize these NPCs are 100 percent superfluous to the game. A different implementation of this type of pledge reward is seen on the "memorial stones" you find throughout the game. They have messages by backers at the $500 level and above. These are less distracting and in some cases poignant. One pays tribute to British game designer Mike Singleton (*War in Middle Earth, Midwinter, Dark Sceptre*): "Mike Singleton: An often forgotten

FIGURE 22.6 Here, a *Pillars of Eternity* Kickstarter backer uses its pledge reward to pay tribute to British game developer Mike Singleton.

visionary, giving the gaming world some of its most brilliant games when video gaming was in its infancy" (Figure 22.6). Sadly, another one contained an offensive joke that created a stir on social media before Obsidian could work with the backer to revise it.

All in all, *Pillars of Eternity* is a good mix of old-fashioned and modern ideas, with good storytelling and all the little fussy details that makes RTwP combat involving without being overly tedious or frenetic. The characters aren't as memorable as the likes of Minsc or Imoen from *Baldur's Gate,* but Edér, Aloth, and Durance—human fighter, elf wizard, and dwarf priest, respectively—are worth getting to know.

> *Shane:* I really liked Durance; he was the standout character for me. He was this crazy fire priest dude who kind of bulged his eye at you and told stories of fighting gods on a bridge. Was it a bridge? Anyway, he said crap blew up good.
> *Matt:* You're making my eye bulge.

Obsidian released "The White March" expansion pack for *Pillars of Eternity* as two separate DLCs in 2015 and 2016. They add a considerable amount of content and some very useful features and improvements to the interface. These features and improvements were backported to the main game.

Pillars of Eternity II: Deadfire

Pillars of Eternity II: Deadfire, Obsidian's first sequel to *Pillars of Eternity,* appeared in 2018 after raising $4.4 million on Fig—nearly four times its original goal (Figure 22.7). Like its predecessor, it won instant acclaim and topped sales charts. I'd characterize it chiefly as a pirate-themed adventure; instead of a Stronghold, you get to captain a sailing vessel, which you can upgrade or even replace as you raise sufficient capital. There's even ship-to-ship combat: a worthy addition even if it does pale in comparison to *Sid Meier's Pirates!* It is great fun to sail around listening to pirate shanties as you search for and make landfall on islands, many of which have their own dungeons, mini-adventures, or just interesting lore or treasure.

The story picks up five years after the first game, and once again you're cast as a Watcher. Eothas, the god of light and rebirth, is on the rampage, and other gods recruit you to hunt him down and put a stop to it—one way or the other. There are a number of factions you can ally with, but you can seldom please one without angering another.

Some of the characters from the first game are back, like Edér, Aloth, and Pallegina, but there are also some great new characters like Xoti, a "Reaper" who carries a lantern to store lost souls. In addition there's a ranger named Maia, an Aumaua—a race of semi-aquatic humanoids. Maia has her own companion, a powerful bird named Ishiza. All of these

FIGURE 22.7 Sailing around in *Pillars of Eternity II: Deadfire* is a sheer delight, thanks in no small part to some rather excellent sea shanties.

characters are well woven into the plot, and, as with the factions, it's hard to keep them all happy.

On January 22, 2019, Obsidian released a patch that adds turn-based combat as an optional combat mode in *Pillars of Eternity II: Deadfire*. According to Sawyer, the move was a response to *Divinity Original Sin 2*. It's too early to say whether the option will be prove a hit with fans, but I'm certainly excited about it—and also hoping that it'll be included and refined for future games in the series.

For my money, the *Pillars* games are the closest approximation yet to the intensely satisfying gameplay of the *Baldur's Gate* series. As of this writing, it's not clear when and whether there will be a third game, but you can count on one thing–I'll be making my pledge as soon as their crowd-funding campaign goes online.

Tyranny

In between its *Pillars* games, Obsidian used the engine for an original game called *Tyranny* (2016). Its key feature concerns its "evil has won" theme: The game starts after an evil overlord has conquered the world, and your character is a high-ranking member of his command. This gets into some murky moral territory rather quickly, and it is disturbing how easily one slips into a nefarious role. The writing is sharp and poignant, but the dark, sinister themes leave some players cold. In short, while its literary and artistic merits are admirable, it lacks the charm and general good-naturedness of the *Pillars* games so it's not for everyone, despite the game receiving favorable reviews.

For some, the most memorable aspect of *Tyranny* wasn't the gameplay or darker setting but instead its almost surprise appearance on the CRPG gaming scene: First announced in March 2016, with a playable demo available at that year's E3 in June and then released in November of the same year, the game was in players' hands very swiftly compared to the usual modern CRPG "announcement to release" cycle (which can easily take years).

It's also interesting to note that *Tyranny* was a combination of ideas and concepts from three previous CRPG projects Obsidian had taken to various stages of pitching or development starting in 2006 but never completed: *Fury*, *Defiance* and *Stormlands*.

Torment: Tides of Numenera

While I'm on the subject of CRPGs that strive to be taken seriously as works of art or literature, inXile's *Torment: Tides of Numenera* certainly

FIGURE 22.8 *Torment: Tides of Numenera* is a spiritual successor to the cult classic *Planescape: Torment* game from Chapter 16.

fits the profile. It's touted as the spiritual successor of *Planescape: Torment*, which we covered back in Chapter 16 (Figure 22.8). However, while that game was set in TSR's *Planescape* universe, for *Torment* inXile licensed Monte Cook Games' *Numenera* tabletop RPG (which in turn uses its Cypher System RPG system). There are, of course, significant differences between these two settings, but they're both surreal, metaphysical, and philosophical yet with enough action to hopefully strike a nostalgic chord among fans of the earlier game.

Numenera is an interesting and creative setting that blends science fiction with fantasy in intriguing ways. Taking sci-fi writer Sir Arthur C. Clarke's famous adage "Any sufficiently advanced technology is indistinguishable from magic" and running like a mad person with it, players find themselves in the Ninth World, a billion years in Earth's future after multiple highly advanced civilizations have risen and collapsed. The majority of humanity is reduced to a quasi-medieval way of life, but one surrounded by the remnants of those much more technologically advanced civilizations. They call the artifacts they find "numenera," and they're sufficiently advanced beyond the understanding of the current era to be regarded as magical.

You take on the role of "The Last Castoff," the last incarnation of "The Changing God," a being who has achieved incredible longevity by virtue of being reborn into new bodies and discarding or "casting off" the old ones, who are then left to their own devices. Meanwhile, "The Sorrow," the Changing God's ancient enemy, is hunting for you and your fellow castoffs. The castoffs can gain insights into each other's experiences via "Meres," or artifacts that store and revive memories. Your character has a unique ability not just to revive these memories but alter them, altering reality in the process.

The game uses an innovation that inXile named the Crisis system: All significant encounters are scripted, turn-based events that can be resolved in a variety of ways depending on the player's preference. This system was designed so that any method of resolving a crisis should be satisfying and meaningful, and provide the player with experience points.

As with *Planescape: Torment*, combat isn't this game's selling point—indeed, you can usually avoid or end them simply by talking your way out, even in the midst of combat. However, you can certainly resort to, or provoke, violence during a crisis event if you'd like. The numenera bring some interesting ideas to the table. Cyphers, for instance, are powerful, one-off magic items that can easily turn the tide in battle. However, carrying them comes with a penalty, and trying to carry too many can even destroy you (the given story reason being the "weird energies" of exotic technology from different eras mixing together).

Torment is quite ambitious in both scope and goals, a fact that ironically might not be readily apparent to a player due to those selfsame goals. As the Crisis system hints at, *Tides of Numenera* was developed as a reactive game that, while telling a similar story, molds itself to the players' style and choices in a smooth, nuanced manner. Two different players can have very different experiences with the game and might even be puzzled when comparing notes. *Torment* might possibly require the most playthroughs of any CRPG to experience everything it has to offer.

To achieve this took a tremendous amount of talent and writing (over a million words!). To bring in more talent to help, and to build more excitement for the Kickstarter campaign, "big names" were added to the already seasoned and experienced inXile core design team as stretch goals (all successfully achieved) including Chris Avellone, Monte Cook, George Ziets, and fantasy author Patrick Rothfuss.

In inXile's own words from a Kickstarter campaign update: "Four years is an extended development timeline for an RPG, and it is a hallmark of our ambition for the game. Torment has the longest script we've ever produced at over 1.2 million words, and provides more nuanced reactivity and more complicated quests and stories than we have ever done before."[3]

The ambitious scope and word count proved to be both a positive and a negative among fans. While some welcomed a CRPG with deep, rich, and nuanced storytelling, others dismissed it as a "novel" that they didn't want to take the time to read. I can only speculate that inXile, having heard complaints for years that modern CRPGs were too shallow and dumbed down, was surprised by this particular reaction.

Perhaps the most interesting aspect of the game is the "Tides" mentioned in the title, which is this game's version of an alignment system. These are emotional currents that flow through humanity's collective unconscious. The Changing God has some power to manipulate these Tides—a dangerous practice since everyone is connected to them. Indeed, the Sorrow itself was created by ancients trying to harness their power. The Tides come in five colors, each representing a set of values and goals. The Silver Tide, for instance, is concerned with power and fame, and is connected most closely to people who want to be remembered or influence other people. Your character's dominance in any particular Tide is established by your actions or dialog choices, resulting in changes to your "Legacy." It's deep stuff, but as creative lead and lead writer Colin McComb (also a designer on *Planescape: Torment*) puts it, "*Torment* explores philosophical themes, but isn't a philosophy class."

In short, *Torment: Tides of Numenera* is a surreal, often haunting game. Whereas *Planescape: Torment* had enough lighthearted humor to keep things from getting too grim—Morte to the rescue—this one is much more disturbing and unsettling, even psychedelic. Obviously, it's not for everyone, but as with *Tyranny*, I applaud any developer willing to pursue a vision to its end, even if the resulting game is more interesting than entertaining.

My co-author Shane has his own perspective: "*Torment: Tides of Numenera* is a magnificent yet unsung achievement among CRPGs and I hope it is rediscovered in time with fresh eyes. I'm partially biased because I'm also under the spell of the Numenera tabletop RPG world and lore, and was thrilled when I first read that *Planescape: Torment*'s spiritual successor would adapt it. Even without that aspect, however, I love its story, its gameplay, and its sheer audacious intent. It may seem strange to say given the almost poetic experience *Torment: Tides of Numenera* delivers, but this game, and the team behind, has some serious stones to put it mildly."

Shane also asked Colin McComb if he had a final thought on the game for posterity. He offered the following: "The central theme of the game is 'what does one life matter?' We choose how to answer that, both in the game and in our own lives. I can't tell you the best answer—that's up to you. Choose wisely, and find your own meaning."

Shadowrun Returns

Yet another of the early Kickstarter triumphs is Harebrained Schemes' *Shadowrun Returns,* a turn-based CRPG set in the science fantasy world of the *Shadowrun* tabletop game (Figure 22.9). Fusing cyberpunk, crime, horror, and industrial espionage themes, these games offer a nice alternative to fantasy or sci-fi games. Here, standard fantasy races like elves and dwarves can employ magic, but also hack computers or control robotic drones. The concept for a turn-based CRPG set in this universe was popular enough to earn nearly $2 million in pledges on Kickstarter in 2012, and the game was shipped a year later.

Other than the uniqueness of its setting, other aspects of *Shadowrun Returns* are relatively familiar to the genre, such as a turn-based mode utilizing "Action Points" and an isometric graphics with prerendered backgrounds. It's a good-looking game, with a nice mix of neon lights, grimy city streets, and cold metallic corridors. If you can imagine *Blade Runner* with fantasy creatures and magic, you wouldn't be far off.

Critics praise the story, which seems to focus on a murder investigation but soon spirals out into conspiracies. A serial killer named the "Emerald City Ripper" has been menacing Seattle, stealing organs from his or her

FIGURE 22.9 *Shadowrun Returns* is an intriguing mesh of cyberpunk and fantasy themes.

victims. Eventually this leads you to the Universal Brotherhood, a cult obsessed with extradimensional insect spirits. However, the relative brevity of the game led some to assigning it middling reviews.

An expansion called *Shadowrun: Dragonfall* followed in 2014, but was later released as a standalone game called *Shadowrun: Dragonfall—Director's Cut*. It offers a longer, more complex story and introduces several companions to get to know in between tossing magical hexes and grenades at enemies. The next full game in the series, *Shadowrun: Hong Kong*, was released on August 20, 2015. In each case, the critics were greatly impressed by the writing, but less thrilled with the linearity and combat mechanics.

Harebrained also took pains to include a fairly sophisticated editor so players can create their own *Shadowrun* scenarios and adventures to share online with other players.

Serpent in the Staglands

The next two games I'd like to discuss are both known for their no-holds-barred difficulty. Indeed, Iron Tower Studio, the maker of *The Age of Decadence*, proudly boasts on its website that it has been "proudly serving the 0.003% of the Global Gaming Market since 2015. The remaining 99.997% need not apply." However, even if both games have something to prove, they go about in very different ways—and I daresay have broader appeal than their marketing suggests.

Let's start with *Serpent in the Staglands*, a charming "Transylvanian-inspired Bronze Age" game by an even more charming husband and wife duo, Joe and Hannah Williams of Whalenought Studios (Figure 22.10). As far as I know, this is the only CRPG inspired by Romanian mythology—but after playing this I hope it won't be the last. You may have played a deity trapped in a mortal's body searching for a way back to their realm before, but you've never played it like this.

The first thing you'll notice about the game is the retro graphics; it looks like something from the *Darklands* era of the early 1990s (it even describes itself as a "90s CRPG in every way but the release date"), with pixelated graphics and almost total reliance on text for narrative purposes. Naturally, some philistines would simply decry these graphics "obsolete" or evidence of shoddy production values, but we know better, and Whalenought is not the only modern studio employing the "retro" look simply because they choose to do so, not because they couldn't do something more realistic. I hate to belabor the point, but as someone who's dabbled in game

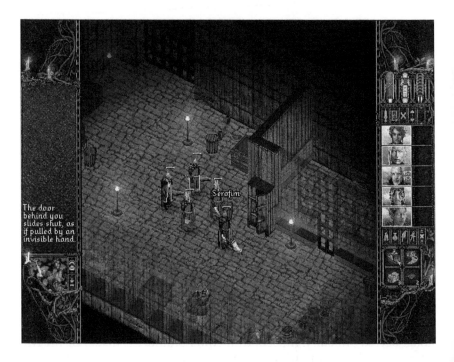

The door behind you slides shut, as if pulled by an invisible hand.

Serofim

FIGURE 22.10 *Serpent in the Staglands* has great retro-style art and truly challenging combat.

development himself, I can tell you that it's infinitely quicker and easier simply to buy realistic 3D models from the Unity Asset Store than to create and animate 2D sprites and backgrounds—yet you might assume the former looks more "commercial." The point is that it might take some knowledge to truly appreciate what it takes to make a retro game; in many ways it's no easier now than it was back in the 1990s.

But I digress. *Serpent in the Staglands* plays something like *Baldur's Gate,* with isometric perspective and RTwP combat. It's party-based, and the developers strive to emphasize "creative party skill combinations." The key here is that the game doesn't use traditional classes; instead, you can create any combination of magic, combat, and other skills as you see fit. The challenge here is that there's a reason why all those other games use classes: It's easier to see how mages, clerics, and fighters work together than a bunch of characters with mixed skills. In other words, you'll have to think strategically here about your party dynamics, not just tactically on the battlefield.

A nice touch is the way the game handles combat. Few developers have ever truly mastered RTwP combat; it always seems to end up feeling like some awkward compromise between *Diablo* and *Neverwinter Nights*—like some annoying hyperactive kid in a *World of Warcraft* instance who keeps yelling "gogogo!!!" at the tank. Sure, you can constantly pause the action to assess the battlefield and issue orders, but to the extent that you do so, you beg the question of why the game isn't turn-based. Whalenought's proposed solution is to focus on prebuffing, positioning, and movement instead of cooldowns and windups. You'll still need to pause occasionally and, let's be honest, die a lot, but it's easier to manage than in most games.

Speaking of combat, *Serpent in the Staglands* absolutely does not hold a player's hand, so much so that some players are unceremoniously slain by a cuddly forest creature near the start of the game. However, this isn't a bug, but a feature: This harsh learning curve provides immense satisfaction as you improve over time.

Another of the game's strengths is its setting and writing. What it lacks in graphical detail it makes up for with detailed descriptions of pretty much everything, including the language of the inhabitants. And you'll need to read it all carefully. The designers intentionally avoid linearity and obvious plot points; you're meant to figure out this stuff on your own. In the extensive manual (of course!) provided with the game, you learn that the developers consider themselves "your GM," a fitting image for the way game creates a narrative—not guide you through one.

Under the hood is a complex stats, leveling, proficiencies, and skill system that'll delight anyone who loves math. You can have up to three active skills, and automatically trigger when specific conditions are met; all you need to do is select which enemy to attack. The Grade 3 skills Poison Weapon and Adrenaline, for instance, is applied on every hit, whereas Mangle works on random attacks and only if you're polymorphed into a wolf. Magic is also designed with minimal pausing in mind. Most spells must be "held" and uninterrupted for maximum effectiveness, obviating the need to constantly cast other spells. The Grade 2 spell Nauseate, for example, degrades a target's immunities and causes sickness: the longer it's held, the weaker the target becomes.

In short, *Serpent in the Staglands* is a wonderfully ambitious game with many innovations that's well worth playing, and it's all the more impressive for being developed by a developer couple instead of a couple hundred developers.

Whalenought is currently working on a futuristic, gritty cyberpunk-espionage game called *Copper Dreams,* which will hopefully be just as successful. In addition, a pending free expansion for *Serpent in the Staglands* called *A Fool's Errand* that takes place following the story of the main game was announced in 2016, utilizing a new ruleset called The Burning Candle (which will also be used to power *Copper Dreams*).

Age of Decadence

Iron Tower Studios is one of the few developers in this chapter who doesn't rely on crowdfunding for support. Indeed, Vince D. Weller, its lead designer, is adamant about refusing to go that route, even when begged to do by his fans on the Iron Tower forums: "There are only two possible futures here: *AoD* sells well and we use the revenues to make another game or *AoD* doesn't sell well and we say 'well, at least we've tried.'" I bring this up because this is precisely the kind of stubbornness you'll need to enjoy *Age of Decadence*—and, by the way, it did sell well enough for Iron Tower to fund two new projects, **Dungeon Rats** and *Colony Ship* (Figure 22.11).

The developers call the game "an experiment, an attempt to explore a different direction, taking you back to the PnP roots of the genre. It doesn't mean that the game is awesome. In fact, there is a good chance that you won't like it, precisely because we took too many liberties with the established design." Whether you admire this brazenness or dismiss it as poor marketing, the game has struck a chord with a certain population of CRPG fans weary of Late Modern games and their perceived dumbed-down gameplay. I often fall prey to this thinking ourselves, but it's often

FIGURE 22.11 *Age of Decadence* is gritty and difficult, but so was life in the late Roman Empire.

just exceptionalism and sour grapes. It's like those types who sneer at Michael Bay's films without ever condescending to watch one. That's not to say that whatever independent film they prefer isn't somehow superior to the latest *Transformers*, but, to quote the game, I'd rather be "tossed still living into a pile of rotting corpses and waste—unable to get up," than suffer through some film snob's itinerary of what I *should* be watching, had I only the proper depth of character.

Anyway, like *Serpent in the Staglands, Age of Decadence* avoids the usual fantasy tropes, this time with a world inspired by the declining Roman Empire. It's not a place where you mindlessly attack whatever gets in your way; this game is more about negotiating your way through the political machinations of three powerful noble houses and four guilds. There's over 600,000 words of dialog, and success is as much about reading comprehension than battlefield tactics. Again, the developer says it best. It's one thing to claim your world is harsh and unforgiving, but all too often CRPGs become tales of overwhelmingly powerful heroes who save the world all on their own. Iron Tower wanted to create a more authentically harsh experience, and to do that, "The game has to be hard, dying should be easy, and you should have reasons to pick your fights." It's far from the only game in this book that makes that point, but *Age of Decadence* may well come closest to living up to this promise.

Of course, the game does have combat. Indeed, it's a well-developed turn-based system based on action points. There are multiple standard attacks, special attacks, and even aimed attacks targeting body parts. Each of the eight weapon types has its own traits, and all kinds of special items like throwing nets to add diversity to the battles.

More than anything, *Age of Decadence* comes across as a commentary on Late Modern CRPGs, especially those that focus solely on action and power fantasy fulfillment. Recall how easy it was to kill a dragon in *Skyrim*? Here, by contrast, is a dark, gritty world where you'll have to do more than just fight to stay alive. In this game, you can Shout all you like—and you probably will; but unlike the brat who always gets what he wants with a well-timed tantrum in the toy store, this time you'll just get your butt spanked.

> *Shane:* I have to admit I always get a certain visceral thrill out of Shouting at things in *Skyrim*.
>
> *Matt:* I have to admit I sometimes find it a little too easy to get to the viscera of *Skyrim*'s things.

BattleTech

On April 24, 2018, Harebrained Schemes (the same company that brought us *Shadowrun Returns*) released *BattleTech* to much anticipation, a game that, like its predecessor, *BattleTech: The Crescent Hawk's Inception* (see Chapter 12), straddles the line between strategy and role-playing games. The easiest way to describe this game, however, is to compare it to *X-Com: Enemy Unknown* (the 2012 game by Firaxis/Feral Interactive). Whereas the *X-Com* game feels more like a hybrid management/strategy game, this one's narrative and dialogue make it feel more like a role-playing game, though not to the extent of the *Crescent Hawk*. At any rate, like *X-Com,* the setup is around individual missions; you fly to one, complete it, and return to base (in this case, your ship). Combat is turn-based and decidedly tactical; careful positioning is crucial.

The story begins on the coronation day of Lady Karmea Arano, set to be new ruler of the Aurigan Reach. However, the throne is usurped, and you barely manage to escape—spending the next three years in the company of a scrappy band of mercenaries. I won't spoil the story for you, but it's probably no surprise that you up in charge of this band, and that you'll soon find yourselves involved with the political struggles for the throne.

Like *X-Com,* there's much more to develop and upgrade than your characters. As you'd expect, most of the focus here is on your "mechs," or giant walking robots piloted by your team (Figure 22.12). However, you can also level up the pilots, and even the ships that carry you from mission to mission. If there's one thing that's missing is a tech tree; it'd be nice if there was a way to learn how to build better parts or even your own mechs. I also miss being able to climb out of the cockpit; once you eject, that mechwarrior is out of the battle.

Harebrained Schemes is currently developing the first expansion for the game, called *BattleTech Flashpoint*. It will add three new mechs, a new mission type, and a tropical biome. The big draw, though, is the titular "Flashpoint," which the developers describe as "high-stakes, branching short stories comprised of procedural mercenary missions linked together with new crew conversations, special events, critical choices, and valuable rewards." It sounds great, but we've seen how often procedurally generated content fails to hold up. In any case, I'm excited just to have new mechs to play with!

FIGURE 22.12 Instead of gearing up individual characters, in *BattleTech* you outfit massive mechs.

Hero U: Rogue to Redemption

Let's turn now from giant robots to giant egos—or at least that's what we find all too often at Hero University, where the students vie to become the head of their class. Designed by Lori and Corey Cole of *Quest for Glory* fame (see Chapter 9) under their Transolar Games company, *Hero U: Rogue to Redemption* is sort of a Hogwarts simulator where every line of text has at least one pun. You play as Shawn, a young scallywag who finds himself enrolled in the school's rogue program—or, as the game would have it, a "Disbarred Bard." Shawn wants to become Rogue of the Year, and that'll mean developing his skill set while socializing with his colorful classmates. Like the *Quest for Glory* series, it seldom takes itself too seriously. Combat is optional and a simple turn-based affair; if you like this game, it'll be because you enjoy the writing, characters, jokes, and endless cringeworthy puns (Figure 22.13).

Perhaps more interesting than the game itself is how it got funded on Kickstarter not only once, but twice! The first campaign (2012) raised $409,150, just a little over its initial goal of $400,000. This turned out to be insufficient, and it returned to Kickstarter (in 2015) to raise another $116,888. This move angered some of those who pledged to the first one, but Corey Cole got into more trouble with a poorly worded update post

FIGURE 22.13 *Hero U: Rogue to Redemption* isn't focused on combat, but don't worry—you'll fight plenty of rats.

where he tries to explain the "real cost of an adventure game." Here's the offending passage:

> Players reasonably ask, "If great games like *Quest for Infamy, The Blackwell Epiphany,* or *Oak Island* can be made for $30K, and *Heroine's Quest* is free, why do you need so much funding to make Hero-U?"
>
> Part of the answer may be that we have higher production standards (graphics, music, etc.).

This sounds like Cole is implying that those games have low production standards. However, he goes on to argue that it's really the cost of the team's time that makes the difference: "Their real cost is a combination of the base expense along with the value of the time spent making them. If three people work on a game for two years, there is a real cost to that time, at least $300K in that case." However, some fixated on what they perceived as an insult to the games he used as examples, so he apologized. In Cole's defense, almost every update, including that one, ends with support for other Kickstarter projects, including the *Oak Island* game mentioned above. In any case, anyone considering running a crowdfunding campaign would do well to study this example.

One aspect that tends to get overlooked in the discussion of *Hero-U*'s development is the Coles' personal commitment to delivering the game that was promised no matter the time or cost involved. Corey shared on *Shane Plays Geek Talk Episode 157* that he has design notes from as far back as July 2008, with the development itself taking about five and a half years (they began active development following their first successful Kickstarter campaign in 2012). The Coles also took steps such as using their personal savings and taking loans to help cover the costs. Some estimates put the final required budget for *Hero-U* at over $1 million[4] compared to a crowdfunding total of just over $500,000 from both campaigns.

Here's an excerpt of an interview with the Coles from *Shane Plays Geek Talk Episode 157*:

Shane: There was some discussion online about, oh they should have just given up on it at some point you know like other devs do.… I've got nothing but respect for people who hang through the ups and downs and deliver what they promise.

Corey: That's what it comes down to. We're not kids, nothing wrong with kids, but we are professionals and when we promise something we're gonna deliver on it.… We wanted to come out with the game we promised people.… During the kickstarters we promised an awful lot.

Lori: We just wanted to make sure we made our fans happy.

Despite all the hubbub, the finished game turned out to be a worthy spiritual successor to the beloved franchise. Nostalgic fans will likely appreciate it more than newcomers, but anyone who likes a good pun— or even better, a bad one—will chuckle at every item description. It's also an ideal CRPG for younger players. The Coles hope to release future games in the *Hero-U* series, each one featuring a different fantasy character archetype now that the Rogue's story has been told (think Wizard, Paladin, etc.).

Undertale

In 2015, an American indie developer named Toby Fox published a game he built with GameMaker Studio, a humble do-it-yourself 2D game engine designed for novices. It's a great tool for learning the rudiments of programming and game design, but it's doubtful even YoYo Games, who makes the software, imagined that someone would use it to build a game as financially successful and influential as Fox's *Undertale*. On the surface, it looks like a charming little JRPG from the NES era, but don't let it fool you—*Undertale* is a deeply moving game that will get you rethinking the very concept of "monsters" in CRPGs.

I suggest you play the game before or instead of reading the commentary here. Indeed, the less you know before going in, the better.

Undertale, like so many games of this Renaissance, was made possible by Kickstarter (Figure 22.14). Fox's pitch was that he wanted to make a game that "utilizes the medium as a storytelling device ... instead of having the story and gameplay abstractions be completely separate." In one line, Fox has captured what is probably the greatest flaw in not just CRPGs, but any game with any narrative whatsoever. Over the course of this book, we've seen CRPGs evolve from simplistic, procedurally generated dungeon crawlers to sophisticated narratives chocked full of feature film-quality cutscenes, endless professionally voiced dialog, and enough lore to fill a bookshelf. It's not that this material is unimportant; it's just that when you look closely at how all of this is fused to the gameplay, you see that it's no better connected than streaming *The Lord of the Rings* in the background as you play solitaire.

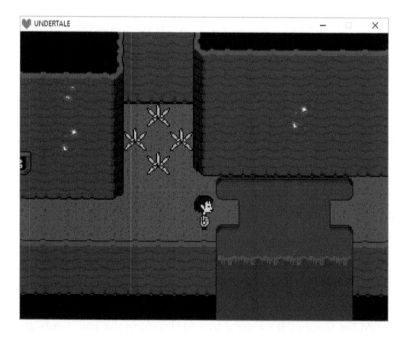

FIGURE 22.14 *Undertale* is essentially a philosophical meta-CRPG that will have you asking as many questions about game design as the meaning of life.

A handy example here is to compare Iron Tower Studios' *Age of Decadence* with the quick and dirty game it later built with its engine, *Dungeon Rats*. The former has a sophisticated narrative and well-developed setting; the latter is a straight-up dungeon crawl. Yet, playing them side-by-side, what difference does it really make? Of course, I'm being facetious here; context is what distinguishes CRPGs (or *D&D*, for that matter) from games of dice to games of dragons. Yet I can't help but shake the feeling that Fox is onto something big, and I'm not alone: Fox asked for a mere $5,000 to make his game. He raised $51,124, and *Undertale* went on to sell over a million copies.

Well, then, how does *Undertale* itself fuse together story and gameplay? Fox's approach is to continuously challenge our expectations, setting us up again and again to anticipate one kind of experience, only to surprise us with another. What results is really a metagame; we start thinking of not just the game we're playing, but the game Fox is playing with us—or, maybe, the game we're playing with ourselves. For example, early in the game Flowey the flower tells you that you need to kill monsters to gain experience, hardly a novel idea. However, this idea is immediately challenged when Flowey tries to kill you. You're saved by a motherly (or perhaps smother-motherly) monster named Toriel, who urges you not to kill; in fact, just stay safe at her place. I suppose you could turn off your PC at this point, but you're more likely to get bored and leave her house anyway. The fact that the game essentially "waits" for you to take this action is what Fox was talking about; a lesser game would've felt compelled to force you to, or at least prod you enough to make it clear what you "should do" next.

Another fascinating contrivance concerns reloading. If you kill a character, perhaps by accident, the natural thing to do is reload. Yet here again Fox shocks us—the game "remembers" and won't let you forget your mistake—old Flowey is there to remind us. Here again, when we try to reduce the game to its nature as a game, Fox makes it part of the story, instead. This is brilliant stuff.

Undertale is unquestionably a great game, but I wonder if its conceits would really translate into more games. Once you "get it," so to speak, do you really want more games like it? Indeed, there's even a petition on Change.org urging Fox not to make a sequel—as if he even wanted to: "I wished I had a way to quell the attention. I felt a strange powerlessness."[5] It's tempting to just roll your eyes at a statement like that; I'm reminded of Notch of *Minecraft* fame expressing a similar sentiment. If games like *Minecraft* and *The Stanley Parable* let us behind the curtain to make a game of game design, *Undertale* does the same for narrative. The problem with both is simply this: Once you bring the audience onstage with you, there's no second act.

Pathfinder: Kingmaker

Two major CRPGs (both, you guessed it, crowdfunded via Kickstarter) were released within one week of each other and not long before work on this book was completed. The first was *Bard's Tale IV*, an eagerly anticipated title discussed below.

The second was *Pathfinder: Kingmaker*, "the first isometric party-based computer RPG set in the Pathfinder fantasy universe" as developer Owlcat Games describes it. The game adapts the popular Pathfinder pen-and-paper RPG's *Kingmaker* "adventure path" (a collection of six interconnected adventures that can be played individually or as one large campaign) with veteran CRPG designer and writer Chris Avellone involved as lead narrative designer (Figure 22.15).

Given the importance of *Dungeons & Dragons* to CRPG history, it's worthwhile to look briefly at *Pathfinder*'s tabletop RPG pedigree. First released in 2009 by Paizo Publishing after a massive open playtest, *Pathfinder* is a modified version of the *D&D* version 3.5 ruleset legally published under Wizards of the Coast's Open Gaming License (OGL) and is often informally referred to as "*D&D* 3.75." The game proved a hit

FIGURE 22.15 A combat with bandits unfolds at Oleg's Trading Post, an early story location in *Pathfinder: Kingmaker*. Beta version shown.

(partly due to player dissatisfaction with *D&D* 4th Edition and partly due to its design innovations, character options and world building), quickly developing a large player base and staking out territory. Usually placing a very solid second in popularity in the tabletop RPG world only to *D&D* itself, *Pathfinder* has even at times outsold *D&D*. Speaking of second, as of this writing *Pathfinder* is currently in the midst of another massive open playtest as Paizo prepares to release *Pathfinder* Second Edition.

Pathfinder: Kingmaker's story finds the player and their companions sent by the nation of Brevoy into the untamed and dangerous Stolen Lands region of Golarion (the default *Pathfinder* RPG setting) to subdue its bandits, beasts, and other threats. Along the way the player will (as the name implies) ultimately establish, manage, and defend a growing kingdom with plenty of sidequests and challenges (not to mention plenty of NPC companions to either delight or despair you) along the way. Although adapting an existing and well-known pen-and-paper adventure, the developer has stated there will be unexpected twists—and those aforementioned companions to create a new experience for all.

Gameplay and user interface-wise, it's hard not to think of BioWare's isometric, party-based Infinity engine (*Baldur's Gate*, for example) while playing *Pathfinder: Kingmaker,* albeit with modern updates and UI innovations on Owlcat's part. One example of these innovations is the "Class" screen for character management. It's a well-designed screen that allows players to easily assess what class abilities they currently have access to as well as quickly review what class abilities are available at each level for planning ahead. Another innovation is a chart showing how a character's alignment shifts (or doesn't) over time based on actions the player takes (Figure 22.16).

The combat system is RTwP. Shane rightfully asks: Why do devs keep doing that when the source rulesets are tactical turn-based combat systems? However, you can set up automatic pauses keyed to certain events, and Owlcat included a helpful Tactical Time Flow option that allows time to move very slowly rather than stop altogether.

Given pen-and-paper *Pathfinder*'s success and the natural fit of *D&D* and CRPGs, it's surprising it took almost a decade for a game like *Pathfinder: Kingmaker* to appear. It seems the wait was worth it, as both reviews and player word of mouth are for the most part favorable and sales are speculated to be outpacing the latest entry in what is practically CRPG royalty, *Bard's Tale IV* (Figure 22.17).

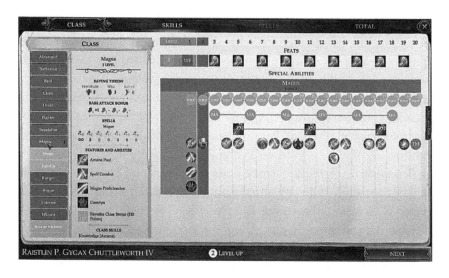

FIGURE 22.16 The "Class" screen (part of the character management UI) is an example of the design sense Owlcat Games has brought to *Pathfinder: Kingmaker*. Beta version shown.

Bard's Tale IV

Shane: Matt, *The Bard's Tale* series means so much to you personally. Why don't you take this one completely.

Matt:

The Song I sing

Will tell the tale

Of my love for CRPGs ...

I want to end this chapter with the series that, for me, started it all: *The Bard's Tale,* or, to be pedantic about it, *Tales of the Unknown Vol. 1* (Figure 22.18). It was the first game I ever bought with my own money, but it wasn't the first time I played it–no, I was one of many kids who was initially a trespasser in Skara Brae. However, my pirated copy lacked a manual, and in those days, there was no internet or in-game tutorials to help a kid out. I spent many happy evenings exploring those dungeons, often racing home after school to resume wherever I'd had to leave off the night before, and it wasn't easy even with the manual and handy map of Skara Brae!

FIGURE 22.17 Hear Matt sing the original *Bard's Tale* opening song (in costume, no less) on *Matt Chat* 71: The Bard's Tale.

Needless to say, when Fargo and inXile launched a Kickstarter to fund the first sequel in thirty years—*Bard's Tale IV*, I immediately readied my credit card for battle. The campaign eventually raised $1.5 million, and *The Bard's Tale IV: Barrows Deep* was launched on September 18, 2018.

As with *Wasteland 2*, inXile didn't attempt simply to update the interface of the older games. Instead, *Bard's Tale IV* switches between two modes. Exploration uses a first-person shooter style mode. During combat, the interface shows your party from behind, facing off against your opponents shown above them. A two-rowed grid across the bottom lets you position your characters; as before, it matters whether they are on the frontline or

FIGURE 22.18 inXile CEO Brian Fargo standing at the site of the actual Skara Brae, Bay of Skaill, Orkney, Scotland. Image by inXile.

FIGURE 22.19 Combat in *Bard's Tale IV* is still turn-based, but it works quite differently than in the original trilogy.

behind someone. There are also quite a few changes to character development and combat that we'll get into momentarily (Figure 22.19).

The game is set 100 years after the earlier games. Once again, dark forces plague Skara Brae. However, rather than turning to the Adventurer's Guild for help, the fanatical followers of The Temple of the Swordfather have turned the city against them, blaming them for the monsters roaming the streets. Naturally, it's your job to uncover the real threat, clear the Guild's name, and restore harmony to the city.

Combat in the original *Bard's Tale* games was a relatively simple affair; you give orders to each member of your party, then kick back and read the results of the round scroll by. It was a fine system for the time, but most of the action had to be imagined; all you saw on screen was a slightly animated portrait of the monster you were fighting. For *Bard's Tale IV*, inXile felt a radical redesign was necessary. Now your characters and each monster are shown on-screen and animated. It's still leaves much to the imagination, but it's a great deal more engaging from an audiovisual perspective.

Another update is a switch to action points, or "opportunity gems" as they're called. However, rather than allocate each character with gems, your party shares from a common pool. Since some abilities cost more gems than others, it's important to weigh them carefully before committing. Each character can have five abilities, divided into five categories:

arcane, battle ready, channel, drunk, and stance. Some require another resource called spell points, and bards must drink to use their abilities. Leveling up grants a skill point to spend on a tiered skill tree. Whereas in the earlier games only magic-users had access to prestige subclasses, now all classes have their own versions.

Sadly, so far the critical reception to the game has been mixed, mostly due to technical issues and bugs. InXile rushed two patches, but as we've seen time and time again, a bad first impression is hard to shake off. As for me, my time writing this book has prevented me from playing it as much as I'd like, but I'm loving the music and witty writing I've seen so far. If some consider it too old school, archaic, or just plain outdated, well, so am I, and damn proud of it.

There are many other games we could talk about in this chapter, but for now, please look at the Bestiary in the appendix for entries on *Avernum* (2000), *Frayed Knights: The Skull of S'makh-Daon* (2014), *Lords of Xulima* (2014), *Legends of Eisenwald* (2015), *Darkest Dungeon* (2016), *Grimoire: Heralds of the Winged Exemplar* (2017; a game that shocked many by actually shipping after twenty years of development), and many more.

NOTES

1. See Nick Horth of Game Watcher's interview with Fargo at https://www.gamewatcher.com/interviews/wasteland-2-interview/11192#.
2. See https://www.polygon.com/2017/5/9/15589492/divinity-original-sin-2-game-master-mode-gameplay-video-dungeons-and-dragons.
3. See https://www.kickstarter.com/projects/inxile/torment-tides-of-numenera/posts/1823045.
4. https://en.wikipedia.org/wiki/Hero-U:_Rogue_to_Redemption.
5. See http://undertale.tumblr.com/post/150397346860/retrospective-on-undertales-popularity.

CHAPTER 23

The Road Ever Ventures Forth

Shane (singing, if you can call it that): The Road goes ever on and on …
Matt (clears throat): Uh, Shane …
Shane: Huh? What?
Matt: That's a great nerd fantasy reference and everything, but shouldn't it, be, you know, well—
Shane: Be what?
Matt: Well, uh—hey, you know what? Just listen. *(He straightens up, brandishes his drinking horn like a total badass rat-killing, CRPG-loving VIKING and then, in a strange, deep, yet somehow familiar voice says)*
YOU MUST GATHER YOUR PARTY BEFORE VENTURING FORTH!
Great. Now my throat has run dry. I'm off to the tavern.
Shane: No problem. I've got this chapter.

The time between the first edition of *Dungeons & Desktops* and this updated version has been practically explosive for CRPGs. One can hope ten years from now we'll look back and see another prolific decade for the genre, necessitating the writing of *Advanced Dungeons & Desktops: Dungeons & Desktops* Third Edition.

It's quite possible. Scanning the near horizon and analyzing data and trends like *Watchmen's* Ozymandius sifting through the various images on the TV wall in his Antarctic retreat, the outlook is positive.

The Kickstarter Renaissance is far from over. Kickstarter currently lists over 1,600 active campaigns under the Video Games category that mention "RPG" across a wide variety of settings and genre. The same search on Indiegogo is healthy as well, although the total campaign count is not readily apparent via its website.

CRPGs UNDER DEVELOPMENT

Crowdfunded or not, here's a small sampling that shows the wide range of CRPGs currently under development (or hoped to soon be by eager devs):

- The "Russian Fallout" is coming in the form of *ATOM RPG*, a postapocalyptic game inspired by *Fallout* and *Wasteland* under development by Russian devs AtomTeam. It's essentially an isometric Fallout-type experience, but set in a postnuke Soviet Union with all of the cultural differences that entails.

- The fantasy genre *Realms Beyond: Ashes of the Fallen* by Ceres Games describes itself as a "classic single-player RPG featuring a party-based character system and tactical turn-based combat evolved from the SRD 3.5e ruleset."

- Not only is *Wasteland 3* slated for 2019 from inXile, but it also claims to offer bold new CRPG multiplayer experiences for a primarily "single-player" game: "Up to two players can each field a unique team of Rangers. When those teams are close together in the game world they'll be able to take part in the same turn-based skirmishes. But when they're apart, each player will have their own chance to move the campaign story forward, at times leading to a cascade of unintended consequences for the other player."[1]

- *Popup Dungeon* is a Roguelike dungeon crawler with a "papercraft" aesthetic that employs turn-based tactical combat. According to the developer Triple B Titles it lets players "create any weapon, ability, enemy, or hero they can imagine."

- Working under his Maverick Games label, one man dev team Don Wilkins is working hard on his labor of love *Stellar Tactics*, an ambitious turn-based procedural sci-fi CRPG with "ground combat, space exploration, deep character customization and a massive living universe with over 160,000 star systems." *Stellar Tactics* already shows a lot of promise based on just the Alpha version.

- Spanish development studio Gato Salvaje (with *Dragon Age* creative director Mike Laidlaw involved) has a project in the works called *The Waylanders*, a classically inspired CRPG that lets players time travel (via reincarnation) between two different historical eras and implements a combat system based around formations.

- Indie duo Shy Snake is currently hard at work on *Spy DNA*, a futuristic tactical squad CRPG involving genetically enhanced spies. *Spy DNA's* physics-model combat strives to be as realistic as possible when it comes to such elements as weapons ballistics, accuracy, range, and armor.

- Brian Fargo himself stirred the online pot on October 4, 2018, with a Twitter post stating simply "I happen to know who is working on BG3 ☺" with no further details offered.[2] Assuming he was referring to *Baldur's Gate III*, CRPG fans of course went into a frenzy of speculation. Assuming a studio *is* working on *Baldur's Gate III* my money would be on Beamdog given its history remastering the previous two *Baldur's Gate* games, creating the "midquel" *Siege of Dragonspear*, and Beamdog CEO Trent Oster publicly discussing vague plans for *Baldur's Gate III* were it to happen.[3]

The list truly goes on and on. As of this writing, Otherside Entertainment's *Underworld Ascendent* (the self-proclaimed spiritual successor to *Ultima Underworld*) is due out soon, CD Projekt Red's open-world *Cyberpunk 2077* is due in 2019 and, who knows, maybe we'll get to play *Star Citizen* before we spontaneously combust from CRPG overload. Not every highly anticipated game will live up to its promise, and there'll be plenty of indies out of nowhere that'll shine all the brighter for it.

PUBLISHERS NEED NOT APPLY

It should be noted that it's not just Kickstarter powering the current Renaissance. Increasingly, development studios both large and small have access to creative and effective ways to either take their pitch directly to the players or else keep a larger cut of game sales.

Let's briefly look at a few examples:

- Richard Garriott's Portalarium-developed *Shroud of the Avatar: Forsaken Virtues* used a variety of funding methods (including Kickstarter, recurring "telethon" style events, early access sales, venture capital funding, and more) to raise over $11 million.[4,5]

- The indie team for *Call of Saregnar* is relying solely on pledges via Patreon and donations from PayPal.

- Robot Cache (with names like Brian Fargo and Nolan Bushnell involved) hopes to be a Steam competitor that takes a much smaller cut per digital game sold (what publisher or developer wouldn't like that?) and will utilize blockchain technology to allow customers to resell their digital game. Resold games will result in an additional payment to the game's publisher or developer. Robot Cache is creating its own cryptocurrency called Iron (a nod to the Iron Bank from *Game of Thrones*).

It will be interesting to see what other paths become available to game developers as the Internet, social media, store fronts, and payment methods continue to change and innovate.

No matter what happens, though, we hope you've enjoyed our own massive dungeon crawl through the CRPG's past. There are countless treasures here to be savored, and if you've a mind to dust off some beloved game from your youth—or just stumble across one at a flea market, thrift shop, or dare we think, library—take the time to try it out for yourself.

Yes, you might struggle at first with the interface, wonder why there's no automapper, or where in blazes you should insert a 5¼" disk into a modern PC, but if you work up a sweat, at least you can wipe your forehead on that handy cloth map.

Now gather your party, venture forth, and go kill those rats menacing that poor farmer's basement!

NOTES

1. See https://www.polygon.com/platform/amp/2016/9/28/13081728/wasteland-3-announcement-fig-kickstarter-crowdfunding-release-date.
2. See https://twitter.com/BrianFargo/status/1047967566168174592.
3. See https://twitter.com/TrentOster/statuses/195534536350765056.
4. See https://kotaku.com/richard-garriott-reassures-shroud-of-the-avatar-backers-1795774769.
5. See https://www.seedinvest.com/portalarium/series.b/product.

Shane's Afterword: Surprise Encounter

Just when you thought the absolute last bit of gameplay was done, your humble co-author Shane offers you this final surprise encounter.

For those with a desire to make your own CRPG, well, that's a tale as old as *Dungeons & Dragons*. Many are the CRPG designers who began by playing *D&D*, moved up to Dungeon Master, and finally made the leap into computer games. They had to learn to master the intricacies of computer programming, but nowadays the only real barrier is your own creativity, ambition, and dedication to getting the job done. If you are serious about doing it yourself, we strongly suggest getting a copy of Neal and Jana Hallford's *Swords & Circuitry: A Designer's Guide to Computer Role-Playing Games*. Powerful game development engines such as Unity, Unreal Engine 4, and Lumberyard are available for free.

Meanwhile, for those who just want to play the games mentioned in this book, be sure to check the Good Old Games website (https://www.gog.com). There are many classic CRPGs available for sale there, already preconfigured and ready to run on a modern PC. Steam is also an option in some cases; however, many players prefer GOG.com since Steam games use DRM. If you're a bit more daring and don't mind hit-or-miss technical experiences, The Internet Archive Software Collection (https://archive.org/details/software) has thousands of software titles and games preserved for posterity.

There are plenty of online discussion boards dedicated to CRPGs old and new, such as *GameBanshee, RPG Watch,* and *RPG Codex* (be warned, Codex is a great resource, but you'll need your flameproof underwear should you venture into the forums).

For those who prefer to experience playing CRPGs vicariously through others, there are a multitude of players who will allow you to do so on platforms like Twitch and YouTube. Another fantastic resource is The CRPG Addict (http://crpgaddict.blogspot.com/) where Chester Bolingbroke (a pseudonym) offers continuing, wonderfully detailed posts documenting his playthroughs of classic CRPGs. In his own words: "This blog is about my personal journey (roughly chronologically) through 40 years of computer role-playing games (CRPGs). I play each game and discuss its strengths and weaknesses, its place in the history of RPGs, its influences, and just what it's like to play the game today."

Matt: Feel free to visit *Matt Chat* on YouTube (https://www.youtube.com/user/blacklily8) where I review CRPGs and interview all manner of professional and amateur CRPG developers.

Shane: Matt's being too modest. It's THE best resource out there for documenting video game history with the people who were there.

Matt: You can reach my co-author, Shane Stacks, at his site shaneplays.com, where he takes listeners on a journey into the things we love with his weekly *Shane Plays Geek Talk* live talk radio show and podcast. Shane is also very active on Twitter (@shaneplays) and does the occasional (and usually a bit clueless) CRPG Let's Play video series on YouTube (https://www.youtube.com/user/goshaneplays).

Appendix:
The CRPG Bestiary

2400 A.D.

Chuck "Chuckles" Bueche's *2400 A.D.* was published in 1987 by Origin. Set in a postapocalyptic sci-fi world called Metropolis, the player takes on the role of a rebel fighting his way to Tzorg Central Control to defeat the alien robots that have taken over. John Romero of *Doom* fame was tasked with porting it to the Commodore 64 and Apple II, but these projects were canceled, likely due to poor sales and unfavorable comparisons to *Ultima*. In any case, it convinced Chuckles to stick with technical work and leave the game design to others (Figure A.1).

ABANDONED PLACES

This is a 1992 *Dungeon Master*–style game by Artgame for Amiga and MS-DOS. It offers cinematic cutscenes and a top-down "bird's eye" display mode for overland travel. It also has a diamond-shaped directional selector for attacking in any direction. It's particularly tough at the beginning: Your party must escape from a monster-infested temple—without any arms or armor! Its publisher, Electronic Zoo, collapsed soon after its release. Its sequel, *Abandoned Places II* (1993), made some improvements to the interface, such as a heartbeat sound that grows louder and more frantic when monsters are nearby—a nice effect borrowed from *Dungeons of Daggorath*.

ADVANCED DUNGEONS & DRAGONS CARTRIDGE

This game for the Mattel Intellivision was made by Tom Loughry and published in 1982, who also did the sequel, *Treasure of Tarmin*, a year later. In the first version, you control a group of three archers exploring

FIGURE A.1 Chuckles is better known for *Autoduel,* but he also did *2400 A.D.,* an early sci-fi CRPG.

monster-infested dungeons. The dungeons are procedurally generated. The bulk of the gameplay amounts to a *Robotron*-esque shoot 'em up; you can fire in eight different directions and move independently. It was later subtitled "Cloudy Mountain" to avoid confusion with the sequel.

ADVANCED DUNGEONS & DRAGONS: TREASURE OF TARMIN CARTRIDGE

Loughry's sequel to "Cloudy Mountain" is much different than the first in all the right ways. This time the perspective is first-person. There's an inventory system, hidden rooms, hunger and thirst mechanics, real-time battles, and 256 procedurally generated mazes. The walls of the dungeons are solid color, too, not just wireframe. There's no leveling system per se, but you can build up your character by collecting weapons, shields, and other items. An enhanced version followed for Mattel's short-lived Aquarius computer. All in all, it's an ambitious game that every Intellivision and Aquarius fans should own, but the lack of a proper leveling system makes us hesitant to christen it the first console RPG (Figure A.2).

AGE OF CONAN

Robert E. Howard's *Conan* stories are among the best of the swords-and-sorcery genre, so it was only a matter of time before someone tried bringing his world of Hyboria online. It finally happened in 2008, thanks to Funcom. It's known for its brutal real-time combat, mature content (including plenty

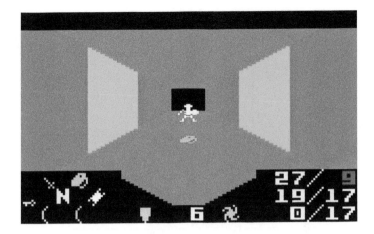

FIGURE A.2 The second *AD&D* game for the Intellivision is a truly impressive feat of programming. Photo by CRPG Addict, who credits it as the first console RPG ported to a PC.

of nudity), and large-scale player-versus-player warfare. There was some speculation that it might be a *"WoW* killer," but a lack of polish in later areas dampened much of this enthusiasm. In 2009, it began offering free-to-play options in a gambit to entice new players, but still hasn't managed to live up to the expectations set by its impressive opening segments.

AION

This hit Korean free-to-play MMORPG was released by NCSoft in 2008. It's known for its "PvPvE," gameplay, which fuses player-versus-player with player-versus-environment combat. Players clash in aerial combat against each other and NPCs to control fortresses, which, when held, allow you to collect taxes and other rewards.

ALIEN FIRES: 2199 A.D.

This 1987 sci-fi-themed CRPG was written by Jeff Simpson and Sky Matthews on a Commodore Amiga and later ported to Atari ST and MS-DOS. It has a first-person perspective and the original version uses the Amiga's speech synthesizer for dialog (think Stephen Hawking). It features a wonderfully diverse cast of characters, fantastic ambience, and an anxiety-inducing heartbeat system similar to *Dungeons of Daggorath*. The story is a mash-up of *Doctor Who* and Conrad's *Heart of Darkness*. Unfortunately, its virtues aren't sufficient to overcome uneven pacing and unbalanced combat (Figure A.3).

FIGURE A.3   *Alien Fires: 2199 A.D.* is one of the weirdest CRPGs ever.

ALIEN LOGIC

In 1994 SSI released this interesting if obscure real-time, top-down and side-by-side game developed by Ceridus Software. It was based on the tabletop *Skyrealms of Journey* RPG. It's set 3,500 years in the future, after Earth has established a colony on a planet already occupied by two civilizations. These civilizations don't object to the new colony as long as it stays in its place and receives regular shipments from Earth. However, the feeding tube from Earth is severed, leaving the colonists to their own devices. Tensions escalate rapidly, and war breaks out between the settlers and the natives. Combat is a furious side-by-side fighter style affair, but otherwise this is a thinking person's game. You'll have to learn a great deal about the two civilizations and their technology, much of which is organic in nature.

ALTERNATE REALITY: THE CITY/THE DUNGEON

Published by Datasoft in 1985, Philip Price's *Alternate Reality: The City* was the first of a planned series of five games based on the same premise: aliens abducting the character and transporting him to different realities. Only the first two were completed; the second part, *The Dungeon*, appeared in 1987. The series has a cult status among fans of the Atari 8-bit computers, where these games originated. It has a first-person perspective and smooth-scrolling 3D graphics that were spectacular on the Atari 800,

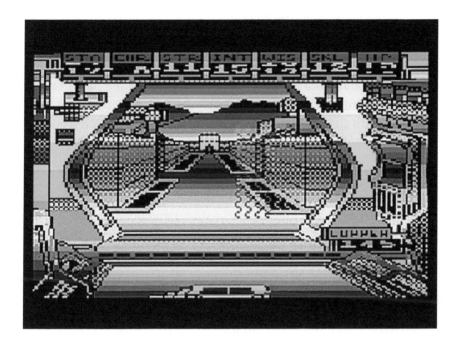

FIGURE A.4 *Alternate Reality* is a cult classic CRPG for Atari 8-bit computers.

with cool effects like darkening for nighttime and flowing water. It also has four-channel sound and a song with synchronized on-screen lyrics. Unless you're into karaoke, the game's main appeals are exploring the city and building up your character (Figure A.4).

AVADON (SERIES)

See *Avernum*.

AVERNUM (SERIES)

This is a massive series of indie CRPGs by Jeff Vogel, a prolific solitary developer called Spiderweb Software. They began as remakes of a shareware series called *Exile* from the mid-1990s, but the later games are original creations with an updated game engine. There are many to choose from, and opinions vary widely about which one's the best or which one a newcomer should play first. *Avernum 6* from 2012 is a fan favorite. In any case, if you're a fan of 1990s isometric games, you should give this series a try, as well as Vogel's other series: *Avadon* and *Geneforge*.

THE BANNER SAGA

This distinctive tactical RPG series was developed by Stoic Studio, a company founded by former BioWare staff. Inspired by Norse mythology, it has turn-based combat and a caravan story reminiscent of the classic *Oregon Trail*. It's rightfully celebrated for its lovely artwork, which reminds me of Ralph Bakshi's classic animations. It was released in 2014, with sequels in 2016 and 2018.

THE BARD'S TALE

This 2004 "spiritual successor" of the classic CRPG series was developed by Brian Fargo's inXile Entertainment studio and published by Vivendi Universal Games for consoles and PC; now there's even versions for mobiles. It's essentially a parody of the genre, and it's effective humor for the most part. There's also more emphasis on your character's role as a bard; it even has singalongs. The gameplay is far removed from the original series, though—this is more of an action game with a single-player character. It's not a bad game, but it disappointed old-school fans hoping for something closer to the original series.

BLACK CRYPT

This *Dungeon Master*–style game was developed by a Wisconsin-based company called Raven Software, who would go on to create many well-known games for the PC. Published in 1992 by Electronic Arts in 1992, *Black Crypt* was available only for the Commodore Amiga, where it maintains a loyal fanbase. Unlike *Dungeon Master,* it lets players create characters rather than select them from a cast of premade heroes. The storyline has the party seeking out an evil cleric named Estoroth Paingiver, who's managed to escape his magically sealed Black Crypt and now threatens the land of Astera. *Black Crypt* was originally envisioned as a conventional tabletop RPG, designed by brothers Brian and Steve Raffel, who ended up doing the art for this computer game instead.

BLACK DESERT ONLINE

RedFox Games published this Korean MMORPG by Pearl Abyss on November 15, 2017. While its narrative qualities may be lacking, it's widely praised for its action-based combat, crafting, and production options. In some ways it's more like *Civilization* than other MMORPGs. If you've ever wanted to build your own brewery in an MMO—even growing your own potatoes—this game's for you. And yes, I know beer isn't typically made with potatoes, but, er, magic.

BLOODWYCH

This game sounds like a product from a truly demented sandwich artist, but it's actually an early *Dungeon Master*–style game noted for its split-screen interface that lets two people enjoy the game simultaneously. It was developed by Mirrorsoft and published by Konami for a variety of systems. Each player controls a four-member party that can move about the dungeons independently of the other. It also has a neat dialog system, which lets you interact with friends and foes even during combat. Spells are chosen from a list rather than made by combining runes. The goal is to destroy the evil Zendick, whose undead minions have been terrorizing the village of Treihadwyl. Only a secret alliance of psychic sorcerers named the Bloodwych can prevent Zendick from ravaging the land of Trazere. Ultimately, the party must confront the Lord of Entropy, a being whose purpose in life is to dissolve the "fabric of the universe" and restore it to its original chaotic state.

CENTAURI ALLIANCE

Though he's much better known for *The Bard's Tale,* Michael Cranford also did this sci-fi-themed CRPG, published in 1989 by Broderbund. The interface is similar to his earlier game, but this one has combat taking place on a hexagonal grid reminiscent of miniatures wargaming. This hexagon theme was even carried over to the box! Both story and setting were excellent, but the game faltered in the marketplace, most likely due to its exclusivity to 8-bit systems (Figure A.5).

CLANS

This *Diablo*-like was developed by Computer House and published by Strategy First in 1999. It was an attempt to blend *Diablo* with a point-and-click adventure game. To that end, it offers puzzles based mostly on the "find object, use object" model. It replaces the experience point-based leveling system with a system based on finding special objects or quaffing magical potions. The main quest is to find the Crown of Peace and destroy an evil demon. It has a fairly robust multiplayer system, but no Battle.net or matchmaking system.

FIGURE A.5 Not even many *Bard's Tale* fans are aware of Cranford's *Centauri Alliance* CRPG.

THE DARK HEART OF UUKRUL

This is an often-overlooked Gold Box–style game developed by Digital Studio and published by Broderbund in 1989. It incorporates *Ultima's* multiple-choice dilemma system for creating up to four characters and features a handy automapper. Magic is based on rings of various metals whose value determines the strength of the spell in question. The story has players seeking out the titular heart, which is the only means of destroying the merciless tyrant. It was never as popular as the games it was inspired by, but it's worth seeking out if you're a fan of the style (Figure A.6).

DARKEST DUNGEON

Red Hook Studios released this Gothic Roguelike in 2016, and it quickly became a cult classic. Featuring a distinctive, hand-drawn art style, it ventures into psychological territory seldom explored in other CRPGs. How would real-life adventurers feel about being exposed to so much killing? How long could they really maintain their sanity under these conditions? If you've ever wondered about such things, you'll find much to love about this award-winning game.

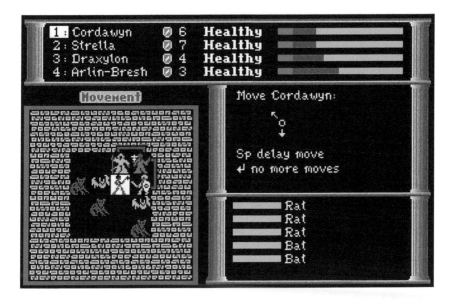

FIGURE A.6   If you like the Gold Box games, check out *Dark Heart of Uukrul* (not to be confused with *The Dark Heart of Steve Urkel*).

DARKSTONE

This *Diablo*-like was designed by Delphine Software and published in 1999 by Gathering for Sony's PlayStation and Windows. Sometimes dismissed as a shameless clone, in reality it differs quite markedly. For one, it has true 3D graphics and the ability to control two characters, though only one at the time (the other is controlled by the computer). Its 3D camera controls were a huge step forward, and it's worth noting that this was a year ahead of *Diablo II*, which still offered only a 2D isometric view. GameSpy declared *Darkstone* the action CRPG of the year for 1999. *Darkstone* also offered a multiplayer option, but no equivalent of Blizzard's Battle.net server. Instead, players set up their own servers using IPX (for LAN parties) or TCP/IP.

DEATH BRINGER

See *Xenomorph*.

DINK SMALLWOOD

One of the earliest *Diablo* clones, this satirical game by Seth Robinson was published in 1998 by Iridon Interactive. *Dink Smallwood* was noted for its irreverent and provocative, quirky humor. It also featured a construction tool named *Dinkedit*. It was later released as freeware and still later as an app for mobiles.

DRAGON'S DOGMA

This 2012 open world action RPG by Capcom (later enhanced and rereleased as *Dragon's Dogma: Dark Arisen*) features real-time combat and was reportedly inspired by *The Elder Scrolls* and *Fable* series. The narrative is rather weak, but the game does have a nice "Pawn" system for controlling the other characters in your party. In addition to helping in combat, the pawns yell advice and can be issued orders.

DRAGONS OF FLAME

Although *Heroes of the Lance* serves more often as the butt of jokes than a source for nostalgia, SSI and U.S. Gold apparently found it successful enough to warrant a sequel. Thus we get *Dragons of Flame* in 1989. It's quite like the first, though now with a special top-down overland travel mode and a new story. This time, the Heroes' mission is to charge into a fortress called Pax Tharkas, recover the sword Wyrmslayer, and free the captives held in the dungeon.

DRAKENSANG: THE DARK EYE

This German import is based on *The Dark* or *Das Schwarze Auge* roleplaying system. It's a third-person, party-based game with real-time with pause combat. Reviews for the game are generally positive, though some unfairly dismiss it as a budget gamer's *Dragon Age: Origins*. If nothing else, it's worth playing just to see how the team adapted "Germany's *D&D*" for the desktop. It was designed by Radon Labs and released in 2009. The second game, a prequel called *Drakensang: The River of Time,* was published in North America in 2011.

DUNGEON RATS

This 2016 game from Iron Tower Studios is a relatively straightforward hack 'n slash game based on the *Age of Decadence* engine. You play as a prisoner in a prison run by gangs, and you have to fight your way out— either on your own or with allies. There's plenty of tactical turn-based excitement here, but don't expect the narrative depth of *Age of Decadence*.

EXILE

See *Avernum*.

EXPEDITION AMAZON

This obscure 1983 game by Williard Phillips for the Apple II and Commodore 64 is set in recent times. Your goal is to send a team of four explorers (medic, field assistant, radio operator, and guard) on an expedition into ancient Incan ruins. Instead of orcs and dragons, players struggle against angry natives, anacondas, and malaria-infected mosquitoes. Gameplay is similar to *Sword of Fargoal*'s, though with fixed rather than randomized dungeons. There's quite a bit of humor; the intro screen shows Flint University as a rundown trailer in a trailer park, with a slow-moving armadillo scuttling past, and items recovered from battles with Amazons include Pac-Man lunch boxes (Figure A.7).

THE FAERY TALE ADVENTURE

Here we have an early action RPG that debuted on the Amiga back in 1987. Its story is about three brothers, Julian, Philip, and Kevin, who are sent after a talisman stolen by an evil necromancer. It features a massive gameworld and truly impressive audiovisuals for the time. It was later ported to several other platforms, including the Sega Genesis. It was designed by David Joiner for MicroIllusions (Figure A.8).

FIGURE A.7 *Expedition Amazon* is an intriguing early title with lots of geeky humor.

FIGURE A.8 It's not much of a stretch to call *The Faery Tale Adventure* a *Diablo*-like before *Diablo* was a thing.

FATE

This 2005 *Diablo*-like by WildStudios/WildTangent was published in 2005 and was successful enough to warrant three sequels. It has randomized dungeon levels, full 3D graphics, pets, fishing, and a retirement option (meaning you can create a new character with special benefits inherited from your old one). There's no multiplayer, but it still sold well and won several awards. Its cutesy style and relaxed difficulty led some to call it "*Diablo* for kids," but it's fun for anyone who likes a good action RPG. Did I mention the pets carry loot for you?

FIGHTING FANTASY

This pre–Golden Age series was published by Puffin Books (an imprint of Penguin) for the Commodore 64 and ZX Spectrum. These games are based on a successful series of printed solo-player "gamebooks" by Steve Jackson (not to be confused with the founder of Steve Jackson Games) and Ian Livingstone. Six games were published between 1984 and 1987, mostly by Puffin, but later by Adventure Soft UK, Ltd. Some, like *The Citadel of Chaos* and *The Forest of Doom* (both 1984), are straightforward adaptations; at critical moments, you select an appropriate course of action from a small, numbered menu. Later games (*Seas of Blood, Rebel Planet*) offer an adventure game–style parser supplemented with graphical illustrations. More recently, Tin Man Games developed and published *The Forest of Doom, Appointment with Fear, Caverns of the Snow Witch, Starship Traveller,* and *House of Hell.* They feature physics-based dice rolling for battles, automapping, automatic adventure sheets, and stat keeping. Highly recommended!

FRAYED KNIGHTS: THE SKULL OF S'MAKH-DAON

My good friend Jay "Rampant Coyote" Barnson wrote this charming throwback title in 2014. His goal was to recreate the social nature of a tabletop game with the exploration and tactical combat of a game like *Wizardry 6.* It's a lighthearted romp with plenty of inside jokes and fourth wall breaking, but the level designs and story arcs make for a surprisingly sophisticated role-playing experience. I highly recommend it.

GEMSTONE WARRIOR/GEMSTONE HEALER

These hybrid shoot 'em up/CRPG games by Peter William Lount and Trouba Gossen were published by SSI in 1984 and 1986, respectively. You control an armor-clad figure who roams about dungeons firing crossbow bolts and fireballs at a variety of enemies. The quest is to find the five pieces of the gemstone, a powerful artifact that once brought peace and prosperity to the land, shooting plenty of enemies who get in the way. The sequel is much the same, though the quest is slightly more complicated (this time, the player is searching for tools to heal the gemstone that was damaged before the first game). Some consider them precursors to the action RPG subgenre, though they lack any sort of class, level, or skill system (Figure A.9).

GENEFORGE

See *Avernum.*

GRIMOIRE: HERALDS OF THE WINGED EXEMPLAR

Fans of old-school *Wizardry* and *Might and Magic* games should check out Blakemore's long-awaited magnum opus from 2017. Twenty years in the making, it's a labor of love with challenging turn-based combat, great retro artwork, clever puzzles, charming MIDI music, and no shortage of Blakemore's unique wit and personality. Incline!

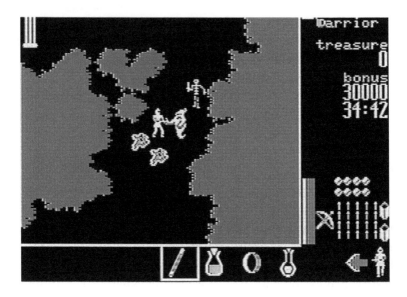

FIGURE A.9 *Gemstone Warrior* is an obscure action RPG, though the "action" component here is reminiscent of a shoot 'em up game.

HARD NOVA

Published in 1990 by Electronic Arts, *Hard Nova* can be thought of as an unofficial sequel to Karl Buiter's earlier game *Sentinel Worlds* (see below). This one has more of a cyberpunk theme but shares most of his earlier game's mechanics. Perhaps the biggest change concerns the role of the main character, who is now a mercenary rather than a military officer. *Hard Nova* is usually considered the better of the two games.

HEIMDALL

As far as I'm concerned, there can never be enough CRPGs based on Norse mythology. Far from a serious take on the setting, this quirky action RPG from 1991 seems to channel *Eric the Viking* (1989). The character creation process is the most interesting bit—instead of the usual rolling for stats, you play minigames like drunken axe-hurling. It was developed by The 8th Day and was successful enough to warrant a sequel, *Heimdall 2*, in 1994.

HERETIC KINGDOMS: THE INQUISITION

This *Diablo*-like was developed by the Slovakian-based 3D People and published in 2005 by Got Game Entertainment. It is notable for several reasons, first for its female protagonist. The backstory is also intriguing, set in a world where those practicing religion are savagely persecuted by the inquisitors. Your character is one of these inquisitors, but you decide whether to follow her mission. The leveling system uses school letter grades instead of hit dice, and the skill system is based on bonuses received from "attunements" from weapons or items. All 100 of these attunements are worth gaining, even though only so many can be active at any given time. Once again, bugs and rough edges tempered reviews, but it's worth seeking out if you're a fan of the subgenre.

HEXX: HERESY OF THE WIZARD

This is a lesser-known Underworld clone developed and published in 1994 by Psygnosis. It's a combination of *Dungeon Master* and *Ultima Underworld* that lets you control a party of four adventurers rather than a lone hero. As with the *Dungeon Master*, the player doesn't create characters but selects them from a pool. *Hexx* doesn't seem to have made much impact on the market, even though it was relatively free of bugs. The interface is somewhat clumsy, particularly when casting spells during the real-time combat segments, but the bigger problem was the overall mediocrity of the game in terms of graphics, story, and characters.

THE INCREDIBLE ADVENTURES OF VAN HELSING

If you ever wanted a *Diablo*-like set in a Gothic noir world with plenty of weird science, check out this 2013 game from NeocoreGames. The game took its name from Bram Stoker's vampire hunter in *Dracula;* your character is his son. You can play it solo or with up to three friends. There are two sequels available and a compilation of all three games called *Final Cut.*

KINGDOMS OF AMULAR: RECKONING

THQ Nordic recently acquired the rights to this 2012 action RPG from 38 Studios and Big Huge Games. Sadly, it was the only game 38 Studios managed to release before going bankrupt. The idea was to create a game that would be a "marriage between *God of War* and *The Elder Scrolls IV: Oblivion,* and to that end we think they succeeded, with just enough RPG mechanics to add weight to the action-based combat. Famed comic book creator and artist Todd McFarlane and fantasy author R. A. Salvatore lent their talents to the project.

LEGEND OF FAERGHAIL

This is a German game that was translated into English and made available for the Amiga, Atari ST, and DOS platforms in 1990. Designed by Electronic Design Hannover, it's similar to *The Bard's Tale* and even allows players to import their characters from that series as well as from SSI's *Phantasie* games. Like many German CRPGs, it is quite complex and best suited for experts—the ninety-five-page manual is essential reading for anyone hoping to master it. The goal is to learn why the normally peaceful elves have suddenly turned violent. Naturally, this simple quest soon spirals into a much thicker plot that'll have the party traipsing all across (and underneath) Faerghail. All in all, it's a well-crafted and highly detailed CRPG that deserves more attention (Figure A.10).

LEGENDS OF EISENWALD

This innovative hybrid of adventure, strategy, and role-playing elements was designed by Aterdux Entertainment, a studio from Minsk, Belarus, and published in 2015. It's set in old Germany, but it avoids the supernatural and other clichés of the genre. It's a bit like the *Heroes of Might and Magic* series, with battles taking place between squads facing off side-by-side on a hexagonal grid. The developers claimed to have solved the "main enemy of turn based battles—lack of dynamics," but it's debatable whether

FIGURE A.10   *Legend of Faerghail* is one of many high-quality German imports that deserves more attention.

its solution—every movement is also an attack—really does the trick. It definitely speeds things up, though.

LEGENDS OF VALOUR

This 1992 game, developed by Synthetic Dimensions and published by SSI, is one of the earliest and most unabashed attempts to mimic the *Ultima Underworld* model. Notably, it was available not only for DOS but also for the Amiga and Atari ST platform, which is quite a feat considering the complexities of porting a 3D graphics engine. It also had day and night cycles, which *The Stygian Abyss* lacked since it was set underground. Finally, there are forty-five quests, multiple endings, and "an unparalleled array of professions" available at guilds and temples. To complete the game, the player's character must join at least four guilds, rising up the ranks in at least one temple and guild to become their master. On the negative side, combat amounts to a simple reflex action (how fast you can click the mouse), and there's plenty of bugs. Nevertheless, it has a dedicated following, especially among Amiga and Atari ST fans.

LORDS OF XULIMA

This underrated 2014 series was funded on Kickstarter and created by Numantian Games, a studio based in Madrid, Spain. It's a charming series that plays something like the *Heroes of Might and Magic* series, but with a turn-based combat system closer to a *Dragon Quest* game. It has a large world to explore, slick production values, and enough combat and leveling mechanics to keep you busy for many weeks.

MARVEL HEROES

This free-to-play massively multiplayer action RPG—sometimes called "Marvel *Diablo*"—launched in 2013 and crashed in 2017. It featured over 100 Marvel characters, including the ever-popular Spider-Man and Iron Man. Problems were numerous; one reviewer compared it to "one of those 80s half-arsed movie tie-in arcade games that would be ported clumsily to home computer." Even with the benefit of Marvel's intellectual property behind it, it compared miserably to the earlier *City of Heroes*.

MOEBIUS: THE ORB OF CELESTIAL HARMONY

This hybrid beat 'em up/CRPG game, published in 1985 by Origin, is an effort to combine the side-by-side fighting mechanics of games like *Karateka* and *Street Fighter* with CRPG elements. It is set in a world

FIGURE A.11   *Windwalker* is the sequel to *Moebius: The Orb of Celestial Harmony,* a sort of proto–*Jade Empire.*

inspired by ancient China and integrates various aspects of Eastern mysticism, such as meditation and reagents such as tiger teeth for spells. You might like the action-based combat or you may not; some critics found the combination "schizophrenic." In any case, it was popular enough to warrant a sequel, *Windwalker,* in 1989 (Figure A.11).

NEVERWINTER

Not to be confused with any of the various *Neverwinter Nights* games, this is a free action-based MMORPG based on the 4th Edition of *Dungeons & Dragons.* Developed by Cryptic Studios and published by the Chinese company Perfect World Entertainment in 2013, its combat gets a lot of praise. Rather than adopt the industry standard of dozens of skills or abilities, *Neverwinter* does more with less. Instead of staring at your action bar waiting for abilities to cool down, you're watching for the enemies' telegraphs to know when to dodge. Likewise, there's no tabbing for targets, but a free aiming or reticle system. On the negative side, it gets repetitive rather quickly, and the developers failed to bring the Forgotten Realms campaign setting to life.

NOX

One of the more popular and charming *Diablo*-likes, this game was developed by Westwood Studios and published by Electronic Arts in 2000. Westwood took Blizzard's lead and set up its own free centralized servers (Westwood Online) to support multiplayer, offering five different game types for up to thirty-two simultaneous players. It was noted for its TrueSight technique, which limits the display to the character's field of view. Another nice feature is an interactive environment; barrels can be smashed, rocks moved to block passages, and fires doused with water. The main character, Jack, is a trailer park resident who gets sucked into his television set and emerges in Nox, a medieval world threatened by an evil sorceress and her minions. Naturally, Jack's mission is to defeat the sorceress and become a great hero. It suffers from a handholding role-playing engine, which automatically improves your stats after each chapter—the same upgrades regardless of how many monsters you slay. Nevertheless, the game sold decently and has since become a cult classic. Westwood developed a free expansion called *Nox Quest.*

PATH OF EXILE

This is an award-winning free-to-play online *Diablo*-like released by Grinding Gear Games in 2013. According to its developers, it was created precisely because they felt the subgenre had fallen into a slump and wanted to do something about it. Although they rely on microtransactions for income, they're quick to point out that you can't pay to win; money gets you only cosmetic items and various conveniences. In any case, the randomized content ensures high replayability, and you can explore on your own if you don't like playing with other people. The developers are also right to resist the MMORPG label for their game; gameplay occurs in small instanced groups.

THE REALM

This early and rather obscure MMORPG was published by Sierra in May 1997. Unlike *Meridian 59*, *The Realm* was a 2D, side-scrolling game, with graphics reminiscent of Sierra's many point-and-click adventure games (*King's Quest*). It had turn-based combat, four classes, and skills for each. While quite simplistic compared to other MMORPGs, it was intended to be accessible even to children. It's now operated by Norseman Games.

REALMS OF DARKNESS

One of SSI's more obscure games, Gary Scott Smith's *Realms of Darkness* was published in 1986 for the Apple II, with a C-64 port in 1987. Like *Rings of Zilfin* (see Chapter 7), *Realms of Darkness* emphasizes puzzles and storyline, but goes a step closer to adventure games by incorporating an actual text parser to simulate dialog with the various characters encountered by the party. It also strays from conventional fantasy with anachronisms like lawnmowers, electric fans, and robots. Perhaps the best way to describe the game is seven interconnected scenarios, with different modes for overland and dungeon exploration (the latter uses a wireframe mode similar to *Wizardry* or *Akalabeth*). Using a text parser to simulate dialog was a promising idea, but it failed to live up to the hype. Also see *Tangled Tales*, another game by Smith (Figure A.12).

SCAVENGERS OF THE MUTANT WORLD

Published in 1988 for MS-DOS, this game borrows *Autoduel*'s postapocalyptic setting and build-a-vehicle concept. However, this time the only purpose in building the vehicle is to escape to a radiation-free zone, hacking and slashing anything or anyone that gets in the way. It might have looked good on paper, but the graphics are terrible and the gameplay hopelessly frustrating: The monsters simply grow tougher as the

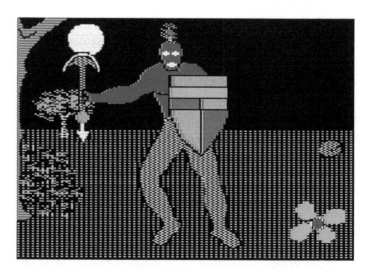

FIGURE A.12 This game is called *Realms of Darkness*. Beware of crazy, axe-wielding purple men in pantyhose.

game progresses, eventually becoming overpowered. In short, there's more disaster here than the one serving as the game's premise, but it's worth seeking out this game just to see how badly developers can bungle a promising concept.

SENTINEL WORLDS

Inspired by *Starflight,* Karl Buiter's *Sentinel Worlds I: Future Magic* is a game Electronic Arts published in 1989. Players assemble a five-person crew, who are then assigned skill points in areas as diverse as gunnery, bribery, and ATV repair. Combat can take place either on the ground or in space, but there is more to this game than who had the bigger gun. Players also must choose the right options from conversation menus, where a few bad choices cam force restoring to an older saved game. The learning curve is steep, which may explain its lack of popularity compared to similar games (Figure A.13).

SPACE WRECKED: 14 BILLION LIGHT YEARS FROM EARTH

This impressively titled game was developed by Celestial Software and released in 1990. It's a *Dungeon Master*–style game quite similar to *Xenomorph,* but lets you program six different droids to assist with your mission.

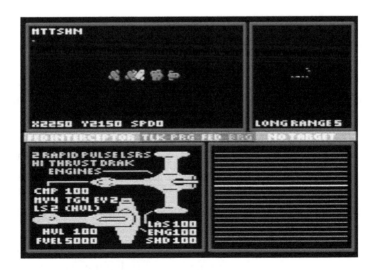

FIGURE A.13 *Sentinel Worlds I: Future Magic* is an ambitious space sim from the late 1980s.

STAR TREK ONLINE

Space, the final frontier! Countless fans of Gene Roddenbury's *Star Trek* franchise have dreamed of joining Starfleet and captaining a starship. On February 2, 2010, Cryptic Studios attempted to give them that chance with this free-to-play MMORPG. Loaded with content and references to the show and movies, *Star Trek Online* offers both ground and space missions, and its space combat is particularly, er, engaging. It's received mixed reviews, mostly concerning its repetitiveness, but others consider it one of the most underrated MMORPGs.

SWORD COAST LEGENDS

Developed by n-Space in conjunction with Digital Extremes and close consultation with Wizards of the Coast, this party-based action RPG adapted the *D&D* 5th Edition rules for a story set in the popular *D&D* setting *Forgotten Realms*. A combination of what many felt was a lackluster story without real choices and a DM mode that failed to deliver on marketing hype ultimately delivered a critical blow to the game with no healing potions left. Released in 2015, sales were suspended at the end of 2017 with multiplayer servers shut down in July 2018 (sadly, n-Space closed its doors in 2016 after twenty-two years of existence). The game received one free DLC in the form of the Underdark-centric *Rage of Demons*.

TANGLED TALES

Designed by Gary Scott Smith and published by Origin for Apple II and other platforms in 1989, this game is a light RPG intended for young people. It features three adventures and some fifty "peculiar" characters and humorous anachronisms such as a rad California surfer dude. You play as an inept young apprentice whose spell book was seized by Eldritch, his angry master. Now the apprentice seeks redemption by completing three interconnected quests with the help of some memorable companions. To better appeal to kids, it uses simple adjectives rather than percentages to describe abilities. For example, speed is described as "lethargic, sluggish, brisk," and so on. Instead of the text parser system introduced in Smith's earlier *Realms of Darkness* (see above), this game uses a predefined menu and tracks known keywords. All in all, it's a cute, accessible, and humorous game with good personality, but not enough challenge for experienced players.

TERA

TERA stands for The Exiled Realm of Arborea, a game designed by a South Korean developer with the charming name of Bluehole. It was released in North America on May 1, 2012, and went to a free-to-play model eight months later. Its main innovation concerns targeting. Rather than clicking or tabbing to target a monster, you must line up a crosshair cursor. Dodging is another crucial mechanic, which has to be timed just right. You may be disturbed by the "Elin" race, which resemble scantily clad young girls. You may be more disturbed to learn that the company has already censored their appearance; apparently, the South Korean version has them running around in panties.

THRONE OF DARKNESS

This game by Click Entertainment, published in 2001 by Sierra On-Line, was a *Diablo* clone in a medieval Japanese setting. Your task is to guide seven samurai in their quest to defeat a wily demon named Zanshin, who's terrorizing the land of Yamato. It innovates on the *Diablo* model in several ways. First, you can control four characters in combat, swapping them in and out of a pool of seven. You only control one character at a time in combat, but the others can be set to one of twelve preset tactics. Another nice touch is a blacksmith and priest, always on hand to repairing equipment and healing fallen characters. The blacksmith can even make new items from unneeded equipment. Multiplayer capability was available via Sierra's servers, which allowed up to seven players to compete or cooperate in a "king of the hill" type game. This all sounded great, but even though some *Diablo* developers were on the team, it failed to dethrone its predecessor.

TORCHLIGHT

This *Diablo*-like was developed and published by Runic Games in 2009. Its key selling point is its hefty procedural generation, which brings us back nicely to the first *Diablo*. It also boasts great support tools for modding or creating new scenarios, pets and fishing to lighten the mood, and an option to retire your hero and pass on a prized item for your next character. It was followed by *Torchlight II* in 2012.

WILDSTAR

This short-lived sci-fi MMORPG from Carbine Studios went online on June 3, 2014, quickly shifting from a subscription to a free-to-play model.

It was quite campy, with a cartoonish aesthetic and action-based combat. It seemed to have a lot going for it, but bugs, poor optimization, tedious leveling, and a lack of options for endgame content seems to have led to its downfall.

XENOMORPH

Pandora's 1990 game *Xenomorph* is much better than its earlier game, *Death Bringer,* an uninspired *Dungeon Master* clone. This one is a sci-fi thriller reminiscent of the film *Aliens.* It's set in a mysteriously abandoned mining station, where the player's character has been forced to dock his heavily damaged ship. The player's primary mission is to gather the parts needed to repair his craft, though along the way he'll learn what happened to the crew of the station—and, of course, battle plenty of fearsome aliens. Unfortunately, as with *Death Bringer,* the game was hampered by poor audiovisuals, lack of automapping, and clumsy difficult navigation.

ZYLL

Scott Edwards and Marshal Linder's *Zyll* is a 1984 game programmed for IBM's short-lived PCjr (though the game will run on any IBM PC compatible). It's a two-player, text-based CRPG in which players either compete or cooperate in a quest to find the Black Orb. It's set in real time and features well-written descriptions of the scenery, and enough of the gameplay was randomly generated to make it fun to play over and over. In effect, it's a MUD playable on a single, non-networked computer. According to Scott Edwards, both he and Linder were IBM employees who wrote the game during their office hours. They submitted it to IBM's employee submissions program and were one of only seven who were accepted.

Index